Coffee and Philosophy

A Conversational Introduction to Philosophy with Readings

Bruce N. Waller

Department of Philosophy & Religious Studies
Youngstown State University

PEARSON
Longman

New York San Francisco Boston
London Toronto Sydney Tokyo Singapore Madrid
Mexico City Munich Paris Capetown Hong Kong Montreal

Vice President and Publisher: Priscilla McGeehon
Executive Marketing Manager: Ann Stypuloski
Production Manager: Denise Phillip
Project Coordination, Text Design,
and Electronic Page Makeup: WestWords, Inc.
Senior Design Manager/Designer : Nancy Danahy
Cover Image: © Getty Images, Inc.
Manufacturing Manager: Mary Fischer
Printer and Binder: R.R. Donnelley & Sons
Cover Printer: Coral Graphic Services

For permission to use copyrighted material, grateful acknowledgment is
made to the copyright holders on p. 587, which are hereby made part of
this copyright page.

Library of Congress Cataloging-in-Publication Data

Waller, Bruce N.,
Coffee and philosophy : a conversational introduction to philosophy with
readings / Bruce N. Waller.
    p. cm.
ISBN 0-321-33093-5 (pbk.)
1. Philosophy. I. Title.
BD31.W28 2005
100–dc22

                                                    2005003150

Please visit our website at http://www.ablongman.com

ISBN 0-321-33093-5

3 4 5 6 7 8 9 10—DOH—08 07 06

Contents

Preface

Coffee and Philosophy is quite different from the usual introductory philosophy text and may require more than the usual introduction. The book is written in dialogue form, and though the dialogue has proved a valuable platform for philosophers as diverse as Plato, Lorenzo de Valla, David Hume, Bishop Berkeley, Denis Diderot, and Raymond Smullyan, it is not common in introductory textbooks. It is, however, an excellent format for that use, allowing the presentation of ideas, arguments, counterarguments, objections, criticisms, questions, and answers in a natural progression; and because it is arranged conversationally, the argument can reach considerable depth while remaining clear and readable. Furthermore, while the dialogue invites the reader into the discussion, it also invites the reader deeper into the issues. It is a natural setting for not merely presenting theories, but also examining their strengths and weaknesses, and comparing them with competing views. Thus, the dialogue both presents the ideas of outstanding philosophers and invites us to think through those ideas, their grounds, their justifications, and their larger contexts. It offers the opportunity to examine major theories and their sources, as well as their supporting arguments, their major criticisms, and their connections with other issues.

The participants to the dialogue don't talk about sex quite as much as Diderot did in his dialogues; but they are contemporary college students, and sex, football, professors, and politics are elements of their conversation. Dialogues are inherently conversational, and that conversational format encourages discussion, humor, the exchange of ideas, and even playfulness. One need only read the dialogues of Plato, Hume, and Diderot to become immediately aware of the banter encouraged by the conversational setting; but while their dialogues are not somber, they are certainly serious. Plato, Hume, and Diderot presented important philosophical arguments in that context, and the present text aims at in-depth examination of philosophical views—and philosophical *arguments.* The style of the book is light, but the goal is very serious: critical, but fair, examination of some very important questions, ideas, theories, and arguments.

Furthermore, the dialogue format has a special advantage for the introductory textbook: It is the natural way to draw out the connections and implications among various philosophical issues. Too often in introductory philosophy courses we discuss epistemology, drop that topic and move on to philosophy of mind, and then leave that to start afresh with ethics. But that is not the way we pursue philosophical issues, and such fragmentation is not the most informative or natural way to examine philosophical questions. When we follow the same characters throughout a lengthy dialogue, the connections among their views become a prominent feature of the discussion: The student in the dialogue who favors an empiricist approach to epistemology naturally brings those ideas to her discussion of mind and ethics, and the rationalist and the pragmatist do the same. The person who favors a Kantian epistemology brings that history to the discussion of free will and ethics. Debates that start in one area reappear in later chapters, and positions that were taken earlier are employed, defended, and modified in light of ideas developed in later discussions.

Finally, the dialogue not only promotes serious discussion of substantive philosophical issues, but also models a style of conversation and debate in which important beliefs are discussed—and attacked, defended, and modified—while avoiding personal attacks, distortions, and antagonism. Too often, serious discussion of conflicting views degenerates into personal animosity. What is presented here, however, is a dialogue among close friends with profoundly different philosophical positions, political stances, and basic perspectives; the participants engage in serious and spirited argument, avoiding both straw-man and ad hominem fallacies—and they remain friends.

In sum, this introductory text aims at drawing readers into systematic philosophical inquiries through dialogues that probe deep into philosophical issues and arguments in a style that is engaging and accessible.

Features of the Text

1. The book is written as a dialogue in conversational style, encouraging students to participate in the arguments and inquiries.

2. Rather than being abstract ideas, the positions discussed are actually championed—and critiqued—by the participants to the dialogue, who take the issues very seriously.

3. Connections among issues in epistemology, ethics, philosophy of mind, and philosophy of religion are a natural part of the discussion, as the participants develop their own comprehensive philosophical perspectives and draw out the implications of their positions for earlier issues.

4. The participants offer positive models of philosophical inquiry: They argue their positions forcefully and critique one another's views vigorously in a pleasant atmosphere of respect, affection, and even playfulness. Students learn that vigorous disagreements can occur without

the use of straw-man fallacies and ad hominem attacks and without compromising friendships.

5. Twelve chapters start from an examination of skills in argumentation and continue through serious discussions of topics in philosophy of religion, epistemology, philosophy of mind, ethics, free will, political philosophy, and personal identity.

6. Extensive exercises draw students further into serious philosophical inquiry.

7. In addition to dozens of brief quotation boxes scattered throughout the text, twenty-four longer primary source readings cover major figures in the history of philosophy as well as a number of contemporary writers.

8. Among the study aids in every chapter are study questions, a glossary, a time line, and an extensive annotated guide to additional resources (including both written and World Wide Web resources).

Acknowledgments

In writing this book, I have received generous help and support from many quarters. My colleagues in the Department of Philosophy and Religious Studies at Youngstown State University have been a rich source of ideas, encouragement, and warm friendship for many years. Tom Shipka encouraged me to write the book and was particularly supportive of the dialogue format; he generously shared a wide variety of articles and ideas, especially in the area of political philosophy. Brendan Minogue read many early versions of articles and offered judicious advice, as well as being a constant source of very valuable information in both ethics and philosophy of science. Chris Bache and I never agree on anything, and for that reason and many others, he is a richly valued colleague. J-C. Smith—in addition to being patient and encouraging when I am attempting to understand some new development in cyberspace—is also a penetrating explorer of issues in epistemology and logic, and has often led me to important material. Linda "Tess" Tessier is a faithful source of wisdom, and her insights are as deep as her integrity. Victor Wan-Tatah has a genuine and infectious joy in ideas and arguments, and he is a wise and warm-hearted colleague. Mustansir Mir has a remarkable breadth and depth of knowledge in philosophy, religion, literature, and history, and he weaves the strands together into fascinating and enlightening conversations. Gabriel Palmer-Fernandez is a wonderfully provocative and splendidly informed source for ideas, arguments, and resources in almost every area of contemporary ethics and political philosophy. Charles Reid knows more obscure and fascinating facts about more subjects than any person I have ever known, and he is most generous in sharing them. Walter Carvin is a wonderful resource for Irish poetry and medieval philosophy, and Stephanie Dost-Barnhizer is my guide for topics in esthetics and literature. Donna Sloan has deep knowledge, both practical and theoretical, of the practice of ethics in very important institutional settings. Vince Lisi offers an interesting perspective on ethical issues and is steadfast and joyful in living by the principles he espouses. Julie Aultmann is a very congenial source for insights into contemporary bioethics.

Joan Bevan finds a way to get the impossible last permission to reprint, discovers the address no one else can locate, completes every task ahead of schedule and often before anyone else even knew there was a task to do, and keeps about a thousand balls juggling in the air while never dropping even one; and she does it all with a smile for everyone, at the same time making it look easy. Describing her as our superb department secretary is as inadequate as calling the Grand Canyon a ditch. Justina Rachella is her invariably cheerful and highly efficient assistant. James Sacco generously takes time from his demanding duties in editing an excellent journal to provide invaluable help with computers and references.

From the Sociology and Anthropology Department offices next door, Robert Weaver invariably leads me to new perspectives and intriguing ideas in medical sociology, death and dying, and many other areas. John White is a delightful colleague, with a vast knowledge of local as well as native American history and excellent suggestions for fascinating books and articles.

Stephen Flora, in psychology, is particularly helpful in keeping me informed of developments in contemporary psychology and their applications to traditional philosophical issues, such as free will.

I am indebted to Charles Singler for many enlightening discussions on topics too broad and various to recount. My friend Homer Warren has provided rich insights on topics ranging from economics to affirmative action; and he is the model for vigorous, courteous, fair, and careful argument that I have attempted to portray through the characters of this book.

I should also like to thank the research librarians at Y.S.U., who again and again find sources from the most obscure clues and in the most improbable places—and approach the task with warm and generous enthusiasm.

Nawal Ammar has been most helpful in increasing both my depth and breadth of understanding of issues in international relations and cultural conflict. Richard Double is the most profoundly insightful philosopher I have ever known, particularly in areas related to free will; and he also personifies how to live gracefully and generously through challenges and hardships. Bryan Hilliard is a valued resource for material in bioethics and particularly for his understanding of the legal aspects of ethical issues. George Graham is the best source for demonstrating the profound philosophical importance of much material in psychology that is too often neglected by philosophers. Robert Kane's provocative views and careful arguments—particularly his absolute fairness in debating philosophical issues—has greatly enhanced my understanding of many very difficult issues related to free will and determinism. Lia Ruttan not only read and critiqued many of the chapters and offered helpful advice, but also led me to many valuable articles and essays—especially in the areas of anthropology, cultural relations, and the ethics of research—that I would have never discovered without her help.

Jack Raver offers a wonderful example of joyous, enthusiastic, and scrupulously fair argument on every topic imaginable.

My Irish-music friends are my main source of restored energy; one raucous Celtic session, and I am recharged for at least a week. I am sincerely grateful for their long and cheerful tolerance of every Irish musician's worst nightmare: a concertina player rich in enthusiasm, but meager in talent.

Thanks to my good friends Fred Alexander, Lauren Schroeder, and Luke Lucas for many fascinating discussions of ethics, politics, religion, the importance of wetlands, the varieties of hawks, the professional privileges of engineers, and the perils of drawing to an inside straight. I just wish the discussions were a bit less expensive.

My model for the perfect coffee shop is The Beat, a friendly and welcoming haven across the street from the Y.S.U. campus. The rich goodness of their coffee is perfectly matched by the constant warm atmosphere provided by Cheri, Gina, Karen, Kevin, Sherrie, Steve, and Tricia.

Priscilla McGeehon is the best editor one can imagine. Always supportive, insightful in her suggestions for improvements, and gentle with her criticisms, she smooths the long, bumpy road of taking a book from proposal to final production. Her associate, Stephanie Ricotta, is remarkably efficient at handling the details and superb at locating excellent and dedicated reviewers for early drafts. Kristi Olson is peerless at taking crude ideas for supplementary materials and turning them into beautifully finished guides.

I am grateful to Brian Baker, the superb copy editor with Write With, Inc., whose keen eye and broad knowledge of philosophy enabled him to correct a multitude of my mistakes. In addition, I would like to thank

Professors Mary Louise Bringle and Margaret L. Brown and their students at Brevard College for class testing the text and providing excellent suggestions for revisions.

Special thanks go to the insightful and thorough reviewers of the book who went far beyond the minimum and made specific excellent suggestions for improving the text: Marina P. Banchetti, Florida Atlantic University; John Bardi, Pennsylvania State University–Mont Alto; W. David Beck, Liberty University; Mary Louise Bringle, Brevard College; Jeremiah Hackett, University of South Carolina; Paul Hodapp, University of Northern Colorado; Andrew Kelley, Bradley University; and Michael F. Patton, Jr., University of Montevallo.

After years of writing journal articles and books published by university presses, it was a question from my wife, Mary Newell Waller, that first stimulated me to write a textbook: "Why don't you write something that makes money?" Her constant loving support through this project—as well as through all the projects that never turned a profit—is deeply appreciated.

I am particularly indebted to my sons, Russell and Adam, who have talked with me for many years about a variety of subjects, including philosophy, ethics, politics, religion, music, baseball, and gymnastics; and to my students at Y.S.U., who have discussed so many issues with me over the past 15 years, both in class and over coffee. If the conversations among the students in this book are believable, that is thanks to Russell and Adam, and Robyn, Tamar, Rich, Mark, Eric, Laura, Daren, David, Andrea, Katie, Courtney, Megan, and their friends, and my many excellent students at Y.S.U. Of course, if the conversations are not believable, then it's all their fault.

Bruce N. Waller

Chapter *1*

Thinking Critically

in which Ben and Selina learn to fight fair

"I just don't understand, Selina. You're always eager to try new ideas in science and politics, delighted to taste new foods and visit exotic places, happy to hear experimental music and meet new people, yet when I ask you to honestly consider just one new argument, you crawl back in your shell like some old snapping turtle." Ben's voice carried above the hiss of the espresso machine. Sarah smiled to herself. It was never difficult to locate Ben and Selina. Ten every morning, an hour between classes, they were here at the coffee shop, getting recharged with caffeine—Selina taking a break after her organic chemistry lecture, Ben arriving from his history of Latin America, and Sarah joining them last of all: The students in her rationalist philosophy seminar always lingered, especially now that the subject was Spinoza. An improbable threesome, but college life seemed to turn improbabilities into actualities at an astonishing rate.

Sarah, Selina, and Ben

Sarah had gotten thrown in with Selina as a result of roommate clashes during their freshman year. Selina's roommate lived to party, and her musical tastes ran to top forty, which Selina found stupid and shallow—and said so. Selina did not suffer fools gladly—or quietly, for that matter. She took few pains to conceal the fact that she thought her roommate a fool, a waste of space at a university Selina loved. Much of that love was focused on the university's outstanding chemistry department: Selina had loved chemistry ever since her uncle had given her a chemistry set for her tenth birthday. So chemistry had attracted her to Ann Arbor—that and spending many fall afternoons sitting with her father, a former Michigan linebacker, cheering for the Wolverines. In any case, Selina hadn't enrolled at Michigan to party: She could damned well party back home in Birmingham, Alabama. Better parties and better music than anything she had found in Michigan.

Not that Selina had anything against partying. Quite the contrary: When she partied, she *partied*; and when she studied, she studied; and she had no patience with those who could not separate one from the other. Selina and her roommate didn't really fight—Selina was small and slender, yet also rather intimidating—but they coexisted in a semester-long cold war.

Across the hall, Sarah and her roommate never argued. They were carefully polite to each other and occasionally shared breakfast at the cafeteria, but there was little sympathy between them. Sarah was quiet, was a voluminous reader, and preferred the company of a few friends. She was far from home, but Ann Arbor immediately seemed like a second home to this Jewish kid from Brooklyn. Sarah's roommate liked crowds and sought out courses that required the least reading and an absolute minimum of writing. Sarah soon found herself spending most of her evenings in the library. That was fine: Sarah loved the huge dusty stacks at University Library and had soon discovered a favorite secluded quiet corner for her long hours of reading. She had friends from her classes and a few more in her dorm—she and Selina had quickly hit it off when Sarah admired a Charley Parker CD Selina was playing one Sunday afternoon.

Selina's roommate had become tight friends with Sarah's roommate, and one evening when she stopped in to complain about the trials of living with Selina, Sarah found herself making a suggestion: "Why don't you move in here? I'll move my stuff across the hall and live with Selina." Within an hour, the room swap was completed. That was two years ago, and Selina and Sarah had been roommates ever since—roommates, soul mates, best friends, sharers of sweaters and jewelry and secrets.

Secrets, including Selina's wild delight in Ben and her frequent anger at Ben. A real anger, since Selina and Ben often had genuine deep disagreements. But an anger that never quite eclipsed the delight. Sarah liked both of them—loved Selina and liked Ben for himself and for his genuine affection for Selina. Not an easy affection. Sarah was easygoing, and she enjoyed Selina's fiery personality. But she knew that Selina was proud, almost arrogant, and that, for all her charms, Selina could be stubborn and difficult to get along with. Ben was long suffering, but he also had very strong beliefs and convictions, and there were more than a few times that they clashed. Selina would cry on one of Sarah's shoulders at night, and Ben would cry on Sarah's other shoulder in the morning, and by that afternoon peace was usually restored. Reconciliations were tempestuous. Sarah suspected that the joy of their reconciliations motivated some of their conflicts.

Selina, Sarah, and Ben almost always had coffee together at ten. Except, of course, on Sunday, when Ben was lifting his voice in praise to God, much to the disgust of Selina. "I can't see how you can deny the existence of God," Ben would entreat. "I do believe in God," Sarah would reply. "His name is Sonny Terry, and he performs blues miracles with a tiny mouth harp." It was an enduring difference between them.

Actually, it was one difference. There were so many differences between Selina and Ben that Sarah had given up trying to sort them into categories of major and minor. Both were very serious about their work. Ben could be lost for hours pursuing his research on the colonial history of the Americas; and Selina often lost all sense of time in the isolation of her laboratory. Yet they seemed to emerge from their respective haunts at compatible times. It was never clear to Sarah how they did it; certainly, neither was capable of making elaborate plans to meet, and if they had, neither would have kept sufficient track of time to keep their engagement. Still, they often showed up at the same place at the same time. Sarah thought they might have the same biological clock.

Of course, at ten it was easy: Leave your first class, head to the coffee shop. Both Ben and Selina often lost track of time—if Sarah was meeting them for dinner, she always brought a book and prepared to wait anywhere from ten minutes to an hour. But morning coffee was an easier schedule. And finding the table where Selina and Ben were sitting was never a problem: Just follow the raised voices. Ben's suggestion that Selina reminded him of a snapping turtle meant that their morning argument was already in progress. If that was the worst thing said so far, then this argument was being conducted at a relatively high level of cordial courtesy.

"Is this a private fight, or can anyone play?"

"Hi, Sarah. Sure, please join us." Ben took his backpack off the third chair and dropped it on the floor, beckoning to Sarah. "Perhaps you can help me persuade Selina to listen to reason."

Selina laughed. "I'd happily listen to reason. It would make a nice change from arguing with you, Benjamin."

"But my arguments *are* based on reason. You won't even consider them."

"Ben, Ben," Selina shook her head, "look, you want to give an argument to prove that God exists. But what you really want is a security blanket: God will take care of everything, we don't have to worry, we'll understand it better by and by. God's a crutch; rise, throw away your crutches, and walk! People who argue for the existence of God are really just trying to escape their own fears of standing on their own two feet."

Ad Hominem Arguments "against the man" personal attack fallacy

"I should know better than to get in the middle of this," Sarah smiled. "But look, Selina, suppose that what you say is true: Ben's arguments for the existence of God are motivated by his own fears, his own desire for security."

Ben rolled his eyes. "Thanks a lot, Selina. I should have known you two would stick together."

"No, Ben, wait," Sarah continued. "I didn't say those actually were your motives. But *suppose* they were. It wouldn't really matter, would it? After all, if you give an *argument* for the existence of God, then the argument has to stand or fall on its own merits: the motives behind the argument don't count."

Selina looked puzzled. "I don't think I follow you. But then, you often don't make much sense when you've recently been in your philosophy seminar."

"It's nothing strange, Selina." Sarah leaned forward. "Look, suppose I give you an *argument* for why the Jews are the chosen people and we should get special treatment: We should get free refills on our coffee and get first choice of the bagels—whatever. Not that I have such an argument: If I think of one, you'll be the first to know. But suppose I did give you an *argument* for that conclusion. Then the argument has to stand or fall on its own merits. It doesn't matter *who* gave the argument, whether it's some Jewish kid from Brooklyn or an atheist from Birmingham. Argument is argument. Whether it comes from Moses Maimonides or Frederick Douglass or Rush Limbaugh, you have to consider the *argument*, not the *source* of the argument. So if you said, 'Well, sure, Sarah's gonna give an argument that Jews should get special treatment; she's just arguing for her own selfish interests; we don't have to pay any attention to her argument,' then you would be *wrong*. You would be committing the *ad hominem fallacy*."

Selina laughed. "I'm surrounded. I've got the preacher on one side of me and the philosopher on the other. What are you talking about, Sarah, 'ad hominem fallacy'?"

"A fallacy is just a standard argument error. An ad hominem fallacy is the fallacy of rejecting an argument on the basis of the *source* of the argument: saying that, because the person who gave the argument is bad, or biased, or hypocritical, or whatever, it follows that her *argument* is bad. But that's not a good reason to dismiss an argument. Suppose you give an *argument* to demonstrate that affirmative action is fair and just. Someone says, 'We don't have to pay any attention to that argument; the argument is obviously no good, since Selina is an African-American woman, so she might benefit from a policy of affirmative action, and that's why she's arguing in favor of it.' That would be an ad hominem fallacy: Even if it's true that you might benefit from an affirmative action policy, your *argument* for that policy has to be evaluated on its own merits. Your *argument* for affirmative action is the same argument, whether you give it, or Ben gives it, or it's given by a talking horse, or it's written on golden tablets by God Herself. Argument is argument, and you can't judge the quality of an argument by the *source* of the argument."

Selina still looked skeptical. "So if you give an argument for why Jews should always be first in line at the coffee shop, it doesn't matter that you will get special benefits: we still have to judge the argument on its own merits, independently of you."

"Of course," Sarah insisted. "Suppose that *Ben* gave the argument. That wouldn't change the argument, would it? I might think more kindly of good old Ben, for trying to establish that I should always be first in line for coffee. But the argument is the same argument, no matter who gives it. Right?"

"Makes sense to me," Ben said, "so you have to listen to my *argument* for the existence of God, and my *motives* for giving that argument are *irrelevant*. Thank you, Sarah, for pointing out Selina's *ad hominem fallacy*. As far as I'm concerned, I think you've earned the right to always be first in line for coffee." Ben gave Sarah a small bow, and Sarah returned it.

"Not quite so fast, Sir Walter Raleigh. I might listen to your arguments, but no way Sarah cuts in line for coffee. Besides," Selina wasn't quite convinced, "it's still not clear to me that the source *never* matters."

"The source of an *argument* doesn't matter. But in some cases, the source matters quite a lot. Suppose someone is giving *testimony*, rather than argument. Like, say I'm *testifying* that I saw Ben rob a convenience store. In that case, you *would* need to know about the source of the testimony: You would want to know that I hate Ben because he is a better philosopher than I am, or that I'm getting a payoff in exchange for my testimony because the District Attorney has agreed to drop my shoplifting charges if I'll testify against Ben. Or that I am a notorious liar. Or that I'm trying to pin the robbery on Ben so that I won't be a suspect. All that would be *relevant*. And if you said, 'Don't believe Sarah's *testimony* because she is a habitual liar and she has a strong motive for lying,' that would be *ad hominem*, but it would be a *legitimate* use of an ad hominem argument. If I give you an *argument* for why Jews are special people who should always be first in line for coffee, then you have to evaluate that argument on its own merits. But if I claim that Jews are special people because *God directly told me so*, and you should accept my *testimony* that God gave me that special privilege, then you can certainly consider my motives and character in evaluating my testimony. For example, Moses comes down from the mountain, and he *testifies* that God told him that only his family could be priests. I think I might have raised some questions about that: 'Are you *sure* you heard right? Only *your* family gets to be priests?' When Moses gives *testimony*, his motives are fair game, and it's legitimate to raise questions about them."

"Not me," Selina replied. "Wasn't that right after God had zapped the Egyptians with all those plagues? Turned the Nile to blood, sent swarms of flies, caused boils all over their bodies, killed all the firstborn children? I wouldn't be taking any chances. If you told me God said, 'Okay, Sarah gets to be judge, and she gets to be first in line for coffee,' I'd be saying, 'Right, God, whatever You say.'"

Ben laughed. "That's probably the only way Selina would be convinced. It would take a plague of locusts, at the very least."

"It'll take more than testimony," Selina agreed. "A plague of locusts might suffice. A moving finger writing on the wall, that might do it, too. Or maybe ten straight wins over Ohio State. But not testimony."

"Of course, testimony is not the *only* place that ad hominem is legitimate," said Sarah. "If someone is running for office, that person's character and truthfulness and integrity can be a legitimate issue. Or if someone is applying for a job: 'Don't hire Richard, because he's a thief and a swindler.' That might be a legitimate reason not to offer Richard the job. But if Richard is offering *argument*, then his history of theft is irrelevant to the quality of his argument. It is still the same argument, whether offered by a villain like Richard or a paragon of virtue like old Ben."

> **"**Argument is argument. You cannot help paying regard to their arguments, if they are good. If it were testimony you might disregard it. . . . Testimony is like an arrow shot from a long bow; the force of it depends on the strength of the hand that draws it. Argument is like an arrow from a cross-bow, which has equal force though shot by a child.**"**
>
> Samuel Johnson, *Life,* May 19, 1784

Fallacy of Appeal to Ignorance

"Speaking of argument," Ben said, "can we get back to my argument for the existence of God?"

"The boy is persistent, isn't he?" Selina shook her head. "What was the proverb from King Solomon? 'As a dog returneth to his vomit, so a fool returneth to his folly.' Solomon must have had Ben in mind. This hope of finding a proof for the existence of God is folly, dear Ben."

"It's folly to argue with you," Ben answered. "But perhaps now you'll listen to reason, Selina, since Sarah has established that you can't just dismiss my argument because of what you think about my *motives*. The argument is a simple one: Many people have been opposed to religious belief, and they have tried to dismiss belief in God as irrational and ill founded. But notice this: No one has offered conclusive proof that God does *not* exist. Maybe they can offer an alternative account of how the world was formed, how the big bang occurred, how evolutionary processes proceed; but none of that demonstrates the *non*existence of God. So since all efforts to *disprove* the existence of God have fallen short, it is obviously more plausible to believe that the existence of God is irrefutable and thus that God does exist."

Selina shook her head. "I can't prove that something doesn't exist, so that must be proof that it does. You can't prove that I don't own a million shares of Microsoft stock, so that's proof that I do! Wow! God exists, and I'm rich! Happy day."

"I'm afraid Selina's right, Ben: That argument has some problems. It commits the fallacy of *appeal to ignorance*."

"It's your lucky day, Ben." Selina was in great spirits. "They named a fallacy after you: the fallacy of appeal to ignorance."

"Now, Selina, play nice. Even very bright people—like our friend Ben—can fall prey to the fallacy of appeal to ignorance. It's a very common fallacy: the fallacy of arguing that because one's claim cannot be proved *false*, that's a reason for thinking it true. But that doesn't work, because it

---

Placing the burden of proof may be a life-or-death question. The 1986 explosion of the Challenger *spacecraft cost the lives of seven people. The accident was traced to problems with the O-rings, which did not function properly in the freezing weather of the launch, allowing fuel to leak and thus causing the deadly explosion. Morton Thiokol was the company that manufactured the O-rings, and prior to the planned launch, engineers from the company raised the possibility of danger from frozen O-rings. In the past, if anyone raised reasonable doubts about the safety of a launch, there had to be solid proof that the supposed danger did not exist before the launch could proceed: The burden of proof was always on those who claimed that it was safe to launch. But in this case, the presumption was reversed: The craft was presumed to be safe, and anyone raising doubts had to conclusively prove that there was genuine risk in order to stop the launch. The Morton Thiokol engineers could show reasonable grounds for concern, but they could not demonstrate that the O-rings actually would malfunction in the cold and cause an explosion. Since the burden of proof was (wrongly) placed on the engineers to prove that the O-rings were dangerous (rather than on the launch team to prove that the O-rings were safe), the launch proceeded; and an appeal to ignorance ended in disaster.*

shifts the burden of proof to the wrong side. The person *making the claim* bears the burden of proving it true. It's not up to anyone else to prove it false. If I claim that there's a subterranean colony of space aliens living two miles directly below Ann Arbor, then I have the burden of proving that claim; and obviously, I can't claim that it *must* be true because no one has dug a hole two miles deep and proved it false. If I accuse you of a crime, then I must prove that you are guilty: You don't have to prove that you didn't do it—you don't have to provide any alibi—because the full burden of proof rests on me to prove the charges. If I claim that Iraq has weapons of mass destruction hidden away, then it's up to me to offer the proof. And if I claim that God exists, then I bear the burden of proving that claim. Trying to shift the burden of proof to the other side commits the fallacy of appeal to ignorance."

> I wish to propose for the reader's favourable consideration a doctrine which may, I fear, appear wildly paradoxical and subversive. The doctrine in question is this: that it is undesirable to believe a proposition when there is no ground whatsoever for supposing it to be true.
>
> Bertrand Russell, *On the Value of Scepticism*

Appeal to Authority

"Alright, forget that argument," Ben conceded, "but still, consider this: Think of all the great teachers and prophets and theologians who have studied the question of God's existence—I'm thinking of people you know well, Sarah—philosophers and theologians and thinkers and mystics, like Aristotle, Lao-Tse, Plotinus, Augustine, Aquinas, Rabia, Anselm, Averroës, Avicenna, Maimonides, Descartes, Leibniz, Spinoza, and Locke. Though they obviously disagree on many details, they agree on one fundamental thing: God exists. Such agreement among so many wise sources is sufficient proof of what they agree on, namely, the existence of God."

"That's an interesting line of argument, Ben," Sarah replied. "It's an *appeal to authority*, and the right kind of appeal to authority can certainly be legitimate."

"Yeah," Selina replied, "but Ben's argument is not the right kind of appeal to authority."

"I gotta agree with Selina on this one, Ben. There are two basic conditions that a legitimate appeal to authority has to meet. First, the authority appealed to must be an authority on the subject in question. For example, if we ask one of the chemistry professors how many electrons there are in a nitrogen atom, then we're appealing to a genuine authority in the appropriate area. But if we ask the same chemistry professor a question about who was the commanding Union general at the battle of Fredericksburg, we are not asking an expert in the right area: We need a Civil War historian, not a chemist. Second, there must be *general agreement* or *consensus* among the authorities. Suppose we ask Dick Vitale who was the greatest college basketball coach in history? Well, Dick Vitale probably counts as a genuine expert on college basketball, and it would be fun to hear his opinion; but we couldn't legitimately conclude that the coach favored by Vitale must be the greatest, because lots of other authorities on college basketball would have a different opinion: Some would say John Wooden, others would favor Dean Smith, and still others would pick John Thompson. In the case you gave, Ben, it's not clear that everyone on your list would count as an authority. Certainly, some of the 'authorities' you cite would not accept the others as legitimate authorities. For example, Spinoza would not accept the authority of Augustine or Aquinas or Anselm, and they would not accept his authority or that of Maimonides or Rabia. And there's another problem: Even if we could find some element of agreement among all those people, it's still not clear that we would have a consensus among authorities. After all, many philosophers—and a significant number of theologians, for that matter—favor atheism or agnosticism. And we can't just count the ones who believe in God as the only real authorities: That would beg the question."

Dilemma Arguments

"Okay, if you don't like that argument, consider this one." Ben was not giving up easily. "I once heard a minister give this argument: Jesus claimed to be God, right? 'You have seen me, you have seen the Father,' meaning God, because 'I and the Father are One.' So *either* Jesus really is God, or Jesus was totally crazy: after all, anyone who claims to be God—and is not God—must be crazy. But Jesus obviously wasn't crazy: no one could read his sermons and parables and suppose he was crazy. So, obviously, Jesus is God. And of course, if Jesus is God, then God must exist!"

"Another interesting argument, Ben." Sarah smiled.

"Don't encourage him, Girl," Selina shook her head. "You let Ben get started on God, and no one will be able to drink a cup of coffee in peace."

"I said it was an interesting argument—but it still doesn't work. It's a dilemma argument: Either A or B must be true; A is certainly false; so B must be true. The argument's structure is good; unfortunately, the first premise is false. So the argument is a *false* dilemma. Come on, Ben, you're a historian. Are those really the only possibilities: Either Jesus really is God, or he's a madman who only claims to be God? As a historian, you

Betsy Hart is a commentator on CNN and the Fox News Channel. In a newspaper column (June 12, 1998), she discussed a resolution passed by the Southern Baptist Convention, a resolution which affirms as a biblical principle the doctrine that "wives must submit to their husbands." The resolution drew widespread criticism, but Hart defended it, claiming that its critics are "elites" who look down on the Southern Baptists; she then offered this answer to all the criticism:

> So, back to the Southern Baptist Convention and the specifics of what's causing all the fuss. I can't imagine elites really would say, for starters, that, contrary to this Scripture, women should always demand their own way. Is that a healthy model for anyone?

Well, no, it's not a healthy model. But are those the only alternatives? Women must either be submissive to their husbands or always demand their own way? Apparently, Betsy Hart considers those the only options. But it doesn't take great insight to recognize that equality is another possibility and that Hart's argument is a false dilemma.

know that sometimes the written historical record is not completely true; and furthermore, the written record is often open to multiple interpretations. Take that line, 'You have seen me, you have seen the Father.' Maybe Jesus was saying that he is the same as God, a special divinity on Earth. Or maybe he was saying something quite different: You've seen me, you've seen all there is of God; we are all equally special, there's no Divine force outside the world. After all, that was how many of the early Christians— the gnostics, for example—interpreted the teachings of Jesus: not that Jesus was some special transcendent divinity who miraculously visited Earth, but rather that there is something special and wonderful and 'divine' in all of us. Or maybe Jesus' words got written down wrong: After all, the written Gospels were not compiled until several decades later, and that's plenty of time for all sorts of sayings to be wrongly attributed to a revered teacher. If we grant your premises—either Jesus is God or he was crazy, and Jesus wasn't crazy—then it certainly follows that Jesus is God. But that first premise is a false dilemma."

"Alright, I never thought much of that argument anyway; just thought I'd give it a shot. Still, I do believe that God exists."

Straw-Man Fallacy

"Ben, really, how can you believe in God?" Selina leaned forward. "God is just a name for our ignorance. It's fine when you're a child and you don't know the answers. And perhaps it's okay before the development of science and scientific inquiry. But now it's just an excuse for laziness. Why did we suffer a drought? God must be punishing us. Why is the moon being eaten by a shadow? God must be angry with us. Why did that person die of disease? God must have decided that it was time for her to die. Why do we have eyes? God must have designed them. Those 'answers' are too easy, and they don't really explain anything, and they keep us from seeking out the real answers through the hard work of scientific study. Besides, it's not a very plausible story, is it? God decides to make a world. Leave aside the absurd idea of an infinite God making something distinct from Himself—if God is infinite, how could there be a world outside of God? So God spends a week making a world: one day to make all the billions of galaxies and stars, and then five full days shaping up this tiny little planet called Earth. And He makes every species of bird and animal and insect—including tens of thousands of distinct species of beetles—and he makes two humans, Adam and Eve. They have two kids, Cain and Abel, and Cain kills Abel. So God sends Cain away and puts a mark on him so that the people in the surrounding cities won't kill him. Wait a minute. There's only three people: Adam, Eve, and their remaining son, Cain. Where did all those people in the cities come from? None of it makes sense. You don't really believe that stuff, do you?"

"Well," Ben replied, "not the way you describe it, Selina. I know some people want to read the Bible as a biology or geology text; but that seems to me to cheapen it. It's not a text on how all the dinosaurs and beetles and bacteria came into being, but instead it tells deep spiritual truths about who we are and our relationship to God. The story of Adam and Eve isn't a literal account of how humans started; but it's a wonderful, inspiring account of how we are all brothers and sisters—one family—and a story of how God still loves us, even after we do terrible things, like killing a brother in a stupid argument. Maybe some people still want to use God as a lazy substitute for scientific reasoning, but it's not fair to attribute that view to me and then declare victory over a position I don't even hold."

"Ooh, nice shot, Ben!" Sarah clapped and smiled. "Hate to go against you on this one, Sister, but I gotta give that point to Ben. You were making a straw-man argument against his view, and he called you on it."

"Yeah, Selina," Ben gloated, "you used a straw-man argument, and I caught you. Uh, what's a straw-man argument, Sarah?"

"Sounds like sexist language to me," Selina said. "Shouldn't it be straw *person?*"

"A straw-man argument is the fallacy that's committed when someone misrepresents or distorts an opposing position, in order to make that position easier to attack," Sarah explained. "For example, if you attribute a more extreme position to your opponent than he or she really takes. Like when there are arguments over abortion, and the pro-life people claim that the pro-choice folks want to kill any unwanted child up to two years old. Maybe there are a few people who favor that, but it's certainly not the view of most people who are pro-choice, and presenting their views that way is a distortion, a straw man. It's much easier to attack than the position that women should have control over their own bodies and not be forced to carry an unwanted fetus; after all, a newborn baby can be put up for adoption, and the mother isn't forced to keep it, but you can't have someone else carry your fetus for you. The distorted straw-man position is easier to knock down than the actual pro-choice view, and that's why the straw-man fallacy is so tempting and so common; but it's still a fallacy. Of course, the pro-choice side also indulges in some straw-man attacks: Some pro-choice advocates portray the pro-life party as wanting to ban not only abortions, but also all forms of artificial contraception. And there are some people in the pro-life movement who favor that. But that's not the main view of the pro-life position; instead, it's an extreme view that is much more vulnerable to attack. Representing the pro-life view in that form is setting up a straw man."

"Oh, I know that fallacy," Selina said. "It's a favorite among politicians."

"It shows up in almost all social debates," Sarah replied, "and it is indeed a common political trick. But what were you saying before, Selina? You think the straw-man fallacy should be renamed the straw-person fallacy?"

"Well, let me think about that. A straw-man argument is a fallacious use of distortion and misrepresentation to score a cheap victory, right? Nah, I guess 'straw *man* is the appropriate word, after all."

In the fall of 2000, a study—performed by a consultant who often works for the U.S. Environmental Protection Agency and called "state of the art" by a spokesperson for the American Lung Association—reported that air pollution from electric power plants in the United States kills more than 30,000 Americans every year. Ralph DiNicola, a spokesperson for FirstEnergy Corporation, had this response to the report: "It is one thing to stand on the sidelines and bark about what the problem is, and a totally different responsibility to produce reliable, affordable electricity in an environmentally responsible manner. While these people would like to grow food in their back yards, and pedal bicycles to power medical diagnostic equipment, that is not what the rest of the world wants to do."[Reported in The Cleveland Plain Dealer, *October 17, 2000]*

But those who worry about deaths due to air pollution obviously don't want to eliminate all electrical power; rather, they want to produce power in a way that causes less pollution (by burning less coal, for example). But that is a more difficult position to attack than DiNicola's straw-man target.

Fallacy of Begging the Question

"Pretty selective in your sexist language, aren't you, sweetheart? Anyway, now that we've got Selina's straw-man fallacy out of the way, let's look at the most basic reason we can know that God exists. It's a simple reason," Ben continued, "that is obvious to everyone: Look closely and you'll see it. Only don't look outside, don't look to some laboratory, don't look at the stars. Look inside yourself, and you will find a clear sense, a deep certainty, of the existence of something greater and stronger than we are. What does the Bible say? 'Be still, and know that I am God.' That special quiet intuition is the best proof you could have of the existence of a Supreme Being."

Selina shook her head. "Ben, I just *knew* that the Cubs were going to win the World Series in '03: I could *feel* it, down to the tips of my toes. This is the year of the Cubs! It was a gut feeling, a fixed certainty. A lot of faithful, long-suffering Cubs fans felt the same way: 'This is our year, the curse of the goat is lifted, we kept the faith, our suffering was not in vain. This is the year of the Cubs!' But we were wrong. We were all wrong. Feelings can't tell you about what exists outside of you or what is going to happen. My feelings can tell me I have a pain in my leg, and I can have that pain even though my leg has been amputated. I might be wrong about where the pain comes from: it feels like it's in my leg, but my leg is no longer there, so obviously it's coming from somewhere else. Perhaps it feels like my leg has been damaged, but the problem is really psychosomatic; it's a problem in my mind, in my brain. Still, I know that I have pain, because I feel it. And I know that I love Ben, because I feel it. I have no idea why—we don't agree on anything; must be purely physical—but still, I know how I feel about him. But my feelings can't tell me who is going to win the World Series, and my feelings can't tell me how many moons Jupiter has, and my feelings can't tell me about the supposed existence of God. If you want to know what exists, you have to do careful scientific investigation. I'm not knocking feelings: They can be very, very nice. But they can't tell you about the existence of moons or mountains or deities."

"But Selina," Ben protested, "that's not a fair comparison. Your feeling about the Cubs winning—that's just a feeling about your hopes; it's just a product of your own desires. But the feeling, the special deep certainty of the existence of God—that's very different. It's an intuition implanted in each of us by God. And God is truth itself, and there is no deception in God, so this deep God-implanted sense cannot be a trick or a deception: It must be accurate. So it's not at all like your very fallible feeling that the Cubs will win."

"Ben, you're making my head spin," Selina laughed. "I feel like I'm riding a carousel, and it keeps going round and round."

"Yeah, I'm afraid Selina's right, Ben." Sarah smiled gently. "It's a clever argument, but it goes in a circle: It begs the question."

"What do you mean, Sarah, 'begs the question'?" Ben was disappointed. "I thought it was a good argument."

"Well, it is a good argument, in one sense," Sarah said. "The conclusion certainly follows from the premises. That is, it's a *valid* argument, as logicians like to say: *If* the premises of the argument are true, then the conclusion *must* also be true. The premises—the reasons given in support of the conclusion—certainly do support the conclusion. But the problem is, you managed to slip the conclusion in among the premises. Once you've done that, it's very easy to 'prove' your conclusion on the basis of your premises. That's why the argument commits the fallacy of begging the question. We have a special feeling that God exists. And the feeling is accurate because it is implanted by God, and God is not a deceiver. The *conclusion* of your argument is that God exists; so you can't say, in one of your premises, that we have a feeling that is implanted by God. Obviously, if God implants feelings, then God exists. But the existence of God is what the argument is supposed to be proving. You can't use a premise that assumes the existence of God without committing the fallacy of *begging the question*."

Some people suggest that chimpanzees have higher intelligence: that they can make plans, solve problems, and even use language. But clearly chimps do not have higher intelligence, because humans are the only animals that have higher intelligence." Indeed, if humans are the only animals with higher intelligence, then no nonhumans (including chimps) have higher intelligence. But of course, the question at issue is whether at least one nonhuman species— chimpanzees—have higher intelligence. This argument begs the question by offering a reason (a premise) that encompasses the argument's conclusion.

Fallacy of Irrelevant Reason

"Ben," said Selina, "you gotta give up this notion of proving the existence of God. It's never going to work. Look around you at all these people who claim to 'know that God exists' and claim that they that have special knowledge of God and God's will. 'God is ready to pour out a special blessing on you; just send cash, check, or credit card number, and I'll whisper your name in God's ear, and your troubles will be over.' 'God has ordered us to smite the infidels; grab your swords and slaughter those wicked people who are now living on the land that God obviously intended us to take as our destiny.' 'I have the power of God, and I can heal what ails you. Give me a special love offering to support this ministry, and you will be healed.' 'That wicked woman is a witch; God orders that she be tortured until she confesses her allegiance to Satan.' The name of God has been used to start more wars and torture more innocents and exploit more sufferers than any other fraud in history."

"Quite true, Selina," Sarah agreed.

Ben shook his head with a rueful smile. "It's bad enough I have to argue against the united sisterhood; now they're marching arm in arm in a fervent cause. God preserve us from evil."

Selina raised her fist in triumph and smiled at Sarah. "What was that slogan from the French Revolution? 'Humanity will not be free until the last king is strangled with the entrails of the last priest.' Tyranny is toppled, and Ben's proofs for the existence of God go down in ignominious and total defeat!"

"I didn't quite finish what I was saying," Sarah replied. "I'm afraid you will remove my banner from the barricade."

"What do you mean, Sarah?" Selina looked disappointed. "I thought you agreed that what I said was *true:* Claims about the will of God have been used to cause enormous suffering and exploitation."

"I did agree that it's true. It's true, but it's completely irrelevant. Look, Selina, people have long claimed that they have a cure for cancer, and if you come to our clinic or take this treatment or swallow these special pills—all for a special price, of course—you will be cured of cancer."

"Yeah, of course," agreed Selina, "those are some of the nastiest people on earth. How could you take advantage of people who are dying of cancer—even children dying of cancer—to steal money from desperate people? And the worst part is, often people who *could* be successfully treated wind up going to these charlatans and quacks, and then the cancer metastasizes and spreads, and by the time they seek legitimate medical treatment it's too late. So they lose not only their savings, but also their lives."

"So because there are lots of charlatans and frauds who falsely *claim* to have found a cure for cancer, does that mean that no cure for cancer is possible?" Sarah asked.

"No, of course not," Selina replied. "We have very effective treatments for many forms of cancer, and I'm confident that further research will reveal treatments for other cancers as well. In fact, I would love to be part of the research effort that finds treatments for cancers that are now untreatable."

"So just because there are many frauds who claim to have discovered a cure for cancer when they have not—that doesn't show that no cure for cancer is possible. And likewise, the fact that many people fraudulently claim to have special knowledge of God doesn't mean that no knowledge or proof of God's existence is possible. In both cases, the facts noted are *true:* There really are medical charlatans, and there really are religious frauds. But that's *irrelevant* to the question of whether we will ultimately find a cure for cancer, and it's *irrelevant* to the question of whether we will ultimately find a proof of the existence of God. It doesn't matter whether it's true or false, since it's irrelevant to the conclusion of the argument. Of course, there are many fraudulent and crooked and hypocritical 'priests' and 'prophets' who falsely claim to know God and speak for God. But that has no bearing on the *conclusion* of your argument: that no proofs for the existence of God are possible."

"Aha!" Ben was delighted. "Sarah dwells in the tents of righteousness, after all. Give it up, Selina; even your roommate is on my side."

"Not exactly, Ben," Sarah shook her head. "Okay, I agree that Selina's argument that there can be no proofs for the existence of God doesn't work: It commits the fallacy of irrelevant reason, or, as some people call it, the *red-herring* fallacy. But that doesn't mean that there *are* legitimate proofs for the existence of God. Selina's argument fails, but that doesn't prove that her conclusion is false; it only shows that her argument fails to establish her conclusion. In fact, if you claim that God exists, the burden of proof still rests on you, Ben."

"Alright, girl," Selina said, "I see your point. The reasons I gave were irrelevant. I guess it's not only the righteous who fall into error."

"Actually, Selina, anyone can fall into these argument errors. They're tricky devils. And anyone can fall *for* them, also: They often sound very convincing, and they can lead you off on the wrong track. That's why the fallacy of irrelevant reason is often called the red-herring fallacy. It got that name from the days of fox hunting in Great Britain. Imagine that you're going on a fox hunt in jolly old England. You're all dressed up in your red jacket and your boots, sitting on your beautiful horse, sipping your tea from fine English bone china, and getting ready to follow the hounds as they chase some unfortunate terrified fox across hill and heather."

"Not me," Selina replied. "That pale British aristocracy didn't encourage us folks of darker hue to sip tea out of fine china and ride on the hunts. I'd probably be holding the tea tray."

"Alright, imagine that His Excellency, Ben, the Duke of Somerset, is up on his horse, sipping his tea and getting ready for the hunt."

"Wrong again, Sarah," Ben said. "I come from good, hardy peasant stock."

Sarah placed her hand on her forehead. "You guys are just trying to make life difficult for a poor embattled philosophy major, aren't you? Alright, *some* people are going on a fox hunt; you two peasants don't get to ride, you're taking care of the dogs, okay? Anyway, the dogs chase the fox,

In 1986, the National Coalition Against Pornography ran advertisements arguing for a national ban on pornography and claiming that such a policy would not *be censorship. One of their arguments went like this (their italics):*

> The effort to eliminate hard-core pornography is *not* censorship. *It is enforcement of the laws passed by our elected officials and interpreted by our duly appointed Supreme Court justices.* That is the very essence of democracy in action! . . . So when judges and juries uphold those laws, it is not censorship. It is responsible democracy!

But that commits the fallacy of irrelevant reason. Democracy is a wonderful thing, but in this argument it is being used as a red herring. Even if antipornography laws were democratically passed, that would have nothing to do with whether they count as censorship. If United States citizens voted in overwhelming numbers to pass a constitutional amendment forbidding anyone from owning, reading, or distributing the Bible, that Bible-banning law would be an example of 'democracy in action,' but it would still be censorship. The fact that something is done democratically is irrelevant to the question of whether it is censorship.

and the horses chase the dogs, and everyone—with the exception of the fox and you peasants—has a great old time. But finally Lord and Lady Twinkletoes get tired of the chase, and they're ready to head back to the manor house for tea and cakes. But you peasants are stuck trying to round up the dogs, and the dogs are still chasing around after the fox, so they are very difficult to catch. So what do you do? Well, being clever and resourceful peasants, you take a bunch of these fish—these herring—that are very oily and have a strong odor. You cook the herring until they turn red and greasy, and then you put the cooked red herring into a cloth bag, and the bag gets all greasy, and it smells to high heaven from the red herring. And then you watch where the fox is going, and you drag the bag of red herring across the trail of the fox just before the dogs arrive. The smell of the red herring is so strong that the dogs quickly lose the scent of the fox they are trailing, so they sort of stand there, sniffing around, trying to find the trail of the fox. And while they're milling around, they're easy to catch, right? So that's why you drag red herring across the trail: It throws the dogs off the scent. And that's why the fallacy of irrelevant reason is often called the red-herring fallacy. The red-herring fallacy does the same thing: It brings up something that catches your interest—the sleazy fraudulent claims of the religious shysters—and you get focused on that, and it takes you off the trail of the argument, and because the new topic is interesting, you forget that it has no relevance to the actual conclusion. Not that it has no relevance at all, of course. It certainly is important, and very unfortunate, that these vile religious frauds use their religious claims to stir up wars and to exploit the gullible and steal money from the vulnerable. But it is *irrelevant* to the question at issue: It is irrelevant to the specific conclusion of the argument, and it is irrelevant to the issue of whether any proof for the existence of God is possible."

"I gotta go to class, guys." Ben finished his coffee and grabbed his book bag. "Besides, I've suffered enough straw-man abuse for one day and been misled by too many of Selina's red herrings. But this fight isn't over. Tomorrow, same time, we'll settle this debate over the existence of God once and for all—and Selina will see the error of her skeptical ways."

"You're going to convert Selina?" Sarah laughed. "That *would* be a miracle; that in itself would be solid proof for the existence of God!"

Ben waved. "Make sure you're here, Sarah. We'll need a referee. No kicking, no eye gouging, and no red herrings."

"And no false dilemmas, either," Selina shot back. "These defenders of the faith will stoop to any trick in their holy wars. You keep an eye on him, girl."

"I'll be here," Sarah replied. "But if I have to referee, you guys have to buy the coffee."

Study Questions

1. When are ad hominem arguments fallacious? When are they legitimate?
2. What is the fallacy of appeal to ignorance? Explain why it is fallacious.
3. What conditions must be met in order for an appeal to authority to be legitimate?
4. When is a dilemma argument a *false* dilemma?
5. What is a straw-man fallacy?
6. What is the fallacy of begging the question?
7. What's another name for the fallacy of irrelevant reason? How does that name fit the fallacy?

Exercises

The arguments that follow are examples of some of the argument forms discussed in this chapter. Some are fallacious, and some are *not* fallacious. Name the form of each argument, and tell whether it is fallacious or legitimate. The argument forms we discussed are as follows:

Appeal to ignorance, always a fallacy
Ad hominem, which is sometimes fallacious, but often legitimate
Appeal to authority, which may be either fallacious or legitimate
False dilemma, always a fallacy (though of course not all dilemmas are false:
 If a dilemma argument actually covers all the genuine possibilities, then
 it is legitimate and nonfallacious)
Begging the question, which is always fallacious
Straw man, always fallacious
Irrelevant reason, or red herring, which is always fallacious

A. Opponents of capital punishment sometimes claim that there is a danger that innocent people will be executed. But that is not really a danger. After all, our society is swamped with violent, vicious crimes, and we must have strong measures in response. Swift and severe punishment is essential to control crime and to properly express society's deep disgust with the most vicious and depraved criminal acts. So there is no real danger of executing the innocent.

B. A philosophy course should be required of all students at Home State University, because, obviously, every university student should have to take at least one course in philosophy.

C. Lisa claims that she saw Anita's boyfriend, Angelo, at a tavern on the west side of town. Lisa says that Angelo was sitting with his old high school girlfriend, in a back booth, and they were being *very* friendly. But frankly, I don't believe a word of what Lisa says. After all, she hates Angelo, and would do anything to break up Angelo and Anita; and besides, Lisa loves to spread rumors, and she's not always very careful about whether the rumors she spreads are actually true.

D. Members of the jury, this is not a difficult case. The defendant, Sandra Banks, shot and killed her husband. Now, either that shooting was an accident, or she is guilty of coldly calculating a first-degree murder. But certainly, it was not an accident: As she herself testified, she intended to shoot him. So it follows that she must be guilty of murder in the first degree.

E. Some folks complain that the United States has a larger percentage of its population in prison than any other Western country; well, that's true. But then they say that we ought to try to reduce the U.S. prison population—that the United States is imprisoning far too many people. But that's just nonsense: Apparently, these people think that murderers and bank robbers and rapists should be free to commit their crimes without any prison time. When people do the crime, they should do the time—and those people who think we should reduce the U.S. prison population haven't really thought enough about how terrible it would really be to turn these vicious criminals loose with little or no punishment.

F. Rachel argues that it is wrong for humans to eat animals for food, since eating meat is a luxury, and not a necessity, for humans, and such indulgence in luxury cannot justify the suffering imposed on the slaughtered animals. But Rachel is wearing leather shoes, a leather belt, and carrying a matching leather handbag—all luxuries, not necessities; and they are all made from slaughtered animals. So Rachel's arguments against eating meat are undermined by her own actions!

G. You keep saying that you don't want to vote guilty, because you still have doubts about whether the defendant is guilty. Okay, Mr. Reasonable Doubt, you say you aren't convinced that the defendant murdered James Finn. Well, I know one thing: James Finn was murdered, and someone murdered him. And there are no other suspects, and the defendant does not have an alibi. So unless you can give me some reason to think that the defendant really is not guilty, then I have to conclude that the defendant is guilty as charged.

H. It is sometimes claimed that persons in prison have a right to private phone calls with their family and friends. But prisoners do not have a right to private phone calls, because people who have been convicted of crimes and are serving time in prison have no rights whatsoever.

I. Senator Zane claims that he has strong and conclusive evidence that his opponent, Lewis Clark, accepted bribes while he was governor. Senator Zane says he can't reveal his evidence, because that would undermine ongoing investigations. But he assures us that he has solid evidence, and he says that he will make it all public as soon as possible. But I see no reason to believe Senator Zane. He is a politician who is trying desperately to defeat Clark in the senatorial election. So, given Senator Zane's strong motives for lying, or at least exaggerating the "evidence" he claims to have against Clark, no one should have any faith in his unsubstantiated claims. Besides, Senator Zane has played this sort of game before: During his first campaign for the Senate, he claimed to have conclusive evidence of serious lawbreaking and moral depravity by his opponent, but he couldn't reveal the evidence. After he won the election, he finally revealed his "conclusive evidence": It showed that his opponent had once been ticketed for driving ten miles over the speed limit and had once paid a small tax penalty for filing his state income tax returns three days late! So we should ignore Senator Zane's claims of "secret evidence" against Clark: Senator Zane should put up or shut up.

J. There are those who favor guaranteed universal health care for every U.S. citizen. But their position is impossible and absurd: They want everyone in the United States to have complete and unlimited access to every medical procedure they want: not just vaccinations and basic health care and needed surgeries, but anything anyone wants in the way of medical services. So if you want seven pairs of designer eyeglasses—one for each day of the week—then that would be completely paid for. If you felt a bit tired, you could go and spend a week or two in a fancy health spa—again, completely paid for by the government and guaranteed for everyone! And if you don't like the way your nose looks, you could have plastic surgery; and if you don't like your new nose, you could try another. How about a face-lift? You could have one every year— twice a year if you wish. But if you think medical costs are high now, just think of the incredible costs that would be involved in providing such services for everyone in the country. We are a wealthy nation, but no country could afford the medical costs of that kind of lavish and extravagant medical care. So the proposal of universal health care is obviously unworkable, impractical, and ridiculous.

K. Students are complaining that the tuition at East State University is too high: They claim that the university is being wasteful and that, by being more careful in its spending and economizing in some simple ways, the university could easily reduce tuition. But obviously, the tuition at East State University is *not* too high. For consider all the tremendous benefits students receive from attending East State: They gain knowledge of literature and art and music, they learn to write better and reason more effectively, and they gain knowledge and skills that will greatly increase their future earning power and more than pay back the cost of their tuition. Thus, when students consider it carefully, it should be clear that East State University tuition is not excessive.

L. Look, I know you are planning to have open heart bypass surgery to correct your heart problems. That's fine. But I heard your surgery is scheduled with Dr. Pangloss, and that's terrible. Dr. Pangloss has been suspended from practice by the Pennsylvania Board for botching several operations while under the influence of alcohol. That's why he moved here to Cleveland. And the Ohio board is currently reviewing his license, because of charges that he caused the death of a surgical patient through gross recklessness. And I know two people in Cleveland who sued Dr. Pangloss for malpractice, and they both received large settlements from his insurance company. And he has had his hospital privileges revoked by at least three area hospitals, reportedly for making his hospital rounds while intoxicated. And his driver's license has been permanently suspended for driving under the influence. So if you want a clumsy, reckless surgeon with a severe drinking problem cutting your heart, then stay with Dr. Pangloss. But I strongly recommend that you find another surgeon and stay as far away from Dr. Pangloss as you can.

M. Criminal acts by juveniles are a serious problem in our country. Children who are 12, 13, 14 years old—and often younger!—are committing assaults, robberies, and even murders. Either we must prosecute those juveniles as full adults and, when they are convicted, lock them up in maximum security prisons or even execute them, or we have to just ignore the problem of juvenile crime and do nothing at all to control violent crime by juvenile offenders. Since we obviously cannot ignore the problem of violent crimes committed by juveniles, it follows that we must start treating juvenile offenders just as we do adults.

N. There may be many opinions about music, but we can settle right now the question "What was the greatest piece of music ever written?" Yesterday I heard a lecture by Fyodor Smirnoff, the music director and conductor of the Moscow Symphony Orchestra. Smirnoff is not only a great conductor, but also a wonderful composer and an expert on musical history. In his lecture, Smirnoff asserted that Mozart's 23rd Symphony is the greatest single piece of music ever written. That should settle the issue once and for all: If Smirnoff says Mozart's 23rd Symphony is the greatest music ever written, then it must be the greatest.

O. The North State University Board of Trustees should be allowed to hold closed meetings when it wishes, because, obviously, the Board of Trustees should be able to meet confidentially when that is its preference.

P. Bruce Waller argues that every college student should be required to take a philosophy course. He says that it is useful for students to examine philosophical systems carefully and critically evaluate the arguments for those systems, no matter what their major: Whether mathematicians or English majors, engineers or historians, sociologists or chemists, they can all benefit from the careful reasoning processes required in philosophical discussion. And Bruce also says that all students should have some study of philosophy because all students are citizens in a democracy, and they must think carefully when they decide how to vote, when they serve on school boards or juries, and as they play their parts as effective, thoughtful, self-governing citizens participating in our democratic society. But you should keep one thing in mind as you listen to Bruce's argument: He wrote a philosophy textbook, and every time a new copy of that text is sold, Bruce picks up a buck or two. So it's not hard to guess why that greedy sleaze wants all students to take philosophy! And when you keep that in mind, it's hard to take seriously Bruce's argument for requiring students to take philosophy.

Q. The U.S. Congress recently passed legislation that allows people to be held in jail for long periods when they have not been convicted of crimes, allows the government to tap into phone lines and listen in on private conversations almost without restriction, and even suspends the basic right of trial by jury for some types of crimes. Some people say that these laws are an assault on our basic rights and that such policies threaten our liberties. But in fact, these policies do not threaten our basic rights and liberties, for these are desperate and dangerous times, and the threat of terrorism is very real. Indeed, we are now in a full *war* against terrorism. So these new policies obviously do not pose a threat to our basic rights and liberties.

R. Some smokers believe that smoking around their children—at home or in the car—and thus exposing them to "secondhand smoke" does not cause any harm to their children. But they are wrong: The National Institutes of Health, the American Cancer Society, the Mayo Clinic, the *Harvard Medical School Newsletter*, and the surgeon general of the United States have all issued clear statements confirming the serious and significant health hazards of second-hand smoke for children.

S. Some animal-rights advocates insist that it is wrong to inflict suffering on animals such as chimpanzees in order to conduct medical research that might provide benefits to humans. But the animal-rights position is obviously wrong, since it can never be wrong to cause the suffering or even death of an animal in order to provide medical benefits for humans.

T. William Bennett is the best-selling author of *The Book of Virtues*. Bennett constantly argues in favor of the traditional virtues, such as honesty, thrift, patriotism, traditional family roles, and self-reliance—the values that Bennett and other social conservatives call "family values." But now comes news that Bill Bennett is a high-stakes gambler, who has lost hundreds of thousands of dollars during gambling sprees at a number of Atlantic City casinos. Well, blowing hundreds of thousands of dollars in sleazy casinos is not exactly practicing thrift, nor is it a great way to spend quality time with your family. So nobody should be fooled by "Blackjack Bill Bennett" and his arguments for "family values."

U. This person is surely a true messenger from God, because he performs wonderful miracles. And clearly, the works he performs are genuine miracles and not cheap deceitful tricks; for no true messenger of God would stoop to using cheap tricks.

V. Naming sports teams Indians or Braves or Redskins cannot really be offensive and demeaning to anyone or any group. After all, spectator sports are good, wholesome family entertainment, sports teams are sources of great school and community pride, and sports teams often enhance the sense of community of the schools or cities that they represent.

Glossary

Ad hominem argument: "Ad hominem" literally means "to the person." An ad hominem argument is an argument that focuses on a person (or group of people), typically attacking the person—for example, "Joe is a liar," "Sandra is a hypocrite," "Republicans are coldhearted." Ad hominem arguments are *fallacious* only when they attack the source of an *argument* in order to discredit the argument—for example, "Joe's argument against drinking and driving doesn't carry much weight, because Joe himself is a lush." When *not* attacking the source of an *argument*, ad hominem arguments do *not* commit the ad hominem *fallacy* and can often be valuable and legitimate arguments. For example, an ad hominem attack on someone giving *testimony* ("Don't believe Sally's testimony; she's a notorious liar") is relevant and *not* an ad hominem fallacy; likewise, it is a legitimate use of ad hominem argument (*not* an ad hominem *fallacy*) if you are attacking a job applicant ("Don't hire Bruce; he's a crook"), a politician ("Don't vote for Sandra; she's in the pocket of the tobacco industry"), and in many other circumstances ("Don't go out with Bill; he's a cheat and a creep").

Appeal to authority: Any attempt to establish a claim by appealing to an expert or to someone who supposedly has special expertise. If the authority to whom the appeal is made is a genuine expert or authority in the *relevant area*, and if there is *consensus* among authorities, then appeal to authority is legitimate; otherwise it is fallacious.

Appeal to ignorance: A fallacious argument that attempts to shift the burden of proof from the person making a claim or assertion by asserting that the claim should be believed because no one has been able to prove it false.

Begging the question: Arguing in a circle—that is, the fallacy of assuming the conclusion as one of the reasons for itself.

Conclusion: What an argument aims at proving; the statement that is supposedly proved by the premises of an argument.

Fallacy: A standard argument error or deception; usually one that is so common that it has been given a special name.

False dilemma: A fallacious argument which claims that there are fewer alternatives than actually exist.

Fallacy of irrelevant reason: An argument which uses premises that have no bearing on the conclusion, but only distract from the real issue. Also known as the *red-herring* fallacy.

Premise: In an argument, a statement that supports or provides justification for the conclusion.

Straw-man fallacy: The fallacy of distorting, exaggerating, or misrepresenting an opponent's position or argument in order to make it easier to attack.

Valid argument: For deductive arguments, a valid argument is an argument in which, *if* all the premises are true, then the conclusion of the argument *must* be true. In a valid argument, it is impossible for all the premises to be true and the conclusion be false. But of course, not all valid arguments actually have true premises. For example, consider this argument: All penguins have six legs; Bill Clinton is a penguin; therefore, Bill Clinton has six legs. That rather ridiculous argument has false premises and a false conclusion, but it is still perfectly *valid*.

Additional Resources

Among the many excellent guides to critical thinking are S. Morris Engel, *With Good Reason*, 6th ed. (New York: St. Martin's, 2000); Theodore Schick, Jr., and Lewis Vaughn, *How to Think About Weird Things*, 3d ed. (Boston: McGraw-Hill, 2002); and Bruce N. Waller, *Critical Thinking: Consider the Verdict*, 5th ed. (Upper Saddle River, NJ: Prentice Hall, 2005).

On the web, EpistemeLinks.com has a particularly extensive and impressive set of links to many sites related to philosophy, and they are very conveniently arranged. *The Internet Encyclopedia of Philosophy* can be found at *www.utm.edu/research/iep/*; has excellent information on a wide range of topics in philosophy, including, of course, ethics, and it is easily searched. *The Stanford Encyclopedia of Philosophy* is well organized, and its articles are consistently high quality. Peter Suber's *Guide to Philosophy on the Internet*, at *www.earlham.edu/~peters/philinks.htm*, has a good search engine, as well as extensive links to information on specific philosophers (click on *philosophers*) and topics in philosophy (click on *topics*).

Some of the quotations in this book were found on the net in the collection of quotations at TPM Online's *The Philosopher's Magazine*. The site has many helpful resources in philosophy, papers and debates on a number of topics, and a wide variety of philosophical amusements. Go to *www.philosophers.co.uk*.

For critical thinking, there are a number of excellent websites. *The Reasoning Page* contains LSAT and MCAT sample tests and a number of good links. It can be found at *pegasus.cc.ucf.edu/~janzb/reasoning*. The Critical Thinking Across the Curriculum Project contains very good material, including a nice section of links to puzzles and games. Go to *www.kcmetro.cc.mo.us/ longview/ctac/toc.htm*.

Douglas Walton is an outstanding writer on critical thinking. He has made a collection of his papers available for downloading at *io.uwinnipeg.ca/~walton*. Go to the site and click on *papers*. The site also contains connections to other valuable sites: Click on *fallacies, evidence*, and *teaching aids*.

Tim van Gelder's *www.austhink.org* is a rich resource for all manner of material related to critical thinking and has excellent connections to other websites.

Chapter 2

Religion and Philosophy

in which three friends don't quite settle
the question of God

"Look, Selina, there has to be a God. Look around you! There are trees, hills, flowers. Go a few miles north, you'll find Lake Michigan. Look farther: You can see the sun. In a few hours, you'll be able to see the vast array of stars. And that's just a start: There are millions of stars you can't even see. In fact, there are millions of *galaxies*. So where did it all come from? You didn't make it. I certainly didn't. Maybe there are highly intelligent extraterrestrials out there, but even they couldn't make millions of galaxies. Besides, something would still have to make the intelligent extraterrestrials. And that something is God."

"Nice explanation, Ben. And how nice for you to have all the answers. That's what God is, right? An answer for everything. How do we explain the trees? God made them. What about the mountains? Well, God made them, too. And the stars. And all the galaxies. God explains it all. How convenient: instant, all-purpose explanation. You remind me of those people who get all excited when a plane crashes and one infant escapes death. 'It's a miracle! God works wonders!' But why did God let all those other people—including all those other infants—die? Well, that must have been God's will. Why bother trying to understand anything? God is the answer."

The Cosmological Argument

"Come on, Selina, you're not playing fair. I don't appeal to God to explain why one person survived when another died. I know some people do, but that's not me. But look, explaining why galaxies exist is hardly the same as explaining why one person survived a plane crash. The question I'm getting at is even bigger than the question about why galaxies exist. It's the

The spacious Firmament on high,
With all the blue Ethereal Sky,
And spangled Heavens, a shining Frame
Their great Original proclaim.
The Unweary'd Sun, from Day to Day,
Does his Creator's power display;
And publishes, to every Land,
The work of an Almighty Hand.

Soon as the evening shades prevail,
The Moon takes up the wondrous tale,
And nightly to the listning earth
Repeats the story of her birth:
Whilst all the Stars that round her burn,
And all the planets, in their turn,
Confirm the tidings as they rowl,
And spread the truth from pole to pole.

What though, in solemn silence, all
Move round the terrestrial ball?
What tho' nor real voice nor sound
Amid their radiant orbs be found?
In Reason's ear they all rejoice,
And utter forth a glorious voice,
For ever singing, as they shine,
"The hand that made us is divine."

Joseph Addison, 1711

question of why *anything* exists. Why is there something, rather than nothing? That's not a question you can answer scientifically. There *is* something, and it had to come into existence somehow. Astronomy studies how the big bang caused the galaxies to form, biology studies what causes species to evolve. But all those causal studies presuppose *something* that set the entire process in motion: a *First Cause*. I'm not talking about some deity that made the world in six days. I'm talking about the foundation of all existence. God, the *ultimate* source, clearly does exist."

"Look, Ben, that argument doesn't work. God doesn't work as an explanation of the details—why one survived when others died, how planets form, what causes bubonic plague. So what makes you think it would work as an explanation for the massive cosmic questions, like why is there something rather than nothing, or what is the *first* cause? I'm not sure those questions even make sense. You're using a concept of cause that makes sense empirically, but I doubt that it's meaningful when you take it *outside* the natural world. But even if the questions do make sense, then 'God caused it' is no answer. It's just a confession of our ignorance."

"Aw, Selina, take it easy on poor Ben. It's not his fault that he's ignorant; it's a common characteristic of members of his gender."

"Oh, Hi, Sarah. When did you get here?"

"Just in time to hear you berating old Ben for his ignorance. Pretty harsh, weren't you?"

"She's vicious, Sarah. Come slay this atheistic dragon, and save a friend in distress."

"Sarah, I'm not being harsh with Ben. I'm just trying to educate him about explanation. He thinks that just by saying 'God did it' you can explain anything. Help me straighten him out, would you?"

The Design Argument

With Sarah arriving, Ben decided to take another arrow from his quiver. "Look, God *does* work as an explanation. Not as an explanation for why one person survived a plane crash when everyone else died, but an explanation of much larger issues. Look at the world around us. We have a sun to warm our days and give us energy. A little closer, the earth is drawn into its gravitational pull and is destroyed. Much farther from the sun, and it becomes too cold for our survival. Now, I'm not giving some old-fashioned design argument: 'Look, I have hands, and eyes, aren't they wonderful, God must have designed them.' Darwin offers a simpler explanation, and the overall evidence for natural selection is overwhelming. Besides, God is a lot larger than some tinkering watchmaker who put together all the parts for lions and tigers and bears and beetles and paramecia and humans and oysters. But look at the larger picture: The world *is* a wonderful place, and

---

Ben is offering an updated version of the design *argument, made famous by the English philosopher William Paley (1743–1805): "Suppose I had found a* watch *upon the ground. . . . When we come to inspect the watch, we perceive . . . that its several parts are framed and put together for a purpose, e.g., that they are so formed and adjusted as to produce motion, and that motion so regulated as to point out the hour of the day. . . . This mechanism being observed . . . the inference we think is inevitable, that the watch must have had a maker . . . who completely comprehended its construction and designed its use." This argument is sometimes called the* teleological *argument for the existence of God, since it endeavors to prove the existence of God on the basis of God's purposive acts in designing a world. Telos, from which the argument takes its name, is a Greek term for goal or purpose.*

Tell me honestly, I challenge you—answer me: imagine that you are charged with building the edifice of human destiny, the ultimate aim of which is to bring people happiness, to give them peace and contentment at last, but that in order to achieve this it is essential and unavoidable to torture just one little speck of creation, that same little child beating her chest with her little fists, and imagine that this edifice, has to be erected on her unexpiated tears. Would you agree to be the architect under those conditions? Tell me honestly!

Fyodor Dostoyevsky, *The Brothers Karamazov*, trans. Ignat Avsey (Oxford University Press: Oxford, 1994), i, part 2, bk. 5, ch. 4. First published in 1879–80

it's well suited for our survival. I can't believe that all of that happened just by chance. Okay, we evolved in this world, and so naturally it suits us. But still, there had to be a world in which our evolution would be successful; and Darwinian evolution can't explain *that*. Sometimes, of course, we have to struggle: It gets too cold or too hot, there are bugs and vipers that kill us, and there are blights that destroy our crops, and floods and tornadoes and hurricanes and earthquakes that ravage our homes and our lands. But God didn't design this to be a world of indolent leisure, devoid of challenges; rather, it is a world of challenges, a world that tests us, a world that requires our best efforts. But it's also a world in which our efforts are generally rewarded, in which improvement is possible, and in which virtue can be exercised; a world where there is suffering, but also opportunities to relieve and overcome suffering; a world where wars occur, but also where peacemakers can succeed; a world of hunger, but also a world in which the hungry can be fed. In sum, it seems a wonderful world, designed by a loving God, Who did not want us to be complacent and incompetent and lazy, but instead wanted us to exercise and develop our talents and capacities, and, above all, to grow in virtue and goodness. This world gives us plenty of opportunities for that sort of exercise, and for such exercise to meet with sufficient success to keep us motivated."

I had no intention to write atheistically. But I own that I cannot see as plainly as others do, and as I should wish to do, evidence of design and beneficence on all sides of us. There seems to me too much misery in the world. I cannot persuade myself that a beneficent and omnipotent God would have designedly created the Ichneumonidae with the express intention of their feeding within the living bodies of caterpillars, or that a cat should play with mice.

Charles Darwin, *Letters*

Selina patted Ben's hand and raised her coffee cup in a toast. "To Ben, who at least does not reject natural selection! If you based your argument on rejecting Darwin, I'm afraid we would just have to drink our coffee at separate tables. Your argument is certainly better than the old 'watchmaker' argument; but I still can't buy it. Think about it: If you just looked around the world objectively, would you conclude that it was designed by an omnipotent God Who is perfectly benevolent? Look at the suffering around the world: the Holocaust, the Palestinians suffering under occupation, the recurrent episodes of starvation in Africa, the misery of the Native Americans who were forced out of their homelands, the purges of Stalin. I suppose that in each case there were opportunities for heroism as well as for compassion, but at what a terrible price! Couldn't an omnipotent and benevolent God have come up with opportunities for compassion and heroism that didn't involve quite so much brutality? Besides, for every person who became more virtuous, there were at least as many who became more vicious: the cowardly collaborators with the Nazis, the greedy land speculators who profited from the misery of the Native Americans, the prison guards and executioners who became callous and brutal as they carried out the policies of Hitler and Stalin. And think of the millions of infants and children who have died, and died horribly. Or think of war and famine and genetic diseases. And don't say, 'Well, but some people learned compassion.' Maybe. But do you call that good design? Causing millions of children terrible suffering in order to improve the virtue of a few? And even if there were some whose virtue was enhanced, I would be willing to wager that there were at least as many who became worse. Looking at it objectively, with no preconceptions, would you conclude that this world was designed by an omnipotent and benevolent God to maximize virtue? Or that this world is the *best possible* world an omnipotent Designer could have contrived?"

Selina sipped her coffee and continued. "David Hume long ago made a powerful case against any form of the design argument for the existence of God: If you examine our world—with all its misery and imperfections—and try to judge what sort of God might have fashioned it, you would never conclude that it was made by an all-powerful and all-benevolent deity. Instead, you would probably conclude—*if* you assumed it *had* to be made by some sort of god—that it was the work of an apprentice god, as a first flawed attempt. Or a doddering old god, who had lost his touch when it comes to creating good worlds. Or a malevolent god, who took delight in human suffering and tribulations. But there is nothing here to suggest that the creator was the omniscient, omnipotent, benevolent God of the Judeo–Christian–Islamic tradition."

Ben threw up his hands and turned to Sarah. "You see what I mean, Sarah? Selina's hopeless. I don't know which is worse: when she argues for atheism or when she suggests that God might be a pathetic old foolish

God, having a last shot at creating a world before He dies. I'm surprised that this entire coffee shop hasn't been consumed by the fire of God's righteous wrath. Selina is mired in atheistic dogma and refuses to even consider the existence of God."

"You're absolutely wrong, Ben. I have indeed considered the existence of God. Considered it and rejected it. I see no reason whatsoever to believe that God exists."

Intuitive Knowledge of God

"No reason at all?" Ben shook his head. "Maybe you're considering the wrong sorts of reasons, Selina."

"So give me some good reasons; I'll gladly consider them. But make them good reasons: Just because you find some ancient scroll written by a bunch of savage desert nomads that proclaims the existence of God, don't expect me to turn into a believer. Belief in God may be an ancient belief, but so is belief in ghosts and belief in evil spirits causing disease and belief that the earth is stationary and the sun revolves around the earth. Their ancient origins don't increase their credibility."

> *I myself believe that the evidence for God lies primarily in inner personal experiences.*
>
> William James, *Pragmatism*, Lecture 3 (1907)

"No, Selina, I'm not appealing to ancient texts," Ben answered. "Those are written to guide believers, not to convince nonbelievers. If you're really a dedicated skeptic, I'm not sure there is any 'proof' of the existence of God that could convince you. But maybe you should consider the direction you're looking. Don't look for proof out there; look for proof in here. Don't you sometimes have a sense, a feeling, maybe an intuitive idea, that there is something greater or deeper than the mundane world of cities and trees and mountains, deeper even than the world of atoms and galaxies and black holes and quasars. Not something we see clearly, not even something we can really argue for or prove scientifically; but something greater, nonetheless. Are sensory observation and reason our only sources of knowledge?"

Selina rolled her eyes and gave an exasperated sigh. "No, you're right, of course: We also know things by consulting the oracles, reading tea leaves, using our psychic powers, and probing our deep feelings that pass all understanding. Oh, and let's throw in divine revelation and profound intuitions while we're at it. And don't forget astrology; that's always a great source of wisdom, as well. Come on, Ben. Once you start counting our 'profound feelings' or 'deep intuitions' as sources of knowledge, where do you draw the line? Not long ago there were some people who just intuitively *knew* that all people of my race were inherently inferior and best suited for slavery. There are *still* people who 'just know' that it's not right for people of my gender to have equal rights and equal opportunities. And there are lots of people who 'intuitively know' that Bill is evil and unnatural because he's gay. Intuitions of a warm fuzzy divine presence—maybe that's not so bad if you really need it. The problem is, once you start counting warm fuzzy feelings as real sources of knowledge, you open the door to all sorts of feelings—racist, sexist, intolerant, bigoted, and homophobic, to name just a few—that are vicious and hateful. So, yes, now that you mention it, observation and reason *are* the ways that we know things. If you want to talk about *knowledge*, then you're talking about what can be confirmed scientifically or logically. I'm sorry if that shuts the door on warm fuzzy feelings of a caring divine presence, but that's the only way I can keep out a lot of feelings that are not at all warm and fuzzy."

"But Selina," Ben objected, "you don't really mean that science and reason are the only ways of knowing things. They're very important, certainly. But Pascal, the brilliant mathematician, perhaps said it best: 'The heart has its reasons that the reason knows not of.' Look, you believe that sexism is wrong. I agree. But do you have scientific proof that sexism is wrong? After all, sociologists report that it is very widespread, and some biologists have even indicated that it might have survival value. I don't count that as scientific proof that sexism is *right*; but I can't imagine what *scientific* proof you could offer that sexism is morally wrong."

"Let's not stray over into morality," Selina protested. "I'm not sure we really have moral knowledge, but that's a topic for another day. I thought we were talking about God. Other than the fact that most of the Gods I've heard about seemed to have very little objection to sexism—in fact, some deities seem to think rather highly of it, at least according to the self-appointed spokespersons for those gods—other than that, I can't see what all this talk about morality has to do with the existence of God."

"There are two ways it's related," Sarah responded. "First, some people use moral knowledge as a proof for the existence of God: There *are* objective moral truths; the only grounds for genuine objective moral truths is God's will; therefore, God must exist as the source of objective morality. But that argument is based on two very controversial premises: One, the claim that there *are* objective moral truths; and two, the claim that moral objectivity requires divine sanction. Leaving aside that argument, there's a second way the discussion of morality could be relevant: *If* you think that there could be moral truths that are not known scientifically, that would open the possibility of knowing truths by nonscientific methods—and among such nonscientific knowledge might be our knowledge of God."

Ben's claim that true faith and reason cannot be in conflict, since God is the source of both, is an echo of the view expressed by St. Thomas Aquinas: "Now, the knowledge of the principles [of reason] that are known to us naturally has been implanted in us by God; for God is the Author of our nature. These principles, therefore, are also contained by the divine Wisdom. Hence, whatever is opposed to them is opposed to the divine Wisdom, and, therefore, cannot come from God. That which we hold by faith as divinely revealed, therefore, cannot be contrary to our natural knowledge."

St. Thomas Aquinas (1225–1274), *On the Truth of the Catholic Faith, Book One: God* (translated by Anton C. Pegis)

"Exactly, Sarah," Ben agreed. "Our basic knowledge of God is too personal to be proved scientifically. It's deeper, more personal. God speaks to us quietly, but quite clearly if we are willing to listen. God then enhances our understanding through special revelations revealed in testimonies and texts. And those we test against our immediate awareness of God, as well as by the use of reason. After all, God gives us our faith as well as our reason, so true faith and true reasoning cannot be in conflict. Still, our best knowledge of God is very personal, very immediate. Not like the knowledge we have of math or science, but still knowledge."

"Special, intimate feelings." Selina shook her head. "Look, dearest, I'm all for special, intimate feelings. But they don't seem to me to reveal evidence of God. Frankly, I just can't imagine how a feeling could provide reason to believe in the existence of some omnipotent deity—or, indeed, of any divinity whatsoever."

"Not everything depends on reasons, Selina." Ben responded. "Look, I know that my mother loves me. How do I know? Well, maybe I could sit down and reason it out: She sends cookies, she listens when I need a shoulder to cry on, she nursed me through chicken pox and measles and high school broken hearts. But reason is *not* how I know that my mother loves me: I just know! Maybe I could find reasons to prove that God exists. But I don't need reasons: I just *know!* Reason is helpful in many ways, certainly; but reason isn't everything, and not everything we know is known by reason."

The Problem of Evil

Selina hesitates, sips her coffee. "If you *know* that God exists, well, okay. Perhaps I'm just not lucky enough to be graced with a special revelation. Or maybe God did reveal himself—himself, herself, itself? I've always been a bit uncomfortable assigning a gender to God—did reveal himself to me, but I was too stupid or stubborn or blind to recognize it. But the analogy with your mother—that's not very convincing. Your Mom loves you; that's certainly true. But you don't know that from some special power of intuition or mystical insight; you know it by her actions over the last two decades: She tucked you in bed and read you stories, even when she was tired from a long day's work; she got up early to cook your favorite breakfast; she was always happy when things went well for you, and she shared your sadness over broken romances and flunked algebra tests and unsuccessful basketball tryouts. When you were sick, she stayed up all night to cool your fevered brow with a damp cloth, and she rushed you to the best doctor she could find, and she spared no expense or effort to get the medicines you needed. Of course, she didn't always let you do everything you wanted: You couldn't eat all your Halloween candy in one night, because she knew it would make you sick; she didn't let you go to Ft. Lauderdale for spring break when you were 14, because she thought it would be too dangerous for you. She wouldn't let you play kickball in the street when you were 7, because she was afraid you would be injured by a car. She didn't buy you a bright new sports car for your 18th birthday, because she just didn't have the resources. In all those cases, you might have been upset, but you could see that your mother was doing the very best she could to keep you safe and healthy and happy. It all fits with the belief that your mother loves you."

Selina frowned, then continued. "But with God, it's a very different story. When you were sick, your Mom did everything in her power to ease your suffering and make you well. But where was God? Did He fail to notice? No, he's omniscient. Did He do the best He could, but He just couldn't help? No, He's omnipotent. Was He indifferent to your suffering? No, He's supposed to be a loving God. Something doesn't add up. And the equation gets more out of whack the further we look. Where was God when millions died from starvation, from plague, from war? Where was God when Hitler murdered millions of Jews and Gypsies and homosexuals and persons with disabilities, and anyone else he judged unfit? Some might say it was God's punishment. We suffer an AIDS epidemic; well, must be God's judgment on those who engage in promiscuous sex. That seems like an awfully ugly image of God to me: You have a romantic fling with a wildly attractive stranger during summer vacation, and wham— God punishes you with a deadly debilitating virus. But it gets worse: What about the people who developed AIDS through blood transfusions? The faithful wife who is infected by her cheating husband? The innocent infant whose HIV infection was passed on from her infected mother? God seems pretty careless about whom He punishes. Did thousands of Jewish children deserve the punishment of such brutal deaths? Did thousands of African babies deserve to be punished through death by starvation? So we have to conclude that God failed to notice and so is not omniscient; or

God noticed, but couldn't help, and so is not omnipotent; or God noticed and could have helped, but did not, so God is *not* a loving God. Or maybe that's the way God shows His love to us: with famine, war, and pestilence. But that's like calling an abusive parent's cruelties a type of loving affection—and that makes nonsense of the whole notion of love. Your mother loves you: That's a reasonable and well-supported and meaningful statement. God loves you: That's either false or nonsense."

God Is Beyond Understanding

"Look, Selina, you're still trying to understand everything rationally," Ben objected. "But God's ways are not our ways, and God's purposes are beyond our puny understanding. God has an answer for the questions you raise." Ben extracted a small Bible from his backpack and quickly found a favorite passage. "It's the same answer He gave to Job when Job wondered why God had allowed such miseries to be inflicted upon him: 'Then the Lord answered Job out of the whirlwind, and said, "Who is this that darkeneth counsel by words without knowledge? Gird up now thy loins like a man; for I will demand of thee, and answer thou me. Where wast thou when I laid the foundations of the earth? Declare, if thou hast understanding."' So where were you, Selina, when God laid the foundations of the earth and scattered the stars in space? What makes you suppose that you could possibly understand God's ways, much less have the right to question God?"

"Okay, it's a mystery," Selina answered. "But of course, if you allow mystery, then you can 'explain' anything. It doesn't strike me as a very satisfactory 'explanation.'"

"I'm not trying to explain. God's ways are beyond explanation. Just like my knowing that God exists and that God loves me. It can't be explained rationally or empirically, but I know it just the same."

"Yeah, and you know that God loved all those children who died in agony. So why did He let them die? It's a mystery; don't ask; we can't understand. Well, I understand this much: An appeal to mystery doesn't explain away the contradiction between a loving, omnipotent, omniscient God and the massive suffering that we see all around us. And appeals to God's punishment make God look a lot more like an *abusive* father than a loving father."

Concepts of God

Ben's cheeks were becoming flushed. Questioning the existence of God, that's one thing. Comparing God to an abusive father: Selina was going way too far. Sarah quickly perceived that a pleasant philosophical discussion over coffee was rapidly escalating toward a hostile confrontation that might end with coffee cups being deployed as weapons. She placed a hand on the shoulder of each and tried to pour a bit of oil on the troubled waters. "Wait a minute, guys, this whole discussion is based on a faulty premise. You're both discussing a God who sits out there making judgments and granting favors. But suppose you think of God somewhat differently: not as some father figure sitting on a golden throne, nor as a divine lawgiver, nor as a deity Who is your ally in your wars against your heathen enemies. I mean, really, if your notion of God is a sort of omniscient Santa Claus Who *really* knows if you've been bad or good—or even worse, some divine Super Weapon Who takes delight in slaughtering various peoples, depending on which side He happens to favor—then don't you think your notion of God needs to grow up? God as a divine comic book superhero, with special powers to bring rain if He likes your prayers, or nudge a basketball through a hoop if you find favor in His sight, or slaughter your enemies if He happens to be on your side. That's a pretty pathetic concept of God, isn't it? The notion of a God out there who intervenes miraculously when we recite the right formulas or perform the right rituals; some distant Deity Who rewards us when we're good (at least in the afterlife) and punishes us for our wrongs; Who heals the sick—at least sometimes, maybe when a saint intervenes with a special request or when some television evangelist in a tailored suit gets the right payoff—and at other times ignores suffering."

Selina was glad to have Sarah's intervention. Ben was special, and she hadn't meant to upset him. No wonder they made Socrates drink the hemlock. Come on, Selina, be nice. You can have a philosophical discussion without laying waste to the belief system of your lover. Got to be a little more careful in challenging people's cherished beliefs. "Alright, Sarah, I'll bite. Enlighten me about God."

"Delighted to do so, Selina. Sarah dispenses wisdom the way Joe dispenses cappuccino. You and Ben were talking about God being omniscient and omnipotent—and a few other qualities, but I don't want to stir up that hornet's nest

Sarah is here developing an idea favored by Benedict Spinoza: that if God is infinite, there can be nothing other than God; everything is in God, everything is One. Spinoza states this in Proposition 14 of his Ethics: *"Besides God no substance can be granted or conceived." And Spinoza's proof is this: "As God is a being absolutely infinite, of whom no attribute that expresses the essence of substance can be denied, and He necessarily exists; if any substance besides God were granted, it would have to be explained by some attribute of God, and thus two substances with the same attribute would exist, which is absurd; therefore, besides God no substance can be granted, or, consequently, be conceived."*

(Trans. R. H. M. Elwes)

again. But you forgot one of the other "omni" qualities: God is *omnipresent.* Right? Now what does that mean? If God is *omni*present, then God is present *everywhere.* Not just as an observer—that's covered under omniscience. To be *omni*present, God must be present everywhere, always, in all things. So we can't say, 'Well, God goes this far, but there's the boundary.' That would make God very large, maybe *mega*present, but not *omni*present. There is no place in this galaxy or any other galaxy, no space whatsoever that is outside God. There can't be *many* gods, because that would mean there are gods outside of God, and God would not be *omni*present. God would have limits and boundaries. There is no god, no galaxy, no thing, nobody outside of God: God is omnipresent—present everywhere and in everything."

Ben wanted to know where this was leading. "So enough with the 'omni' stuff, Sarah. What's your point?"

"Well, if God is everywhere, it makes no sense to think of God being *out there*, looking over His creation. In fact, it makes no sense to think of God *creating* something apart from God. And God couldn't *intervene* in the world—nor fail to intervene, for that matter."

Ben was skeptical. "But if everything is God, then nothing is God."

"Works for me," Selina responded.

"Yeah, it would, wouldn't it," Ben agreed. "That doesn't explain God, Sarah; it explains God right out of existence. Your view is just a backdoor route to atheism."

"No, it's not the same at all. Just because God isn't sitting out there somewhere on His throne doesn't mean that God doesn't exist. After all, this isn't some weird notion of God, Ben. It follows directly from a characteristic you yourself attribute to God: God is *omnipresent.*"

"Look, Sarah, I prefer your idea of God to Selina's. But it's still a bit mystifying. If God is omnipresent in the way you suggest, then you, me, this table, this cup of cappuccino, and all the moons of Jupiter are part of God."

"Exactly right. So what's your problem?"

"Well, my problem, Sarah, is that I'm not a table. I've got legs, but not the legs of the table. And I'm not a moon. And I'm not a galaxy. When I move, the world doesn't move. I'll drink the cappuccino, and it will be in me—at least temporarily—but *I* am not the cappuccino."

"No one said you were a cup of cappuccino, Ben, though I confess, the idea has its charms: If you were a cup of cappuccino, we could order you to go and then put a lid on you. You, Selina, the cup of cappuccino, and the moons of Jupiter are all part of one great whole: all part of the One, since there is only the One. An elephant's trunk and elephant's ears are all part of one elephant; that doesn't transform the trunk into an ear."

Ben was struggling. "Sarah, I still can't quite grasp this notion of the One. And in particular, I can't see how it gets you any closer to belief in God. Suppose I agreed with you, that somehow everything was part of a larger whole. I still don't see why we should consider that larger whole to be God. Okay, everything is connected in some wondrous manner. Why suppose that everything together counts as God? The One is everything there is. Okay, cool. I look around, I see Selina, the table, the Sun, the cup of cappuccino: Don't any of 'em look like God to me. No offense intended, but none of you look like *part* of God, either."

"Ah, Ben, you still want to find something that you can label as God. Somebody sitting on a celestial throne, or someone walking on water, or a huge moving finger writing cryptic messages on a wall. A God you can set apart, place on a map, fit in a clear, distinct category. But you already acknowledged the inadequacy of that concept of God: It lacks omnipresence. Not to mention the fact that it runs into the problem Selina so vigorously asserts: the problem of evil, the problem of how to reconcile vast suffering with the existence of an all-powerful and benevolent God. God isn't merely the One—though it sounds a little funny to speak of the entire Cosmos as *merely* anything. Everything is changing, moving, evolving. But it's not like Darwinian evolution, evolution through natural selection, that simply responds to environmental pressures and adapts in whatever way promotes survival—survival, not progress. This view of God includes a process of slow, but steady, progress toward a better end state, a wiser end. Not unbroken progress: there are some backward steps. And in cosmic time, a backward step might last a century or two. Still, there is long, slow, overall progress. It is like Darwinian evolution in one respect: It's very slow and very lengthy."

"Why doesn't God speed it up?"

"There you go again, Ben, putting God outside the world, outside the process. God doesn't *control* the process; it would be closer to say that God *is* the process. But don't start thinking of the process as *separate* from the One."

Ben found this troubling. "But look, Sarah, if God is part of the process, or is the process, or is the One going through the process, or whatever, then you can't speak of this evolving into a higher or better or wiser state. After all, God is perfect, and thus God changeth not. If God changed and *became* perfect, that would imply that God is not *now* perfect. And if God were perfect, then God could not change, for any change would be a change to imperfection."

Sarah raised her eyebrows. "I can hardly believe what I'm hearing, Ben. You, a devoted worshipper of the Judeo-Christian God, telling me that God can't change? Your God changes His mind more often than my first roommate changed boyfriends. One day He creates humankind, puts them in the Garden of Eden. Then He changes His mind and kicks them out of the Garden of

Eden. (Okay, I know, Adam and Eve ate the apple—that was the reason for the change; but your God is omniscient, right? So He had to know that they would eat the apple. He's still changing His mind.) Then he gets disgusted with humankind, sorry He ever made us, and resolves to kill us all. And He changes His mind and saves a few, lets them start over. And then He decides to kill all the children of Israel, but He talks with Moses and changes His mind and only kills a fifth of them. And you're telling me that God can't change?"

"Alright, forget about the change problems. But I don't see how you avoid Selina's problem of evil. If everything is constantly changing for the better, how come there is so much bad in the world, so much suffering?"

"I know what she's going to say," Selina interjected. "It's all an illusion. There's no real suffering. On this point, Ben, I'm closer to your view than to Selina's: There certainly is real suffering in the world. Don't try to tell the people who've lost their jobs, the folks who can't afford health care for their children, the people dying of AIDS in Africa and from violence in the Middle East. Don't tell them it's all an illusion. I haven't suffered like they have, but I've had some suffering in my life, and don't try to tell me it's an illusion. If it's all a dream, it's a painful dream; and a painful dream is still genuinely painful."

Sarah shook her head. "It's kind of you to speak for me, Selina, and describe the view I hold. If you would just get it right, you would save me a lot of trouble. But in fact, that's not my view at all. Of course, there is suffering—real suffering, terrible suffering, ages of suffering. I wouldn't try to answer the problem of suffering—the problem of evil— by denying that there is real suffering or real evil. They exist, and they are all too real. But that's a problem only if you think of God as some stand-apart omnipotent Deity Who controls everything. That's not what God is, at least not on my view. The evolution to a higher, better world is a long, slow, grinding process. It follows its own pace, and we can't speed it up."

"You mean there's nothing we can do about it? We don't have any influence over what happens?" Selina did not like the sound of this.

"Of course, you have influence—of course, there are things that you can do and things you can change," Sarah answered. "But that's not separate from the process: It's part of the process; *you* are part of the process. As you become wiser, wisdom increases. Your acts of kindness and generosity, your struggles against cruelty and suffering—all are vital elements of the long process toward a more enlightened state."

"But why must it be so slow?" Patience was not Selina's strongest virtue.

"Because the acquisition of wisdom just is a slow process. Information may be gained swiftly, and the pace at which it is acquired may be hastened, but wisdom comes slowly."

Selina remained skeptical. "It all sounds rather lovely. We are all part of a great whole, and we all make our contributions to a steady and inevitable progress toward enlightenment. Okay, but how do you know any of this is true? By revelation? Intuition? The testimony of someone who had the revelation directly? That takes us right back to where we started."

The Benefits of Belief in God

"No, not through revelation or intuition," Sarah said. "More by observation."

"You mean your observation that the world is getting constantly better?" Selina was not impressed. "Sorry, you and I seem to be looking at different worlds. The one I see seems to be going to hell in a handcart, as my grandmother used to say. In any case, I see scant evidence of this steady improvement you anticipate. Seems as reliable as a politician's promise."

Sarah had a ready answer, though she suspected not one that would satisfy either Selina or Ben. "No, not by observation of a constant stream of improvements in the world. I told you, it's a slow process. I no more expect to look around and see improvements than I expect to look around and observe the evolution of a new species. Both take much too long. The best evidence is found in how this view changes the people who embrace it. Not that it transforms them into saints, certainly. But it does enable them to live with more confidence, greater patience, stronger resolve. In short, the view works. That's the best proof you could have of its truth. Try it and see."

"Thanks for the invitation, but I must decline." Selina was unconvinced. "I like to have proof *before* I believe something, not as a promissory note. Besides, believing something doesn't make it true, even if the belief makes you very happy. For example, it would make me happy to believe that there were no nuclear weapons in the world. But even if I could manage such a belief, and lived a more confident and contented life because of holding that belief, it would still be a *false* belief. Whatever it might be that makes a belief true, it's *not* whether the belief makes us *happy.*"

"You're oversimplifying, Selina." Sarah was undaunted. "Sure, it would be great if there were no nuclear weapons; probably all of us wish we could make that genie go back in the bottle. But if you tried to believe that there were no nuclear weapons, your belief would soon cause all sorts of problems. For a start, you would have problems every time you studied the history of World War II. Believing that I'm wealthy would be quite pleasant, but that belief would cause major problems when I tried to write a check to pay for my new sports car. Those beliefs just won't work. But believing that ultimately everything will move in the right direction—that belief doesn't cause such problems; to the contrary, it helps me live more confidently and hopefully, and avoid depression and despair. In my book, that's a belief that *works.*"

"Yeah, it works, just as it works to hide your eyes when there's a gruesome scene at the movies. You think happy thoughts, and the chain-saw murderer goes away in the next scene." Selina was unconvinced. "But that doesn't work when you step outside the fantasy world. Thinking happy thoughts won't get it done. There really is a lot of sorrow and brutality and pain in the world, and the only way to change that is to recognize it as a cold, hard, sad fact and then try to change it. 'Don't worry, it will all work out in the end.' That's not the way to fix what's wrong and make things better."

"Of course, it's not; but I never suggested that it was," Sarah replied. "You have to work at things to change them and make them better. But if you have confidence that your efforts will succeed, that the problems can be solved, then you will work with more energy and confidence and success."

"Okay, God gives me hope for the future, but not because that hope is useful, but because God exists. You're turning everything on it's head." Ben was attacking from the other quarter. "I have confidence *because* God exists. That's very different from believing that God exists because that belief gives me confidence. Besides, I can't buy this idea of 'choosing' to believe. Look, I believe in God. But it's not because I chose to believe in God. It's like people who condemn homosexuality as a 'sexual preference.' Choice has nothing to do with it. I didn't wake up one morning when I was 13 and say, 'Oh, I think I would like to be a heterosexual.' I discovered a powerful sexual attraction for girls—fact is, I don't think I thought about anything else until I was about 17—and that was that. Same thing with believing in God: Maybe some day I'll lose my faith, and maybe someday Selina will come to believe in God (though I wouldn't want to bet on it). But neither of us will *choose* to believe or not to believe. I choose what shirt to wear in the morning, and I choose whether to go to the football game or take a nap or study at the library. But I don't choose what I believe. Even if I could, I don't think I would find it a very satisfying sort of faith. 'I believe in God because it's useful, because it makes me feel good'—that statement of faith hardly inspires devotion, does it?"

Pascal's Wager

Selina was laughing. "You've performed a miracle, Sarah: You've found something that old Ben and I agree on. It's like Pascal's wager argument: Believe, because you've got more to gain by believing. A tyrant might terrorize his subjects into submission with such threats and rewards, but it seems an awfully sad way to promote devotion to a God Who is supposed to be just and loving."

"Hey, you guys are ganging up on me, no fair. And you're distorting and misrepresenting what I said: Double unfair. And you're not being totally fair to Pascal, Selina. Okay, he did devise the wager argument for belief in God: You get better odds by believing, so believe."

"The wager argument? What's that? Betting on belief?" Ben found this a disturbing notion. "Maybe your Oneness God would approve, but not the God I worship."

"Okay, guys, to be perfectly honest, Pascal's wager never struck me either as a very strong argument for belief in God. It goes like this, Ben: What are the possibilities? Either you believe in God or you don't. This is one of those situations where you have to choose: By not deciding whether to believe, you effectively choose not to believe. So what are the possibilities if you believe? Well, maybe you believe wrongly, and no God exists. But that's not so bad: You still live in hope and try to live a good, positive life; and when you die, you become nothing. Suppose you believe, and you're right. Well, then you hit the jackpot: eternal bliss with God's angels, right? Now consider the other possibility, that you don't believe: Okay, it turns out you're right. Big deal. You still die, and that's the end of it. But what if you're wrong? Then you get eternal damnation, and that's a rather nasty prospect. So add it up, Pascal says: Belief has all the advantages. If you believe, the worst that can happen is that you were wrong, and you pass into nothingness anyway; and the best that can happen is eternal bliss. But if you *reject* belief, then the *best* that can happen is nothingness, and the worst that can happen is eternal damnation, which is very bad, indeed. So which way should you wager, belief or disbelief? It doesn't take much of a statistician to see that the odds are much better on the belief side."

Blaise Pascal (1623–1662), a French physicist, philosopher, and theologian, was also a superb mathematician and statistician. His famous Pensées *is a collection of his thoughts, not systematically organized. For example, he says, "What kind of a chimera then is man? What novelty, what monster, what chaos, what subject of contradiction, what prodigy? Judge of all things, imbecile worm of the earth, depository of truth, sink of uncertainty and error, glory and scum of the world."*

"I believe because the odds are better . . ." Selina shook her head. "Not very inspiring. Maybe we could write a hymn about it. "Amazing odds, how sweet the spread, that saved a sport like me."

Sarah laughed. "As I said, I'm not crazy about it. In the first place, given my own conception of God, it doesn't make sense to think of God handing out rewards and punishments. But even on traditional Judeo–Christian–Islamic conceptions of God, the argument seems a bit

Rabi'a was an Islamic teacher in the Sufi tradition. She once rushed through the marketplace with a torch in one hand and a jug of water in the other. When asked why she was carrying a torch and a jug of water, she answered that she was going to burn Paradise and put out the fires of Hell, so that people would do good acts from love of doing good and love of kindness and love of God, and not from hope of reward or fear of punishment.

Faith is not a question of the existence or non-existence of God. It is believing that love without reward is valuable.

Emmanuel Levinas
(1905–1995)

dicey. Who knows, maybe God is vehemently opposed to gambling and reserves His harshest punishments for those who believe on the basis of the best odds. But even Pascal didn't suppose you could just *choose* to believe because it seemed the safest course. Instead, he recommended that you associate with believers, attend services, act as the believers act—and, gradually, belief will come. That part of his view seems plausible to me. *Try* believing, try living with the strong hope that things will ultimately turn out for the good, and you'll see that it works well for you and enables you to live better. And a belief that helps you live better—that seems to me the best measure of a good belief. And it doesn't *have* to be belief in the traditional creator–harsh-judge God of the Judeo–Christian–Islamic tradition: You might try belief in God as a sense of Oneness, of ultimate unity and ultimate goodness."

"Frankly, Sarah, your concept of God is warm and fuzzy," Selina said, "but I haven't cared much for warm and fuzzy since I was six years old and stopped sleeping with Bartholomew Bear, my childhood stuffy. Warm and fuzzy is fine for childhood comforts, but for adult beliefs, I prefer cold and calculating. And not calculating the way Pascal does it: That strikes me as cowardly. Stand on your own two feet, think clearly about things, and try to see the world as it is, rather than as how you might like it to be. Religious fantasies offer comfort; but the comfort comes at too high a price: They distort your view of the world and get in the way of real changes that would actually improve things. Forget about a better afterlife, and focus on improving this life: There are lots of improvements to be made, and God won't do it for us. We have to do it ourselves."

God and Science

Ben was bothered, as he often was when Selina spoke of the benefits of life without God. "Sarah, I'm not much impressed by Pascal's argument myself. But I do think belief in God is important—and belief in a personal God, not this Oneness God you spoke of. Is there any way to reconcile it with the world of science? Selina always thinks I'm antiscience. I'm not. I want both: God *and* science. Is that possible?"

"No way, Ben." Selina was uncompromising. "They are completely different systems of explanation, and they can't fit together. Christians say God designed the world; scientists say it developed through natural selection and natural laws, and Divine purpose is not required. Once you have scientific explanations, you no longer have need of the God hypothesis. In fact, you no longer have room for it."

"Maybe not, Selina." Sarah was still seeking a reconciliation between Ben and Selina, no matter how improbable it looked. "Maybe they belong to different spheres, serving different purposes. You seem to think that the only possible notion of God is a 'God of the gaps': a God that fills in the gaps in our scientific knowledge—or better, *hides* in those gaps; and as the gaps get smaller, God gets squeezed tighter and tighter. Once God was the Ruler of everything—kept the stars on their course, guided the comets, moved the oceans, shaped each species. But as we learned more about the natural forces that controlled the planets and comets and evolutionary processes, there was less for God to do, and less reason for God to exist."

"Exactly, Sarah." Selina liked this story so far. "When science gives us real explanations and real answers, we don't need gods and miracles to fill in the gaps and cover our ignorance."

"But maybe that's the wrong concept of God, Selina," Sarah continued. "Appealing to God to explain what science can better explain is bad science, certainly; but it's bad theology also. God is not a competing scientific hypothesis: It's not as if we have to choose between God and Newton. The Bible isn't an alternative biology textbook that offers its own scientific hypotheses about the origins of life—no matter what creationists and fundamentalists may suppose. If you treat it like that, it's ridiculous. I mean, you not only have to reject Darwin's natural selection, you also have to reject the Copernican theory and suppose that the Earth is the center of the universe and the Sun revolves around the

Selina's view is shared by psychologist B. F. Skinner:

> Krutch has argued that whereas the traditional view supports Hamlet's exclamation, "How like a god!," Pavlov, the behavioral scientist, emphasized "How like a dog!" But that was a step forward. A god is the archetypal pattern of an explanatory fiction, of a miracle-working mind, of the metaphysical. Man is much more than a dog, but like a dog he is within range of a scientific analysis.
>
> B. F. Skinner, *Beyond Freedom and Dignity*, p. 201

To invoke God as a blanket explanation of the unexplained is to make God the friend of ignorance. If God is to be found, it must surely be through what we discover about the world, not what we fail to discover.

Paul Davies, physicist; quoted in Chet Raymo, *Skeptics and True Believers*

Earth. That's literally what the biblical account teaches. Joshua and his armies were fighting against the Amorites, and the Amorites were utterly defeated, partially because God pounded the Amorites with huge hailstones that killed most of them. Anyway, the Amorites were in full retreat, and darkness was falling, and Joshua was afraid some of them would get away; and of course, Joshua had been ordered by God to slay absolutely all his enemies: soldiers, old men, women, and children. So"— Sarah paused for a moment, reached over for Ben's Bible, and turned swiftly through the pages—"rather than let a few escape into the darkness, God ordered the Sun to stand still." Sarah ran her finger down a page, then smiled in triumph. "Here it is: '[T]he sun stood still, and the moon stayed, until the people had avenged themselves upon their enemies. . . . So the sun stood still in the midst of heaven, and hasted not to go down about a whole day." Notice it does *not* say the Earth stopped turning; rather, the Sun stopped in its motion around the Earth. So if you treat it literally, you not only get lousy biology, but an obsolete astronomy as well. Not to mention a view that seems to me much more profoundly mistaken: a view of God encouraging war and ordering mass slaughter."

"That's what I keep telling Ben," agreed Selina.

"What's all this, Sarah? You've joined forces with Selina. I thought you were going to be a peacemaker."

"Patience, Ben. Keeping the peace between you and Selina is no small challenge. But I'm not attacking your view—or Selina's view, either. I think there's common ground."

"How can there be common ground, Sarah? I'm a scientist; and as you just noted, the biblical account is simply wrong: It won't pass either scientific or logical muster."

Though I have asserted . . . that in truth a legitimate conflict between religion and science cannot exist I must nevertheless qualify this assertion . . . on an essential point, with reference to the actual content of historical religions. This qualification has to do with the concept of God. During the youthful period of mankind's spiritual evolution human fantasy created gods in man's own image, who, by the operations of their will were supposed to determine, or at any rate to influence the phenomenal world. Man sought to alter the disposition of these gods in his own favor by means of magic and prayer. The idea of God in the religions taught at present is a sublimation of that old conception of the gods. Its anthropomorphic character is shown, for instance, by the fact that men appeal to the Divine Being in prayers and plead for the fulfillment of their wishes.

Albert Einstein, "Science and Religion," 1941 (in *Out of My Later Years*)

If the provinces of faith and reason are not kept distinct by these boundaries, there will, in matters of religion, be no room for reason at all; and those extravagant opinions and ceremonies that are to be found in the several religions of the world will not deserve to be blamed. For, to this crying up of faith, in opposition to reason, we may, I think, in good measure ascribe those absurdities that fill almost all the religions which possess and divide mankind. For men, having been principled with an opinion that they must not consult reason in the things of religion, however apparently contradictory to common sense and the very principles of all their knowledge, have let loose their fancies and natural superstition; and have been by them let into so strange opinions, and extravagant practices in religion, that a considerate man cannot but stand amazed at their follies, and judge them so far from being acceptable to the great and wise God, that he cannot avoid thinking them ridiculous, and offensive to a sober good man. So that in effect religion, which should most distinguish us from beasts, and ought peculiarly to elevate us, as rational creatures, above brutes, is that wherein men often appear most irrational and more senseless than beasts themselves.

John Locke (1632–1704), *Essay Concerning Human Understanding* (1690), Book IV, Chapter 18

"But Selina, maybe you should think of it differently," Sarah responded. "It's not a biology text, it's not an alternative scientific hypothesis. That misses the whole point. It's a *myth*. But not a myth like the tooth fairy or the Loch Ness monster. It's a myth in the sense of being a story that is not literally true, but that nonetheless expresses a deep truth or a profound idea."

"What kind of truth are you talking about, Sarah?" Selina was still skeptical.

"Okay, think about the Genesis account of human creation. God creates a world, divides night from day, hangs the stars in space, separates the oceans from the continents, creates the fishes of the sea and the fowls of the air and all that creepeth upon the land, and then He creates man: shapes him out of clay, breathes life into him—finally takes a rib from him and fashions a woman. Now, obviously, that can't literally be true, not even on good Christian and Jewish and Muslim principle. After all, God is supposed to be perfect, right? So a perfect God can't be tinkering around with creating a world. That would imply that God is somehow incomplete without such a creation—that God needs something to do, or is bored, or lonely, or insufficient in Himself. But a perfect God could not have any inadequacies. Besides, if an omnipotent God decided to create a world, it wouldn't take Him six days, and He wouldn't need a day of rest following his labors. But think about what the story *means*. It is a world created for human use. Of course, you can take that to mean that humans have dominion over the world to exploit and destroy it as they wish. But that's a shallow reading. Taking it at a deeper level, it means that the world is *suited* to us. And it means that the world is special, a divine creation that God saw as good; and we should appreciate its beauties and delights, and not trash it. Of course the rose has thorns, but it also has beautiful petals, and we should enjoy them."

"Well, of course we shouldn't trash the world. It's the only one we have. And we hardly need some great myth to understand why we are well suited for this world: We evolved in it, we adapted to it." Selina was not convinced of the joy of myth. "The world wasn't made to suit us; rather, we survived because we were a good fit to our environment. With apologies to A. E. Housman, I would say that 'Darwin does more than Genesis can, to justify God's ways to man.' If you want to understand why we are suited for this environment, study biology, not myth."

"Yes, of course," Sarah agreed. "Biology does answer that question better. But that's exactly my point. That's *not* the purpose of the Genesis story: It's not a competing account with Darwinian biology. The story of Genesis helps us to *appreciate* the world; biology helps us to *understand* it. I'm not saying that there is no beauty or deep meaning in science; many scientists find great meaning and delight and satisfaction in the scientific understanding of the world. But that doesn't rule out also gaining the enjoyment of a mythic appreciation of the world as well. Look, Selina, I know you love painting. Think of Monet's paintings of water lilies. Those are not the paintings that a botanist might make for a scientific classification; but neither are they in *conflict* with what the botanist might draw. Rather, they serve different functions. Here's another one: What does Ben whisper in your ear when he's nibbling on your earlobes? 'Your skin is like a deep brown river, lighted with torches, mysterious in its depths, wondrous in its shadows.' I know, I've heard him. I have to go suck on a lemon for half an hour every time I hear that boy talk."

Selina smiled at Ben, took one of his fingers in her hand, and lightly kissed it. "Hey, Sarah, that's personal!" Ben blushed slightly.

"Sorry, guys, but look, here's my point. Ben's descriptions aren't exactly the descriptions you would get in an anatomy textbook. Still, they have their own special worth. It's a different category from scientific investigation, right?"

Ben was eager to change the subject. "Sarah, let's get back to Genesis, okay? This is starting to sound more like the Song of Solomon."

"Okay, Ben. Actually, there's a second deep truth in the Genesis story, and I think it's very special. In fact, it's the deep truth you yourself mentioned yesterday. We are all one family, we all have the same mother and father. Black or white, gay or straight, rich or poor, woman or man, we are all part of one family. That's the really important truth told by the story. And if you try to take it literally, you miss that important truth. That's why you see all these people who insist that the Bible is God's word, that the Bible is perfect truth; and they get obsessed with the literal truth of the Bible and miss the deeper truth. Some of them are deeply prejudiced against other races or ethnic groups: They despise gays, discriminate against women, are indifferent to the suffering of the poor; but they insist that they believe the Bible, they follow the Bible. If you try to read it literally, it ties you in logical knots; and even worse, you miss the real truths that it expresses. We are all one family. That's a lot more important than whether God literally created every species of beetle. And it's not in conflict with science. In fact, the more science studies it, the more scientists recognize how closely related all humans are and how insignificant racial differences are. That's an important scientific truth. But if you want to celebrate and affirm that truth—that we are all one wonderful family—then religious myth is an excellent way of doing that."

"Look, Sarah, I agree with you, Sister, you know that. I'm an African-American atheist from Alabama, you're a Jewish kid from Long Island, and Ben's a good Christian boy from the Michigan heartland. But we're all just one big happy family. And maybe that creation myth you celebrate affirms that, and that's fine. But there's myths and then there's myths, right? You remember that course in ancient philosophy you were taking last semester? You were telling me about some of the myths that Plato liked. Wasn't there one that promoted the belief that some folks were natural rulers and others were natural slaves? And that's not just ancient history: There are people today—go online and you can find them—they promote a myth that all folks who are my skin color are 'mud people,' and we're inferior and ought to be killed or herded into ghettoes or banished from the country. And your folks know something about that as well, right? Lots of myths some people like to celebrate about the evil Jews, and how they have secret plans to rule the world, and they have to be stopped. For every myth that gives me a warm fuzzy feeling, there seem to be two or three that terrify me. What's the saying? Anyone can be bad, but to be really evil, you need religion. If everyone had Sarah's warm heart and generous spirit and celebrated *her* myths, well, that would be fine. But I'm not comfortable leaving it to whatever myths happen to catch people's fancy, 'cause some of the myths they fancy are vicious. We are one family, and there's not enough genetic difference, much less 'racial purity,' to really separate us. But the best way of knowing and affirming that is through solid scientific evidence, not through mythic hopes."

"Yeah, Sarah, I don't think it quite works for me, either," said Ben. "Don't get me wrong. I love to celebrate the stories and ideas of my religion, and I don't think of Genesis as a biology textbook. It teaches us about *God*, not about single-celled or multicelled organisms and not about astronomy or physics. Still, those stories and principles are worth celebrating not just because they feel good, but because they are *true*. Not true as biology or astronomy textbooks, but as sacred God-given truths. Otherwise they're a pious fraud, whether they make us feel good or not. So I still don't see how you can square Selina's views with mine. I think those basic principles—God loves us and cares about us, and God wants us to love one another—are true; Selina thinks they are false, because she doesn't believe in God. That seems to me a basic conflict."

"Okay, maybe you guys are right, maybe there is a conflict," Sarah said. "But on the other hand, maybe the conflict is not as deep as it looks. Selina, scientists have learned that if we continue to cut down rain forests, we will cause mass extinctions of species. So, should we stop destroying rain forests?"

"Of course we should," Selina agreed. "It's a terrible waste. We cut down rain forests in South and Central America so we can use the land to raise more beef animals—or build more huge, heavy mahogany dressers and dining room tables—and that impoverishes the people who were living in the forests and destroys many species we will never replace and never even know existed. And the result is a lot of hamburgers that cause high cholesterol and obesity and shorten life. Certainly, we should stop it. It's no benefit to anyone, except maybe a few major investors in multinational corporations."

"Is that a scientific conclusion you're drawing, Selina? After all, obviously, *some* people enjoy eating greasy cheeseburgers, and *some* people like to eat them on mahogany tables. Is it a scientific fact that we morally *should* stop cutting down rain forests?"

"Okay, maybe science can't really lay down moral principles that you should follow; but science can give you the facts for the application of moral principles."

"Exactly so. And that leaves an important role for religion, right?"

"What, you think we get our ethical principles from what God commands? No way, Sarah. Even if there were a God, I don't see why His ethical commandments would carry any special weight. What's the great commandment that God gave to Father Abraham, Father of your whole tribe, great righteous man, right, Sarah? Go and kill your beloved son Isaac as a sacrifice—that was God's command. When Abraham actually takes up the knife, and Isaac is lying there in terror of being killed by his father, then God says no, it was just a test. In some ways, that seems worse than actually demanding the killing. And go back to that story you were telling about God making the Sun stand still, so that Joshua can slay all his enemies. That story is right in the middle of page after page of detailed descriptions of Joshua and his armies—under orders from God—conquering the cities of all these people whose only crime was that they happened to be living in the land God had decided to give to His chosen people. And what does God order that they do with the cities they conquer, time after time, city after city?" It was Selina's turn to reach for the Bible. She quickly found the passage she wanted and stabbed it with her finger as she read: "'And they utterly destroyed all that was in the city, both man and woman, young and old, and ox, and sheep, and ass, with the edge of the sword.' Thanks, but I'll seek ethical principles elsewhere."

"But Selina, you're back to that notion of God sitting on a throne and issuing orders. If you think of God more as the unity of all that exists and the hope of a better future, wouldn't that be a better perspective for thinking about ethics and values? Then there would be important roles for both science *and* religion, and they wouldn't conflict."

Selina shook her head. "Sarah, I'm not sure where we get our ethical principles. Frankly, I'm not sure that any objective ethical principles exist, at least not in the way objective scientific principles exist. But in any case, I'm not ready to isolate science and agree that, when it comes to values and ethics, we have to take off our lab coats and take up our beads and incense—or our deep spiritual meditations, or profound myths, or whatever you do in your religion."

Ben was also in opposition. "I can't live with that 'compromise' either, Selina. What are you saying? Religion is the realm of values, and science is the realm of facts. Certainly, I would agree that religion deals with values; but religion also deals with its share of facts. Maybe not the facts of science, but no less facts for all that."

"Well, guys, blessed are the peacemakers. But I fear I am not among that blessed number. I tried my best to find common ground for you. I'm not sure there's any to be found. But maybe there is some hope if you would both just enlarge your ideas: Selina, if you could recognize that there is a larger force that binds all these things together into one; and if Ben would realize that his conception of God is too narrow and needs to be larger and all inclusive. Then you guys could meet in the middle. As it stands, I guess I get to keep all the enlightenment for myself. And on that note of serenity, I must leave you. My philosophy-of-mind seminar starts in three minutes, and Professor Stein insists on punctuality: Obviously, he has not come to the full understanding that all time and place are one. Maybe I'll go enlighten him."

READINGS

David Hume (1711–1776) was born in Edinburgh and attended Edinburgh University. He became a leading figure of the Enlightenment. His earliest writings were largely ignored. He published A Treatise of Human Nature *anonymously in 1739 and expected it to be greeted with furious criticism; instead, to his great disappointment, by his own description, it "fell deadborn from the press." Hume then wrote a more popular version under the title* An Enquiry Concerning Human Understanding *that was warmly received. Hume was delighted by the literary fame he won, both for his philosophical work and for his writings on English history and politics. A popular and greatly respected figure during his years in Paris (part of that time he held positions with the British ambassador in Paris), he had many friends (including the American ambassador to Paris, Benjamin Franklin) and was welcome at the most fashionable parties. Though Hume was rather careful in his published writings to avoid offending religious sensibilities—after attacking any rational grounds for religious belief, he often inserted suggestions that the matter is beyond reason and must be accepted by faith—he was nonetheless widely regarded as an enemy of Christianity and was known to the Scottish clergy as "the great infidel." In contrast, Hume's close friend and fellow Scot, the economist Adam Smith, said of Hume, "Upon the whole, I have always considered him, both in his lifetime and since his death, as approaching as nearly to the idea of a perfectly wise and virtuous man as perhaps the nature of human frailty will permit." The selection that follows is taken from* Dialogues Concerning Natural Religion, *which was published after Hume's death. (A good source for those wishing to read the entire work is the edition edited by Richard H. Popkin, published by Hackett Publishing Company, Indianapolis, 1980.) In the selection, Cleanthes is presenting the design argument, while Philo—in response—draws out problematic implications of that argument.*

Dialogues Concerning Natural Religion

Cleanthes: Not to lose any time in circumlocutions, said *Cleanthes*, I shall briefly explain how I conceive this matter. Look round the world: Contemplate the whole and every part of it: You will find it to be nothing but one great machine, subdivided into an infinite number of lesser machines, which again admit of subdivisions to a degree beyond what human senses and faculties can trace and explain. All these various machines, and even their most minute parts, are adjusted to each other with an accuracy which ravishes into admiration all men who have ever contemplated them. The curious adapting of means to ends, throughout all nature, resembles exactly, though it much exceeds, the productions of human contrivance; of human design, thought, wisdom, and intelligence. Since therefore the effects resemble each other, we are led to infer, by all the rules of analogy, that the causes also resemble, and that the Author of Nature is somewhat similar to the mind of man, though possessed of much larger faculties, proportioned to the grandeur of the work which he has executed. By this argument *a posteriori*, and by this argument alone, do we prove at once the existence of a Deity and his similarity to human mind and intelligence.

• • •

Philo: But to show you still more inconveniences in your anthropomorphism, please to take a new survey of your principles. *Like effects prove like causes.* This is the experimental argument; and this, you say too, is the sole theological argument. Now it is certain that the liker the effects are which are seen and the liker the causes which are inferred, the stronger is the argument. Every departure on either side diminishes the probability and renders the experiment less conclusive. You cannot doubt of the principle; neither ought you to reject its consequences.

All the new discoveries in astronomy which prove the immense grandeur and magnificence of the works of nature are so many additional arguments for a Deity, according to the true system of theism; but, according to your hypothesis of experimental theism, they become so many objections, by removing the effect still farther from all resemblance to the effects of human art and contrivance. For if *Lucretius*, even following the old system of the world, could exclaim:

Who is strong enough to rule the sum, who to hold in hand and control the mighty bridle of the unfathomable deep? who to turn about all the heavens at one time, and warm the fruitful worlds with ethereal fires, or to be present in all places and at all times.[1]

If Tully[2] esteemed this reasoning so natural as to put it into the mouth of his Epicurean:

What power of mental vision enabled your master Plato to descry the vast and elaborate architectural process which, as he makes out, the deity adopted in building the structure of the universe? What method of engineering was employed? What tools and levers and derricks? What agents carried out so vast an understanding? And how were air, fire, water, and earth enabled to obey and execute the will of the architect?[3]

---

[1][*On the Nature of Things*, II, 1096–1099 (trans. by W. D. Rouse).]

[2][Tully was a common name for the Roman Lawyer and philosopher, Marcus Tullius Cicero, 106–43 B.C.]

[3][Cicero, *The Nature of the Gods*, I, viii, 19 (trans. by H. Rackham).]

If this argument, I say, had any force in former ages, how much greater must it have at present when the bounds of nature are so infinitely enlarged and such a magnificent scene is opened to us? It is still more unreasonable to form our idea of so unlimited a cause from our experience of the narrow productions of human design and invention.

The discoveries by microscopes, as they open a new universe in miniature, are still objections, according to you; arguments, according to me. The farther we push our researches of this kind, we are still led to infer the universal cause of all to be vastly different from mankind, or from any object of human experience and observation.

And what say you to the discoveries in anatomy, chemistry, botany? . . . **Cleanthes:** These surely are no objections, replies *Cleanthes;* they only discover new instances of art and contrivance. It is still the image of mind reflected on us from innumerable objects. **Philo:** Add a mind *like the human,* said *Philo.* **Cleanthes:** I know of no other, replied *Cleanthes.* **Philo:** And the liker, the better, insisted *Philo.* **Cleanthes:** To be sure, said *Cleanthes.*

Philo: Now, *Cleanthes,* said *Philo,* with an air of alacrity and triumph, mark the consequences. *First,* by this method of reasoning you renounce all claim to infinity in any of the attributes of the Deity. For, as the cause ought only to be proportioned to the effect, and the effect, so far as it falls under our cognizance, is not infinite: What pretensions have we, upon your suppositions, to ascribe that attribute to the Divine Being? You will still insist that, by removing him so much from all similarity to human creatures, we give in to the most arbitrary hypothesis, and at the same time weaken all proofs of his existence.

Secondly, you have no reason, on your theory, for ascribing perfection to the Deity, even in his finite capacity; or for supposing him free from every error, mistake, or incoherence, in his undertakings. There are many inexplicable difficulties in the works of Nature which, if we allow a perfect author to be proved *a priori,* are easily solved, and become only seeming difficulties from the narrow capacity of man, who cannot trace infinite relations. But according to your method of reasoning, these difficulties become all real; and, perhaps, will be insisted on as new instances of likeness to human art and contrivance. At least, you must acknowledge that it is impossible for us to tell, from our limited views, whether this system contains any great faults or deserves any considerable praise if compared to other possible and even real systems. Could a peasant, if the *Aeneid* were read to him, pronounce that poem to be absolutely faultless, or even assign to it its proper rank among the productions of human wit, he who had never seen any other production?

But were this world ever so perfect a production, it must still remain uncertain whether all the excellences of the work can justly be ascribed to the workman. If we survey a ship, what an exalted idea must we form of the ingenuity of the carpenter who framed so complicated, useful, and beautiful a machine? And what surprise must we feel when we find him a stupid mechanic who imitated others, and copied an art which, through a long succession of ages, after multiplied trials, mistakes, corrections, deliberations, and controversies, had been gradually improving? Many worlds might have been botched and bungled, throughout an eternity, ere this system was struck out; much labor lost; many fruitless trials made; and a slow but continued improvement carried on during infinite ages in the art of world-making. In such subjects, who can determine where the truth, nay, who can conjecture where the probability lies, amidst a great number of hypotheses which may be proposed, and a still greater which may be imagined?

And what shadow of an argument, continued Philo, can you produce from your hypothesis to prove the unity of the Deity? A great number of men join in building a house or ship, in rearing a city, in framing a commonwealth; why may not several deities combine in contriving and framing a world? This is only so much greater similarity to human affairs. By sharing the work among several, we may so much further limit the attributes of each, and get rid of that extensive power and knowledge which must be supposed in one deity, and which, according to you, can only serve to weaken the proof of his existence. And if such foolish, such vicious creatures as man can yet often unite in framing and executing one plan, how much more those deities or demons, whom we may suppose several degrees more prefect?

To multiply courses without necessity is indeed contrary to true philosophy, but this principle applies not to the present case. Were one deity antecedently proved by your theory who were possessed of every attribute requisite to the production of the universe, it would be needless, I own (though not absurd), to suppose any other deity existent. But while it is still a question whether all these attributes are united in one subject or dispersed among several independent beings; by what phenomena in nature can we pretend to decide the controversy? Where we see a body raised in a scale, we are sure that there is in the opposite scale, however concealed from sight, some counterpoising weight equal to it; but it is still allowed to doubt whether that weight be an aggregate of several distinct bodies or one uniform united mass. And if the weight requisite very much exceeds anything which we have ever seen conjoined in any single body, the former supposition becomes still more probable and natural. An intelligent being of such vast power and capacity as is necessary to produce the universe, or, to speak in the language of ancient philosophy, so prodigious an animal, exceeds all analogy and even comprehension.

But further, *Cleanthes*, men are mortal, and renew their species by generation; and this is common to all living creatures. The two great sexes of male and female, says *Milton*, animate the world. Why must this circumstance, so universal, so essential, be excluded from those numerous and limited deities? Behold, then, the theogeny of ancient times brought back upon us.

And why not become a perfect anthropomorphite? Why not assert the deity or deities to be corporeal, and to have eyes, a nose, mouth, ears, etc.? *Epicurus* maintained that no man had ever seen reason but in a human figure; therefore, the gods must have a human figure. And this argument, which is deservedly so much ridiculed by *Cicero*, becomes, according to you, solid and philosophical.

In a word, *Cleanthes*, a man who follows your hypothesis is able, perhaps, to assert or conjecture that the universe sometime arose from something like design: But beyond that position he cannot ascertain one single circumstance, and is left afterwards to fix every point of his theology by the utmost license of fancy and hypothesis. This world, for aught he knows, is very faulty and imperfect, compared to a superior standard; and was only the first rude essay of some infant deity who afterwards abandoned it, ashamed of his lame performance: It is the work only of some dependent, inferior deity, and is the object of derision to his superiors: It is the production of old age and dotage in some superannuated deity; and ever since his death has run on at adventures, from the first impulse and active force which it received from him. . . . You justly give signs of horror, *Demea*, at these strange suppositions; but these, and a thousand more of the same kind, are *Cleanthes'* suppositions, not mine. From the moment the attributes of the Deity are supposed finite, all these have place. And I cannot, for my part, think that so wild and unsettled a system of theology is, in any respect, preferable to none at all.

Cleanthes: These suppositions I absolutely disown, cried *Cleanthes:* They strike me, however, with no horror, especially when proposed in that rambling way in which they drop from you. On the contrary, they give me pleasure when I see that, by the utmost indulgence of your imagination, you never get rid of the hypothesis of design in the universe, but are obliged at every turn to have recourse to it. To this concession I adhere steadily; and this I regard as a sufficient foundation for religion.

Demea: It must be a slight fabric, indeed, said *Demea*, which can be erected on so tottering a foundation. While we are uncertain whether there is one deity or many, whether the deity or deities, to whom we owe our existence, be perfect or imperfect, subordinate or supreme, dead or alive; what trust or confidence can we repose in them? What devotion or worship address to them? What veneration or obedience pay them? To all the purposes of life the theory of religion becomes altogether useless; and even with regard to speculative consequences its uncertainty, according to you, must render it totally precarious and unsatisfactory.

Walter Terence Stace was born in 1886. He worked in the British Civil Service for twenty-two years. At the age of 46, he retired from the British Civil Service and joined the philosophy department at Princeton University. Stace published on many topics, including politics, epistemology, ethics, and Greek philosophy. The passage that follows is excerpted from Chapter 8 of Time and Eternity *(Princeton, NJ: Princeton University Press, 1952). In it, Stace argues that it is a mistake to attempt arguments either for or against religious belief, since religion belongs to a realm quite different from the realm of reason and science.*

Time and Eternity

The pure religious consciousness lies in a region which is forever beyond all proof or disproof.

This is a necessary consequence of the "utterly other" character of God from the world, and of the "utterly other" character of the world from God. The eternal order is not the natural order, and the natural order is not the eternal order. The two orders intersect, but in the intersection each remains what it is. Each is wholly self-contained. Therefore it is impossible to pass, by any logical inference, from one to the other. This at once precludes as impossible any talk either of the proof or disproof of religion.

When philosophers and theologians speak of "proofs of the existence of God," or "evidences of Christianity," what they have in mind is always a logical passage from the natural order, or some fact in the natural order, to the divine order. They may, for instance, argue in the following way. Here is the world. That is a natural fact. It must have had a cause. Other natural facts are then pointed out which are supposed to show adaptations of means to end in nature. Bees pollinate flowers. Surely not by chance, nor following any purpose of their own. Or the heart has the function—which is interpreted as meaning the purpose—of pumping the blood. This teleological mechanism was not made by us, and the purpose evident in it is not our purpose. Therefore the cause of the world must have been an intelligent and designing mind. Doubtless I have much over-simplified the argument, and this version of it might not be accepted by the theologian as a statement of it which is to his liking. Certainly it is not a full statement. That, however, is not the point. The point is that, however the argument is stated, it necessarily starts from the natural order, or from selected facts in the natural order, and ends with a conclusion about the divine reality.

In other cases the natural fact from which the argument starts may be some very astonishing occurrence, which we do not yet know how to explain, and which we therefore call a miracle. This is evidence, it is believed, of a divine intervention.

In all cases we use some fact or facts of the natural order as premises for our argument, and then leap, by an apparently logical inference, clear out of the natural order into the divine order, which thus appears as the conclusion of the argument. The point is that the premise is in the natural world, the conclusion in the divine world.

But an examination of the nature of inference shows that this is an impossible procedure. For inference proceeds always along the thread of some relation. We start with one fact, which is observed. This bears some relation to another fact, which is not observed. We pass along this relation to the second fact. The first fact is our premise, the second fact our conclusion. The relation, in the case of the deductive inference, is that of logical entailment. In non-deductive inferences other relations are used, of which the most common is that of causality. Thus, although the sun is now shining, and the sky is cloudless, I see that the ground is wet, and the trees are dripping with water. I infer that an April shower has passed over, and that it rained a few minutes ago. My inference has passed along the thread of a causal relation from an effect as premise to a cause as conclusion. To pass in this way from facts which are before my eyes, along a relational link, to other facts which are not before my eyes—which are inferred, not seen—is the universal character of inference.

But the natural order is the totality of all things which stand to each other in the one systematic network of relationships which is the universe. Therefore no inference can ever carry me from anything in the natural order to anything outside it. If I start from a natural fact, my inferential process, however long, can end only in another natural fact. A "first cause," simply by virtue of being a cause, would be a fact in the natural order. It is not denied that it might conceivably be possible to argue back from the present state of the world to an intelligent cause of some of its present characteristics—although I do not believe that any such argument is in fact valid. The point is that an intelligent cause of the material world, reached by any such inference, would be only another natural being, a part of the natural order. The point is that such a first cause *would not be God*. It would be at the most a demi-urge. I shall return to this point later.

If God does not lie at the end of any telescope, neither does He lie at the end of any syllogism. I can never, starting from the natural order, prove the divine order. The proof of the divine order must lie, somehow, within itself. It must be its own witness. For it, like the natural order, is complete in itself, self-contained.

But if, for these reasons, God can never be proved by arguments which take natural facts for their premises, for the very same reason He can never be disproved by such arguments. For instance, He cannot be disproved by pointing to the evil and pain in the world.

But if, by arguments of the kind we are considering, the divine order can never be proved, nevertheless God is not without witness. Nor is His being any the less a certainty. But the argument for anything within the divine order must start from within the divine order. The divine order, however, is not far off. It is not beyond the stars. It is within us—as also within all other things. God exists in the eternal moment which is in every man, either self-consciously present and fully revealed, or buried, more or less deeply, in the unconscious. We express this in poetic language if we say that God is "in the heart." It is in the heart, then, that the witness of Him, the proof of Him, must lie, and not in any external circumstance of the natural order. So far as theology is concerned, we had better leave the bees and their pollination of flowers alone.

Denis Diderot (1713–1784) was a leader among the French philosophes in 18th-century Paris, a group—including Voltaire, Rousseau, Montesquieu, and La Mettrie—with many diverse views, but whose revolutionary ideas in religion, politics, and science marked the height of the French Enlightenment and contributed to both the American and the French Revolutions. Some of Diderot's works were considered too radical by both the religious and civil authorities in France, and he spent several months in prison for his writings. As editor of the great Encyclopedia, *Diderot aimed at collecting all the world's knowledge, both theoretical and practical, in a single work; it was finally published in 1772. The short piece that follows was published in 1777. Though its purpose is serious, it was written with all the style, wit, and playfulness which characterized that period of French culture. Translated by Bruce N. Waller; thanks to Adam N. Waller, Mary N. Waller, and particularly to Myrande Brooks for their generous help.*

Conversation of a Philosopher with Maréchale de * * *

Having something to discuss with the Maréchal de * * *, I went to his home one morning. He was not home, but I paid my respects to Madame la Maréchale. She is a charming woman, beautiful and pious as an angel. Her sweetness is apparent on her face, and her gentle voice and ingenuous speech match her bodily appearance. She was at her dressing table. A chair was set out for me; I sat down, and we talked. I made several remarks that edified and surprised her (for she held the opinion that anyone who denies the Holy Trinity must be a villain, and suited only for the gallows), and she said to me:

La Maréchale: Aren't you Monsieur Diderot?

Diderot: Yes, Madame.

La Maréchale: Then you are the man who believes nothing?

Diderot: That is me, Madame.

La Maréchale: But your moral views are the same as those of a believer.

Diderot: Why not, so long as he is an honest man?

La Maréchale: And your moral principles, do you follow them?

Diderot: As well as I can.

La Maréchale: What? You don't steal from people, you don't kill them, you don't rob them?

Diderot: Very rarely.

La Maréchale: Then what do you gain by not believing?

Diderot: Nothing at all, Madame La Maréchale. Is one a believer in order to gain benefits?

La Maréchale: I can't say; but concern for our own interests does us no harm in this world or in the next.

Diderot: That reflects poorly on humanity. I am sorry for that.

La Maréchale: What, you really do not steal?

Diderot: No, upon my honor.

La Maréchale: Then if you neither steal nor kill, you must admit that you are not being consistent.

Diderot: Why so?

La Maréchale: It seems to me that if I had nothing to hope for or fear in the next world, there are many little treats I should not deny myself in the present world. I confess that I expect God to reward me well for my virtuous life.

• • •

Diderot: Madame La Maréchale, it is very easy to sin grievously against your law?

La Maréchale: I must agree.

Diderot: The justice that will decide your fate is extremely rigorous.

La Maréchale: That is true.

Diderot: And if you believe what is said by the oracles of your religion, the number of the elect is extremely small.

La Maréchale: Oh, I am not a Jansenist; I look only at the side that is consoling. The blood of Jesus Christ can cover a great many sins; and it seems clear to me that the Devil, who did not give up his only son to death, is unlikely to gain most of the souls.

Diderot: Are Socrates, Phocion, Aristides, Cato, Trajan, and Marcus Aurelius all damned?

La Maréchale: Certainly not! Only a wild beast could think that. Saint Paul says that each will be judged by the law he has known; and Saint Paul is right.

Diderot: And by what law will the unbeliever be judged?

La Maréchale: Your case is a bit different. You are one of those accursed inhabitants of Chorazin and Bethsaida, who closed their eyes to the light that shone on them, and who stopped their ears to avoid hearing the voice of truth as it spoke to them.

Diderot: Madame La Maréchale, those persons of Chorazin and Bethsaida were unlike all others in the world if they were masters of whether they believed or did not believe.

La Maréchale: But they saw miracles that would have caused the price of sackcloth and ashes to soar had the miracles occurred in Tyre and Sidon.

Diderot: But the residents of Tyre and Sidon were brilliant, and those of Chorazin and Bethsaida were fools. But do you think that the one who made them fools will punish them for being fools? . . . I would like to tell you a story. . . . A young Mexican, tired after his day's work, was walking along the seashore. He saw a plank, one end of it in the ocean and the other lying on the beach. He rested on this plank, and as he gazed upon the vast waters before him, he said to himself: It is clear that my grandmother's mind has become muddled by her old age. Those stories she tells of people who, from some unknown time, coming here from some unknown place across the sea: That goes against common sense. Can't I see that the sea and sky meet out there? So how should I believe, contrary to the evidence of my senses, an old fable that no one knows the date of, that everyone tells differently, that is nothing but a tissue of absurdities, and that causes everyone to eat out their own hearts and scratch out one another's eyes? As he thought about these things, the waves rocked the plank on which he was resting and he fell asleep. While he was sleeping the wind rose and the tide floated the plank on which he rested, and soon our young philosopher was out to sea.

La Maréchale: Alas! Your picture is true: We are all of us floating on that plank; the wind blows, and the tide carries us out.

Diderot: He was far from land when he awakened. Who was surprised to find himself out on the ocean? It was our young Mexican. But what did he find even more amazing? Now that the shore on which he had been walking a little while ago had disappeared from view, the sea met the sky all around him. Seeing this, he began to think he had been wrong;

and that, if the wind continued blowing him in the same direction that he might meet the inhabitants that his grandmother had told him about so often.

La Maréchale: But his care and fear, you have said nothing of it.

Diderot: He had none. He said to himself: What difference does it make, so long as I reach land? I have reasoned stupidly, true; but I was honest with myself; and that is all that anyone can demand of me. If it is not virtuous to be clever, then it cannot be a crime to be dull. Meanwhile the wind continued, the young man and the plank drifted onward, and the unknown land loomed on the horizon. He touched the land, and came ashore.

La Maréchale: We shall meet there one day, Monsieur Diderot.

Diderot: I hope so, Madame La Maréchale; wherever that may be, I shall always be honored to court you. As soon as he had left the plank and set foot upon the sand, he noticed a venerable old man standing next to him. The young Mexican asked where he was, and with whom he had the honor of speaking. "I am the sovereign of this land," replied the old man. Immediately the young man bowed to the ground. "Stand up," said the old man. "You have denied my existence?" "That is true." "And the existence of my empire?" "That is true." "I pardon you, because I am the one who sees the heart, and I have looked in yours and have seen that you acted in good faith; but the rest of your thoughts and your actions have not been equally innocent." Then the old man took him by the ear, and reminded him of all the errors in his life; and at each one, the young Mexican bowed down, beat his breast, and asked forgiveness. Now, Madame La Maréchale, put yourself for a moment in the place of the old man, and tell me, what would you have done? Would you have seized the foolish young man by the hair, and happily dragged him around for all eternity on the shore?

La Maréchale: In truth, no.

Diderot: What if one of your lovely children ran away from your home and did many stupid acts, and returned repentant?

La Maréchale: Me, I should hurry to meet him; I would take him in my arms, and I would cover him with my tears; but Monsieur le Maréchal, his father, is not so tender.

Diderot: Monsieur le Maréchal is not a tiger.

La Maréchale: Not at all.

Diderot: He would have to be coaxed a while, but he would eventually give his pardon.

La Maréchale: Certainly.

Diderot: Particularly if he considered that before the child was born he knew the child's whole life, and that punishing the child would be of no help to himself, nor to the child, nor to the child's brothers.

La Maréchale: The old man and Monsieur Le Maréchal are two different individuals.

Diderot: Are you saying that Monsieur Le Maréchal is better than the old man?

La Maréchale: God forbid! I mean that just as my justice is not the same as Monsieur Le Maréchal's, the justice of Monsieur Le Maréchal may not be the same as that of the old man.

Diderot: Ah! Madame! You do not see the implications of that response. Either the general definition of justice applies equally to you, to Monsieur Le Maréchal, to me, to the young Mexican and to the old man; or I no longer know what justice means, and I am completely ignorant of what will please or displease the old man.

Study Questions

1. What is the cosmological argument, and what are some objections to it?
2. Describe the design argument for the existence of God, and discuss some objections to that argument (including at least one objection from Hume's *Dialogues*).
3. What is the problem of evil? What are some of the traditional answers to the problem?
4. On the orthodox Judeo–Christian–Muslim view, God is *omnipresent*. What further specific implications might that quality have for the nature of God?
5. What is Pascal's wager?
6. Describe an attempt (such as Sarah's) to reconcile science with religious belief.
7. Compare and contrast the views of Stace and Diderot on our understanding of God and of the ways of God.

Exercises

1. "Why is there something rather than nothing?" That is the question Ben poses for Selina. It is posed in many ways: Suppose science explains what happened after the Big Bang; still, what happened *before* that? Where did all the matter and energy that exploded outward originate? According to Ben, that is a question science can't answer. Religion can: God is the ultimate Source, the first Foundation.

   Why is there something rather than nothing? Could science ever answer that question? Is it even the type of question science might *attempt* to answer?

   Some people argue that, although the question sounds meaningful and legitimate (similar in form to "Why did you take philosophy rather than political science?") it is actually *not* meaningful, not a question that really makes sense. They say that it is like asking "Why is a circle happier than purple?" It may sound like a meaningful question, but it is not. *Is* it a meaningful question?

2. Joseph Addison's poem (on the first page of this chapter) was written the year David Hume was born. Based on the reading from Hume's *Dialogues*, what do you think Hume would say about the poem?

3. Ben ultimately gives up on standard arguments to prove the existence of God and turns instead to the internal perspective:

> Don't look for proof out there; look for proof in here. Don't you sometimes have a sense, a feeling, maybe an intuitive idea, that there is something greater or deeper than the mundane world of cities and trees and mountains, deeper even than the world of atoms and galaxies and black holes and quasars. Not something we see clearly, not even something we can really argue for or prove scientifically; but something greater, nonetheless.

That is also the view favored by Walter Terence Stace, in the essay from which the second reading was excerpted:

> God is either known by revelation—that is to say, by intuition—or not at all. And revelation is not something which took place in the past. It takes place in every moment of time, and in every heart. . . .

If Ben and Walter Stace are correct, is it then hopeless to try to convince anyone else of the existence of God? That is, would evangelism be futile? If they are correct, does real *argument* concerning the existence of God become impossible?

4. Drawing on Spinoza as well as Taoism, Sarah concludes there can be *nothing* outside of God; in fact, there can be only one substance, in which God and the world and all that exists has its being. Of course this radical *monism* is a very unorthodox view of God for Jews and Christians: Spinoza was excommunicated from the Jewish community in Amsterdam because of his views, and orthodox Christianity also rejects the position. *Is* this an implication of the principle (held by both Jews and Christians) that God is omnipresent and omnipotent?

5. "Nothing that is contrary to, and inconsistent with, the clear and self-evident dictates of reason has a right to be urged or assented to as a matter of faith." So John Locke insists; and St. Thomas Aquinas (in another boxed passage) seems to agree. And yet the book of Job (in a passage quoted by Ben) seems to suggest a very different view: The ways of God are beyond our understanding, God's justice is not our justice. God challenges Job, implying that Job's knowledge and reason are completely inadequate to judge anything concerning God: "Where wast thou when I laid the foundations of the earth? Declare, if thou hast understanding." On this view, human understanding is woefully inadequate to judge concerning matters of faith. Which view seems more plausible to you?

   Now, look back at the question you just answered: "Which view seems more plausible to you?" That is basically a question of which view is more *reasonable.* But the very question is one of whether *reason* or faith should be our guide. Does the question itself *beg the question* in favor of reason? If you think so, is there any way to frame the issue *without* begging the question?

6. Diderot's dialogue discusses a view that is similar to the one found in Job: God's ways, and God's *justice*, cannot be understood by humans. Diderot claims that such a view makes all our talk of justice incoherent. Is he right?

Glossary

Cosmological argument: An argument for the existence of God, based on the claim that the very existence of the universe (the cosmos) requires something that brought it into existence, since it could not have come into existence without a cause; and that ultimate cause must be God.

Design argument: An argument for the existence of God, based on the claim that observation of the world shows evidence that it was created by an intelligent and purposeful Designer, and only God could carry out such a design. Sometimes called the teleological argument.

Pascal's wager: An argument for belief in the existence of God, based on Pascal's claim that we have more to gain by believing, so belief is a "better bet."

Problem of evil: A problem that confronts believers in an omnipotent, omniscient, and benevolent God. If God has the power and wisdom to stop suffering and prevent evil, then how can God be considered kind and benevolent if He allows these to exist?

Additional Resources

One of the best general collections of articles on the philosophy of religion is John Hick, *Classical and Contemporary Readings in the Philosophy of Religion*, 2d ed. (Englewood Cliffs, NJ: Prentice Hall, 1970). Philip L. Quinn and Charles Taliaferro, eds., *A Companion to Philosophy of Religion* (Oxford, U.K.: Blackwell, 1997), is a superb collection of essays, specially commissioned for the book, by experts on a wide range of issues in philosophy of religion. *Philosophy of Religion: Selected Readings*, 2d ed., edited by Michael Peterson, William Hasker, Bruce Reichenbach, and David Basinger (Oxford, U.K.: Oxford University Press, 2001) is a particularly good collection, bringing together key essays on almost every major issue. *Philosophy of Religion: A Guide and Anthology*, edited by Brian Davies (Oxford, U.K.: Oxford University Press, 2000) contains excellent sections on arguments for the existence of God and covers other topics as well. The essays included cover a wide range of perspectives. A very good collection of essays by contemporary writers is offered by Steven M. Cahn and David Shatz, eds., *Contemporary Philosophy of Religion* (Oxford, U.K.: Oxford University Press, 1982). *Readings in the Philosophy of Religion: An Analytic Approach*, 2d ed., edited by Baruch A. Brody (Englewood Cliffs, NJ: Prentice Hall, 1992), contains important writings ranging from Plato, through Aquinas, to Locke and Hume and including good contemporary essays as well. A good brief introduction to some of the key issues in the philosophy of religion is presented by Brian Davies in *An Introduction to the Philosophy of Religion* (Oxford, U.K.: Oxford University Press, 1982). All of these books discuss most, if not all, of the issues discussed in what follows.

While arguments for the existence of God go back at least to Plato (*The Laws*, Book X) and Aristotle (*Metaphysics*), the best known early systematic source of such arguments is St. Thomas Aquinas, in his "Five Ways," in the *Summa Theologica*, Part I. Criticism of those arguments can be found in Hume's *Dialogues Concerning Natural Religion*, as well as in Section XI of Hume's *Inquiry*

Concerning Human Understanding. Immanuel Kant's critique of traditional arguments for the existence of God can be found in the *Critique of Pure Reason.* (See the chapter on "The Ideal of Pure Reason.") One of the best known 20th-century critics of religious belief and arguments for the existence of God was Bertrand Russell. A systematic, but difficult, presentation of his views on religion can be found in his book on Leibniz: *A Critical Exposition of the Philosophy of Leibniz,* 2d ed.(London: Allen & Unwin, 1937); more accessible accounts of Russell's views are found in his paperback *Religion and Science* (London: Oxford University Press, 1935); and his *Why I Am Not a Christian and Other Essays* (London: Allen & Unwin, 1957).

The design argument has a long history, and it never seems to go away. Recently, it has been revived by "creationists" and "intelligent design" theorists, who campaign to have the biblical creation account or the thesis of a "Designer God" taught as a scientific concept in public schools, as a "scientific alternative" to Darwin's theory of natural selection. One of the better known critics of this view is Richard Dawkins; see his book, *The Blind Watchmaker* (London: Longman, 1986). For a debate on intelligent design, based on a set of articles in *Natural History* magazine (April 2002), go to *http://www.actionbioscience.org/evolution/nhmag.html.* The site contains papers favoring intelligent design as well as critiquing the view, and each author lists his or her favorite web links to other resources. Darwin's own views can be found in *The Autobiography of Charles Darwin* (London: Collins, 1958). Asa Gray, an American botanist who was a contemporary of Darwin's, argued that there was no conflict between natural theology and Darwinism; Gray's work can be found in *Darwinia,* edited by A. H. Dupree (Cambridge, U.K.: Cambridge University Press, 1963).

For a very interesting and beautifully written view of the contrast between science and religion, as seen by a distinguished contemporary biologist, see the final chapter of E.O. Wilson's *Consilience.* Wilson summarizes the problem thus: "The essence of humanity's spiritual dilemma is that we evolved genetically to accept one truth and discovered another." (p. 264) Chet Raymo is a physicist–astronomer who tries to build bridges between the scientific and the spiritual; see his *Skeptics and True Believers: The Exhilarating Connection Between Science and Religion* (New York: Walker and Company, 1998). Kenneth R. Miller is a professor of biology at Brown University who follows the Christian religion; he explains his own reconciliation of his scientific and religious views in *Finding Darwin's God: A Scientist's Search for Common Ground Between God and Evolution* (New York: HarperCollins, 1999).

The "problem of evil" is one of the most intractable in the philosophy of religion. There is a fascinating debate on the subject among three distinguished British philosophers: Antony Flew, R. M. Hare, and Basil Mitchell. It was first published in 1955, in *New Ideas in Philosophical Theology,* edited by Antony Flew and Alasdair MacIntyre (New York: The Macmillan Co.), and has been widely anthologized. An interesting answer to the problem, proposed from the perspective of process theology, is offered by John B. Cobb and David Ray Griffin in *Process Theology: An Introductory Exposition* (Philadelphia: Wesminster Press, 1976), pp. 69–75.

Pascal's wager originates in Pascal's *Pensées*. An English translation is available by F. W. Trotter (New York: E. P. Dutton & Co., 1932), No. 233. William James discussed the argument in his essay "The Will to Believe," which formed part of *The Will to Believe and Other Essays in Popular Philosophy* (Longmans, Green & Co., 1897) and is now available in *The Will to Believe and Other Essays in Popular Philosophy* (New York: Dover, 1957). Pascal's wager is also the subject of a lively and interesting paper by William Lycan and George Schlesinger, "You Bet Your Life," which can be found in Joel Feinberg, ed., *Reason and Responsibility*, 7th ed. (Belmont, CA: Wadsworth, 1989), also available in 8th, 9th, and 10th editions. The paper has been anthologized elsewhere as well. *Gambling on God* (Lanham, MD: Rowman & Littlefield, 1994) is a good collection of articles on Pascal's wager. (Schlesinger restates the "You Bet Your Life" argument in this anthology.)

Spinoza's *Ethics* is available in an excellent translation by R. H. M. Elwes. Originally done in 1883, the translation is now published in a Dover edition (New York: Dover, 1955) under the title *The Chief Works of Benedict de Spinoza*. Stuart Hampshire provides an excellent and very readable study of Spinoza's philosophy in his *Spinoza* (London: Penguin, 1951). A wonderful study of Spinoza's life and the era in which he lived is Lewis Samuel Feuer's *Spinoza and the Rise of Liberalism* (Boston: Beacon Press, 1958).

The issue of direct experience of God is taken up by Michael Martin in *Atheism: A Philosophical Justification* (Philadelphia: Temple University Press, 1990). For a more positive perspective, see William James, *Varieties of Religious Experience* (New York: Longmans, Green and Co., 1923).

A charming set of essays written from a Taoist perspective can be found in Raymond Smullyan's book, *The Tao is Silent* (Harper & Row, 1977). Smullyan is a logician, and among his many fascinating books of logical puzzles are *What Is the Name of This Book?*

Chapter 3

What Can We Know?

In which Ben and Selina pit reason against experience

"Hi, Sarah, can I join you? If you have work to finish before class and need to be alone, that's okay, I don't mind, there's an empty table over there."

"No, sit down, Selina. My seminar doesn't meet until Friday; I was just getting ahead. Sit down, I would love the company."

"Oh, good, I need to talk with my best friend. Ben is driving me crazy. He's such a bright guy, but he has all these crazy ideas. He's a skeptic about everything. Except religion, of course. On that he's absolutely certain, no doubt whatsoever. Me, I believe we have all kinds of knowledge, through science, mathematics, observation. In fact, about the only thing I'm really skeptical of is religion! God is the one thing it makes no sense to claim certainty about; and sure enough, that's the one thing Ben *is* certain of. I just can't understand that man."

Today's discussion focuses on the theory of knowledge: what *can we* know, *and* how *do we* know it? *This branch of philosophy is often called* epistemology. *The name is derived from the Greek word for knowledge:* episteme.

"The two of you are amazing, Selina. You never agree on anything at all. One thing I can be certain of: If I see my friends Selina and Ben sitting together in the coffee shop, they'll soon be engaged in a lengthy philosophical dispute. How do you two stay together?"

"Oh, that's no mystery, Sarah. There are things in this life other than philosophy, right?"

"Spare me the sordid details. . . . Oh, speak of the devil and he shall appear! Hi, Ben. Pull up a chair. Selina was just explaining to me what an impossible person you are."

"Me, impossible? You've obviously been getting the wrong side of that story, Sarah. I'm the most reasonable person you can imagine."

"Yeah, you're reasonable," Selina responded, "and the Easter Bunny is a terrorist. How can it be reasonable to *doubt* the evidence of your senses and the discoveries of science and the proofs of mathematics, and have *no* doubt about your religious convictions. You're looking through the wrong end of the telescope, Ben."

"Wait a minute, Selina. You don't *always* trust the evidence of your senses, right?" Sarah was somewhat hesitant to be drawn into this dispute. Still, it looked like fun; and though a dispute between lovers, it really didn't seem like a lovers' spat. At least, Sarah had never heard of a lovers' spat over the question of knowledge and skepticism—though, with Selina and Ben, anything was possible. "You see a stick in the water, your senses tell you it's bent, but you know that in fact it is straight. Your senses tell you that you are standing on an immobile Earth, while the Sun orbits around us; but you don't doubt that our senses deceive us on that, and that the Copernican theory is true and the Earth is now spinning on its axis as it makes its long orbit around the Sun. And the table on which you just placed your coffee cup seems quite solid, at least according to your senses; but you have good scientific grounds for believing it to be a collection of atoms, made up of considerably more space than solid substance."

Empiricism

"Of course, science can correct and refine our sensory observations," Selina replied. "That's why we use microscopes. But science is still *founded* on our sensory observations. We recognize that some are unreliable; but if we could never trust our sensory observations, then scientific knowledge would be impossible. After all, how did we finally recognize that we were mistaken in our commonsense belief that the Earth is stationary? It was through careful sensory observations of the motions of the planets. Obviously, a lot of mathematical reasoning was also involved, but the observations of astronomers were essential, too. We do indeed discover that some of our sensory observations are wrong, but we discover that through *other* sensory observations. So there is no reason for general skepticism about either our senses or the scientific results based on them."

"Yeah, well, science corrects our sensory observations; and then later, science corrects earlier science; and so on. But where's the stopping point?" Ben was adamant in his skepticism. "Sure, Copernicus taught us that the Earth moves around the Sun, and our senses deceive us. But that was a rejection of Ptolemaic theory, which insisted that the Sun and all the planets revolve around the Earth. And there was a period in between, when most astronomers favored Tycho Brahe's theory: The Earth is stationary, the Sun revolves around the Earth, and all the other planets revolve around the Sun. And someday there will be the Selinian theory, with the Sun revolving around a black hole and all the planets dancing the tango. Aristotle develops a physics, it lasts almost two thousand years, and every scientist believes it. Then along comes Newton, and everyone thinks that Newton is eternal scientific truth. Then Einstein revealed some problems in Newtonian theory. And in just a few decades, Einstein was left in the background, and his views were corrected by quantum mechanics. Now we've got string theory, and loop quantum gravity, and the next bright new theory of the year. Pay your money and take your choice. Well, for my money, when I talk about genuine knowledge—*real* knowledge—I want something that lasts, something that changeth not; and that is God, not science."

Selina was eager to offer a cutting refutation, but Sarah edged in first. Their argument was likely to take on speed and steam, and she wanted time to finish her coffee before it totally erupted. "What about mathematics, Ben? That changeth not, right?"

"No, it changes also, Sarah. Maybe not as much as science, and it's not as unreliable as our senses, perhaps. But it certainly changes. Isaac Newton thought that Euclidean geometry was eternal truth; but Einstein showed that non-Euclidean geometries were more useful in some respects. But look, Selina thinks I'm out to reject all of science. I'm not. Nor mathematics and geometry either, for that matter. I like science, I like reading about contemporary work in science, and I particularly like the history of science: I guess that's why I majored in history. But if you want to talk about what we really *know*, what we know with bedrock certainty, then neither science nor mathematics is the best foundation. Batten down the hatches, Selina is gonna storm at me, but the only real foundation is God. That is unchanging, indubitable certainty."

"But Ben, why does it have to be absolutely and eternally certain in order to count as real knowledge? Couldn't it still be knowledge, even if we aren't absolutely certain of its truth, or its eternal duration?" Selina was pushing hard. "Of course some of our scientific beliefs prove false; that's the way it is with a living, growing body of knowledge. But that doesn't mean it doesn't count as knowledge. You set the standards way too high. Besides, there's nothing wrong with some uncertainty: It's what leaves us open to new ideas and prompts our explorations. Nothing wrong with a little skepticism. There's a great line from one of your philosophers, Sarah: George Santayana. Santayana said something like this: 'Scepticism is the chastity of the intellect, and it is shameful to surrender it too soon or to the first comer.'"[1]

George Santayana (1863–1952) was a philosopher, essayist, poet, and novelist. Born in Spain, he moved to Boston with his mother when he was eight. He did his doctorate at Harvard and taught at Harvard until 1912. He then moved to England and on to Paris, and in 1925 he moved to Rome. During World War II, he took refuge in a convent of English nuns, where he remained until his death. Though he was an atheist, he was also—paradoxical as this will sound—deeply religious and a practicing Catholic. Santayana once said that religion is composed of poetry and dogma—and that the Catholic Church keeps both, the Church of England attempts to keep the poetry and drop the dogma, and the Protestants keep the dogma and eliminate the poetry. Santayana's deep devotion to the Catholic Church, his atheism notwithstanding, led Robert Lowell to say that Santayana believed "there is no God and Mary is His Mother."

Sarah laughed. "Oh, that's rich—Selina celebrating the virtue of chastity."

Selina smiled. "Hey, girl, watch it there. Okay, I admit, I see more virtue in intellectual chastity than in physical chastity. But I seem to remember some saying about people who live in glass houses?"

"Alright, let's drop the discussion of chastity," Sarah agreed. "Anyway, I want to get back to old Ben's ideas. Actually, Ben comes from a long and glorious tradition. Goes back at least to Plato, maybe even older. He's a rationalist."

Rationalism

"Yeah, Selina, I'm part of a long and glorious tradition. So Sarah, tell me more about this great rationalist tradition that I'm part of."

"Plato was certainly one of your number, Ben. Maybe the founding father. Rationalism has at least three key factors: First, all real knowledge has to be absolutely certain, eternal, unchanging. Second, appearances and sensory observations are inherently untrustworthy. Third, reason is the best—perhaps the only—path to genuine knowledge."

"But am I really a rationalist, Sarah? I believe the first two, but I'm not sure about the third. I think faith and revelation may be perfectly legitimate paths to the most important knowledge of all: knowledge of God."

"That might compromise your status as a rationalist, true enough. But perhaps not fatally: After all, you believe that the existence of God can also be known through reason, right? Or at least by special intuition. Perhaps that's enough to let you keep your membership in the rationalist club."

"Seems a pretty small club. Sometimes I feel like I'm the only member. Most of the people I know—starting with Selina—seem to think that science is the only path to truth."

Selina nodded. "Absolutely right. If you want truth, science is the best source I know of. I have nothing against reason: Careful design of experiments and interpretation of results requires lots of reasoning. But reason must be combined with experiment and observation and testing in order for us to gain real knowledge."

"See what I mean, Sarah? We rationalists seem to be the smallest club on campus."

"Perhaps so, Ben. But you have a glorious history, all the way back to the Ancient Greeks."

"Good point, Sarah. I don't know that much about philosophy, but I remember reading Plato in my History of Ancient Greece course. I really liked it—especially Plato's story of the cave."

"What cave? What story?" Selina was feeling a bit left out of the conversation.

"It's a story Plato tells, a sort of allegory, that represents his conception of human experience and genuine knowledge," Ben explained. "We're like people who are trapped in a cave, on a narrow ledge, and we can't get out. Except we don't even know we're in a cave: We were born there, and we have no idea that there's anything other than the shadowy world we see. Down below our little ledge there is a fire burning; but we can't see the fire, and we can't see the people who built the fire. All we can see are the shadows cast by the fire, shadows that flicker on the wall opposite us. The hidden people, down below, put up objects in front of the fire, and we see the shadows of those objects on the wall. And we believe that the shadows we are observing are the real world."

Sarah continues. "Yeah, and then finally someone escapes and climbs out of the cave into the bright sunlight. Of course, for a while he is almost blinded, and it takes him some time to understand the reality he is seeing. When he returns to tell his companions what he has seen, and to help lead them out of the cave, they refuse to follow: They think he is crazy, since he is describing a bright reality so far beyond their world of dark shadows that they can hardly imagine it, much less believe it."

"Okay, nice story, guys," Selina said, "but what's the point?"

Ben teases her. "You scientists, you want everything so literal. The cave and the shadows represent our world of observation and sensory experience. It's a shadow world, but we take it for the real world. If we want to understand the real world, we must escape the world of the senses and their deceptions and shadows, and use our reason to look deeper for the reality behind the sensory shadows."

"That's a nice story, guys," said Selina, though her tone indicated it was hardly one of her favorites. "But if we actually want to get at the reality, we have to deal with those shadows: We have to take the sensory experiences we have, examine them as carefully as we can, develop our best hypotheses, and then test them scientifically. You escape from the cave, and you find the bright light of truth. Great. But *how* do you accomplish that? You need more than reason. And you need a *lot* more than blind faith, Ben. You have to do the hard, gritty work of testing and observing and measuring and examining. It would be nice if we could just sit in our armchairs and let pure reason—or pure faith—lift us to the glorious truth. That has some advantages; to quote one of *my* favorite philosophers, Bertrand Russell, it has all the advantages of theft over honest labor. And getting the truth *does* require honest labor: the labor of rigorous scientific research."

"I agree it's hard work, and what scientists discover is valuable, sure. But it's not bedrock certainty, and that's what I want when I count something as genuine knowledge." Ben was taking his stand and staking his claim for rationalist certainty. "I want a truth that doesn't change, a truth that is beyond question, a truth I cannot doubt."

"You're an amazing and pure rationalist, Ben." Sarah was working hard to postpone Selina's inevitable eruption. "You start with Platonic rationalism, and you wind up with a position that is similar to that of René Descartes, the great French philosopher and leading rationalist of the 17th century."

Ben brightened. "Yeah, Sarah? So on my own I came up with a view that matches one of the great philosophical systems?"

"Almost matches, Ben. Descartes added a few details. But just like you, Descartes was looking for certainty, some absolutely indubitable truth on which he could build. You're a historian, Ben. When we think about the 17th century, the early Enlightenment, we think of a period of great artistic and literary and scientific achievement. And of course, in some ways it was. Shakespeare and Moliere were writing plays, Cervantes was writing novels, Rembrandt and Rubens were painting. The Blue Mosque was completed in Istanbul, the Taj Mahal was built, so was the Salzburg Cathedral, and Bernini designed St. Peter's. Galileo was looking through his telescope and devising his theories, while William Harvey described the circulation of the blood and Francis Bacon proposed a massive new enterprise for science. And it was all accompanied by brand new musical forms: concertos, sonatas, oratorios, operas. A wonderful period, the opening of the Enlightenment, right? Except it wasn't all glorious music and Shakespearean comedies. There were waves of bubonic plague, epidemics that emptied out whole cities, with many dying and the others fleeing. The Thirty Years War swept across Europe, and many people lived their entire lives in a state of brutal conflict. Witchcraft was widely suspected, and many innocent people were tortured to death. The effects of

---

In 1611, the poet John Donne published a poem that captures the confusion and uncertainty and skepticism that was then dominant:

New philosophy calls all in doubt
The element of fire is quite put out;
The sun is lost, and the earth, and no man's wit
Can well direct him where to look for it.
And freely men confess that this world's spent,
When in the planets, and the firmament
They seek so many new; then see that this
Is crumbled out again to his atomies.
'Tis all in pieces, all coherence gone;
All just supply, and all relation:
Prince, subject, Father, Son, are things forgot.

John Donne, *An Anatomy of the World. the First Anniversary,* 1611, 1. 205

---

the Protestant Reformation and Catholic Counter-Reformation were being felt, and everyone lived in constant fear of being branded a heretic, if not by one side, then by the other. The 17th century opened with the astronomer Giordano Bruno being burned at the stake in Rome. And even though great scientific discoveries were being made by Galileo and Harvey, there was also great scientific uncertainty. After all, lots of people now believed in the Copernican theory—though, as Bruno and Galileo learned, it was not wise to say so openly—but the Copernican theory completely undermined Aristotelian physics, which depended on everything in the universe seeking its proper place: Rocks fell to the earth because they were seeking their proper sphere, and heat rose for the same reason. But now the Earth was hurtling through space (at least, according to Copernicus), so who could tell where *anything* was supposed to be, and where anything's 'proper place' would be? So Aristotelian physics, which had worked for two thousand years, was now useless. And Ptolemaic astronomy, which had served for many centuries, was under challenge. And the most obvious and certain truths—that the Earth is stationary and that the Sun travels over our heads and around the Earth—were now in doubt. And if you can't believe the clear evidence of all your senses and the most solid commonsense truth—that the Earth is stationary beneath your feet—then what *can* you believe? So the early 17th century was a period of great doubt and turmoil and uncertainty and skepticism."

"Wow, Sarah, you know your history!" Selina was impressed.

"No, not really. I just happen to like that period of history. I love Rembrandt's portraits, and I really like Spinoza, so I started reading some about 17th century Dutch history, and that led to lots of other stuff. But really, most of it I learned in Professor Stanislaw's 17th-century European history class."

"Yeah, I'm registered for that next semester." Ben was delighted to find another person with an interest in history. "Everyone says she's a great professor. I hope I learn half as much from the course as you did. But anyway, how does all that relate to Descartes? I still want to know how my views are similar to his."

> *"When I play with my cat, who knows if I am not a pastime to her more than she is to me?"*
>
> Michel de Montaigne (1533–1592), *Essays*, Book II, Chapter 12

"Well, here's Descartes, living in the midst of this incredible skepticism. I mean, even the Catholic Church was willing to make use of skepticism in its struggle against the Protestants. The great Catholic philosopher Michel de Montaigne argues for skepticism and then concludes that, since we can't really know anything, the most prudent choice is simply to stay where God put us; that is, God saw fit to make us Catholics, so we should just remain Catholics, since we can't possibly have any reliable reason for following some other view. Well, Descartes didn't like it. He was convinced that we *could* gain real knowledge if only we used the right *method*. And that's what Descartes set out to find: a method that would give us certain, reliable truth. And the method he used, rather ironically, was what he called the *method of doubt*. He would doubt everything that he could, until he discovered something that was absolutely indubitable. Except he went a step beyond you, Ben: He even doubted the existence of God."

"Go, Descartes!" Selina liked this turn in Sarah's story. "That's where doubt ought to start! How can anyone reject science as doubtful and still cling to belief in God? If you consider the evidence for science weak, you ought to rate the evidence for God a lot weaker."

"Actually, Descartes first questioned our sensory knowledge. Our senses are often deceived, that's easy enough. I have vivid experiences that seem very real, and then I awake to discover that they were merely a dream. So sensory experience is out as a source of indubitable knowledge. Then he noted that it was possible to doubt the existence of God—after all, God might be something very different from what we suppose. Of course, Descartes made it clear that he wasn't *really* doubting the existence of God, since the Catholic Inquisition did nasty things to people who said they doubted the existence of God; and on that score, the Protestants were no more tolerant than the Catholics. But Descartes was simply stating that it was *possible* to doubt the existence of God, so certainty of God could not be the indubitable starting point Descartes was seeking. What about mathematics? The truths of mathematics don't depend on our

I shall then suppose, not that God who is supremely good and the fountain of truth, but some evil genius not less powerful than deceitful, has employed his whole energies in deceiving me; I shall consider that the heavens, the earth, colours, figures, sound, and all other external things are nought but the illusions and dreams of which this genius has availed himself in order to lay traps for my credulity; I shall consider myself as having no hands, no eyes, no flesh, no blood, nor any senses, yet falsely believing myself to possess all these things; I shall remain obstinately attached to this idea, and if by this means it is not in my power to arrive at the knowledge of any truth, I may at least do what is in my power [that is, suspend my judgment], and with firm purpose avoid giving credence to any false thing, or being imposed upon by this arch deceiver, however powerful and deceptive he may be.

Descartes, *Meditations One*, p. 148, translated by
Elizabeth S. Haldane and G. R. T. Ross

senses: Two plus two still equals four, no matter how many times a magician deceives our senses and shows us two balls and two more balls, and then opens his hands and reveals that there are only three balls. A good trick, we might say, but we won't suppose that two plus two no longer equals four. We might even conclude that somehow the magician made one of the balls vaporize into thin air—that would be a really good trick—but that won't change the fact that two plus two equals four. But even mathematics won't give us the indubitable starting point that Descartes wants. Because if he can doubt the existence of God, then he can imagine that God is a deceiving demon who uses all his powers to confuse us. And such a powerful demon could slip into our minds and muddle them so that we would believe that two plus two equals five. Actually, Descartes's demon is one of the most famous philosophical creations: It raises skepticism to new heights."

"And it raises philosophy to new heights of silliness if you ask me." Selina could only stand so much philosophical speculation at one sitting. "Look, Sarah, there's no reason whatsoever to believe there is some demon deceiver who is dedicated to confusing us about the truths of mathematics. If there were such a demon, he could find better ways to occupy his time. And besides, the notion of an all-powerful malicious demon is just as implausible as the notion of an all-powerful benevolent God. Maybe more implausible—though I'm not sure that anything is really more implausible than belief in God. Why is Descartes giving us this demon deceiver fantasy?"

Sarah smiled, sipped her coffee, waved her hand at Selina. "No, Selina, Descartes wasn't suggesting that some such demon, this 'arch deceiver,' really exists. He was trying to doubt everything that could *conceivably* be doubted, and the demon was just a very useful way to do that. Such a demon is *possible*, even though it's hardly likely and not even plausible. But if it's *possible* that such a demon deceives us about mathematics, then mathematics is not the indubitable foundation of truth that Descartes is searching for."

"So what was?" Ben was enjoying this story.

"Descartes continued his quest, until he tried to doubt one last thing: his own existence. And there he finally found something he could not doubt. Even if a powerful demon tried to deceive him about that, he could still be sure that he existed; after all, the demon would have to be deceiving someone, and that someone would be him. Now, exactly who was it that Descartes was sure existed? Well, not the Descartes known by his friends—not the Descartes they would recognize by his face and other bodily characteristics. After all, it would still be possible to *doubt* that he had a body: His sense of having a body might all be illusion, dream, deception. Descartes didn't actually put it this way, but you *could* be just a brain in a vat, hooked up to a computer on which some mad scientist programs all your experiences. All your thoughts, and all your sensory experiences, are being fed into your brain by the mad scientist's computerized electrical inputs. Or maybe you're not even a brain—just an experiencing spirit. Anyway, when Descartes applied his method of systematic doubt, what he ultimately concluded was this: All I really know—all that I know *indubitably*—is that I exist as a thinking thing. That is, *I think, therefore I am.* Or, in Descartes' famous line, *Cogito, ergo sum.* So Descartes concludes that he can *know*, with absolute indubitable certainty, that he *exists as a thinking thing.* A thing that may be deceived, tricked, mistaken, deluded—but without doubt, an existing thing that thinks. You can't trick or deceive a nonthinking, nonconscious being."

Ben had a question. "I'm still confused, Sarah. It would be neat to suppose that I'm thinking along the same pattern as some famous philosopher, but I don't see how my view corresponds to Descartes's. I start from absolute certainty about God; Descartes doubts the existence of God—maybe not really, but in applying his method of doubt, he does—and instead is certain that he exists as a thinking thing. Those seem like very different views to me."

"Not really as different as you suppose, Ben. What you and Descartes have in common is that you both want to start from some absolute, indubitable truth. For you it's God; for Descartes, it's *cogito, ergo sum.* And actually, Descartes's very next step is trying to prove—absolutely and indubitably, which is what all genuine *knowledge* has to be, according to him—that God exists and that God is no deceiver. From there, Descartes moves on to prove the truth of mathematics, and before long he has a whole range of knowledge built up from this absolute starting point."

"Okay, I see at least this much that I have in common with Descartes: When we talk about knowledge, we're talking about what we *know to be true*. I know that the existence of God is true—eternally true, permanent and unchanging truth, the way all genuine truth has to be. The 'truths' of science, well, they're here today and gone tomorrow. So we can't really *know* them today. It's like my roommate, Walt. Today he's in love with Marsha, tomorrow it's Sharon, and last week the great love of his life was Stacy. That's not love. Shakespeare had it right:

Let me not to the marriage of true minds
Admit impediments. Love is not love
Which alters when it alteration finds,
Or bends with the remover to remove:
O, no! it is an ever-fixed mark,
That looks on tempests and is never shaken,
It is the star to every wandering bark,
Whose worth's unknown, although his height be taken."

It is difficult to know exactly what views Descartes actually held, although, in his writings, he always expressed perfectly orthodox Christian religious beliefs. However, Descartes lived in an era when it was dangerous to express ideas that were in conflict with religious orthodoxy; and, desiring a quiet life and wishing to avoid strife or persecution, he was very cautious about what he wrote. His motto (which is carved on his tomb) is "He who hides well, lives well." So what Descartes's hidden beliefs might have been we may never know.

Selina leaned across the table and kissed him passionately. "The boy's a little crazy, Sarah, but I do love it when he does that poetry stuff."

"Hey, guys, I'm trying to eat my breakfast here. Get a room." Sarah sipped her coffee. "Anyway, I guess it's a good thing that Ben can look on tempests and not be shaken; Selina is a woman full of tempests."

Selina laughed. "Well, maybe a summer cloudburst, occasionally. Tempests is a bit strong, Sarah. But I have every right to a tempest or two. How can a man who is so sexy be so confused? If you want the starting point of knowledge, you don't turn to some private intuition about your own existence, much less to faith in God. Descartes is entertaining, with that demon-of-doubt stuff. But Cartesian rationalism is not the high road to knowledge: Knowledge requires more than reasoning. Real knowledge requires getting your hands dirty, running the experiments, making the observations. Right, Sarah?"

"Come on, Selina, don't try to get me to take sides between you two. That's a tempest I plan to avoid. Actually, it's a tempest that has raged for centuries. Of course, the two of you are more charming combatants than Descartes and Locke, or Hume and Kant, but it's still basically the same conflict."

"You mean this argument between Selina and me has been going on for centuries?" This caught Ben's attention. "I don't know if that's a comfort or a horror. On the one side, at least it's not just between us. But on the other side, if the controversy has raged for centuries, then what chance do I have of ever convincing Selina to listen to reason?"

"Ho, boy, Sarah. Isn't that just like a man? No matter how unreasonable and stubborn they are, they're always convinced they have a monopoly on reason."

"I don't think I have a monopoly on reason, Selina," answered Ben. "We all have the ability to reason; that's the distinguishing mark of humans. I think that's what the Bible means when it says we were made in the image of God. In any case, reason is much better than our senses as a source of genuine knowledge—reason, when properly combined with our intuitive, immediate knowledge of God."

"Ben, that's amazing." Sarah smiled. "You really are the second coming of Descartes. He would agree with you about reason being the best guide, of course. Descartes did think we could know things through the senses, but only after laying an elaborate foundation in reason. And knowledge gained through the senses could never be as reliable as knowledge gained through pure reason. But he also believed in innate ideas: ideas similar to the ideas that Ben was talking about—what Ben called the intuitive immediate knowledge of God. Except that, for Descartes, our innate idea was the idea of the infinite. Descartes was convinced that we could never develop such an idea from observation, since everything we observe is finite. So the idea had to be in us innately, part of our original makeup. In fact, Descartes believed that the idea was given to us by God, stamped into us by God, as a sort of maker's mark or artist's signature: We are God's special creation, and we are stamped with this special idea of the infinite, which could come only from something infinite and thus could come only from God. In fact, that was the cornerstone of one of Descartes's proofs of the existence of God."

"Wow, Sarah, I like it." Ben gave it his stamp of approval. "Descartes is my kind of philosopher."

"Come on, Sarah, this is ancient history." Selina shook her head. "I mean, I like history fine—no knock on Ben's major. But what does this have to do with contemporary ideas about knowledge? Lot of water under the bridge since Descartes wrote in the 17th century. Just because *some people* haven't made any progress since then"—Selina indicated Ben with a nod of her head—"doesn't mean that the rest of us should be stuck in 17th-century dogma."

"Actually, Selina, this controversy stretches back at least to the 17th century, but it's not just philosophical history." Sarah was getting into the idea. "It was a huge issue in the 17th and 18th centuries: Descartes argued for *reason* as the key to knowledge, and he argued for the existence of innate ideas. And on Descartes's *rationalist* side—though, obviously, they didn't agree with him on everything—you had the great Dutch philosopher Benedict Spinoza, who is one of my favorites, and Gottfried Wilhelm Leibniz, who developed an elaborate rationalist metaphysics he called the monadology and who also worked out his theodicy, in which he endeavored to prove that this is the best of all possible worlds and thus answer the problem of evil—the problem we talked about before, remember, about why there is suffering in a world created by an omnipotent and omnibenevolent God. And in his spare time he worked out the calculus, at roughly the same time that Isaac Newton was doing calculus in England. And then there's Immanuel Kant, whom many consider a rationalist, and certainly in many ways he was. But Kant sort of fits into his own category. Anyway, on the other side, you get the *empiricists*, mainly in Great Britain. John Locke was a fierce opponent of Descartes, arguing that there are no innate ideas and that all our ideas—and, ultimately, all our knowledge of the world—are based in *sensory experience*. Locke coined a famous phrase, calling the human mind a *tabula rasa*—a blank slate—that experience then "writes upon." According to Locke, all our ideas must ultimately be rooted in our experiences. Of course, we can combine them in novel ways: He used the example of a golden mountain, in which we combine our ideas—that we gained from experience—of gold and mountain, even though we have never experienced an actual golden mountain. And David Hume—the great Scottish philosopher of the 18th century, who spent most of his life in France—was perhaps the most forceful and resourceful advocate of empiricist thought. He believed in

G. W. Leibniz (1646–1716) was a famous philosopher, mathematician, and scientist. He was caricatured by Voltaire in his novel Candide: *Leibniz is the model for Candide's friend, Dr. Pangloss, who— no matter what terrible disaster occurs—constantly assures Candide that there can be no doubt that this is "the best of all possible worlds." As a result of Voltaire's satirical depiction, Leibniz remains the stereotypical image of a philosopher spinning out metaphysical systems that have little relation to the actual world.*

John Locke (1632–1704) is famous for his work in philosophy as well as his writings on government. He supported the restoration of a constitutional monarchy in Britain, and his writings on the proper structure of government influenced the American debate concerning the U. S. Constitution.

mathematical truths, of course: He called them relations of ideas; but he also believed that the only source of knowledge of the real world, of "matters of fact," was experience. There's a great passage from Hume"—Sarah reached in her backpack for a battered paperback copy of Hume's *Enquiry* and turned to a passage she had highlighted in yellow—"that sums up his empiricist principles rather nicely:

> When we run over libraries, persuaded of these principles, what havoc must we make? If we take in our hand any volume; of divinity or school metaphysics, for instance; let us ask, *Does it contain any abstract reasoning concerning quantity or number?* No. *Does it contain any experimental reasoning concerning matter of fact and existence?* No. Commit it then to the flames: for it can contain nothing but sophistry and illusion."[2]

"Hooray for Hume! That's a great passage, Sarah. I want to get that printed on a poster and hang it up in our dorm room. We ought to have it engraved over the entrance to the library." Selina was delighted, but puzzled. "Still," said Selina, "isn't this just a chapter in the history of philosophy? Hume against Descartes, empiricism vs. rationalism: a fascinating jaunt into the 17th and 18th centuries, but not really an issue today, is it? Except for maybe one reactionary throwback who thinks he's the reincarnation of Descartes and whose name I will not mention out of courtesy."

"Actually, Selina," Sarah answered, "the controversy is far from dead. It seems to get played out in every generation. You ever read Noam Chomsky?"

"Sure, I love his stuff. I thought his book *9–11* was the best analysis of what actually led to the terrorist attacks and the best guide to preventing more of them. And his writings about the U.S. treatment of people in Latin America is wonderful, along with his work on the distortions made by the media. Great writer."

"Yeah," responded Sarah, "Chomsky's great on contemporary social and political issues. But that wasn't what I was thinking of, actually. Chomsky is also famous as a linguist: He was one of the major forces behind the 'transformational grammar' theories, and his writings on how children learn language had a great influence. Chomsky basically argued that learning a language is too difficult for children to accomplish in a relatively short period—just a few years, generally—simply by being exposed to people speaking the language. And of course, we are the only species that uses language, and chimpanzees raised from birth with humans don't start speaking a language. So human children must be starting with an innate advantage—some innate ideas of language. In other words, we do *not* start as a *tabula rasa*, as Locke claimed. Actually, Chomsky thinks we start with a fairly elaborate language *theory*, or language framework, and

A theory of linguistic structure that aims at explanatory adequacy incorporates an account of linguistic universals, and it attributes tacit knowledge of these universals to the child. It proposes, then, that the child approaches the data with the presumption that they are drawn from a language of a certain antecedently well-defined type, his problem being to determine which of the (humanly) possible languages is that of the community in which he is placed. Language learning would be impossible unless this were the case. The important question is: What are the initial assumptions concerning the nature of language that the child brings to language learning, and how detailed and specific is the innate schema . . . that gradually becomes more explicit and differentiated as the child learns the language?

Noam Chomsky, *Aspects of the Theory of Syntax*,
(Cambrigdge, MA: MIT Press, 1965), p. 27

then we fill in the parts of the theory as we are exposed to one particular language or another."

Selina was not pleased. "Hey, Sarah, that's dreadful news. Chomsky is on the side of the rationalists? How could anyone who writes so insightfully about politics and world affairs be a rationalist?"

"There are lots of very bright and insightful rationalists, Selina." Ben was enjoying this turn of events. "Just look around you."

"Yes, Chomsky would be classified a rationalist, I suppose. Actually, in one of his books he refers to his own position as *Cartesian*, and Descartes is the prototype of the species. Anyway, what I was going to ask, you know of the psychologist, B. F. Skinner, right?"

"Sure, we studied him in intro psychology. He was a behaviorist, right? He maintained that the best way to study psychology was to study behavior and the environment that shaped it, rather than speculating about mysterious unconscious thoughts and hidden feelings and miracle-working minds. And of course, he was a strict empiricist, who insisted that all claims about psychology had to be empirically testable. I really liked his *Beyond Freedom and Dignity*."

"Yeah, that's the guy, Selina. He and Chomsky had a long controversy over language and language acquisition, and about psychology generally. There were other issues involved, of

The growth of language in a child is easily compared with the growth of an embryo, and grammar can then be attributed to rules possessed by the child at birth. A program in the form of a genetic code is said to "initiate and guide early learning . . . as a child acquires language." But the human species did not evolve because of any inbuilt design: it evolved through selection under contingencies of survival, as the child's verbal behavior evolves under the selective action of contingencies of reinforcement.

B. F. Skinner, *About Behaviorism*, p. 99

course, but at the root of the conflict was the controversy between Chomsky's rationalism and Skinner's empiricism. So the rationalist–empiricist struggle continues—it's not just a matter of philosophical history."

"If the battle is still raging," Ben interjected, "then I want to march under the banner of rationalism."

"And I'll stand at the barricades with the empiricists," Selina replied.

Ben frowned. "Look, Sarah, I like rationalism, and I like Descartes. I do believe there is something special and distinct about humans and human powers and human reason. And I believe that the special human powers of reason and logic and principle are the best means of gaining genuine knowledge—certainly better than the fallible sensory capacities that we share with other animals, which often have more acute sensory powers—of hearing, sight, and smell—than humans do. We should use our distinctive strength to gain knowledge, and our distinctive strength is our power of reason. Still, I don't really believe that our knowledge is limited to our knowledge of God, and of math and geometry—oh, and my knowledge that I exist. Can't we know, with certainty, some things about this world?"

"Sure you can, Ben." Selina took her turn. "Just become a scientist. Science teaches us a great many solid truths about the world."

"No, I still can't buy that, Selina. Science is too transitory: Today's scientific wisdom is tomorrow's rejected scientific history. No, I mean solid, unchanging certain truths about this world. Do any philosophers believe such truths can be known, Sarah?"

Kant

"There was another philosopher who might interest you, Ben," answered Sarah. "In fact, he struggled with exactly the question you're asking. Immanuel Kant firmly believed that there was special certain knowledge of the world. In fact, he believed that we could know some things about the world without depending on experience."

Selina was skeptical. "Sounds like just another version of the rationalist mysteries, the amazing power of reason."

"Not quite the same, Selina, though Kant was certainly closer to rationalism than to empiricism. Anyway, to get a full picture of the position Kant favored, we'll need to look at some special terminology: terminology that Kant didn't invent, though he made great use of it. First, there's the *analytic–synthetic* distinction. *Analytic* statements are matters of definition, in which the predicate is part of the definition of the subject. For example, if we say, 'A bachelor is unmarried,' that's *true*, though perhaps not very informative. For after all, 'unmarried' is part of the definition of bachelor. 'Cats are animals.' That's an analytic truth, too, because if something is a plant, then, by definition, you know it's not a cat. But synthetic statements are different: In synthetic statements, the predicate adds something to the subject—something not contained in the definition of the subject. For example, 'Cats are good hunters.' That tells us something about cats, something that goes beyond the definition of cats."

"Or like 'Selina is beautiful.' That's a true synthetic statement, since beauty is not part of the definition of Selina, though maybe it should be."

"God, he's a silver-tongued devil, isn't he, Sarah? I'm sure Ben's the first guy who ever whispered into a girl's ear, 'It's a synthetic truth that you are beautiful.'"

Sarah sighed. "If we're finished whispering sweet nothings, perhaps we can consider the second distinction: *a priori–a posteriori*."

Immanuel Kant (1724–1804) lived his entire life in East Prussia, never leaving it during his lifetime. His great work, the Critique of Pure Reason *(1781), was aimed at nothing less than establishing the powers, as well as the limits, of reason. It was followed by his major works in ethics:* The Foundations of the Metaphysics of Morals *(1785) and* Critique of Practical Reason *(1788). His writings have had an enormous impact on the ethical and epistemological thought of the last two centuries.*

"Where *do* you philosophers come up with these terms, Sarah?" Ben had the feeling the discussion was going on in another language. "I thought scientists used strange terms—quark, neutralino, muon neutrino—but philosophers are just as bad."

"We philosophers have been around for a long time, Ben, and we have a glorious history. Philosophy was already two thousand years old when chemistry was still trying to transmute lead into gold. So many of our terms were developed in other eras and in other languages. Like *a priori–a posteriori*—that goes back to the centuries when most scholarly writing was in Latin."

"Well, wherever it came from, what does it mean?"

"It's just a distinction between the ways we gain knowledge. *A priori* knowledge is knowledge we have *prior* to experience, or, more precisely, knowledge that is based on *reason* rather than observation. It doesn't really come *prior* to experience—unless you believe in pure innate ideas that were placed in us prior to birth. I guess Descartes thought we had a few such ideas, and Plato thought we had lots of them. But leaving innate ideas aside, there is a whole range of knowledge that seems to come from *reason* rather than experience. Remember when your first-grade teacher held up two red balls and then two green balls and asked how many balls was that altogether? Then she put them down on the desk, and you all counted out four, right? Looking at the brightly colored balls helped you to grasp the concept, but mathematical knowledge isn't *really* based on experience, is it? Think about it: What sort of experiment would convince you that two plus two equals five? Suppose I took two balls in this hand and then two in the other hand, put them together, and *voila:* five balls. What would you say?"

"I'd say you were a great magician, Sarah," replied Ben.

"Exactly! But suppose you were convinced that I wasn't using sleight of hand. Then what?"

"Then somehow the four balls together are generating another ball: Maybe four balls together in a dark space can reproduce. Or maybe the fifth ball materialized out of subatomic particles drawn randomly together. Or maybe God created it out of nothingness."

"Rather wild scenarios, Ben. But while you might consider even such bizarre events, you would *not* consider the possibility that two plus two actually equals five. If the number were larger, you might consider the possibility that you made an error in calculation. You might even consider the possibility that you were losing your rational faculties and could no longer do mathematics. But there is no experiment that would refute mathematical truths. Of course, we might decide that a different set of mathematical or geometrical principles is more convenient for some applications. For example, Einstein found non-Euclidean geometry very useful for some of his theoretical work. But that was not experimental proof that Euclidean geometry was wrong; it only showed that other sets of geometrical axioms might also have uses. And clearly, a mathematician might prove that some mathematical principle we had always thought true was in fact false; but the proof would be a proof *within* mathematics, not an empirical or experimental proof that some mathematical principle is false. That couldn't happen, because mathematics and geometry are not based on experience; rather, they are based purely on *reason*. That is, they are *a priori* truths. Now, obviously, if some monster had locked you in a dark closet at birth, in a situation of total sensory deprivation, yet somehow kept you nourished and alive, then you never would have understood anything about mathematics and geometry. Being the sorts of social animals we are, we need social interaction and experience to become healthy, competent reasoners. But our reasoning about mathematics is not *based* on such experiences. The experiences may be a necessary condition for our reasoning powers to develop; but once those powers are mature, we can know truths of reason, *a priori* truths, that are independent of our experience—truths that no experience or experiment could refute."

Ben nodded. "Okay, I think I've got some idea of *a priori* knowledge—though it's still a bit fuzzy around the edges. What about *a posteriori* knowledge?"

"Oh, that's Selina's side of the shop. *A posteriori* knowledge is knowledge based on experience. You know that snow is cold because you have played in it without your mittens. You know that robins fly because you chased one you saw hopping along, and when you got close, it soared into the air. Selina knows that oxygen is essential for combustion because she's run the experiment. And she knows that salt is a combination of sodium and chloride because she's pulled it apart in her laboratory. Of course, she may have used mathematical reasoning in her research, but her research is still based on observational experience: Her results are known *a posteriori*. No matter how long you sit and think about it, you couldn't know those truths without experience. Obviously, once you have gained some *a posteriori* knowledge, you can apply it to other cases through reasoning: I've never dropped a bowling ball on my foot, but I have good grounds for believing it would be unpleasant, rather than delightful. After all, I once dropped a large dictionary on my foot, and it was very unpleasant. So even without running the experiment with the bowling ball, I know that dropping one on my foot is not likely to bring me joy. Still, that's *a posteriori* knowledge, based on painful experience."

Selina was growing restless. "Alright, Sarah, you've got this distinction between analytic and synthetic statements, and another distinction between stuff that's known *a priori* and stuff that's known *a posteriori*. What are you going to do with them?"

"Actually, it's what *Immanuel Kant* did with them. He used them to set up a sort of grid, with four distinct categories: analytic *a priori*, analytic *a posteriori*, synthetic *a priori*, and synthetic *a posteriori*. So consider each category: What do we find under analytic *a priori*? Well, we find statements like 'A bachelor is unmarried,' right? That's a standard analytic statement, and certainly we don't require experience to know that it's true. Maybe mathematics and geometry belong here, also, but that gets into considerable controversy. Are the truths of mathematics based purely on definitions, and the working out of the implications

Mathematics is a natural part of being human. It arises from our bodies, our brains, and our everyday experiences in the world. Cultures everywhere have some form of mathematics. There is nothing mysterious, mystical, magical, or transcendent about mathematics. It is an important subject of human study. It is a consequence of human evolutionary history, neurobiology, cognitive capacities, and culture.

George Lakoff and Rafael E. Núñez, *Where Mathematics Comes From* (New York: Basic Books, 2000)

The propositions of mathematics have . . . the same unquestionable certainty which is typical of such propositions as "All bachelors are unmarried," but they also share the complete lack of empirical content which is associated with that certainty: The propositions of mathematics are devoid of all factual content; they convey no information whatever on any empirical subject matter.

Carl Hempel, "On the Nature of Mathematical Truth," *American Mathematical Monthly*, 52 (1945)

of those definitions? Let's leave that for another day; better yet, let's leave it to the mathematicians. Consider the second category: analytic *a posteriori*. What do we find there? Nothing. That's an empty category. If something is an analytic truth—a truth based purely on definition—then, obviously, it's not known by experience, right? Okay, skip down to the last category: synthetic *a posteriori*. That one's easy: It's chock full of all kinds of stuff. Water turns into steam when it boils, eagles can fly, penguins cannot fly, Michael Jordan is a great jumper, Ben loves Selina, continents shift on tectonic plates, an oxygen atom contains two electrons, tadpoles turn into frogs, and frogs do not become handsome princes when you kiss them. None of those statements are matters of definition, and none can be known purely by reason. It would be very surprising if frogs turned into princes when you kiss them, but we didn't know that they wouldn't until we tried. Actually, we already knew, on the basis of other stuff we know about biology: Animals don't change species that easily, but that's something we know by scientific experience. So, anyway, the synthetic *a posteriori* category is crammed full. The interesting question arises when we examine the third category: the synthetic *a priori*. Is it occupied? That is, are there any real synthetic truths (not merely analytic truths by definition) that can be known *a priori*—known purely by reason? Can we know things about the world—not merely definitions—by means of pure *a priori* reasoning? *That* question has caused controversy ever since Kant asked it, way back in the 18th century."

Selina laughed. "So *that* is the sort of question that gets philosophers excited: Are there any synthetic *a priori* truths? What happened to all those other famous philosophical questions? What's the meaning of life? If a tree falls in the forest and no one hears it, does it make a sound? Why is there something rather than nothing? I don't know, Sarah: Those sound like sexier questions than 'Are there any synthetic *a priori* truths?'"

"But it's a very important question, Selina." Sarah leaned forward. "It's the question of whether there is any factual truth about the world that can be known strictly through reason and that is not derived from experience. What question could be more important than that? In fact, it's the way Kant posed that question that has made him generally regarded as one of the great philosophers in Western history. I'm guessing that if you asked fifty philosophers to name their top five philosophers, at least forty of them would have Kant in the top five. And that's about as much agreement as you are likely to find among philosophers: We are a charming, but somewhat contentious, lot. Much like some couples I know."

Selina poked playfully at Sarah. "Hey, girl, that's a low blow. Ben, are you gonna sit there and let Sarah demean us? Listen, you can insult our manners and deplore our morals, but don't go comparing us with philosophers."

Sarah raised her hands. "Sorry, guys. That was a vicious shot. Anyway, what made Kant a great philosopher was not so much the answer he gave to that question—though he gave a very interesting and profoundly influential answer—but the way he posed the question; or maybe it was the fact that he recognized that there was a question to be posed at all. Anyway, that's Kant's question: Are there any synthetic *a priori* truths? Are there truths about the world that can be known purely by reason? Is there anything about the world that we could know just by sitting quietly in a darkened room and *reasoning?*"

"That's the trouble with philosophers, Sarah. They're great at asking questions, but lousy at answering them." Selina was ready to move along. "Scientists, on the other hand, not only ask questions: they answer them as well. And the answer is clear: No. That is, if you leave math and geometry out of it, then the synthetic *a priori* category is *empty*. If you want to know real, substantial truths about the world, you have to get out there and do the hard, grubby work: Set up the laboratory, design the equipment, run the experiments, make the observations. It's hard work; but sitting and reasoning won't give you the answers. Reason is fine, I'm not knocking it; scientists have to make good use of it. But reason alone, without experience and experiment and careful observation, can never tell you truths about the world. You have to get your hands dirty. There is no pure rational shortcut to knowledge of the world."

"Spoken like a good empiricist, Selina," said Sarah. "Hold that empiricist banner high. But are you really so sure that there are *no* synthetic *a priori* truths? What can you know about what will happen tomorrow? I mean, just by sitting and thinking and reasoning—not on the basis of any experience or observation—what can you *know* about tomorrow? You don't know what direction the stock market will go, or which football teams will win, or what discoveries will be made, or what wars might break out. But is there anything you *do* know about what will happen tomorrow, entirely on the basis of your reason?"

"She knows what I'll do tomorrow," interjected Ben. "Selina can read me like a book."

"And a fascinating book it is, Ben. But Selina's knowledge is based on past experience. Without that *a posteriori* knowledge of your habits and desires and inclinations, she couldn't tell what you're going to do tomorrow; that is, she couldn't know purely by *a priori* reasoning."

"What are you getting at, Sarah?" Selina wore a puzzled look. "Are you claiming to be some sort of clairvoyant? You can see into the future purely by your use of reason? Call Miss Sarah on her 900 number, she knows all and tells all."

"No, nothing like that, Selina. But there is something I know about what will happen in the future, about all events in the future: They will occur in space and time.

"Well, la de da, Sarah, that's certainly exciting news." Selina shook her head. "If I had paid you to read my future, I'd be demanding my money back."

"Maybe it's more exciting than it looks at first glance, Selina. It may not provide any hot tips for the stock market or the race track, but it *does* provide something important: synthetic *a priori* knowledge—knowledge about the world that is derived purely from reason. All the events that occur tomorrow will occur in space and time. And notice, that's not just some handy generalization based on the past: It's an absolute truth, a universal truth, something we know with *certainty*. And that's a clear mark of *a priori* truth, because anything we know from experience is based on very high probability, not absolute certainty: Dr. Reichard will assign a heavy load of reading for my philosophy of mind class because she has assigned a heavy load every class she has taught for the past twenty-five years; that's very likely, but it could be false. Ben is going to run this afternoon because he has run every single day for the last three years; again highly likely, but today might be the exception. But whatever Dr. Reichard and Ben do, their acts—and *all* the events that occur—will occur in space and time. That's certain, *a priori* knowledge. And it's synthetic, not analytic: There's nothing in the *definition* of Ben's running that says it must occur in space and time. That is something we *add*, and we add it by pure reason. So the synthetic *a priori* category is *not* empty, as you suggested it was."

Selina was shaking her head. "Look, Sarah, even if I grant that this stuff about everything occurring in space and time is a synthetic *a priori* truth, it doesn't seem very significant. Those are pretty trivial—not to say pathetic—examples of truths."

"Not trivial at all, Selina. Amazing, actually. How could we know something about the *world*, something about the world *out there*, not just about our ideas—how could we know something about that world by *pure reason?* How do we *know* that every event that occurs will occur in space and time? Not because we have seen space and time operate in the past. That might tell us that events in the past occurred in space and time, and it might give us good reason to believe that all future events will also occur in space and time. But this is different. I don't just *project*, on the basis of past experience, that all future events will also occur in space and time; I *know* that all future events—and all past and present events, for that matter, including those I did not observe—will occur in space and time. That has to be a very special sort of knowledge. How do I know that all the events *out there* in the world will conform to that belief? It's because space and time are a necessary element of my thought process, of the way I perceive and conceptualize the world. It tells me something very important about the system of ideas and categories that we use in ordering our experience of the world. In fact, it tells us about the basic way we order our experience—so basic that it is very difficult to pull it apart from what is experienced, because it is always there, the lens through which we experience the world."

"But Sarah," Ben asked, "if space and time are parts of my thought processes, then when I say that all events occur in space and time, I'm not really saying anything about the world; instead, I'm merely saying something about me."

"In one sense, Kant would agree with you, Ben. He said that space and time were 'empirically real, but transcendentally ideal.' That is, space and time are not part of the world as it is—the world as perhaps God would understand it in perfect unmediated understanding. But don't say that it's *merely* what we bring to experience. Experience is impossible without such categorizations. Trying to dismiss them would be like trying to have experience without having experience. They are an essential element of all our empirical observations, not just something we add on as an option, like deciding to look at everything through tinted glasses for a couple of hours."

"But really, Kant didn't discover any essential categories after all." Selina shook her head. "What he thought were absolutely essential and necessary elements of our conceptual system turned out to be just the Newtonian concept of space and time. We now know that there are other ways to conceptualize the world: Newton thought Euclidean geometry eternal and absolute, and Kant followed him; but in fact, other systems of *non*-Euclidean geometry can also offer valuable perspectives, as Einstein's work made clear. And quantum mechanics offers new conceptual systems as well."

"Ah, yes, good point, Selina." Sarah nodded. "The conception of space and time that Kant thought universal and eternal for all human perception of the world was actually the conception that Newton used. Kant was convinced that the conception of space and time held by Newton was fixed and unchanging, at least for creatures like ourselves. Newton had just formulated his laws of motion, which transformed a world of chaotic confusion into one of sublime order. The poet Alexander Pope expressed the view of most people when he proposed this as Newton's epitaph:

> *Nature and Nature's laws lay hid in night;*
> *God said, Let Newton be, and all was light.*

Newton had pulled together physics and astronomy, and shown how they all fit together: The same simple laws that govern the orbit of the earth around the sun, and the moon around the earth, and even the path of a comet, also explain the motion of a ball dropping from a tower or thrown from one person to another. Newton had found the key to the universe, read the mind of God, discovered the ultimate principles of physics; or so it seemed to Newton's contemporaries. So it was hardly surprising that Kant thought Newton's conception of space and time was the last word on the subject."

"And Kant was wrong," Selina said. "Typical philosophical arrogance: Philosophers always believe they've discovered the eternal truth. Mathematicians and scientists now recognize that there are many conceptions of space and time and many systems of geometry. Einstein showed quite clearly that Newton's conception of space and time is not essential for us. And contemporary physicists are suggesting still other alternatives."

"Okay, Kant's belief about the eternal truth of the Newtonian model was wrong. But the point is, there will *always* be the influence of our own perspective. And it is there we find synthetic *a priori* truths: in our own way of conceptualizing the world. That essential framework sets the framework in which we see the world and so is assumed in all our empirical observations. Thus, we can know *a priori*, necessary, universal truths about the world. There are synthetic *a priori* truths because we use categories and impose perceptual structure when we have experiences; with apologies to William James, without such structure, our experiences would be a 'blooming buzzing confusion.' They are neither arbitrary nor optional, according to Kant: They are necessary for our intelligible experience of the world. And by recognizing the synthetic *a priori*, we can come to understand the importance of what we bring to our experience of the world. Kant made us look more carefully at what elements of our experience are there because of our conceptual and perceptual apparatus. Look, you've had the experience of being in a car, or maybe on a train or ship, and for a second the world around you seems to move backward; but then you realize it's because your car is moving. Kant's insight into the synthetic *a priori* helps us recognize the importance of what we contribute to experience: the necessary contribution we make and the universal necessity of that contribution. Maybe the categories and conceptual framework are not absolute and eternal, as Kant thought; but the importance of recognizing the framework we impose upon our experiences remains."

"I don't know, Sarah." Selina was still skeptical. "Seems to me Kant has a lot more rationalism than empiricism. But speaking of empiricism, it's time for my lab. Kant will have to wait." Selina gathered her books, while Ben quickly finished his coffee.

"No problem," Sarah replied, "Kant is very patient. It's a common virtue among philosophers."

"You go cultivate your virtue, Sarah. While you're at it, you might work on the virtue of neatness. Our room is starting to look like a wing of University Library. I know you philosophers love books, but don't you ever return them? Between you and Ben, I live in fear of being buried under an avalanche of history and philosophy books. What an ignominious demise for a brilliant young chemistry researcher: Instead of getting blown up in my lab, I'm crushed under heavy volumes of metaphysics. Ciao, y'all; see you at dinner."

READINGS

René Descartes (1596–1650) is sometimes referred to as the "father of modern philosophy." His claim to that title is based on his shift of emphasis from what we know to the question of how we know. Though he was a firm and orthodox Christian, Descartes's emphasis on what can be known through the use of reason (without the use of sacred texts or religious faith) also marks him as modern in outlook. Descartes lived in an age of great skepticism: Copernican astronomy was still strongly condemned by the Church, but it had gained sufficient influence to call into question both the Ptolemaic astronomy and Aristotelian physics that had dominated thought for more than a millennium and also to cast doubt on the most basic of commonsense beliefs (that we are stationary at the center of the universe and the Sun moves over our heads) and to threaten the Aristotelian–Christian cosmological view that had been fashioned throughout the medieval period. Descartes himself favored the Copernican view, though he was very cautious not to express that opinion openly (since the Church had publicly condemned and imprisoned Galileo when Descartes was thirty-eight). Descartes's strong insistence that knowledge and science must be based on certainty, and his methodical argument that such certainty can be found only through reason, established him as a leading and profoundly influential rationalist philosopher.

Descartes spent most of his adult life in Holland, where there was less danger that radical thinkers would be persecuted by the religious and civil authorities. Even so, he was always very cautious in his writings, and his support for the Copernican perspective is at most suggested, never explicitly stated. After a long correspondence with Queen Christina of Sweden, he was finally persuaded in 1649 to move to Stockholm to instruct her further in philosophy. Descartes had always preferred to sleep late and then work in his dressing gown before a warm fire. The harsh winter climate of Sweden, as well as the very early tutorial hours demanded by the energetic queen, may have done him no good, and he died of pneumonia the next year.

The passage that follows is from the first two of Descartes's famous Meditations on First Philosophy, *in which he develops his method of extreme doubt, to then reach a bedrock of rational certainty that is indubitable.*

Meditations on the First Philosophy in Which the Existence of God and the Distinction Between Mind and Body are Demonstrated

Meditation I

Of the things which may be brought within the sphere of the doubtful.

It is now some years since I detected how many were the false beliefs that I had from my earliest youth admitted as true, and how doubtful was everything I had since constructed on this basis; and from that time I was convinced that I must once and for all seriously undertake to rid myself of all the opinions which I had formerly accepted, and commence to build anew from the foundation, if I wanted to establish any firm and permanent structure in the sciences. But as this enterprise appeared to be a very great one, I waited until I had attained an age so mature that I could not hope that at any later date I should be better fitted to execute my design. This reason caused me to delay so long that I should feel that I was doing wrong were I to occupy in deliberation the time that yet remains to me for action. To-day, then, since very opportunely for the plan I have in view I have delivered my mind from every care [and am happily agitated by no passions] and since I have procured for myself an assured leisure in a peaceable retirement, I shall at last seriously and freely address myself to the general upheaval of all my former opinions.

Now for this object it is not necessary that I should show that all of these are false—I shall perhaps never arrive at this end. But inasmuch as reason already persuades me that I ought no less carefully to withhold my assent from matters which are not entirely certain and indubitable than from those which appear to me manifestly to be false, if I am able to find in each one some reason to doubt, this will suffice to justify my rejecting the whole. And for that end it will not be requisite that I should examine each in particular, which would be an endless undertaking; for owing to the fact that the destruction of the foundations of necessity brings with it the downfall of the rest of the edifice, I shall only in the first place attack those principles upon which all my former opinions rested.

All that up to the present time I have accepted as most true and certain I have learned either from the senses or through the senses; but it is sometimes proved to me that these senses are deceptive, and it is wiser not to trust entirely to any thing by which we have once been deceived.

But it may be that although the senses sometimes deceive us concerning things which are hardly perceptible, or very far away, there are yet many others to be met with as to which we cannot reasonably have any doubt, although we recognise them by their means. For example, there is the fact that I am here, seated by the fire, attired in a dressing gown, having this paper in my hands and other similar matters. And how could I deny that these hands and this body are mine, were it not perhaps that I compare myself to certain persons, devoid of sense, whose cerebella are so troubled and clouded by the violent vapours of black bile, that they constantly assure us that they think they are kings when they are really quite poor, or that they are clothed in purple when they are really without covering, or who imagine that they have an earthenware head or are nothing but pumpkins or are made of glass. But they are mad, and I should not be any the less insane were I to follow examples so extravagant.

At the same time I must remember that I am a man, and that consequently I am in the habit of sleeping, and in my dreams representing to myself the same things or sometimes even less probable things, than do those who are insane in their waking moments. How often has it happened to me that in the night I dreamt that I found myself in this particular place, that I was dressed and seated near the fire, whilst in reality I was lying undressed in bed! At this moment it does indeed seem to me that it is with eyes awake that I am looking at this paper; that this head which I move is not asleep, that it is deliberately and of set purpose that I extend my hand and perceive it; what happens in sleep does not appear so clear nor so distinct as does all this. But in thinking over this I remind myself that on many occasions I have in sleep been deceived by similar illusions, and in dwelling carefully on this reflection I see so manifestly that there are no certain indications by which we may clearly distinguish wakefulness from sleep that I am lost in astonishment. And my astonishment is such that it is almost capable of persuading me that I now dream.

Now let us assume that we are asleep and that all these particulars, e.g. that we open our eyes, shake our head, extend our hands, and so on, are but false delusions; and let us reflect that possibly neither our hands nor our whole body are such as they appear to us to be. At the same time we must at least confess that the things which are represented to us in sleep are like painted representations which can only have been formed as the counterparts of something real and true, and that in this way those general things at least, i.e. eyes, a head, hands, and a whole body, are not imaginary things, but things really existent. For, as a matter of fact, painters, even when they study with the greatest skill to represent sirens and satyrs by forms the most strange and extraordinary, cannot give them natures which are entirely new, but merely make a certain medley of the members of different animals; or if their imagination is extravagant enough to invent something so novel that nothing similar has ever before been seen, and that then their work represents a thing purely fictitious and absolutely false, it is certain all the same that the colours of which this is composed are necessarily real. And for the same reason, although these general things, to wit, [a body], eyes, a head, hands, and such like, may be imaginary, we are bound at the same time to confess that there are at least some other objects yet more simple and more universal, which are real and true; and of these just in the same way as with certain real colours, all these images of things which dwell in our thoughts, whether true and real or false and fantastic, are formed.

To such a class of things pertains corporeal nature in general, and its extension, the figure of extended things, their quantity or magnitude and number, as also the place in which they are, the time which measures their duration, and so on.

That is possibly why our reasoning is not unjust when we conclude from this that Physics, Astronomy, Medicine and all other sciences which have as their end the consideration of composite things, are very dubious and uncertain; but that Arithmetic, Geometry and other sciences of that kind which only treat of things that are very simple and very general, without taking great trouble to ascertain whether they are actually existent or not, contain some measure of certainty and an element of the indubitable. For whether I am awake or asleep, two and three together always form five, and the square can never have more than four sides, and it does not seem possible that truths so clear and apparent can be suspected of any falsity [or uncertainty].

Nevertheless I have long had fixed in my mind the belief that an all-powerful God existed by whom I have been created such as I am. But how do I know that He has not brought it to pass that there is no earth, no heaven, no extended body, no magnitude, no place, and that nevertheless

[I possess the perceptions of all these things and that] they seem to me to exist just exactly as I now see them? And, besides, as I sometimes imagine that others deceive themselves in the things which they think they know best, how do I know that I am not deceived every time that I add two and three, or count the sides of a square, or judge of things yet simpler, if anything simpler can be imagined? But possibly God has not desired that I should be thus deceived, for He is said to be supremely good. If, however, it is contrary to His goodness to have made me such that I constantly deceive myself, it would also appear to be contrary to His goodness to permit me to be sometimes deceived, and nevertheless I cannot doubt that He does permit this.

There may indeed be those who would prefer to deny the existence of a God so powerful, rather than believe that all other things are uncertain. But let us not oppose them for the present, and grant that all that is here said of a God is a fable; nevertheless in whatever way they suppose that I have arrived at the state of being that I have reached—whether they attribute it to fate or to accident, or make out that it is by a continual succession of antecedents, or by some other method—since to err and deceive oneself is a defect, it is clear that the greater will be the probability of my being so imperfect as to deceive myself ever, as is the Author to whom they assign my origin the less powerful. To these reasons I have certainly nothing to reply, but at the end I feel constrained to confess that there is nothing in all that I formerly believed to be true, of which I cannot in some measure doubt, and that not merely through want of thought or through levity, but for reasons which are very powerful and maturely considered; so that henceforth I ought not the less carefully to refrain from giving credence to these opinions than to that which is manifestly false, if I desire to arrive at any certainty [in the sciences].

But it is not sufficient to have made these remarks, we must also be careful to keep them in mind. For these ancient and commonly held opinions still revert frequently to my mind, long and familiar custom having given them the right to occupy my mind against my inclination and rendered them almost masters of my belief; nor will I ever lose the habit of deferring to them or of placing my confidence in them, so long as I consider them as they really are, i.e. opinions in some measure doubtful, as I have just shown, and at the same time highly probable, so that there is much more reason to believe in than to deny them. That is why I consider that I shall not be acting amiss, if, taking of set purpose a contrary belief, I allow myself to be deceived, and for a certain time pretend that all these opinions are entirely false and imaginary, until at last, having thus balanced my former prejudices with my latter [so that they cannot divert my opinions more to one side than to the other], my judgment will no longer be dominated by bad usage or turned away from the right knowledge of the truth. For I am assured that there can be neither peril nor error in this course, and that I cannot at present yield too much to distrust, since I am not considering the question of action, but only of knowledge.

I shall then suppose, not that God who is supremely good and the fountain of truth, but some evil genius not less powerful than deceitful, has employed his whole energies in deceiving me; I shall consider that the heavens, the earth, colours, figures, sound, and all other external things are nought but the illusions and dreams of which this genius has availed himself in order to lay traps for my credulity; I shall consider myself as having no hands, no eyes, no flesh, no blood, nor any senses, yet falsely believing myself to possess all these things; I shall remain obstinately attached to this idea, and if by this means it is not in my power to arrive at the knowledge of any truth, I may at least do what is in my power [i.e. suspend my judgment], and with firm purpose avoid giving credence to any false thing, or being imposed upon by this arch deceiver, however powerful and deceptive he may be. But this task is a laborious one, and insensibly a certain lassitude leads me into the course of my ordinary life. And just as a captive who in sleep enjoys an imaginary liberty, when he begins to suspect that his liberty is but a dream, fears to awaken, and conspires with these agreeable illusions that the deception may be prolonged, so insensibly of my own accord I fall back into my former opinions, and I dread awakening from this slumber, lest the laborious wakefulness which would follow the tranquillity of this repose should have to be spent not in daylight, but in the excessive darkness of the difficulties which have just been discussed.

Meditation II

Of the Nature of the Human Mind; and that it is more easily known than the Body.

The Meditation of yesterday filled my mind with so many doubts that it is no longer in my power to forget them. And yet I do not see in what manner I can resolve them; and, just as if I had all of a sudden fallen into very deep water, I am so disconcerted that I can neither make certain of setting my feet on the bottom, nor can I swim and so support myself on the surface. I shall nevertheless make an effort and follow anew the same path as that on which I yesterday entered, i.e. I shall proceed by setting aside all that in which the least doubt could be supposed to exist, just as if I had discovered that it was absolutely false; and I shall ever follow in this road until I have met with something which is certain, or at least, if I can do nothing else, until I have learned for certain that there is nothing in the world that is certain. Archimedes, in order that he might draw the terrestrial globe out of its place, and transport it elsewhere, demanded only that one point should be fixed and immoveable; in the same way I shall have the right to conceive high hopes if I am happy enough to discover one thing only which is certain and indubitable.

I suppose, then, that all the things that I see are false; I persuade myself that nothing has ever existed of all that my fallacious memory represents to me. I consider that I possess no senses; I imagine that body, figure, extension, movement and place are but the fictions of my mind. What, then, can be esteemed as true? Perhaps nothing at all, unless that there is nothing in the world that is certain.

But how can I know there is not something different from those things that I have just considered, of which one cannot have the slightest doubt? Is there not some God, or some other being by whatever name we call it, who puts these reflections into my mind? That is not necessary, for is it not possible that I am capable of producing them myself? I myself, am I not at least something? But I have already denied that I had senses and body. Yet I hesitate, for what follows from that? Am I so dependent on body and senses that I cannot exist without these? But I was persuaded that there was nothing in all the world, that there was no heaven, no earth, that there were no minds, nor any bodies: was I not then likewise persuaded that I did not exist? Not at all; of a surety I myself did exist since I persuaded myself of something [or merely because I thought of something]. But there is some deceiver or other, very powerful and very cunning, who ever employs his ingenuity in deceiving me. Then without doubt I exist also if he deceives me, and let him deceive me as much as he will, he can never cause me to be nothing so long as I think that I am something. So that after having reflected well and carefully examined all things, we must come to the definite conclusion that this proposition: I am, I exist, is necessarily true each time that I pronounce it, or that I mentally conceive it.

But I do not yet know clearly enough what I am, I who am certain that I am; and hence I must be careful to see that I do not imprudently take some other object in place of myself, and thus that I do not go astray in respect of this knowledge that I hold to be the most certain and most evident of all that I have formerly learned. That is why I shall now consider anew what I believed myself to be before I embarked upon these last reflections; and of my former opinions I shall withdraw all that might even in a small degree be invalidated by the reasons which I have just brought forward, in order that there may be nothing at all left beyond what is absolutely certain and indubitable.

What then did I formerly believe myself to be? Undoubtedly I believed myself to be a man. But what is a man? Shall I say a reasonable animal? Certainly not; for then I should have to inquire what an animal is, and what is reasonable; and thus from a single question I should insensibly fall into an infinitude of others more difficult; and I should not wish to waste the little time and leisure remaining to me in trying to unravel subtleties like these. But I shall rather stop here to consider the thoughts which of themselves spring up in my mind, and which were not inspired by anything beyond my own nature alone when I applied myself to the consideration of my being. In the first place, then, I considered myself as having a face, hands, arms, and all that system of members composed of bones and flesh as seen in a corpse which I designated by the name of body. In addition to this I considered that I was nourished, that I walked, that I felt, and that I thought, and I referred all these actions to the soul: but I did not stop to consider what the soul was, or if I did stop, I imagined that it was something extremely rare and subtle like a wind, a flame, or an ether, which was spread throughout my grosser parts. As to body I had no manner of doubt about its nature, but thought I had a very clear knowledge of it; and if I had desired to explain it according to the notions that I had then formed of it, I should have described it thus: By the body I understand all that which can be defined by a certain figure: something which can be confined in a certain place, and which can fill a given space in such a way that every other body will be excluded from it; which can be perceived either by touch, or by sight, or by hearing, or by taste, or by smell: which can be moved in many ways not, in truth, by itself, but by something which is foreign to it, by which it is touched [and from which it receives impressions]: for to have the power of self-movement, as also of feeling or of thinking, I did not consider to appertain to the nature of body: on the contrary, I was rather astonished to find that faculties similar to them existed in some bodies.

But what am I, now that I suppose that there is a certain genius which is extremely powerful, and, if I may say so, malicious, who employs all his powers in deceiving me? Can I affirm that I possess the least of all those things which I have just said pertain to the nature of body? I pause to consider, I revolve all these things in my mind, and I find none of which I can say that it pertains to me. It would be tedious to stop to enumerate them. Let us pass to the attributes of soul and see if there is any one which is in me? What of nutrition or walking [the first mentioned]? But if it is so that I have no body it is also true that I can neither walk nor take nourishment. Another attribute is sensation. But one cannot feel without body, and besides I have thought I perceived many things during sleep that I recognised in my waking moments as not having been experienced at all. What of thinking? I find here that thought is an attribute that belongs to me; it alone cannot be separated from me. I am, I exist, that is certain. But how often? Just when I think; for it might possibly be the case if I ceased entirely to think, that I should likewise cease altogether to exist. I do not now admit anything which is not necessarily true: to speak accurately I am not more than a thing which thinks, that is to say a mind or a soul, or an understanding, or a reason, which are terms whose significance was formerly unknown to me. I am, however, a real thing and really exist; but what thing? I have answered: a thing which thinks.

And what more? I shall exercise my imagination [in order to see if I am not something more]. I am not a collection of members which we call the human body: I am not a subtle air distributed through these members, I am not a wind, a fire, a vapour, a breath, nor anything at all which I can imagine or conceive; because I have assumed that all these were nothing. Without changing that supposition I find that I only leave myself certain of the fact that I am somewhat. But perhaps it is true that these same things which I supposed were non-existent because they are unknown to me, are really not different from the self which I know. I am not sure about this, I shall not dispute about it now; I can only give judgment on things that are known to me. I know that I exist, and I inquire what I am, I whom I know to exist. But it is very certain that the knowledge of my existence taken in its precise significance does not depend on things whose existence is not yet known to me; consequently it does not depend on those which I can feign in imagination. And indeed the very term *feign* in imagination[1] proves to me my error, for I really do this if I image myself a something, since to imagine is nothing else than to contemplate the figure or image of a corporeal thing. But I already know for certain that I am, and that it may be that all these images, and, speaking generally, all things that relate to the nature of body are nothing but dreams [and chimeras]. For this reason I see clearly that I have as little reason to say, 'I shall stimulate my imagination in order to know more distinctly what I am,' than if I were to say, 'I am now awake, and I perceive somewhat that is real and true: but because I do not yet perceive it distinctly enough, I shall go to sleep of express purpose, so that my dreams may represent the perception with greatest truth and evidence.' And, thus, I know for certain that nothing of all that I can understand by means of my imagination belongs to this knowledge which I have of myself, and that it is necessary to recall the mind from this mode of thought with the utmost diligence in order that it may be able to know its own nature with perfect distinctness.

---

[1]Or 'form an image' (effingo).

But what then am I? A thing which thinks. What is a thing which thinks? It is a thing which doubts, understands, [conceives], affirms, denies, wills, refuses, which also imagines and feels.

Certainly it is no small matter if all these things pertain to my nature. But why should they not so pertain? Am I not that being who now doubts nearly everything, who nevertheless understands certain things, who affirms that one only is true, who denies all the others, who desires to know more, is averse from being deceived, who imagines many things, sometimes indeed despite his will, and who perceives many likewise, as by the intervention of the bodily organs? Is there nothing in all this which is as true as it is certain that I exist, even though I should always sleep and though he who has given me being employed all his ingenuity in deceiving me? Is there likewise any one of these attributes which can be distinguished from my thought, or which might be said to be separated from myself? For it is so evident of itself that it is I who doubts, who understands, and who desires, that there is no reason here to add anything to explain it. And I have certainly the power of imagining likewise; for although it may happen (as I formerly supposed) that none of the things which I imagine are true, nevertheless this power of imagining does not cease to be really in use, and it forms part of my thought. Finally, I am the same who feels, that is to say, who perceives certain things, as by the organs of sense, since in truth I see light, I hear noise, I feel heat. But it will be said that these phenomena are false and that I am dreaming. Let it be so; still it is at least quite certain that it seems to me that I see light, that I hear noise and that I feel heat. That cannot be false; properly speaking it is what is in me called feeling[2]; and used in this precise sense that is no other thing than thinking.

From this time I begin to know what I am with a little more clearness and distinction than before; but nevertheless it still seems to me, and I cannot prevent myself from thinking, that corporeal things, whose images are framed by thought, which are tested by the senses, are much more distinctly known than that obscure part of me which does not come under the imagination. Although really it is very strange to say that I know and understand more distinctly these things whose existence seems to me dubious, which are unknown to me, and which do not belong to me, than others of the truth of which I am convinced, which are known to me and which pertain to my real nature, in a word, than myself. But I see clearly how the case stands: my mind loves to wander, and cannot yet suffer itself to be retained within the just limits of truth. Very good, let us once more

---

[2]Sentire.

give it the freest rein, so that, when afterwards we seize the proper occasion for pulling up, it may the more easily be regulated and controlled.

Let us begin by considering the commonest matters, those which we believe to be the most distinctly comprehended, to wit, the bodies which we touch and see; not indeed bodies in general, for these general ideas are usually a little more confused, but let us consider one body in particular. Let us take, for example, this piece of wax: it has been taken quite freshly from the hive, and it has not yet lost the sweetness of the honey which it contains; it still retains somewhat of the odour of the flowers from which it has been culled; its colour, its figure, its size are apparent; it is hard, cold, easily handled, and if you strike it with the finger, it will emit a sound. Finally all the things which are requisite to cause us distinctly to recognise a body, are met with in it. But notice that while I speak and approach the fire what remained of the taste is exhaled, the smell evaporates, the colour alters, the figure is destroyed, the size increases, it becomes liquid, it heats, scarcely can one handle it, and when one strikes it, no sound is emitted. Does the same wax remain after this change? We must confess that it remains; none would judge otherwise. What then did I know so distinctly in this piece of wax? It could certainly be nothing of all that the senses brought to my notice, since all these things which fall under taste, smell, sight, touch, and hearing, are found to be changed, and yet the same wax remains.

Perhaps it was what I now think, viz. that this wax was not that sweetness of honey, nor that agreeable scent of flowers, nor that particular whiteness, nor that figure, nor that sound, but simply a body which a little while before appeared to me as perceptible under these forms, and which is now perceptible under others. But what, precisely, is it that I imagine when I form such conceptions? Let us attentively consider this, and, abstracting from all that does not belong to the wax, let us see what remains. Certainly nothing remains excepting a certain extended thing which is flexible and movable. But what is the meaning of flexible and movable? Is it not that I imagine that this piece of wax being round is capable of becoming square and of passing from a square to a triangular figure? No, certainly it is not that, since I imagine it admits of an infinitude of similar changes, and I nevertheless do not know how to compass the infinitude by my imagination, and consequently this conception which I have of the wax is not brought about by the faculty of imagination. What now is this extension? Is it not also unknown? For it becomes greater when the wax is melted, greater when it is boiled, and greater still when the heat increases; and I should not conceive [clearly] according to truth what wax is, if I did not think that even this piece that we are considering is capable of receiving more variations in extension than I have ever imagined. We must then grant that I could not even understand through the imagination what this piece of wax is, and that it is my mind alone which perceives it. I say this piece of wax in particular, for as to wax in general it is yet clearer. But what is this piece of wax which cannot be understood excepting by the [understanding or] mind? It is certainly the same that I see, touch, imagine, and finally it is the same which I have always believed it to be from the beginning. But what must particularly be observed is that its perception is neither an act of vision, nor of touch, nor of imagination, and has never been such although it may have appeared formerly to be so, but only an intuition[3] of the mind, which may be imperfect and confused as it was formerly, or clear and distinct as it is at present, according as my attention is more or less directed to the elements which are found in it, and of which it is composed.

Yet in the meantime I am greatly astonished when I consider [the great feebleness of mind] and its proneness to fall [insensibly] into error; for although without giving expression to my thoughts I consider all this in my own mind, words often impede me and I am almost deceived by the terms of ordinary language. For we say that we see the same wax, if it is present, and not that we simply judge that it is the same from its having the same colour and figure. From this I should conclude that I knew the wax by means of vision and not simply by the intuition of the mind; unless by chance I remember that, when looking from a window and saying I see men who pass in the street, I really do not see them, but infer that what I see is men, just as I say that I see wax. And yet what do I see from the window but hats and coats which may cover automatic machines? Yet I judge these to be men. And similarly solely by the faculty of judgment which rests in my mind, I comprehend that which I believed I saw with my eyes.

A man who makes it his aim to raise his knowledge above the common should be ashamed to derive the occasion for doubting from the forms of speech invented by the vulgar; I prefer to pass on and consider whether I had a more evident and perfect conception of what the wax was when I first perceived it, and when I believed I knew it by means of the external senses or at least by the common sense[4] as it is called, that is to say by the imaginative faculty, or whether my present conception is clearer now that I have most carefully examined what it is, and in what way it can be known. It would certainly be absurd to doubt as to this. For what was there in this first perception which was distinct? What was there which might not as well have been perceived by any of the animals? But when I distinguish the wax from its external forms, and when, just as if I had taken from it its vestments, I consider it quite naked, it is certain that

---

[3]inspectio.

[4]sensus communis.

although some error may still be found in my judgment, I can nevertheless not perceive it thus without a human mind.

But finally what shall I say of this mind, that is, of myself, for up to this point I do not admit in myself anything but mind? What then, I who seem to perceive this piece of wax so distinctly, do I not know myself, not only with much more truth and certainty, but also with much more distinctness and clearness? For if I judge that the wax is or exists from the fact that I see it, it certainly follows much more clearly that I am or that I exist myself from the fact that I see it. For it may be that what I see is not really wax, it may also be that I do not possess eyes with which to see anything; but it cannot be that when I see, or (for I no longer take account of the distinction) when I think I see, that I myself who think am nought. So if I judge that the wax exists from the fact that I touch it, the same thing will follow, to wit, that I am; and if I judge that my imagination, or some other cause, whatever it is, persuades me that the wax exists, I shall still conclude the same. And what I have here remarked of wax may be applied to all other things which are external to me [and which are met with outside of me]. And further, if the [notion or] perception of wax has seemed to me clearer and more distinct, not only after the sight or the touch, but also after many other causes have rendered it quite manifest to me, with how much more [evidence] and distinctness must it be said that I now know myself, since all the reasons which contribute to the knowledge of wax, or any other body whatever, are yet better proofs of the nature of my mind! And there are so many other things in the mind itself which may contribute to the elucidation of its nature, that those which depend on body such as these just mentioned, hardly merit being taken into account.

But finally here I am, having insensibly reverted to the point I desired, for, since it is now manifest to me that even bodies are not properly speaking known by the senses or by the faculty of imagination, but by the understanding only, and since they are not known from the fact that they are seen or touched, but only because they are understood, I see clearly that there is nothing which is easier for me to know than my mind. But because it is difficult to rid oneself so promptly of an opinion to which one was accustomed for so long, it will be well that I should halt a little at this point, so that by the length of my meditation I may more deeply imprint on my memory this new knowledge.

John Locke (1632–1704) was a British philosopher and a leader of the empiricist movement (in opposition to the rationalism of Descartes). Locke was also active in the Parliamentary movement (in opposition to the Stuart monarchy), and in 1683, fearing prosecution by the forces then in power, he fled to Holland. He was denounced as a traitor by King James II following a failed rebellion, and the king demanded that the Dutch authorities turn him over—a request that was essentially ignored. While in Holland, Locke became involved in the plot to place William of Orange and Mary, the princess of Orange (later Queen Mary) on the throne of England. The "Glorious Revolution" of 1688 gave William the throne, and in 1689 Locke returned to England as part of the escort for Princess Mary. Locke's Essay Concerning Human Understanding, *which established his importance as an empiricist philosopher, and from which the excerpt that follows is taken, was published in 1689. His great work on political philosophy,* Two Treatises of Government, *was published in 1690.*

Essay Concerning Human Understanding

Of Ideas in General and Their Original

1. *Idea is the object of thinking.*—Every man being conscious to himself that he thinks, and that which his mind is applied about whilst thinking being the ideas that are there, it is past doubt that men have in their minds several ideas, such as are those expressed by the words, 'whiteness, hardness, sweetness, thinking, motion, man, elephant, army, drunkenness', and others. It is in the first place then to be enquired, How he comes by them? I know it is a received doctrine, that men have native ideas and original characters stamped upon their minds in their very first being. This opinion I have at large examined already; and, I suppose, what I have said in the foregoing Book will be much more easily admitted, when I have shown whence the understanding may get all the ideas it has, and by what ways and degrees they may come into the mind; for which I shall appeal to every one's own observation and experience.

2. *All ideas come from sensation or reflection.*—Let us then suppose the mind to be, as we say, white paper, void of all characters, without any ideas; how comes it to be furnished? Whence comes it by that vast store, which the busy and boundless fancy of man has painted on it with an almost endless variety? Whence has it all the materials of reason and knowledge? To this I answer, in one word, from EXPERIENCE; in that all our knowledge is founded, and from that it ultimately derives itself. Our observation employed either about external sensible objects, or about the internal operations of our minds, perceived and reflected on by ourselves, is that which supplies our understandings with all the materials of thinking. These two are the fountains of knowledge, from whence all the ideas we have, or can naturally have, do spring.

3. *The objects of sensation one source of ideas.*—First, our senses, conversant about particular sensible objects, do convey into the mind several distinct perceptions of things, according to those various ways wherein those objects do affect them; and thus we come by those *ideas* we have of yellow, white, heat, cold, soft, hard, bitter, sweet, and all those which we call sensible qualities; which when I say the senses convey into the mind, I mean, they from external objects convey into the mind what produces there those perceptions. This great source of most of the ideas we have, depending wholly upon our senses, and derived by them to the understanding, I call, SENSATION.

4. *The operations of our minds the other source of them.*—Secondly, the other fountain, from which experience furnisheth the understanding with ideas, is the perception of the operations of our own minds within us, as it is employed about the ideas it has got; which operations, when the soul comes to reflect on and consider, do furnish the understanding with another set of ideas which could not be had from things without; and such are perception, thinking, doubting, believing, reasoning, knowing, willing, and all the different actings of our own minds; which we being conscious of, and observing in ourselves, do from these receive into our understanding as distinct ideas, as we do from bodies affecting our senses. This source of ideas every man has wholly in himself: and though it be not sense, as having nothing to do with external objects, yet it is very like it, and might properly enough be called internal sense. But as I call the other Sensation, so I call this REFLECTION, the ideas it affords being such only as the mind gets by reflecting on its own operations within itself. By Reflection, then, in the following part of this discourse, I would be understood to mean that notice which the mind takes of its own operations, and the manner of them, by reason whereof there come to be ideas of these operations in the understanding. These two, I say, viz., external material things as the objects of Sensation, and the operations of our own minds within as the objects of Reflection, are, to me, the only originals from whence all our ideas take their beginnings. The term *operations* here, I use in a large sense, as comprehending not barely the actions of the mind about its ideas, but some sort of passions arising sometimes from them, such as is the satisfaction or uneasiness arising from any thought.

5. *All our ideas are of the one or the other of these.*—The understanding seems to me not to have the least glimmering of any ideas which it doth not receive from one of these two. *External objects* furnish the mind with the ideas of sensible qualities, which are all those different perceptions they produce in us; and *the mind* furnishes the understanding with ideas of its own operations. These, when we have taken a full survey of them, and their several modes, combinations, and relations, we shall find to contain all our whole stock of ideas; and that we have nothing in our minds which did not come in one of these two ways. Let any one examine his own thoughts, and thoroughly search into his understanding, and then let him tell me, whether all the original ideas he has there, are any other than of the objects of his senses, or of the operations of his mind considered as objects of his reflection; and how great a mass of knowledge soever he imagines to be lodged there, he will, upon taking a strict view, see that he has not any idea in his mind but what one of these two have imprinted, though perhaps with infinite variety compounded and enlarged by the understanding, as we shall see hereafter.

6. *Observable in children.*—He that attentively considers the state of a child at his first coming into the world, will have little reason to think him stored with plenty of ideas that are to be the matter of his future knowledge. It is by degrees he comes to be furnished with them: and though the ideas of obvious and familiar qualities imprint themselves before the memory begins to keep a register of time and order, yet it is often so late before some unusual qualities come in the way, that there are few men that cannot recollect the beginning of their acquaintance with them: and if it were worth while, no doubt a child might be so ordered as to have but a very few even of the ordinary ideas till he were grown up to a man. But all that are born into the world being surrounded with bodies that perpetually and diversely affect them, variety of ideas, whether care be taken about it or no, are imprinted on the minds of children. Light and colours are busy and at hand everywhere when the eye is but open; sounds and some tangible qualities fail not to solicit their proper senses, and force an entrance to the mind; but yet I think it will be granted easily, that if a child were kept in a place where he never saw any other but black and white till he were a man, he would have no more ideas of scarlet or green, than he that from his childhood never tasted an oyster or a pine-apple has of those particular relishes.

David Hume (see Chapter two) holds an empiricist position that is certainly much closer to Locke than to the rationalism of Descartes. Nonetheless, his more skeptical empiricism is different from both, and he raises important criticisms of both perspectives. The following passage is from An Inquiry Concerning Human Understanding, *Sections 2 and 12:*

An Inquiry Concerning Human Understanding

OF THE ORIGIN OF IDEAS

Everyone will readily allow that there is a considerable difference between the perceptions of the mind when a man feels the pain of excessive heat or the pleasure of moderate warmth, and when he afterwards recalls to his memory this sensation or anticipates it by his imagination. These faculties may mimic or copy the perceptions of the senses, but they never can entirely reach the force and vivacity of the original sentiment. The utmost we say of them, even when they operate with greatest vigor, is that they represent their object in so lively a manner that we could *almost* say we feel or see it. But, except the mind be disordered by disease or madness, they never can arrive at such a pitch of vivacity as to render these perceptions altogether undistinguishable. All the colors of poetry, however splendid, can never paint natural objects in such a manner as to make the description be taken for a real landscape. The most lively thought is still inferior to the dullest sensation.

We may observe a like distinction to run through all the other perceptions of the mind. A man in a fit of anger is actuated in a very different manner from one who only thinks of that emotion. If you tell me that any person is in love, I easily understand your meaning and form a just conception of his situation, but never can mistake that conception for the real disorders and agitations of the passion. When we reflect on our past sentiments and affections, our thought is a faithful mirror and copies its objects truly, but the colors which it employs are faint and dull in comparison of those in which our original perceptions were clothed. It requires no nice discernment or metaphysical head to mark the distinction between them.

Here, therefore, we may divide all the perceptions of the mind into two classes or species, which are distinguished by their different degrees of force and vivacity. The less forcible and lively are commonly denominated "thoughts" or "ideas." The other species want a name in our language, and in most others; I suppose, because it was not requisite for any but philosophical purposes to rank them under a general term or appellation. Let us, therefore, use a little freedom and call them "impressions," employing that word in a sense somewhat different from the usual. By the term "impression," then, I mean all our more lively perceptions, when we hear, or see, or feel, or love, or hate, or desire, or will. And impressions are distinguished from ideas, which are the less lively perceptions of which we are conscious when we reflect on any of those sensations or movements above mentioned.

Nothing, at first view, may seem more unbounded than the thought of man, which not only escapes all human power and authority, but is not even restrained within the limits of nature and reality. To form monsters and join incongruous shapes and appearances costs the imagination no more trouble than to conceive the most natural and familiar objects. And while the body is confined to one planet, along which it creeps with pain and difficulty, the thought can in an instant transport us into the most distant regions of the universe, or even beyond the universe into the unbounded chaos where nature is supposed to lie in total confusion. What never was seen or heard of, may yet be conceived, nor is anything beyond the power of thought except what implies an absolute contradiction.

But though our thought seems to possess this unbounded liberty, we shall find upon a nearer examination that it is really confined within very narrow limits, and that all this creative power of the mind amounts to no more than the faculty of compounding, transposing, augmenting, or diminishing the materials afforded us by the senses and experience. When we think of a golden mountain, we only join two consistent ideas, "gold" and "mountain," with which we were formerly acquainted. A virtuous horse we can conceive, because, from our own feeling, we can conceive virtue; and this we may unite to the figure and shape of a horse, which is an animal familiar to us. In short, all the materials of thinking are derived either from our outward or inward sentiment; the mixture and composition of these belongs alone to the mind and will, or, to express myself in philosophical language, all our ideas or more feeble perceptions are copies of our impressions or more lively ones.

• • •

Here, therefore, is a proposition which not only seems in itself simple and intelligible, but, if a proper use were made of it, might render every dispute equally intelligible, and banish all that jargon which has so long taken possession of metaphysical reasonings and drawn disgrace upon them. All ideas, especially abstract ones, are naturally faint and obscure. The mind has but a slender hold of them. They are apt to be confounded with other resembling ideas; and when we have often employed any term, though without a distinct meaning, we are apt to imagine it has a determinate idea annexed to it. On the contrary, all impressions, that is, all sensations either outward or inward, are strong and vivid. The limits between them are more exactly determined, nor is it easy to fall into any error or mistake with regard to them. When we entertain, therefore, any suspicion that a philosophical term is employed without any meaning or idea (as is but too frequent), we need but inquire, *from what impression is that supposed idea derived?* And if it be impossible to assign any, this will serve to confirm our suspicion. By bringing ideas in so clear a light, we may reasonably hope to remove all dispute which may arise concerning their nature and reality.

• • •

Part III

There is, indeed, a more *mitigated* skepticism or *academical* philosophy which may be both durable and useful, and which may, in part, be the result of this Pyrrhonism or *excessive* skepticism when its undistinguished doubts are, in some measure, corrected by common sense and reflection. The greater part of mankind are naturally apt to be affirmative and dogmatical in their opinions, and while they see objects only on one side and have no idea of any counterpoising argument, they throw themselves precipitately into the principles to which they are inclined, nor have they any indulgence for those who entertain opposite sentiments. To hesitate or balance perplexes their understanding, checks their passion, and suspends their action. They are, therefore, impatient till they escape from a state which to them is so uneasy, and they think that they can never remove themselves far enough from it by the violence of their affirmations and obstinacy of their belief. But could such dogmatical reasoners become sensible of the strange infirmities of human understanding, even in its most perfect state and when most accurate and cautious in its determinations—such a reflection would naturally inspire them with more modesty and reserve, and diminish their fond opinion of themselves and their prejudice against antagonists. The illiterate may reflect on the disposition of the learned, who, amidst all the advantages of study and reflection, are commonly still diffident in their determinations. And if any of the learned be inclined, from their natural temper, to haughtiness and obstinacy, a small tincture of Pyrrhonism might abate their pride by showing them that the few advantages which they may have attained over their fellows are but inconsiderable if compared with the universal perplexity and confusion which is inherent in human nature. In general, there is a degree of doubt and caution and modesty which, in all kinds of scrutiny and decision, ought forever to accompany a just reasoner.

Another species of *mitigated* skepticism which may be of advantage to mankind, and which may be the natural result of the Pyrrhonian doubts and scruples, is the limitation of our inquiries to such subjects as are best adapted to the narrow capacity of human understanding. The *imagination* of man is naturally sublime, delighted with whatever is remote and extraordinary, and running, without control, into the most distant parts of space and time in order to avoid the objects which custom has rendered too familiar to it. A correct *judgment* observes a contrary method and, avoiding all distant and high inquiries, confines itself to common life and to such subjects as fall under daily practice and experience, leaving the more sublime topics to the embellishment of poets and orators or to the arts of priests and politicians. To bring us to so salutary a determination, nothing can be more serviceable than to be once thoroughly convinced of the force of the Pyrrhonian doubt and of the impossibility that anything but the strong power of natural instinct could free us from it. Those who have a propensity to philosophy will still continue their researches, because they reflect that, besides the immediate pleasure attending such an occupation, philosophical decisions are nothing but the reflections of common life, methodized and corrected. But they will never be tempted to go beyond common life so long as they consider the imperfection of those faculties which they employ, their narrow reach, and their inaccurate operations. While we cannot give a satisfactory reason why we believe, after a thousand experiments, that a stone will fall or fire burn, can we ever satisfy ourselves concerning any determination which we may form with regard to the origin of worlds and the situation of nature from and to eternity?

This narrow limitation, indeed, of our inquiries is in every respect so reasonable that it suffices to make the slightest examination into the natural powers of the human mind, and to compare them with their objects, in order to recommend it to us. We shall then find what are the proper subjects of science and inquiry.

It seems to me that the only objects of the abstract sciences, or of demonstration, are quantity and number, and that all attempts to extend this more perfect species of knowledge beyond these bounds are mere sophistry and illusion. As the component parts of quantity and number are entirely similar, their relations become intricate and involved, and nothing can be more curious, as well as useful, than to trace, by a variety of mediums, their equality or inequality through their different appearances. But as all other ideas are clearly distinct and different from each other, we can never advance further, by our utmost scrutiny, than to observe this diversity and, by an obvious reflection, pronounce one thing not to be another. Or if there be any difficulty in these decisions, it proceeds entirely from the undeterminate meaning of words, which is corrected by juster definitions. That *the square of the hypotenuse is equal to the squares of the other two sides* cannot be known, let the terms be ever so exactly defined, without a train of reasoning and inquiry. But to convince us of this proposition, *that where there is no property there can be no injustice*, it is only necessary to define the terms and explain injustice to be a violation of property. This proposition is, indeed, nothing but a more imperfect definition. It is the same case with all those pretended syllogistical reasonings which may be found in every other branch of learning except the sciences of quantity and number; and these may safely, I think, be pronounced the only proper objects of knowledge and demonstration.

All other inquiries of men regard only matter of fact and existence, and these are evidently incapable of demonstration. Whatever *is* may *not be*. No negation of a fact can involve a contradiction. The nonexistence of any being, without exception, is as clear and distinct an idea as its existence. The proposition which affirms it not to be, however false, is no less conceivable and intelligible than that which affirms it to be. The case is different with the sciences, properly so called. Every proposition which is not true is there confused and unintelligible. That the cube root of 64 is equal to the half of 10 is a false proposition and can never be distinctly conceived. But that Caesar, or the angel Gabriel, or any being never existed may be a false proposition, but still is perfectly conceivable and implies no contradiction.

The existence, therefore, of any being can only be proved by arguments from its cause or its effect, and these arguments are founded entirely on experience. If we reason *a priori*, anything may appear able to produce anything. The falling of a pebble may, for aught we know, extinguish the sun, or the wish of a man control the planets in their orbits. It is only experience which teaches us the nature and bounds of cause and effect and enables us to infer the existence of one object from that of another. Such is the foundation of moral reasoning, which forms the greater part of human knowledge and is the source of all human action and behavior.

Moral reasonings are either concerning particular or general facts. All deliberations in life regard the former; as also all disquisitions in history, chronology, geography, and astronomy.

The sciences which treat of general facts are politics, natural philosophy, physics, chemistry, etc., where the qualities, causes, and effects of a whole species of objects are inquired into.

Divinity or theology, as it proves the existence of a deity and the immortality of souls, is composed partly of reasonings concerning particular, partly concerning general facts. It has a foundation in *reason* so far as it is supported by experience. But its best and most solid foundation is *faith* and divine revelation.

Morals and criticism are not so properly objects of the understanding as of taste and sentiment. Beauty, whether moral or natural, is felt more properly than perceived. Or if we reason concerning it and endeavor to fix the standard, we regard a new fact, to wit, the general taste of mankind, or some such fact which may be the object of reasoning and inquiry.

When we run over libraries, persuaded of these principles, what havoc must we make? If we take in our hand any volume—of divinity or school metaphysics, for instance—let us ask, *Does it contain any abstract reasoning concerning quantity or number?* No. *Does it contain any experimental reasoning concerning matter of fact and existence?* No. Commit it then to the flames, for it can contain nothing but sophistry and illusion.

Study Questions

1. What are some of the main arguments in favor of empiricism?
2. What are some arguments for rationalism?
3. Describe some key differences between the views of rationalists and of empiricists.
4. What is Plato's famous story of the cave, and what is the *moral*, or point, of that story?
5. What is Descartes's "method of doubt"?
6. On what grounds does Descartes maintain that even truths of mathematics are subject to doubt?
7. What is the first truth that Descartes believes he can know without any doubt?
8. What is the distinction between *a priori* and *a posteriori* knowledge?
9. Why did Kant regard the category of synthetic *a priori* knowledge as so important?
10. According to Kant, why is it possible for us to have synthetic *a priori* knowledge? That is, where do we get such knowledge?

Exercises

1. The question of what sort of *foundation* we require for knowledge is a controversial one (and some reject any need for foundations at all). But if you believe that knowledge requires a foundation, then how solid does that foundation have to be? Many foundationalists insist (with Descartes) that the foundation must be rock solid and indubitable. Others propose a different model: We can build very solid structures on marshy ground; instead of looking for bedrock, we drive in a number of pilings, deep into the marsh, and those pilings are sufficiently strong to hold up a structure of knowledge, even though there is no point in the foundation that is solid, indubitable bedrock. Which model would you favor?

2. How would you define knowledge? That is, what are the defining characteristics of genuine knowledge? The classic definition sets three conditions for genuine knowledge: It must be *true justified belief*. Thus, if you *believe* something to be true, and you are *justified* in your belief (you have good reason for your belief), and what you believe actually is *true*, then it is legitimate to claim that your belief counts as *knowledge*. Each of the three conditions is necessary for knowledge, and jointly they are sufficient. First, if I claim—following a traffic accident—that I *knew* we were going to have an accident on our drive to campus, then you could legitimately reject my claim of knowledge by denying that I really believed it: "You certainly did not *know* any such thing, because you didn't really believe it was going to happen: If you had, you wouldn't have ridden with me." Second, knowledge requires that my belief be *true*. I can't *know* that Venus is the largest planet in our solar system, because that is false. And finally, in order to be *knowledge*, my belief must be *justified*. If every year I make a wild stab at

who will win the Kentucky Derby, and finally one year I get it right (after twenty years of getting it wrong), you would dispute my claim to have *known* before the race which horse was going to win. "You didn't *know*," you might say; "you were just guessing." But if I have a genuine *belief*, and have *justification* for that belief, and the belief is *true*, then my belief counts as *knowledge*.

Or so it would seem. But a philosopher named Edmund Gettier posed a problem for the "true justified belief" account of knowledge: a problem that has become known as the *Gettier paradox*. The problem can be posed in many ways. Here's an example: My friend Alice owns a blue VW bug, 1965 model. I've seen her ownership papers, I've ridden with her in her car, I've seen her at school in her car many times. Someone asks me if I know what kind of car Alice has. "Yes," I reply, "she owns a 1965 blue VW bug." "Are you sure?" "Of course I'm sure," I reply; "I rode to school with her in her blue '65 bug this very morning." Okay, I firmly *believe* that Alice owns such a car, and I have *justification* for that belief, and, in fact, Alice does own a blue '65 VW bug. So my belief counts as *knowledge*, right? But suppose— unbeknownst to me—Alice got into a poker game between classes, and she had a run of bad luck, and she wound up losing her beloved bug in the last hand of the game. She hands over the keys and registration, and no longer owns a blue '65 bug. But thirty minutes later her favorite uncle dies, and he leaves to Alice—you guessed it—his blue '65 VW bug. Alice now owns a blue '65 bug, but she doesn't yet know it. When I claimed to know that Alice owned a '65 blue VW bug, I had no knowledge of the poker game or the will. Still, what I claimed was *true*; and I certainly *believed* it to be true; and I had strong *justification* for that belief. But it seems strange to say that I had *knowledge* that Alice owned a '65 bug; after all, at that point even Alice herself didn't know it. Of course, if I had claimed to know that Alice owns the '65 bug her uncle left her, that would have been false. But that was not my claim. I only claimed to know that Alice owned a '65 bug. And that claim is true, I believed it to be true, and I had justification for my belief: I just rode with Alice in a '65 bug that I knew to be her own. So I have true justified belief; but it's not clear that in this case true justified belief is sufficient for genuine *knowledge*.

The Gettier paradox has been the subject of long philosophical debate, and many solutions have been proposed: Some people think we should reject the classical standard for knowledge (knowledge as true justified belief) and find something else. Others believe that the solution lies in modifying the standards to avoid cases like the one above. (For example, we need a stronger standard for what counts as *justified* belief.) What do you think?

3. Are there any (nondefinitional, synthetic) truths that can be known *a priori*?

4. Suppose that highly intelligent extraterrestrials arrive on Earth. Their technology and science are obviously far more advanced than ours. (For one thing, they can easily travel the distances between stars, which are so vast that we can hardly imagine them). Are there any "laws of thought" that those intelligent extraterrestrials—and *any* rational being, including humans— would have to believe?

5. Many different methods have been proposed for knowing God or knowing of God's existence. Some claim that that knowledge is available only through revelation (such as is revealed in a sacred text). Others believe that there can be empirical proof of the existence of God—for example, the argument from design. (William Paley, its most famous proponent, claimed that the world we observe is like a watch, and therefore there must be a watchmaker.) But one famous proof for the existence of God seems to claim that we can have synthetic *a priori* knowledge of the existence of God. Consider the *ontological* proof of God's existence, proposed by St. Anselm (1033–1109) of Canterbury (and offered in revised versions ever since—Descartes had his own version of the proof). Anselm argued that God is necessarily the greatest being that can be conceived: Anything less would simply not be God. (If you think of some splendid being, but then think of something even greater, then the former could not be God.) So suppose you think of a being having all the possible perfections to the greatest conceivable degree—but it's an imaginary, nonexistent being. Obviously this *non*existent being cannot be God, because we can conceive of something greater: a being with all the same perfections, but that *does* exist. Thus, God's essence is such that God *must* exist. God (and God alone) *necessarily* exists. God is the greatest conceivable being, and the very conception of such a being must involve its existence. You can imagine many things that do not exist: a mountain of gold, for example. But God is different, for only God is necessarily the *greatest* of all beings, and being the greatest must include existing. An *existing* mountain of gold is much more valuable than an *imaginary* mountain of gold, but there is no necessity that any mountain of gold, real or imaginary, be as great as it can conceivably be; with God, and only God, there *is* such a necessity, since anything less than the greatest of all beings is not God.

Anselm's ontological proof has generated controversy for almost a millennium. Two questions: First, *if* Anselm's proof works, would it establish a synthetic *a priori* truth? Second, *does* his proof work?

Glossary

A posteriori **knowledge:** Knowledge that comes from experience and observation; empirical knowledge.

A priori **knowledge:** Knowledge gained "prior to" or independently of experience; knowledge based on pure reason.

Analytic statement: A statement that is true by definition; more precisely, a statement in which the predicate term is contained in the subject term.

Empiricism: The view that all our knowledge of the world must be gained through experience, observation, or scientific research.

Rationalism: The view that our most important source of knowledge is reason; the senses are deceptive, and knowledge based on the senses cannot give certainty.

Synthetic statement: A statement in which the predicate term is not contained in the subject; the predicate term adds one or more characteristics to the subject.

Additional Resources

Descartes's *Meditations on First Philosophy* was originally published in 1641; a good English translation is offered by Hackett Publishing (Indianapolis: 1979). Norman Kemp Smith's *New Studies in the Philosophy of Descartes* (London: Macmillan, 1963) is very good; see also J. Cottingham, *Descartes* (Oxford: Blackwell, 1986), and Bernard Williams, *Descartes: The Project of Pure Enquiry* (Hammondsworth: Penguin, 1978). A careful assessment of Descartes's method of doubt is offered by Harry G. Frankfurt in *Demons, Dreamers, and Madmen: The Defense of Reason in Descartes's Meditations* (Indianapolis: Bobbs-Merrill, 1970). Plato's rationalism is evident in *The Republic*, available in many translations and editions, as well as in other dialogues; for example, see *Five Dialogues (Euthyphro, Apology, Crito, Meno, Phaedo* (Indianapolis: Hackett, 1981).

Classical empiricist sources include Bishop Berkeley's *The Principles of Human Knowledge* and *Three Dialogues Between Hylas and Philonous;* David Hume's *Treatise of Human Nature* (especially Book I, Part IV); and John Locke's *An Essay Concerning Human Understanding. Berkeley*, by G. J. Warnock (Hammondsworth, U.K.: Penguin, 1953) is a very good account of Berkeley's position. On Hume, see *Hume's Theory of the External World* (Oxford, U.K.: Clarendon Press, 1940), by H. H. Price; Norman Kemp Smith, *The Philosophy of David Hume* (London: Macmillan, 1964); and (a very clear and readable account) *Hume*, by Barry Stroud (London and Boston: Routledge & Kegan Paul, 1977). More recent empiricist views are represented by A. J. Ayer, *The Foundations of Empirical Knowledge* (London: Macmillan, 1940), and *The Problem of Knowledge* (Baltimore: Penguin Books, 1956); and Carl G. Hempel, *Aspects of Scientific Explanation* (New York: Free Press, 1965). A good introduction to and comparison of the major traditional epistemological views is Bruce Aune's *Rationalism, Empiricism, and Pragmatism: An Introduction* (New York: Random House, 1970).

Kant's key works on epistemology are *The Critique of Pure Reason*, 2d ed., translated by Norman Kemp Smith (London: Macmillan, 1964), and *Prolegomena to Any Future Metaphysics*, translated by Lewis White Beck (Indianapolis: Bobbs-Merrill, 1950). Among the many excellent studies of Kantian epistemology are Richard Aquila, *Representational Mind: A Study of Kant's Theory of Knowledge* (Bloomington, IN: Indiana University Press, 1983); Jonathan Bennett, *Kant's Analytic* (Cambridge, U.K.: Cambridge University Press, 1966); C. D. Broad, *Kant: An Introduction* (Cambridge, U.K.: Cambridge University Press, 1978); Norman Kemp Smith, *A Commentary on Kant's Critique of Pure Reason*, 2d ed. (London: Macmillan, 1923); and P. F. Strawson, *The Bounds of Sense* (London: Methuen, 1966).

A very interesting book on the origins of mathematics (that seeks the basic psychological sources of mathematics and denies that mathematics is based in intuition or definition or pure *a priori* insight) is *Where Mathematics Comes From: How the Embodied Mind Brings Mathematics into Being*, by George Lakoff and Rafael E. Núñez (New York: Basic Books, 2000).

For more on the "rationalist–empiricist" conflict between Noam Chomsky and B. F. Skinner, see Skinner's *Verbal Behavior* (New York: Appleton-Century-Crofts, 1957), and *Contingencies of Reinforcement* (New York: Appleton-Century-Crofts, 1969); and Chomsky's "Review of Skinner's *Verbal Behavior*," in *Language*, 1959, vol. 35, pp. 26–58, and *Cartesian Linguistics* (New York: Harper & Row, 1966). For a response to Chomsky on behalf of Skinner, see Kenneth MacCorquodale, 1970, "On Chomsky's Review of Skinner's *Verbal Behavior*," *Journal of the Experimental Analysis of Behavior*, vol. 13, pp. 83–99.

An excellent overview of contemporary issues in epistemology is offered by the writers contributing to *The Oxford Handbook of Epistemology*, edited by Paul K. Moser (Oxford, U.K.: Oxford University Press, 2002).

EpistemeLinks.Com covers many topics in philosophy, but is particularly good in epistemology; go to *http://www.epistemlinks.com*. There are also a couple of excellent websites devoted to epistemology. See "The Epistemology Page," developed by Keith De Rose of Yale University, for very good material on contemporary epistemologists; it's at *http://Pantheon.yale.edu/~kd47/e-page.htm*. Also, a particularly entertaining site is "Certain Doubts: A Blog Devoted to Matters Epistemic," at *http://ww.missouri.edu/~kvanvigj/certain_doubts/*.

Notes

1. George Santayana, *Scepticism and Animal Faith*, 1923, Chapter 9.
2. *An Enquiry Concerning Human Understanding*, Section XII, Part 3.

Chapter *4*

The Foundations of Knowledge

in which Sarah considers scientific knowledge

The coffee shop was crowded: a few people just awakening, or trying to with the help of caffeine; several others who looked as if they had been there for hours already, books and notes strewn across their tables and the distinctive worried look of an impending exam on their brows; and the usual crowd rushing in from early classes, in search of friends, coffee, scones, or muffins. Ben had located a small table in the corner and was busily wiping it clean with a napkin, while Selina settled a tray of coffee and scones on the corner Ben had just cleaned and Sarah borrowed an unused chair from a nearby table. As Ben tossed aside the dirty napkin and stirred his coffee, he immediately took up the discussion where they had left it the day before.

"Okay, Sarah, I was thinking about Kant's view that we know these special universal truths because of the way we conceptualize the world—the systematic perspective we bring with us. That's interesting, certainly, but it doesn't quite work for me. God exists. That's a solid fact. We know it intuitively, rationally, whatever. But I know it's true. Now suppose we were made in such a way that we invariably believe in God, and belief in God is an essential element of the way we conceptualize the world. Well, fine. But when I say that God really exists, I mean more than just that all people think in such a way that they believe in the existence of God, like the way everyone thinks that things occur in space. If space is empirically real, but transcendentally ideal, that's not enough for our belief in God. God is empirically real *and* transcendentally real. At least that's what this rationalist means when he says he knows that God exists."

"Actually, Ben, Kant did believe that God exists in the way you describe," Sarah answered. "But of course, Kant didn't think we could perceive God through our senses; and for Kant, it is in making sensory observations and representations of the world that we impose the patterns of space and time. In fact, Kant didn't believe we could give rational universal proofs of the existence of God. Rather, God is known to us more directly, in our moral lives: When we commit ourselves to act morally and aim at morally good results even though we know that we lack the power to achieve those results, by our act of commitment we demonstrate our own individual moral certainty of the existence of a moral creator of the universe."

"Hey, Sarah, that's very nice!" Ben was delighted. "Our knowledge of God comes individually and is found through our own efforts toward acting morally. Actually, that seems to fit our awareness of God better than any of the rationalist proofs. Knowledge of God seems more than merely intuition, but on the other hand, it is also more a matter of commitment than rational deliberation. Certain knowledge of God comes from our dedicated efforts to act morally and our full awareness of what that involves. I think Kant is dead right!"

"I knew there was something I didn't like about Kant," Selina joined in. "Let's see, we commit ourselves to achieving a moral end, even though we know we aren't capable of achieving it. And this proves that God exists, as the moral author of the universe. Maybe I'm missing something, but I don't find that a very convincing proof of the existence of God."

"It's not really intended as a general proof, Selina," Sarah answered. "For Kant, it's more a matter of individual moral certainty of God as a power for moral good—a certainty that you recognize in yourself when you commit to a moral task."

"Sorry, I just can't buy it. I have made strong commitments to moral action, and sometimes I knew that the chances of that moral action achieving success—creating a just result—were far from certain, and the result was not something I could control. Often, the success of the enterprise would depend on other factors, such as the efforts of others who were also part of the struggle and whose efforts were not under my control. I made the commitment to action, and I recognized that the ultimate success of my moral project was not within my control; but that did not awaken in me some deep understanding of my own belief in a moral creator of the universe."

"Perhaps it would," Ben responded, "if you would let yourself be open to it."

Selina shook her head. "That sounds like a question-begging argument to me, Ben. The question is whether there is some deep understand-

---

There can be no doubt that all our knowledge begins with experience. For how should our faculty of knowledge be awakened into action did not objects affecting our senses partly of themselves produce representations, partly arouse the activity of our understanding to compare these representations, and, by combining or separating them, work up the raw material of the sensible impressions into that knowledge of objects which is entitled experience? In the order of time, therefore, we have no knowledge antecedent to experience, and with experience all our knowledge begins.

But though all our knowledge begins with experience, it does not follow that it all arises out of experience. For it may well be that even our empirical knowledge is made up of what we receive through impressions and of what our own faculty of knowledge . . . supplies from itself. If our faculty of knowledge makes any such addition, it may be that we are not in a position to distinguish it from the raw material, until with long practice of attention we have become skilled in separating it.

Immanuel Kant, *Critique of Pure Reason*, Introduction (1781).
Trans. by Norman Kemp Smith

---

ing there; if you assume that I would see it if I 'opened myself' to it, that assumes the existence of what is at issue."

Kant and the Importance of Perspective

Sarah laughed. "Okay, Selina, I didn't have any illusions that you would embrace Kant's position on personal knowledge of God. Still, there are some elements of Kant's work that you might appreciate. Kant turned our attention to the importance of considering our own perspective in determining the nature of the world: We can't just suppose that we directly observe the world as it is in itself, from some absolute neutral detached standpoint; rather, we must always consider the impact of our own perspectives, assumptions, and orientation on our perceptions and judgments. And that insight inspired Einstein and much work in contemporary philosophy of science. Kant would probably disagree with most of it, but he helped lay the foundations for it, nonetheless."

"Alright, Sarah," replied Selina, "I'm not impressed by Kant's theology, but there is something to his account of knowledge. It's true, when you run an experiment, you have to be careful about your own perspective and your own expectations. After all, that's why we run double blind experiments. But still, after you control for such influences, your experiment—if it's well designed—leads you to objective scientific truth. It leads you to the way the world is, and it's not always what we thought and not always what we wanted. For every famous experiment that works out the way the scientist had predicted, there are many you never hear about, because they failed. The scientist's cherished hypothesis was wrong, the hoped-for cure didn't work. And that's what science does: It is *not* faith and hope, *not* the 'evidence of things hoped for'; it provides evidence of what is real."

"Kant doesn't deny that what you discover is empirically real," answered Sarah. "He insists only that some of what you discover is the framework you bring to the whole process of discovery, a framework that is inseparable from the entire enterprise of empirical discovery. That doesn't make science less real; it just gives us a better sense of what that process actually involves. We can't step outside our own perspective and theoretical framework and see the world 'as it is in itself,' *independent* of us. That shouldn't be such a weird idea to you, Selina. After all, you've studied quantum mechanics, and under at least one interpretation, the indeterminacy inherent in that discipline is imposed by the observer. And earlier, of course, the possibility of various perspectives was a fundamental element of Einstein's relativity theory."

"Alright," Selina agreed, "I already said there is something valuable in Kant. But it still seems to me that science *does* arrive at objective reality. Some people may view it from a distorted or biased perspective and get it wrong; but the actual objective reality remains a constant."

Sarah stopped and sipped her coffee. "Let me try a different approach. Let's go back to the rationalist–empiricist conflict that has raged for centuries in the history of philosophy—and has raged for a shorter duration, but with fervent intensity, between Ben and Selina. I'm offering an olive branch to the opposing forces. It's risky, though: Peacemakers often get caught in the cross fire."

Ben was doubtful. "How long did you say this dispute has gone on? At least four centuries, right, Sarah? If you can make peace on this one, you ought to drop philosophy and apply to the State Department."

"Perhaps it won't really be a permanent peace treaty. A temporary truce, as you both attack my view; and then you'll become allies, on the theory that the enemy of my enemy is my friend."

"It would take a seriously dreadful enemy to make me join forces with the rationalists, Sarah." Selina frowned. "What sort of theory are you proposing?"

"Look, guys, all the differences between your rationalist and empiricist views notwithstanding, you have one significant point of agreement."

"Yeah, we do," Ben agreed: "We both love sushi. But I don't see that as grounds for reconciling empiricism with rationalism."

"Clever, Ben." Sarah arched her eyebrows. "No, I meant there's a point of agreement between empiricism and rationalism. And it's an important point of agreement. It's this: Both rationalists and empiricists believe in fixed truths, solid facts, principles that are true *independently* of our knowing them. Now, obviously, you differ on what those facts are and how they are known. Maybe you also differ on how certain and absolute they are. After all, Ben believes that it is a plain fact that God exists, and that's an eternal and unchanging truth, and we have knowledge of it by special powers of intuition or perhaps through special revelation. And Selina believes that water is made up of two hydrogen atoms and one oxygen atom, and that the earth is in orbit around the sun, and that our sun is one star among many in a spiral galaxy, and that continental drift occurs. And Ben believes that God exists regardless of whether any human ever has or ever will recognize that fact. If everyone became an atheist, that would have no bearing whatsoever on the existence of God. And Selina believes that if the Catholic Church had been successful in suppressing Copernican astronomy, and everyone now believed that the earth is stationary and that the sun orbits the earth and that all the other stars we see are attached to a single sphere which spins around the earth, that wouldn't change the fact that the earth is actually spinning around the sun and the sun is one of many millions of stars scattered around our galaxy. Right?"

"Yeah, sure," Ben agreed. "God doesn't exist because I or anyone else believes He exists; rather, my belief in God is right because He exists."

"Why does God have to be 'He'? If I were going to believe in God, I think I'd at least pick a female God. Sorry, Ben. I don't guess you're going to convert your Selina to Christianity anytime soon. I got sidetracked, Sarah. Yeah, sure, the fact that the earth orbits the sun doesn't depend on our recognizing it as true. It was true during the many centuries when everyone believed the Ptolemaic theory and thought the Earth was stationary. And it would still be true if everyone went crazy and decided to reject scientific astronomy. There are all these people who want 'intelligent design' and 'creationism' taught to schoolchildren and who reject Darwin's account of natural selection. Maybe someday they'll succeed, and no one will believe Darwin's account. But that won't change the plain fact of Darwinian evolution."

"But consider it carefully," Sarah said. "Do you really think we can just gather facts, the way you pick up seashells at the beach? That there

> *Science is built up with facts, as a house is with stones. But a collection of facts is no more a science than a heap of stones is a house.*
>
> Henri Poincaré, *Science and Hypothesis*

are 'facts' or 'truths' out there we simply see as they are in themselves, in their pristine purity?"

"What are you talking about, Sarah?" Selina found this a very confusing question.

"Look, Selina, here's a coffee cup, right? Describe it as it really is, as it is in itself, totally independent of us and our perceptions of it."

"It's a coffee cup, alright. Okay, I'll play. It's cylindrical, with a handle sticking out, blue, solid, smooth, made of some sort of clay, I suppose. How's that?"

"That's fine, Selina. But is the cup really blue?"

"Of course the cup's blue. Are you color blind, Sarah?"

"No, the cup looks blue to me, just as it does to you. But is the coffee cup *in itself* blue?"

Ben was sharing Selina's perplexity. "Of course it's a blue coffee cup, Sarah. Either that, or we're all wearing blue-tinted glasses."

"That's just it, Ben! In a sense, all of us *are* wearing blue-tinted glasses. Because the blue isn't really there in the coffee cup; rather, the coffee cup has the property of causing us to perceive it as blue because of the way light reflects off the cup. But the blueness is in our perception, not in the coffee cup itself. Is the coffee in the cup hot? Well, sure, you can see the steam rising from it; and if you drink it too quickly, it will burn you and cause you to feel pain. But there is no *heat* in the coffee cup, any more than there is *pain*. Instead, the molecules are moving very rapidly in the liquid, and that causes us to experience heat, and pain as well. If you add sugar, the coffee will taste sweet; but the sweetness is not in the sugar itself, it's in our perception. And that coffee cup you described as a solid cylinder: It's made up of atoms, with enormous amounts of space between them. We perceive it as solid; but if you want something really solid, you should talk about a black hole, not a coffee cup."

Selina waved her hand for Sarah to stop. "Okay, thanks for the lesson in introductory physics, Sarah. But I'm a chemistry major, remember? I've already taken physics. Anyway, what's your point?"

Thomas Kuhn and Scientific Theory

"I know you've taken physics, Selina, and you know a lot about science—a lot more than I'll ever know. But it's brilliant scientists like you, Selina, who sometimes overlook a very important point. It was a point noted by a *historian* of science, Thomas Kuhn. Kuhn recognized that science didn't always work the way textbook writers said it was supposed to work: Just the facts, the cold hard facts, that's what scientists deal with. But that's not quite accurate."

"Well, we scientists *do* rely on cold hard facts," Selina responded. "Not to cast aspersions on philosophers, Sarah, but if you're looking for cold hard facts, don't you think maybe you picked the wrong major? Come over to chemistry: We've got bushels of them. Seems to me I've memorized at least a million cold hard facts in my organic chemistry course, and we're not even finished with the semester."

"Sarah, I don't wish to speak ill of Kuhn, since he was a fellow historian, and we are, by and large, a splendid lot." Ben was skeptical. "Still, I think I agree with Selina on this one. True, the only physics course I ever took was physics for poets; but even there, we seemed to get an awful lot of cold hard facts."

"Wow, Ben and Selina in agreement! Maybe I should just leave it there and figure I've done enough for one day. But actually, I'm not denying that there are facts: Physics and chemistry are full of them, Selina, as you point out; and history has its share as well, to give Ben his due. But facts are perhaps not as simple and straightforward as many people—rationalists or empiricists, chemists or historians—suppose. Here's one of Kuhn's favorite examples: Think about the conflict between the Ptolemaic and Copernican theories in the 16th century. Ptolemy had said that the earth is stationary, and the moon and the sun and all the planets and even the realm of fixed stars all orbit around the earth. Copernicus comes along, he claims that the sun is the center and the earth is just one of the planets spinning around the sun. So who's right? Here's the Ptolemaic theory, it's worked well for hundreds of years in mapping the heavens and charting the motions of the planets, not to mention the fact that it fits our commonsense observation that we are not moving and the sun is. Of course, they didn't have telescopes, so they couldn't tell that much about the stars; but they did make very careful studies of the moon and the planets and the constellations and the pattern of solar and lunar eclipses, and they knew a great deal, including knowing enough to use the stars in their navigation—all of this using the Ptolemaic theory. True, the Ptolemaic theory had its problems. It required a rather complicated mechanism to account for some astronomical observations, particularly the observation of the retrograde motion of the planets."

"What was that last part, Sarah?" Ben was getting a bit lost.

"The retrograde motion of the planets. Look, suppose you and Selina go out every night with a blanket and lie out under the stars." Selina smiled and ruffled Ben's hair; he leaned toward her and they kissed. "Alright, so that idea has already occurred to you. Well, focus on astronomy for a moment; the biology can come later. Okay, you're looking up at the stars. You notice that they are traveling over your head, just as the sun does during the day, right? And just as the sun rises and sets lower in the sky as winter approaches, and then the days again start to get longer and the sun rises higher in the sky—in the same way, the great panorama of stars shifts as well. Some constellations are visible only in summer, others only in winter. As the weeks go by, all the stars shift together. Except for a few special exceptions. While all the other stars are rising lower on the horizon, one star seems to be rising higher. And it goes like that for a few days, sort of against the grain. And then it swings back into the pattern. The Greeks gave these strange stars a special name: They called them wanderers, or *planets*. And the motion just described is the retrograde motion of the planets."

Selina took up the story. "So why do the planets appear to wander in that manner? It's because the earth is also moving, of course, and when the earth overtakes the orbit of another planet, it looks as if the other planet is moving backwards against the pattern. But of course the backwards-appearing motion is not really because of the special motion of the other planet, which is simply following its own orbit around the sun. Instead, it's because of the motion of the earth relative to the orbit of that planet."

"Very nice, Selina. You chemistry majors know your astronomy, I see. That's exactly the explanation Copernicus gave. In fact, that aspect of the Copernican theory was very important to Kant. He claimed to have carried out a sort of Copernican Revolution in philosophy: Just as Copernicus recognized that the reason the planets seem to wander is because of the (moving) position from which we view them, likewise space and time seem universal because of the perceptual system we use to view the world. But let's get back to astronomy. The Ptolemaic astronomers had a different explanation. After all, they had known about the retrograde motion of the planets for a long time: It was the ancient Greeks who named the wanderers "planets," and that was more than a millennium before Copernicus. According to the Ptolemaic theory, the majestic clockwork of the heavens is governed by an elaborate set of spheres, and spheres within those spheres, and even spheres within the second spheres. Think of a planet as being like a light attached to the rim of a very large bicycle tire, and the bicycle is moving in a circle around us: but all we can see is the light attached to the wheel, okay? As the bicycle circles our stationary position, the light generally seems to be moving forward, right? But sometimes the light briefly moves backward, as the bicycle wheel turns and the light moves with the wheel toward the back. But of course the bicycle itself, following its orbit, is always moving in a constant circle. In the same manner, Ptolemaic astronomers said, the planet is on a wheel within a wheel, and that explains why it sometimes appears to be moving backwards—why it sometimes appears to have a retrograde motion relative to the stars."

Ben was impressed. "That's a beautiful theory, Sarah. Ptolemy must have been brilliant!"

Selina was not quite so impressed. "Yeah, brilliant, sure. Magnificent clockwork. But brilliantly wrong. I'm not surprised that a philosopher would like it, Sarah. You philosophers seem to love complicated theories that are brilliantly false."

"Ah, Selina, just simple lovers of wisdom, that's us. *Philo*, the Greek for love, *sophia*, the Greek for wisdom. Sometimes wisdom is rather complicated. In fact, the Copernican theory wasn't much simpler than the Ptolemaic, at least when Copernicus first proposed it, because Copernicus and Ptolemy and everyone else had agreed on what seemed to be an obvious truth: The motion of the heavens—all of the orbits—had to be perfect circles, or at least perfect circles within perfect circles. The idea that the orbits of the planets might actually be elliptical didn't come along until Johannes Kepler, the brilliant astronomer and mathematician, proposed it many decades later. So Copernicus needed circles within circles, just as Ptolemy did."

"Yeah, well, let's get back to a plain matter of scientific fact, Sarah," said Selina. "Maybe Copernicus didn't have all the details worked out when he proposed the Copernican theory. But it's a plain scientific fact that Copernicus was *right* and Ptolemy was *wrong*."

"But was it such a plain scientific fact, Selina? Imagine that we are living in 1575 and we are trying to decide whether the Copernican theory or the Ptolemaic theory is correct." Sarah leaned forward and spoke quietly. "We have to keep our voices low, because if anyone hears us saying that the Copernican theory might be correct, both the Protestants and the Catholics will probably want to draw and quarter us."

"Draw and quarter?" Selina was lost. "What's that?"

Ben was back on solid historical ground. "That was something they did to condemned prisoners. The executioner would make a slit beneath your stomach, and then draw out your intestines through the hole, and then. . . ."

"Hey, Ben! I'm trying to drink my coffee here!" Selina had heard more than enough.

"Well, you asked."

"Yeah, but I didn't really want to know. Let's get back to the stars and planets. Okay, it's 1575, and we're trying to decide between the Copernican and the Ptolemaic theories. What sort of scientific instruments can we use, Sarah?"

"No orbiting telescopes, of course. In fact, no telescopes at all. But you can use the navigational tools of the 16th century, which were not bad. No clocks—though they did have some means of determining time—and fairly good instruments for sighting the stars."

"Actually, they did have clocks, Sarah." Ben insisted on historical accuracy. "They weren't very good, not until they added pendulums in the mid-17th century. They were spring driven. But still, they were clocks."

"Thanks, Ben. Okay, Selina, it's 1575, you've got crude clocks and decent star-sighting equipment, though no telescopes. Both the Ptolemaic and Copernican theories can account for all the celestial phenomena we have so far observed: eclipses, of course, and also the retrograde motion of the planets. How do you decide which theory is correct?"

"Well, as a good scientist, I'd apply the scientific method. First I'd have to think of some difference between the theories and then some testable implication of that difference."

"The difference is easy, Selina." Ben was eager to help. "The Ptolemaic theory says we are stationary, sitting here on earth, dead center of the whole universe. And according to the Copernican theory, we're hurtling through space, traveling all the way around the sun in the course of a year."

"Isn't he brilliant, Sarah? And you thought I kept him around just for his sexy bod. Okay, now all we need is some testable implication of that difference. Well, according to the Copernican theory, six months from now we'll be way over on the other side of the sun, right? And according to the Ptolemaic theory, we'll be exactly where we are now, since the earth is stationary. If we take a sighting on a couple of stars today and then six months from now we take a careful sighting on the same two stars, then, according to the Copernican theory, we should be able to detect a difference in the angle. Just the same way as when I look at those two tables over in the corner and then move around to where Sarah is sitting and look again, the angle between the two tables will have changed."

"Bravo! You guys are a great team!" Sarah was still trying to maintain the always tenuous harmony between Selina and Ben. "That's exactly the experiment they did in the 16th century. What they were attempting to measure is called the stellar parallax: the change in the angles between two stars caused by the change in the position of the earth."

"And that's how they proved the truth of the Copernican theory!" Selina clapped her hands. "They were clever back in the 16th century, weren't they?"

"So they were, Selina," replied Sarah. "It was a wonderful experiment. Just one problem: They never found any stellar parallax."

"Get out of here, Sarah!" Selina was astonished. "Of course there was stellar parallax. Had to be. Don't tell me the Copernican theory is wrong and the earth doesn't move! You philosophers believe some strange things, but you don't believe that!"

"Look, Selina, I'm just telling you about the history of astronomy. They did the experiment you described, took their readings, and found no stellar parallax. Now suppose you are an astronomer in the 16th century.

You devised a brilliant experiment, ran your experiment carefully, got your results, and your prediction turned out to be *false:* You predicted stellar parallax and there isn't any. So what do you conclude? The Ptolemaic theory is correct and the Copernican theory is wrong. Copernicus, Bruno, Galileo—they were all wrong. Ptolemy, and the Catholic Church—which condemned the Copernican theory as false—were correct."

"No, that can't be right. I know the Copernican theory is true. Something must have gone wrong."

"Selina's right, Sarah," added Ben. "I'm just a humble historian, but even I know that the Copernican theory is true. Something must have been wrong with their experiment."

Sarah was delighted. "That's exactly what the Copernicans said in the 16th century! They didn't give up the Copernican theory, even though their brilliant experiment seemed to show that the theory was false. Instead, they decided that something else was wrong. Could have been the measurements; but no, they had done those very carefully, and several people had done them independently, and they all got the same results. So what could it be?"

"Oh, I know. How stupid of me!" Ben struck himself on the forehead. "That example of measuring the angles between the tables on the other side of the room threw me off. It's always hard to remember how great the distances are when we talk about the stars. Going from one side of the sun to the other, that's a long way, sure. But when we're talking about the distances to the stars, it's insignificant. It would be like we moved about one-thousandth of an inch and then tried to detect a difference in the angles between those two tables. The distance to the stars is so incredible, that even if we move from one side of the sun to the other, it would be very difficult to detect any difference in the angles between the stars; that is, we still couldn't detect the stellar parallax, not unless we had much more sophisticated measuring instruments than they had in the 16th century."

"Wow, nice job, Ben. You were right, Selina: This boy's not just another pretty face. He nailed it. In fact, it wasn't until *1838* that someone actually measured any stellar parallax. But think about what that means: Scientists devised a theory, derived an experimental implication of that theory, ran an experiment, and when the result turned out to be *not* what the theory predicted, they didn't reject the theory; instead, they decided that something else must have happened, something that would explain away the problematic results—even though they had no reason whatsoever to believe that was actually the case, other than that it was needed to save the theory. The crux of the matter is that scientific theories aren't just sets of individual, isolated facts that are each proved true or false. Rather, they succeed or fail as a system: When something goes wrong, there are lots of places where adjustments can be made. When the Copernican

---

The physicist can never subject an isolated hypothesis to experimental test, but only a whole group of hypotheses; when the experiment is in disagreement with his predictions, what he learns is that at least one of the hypotheses constituting this group is unacceptable and ought to be modified; but the experiment does not designate which one should be changed. . . . Physics is not a machine which lets itself be taken apart; we cannot try each piece in isolation and, in order to adjust it, wait until its solidity has been carefully checked. Physical science is a system that must be taken as a whole; it is an organism in which one part cannot be made to function except when the parts that are most remote from it are called into play. . . .

Pierre Duhem, *The Aim and Structure of Physical Theory* (1914), trans. by Philip P. Wiener, p. 187.

---

theory predicts stellar parallax and we fail to find it, we can decide that the basic Copernican idea is wrong, and the earth is actually stationary; or that the stars must be at a much greater distance than we had previously believed; or that our instruments are too crude to make the measurement; or that all the astronomers involved fouled up their readings."

Karl Popper

"Sure, Sarah, you can save a theory at all costs," Selina agreed. "There's that old story about when Galileo discovered the moons of Jupiter, by searching with his telescope. That would have undercut some opposing views, and those who didn't like the results refused to look through the telescope, because they knew that its results were false and would just cause confusion. But their obstinate views led nowhere; they made no new discoveries. Galileo, on the other hand, made discoveries and contributions that led to Newton's principles. When the Copernicans argued that the stars were too far away for stellar parallax to be detectable, they weren't just making some *ad hoc* adjustment to save their theory; they were proposing a major modification in astronomical views, a modification that could be tested, a modification that would lead to other hypotheses and more discoveries. It was a proposal that could have been *wrong*. That's how science proceeds: Formulate a hypothesis that is *testable*, that could be mistaken. And some of them *will* be mistaken. And sometimes some of the background assumptions made by the theory will be mistaken, as in the case of Copernicus. But proposing testable hypotheses, making mistakes, and rejecting our errors is the way science proceeds. And as it proceeds, it discovers *truths* about our universe. They aren't always truths that make us happy: Maybe it would make us happy to believe that we're the center of the universe and everything revolves around us. Or maybe it would be neat to think that humans are unique and distinct and unrelated to all the other life-forms that have evolved. Neat or not, those beliefs are false. And by developing better hypotheses, we have made great discoveries: in astronomy, in biology, in geology."

"Exactly right, Selina!" Sarah applauded. "What you're describing is Karl Popper's account of how science develops."

"Karl Popper." Selina thought for a moment. "Yeah, I've heard of him. Professor Viden, in physics, talked about Popper. 'Don't be afraid to fail,' Professor Viden used to say. 'That's how science makes progress: through bold, testable theories that may eventually prove false. Bold, testable theories that are proven false contribute much more to our scientific understanding than cautious, safe theories that do not make clear, testable claims.' Professor Viden said she learned that from Karl Popper."

"And so she did," Sarah agreed. "Science isn't just a gathering of facts. Rather, it's the organizing of ideas into testable hypotheses that generate interesting predictions. Sometimes we can't really see things, we fail to notice them, until we have a theory that predicts them. I mean, maybe we see them, but we ignore them: They look like static, something irrelevant, until a theory reveals their significance. With the aid of theory, we see a pattern, where before there was only 'blooming, buzzing confusion.' With a theory of insect communication, we see honeybees doing an elaborate signaling that reveals precise directions for other members of the hive; before, we saw only random, confused motion. With a germ theory of disease, we see patterns of infection, where before there was only haphazard disease."

"Yeah, that's right," Ben agreed. "Last summer I was visiting my older brother, Sam. He and Debbie have a baby, little Luke, he wasn't quite a year old. They were having all sorts of problems: Luke would cry when they put him to bed, then wake up and cry, and the problem kept getting worse. Doctor said there was nothing wrong with him. They would feed him, put him down, Luke would cry, they would try to hold out until he went to sleep, but one of them would eventually give in and go pick him up and rock him and walk him. Well, Sam and Debbie were beginning to look like the living dead, never getting any sleep. But I had just finished a psychology course, and we had been discussing B. F. Skinner's schedules of reinforcement. According to Skinner, one of the best ways to shape dedicated behavior is to reward it on a stretched-interval or variable-interval reinforcement schedule. That is, first you give the hungry pigeon food every time it presses the bar, then only after every second press, then after three, then five, and so on. By stretching the intervals between reinforcement, eventually the pigeon will peck the bar hundreds of times between reinforcers. And if you really want the behavior to endure, you then reward it on a variable schedule: sometimes after only a few pecks, other times after dozens. In those cases, the pigeon will continue pecking for very long periods with no reward. Without Skinner's theory, Luke's crying seemed inexplicable: Sam and Debbie just happened to get a kid who cried a lot; tough luck, these things happen. But with Skinner's theory in hand, the behavior takes on a whole new significance: Sam and Debbie were inadvertently setting up a perfect combination of stretched and variable interval reinforcement. And once you understand the causes, then you can change things."

Sarah nodded. "Popper liked to divide theories of knowledge and theories of science into two categories: *searchlight* theory (his own view), as contrasted with the *bucket* theory (which he opposed). According to the bucket theory, we gain knowledge simply by collecting lots and lots of plain facts, and eventually we organize them into more and more comprehensive theoretical structures."

There are and can be only two ways of searching into and discovering truth. The one flies from the senses and particulars to the most general axioms. . . . The other derives axioms from the senses and particulars, rising by a gradual and unbroken ascent, so that it arrives at the most general axioms last of all. This is the true way, but as yet untried.

Francis Bacon, *Novum Organum*, 1620

"Like Francis Bacon!" Ben was delighted. "Yeah, Bacon would be a perfect example of someone with a bucket theory of knowledge. We studied Bacon last year in our 17th-century British history class. He became lord chancellor in 1618, but was removed from office for accepting bribes. He admitted taking money, but argued that the gifts he received—receiving gifts was a common practice during those times—did not influence his judgments. Sounds a lot like today's politicians when they talk about campaign contributions, doesn't it? Anyway, after he was kicked out of office, he spent the rest of his life working on philosophy and writing books and trying to develop a systematic procedure for scientific investigation."

"Yeah," Sarah added, "he died after becoming severely chilled while doing an experiment on refrigeration: He was out in the London winter stuffing a chicken full of snow."

Selina laughed: "Yeah, he sounds like a philosopher."

"You're a fine one to talk," Sarah replied. "Didn't you tell me you blew up your grandmother's glass punch bowl when you were using it as a cover for one of your experiments?"

"Yeah, lucky I didn't kill myself. There was glass all over that kitchen. Grandma was not pleased."

"Anyway," Ben continued, "Bacon's basic method of doing science was to collect all the samples that he could and then look for what was common to them. For example, if he was studying heat, he would make a list of all the hot things he could find, and a list of all the cold things, and then compare the lists to see if there was any distinctive feature to each. That's the key to the scientific method for Bacon: Collect more and more facts, and then draw your conclusion from them."

"Exactly, Ben, that's the bucket theory Popper is describing. But Popper rejects the bucket theory. For one thing, as you already noted, many facts can't even be recognized—they escape our notice, or we don't know where to look, or we don't know *how* to look—without a theory to guide us. It's difficult to imagine that we would have looked for stellar parallax without a theory to guide our search: It's not the sort

> *It is often said that experiments should be made without preconceived ideas. That is impossible.*
>
> Henri Poincaré, *Science and Hypothesis*

of thing you stumble over. And it's not likely that we would have discovered the distinctive trails made by subatomic particles in cloud chambers without a theory to guide our research and without the building of a particle accelerator. And before we had gas theory, some chemists managed to isolate oxygen, but they had a very distorted concept of what it was. And without Newtonian theory, we could certainly observe the appearance of a comet; but we could not see the *return* of Halley's comet, but instead could observe only strange, erratic fiery phenomena in the firmament. So the idea that we can simply collect all our observations without the guidance of theory is not very plausible. But even if we could, there would be no way to proceed from the mass of collected data to a plausible scientific theory that would account for the data. The problem, as Popper and many other scientists and philosophers of science have recognized, is not that we cannot formulate a theory which is consistent with all the observed data. The problem is precisely the opposite: It is *too easy* to develop a theory that will account for all the data. We can formulate *dozens* of theories that will equally well fit all the data and observations we have collected. The challenge is not in developing a theory that will account for everything; rather, the challenge is to determine which of the many possible theories is the right one. But on the searchlight account, we have a solution: A theory is plausible if it *leads* to observational results that we would not have found otherwise. The Copernican theory is plausible because it tells us to look for stellar parallax, which we would not have discovered without that theory. Newtonian theory gained great support from the fact that it could successfully guide us to look for a comet—on a particular date, at a specific astronomical location—that we would not otherwise have expected. The theory of plate tectonics is plausible because it guides us to fossil remains of a specific sort in a specific location, remains that we would otherwise not have easily discovered. So Popper's searchlight account helps us in both ways: First, it guides us to better and more systematic and more thorough collection of observational data; and second, it gives us a standard of theoretical plausibility. What's the best way of gaining knowledge? Don't wander around aimlessly picking up interesting baubles and adding them to your collection; rather, develop an interesting hypothesis that generates specific, important, testable predictions, and then run your experiments and test your hypothesis. If your hypothesis fails, then you have at least learned something. Hypotheses that cannot be refuted are not powerful hypotheses; instead, they are useless: They guide us nowhere."

"Alright, Sarah, you're preaching to the choir, girl. I like Popper: Forget about buckets, shine that theoretical searchlight. But Popper is very different from your philosophical buddy Immanuel Kant. Kant acknowledged the importance of theoretical frameworks to guide our observations and inquiries but he thought he had discovered the eternal framework—the fixed and immutable laws of reason and observation. Popper, on the other hand, wants to develop many exciting new hypotheses, try them out, and reject them when they fail. And rather than being fixed theories, they are useful tools that guide our research and yield new information, but are themselves replaced by better theories in their turn."

"You're right, of course, Selina." Sarah raised her coffee mug in salute. "As you so often are."

Selina bowed. "Don't you mean, as I *invariably* am?"

"No," Ben said, "as you *often* are. Remember, if you could not be wrong, you would not be a very interesting hypothesis; and whatever else Selina may be, she is *always* a very interesting hypothesis."

"Well said!" Selina lifted her coffee cup. "A toast to Ben, science, and Popper's searchlight."

"Alright, Selina," Sarah nodded, "To Ben, and Popper's searchlight. But notice this: There's no solid foundation for anchoring Popper's spotlight."

Selina frowned. "What *are* you raving about, roommate?"

Belief Systems

"Remember how this discussion got started? You and Ben were arguing about the best foundation for knowledge. But," Sarah continued, "does your contemporary view of science really leave any room for foundations? Kant thought that the Newtonian notion of space, together with Euclidean geometry, could serve as a permanent, fixed starting point. But as you already noted, Einstein rejected both Euclidean geometry and Newtonian concepts of space in developing relativity theory. And when Copernican theorists ran an experiment to detect stellar parallax—which their theory predicted—they did not reject Copernican theory because no stellar parallax appeared; instead, they made revisions elsewhere: They changed the background assumption that the stars are relatively close to us, and they concluded that the stars must be an immense distance away and that the Copernican theory was still true. If researchers at Loch Ness finally drag some reclusive creature out of the depths and pose her before the television cameras, then scientists might add Nessie to their taxonomy. That would be surprising, certainly: Not only would we discover an animal we had long thought extinct, but we would have to conclude that an entire breeding population survived for many centuries, with very few believable sightings. Still, that wouldn't be the first time we discovered that a sea creature we had thought extinct was still in existence. We have a place for Nessie in our system of biology, even though we seriously doubt that that niche is going to be filled. But suppose someone shows up with Medusa, the remarkable creature we had thought to be mythic: a woman with snakes—rather than hair—growing out of her skull."

"No way, Sarah!" Selina was laughing.

"What if you looked at her yourself, shook her hand, heard the snakes hissing?" Sarah persisted.

"No, not even then." Selina shook her head. "Seeing isn't always believing. It would have to be a fraud, a trick, some circus sideshow scam."

"You mean," Sarah asked, "you wouldn't believe it even if you saw it? Why not? I thought science was supposed to be based on empirical observations."

"It *is* based on empirical observations," Selina replied. "But that doesn't mean you *always* take observations at face value. If you take one ball in your right hand and one in your left, place a scarf over your hands, and then produce three balls, I'm not going to conclude that one ball plus another ball makes three. I'll say it was a good trick. And the same for Medusa: good trick, but there's no real Medusa."

"But why are you so sure?"

"Look, Sarah," Selina replied, "think about what it would involve: in the first place, the combination of two distinct species to form one individual—and at that, two species very far apart on the evolutionary scale. The branch that led to humans diverged from the branch leading to snakes a *very* long time ago. It would contradict everything we know about biology: For a start, how could you have a single animal that is both warm blooded (the human part) and cold blooded (the snakes)? We would have to throw out all our biological research and start over from scratch. It's a lot easier to believe that someone is playing a trick or running a scam than to believe that decades of biological research are completely false."

The totality of our so-called knowledge or beliefs, from the most casual matters of geography and history to the profoundest laws of atomic physics or even of pure mathematics and logic, is a man-made fabric which impinges on experience only along the edges. Or, to change the figure, total science is like a field of force whose boundary conditions are experience. A conflict with experience at the periphery occasions readjustments in the interior of the field. Truth values have to be redistributed over some of our statements. . . . Reevaluation of some statements entails reevaluation of others . . . because of their logical interconnections. . . . But the total field is so underdetermined by its boundary conditions, experience, that there is much latitude of choice as to what statements to reevaluate in the light of any single contrary experience. No particular experiences are linked with any particular statements in the interior of the field, except indirectly through considerations of equilibrium affecting the field as a whole.

If this view is right, it is misleading to speak of the empirical content of an individual statement. . . . Any statement can be held true come what may, if we make drastic enough adjustments elsewhere in the system. . . . Conversely, by the same token, no statement is immune to revision.

Willard Van Orman Quine, "Two Dogmas of Empiricism," 1951

"Exactly right, Selina. So what's the moral of the story?" Sarah leaned forward. "It's just this: When we have new phenomena that we hadn't anticipated, or when an experiment gives us the 'wrong' results, or when we make an observation that seems to conflict with our theoretical views, what happens? Well, sometimes we decide our theory was wrong, and we reject it in favor of another. For example, the unanticipated major irregularities of physical features of the Earth's surface led to the rejection of old geological theory in favor of plate tectonics. And sometimes we decide that one of our background assumptions was questionable, and we change it. For example, when Copernican theorists failed to detect stellar parallax, they held onto the Copernican theory and rejected the common assumption that the stars are relatively close to the Earth. And sometimes we decide that the observation was flawed—as we would likely do if someone showed us Medusa. The point is that changes can be made in lots of different places, and there is *no* privileged area of knowledge that serves as the fixed foundation. Our theories and beliefs and observations fit together as a whole, and they are judged as a whole; and if something goes wrong, adjustments and changes can occur anywhere in the system. Observation is obviously a crucial element of science; but observations are guided by theory, rather than being the independent, privileged foundation on which theory builds. There is no privileged foundation; instead, there is a system of theory and observational data and background assumptions and mathematical processes that work well as a whole, that guide us effectively, that open up new and fruitful paths of inquiry. But when there are problems, we can make adjustments or changes at many different points. In fact, we can make changes anywhere—even to the principles of geometry. Simply put, there is no fixed foundation that is immune to change."

Pragmatism

"Okay," Selina said, "science is somewhat messier than the textbooks suggest. Kuhn is probably right about that. Still, that messy scientific process results in scientific *knowledge.*"

"Exactly so, Selina." Sarah nodded. "It's not quite the way either the rationalists or the empiricists picture it: knowledge built up from secure foundations. But it's still knowledge: knowledge as *pragmatists* understand knowledge."

"Ah, pragmatism." Ben smiled. So that's the path you've been leading us down: Whatever works is true."

"That's basically it, Ben," Sarah answered, "though pragmatists would add a few details. In particular, pragmatists reject the idea of truth as that which *copies* reality. Instead, true beliefs and true theories *lead* us effectively, guide us to beneficial results, yield new discoveries, and prove their worth as good instruments. And beliefs can't be tested individually, but only as part of a system."

"I'm not so sure about this pragmatism thing, Sarah." Ben looked puzzled. "Aren't there some simple facts that make our claims true or false? Caesar crossed the Rubicon. Well, that's true just in case Caesar actually crossed the Rubicon River."

"What is it that historians say, Ben? Why do the good guys always win the wars? It's because the winners write the history."

"Yeah, Sarah, like that other saying: Why does treason never succeed? Because if it succeeds, none dare call it treason. If the Battle of Saratoga had gone the other way, George Washington would probably be remembered as a vile traitor and Benedict Arnold as a patriotic hero. Okay, there's some truth to that, Sarah." Ben paused, then continued. "Still, that's a bit oversimplified. For years, many U.S. history textbooks taught that freedom-loving Texans won the 'War for Texas Independence' against a vicious band of cutthroat Mexicans who wanted to deny Texans their basic rights. A very convenient story to tell U.S. schoolchildren. But truth crushed to earth will rise again: Historians now note that one of the key causes of that war was the Mexican refusal to allow slavery in their country; so the Texas slave owners wanted to break away from Mexico in order to promote slavery. Not as nice a story as the 'desire for freedom' version; but truth isn't always convenient."

"Look, pragmatists don't deny that there's a truth of the matter," Sarah answered. "Of course there is. But truth is not as simple a notion as we sometimes like to think. In particular, it's not a matter of matching a claim with a corresponding fact. Here's our friend Ben; what simple fact does his presence indicate? From the perspective of physics, we might say that he is a solid object—or perhaps a collection of particles. Biologists would see a male member of the species *Homo sapiens*, while sociologists observe a white Anglo–Saxon Protestant male from the middle class. Historians would see a brilliant historical writer. Selina sees a studmuffin. And so on. Of course Ben is there: Good old lovable Ben. But what that amounts to is very much a function of what approach we are using, what theoretical system we are working in. The notion that we can have some privileged 'view from nowhere' that gives us the truth 'as it is in itself'—that our theories are true just in case they 'match plain reality'—just doesn't work. Kant thought we needed that concept: We have to distinguish phenomena from noumena, distinguish the appearances and theories from the 'thing-in-itself.' But it really isn't a very useful concept. What we've got are phenomena, all the way down. Maybe God can see things as they are "in-themselves," in their noumenal purity. But we aren't gods. The Copernican theory isn't true because it matches or maps reality; rather, it's true because it leads us well, to a better understanding of the vastness of the universe, and because it contributes to Newton's theories: because it leads us well in many respects, whereas Ptolemy leads us to dead ends."

"No way, Sarah." Selina objected. "I'm a scientific realist. Newtonian theory leads us well—it works well—because it's true, and not the other way around."

"But Selina," Sarah answered, "what does saying that it's true really amount to, other than that it works, it leads us to better predictions and new and productive paths. And that's the pragmatist point. Forgive me, you might consider this a nasty shot, but your view is still mired in the old absolutism which insists that we can stand outside the world, from no perspective, in some privileged view from nowhere, and map the world as it absolutely is. It doesn't work. We're not detached, absolute observers, looking down from our privileged position on Mt. Sinai. We are instead grubby animals that have to survive in a challenging world. It's not an alien world—we were born into it and bred to it—but it isn't an easy world either. Think like a Darwinian, not a Platonic absolutist: Knowledge is what helps us forage more effectively. Knowledge is good practice that leads us well and works, and that's an end to it; it's not some detached exercise in pure world-mapping metaphysics."

"Whoa, Sarah, them's fighting words. You can insult my tastes, slander my major, and question my parentage, but don't go calling me a Platonic absolutist! I'm an empiricist—a scientist through and through. But science isn't just making up stories we happen to like. And it's not just grubbing for practical benefit, for that matter. Science is learning how the world really is, on the basis of systematic examination and experimentation that works from solid observational evidence, not absolutist speculation."

"I'm not pushing for absolutism, Selina; maybe Ben will, but I don't. But just because I reject absolutism, that doesn't mean I have to accept some simplistic view of fixed, simple observational facts. The way we know the world and interact with the world is more complex than that. The idea that we require some fixed and certain resting point in order to have genuine knowledge, that's a remnant of absolutism. I'm just trying to help you clear the absolutist remnants out of your scientific outlook. You can't have fixed certainties; everything is open to question."

"I don't need absolute facts or fixed eternal verities," Selina answered. "But I do believe there are factual truths: The Copernican theory is true, and the Ptolemaic theory is false. Facts. Convenient or not, Catholic or pagan, those are facts."

"Look, Selina," Sarah said, "I'm not denying the existence of scientific facts. But I'm not sure that they are quite as neat and clean as the empiricist tradition made them out to be: Formulate a hypothesis, make the observational tests, confirm or defeat the hypothesis. But it may not be that straightforward. First, as Willard Quine points out, and as we noted with the Medusa example and the failure of the Copernicans to discover stellar parallax, theories don't map onto 'physical reality' quite that neatly; instead, our theories tend to confront the world in a more systematic manner. And second, as the historian Thomas Kuhn noted, theoretical scientific systems are neither adopted nor rejected because of their perfect mapping of the empirical world; rather, they win or lose in competition

---

The trail of the human serpent is . . . over everything. Truth independent; truth that we find merely; truth no longer malleable to human need; truth incorrigible, in a word; such truth exists indeed superabundantly—or is supposed to exist by rationalistically minded thinkers; but then it means only the dead heart of the living tree, . . . petrified in men's regard by sheer antiquity. But how plastic even the oldest truths nevertheless really are has been vividly shown in our day by the transformation of logical and mathematical ideas, a transformation which seems even to be invading physics.

William James, *Pragmatism*, Lecture Two, 1907

with some alternative theoretical system. They win or lose not because they offer better maps of reality, but because they make better predictions and solve quandaries the other model can't handle, and because they guide other scientists into useful and fruitful research projects based on that system. That doesn't mean that scientific theories can't be true; but it does raise doubts about whether any simple 'matching with observational reality' is an adequate picture of the truth of scientific theories. If we say that a theory guides us well and leads us to useful research and profitable predictions—well, what do you really add when you say, oh, and also, it's *objectively true.* Not that I'm denying empirical truth; neither is Kuhn or Quine. But we may need to think about empirical truth in a more sophisticated manner."

"Or maybe," Ben said, "we need to try an altogether different approach. Look, I like Popper. But there's another side to that story. William Butler Yeats said it beautifully: 'Wisdom is a butterfly, and not a gloomy bird of prey.'"

"Yeah," Selina shook her head, "just go with the flow, man, wisdom will come to you, you just have to open your heart and your soul to it; relax, dude, chill out, get high, you'll see the truth."

Ben smiled, turned to Sarah. "God, she's a wicked woman. Why do I put up with her, Sarah?" He turned back toward Selina, and shook a finger at her. "That's not what I meant at all, Selina: Let's not slide back into the straw-man fallacy. Just because I think science is not the only source of wisdom, that doesn't make me a flower child."

"Look, Ben," Selina replied, "I like poetry as much as the next girl, especially accompanied by wine and candlelight. But wine, poetry, and candlelight, delightful as they are, can't lead you to knowledge. If you want knowledge, you gotta snuff out that candle and turn on the searchlight. Yeats is fine in the moonlight, but the light of knowledge is Popper's searchlight."

"But Popper's searchlight will never shine brightly enough to reveal fixed certainty, a secure foundation," Ben said, "and that's why we need religion and faith: It offers the certainty that science can never supply. That doesn't make science any worse; it just shows that the two belong to different realms. If you try to have science take the place of religion, then you get a sorry substitute. And if religious claims usurp the role of science—in the form of 'creation science,' for example—then they not only venture into territory where they have nothing legitimate to add, but they also place their own special features at risk. Science is always questioning and open to change; even its most central principles can be tossed out in a paradigm shift, as Kuhn makes clear. So in the improbable event that 'creation science' actually became a scientific theory, it would have to renounce the fixed certainty that is vital to religious faith. If you're look-ing for something that changeth not, faith is a better foundation than sci-ence. And rationalism is a better foundation than empiricism."

"Oh well," Sarah sighed. "I suppose I didn't quite establish harmony between the empiricists and rationalists. William James, the American pragmatist of the early 20th century, claimed that pragmatism could be a 'happy harmonizer,' making peace between empiricists and rationalists by integrating the best elements of both. But William James would not have been so optimistic had he encountered the battles between Selina and Ben. Next time I'll try something easier: like bringing peace to the Middle East."

Selina laughed. "Don't take it so hard, Sarah. You certainly made me think hard about the nature of scientific inquiry. Maybe you philosophers are worth having around after all. And Thomas Kuhn is an interesting historian, Ben. But right now I'm off to my chemistry lab. Doesn't Kuhn make a distinction between, on the one hand, *revolutionary* science, in which major theoretical systems are being challenged and sometimes replaced by new paradigms, and, on the other hand, *normal* science, which involves working out the problems that are generated within an accepted scientific paradigm or framework? Well, I want to go spend a few contented hours doing *normal* science: A morning of philosophical debate wears me out; a few hours of normal productive scientific research should restore my soul."

"Excellent, Selina," Sarah answered. "I hope you get your soul thor-oughly restored, because souls are one of the things I want to discuss at tomorrow's coffee break."

"Sounds great, Sarah," Ben said. "Souls are right up my alley. But it may not be Selina's favorite topic."

Selina shook her head. "If you get here first, Sarah, order me a large Colombian with a double shot of espresso. I'm going to need all the strength I can get."

READINGS

Charles Sanders Peirce (1839–1914) was a brilliant mathematician and philosopher, and perhaps the earliest advocate of pragmatism. His personality was somewhat abra-sive, and he never received the university appointment he much desired, but he had great influence on such philosophers as William James—though Peirce himself did not approve of how other pragmatists developed his ideas. Peirce was clearly influenced by Darwin's development of the theory of evolution by natural selection, although Peirce's ideas are quite different from Darwin's.

Peirce's paper "The Fixation of Belief" was published in Popular Science Monthly *in 1877. In it, Peirce discusses several methods of "fixing," or establishing, beliefs. The "method of tenacity" and the "method of authority" are both quite common and have some advantages, but ultimately fail; the "a priori method," which depends exclusively on intuition and reason, also has appeal, but, like the others, has no way of correcting itself. The method of science, while not as comfortable and easy as the others, offers better long-term results and the possibility of correcting its mistakes.*

The Fixation of Belief

V

If the settlement of opinion is the sole object of inquiry, and if belief is of the nature of a habit, why should we not attain the desired end, by taking any answer to a question, which we may fancy, and constantly reiterating it to ourselves, dwelling on all which may conduce to that belief, and learning to turn with contempt and hatred from anything which might disturb it? This simple and direct method is really pursued by many men. I remember once being entreated not to read a certain newspaper lest it might change my opinion upon free-trade. "Lest I might be entrapped by its fallacies and misstatements" was the form of expression. "You are not," my friend said, "a special student of political economy. You might, therefore, easily be deceived by fallacious arguments upon the subject. You might, then, if you read this paper, be led to believe in protection. But you admit that free-trade is the true doctrine; and you do not wish to believe what is not true." I have often known this system to be deliberately adopted. Still oftener, the instinctive dislike of an undecided state of mind, exaggerated into a vague dread of doubt, makes men cling spasmodically to the views they already take. The man feels that if he only holds to his belief without wavering, it will be entirely satisfactory. Nor can it be denied that a steady and immovable faith yields great peace of mind. It may, indeed, give rise to inconveniences, as if a man should resolutely continue to believe that fire would not burn him, or that he would be eternally damned if he received his *ingesta* otherwise than through a stomach-pump. But then the man who adopts this method will not allow that its inconveniences are greater than its advantages. He will say, "I hold steadfastly to the truth and the truth is always wholesome." And in many cases it may very well be that the pleasure he derives from his calm faith overbalances any inconveniences resulting from its deceptive character. Thus, if it be true that death is annihilation, then the man who believes that he will certainly go straight to heaven when he dies, provided he have fulfilled certain simple observances in this life, has a cheap pleasure which will not be followed by the least disappointment. A similar consideration seems to have weight with many persons in religious topics, for we frequently hear it said, "Oh, I could not believe so-and-so, because I should be wretched if I did." When an ostrich buries its head in the sand as danger approaches, it very likely takes the happiest course. It hides the danger, and then calmly says there is no danger; and, if it feels perfectly sure there is none, why should it raise its head to see? A man may go through life, systematically keeping out of view all that might cause a change in his opinions, and if he only succeeds—basing his method, as he does, on two fundamental psychological laws—I do not see what can be said against his doing so. It would be an egotistical impertinence to object that his procedure is irrational, for that only amounts to saying that his method of settling belief is not ours. He does not propose to himself to be rational, and indeed, will often talk with scorn of man's weak and illusive reason. So let him think as he pleases.

But this method of fixing belief, which may be called the method of tenacity, will be unable to hold its ground in practice. The social impulse is against it. The man who adopts it will find that other men think differently from him, and it will be apt to occur to him in some saner moment that their opinions are quite as good as his own, and this will shake his confidence in his belief. This conception, that another man's thought or sentiment may be equivalent to one's own, is a distinctly new step, and a highly important one. It arises from an impulse too strong in man to be suppressed, without danger of destroying the human species. Unless we make ourselves hermits, we shall necessarily influence each other's opinions; so that the problem becomes how to fix belief, not in the individual merely, but in the community.

Let the will of the state act, then, instead of that of the individual. Let an institution be created which shall have for its object to keep correct doctrines before the attention of the people, to reiterate them perpetually, and to teach them to the young; having at the same time power to prevent contrary doctrines from being taught, advocated, or expressed. Let all possible causes of a change of mind be removed from men's apprehensions. Let them be kept ignorant, lest they should learn of some reason to think otherwise than they do. Let their passions be enlisted, so that they may regard private and unusual opinions with hatred and horror. Then, let all men who reject the established belief be terrified into silence. Let the people turn out and tar-and-feather such men, or let inquisitions be made into the manner of thinking of suspected persons, and, when they are found guilty of forbidden beliefs, let them be subjected to some signal punishment. When complete agreement could not otherwise be reached, a general massacre of all who have not thought in a certain way has proved a very effective means of settling opinion in a country. If the power to do this be wanting, let a list of opinions be drawn up, to which no man of the least independence of thought can assent, and let the faithful be required to accept all these propositions, in order to segregate them as radically as possible from the influence of the rest of the world.

This method has, from the earliest times, been one of the chief means of upholding correct theological and political doctrines, and of preserving their universal or catholic character. In Rome, especially, it has been practiced from the days of Numa Pompilius to those of Pius Nonus. This is the most perfect example in history; but wherever there is a priesthood—and no religion has been without one—this method has been more or less made use of. Wherever there is aristocracy, or a guild, or any association of a class of men whose interests depend or are supposed to depend on certain propositions, there will be inevitably found some traces of this natural product of social feeling. Cruelties always accompany this system; and when it is consistently carried out, they become atrocities of the most horrible kind in the eyes of any rational man. Nor should this occasion surprise, for the officer of a society does not feel justified in surrendering the interests of that society for the sake of mercy, as he might his own private interests. It is natural, therefore, that sympathy and fellowship should thus produce a most ruthless power.

In judging this method of fixing belief, which may be called the method of authority, we must, in the first place, allow its immeasurable mental and moral superiority to the method of tenacity. Its success is proportionally greater; and in fact it has over and over again worked the most majestic results. The mere structures of stone which it has caused to be put together—in Siam, for example, in Egypt, and in Europe—have many of them a sublimity hardly more than rivaled by the greatest works of nature. And, except the geological epochs, there are no periods of time so vast as those which are measured by some of these organized faiths. If we scrutinize the matter closely, we shall find that there has not been one of their creeds which has remained always the same; yet the change is so slow as to be imperceptible during one person's life, so that individual belief remains sensibly fixed. For the mass of mankind, then, there is perhaps no better method than this. If it is their highest impulse to be intellectual slaves, then slaves they ought to remain.

But no institution can undertake to regulate opinions upon every subject. Only the most important ones can be attended to, and on the rest men's minds must be left to the action of natural causes. This imperfection will be no source of weakness so long as men are in such a state of culture that one opinion does not influence another—that is, so long as they cannot put two and two together. But in the most priest-ridden states some individuals will be found who are raised above that condition. These men possess a wider sort of social feeling; they see that men in other countries and in other ages have held to very different doctrines from those which they themselves have been brought up to believe; and they cannot help seeing that it is the mere accident of their having been taught as they have, and of their having been surrounded with the manners and associations they have, that has caused them to believe as they do and not far differently. And their candor cannot resist the reflection that there is no reason to rate their own views at a higher value than those of other nations and other centuries; and this gives rise to doubts in their minds.

They will further perceive that such doubts as these must exist in their minds with reference to every belief which seems to be determined by the caprice either of themselves or of those who originated the popular opinions. The willful adherence to a belief, and the arbitrary forcing of it upon others, must, therefore, both be given up and a new method of settling opinions must be adopted, which shall not only produce an impulse to believe, but shall also decide what proposition it is which is to be believed. Let the action of natural preferences be unimpeded, then, and under their influence let men conversing together and regarding matters in different lights, gradually develop beliefs in harmony with natural causes. This method resembles that by which conceptions of art have been brought to maturity. The most perfect example of it is to be found in the history of metaphysical philosophy. Systems of this sort have not usually rested upon observed facts, at least not in any great degree. They have been chiefly adopted because their fundamental propositions seemed "agreeable to reason." This is an apt expression; it does not mean that which agrees with experience, but that which we find ourselves inclined to believe. Plato, for example, finds it agreeable to reason that the distances of the celestial spheres from one another should be proportional to the different lengths of strings which produce harmonious chords. Many philosophers have been led to their main conclusions by considerations like this; but this is the lowest and least developed form which the method takes, for it is clear that another man might find Kepler's [earlier] theory, that the celestial spheres are proportional to the inscribed and circumscribed spheres of the different regular solids, more agreeable to *his* reason. But the shock of opinions will soon lead men to rest on preferences of a far more universal nature. Take, for example, the doctrine that man only acts selfishly—that is, from the consideration that acting in one way will afford him more pleasure than acting in another. This rests on no fact in the world, but it has had a wide acceptance as being the only reasonable theory.

This method is far more intellectual and respectable from the point of view of reason than either of the others which we have noticed. But its failure has been the most manifest. It makes of inquiry something similar to the development of taste; but taste, unfortunately, is always more or less a matter of fashion, and accordingly, metaphysicians have never come to any fixed agreement, but the pendulum has swung backward and forward between a more material and a more spiritual philosophy, from the earliest times to the latest. And so from this, which has been called the *a priori* method, we are driven, in Lord Bacon's phrase, to a true induction. We have examined into this *a priori* method as something which promised to deliver our opinions from their accidental and capricious element. But development, while it is a process which eliminates the effect of some casual circumstances, only magnifies that of others. This method, therefore, does not differ in a very essential way from that of authority. The government may not have lifted its finger to influence my convictions; I may have been left outwardly quite free to choose, we will say, between monogamy and polygamy, and appealing to my conscience only, I may have concluded that the latter practice is in itself licentious. But when I come to see that the chief obstacle to the spread of Christianity among a people of as high culture as the Hindoos has been a conviction of the immorality of our way of treating women, I cannot help seeing that, though governments do not interfere, sentiments in their development will be very greatly determined by accidental causes. Now, there are some people, among whom I must suppose that my reader is to be found, who, when they see that any belief of theirs is determined by any circumstance extraneous to the facts, will from that moment not merely admit in words that that belief is doubtful, but will experience a real doubt of it, so that it ceases in some degree at least to be a belief.

To satisfy our doubts, therefore, it is necessary that a method should be found by which our beliefs may be caused by nothing human, but by some external permanency—by something upon which our thinking has no effect. Some mystics imagine that they have such a method in a private inspiration from on high. But that is only a form of the method of tenacity, in which the conception of truth as something public is not yet developed. Our external permanency would not be external, in our sense, if it was restricted in its influence to one individual. It must be something which affects, or might affect, every man. And, though these affections are necessarily as various as are individual conditions, yet the method must be such that the ultimate conclusion of every man shall be the same, or would be the same if inquiry were sufficiently persisted in. Such is the method of science. Its fundamental hypothesis, restated in more familiar language, is this: There are real things, whose characters are entirely independent of our opinions about them; those realities affect our senses according to regular laws, and, though our sensations are as different as our relations to the objects, yet, by taking advantage of the laws of perception, we can ascertain by reasoning how things really are, and any man, if he have sufficient experience and reason enough about it, will be led to the one true conclusion. The new conception here involved is that of reality. It may be asked how I know that there are any realities. If this hypothesis is the sole support of my method of inquiry, my method of inquiry must not be used to support my hypothesis. The reply is this: (1) If investigation cannot be regarded as proving that there are real things, it at least does not lead to a contrary conclusion; but the method and the conception on which it is based remain ever in harmony. No doubts of the method, therefore, necessarily arise from its practice, as is the case with all the others. (2) The feeling which gives rise to any method of fixing belief is a dissatisfaction at two repugnant propositions. But here already is a vague concession that there is some *one* thing to which a proposition should conform. Nobody, therefore, can really doubt that there are realities, or, if he did, doubt would not be a source of dissatisfaction. The hypothesis, therefore, is one which every mind admits. So that the social impulse does not cause men to doubt it. (3) Everybody uses the scientific method about a great many things, and only ceases to use it when he does not know how to apply it. (4) Experience of the method has not led us to doubt it, but, on the contrary, scientific investigation has had the most wonderful triumphs in the way of settling opinion. These afford the explanation of my not doubting the method or the hypothesis which it supposes; and not having any doubt, nor believing that anybody else whom I could influence has, it would be the merest babble for me to say more about it. If there be anybody with a living doubt upon the subject, let him consider it. . . .

This is the only one of the four methods which presents any distinction of a right and a wrong way. If I adopt the method of tenacity and shut myself out from all influences, whatever I think necessary to doing this is necessary according to that method. So with the method of authority: the state may try to put down heresy by means which, from a scientific point of view, seems very ill-calculated to accomplish its purposes; but the only test *on that method* is what the state thinks, so that it cannot pursue the method wrongly. So with the *a priori* method. The very essence of it is to think as one is inclined to think. All metaphysicians will be sure to do that, however they may be inclined to judge each other to be perversely wrong. The Hegelian system recognizes every natural tendency of thought as logical, although it is certain to be abolished by counter-tendencies. Hegel thinks there is a regular system in the succession of these tendencies, in consequence of which, after drifting one way and the other for a long time, opinion will at last go right. And it is true that metaphysicians get the right ideas at last; Hegel's system of Nature represents tolerably the science of his day; and one may be sure that whatever scientific investigation has put out of doubt will presently receive *a priori* demonstration on the part of the metaphysicians. But with the scientific method the case is different. I may start with known and observed facts to proceed to the unknown; and yet the rules which I follow in doing so may not be such as investigation would approve. The test of whether I am truly following the method is not an immediate appeal to my feelings and purposes, but, on the contrary, itself involves the application of the method. Hence it is that bad reasoning as well as good reasoning is possible; and this fact is the foundation of the practical side of logic.

It is not to be supposed that the first three methods of settling opinion present no advantage whatever over the scientific method. On the contrary, each has some peculiar convenience of its own. The *a priori* method is distinguished for its comfortable conclusions. It is the nature of the process to adopt whatever belief we are inclined to, and there are certain flatteries to one's vanities which we all believe by nature, until we are awakened from our pleasing dream by rough facts. The method of authority will always govern the mass of mankind; and those who wield the various forms of organized force in the state will never be convinced that dangerous reasoning ought not to be suppressed in some way. If liberty of speech is to be untrammeled from the grosser forms of constraint, then uniformity of opinion will be secured by a moral terrorism to which the respectability of society will give its thorough approval. Following the method of authority is the path of peace. Certain non-conformities are permitted; certain others (considered unsafe) are forbidden. These are different in different countries and in different ages; but, wherever you are let it be known that you seriously hold a tabooed belief, and you may be perfectly sure of being treated with a cruelty no less brutal but more refined than hunting you like a wolf. Thus, the greatest intellectual benefactors of mankind have never dared, and dare not now, to utter the whole of their thought; and thus a shade of *prima facie* doubt is cast upon every proposition which is considered essential to the security of society. Singularly enough, the persecution does not all come from without; but a man torments himself and is oftentimes most distressed at finding himself believing propositions which he has been brought up to regard with aversion. The peaceful and sympathetic man will, therefore, find it hard to resist the temptation to submit his opinions to authority. But most of all I admire the method of tenacity for its strength, simplicity, and directness. Men who pursue it are distinguished for their decision of character, which becomes very easy with such a mental rule. They do not waste time in trying to make up their minds to what they want, but, fastening like lightning upon whatever alternative comes first, they hold to it to the end, whatever happens, without an instant's irresolution. This is one of the splendid qualities which generally accompany brilliant, unlasting success. It is impossible not to envy the man who can dismiss reason, although we know how it must turn out at last.

Such are the advantages which the other methods of settling opinions have over scientific investigation. A man should consider well of them; and then he should consider that, after all, he wishes his opinions to coincide with the fact, and that there is no reason why the results of those first three methods should do so. To bring about this effect is the prerogative of the method of science. Upon such considerations he has to make his choice—a choice which is far more than the adoption of any intellectual opinion, which is one of the ruling decisions of his life, to which when once made he is bound to adhere. The force of habit will sometimes cause a man to hold on to old beliefs after he is in a condition to see that they have no sound basis. But reflection upon the state of the case will overcome these habits, and he ought to allow reflection full weight. People sometimes shrink from doing this, having an idea that beliefs are wholesome which they cannot help feeling rest on nothing. But let such persons suppose an analogous though different case from their own. Let them ask themselves what they would say to a reformed Mussulman who should hesitate to give up his old notions in regard to the relations of the sexes; or to a reformed Catholic who should still shrink from the Bible. Would they not say that these persons ought to consider the matter fully, and clearly understand the new doctrine, and then ought to embrace it in its entirety? But, above all, let it be considered that what is more wholesome than any particular belief is integrity of belief; and that to avoid looking into the support of any belief from a fear that it may turn out rotten is quite as immoral as it is disadvantageous. The person who confesses that there is such a thing as truth, which is distinguished from falsehood simply by this, that if acted on it should, on full consideration, carry us to the point we aim at and not astray, and then, though convinced of this, dares not know the truth and seeks to avoid it, is in a sorry state of mind, indeed.

Yes, the other methods do have their merits: a clear logical conscience does cost something—just as any virtue, just as all that we cherish, costs us dear. But, we should not desire it to be otherwise. The genius of a man's logical method should be loved and revered as his bride, whom he has chosen from all the world. He need not condemn the others; on the contrary, he may honor them deeply, and in doing so he only honors her the more. But she is the one that he has chosen, and he knows that he was right in making that choice. And having made it, he will work and fight for her, and will not complain that there are blows to take, hoping that there may be as many and as hard to give, and will strive to be the worthy knight and champion of her from the blaze of whose splendors he draws his inspiration and his courage.

Karl R. Popper (1902–94) was one of the most original and influential philosophers of science of the 20th century. He opposed foundationalism, and his account of scientific reasoning emphasized the importance of bold, testable hypotheses and the open, systematic effort to falsify them. His books (especially The Logic of Scientific Discovery, *published in 1934) made a great impression on working scientists as well as on philosophers. "The Bucket and the Searchlight: Two Theories of Knowledge," was originally given as a lecture in 1948. It can be found in the appendix of Popper's* Objective Knowledge: An Evolutionary Approach *(Oxford, U.K.: Oxford University Press, 1972). In this paper, Popper sets out the searchlight theory that Sarah briefly described.*

The Bucket and the Searchlight: Two Theories of Knowledge

The purpose of this paper is to criticize a widely held view about the aims and methods of the natural sciences, and to put forward an alternative view.

I

I shall start with a brief exposition of the view I propose to examine, which I will call '*the bucket theory of science*' (or '*the bucket theory of the mind*'). The starting point of this theory is the persuasive doctrine that before we can know or say anything about the world, we must first have had perceptions—sense experiences. It is supposed to follow from this doctrine that our knowledge, our experience, consists either of accumulated perceptions (naïve empiricism) or else of assimilated, sorted, and classified perceptions (a view held by Bacon and, in a more radical form, by Kant).

The Greek atomists had a somewhat primitive notion of this process. They assumed that atoms break loose from the objects we perceive, and penetrate our sense organs, where they become perceptions; and out of these, in the course of time, our knowledge of the external world fits itself together like a self-assembling jigsaw puzzle. According to this view, then, our mind resembles a container—a kind of bucket—in which perceptions and knowledge accumulate. (Bacon speaks of perceptions as 'grapes, ripe and in season' which have to be gathered, patiently and industriously, and from which, if pressed, the pure wine of knowledge will flow.)

Strict empiricists advise us to interfere as little as possible with this process of accumulating knowledge. True knowledge is pure knowledge, uncontaminated by those prejudices which we are only too prone to add to, and mix with, our perceptions; these alone constitute experience pure and simple. The result of these additions, of our disturbing and interfering with the process of accumulating knowledge, is error. Kant opposes this theory: he denies that perceptions are ever pure, and asserts that our experience is the result of a process of assimilation and transformation—the combined product of sense perceptions and of certain ingredients added by our minds. The perceptions are the raw material, as it were, which flows from outside into the bucket, where it undergoes some (automatic) processing—something akin to digestion, or perhaps to systematic classification—in order to be turned in the end into something not so very different from Bacon's 'pure wine of experience'; let us say, perhaps, into fermented wine.

I do not think that either of these views suggests anything like an adequate picture of what I believe to be the actual process of acquiring experience, or the actual method used in research or discovery. Admittedly, Kant's view might be so interpreted that it comes much nearer to my own view than does pure empiricism. I grant, of course, that science is impossible without experience (but the notion of 'experience' has to be carefully considered). Though I grant this, I nevertheless hold that perceptions do not constitute anything like the raw material, as they do according to the 'bucket theory', out of which we construct either 'experience' or 'science'.

II

In science it is *observation* rather than perception which plays the decisive part. But observation is a process in which we play an intensely *active* part. An observation is a perception, but one which is planned and prepared. We do not 'have' an observation as we may 'have' a sense experience but we 'make' an observation. A navigator even 'works' an observation. An observation is always preceded by a particular interest, a question, or a problem—in short, by something theoretical. After all, we can put every question in the form of a hypothesis or conjecture to which we add: 'Is this so? Yes or no?' Thus we can assert that every observation is preceded by a problem, a hypothesis (or whatever we may call it); at any rate by something that interests us, by something theoretical or speculative. This is why observations are always selective, and why they presuppose something like a principle of selection.

• • •

IV

. . . An observation always presupposes the existence of some system of expectations. These expectations can be formulated in the form of queries; and the observation will be used to obtain either a confirming or a correcting answer to expectations thus formulated.

My thesis that the question, or the hypothesis, must precede the observation may at first have seemed paradoxical; but we can see now that it is not at all paradoxical to assume that expectations—that is, dispositions to react—must precede every observation and, indeed, every perception: for certain dispositions or propensities to react are innate in all organisms whereas perceptions and observations clearly are not innate. And although perceptions and, even more, observations, play an important part in the process of *modifying* our dispositions or propensities to react, some such dispositions or propensities must, of course, be present first, or they could not be modified. . . .

At every instant of our pre-scientific or scientific development we are living in the centre of what I usually call a *'horizon of expectations'*. By this I mean the sum total of our expectations, whether these are subconscious or conscious, or perhaps even explicitly stated in some language. Animals and babies have also their various and different horizons of expectations though no doubt on a lower level of consciousness than, say, a scientist whose horizon of expectations consists to a considerable extent of linguistically formulated theories or hypotheses.

The various horizons of expectations differ, of course, not only in their being more or less conscious, but also in their content. Yet in all these cases the horizon of expectations plays the part of a frame of reference: only their setting in this frame confers meaning or significance on our experiences, actions, and observations.

Observations, more especially, have a very peculiar function within this frame. They can, under certain circumstances, destroy even the frame itself, if they clash with certain of the expectations. In such a case they can have an effect upon our horizon of expectations like a bombshell. This bombshell may force us to reconstruct, or rebuild, our whole horizon of expectations; that is to say, we may have to correct our expectations and fit them together again into something like a consistent whole. We can say that in this way our horizon of expectations is raised to and reconstructed on a higher level, and that we reach in this way a new stage in the evolution of our experience; a stage in which those expectations which have not been hit by the bomb are somehow incorporated into the horizon, while those parts of the horizon which have suffered damage are repaired and rebuilt. This has to be done in such a manner that the damaging observations are no longer felt as disruptive, but are integrated with the rest of our expectations. If we succeed in this rebuilding, then we shall have created what is usually known as an *explanation* of those observed events which created the disruption, the problem.

As to the question of the temporal relation between observation on the one hand and the horizon of expectations or theories on the other, we may well admit that a new explanation, or a new hypothesis, is generally preceded in time by *those* observations which destroyed the previous horizon of expectations and thus were the stimulus to our attempting a new explanation. Yet this must not be understood as saying that observations generally precede expectations or hypotheses. On the contrary, each observation is preceded by expectations or hypotheses; by those expectations, more especially, which make up the horizon of expectations that lends those observations their significance; only in this way do they attain the status of real observations.

The question, 'What comes first, the hypothesis (H) or the observation (O)?' reminds one, of course, of that other famous question: 'What came first, the hen (H) or the egg (O)?' Both questions are soluble. The bucket theory asserts that just as a primitive form of an egg (O), a unicellular organism, precedes the hen (H) observation (O) always precedes every hypothesis (H); for the bucket theory regards the latter as arising from observations by generalization, or association, or classification. By contrast, we can now say that the hypothesis (or expectation, or theory, or whatever we may call it) precedes the observation, even though an observation that refutes a certain hypothesis may stimulate a new (and therefore a temporally later) hypothesis.

All this applies, more especially, to the formation of scientific hypotheses. For we learn only from our hypotheses what kind of observations we ought to make: whereto we ought to direct our attention; wherein to take an interest. Thus it is the hypothesis which becomes our guide, and which leads us to new observational results.

This is the view which I have called the '*searchlight theory*' (in contradistinction to the '*bucket theory*'). According to the searchlight theory, observations are secondary to hypotheses. Observations play, however, an important role as *tests* which a hypothesis must undergo in the course of our critical examination of it. If the hypothesis does not pass the examination, if it is falsified by our observations, then we have to look around for a new hypothesis. In this case the new hypothesis will come after those observations which led to the falsification or rejection of the old hypothesis.

Yet what made the observations interesting and relevant and what altogether gave rise to our undertaking them in the first instance, was the earlier, the old and now rejected hypothesis.

In this way science appears clearly as a straightforward continuation
of the pre-scientific repair work on our horizons of expectations. Science
never starts from scratch; it can never be described as free from assumptions; for at every instant it presupposes a horizon of expectations—
yesterday's horizon of expectations, as it were. Today's science is built
upon yesterday's science and so it is the result of yesterday's searchlight;
and yesterday's science, in turn, is based on the science of the day before.
And the oldest scientific theories are built on pre-scientific myths, and
these, in their turn, on still older expectations. Ontogenetically (that is,
with respect to the development of the individual organism) we thus
regress to the state of the expectations of a newborn child; phylogeneti-
cally (with respect to the evolution of the race, the phylum) we get to the
state of expectations of unicellular organisms. (There is no danger here of
a vicious infinite regress—if for no other reason than that every organism
is born with *some* horizon of expectations.) There is, as it were, only one
step from the amoeba to Einstein.

Now if this is the way science evolves, what can be said to be the characteristic step which marks the transition from pre-science to science?

V

The first beginnings of the evolution of something like a scientific method
may be found, approximately at the turn of the sixth and fifth centuries
B.C., in ancient Greece. What happened there? What is new in this evolution? How do the new ideas compare with the traditional myths, which
came from the East and which, I think, provided many of the decisive
suggestions for the new ideas?

Among the Babylonians and the Greeks and also among the Maoris in
New Zealand—indeed, it would seem, among all peoples who invent cosmological myths—tales are told which deal with the beginning of things,
and which try to understand or explain the structure of the Universe in
terms of the story of its origin. These stories become traditional and are
preserved in special schools. The tradition is often in the keeping of some
separate or chosen class, the priests or medicine men, who guard it jeal-
ously. The stories change only little by little—mainly through inaccuracies
in handing them on, through misunderstandings, and sometimes through
the accretion of new myths, invented by prophets or poets.

Now what is new in Greek philosophy, what is newly added to all this,
seems to me to consist not so much in the replacement of the myths by
something more 'scientific', as in a *new attitude towards the myths*. That

their character then begins to change seems to me to be merely a consequence of this new attitude.

The new attitude I have in mind is *the critical attitude. In the place of a dogmatic handing on of the doctrine* in which the whole interest lies in the preservation of the authentic tradition *we find a critical discussion of the doctrine.* Some people begin to ask questions about it; they doubt the trustworthiness of the doctrine: its *truth.*

Doubt and criticism certainly existed before this stage. What is new, however, is that doubt and criticism now become, in their turn, part of the tradition of the school. A tradition of a higher order replaces the traditional preservation of the dogma: in the place of traditional theory—in place of the myth—we find the tradition of criticizing theories (which at first themselves are hardly more than myths). It is only in the course of this critical discussion that observation is called in as a witness. . . .

Thus it seems to me that it is the tradition of criticism which constitutes what is new in science, and what is characteristic of science. On the other hand it seems to me that the task which science sets itself (that is, the explanation of the world) and the main ideas which it uses, are taken over without any break from prescientific mythmaking.

VI

What is the task of science? . . .

The task of science is partly theoretical—*explanation*—and partly practical—*prediction and technical application.* I shall try to show that these two aims are, in a way, two different aspects of one and the same activity.

I will first examine the idea of an explanation.

One often hears it said that an explanation is the reduction of the unknown to the known; but we are rarely told how this is to be done. At any rate, this notion of explanation is not one that was ever used in the actual practice of explanation in science. If we look at the history of science in order to see what kinds of explanation were used and accepted as satisfactory at one time or another, then we find a very different notion of explanation in practical use. . . .

In the course of the historical development of science many different methods and kinds of explanation have been regarded as acceptable; but they all have one aspect in common: the various methods of explanation all consist of a *logical deduction;* a deduction whose conclusion is the *explicandum*—a statement of the thing to be explained—and whose premisses consist of the *explicans,* a statement of the explaining laws and conditions. The main changes that have occurred in the course of the history of science consist in the silent abandonment of certain implicit

demands regarding the character of the *explicans* (that it can be intuitively grasped, that it is to be self-evident, etc.); demands which turn out
not to be reconcilable with certain other demands whose crucial significance becomes more and more obvious as time goes on; in particular the
demand for the independent testability of the *explicans* which forms the
premises and thus the very heart of the explanation.

Thus an explanation is always the deduction of the *explicandum* from
certain premises, to be called the *explicans*.

Here is a somewhat gruesome example, just for the purpose of
illustration.

A dead rat has been discovered and we wish to know what has happened to it. The *explicandum* may be stated thus: 'This rat here has died
recently.' This *explicandum* is definitely known to us—the fact lies before
us in stark reality. If we want to explain it, we must try out some conjec-
tural or hypothetical explanations (as the authors of detective stories do);
that is to say, explanations which introduce something *unknown*, or at any
rate much less known, to us. Such a hypothesis may be, for instance, that
the rat died of a large dose of rat poison. This is useful as a hypothesis in
so far as, firstly, it helps us to formulate an *explicans* from which the
explicandum can be deduced; secondly, it suggests to us a number of
independent tests—tests of the *explicans* which are quite independent of
whether the *explicandum* is true or not.

Now the *explicans*—which is our hypothesis—does not only consist of
the sentence 'This rat has eaten some bait containing a large dose of rat
poison', for from this statement alone one cannot validly deduce the
explicandum. Rather, we shall have to use, as *explicans*, two different
kinds of premises—*universal laws* and *initial conditions*. In our case the
universal law might be put like this: 'If a rat eats at least eight grains of
rat poison it will die within five minutes.' The (singular) initial condition
(which is a singular statement) might be: 'This rat ate at least eighteen
grains of rat poison, more than five minutes ago.' From these two premises together we may now indeed deduce that this rat recently has died
(that is, our *explicandum*).

Now all this may seem somewhat obvious. But consider one of my
theses—the thesis, namely, that what I have called the *'initial conditions'*
(the conditions pertaining to the individual case) never suffice by themselves as an explanation, and that we always need a general law as well.
Now this thesis is by no means obvious; on the contrary, its truth is often
not admitted. I even suspect that most of you would be inclined to accept
a remark like 'this rat has eaten rat poison' as quite sufficient to explain
its death, even if no explicit statement of the universal law regarding the

effects of rat poison is added. But suppose for a moment that we were living in a world in which anybody (and also any rat) who eats a lot of that chemical called 'rat poison' will feel especially well and happy for a week to come and more lively than ever before. If a universal law like this were valid, could the statement 'This rat has eaten rat poison' still be acceptable as an explanation of death? Obviously not.

Thus we have reached the important result, often overlooked, that any explanation that utilizes the singular initial conditions alone would be incomplete, and that *at least one universal law* is needed besides, even though this law is, in some cases, so well known that it is omitted as if it were redundant.

To sum up this point. We have found that an explanation is a deduction of the following kind:

U	(Universal Law)	⎱Premisses
I	(Specific Initial Conditions)	⎰(constituting the *Explicans*)
E̅	(*Explicandum*)	Conclusion

VII

But are all explanations of this structure *satisfactory*? Is, for instance, our example (which explains the death of the rat by reference to rat poison) a satisfactory explanation? We do not know: the tests may show that whatever the rat may have died of, it was not rat poison.

If some friend should be sceptical of our explanation and ask, 'How do you know that this rat ate poison?', it will obviously not be sufficient to answer, 'How can you doubt it, seeing that it is dead?'. Indeed, any reason which we may state in support of any hypothesis must be other than, and independent of, the *explicandum*. If we can only adduce the *explicandum* itself as evidence, we feel that our explanation is circular, and therefore quite *unsatisfactory*. If, on the other hand, we are able to reply, 'Analyse the contents of its stomach, and you will find a lot of poison', and if this prediction (which is new—that is, not entailed by the *explicandum* alone) proves true, we shall at least consider our explanation a fairly good hypothesis.

But I have to add something. For our sceptical friend may also question the truth of the universal law. He may say, for instance, 'Granted, this rat has eaten a certain chemical; but why should it have died of it?'. Again, we must not answer: 'But don't you see it is dead? That just shows you how dangerous it is to eat this chemical.' For this again would make our explanation circular and unsatisfactory. In order to make it satisfactory we should have to submit the universal law to test cases which are independent of our *explicandum*.

With this, my analysis of the formal schema of explanation may be regarded as concluded, but I shall add some further remarks and analyses to the general schema I have outlined.

First, an observation about the ideas of cause and effect. The state of affairs described by the singular *initial conditions* can be called the '*cause*', and the one described by the *explicandum* the '*effect*'. I feel, however, that these terms, encumbered as they are with associations from their history, are better avoided. If we still want to use them, we should always remember that they acquire a meaning only relative to a theory or a universal law. It is the theory or the law which constitutes the *logical link* between cause and effect, and the statement '*A* is the cause of *B*' should be analysed thus: 'There is a theory *T* which can be, and has been, independently tested, and from which, in conjunction with an independently tested description *A*, of a specific situation, we can logically deduce a description, *B*, of another specific situation.' (That the existence of such a *logical* link between 'cause' and 'effect' is presupposed in the very use of these terms has been overlooked by many philosophers, including Hume.)

VIII

The task of science is not confined to searching for purely theoretical explanations; it also has its practical sides: prediction-making as well as technical applications. Both of these can be analysed by means of the same logical schema which we introduced to analyse explanation.

(1) *The derivation of predictions.* Whereas in the search for an explanation the *explicandum* is given—or known—and a suitable *explicans* has to be found, the derivation of predictions proceeds in the opposite direction. Here the theory is given, or assumed to be known (perhaps from textbooks), and so are the specific initial conditions (they are known, or assumed to be known, by observation). What remain to be found are the logical consequences: certain logical conclusions which are not yet known to us from observation. These are the *predictions*. In this case, the prediction *P* takes the place of the *explicandum E* in our logical schema.

(2) *Technical application.* Consider the task of building a bridge which has to comply with certain practical requirements, laid down in a list of specifications. What we are given are the specifications, *S*, which describe a certain required state of affairs—the bridge to be built. (*S* are the customer's specifications, which are given prior to, and are distinct from, the architect's specifications.) We are given, further, the relevant physical theories (including certain rules of thumb). What are to be found are certain initial conditions which may be realized technically and which

are of such a nature that the specifications may be deduced from them, together with the theory. So in this case, S takes the place of E in our logical schema.

This makes it clear how, from a logical point of view, both the derivation of predictions and the technical application of scientific theories may be regarded as mere inversions of the basic schema of scientific explanation.

The use of our schema, however, is still not exhausted: it may also serve to analyse the *procedure of testing our explicans*. The testing procedure consists in the derivation from the *explicans* of a prediction, P, and in comparing it with an actual, observable, situation. If a prediction does not agree with the observed situation, then the *explicans* is shown to be false; it is falsified. In this case we still do not know whether it is the universal *theory* which is false, or whether the *initial conditions* describe a situation which does not correspond with the real situation—so that the initial conditions are false. Of course, it may well be that the theory *and* the initial conditions are false.

The falsification of the prediction shows that the *explicans* is false, yet the reverse of this does not hold: it is incorrect and grossly misleading to think that we can interpret the 'verification' of the prediction as 'verifying' the *explicans* or even a part of it. For a true prediction may easily have been validly deduced from an *explicans* that is false. It is even quite misleading to regard *every* 'verification' of a prediction as something like a practical *corroboration* of the *explicans:* it would be more correct to say that only such 'verifications' of predictions which are 'unexpected' without the theory under examination may be regarded as corroborations of the *explicans*, and so of the theory. This means that a prediction can be used to corroborate a theory only if its comparison with observations might be regarded as a serious attempt at testing the *explicans*—a serious attempt at refuting it. A 'risky' prediction of this kind may be called 'relevant to a test of the theory'. After all, it is fairly obvious that the passing of an examination can give an idea of the qualities of the student only if the examination which he passes is sufficiently severe, and that an examination can be designed which even the weakest student will pass easily.

• • •

IX

Earlier I have tried to show that an explanation will be *satisfactory* only if its universal laws, its theory, can be tested independently of the *explicandum*. But this means that any satisfactory explanatory theory must always assert *more* than what was already contained in the *explicanda* which originally led us to put it forward. In other words, satisfactory theories must, as a matter of principle, transcend the empirical instances which gave rise to them; otherwise they would, as we have seen, merely lead to explanations which are circular.

Here we have a methodological principle which stands in direct contradiction to all positivistic and naïvely empiricist or inductivist tendencies. It is a principle which demands that we should dare to put forward bold hypotheses that open up, if possible, new domains of observations, rather than those careful generalizations from 'given' observations which have remained ever since Bacon the idols of all naïve empiricists.

Our view that it is the task of science to put forward explanations, or (what leads essentially to the same logical situation) to create the theoretical foundations for predictions and other applications—this view has led us to the methodological demand that our theories should be testable. Yet there are *degrees of testability*. Some theories are *better* testable than others. If we strengthen our methodological demand and aim at *better and better testable* theories, then we arrive at a methodological principle—or a statement of the task of science—whose unconscious adoption in the past would rationally explain a great number of events in the history of science: it would explain them as steps towards carrying out the task of science. (At the same time it gives us a statement of the task of science, telling us what should in science be regarded as *progress;* for in contrast to most other human activities—art and music in particular—there really is, in science, such a thing as progress.)

An analysis and comparison of the degrees of testability of different theories shows that the testability of a theory grows with its *degree of universality* as well as with its *degree of definiteness, or precision*.

The situation is fairly simple. Along with the degree of universality of a theory goes an increase in the range of those events about which the theory can make predictions and thereby also the domain of possible falsifications. But a theory which is more easily falsified is at the same time one that is better testable.

We find a similar situation if we consider the degree of definiteness or precision. A precise statement can be more easily refuted than a vague one, and it can therefore be better tested. This consideration also allows us to explain the demand that qualitative statements should if possible be replaced by quantitative ones by our principle of increasing the degree of testability of our theories. (In this way we can also explain the part played by *measurement* in the testing of theories; it is a device which becomes increasingly important in the course of scientific progress, but which should not be used (as it often is) as a characterizing feature of science, or the formation of theories, in general. For we must not overlook the fact that measuring procedures began to be used only at a fairly late stage in the development of some of the sciences, and that they are even now not used in all of them; and we must also not overlook the fact that all measurement is dependent on theoretical assumptions.)

X

A good example from the history of science that may be used to illustrate my analysis is the transition from the theories of Kepler and Galileo to the theory of Newton.

That this transition has nothing whatever to do with induction, and that Newton's theory cannot be regarded as anything like a generalization of those two earlier theories may be seen from the undeniable and important fact that Newton's theory *contradicts* them. *Thus Kepler's laws cannot be deduced from Newton's* although it has been often asserted that they can be so deduced, and even that Newton's can be deduced from Kepler's: Kepler's laws can be obtained from Newton's only *approximately*; by making the false assumption that the masses of the various planets are negligible compared with the mass of the sun. Similarly, Galileo's law of free falling bodies cannot be deduced from Newton's theory: on the contrary, it contradicts it. Only by making the false assumption that the total length of all falls is negligible compared with the length of the radius of the earth can we obtain Galileo's law *approximately* from Newton's theory.

This shows, of course, that Newton's theory cannot be a generalization obtained by induction or deduction but that it is a new hypothesis which can irradiate the way to the falsification of the old theories: it can irradiate, and point the way to those domains in which, according to the new theory, the old theories fail to yield good approximations. (In Kepler's case this is the domain of the theory of perturbations, and in Galileo's case it is the theory of variable accelerations, since according to Newton gravitational accelerations vary inversely with the square of the distance.)

Had Newton's theory achieved no more than the union of Kepler's laws with Galileo's, it would have been only a *circular explanation of these laws* and therefore unsatisfactory as an explanation. Yet its power of illumination and its power of convincing people consisted just in its power to throw light on the way to independent tests, leading us to successful predictions which were incompatible with the two older theories. It was the way to new empirical discoveries.

Newton's theory is an example of an attempt to explain certain older theories of a lower degree of universality, which not only leads to a kind of unification of these older theories but at the same time to their falsification (and so to their correction by restricting or determining the domain within which they are, in good approximation, valid). A case which occurs perhaps more often is this: an old theory is first falsified; and the new theory arises later, as an attempt to explain the partial success of the old theory as well as its failure.

• • •

XII

I hope that some of my formulations which at the beginning of this lecture may have seemed to you far-fetched or even paradoxical will now appear less so.

There is no road, royal or otherwise, which leads of necessity from a 'given' set of specific facts to any universal law. What we call 'laws' are hypotheses or conjectures which always form a part of some larger system of theories (in fact, of a whole horizon of expectations) and which, therefore, can never be tested in isolation. The progress of science consists in trials, in the elimination of errors, and in further trials guided by the experience acquired in the course of previous trials and errors. No particular theory may ever be regarded as absolutely certain: every theory may become problematical, no matter how well corroborated it may seem now. No scientific theory is sacrosanct or beyond criticism. This fact has often been forgotten, particularly during the last century, when we were impressed by the often repeated and truly magnificent corroborations of certain mechanical theories, which eventually came to be regarded as indubitably true. The stormy development of physics since the turn of the century has taught us better; and we have now come to see that it is the task of the scientist to subject his theory to ever new tests, and that no theory must be pronounced final. Testing proceeds by taking the theory to be tested and combining it with all possible kinds of initial conditions as well as with other theories, and then comparing the resulting predictions with reality. If this leads to disappointed expectations, to refutations, then we have to rebuild our theory.

The disappointment of some of the expectations with which we once eagerly approached reality plays a most significant part in this procedure. It may be compared with the experience of a blind man who touches, or runs into, an obstacle, and so becomes aware of its existence. *It is through the falsification of our suppositions that we actually get in touch with 'reality'.* It is the discovery and elimination of our errors which alone constitute that 'positive' experience which we gain from reality.

It is of course always possible to save a falsified theory by means of supplementary hypotheses (like those of epicycles). But this is not the way of progress in the sciences. The proper reaction to falsification is to search for new theories which seem likely to offer us a better grasp of the facts. Science is not interested in having the last word if this means shutting off our minds from falsifying experiences, but rather in learning from our experience; that is, in learning from our mistakes.

There is a way of formulating scientific theories which points with particular clarity to the possibility of their falsification: we can formulate them in the form of prohibitions or *negative existential statements* such as, for example, 'There does not exist a closed physical system, such that energy changes in one part of it without compensating changes occurring in another part' (first law of thermodynamics). Or, 'There does not exist a machine which is 100 per cent efficient' (second law). It can be shown that universal statements and negative existential statements are logically equivalent. This makes it possible to formulate all universal laws in the manner indicated; that is to say, as prohibitions. However, these are prohibitions intended only for the technicians and not for the scientist. They tell the former how to proceed if he does not want to squander his energies. But to the scientist they are a challenge to test and to falsify; they stimulate him to try to discover those states of affairs whose existence they prohibit, or deny.

Thus we have reached a point from which we can see science as a magnificent adventure of the human spirit. It is the invention of ever new theories, and the indefatigable examination of their power to throw light on experience. The principles of scientific progress are very simple. They demand that we give up the ancient idea that we may attain certainty or even a high degree of 'probability' in the sense of the probability calculus with the propositions and theories of science (an idea which derives from the association of science with magic and of the scientist with the magician): the aim of the scientist is not to discover absolute certainty, but to discover better and better theories or to invent more and more powerful searchlights capable of being put to more and more severe tests and thereby leading us to, and illuminating for us, ever new experiences. But this means that these theories must be falsifiable: it is through their falsification that science progresses.

Study Questions

1. Though rationalism and empiricism are very different views, some people suggest that they share some important assumptions. According to that suggestion, what basic assumptions are common to both rationalists and empiricists?
2. In the early debate between Ptolemaic and Copernican theorists, what did they regard as the "crucial experiment"?
3. For Kuhn, what would the main *point* of the "crucial experiment" story be concerning the Copernican theory?

4. What is Karl Popper's "searchlight" theory of knowledge? How does it contrast with the "bucket" theory?
5. Describe the pragmatic account of truth.
6. What are the different methods that Peirce describes for "fixing" or establishing belief? What are their advantages and disadvantages? Which method does Peirce favor, and why?

Exercises

1. Kant is concerned to distinguish *noumena*—things as they are in themselves—from the phenomena we observe. He insists on the importance of factoring in our observational stance in considering our observations; but he also believes that he can ultimately separate what our conceptualization brings to our experiences from the nature of the thing-in-itself (the noumenon), and thus get a clearer grasp of what the thing-in-itself actually is. Some contemporary empiricists believe (with Kant) that the distinction remains important, while many others—such as Kuhn, Duhem, and Quine—have doubts about its usefulness or plausibility. Which side of that debate would you favor?

2. Immanuel Kant believed that geometry is a source of fixed and final truth. Henri Poincaré, the great French mathematician and scientist, held a very different view:

   > *The geometrical axioms are . . . neither synthetic a priori intuitions nor experimental facts.* They are conventions. Our choice among all possible conventions is *guided* by experimental facts; but it remains *free*, and is only limited by the necessity of avoiding every contradiction. . . . In other words, *the axioms of geometry . . . are only definitions in disguise.* What, then, are we to think of the question: Is Euclidean geometry true? It has no meaning. We might as well ask if the metric system is true, and if the old weights and measures are false. . . . One geometry cannot be more true than another; it can only be more convenient. Henri Poincaré, *Science and Hypothesis*, p. 142.

   Of course, these are not the only options—eternal *a priori* truth (Kant) or convention (Poincaré)—so you might disagree with both Kant and Poincaré and opt for another interpretation of geometry. But if you had to choose between Kant and Poincaré on this question, which view seems more plausible to you?

3. Suppose an expedition returns from deep in a South American rain forest, and the members bring Medusa with them. Or at least, it certainly looks like Medusa: She appears to be a woman, with fierce vipers growing from her scalp instead of hair. Is there any possibility that biologists would eventually rule that they have discovered a genuine new species—call it homo viperous—that is another member of the primate family? Why would that be so much more difficult than adding a new species of beetle? Does that added difficulty provide support for the Quine–Duhem–Kuhn account?

4. Charles Sanders Peirce was a pragmatist who rejected the notion of simple, direct truths that are known either empirically or rationally. But he strongly insisted on the importance of a concept of final truth; the truth, according to

Peirce, is that set of beliefs on which scientific inquiry will ultimately converge. Is that a useful standard for objective truth?

5. To what extent do Sarah's epistemological views match or conflict with her religious perspective (Chapter two)?

6. Ben's rationalist epistemology seems a good fit with his religious beliefs (Chapter two); but would it surprise you if Ben were a strict empiricist in his epistemological position? Would an empiricist view be *compatible* with his religious views, or would they be in irreconcilable conflict?

Glossary

Copernican theory: The astronomical theory, developed by Copernicus, asserting that the sun is the center of the solar system, that all the planets (including earth) orbit the sun, and that the earth spins daily on its axis.

Pragmatism: A philosophical position that the meaning of a concept is set by the practical consequences of its application and that the truth of a theory or claim is based on its usefulness in guiding us (rather than on whether it matches or accurately copies reality).

Ptolemaic theory: The astronomical system, developed by Ptolemy and generally accepted until late in the 16th century, according to which the earth is stationary in the center of the cosmos, and the sun, moon, planets, and realm of fixed stars all orbit around the earth.

Additional Resources

N. R. Hanson's *Patterns of Discovery* (Cambridge, U.K.: Cambridge University Press, 1958) used research in Gestalt psychology to challenge the traditional empiricist distinction between observation and theory. Willard van Orman Quine raised serious questions concerning the traditional distinctions between analytic and synthetic, between *a priori* and *a posteriori*, and between theory and observation. His work can be found in *From a Logical Point of View*, revised ed. (Cambridge, MA: Harvard University Press, 1961); *Word and Object* (Cambridge, MA: M.I.T. Press, 1960); *The Ways of Paradox and Other Essays* (New York: Random House, 1966); and *Ontological Relativity and Other Essays* (New York: Columbia University Press, 1969).

The French mathematician Henri Poincaré and the French scientist Pierre Duhem had a significant influence on the development of views such as Kuhn's and Quine's. Duhem's *The Aim and Structure of Physical Theory*, 2d ed., trans. by Philip P. Wiener (Princeton, NJ: Princeton University Press, 1954), originally published in Paris in 1914; and Poincaré's *Science and Hypothesis*, first published in English translation in 1905, currently available in a 1952 Dover edition of that translation (New York: Dover Publications, 1952).

Historian Thomas Kuhn's fascinating and enormously influential *The Structure of Scientific Revolutions*, 2d ed. (Chicago: University of Chicago Press, 1970) is a very readable book that should interest anyone who likes either science or history. An excellent examination of Kuhn's views—including Kuhn's response to some key criticisms—is *Criticism and the Growth of Knowledge*, edited by Imre Lakatos and Alan Musgrave (Cambridge, U.K.: Cambridge University Press, 1970).

Karl Popper's work has been highly influential in both science and philosophy. See *The Logic of Scientific Discovery* (London: Hutchinson, 1959); *Conjectures and Refutations*, 3d ed. (London: Routledge and Kegan Paul, 1969); and *Objective Knowledge: An Evolutionary Approach* (Oxford, U.K.: Oxford University Press, 1972). An excellent book on Popper containing a brief autobiography by Popper and his response to various critics is by Paul A. Schilpp, *The Philosophy of Karl Popper* (La Salle, IL: Open Court Publishing, 1974); this is a volume in Schilpp's superb Library of Living Philosophers series.

Ludwig Wittgenstein's work has had great influence on contemporary philosophy of language and epistemology. See particularly his *Philosophical Investigations*, 3d ed. (London: Macmillan, 1958); and *On Certainty*, originally published by Basil Blackwell, 1969, and now available in paperback from Harper & Row (New York, 1972). *Wittgenstein's Poker*, by David Edmonds and John Eidinow, is the dramatic story of a brief confrontation between Wittgenstein and Popper in 1946, when Popper came to Cambridge to give a lecture that Wittgenstein attended. The book not only gives a nice account of their competing positions, but also offers a superb study of the intellectual and historical background of their debate.

Wilfrid Sellars is not an easy read, but his work on epistemology and philosophy of science has had great influence. For a collection of some of his most important essays, see *Science, Perception and Reality* (London: Routledge and Kegan Paul, 1963). Nicholas Rescher, *The Coherence Theory of Truth* (Oxford: Clarendon Press, 1973), offers a strong alternative to the traditional correspondence account of truth. Thomas Nagel, *The View from Nowhere* (Oxford, U.K.: Oxford University Press, 1986), offers a very insightful analysis of our tendency to suppose we can take a detached, "purely objective" view of the world, independent of our own perspective, and the problems generated by that assumption.

Charles S. Peirce is the primary source for classical pragmatism. The best source for his work is a collection edited by Charles Hartshorne and Paul Weiss, the *Collected Papers of Charles Sanders Peirce* (Cambridge, MA: The Belknap Press of Harvard University Press, 1965). There is also a good collection by Philip P. Weiner, entitled *Charles S. Peirce: Selected Writings*. Originally published by Doubleday in 1958, it is now available in a Dover Edition (New York: Dover, 1966). William James is perhaps the best known pragmatist, and his work is always interesting. His *Pragmatism* was originally published in 1907 and is available in many editions. See also *The Will to Believe and Other Essays in Popular Philosophy*, originally published in 1897, and also widely available. John Dewey was well known as a pragmatist and public philosopher in the mid-20th century, writing extensively on philosophy, education, and political issues. Among his many books, see *Human Nature and Conduct* (New York: Henry Holt, 1922); *Reconstruction in Philosophy* (New York: Henry Holt, 1920); and, especially, *The Quest for Certainty*, the text of Dewey's Gifford Lectures in 1929, available as a Putnam Capricorn paperback (New York: G. P. Putnam's Sons, 1960).

Richard Rorty champions contemporary pragmatism, and his writings are always interesting as well as controversial. His spirited challenge to traditional correspondence views of knowledge can be found in *Philosophy and the Mirror of Nature* (Princeton, NJ: Princeton University Press, 1979); see also the three volumes of his Philosophical Papers, published by Cambridge University Press (Cambridge, U.K.): *Objectivity, Relativism, and Truth*, 1991; *Essays on Heidegger and Others*, 1991; and *Truth and Progress*, 1998; as well as his *Philosophy and Social Hope* (London: Penguin, 1999). Another influential contemporary pragmatist— whose views differ from Rorty's on some interesting points—is Hilary Putnam; a good introduction to his work is *The Many Faces of Realism* (Chicago: Open Court, 1987); see also his *Realism with a Human Face* (Cambridge, MA: Harvard University Press, 1990).

Cornel West is a very engaging writer, and his "prophetic pragmatism" is clearly presented in *The American Evasion of Philosophy: A Genealogy of Pragmatism* (Madison, WI: University of Wisconsin Press, 1987).

Evolutionary epistemology is a fascinating recent development in epistemology. An excellent introduction to the issues raised by this approach can be found in Gerard Radnitzky and W. W. Bartley, III, eds., *Evolutionary Epistemology, Theory of Rationality, and the Sociology of Knowledge* (La Salle, IL: Open Court, 1987).

An excellent site for information on Thomas Kuhn, including a brief biography and a number of links, as well as papers on Kuhn's work, can be found at *www.emory.edu/EDUCATION/mfp/Kuhnsnap.html*. An interesting RealAudio discussion of Kuhn's work from the NPR program Science Friday can be heard at *www.sciencefriday.com/pages/1996/Aug/hour2_081696.html*. A number of links to articles and sites related to Kuhn and the philosophy of science have been developed by Michael Austin at Shepherd College; go to *http://webpages.shepherd.edu/maustin/kuhn/kuhn.htm*. A nice essay on the significance of Kuhn's work can be found at *www.people.fas.harvard.edu/~nagiel/99_hsr_webpage/hsr/winter97/kuhn.html*.

For information on pragmatism, visit *www.pragmatism.org*, the superb site of the Pragmatism Cybrary. See also *radicalacademy.com/amphilosophy7a.htm*. A good site on William James can be found at *www.emory.edu/EDUCATION/mfp/james.html*. It is part of the Welcome to the Middle Website, which is a bit offbeat, but very entertaining.

Chapter 5

The Nature of Mind

in which the friends explore some amazing theories

Sarah hooked her book bag over her shoulder and picked up the steaming mug of coffee in one hand, the scone in the other. She didn't have to look for Selina and Ben: She had heard their voices as she paid the cashier.

"No way, Ben. No one could believe that."

"Yes they could, Selina. Descartes believed it. And so do I. In fact, lots of great philosophers have believed it, Descartes and myself being the first two who spring to mind. Hear that, Selina? The first two who spring to *mind*; not the first who spring to *body*. They're separate things."

"That's ridiculous, Ben. There's no mind apart from the body. What, do you believe in ghosts? Give me a break."

Sarah dropped her book bag in an empty chair, placed her coffee and scone on the table. "Hi, guys. Is this a private fight, or can anyone play?"

Descartes and Mind–Body Dualism

"Oh, hi, Sarah," said Ben. "I'm glad to see you! Remember we were talking about Descartes? I went to the library and read some more about the guy. He believed that the mind is distinct from the body, right? They are two separate substances."

Selina added her own greeting and appeal. "Yeah, sit down and drink your coffee. I'll need a shot of bourbon in mine if I keep talking with Ben. I admit, Descartes sounded a bit crazy when you talked about him before— all the rationalist stuff. But no serious thinker could be that crazy, not even a philosopher—no offense intended, Sarah. Descartes didn't really think that, did he? He didn't believe the mind is separate from the body, no way."

"Yeah," Sarah nodded, "he did, Selina. I mean, not completely separate; but distinct, certainly. He thought the mind was lodged inside the body. As he put it, not like a pilot in a ship—there's a more intimate connection than that. It's not like your mind can just switch from one body to another, the way a pilot guides one ship and then another. But he did think they were distinct. In fact, he believed they were two distinct types of substances. The mental and the physical are different stuff altogether."

"See, I was right, Selina. Descartes did believe that."

"You and Descartes are both crazy, Ben. Sarah, too, for that matter. You should be ashamed of yourself, Sarah: corrupting Ben's innocent young mind with all this philosophical gibberish."

Sarah laughed. "It's only fair, Selina. I corrupt his innocent young mind, and you corrupt his innocent young body. But look, see how natural it is to divide the two? Body and mind, the two parts that make up Ben. It's not really such a weird idea. Some would say it's the plainest common sense."

"Plain and common it may be," Selina answered, "but it makes no sense at all. What, our minds float around somewhere in our bodies? Or are they merely in the general vicinity of our bodies, like some New Age aura? Look, the mind is simply the brain and its activities—or maybe the whole central nervous system. But it's not some separate substance."

"Actually, this mind–brain division doesn't seem like such a weird idea to me." Ben was ready for battle. "After all, there must be something distinct from the physical body. Otherwise, how could I survive the death of my body?"

"I've got some sad news for you, Ben," Selina replied. "You don't. When you die, you're dead. That's it. Period. So 'Gather ye rosebuds while you may,' for this life is fleeting. Or better"—Selina pulled a beat-up paperback copy of *The Rubáiyát of Omar Khayyám* from her backpack—"listen to old Omar Khayyám:

> *Oh, threats of Hell and Hopes of Paradise!*
> *One thing is certain—This Life flies;*
> > *One thing is certain and the rest is Lies;*
> *The Flower that once has blown for ever dies.*[1]

It's just another of those religious or philosophical mysteries: The soul, or the mind, or whatever it is, is somehow distinct from the body, and it survives the body, and gives you godlike immortality. Forget about it. Enjoy life while you can, for this is all you get. As for me, it's quite enough. I don't think I would want to float around in Heaven as a disembodied soul or mind. Sounds boring. I can't imagine that those disembodied spirits have a lot of fun. Take away the body, a lot of the pleasure goes with it."

Ben laughed and shook his head. "Ah, Selina, you are a wicked woman."

"I don't recall you ever objecting before. Anyway, all this separate soul or mind stuff, it's a lot of Judeo–Christian nonsense to try to make sense of what doesn't make any sense: the notion of life after death. The body dies, and something must survive. Bingo, we've got a soul, a mind, a separate nonphysical substance."

"Actually, Selina," said Sarah, "the Jewish tradition isn't big on the notion of life after death. And those who do believe in it tend to think in terms of a bodily resurrection. That was the early Christian idea as well. All this stuff about distinct souls—that comes from the ancient Greeks. Plato talks about it in one of the Socratic dialogues: The soul separates from the body and crosses the river Styx—the Greeks always buried their dead with a coin for the boatman—and then each soul selects a new body for its next life. I don't know how much Plato literally believed in it; I think it was more a story—a myth, remember?—to express other ideas. The Christians seemed to borrow the idea from the Greeks. But they take it very seriously. Just ask Ben."

Ben happily took the opening. "But it's not only the afterlife, guys. Forget about souls for a minute. Let's just look at the mind. After all, that was Descartes's focus. Is the *mind* separate from the body? Or is the mind just the brain, or the central nervous system? Well, really, Selina, they can't just be the same thing. For one thing, the mind is creative, and inventive, and unlimited. The brain, for all its wonderful complexity, is still a physical system, with all the limits inherent in physical systems."

"Are our minds actually unlimited, Ben?" Sarah was a bit skeptical. "I think my mind hit its limit when I took calculus two."

Ben was not deterred. "It's also our special powers of mind, distinct from the physical world, that enables us to exercise free will."

Selina sighed. "Earth to Ben: There is no free will."

"Get serious, Selina. Of course we have free will: We're not robots, not zombies, not destined. You exercised free will when you ordered your latté with a double shot of espresso. And when you chose to attend Michigan rather than Columbia or U.C.L.A. And when you chose to major in chemistry."

"No way, Ben. Those choices were part of the natural universe, and they followed their course, just as the planets do. The causes are more complex and less obvious; but they are there nonetheless. And many of the causes operate in the brain. And none of them operate in that mystical mental separate realm of nonphysical mind."

Sarah raised a hand. "Look, guys, nothing's more interesting than the question of free will. But can't we save that for another day? I want to get back to the question about the mind—and if we take up free will, then we'll be on that for the rest of the hour, maybe the rest of the year."

Selina agreed. "Fine, Sarah. I can't see what free will has to do with the question about the mind and the brain anyway. If we had free will—a very unlikely scenario—that would simply show that purely physical systems *can* exercise free will; because clearly, we, including our brains, *are* purely physical systems. This mental stuff, separate from our brains, is utter nonsense. So why should the question of free will even come up?"

"Actually, Selina, it may have been the question of free will that prompted Descartes to develop his system of mind distinct from body." Sarah sipped her coffee and continued. "Think back to the early 17th century again, when Descartes was writing. You remember, it was a period of great scientific change; that was one of the reasons Descartes was seeking some level of bedrock certainty. Anyway, one of the most important and exciting scientific developments of the period was Harvey's discovery of the circulation of the blood, with the heart as a pump. That was exciting, certainly, but also rather disturbing. After all, if the blood is being pumped through the body, it makes the body seem very much like a machine. And if the body is a machine, then it follows physical laws—the sort of mechanical laws that scientists were beginning to work out and that Newton would soon publish to great acclaim. But if we're just complex machines, governed by fixed laws, then what happens to our free will? What becomes of our special ability to make ourselves as we wish, to rise above nature and exercise reason and be creative and godlike? It seems to get squeezed out of the physical world. So Descartes proposed another alternative: There is a physical, mechanical world, governed and determined by the laws of nature; but there is also a separate, special, *mental* world, the world of our *minds* and ideas and reasoning. And that special mental world is not bound by the laws of physical nature."

"So Descartes starts with a silly idea of free will," Selina said, "and then adds an even sillier notion of a special mental realm in order to save the original silly idea."

Sarah smiled. "Rather harsh on old Descartes, aren't you, Selina?"

"Well, the truth *can* be rather harsh, Sarah. As I believe I have mentioned before, truth is not always sweet and agreeable."

Ben put his hand on Selina's. "If truth is not sweet and agreeable, then it's obviously not like Selina."

"Bite your tongue, Ben. Your Selina is fascinating, fabulously beautiful, and frequently brilliant—but sweet and agreeable are not among my virtues."

"Neither is modesty," responded Sarah. "But fairness certainly is. So be fair to old Descartes. Is the notion of separate realms of mind and body, distinct mental and physical substances, really such a silly idea? After all, they certainly *seem* different: The brain is a mass of nerves, all this gray matter bundled together; and the mind, it's filled with ideas racing along, and they don't seem to be physical. Look, Selina, you have strong ideas about justice and human rights. How much do they weigh? What shape are they? What density?"

"Come on, Sarah, those are silly questions."

"Of course they're silly questions: that's exactly the point. Physical things have weight and shape; we can measure their density. But ideas and thoughts, it doesn't make sense to apply the same terms to them. Besides, I know my own thoughts and ideas—I know them immediately and directly; but my brain states, that's another matter altogether: for that, I would need some sort of brain scan. Doesn't that indicate that the mind and its ideas are in a different category from the brain? That maybe they are even a completely different *kind* of substance? That mental substance and physical substance are different things altogether?"

Are Thoughts Private?

Selina shook her head. "No way. For one thing, you don't really know your own ideas that well. Ben's sitting in my room, saying how what he really wants to do tonight is finish reading this book on the Iroquois Federation, and he really thinks that's what he wants, and I know perfectly well what the boy *really* wants. And what are you laughing about, Sarah? I remember when you and David broke up, how you were saying you were glad, how you really didn't care about him at all—and I think you really convinced yourself. But old Selina knew the truth about that, didn't she, Sister?"

"Yeah, well, let's not exaggerate Selina's psychological insights," Sarah responded. "When you and Ben started studying together, what was it you said? 'Oh, we're just friends, Sarah. That's all. He's in my government class, and it's pleasant to study with him, but there's nothing more than that.' Yeah, you really thought that's what you thought. But your roommate knew what was really going on."

"Okay, that's enough examples." Selina laughed. "But see, that's exactly what I was saying. This notion that we know our thoughts immediately and certainly, that's not really always true, is it? I'm not sure it's ever true. Anyway, this claim that we have special, immediate knowledge of our thoughts, but not of our brain states, and so they must be different: That's a weak argument, guys. Even if it were true that we have special, immediate access to our thoughts, what would that prove? Not

I once knew a Christian Scientist who had a raging toothache; he was frantically groaning and moaning all over the place. When asked whether a dentist might not cure him, he replied that there was nothing to be cured. Then he was asked, "But do you not feel pain?" He replied, "No, I do not feel pain; nobody feels pain, there is no such thing as pain, pain is only an illusion." So here is a case of a man who claimed not to feel pain, yet everyone present knew perfectly well that he did feel pain. I certainly don't believe he was lying, he was just simply mistaken.

Raymond M. Smullyan, "An Epistemological Nightmare,"
from *Philosophical Fantasies* (1982)

that they are different in kind, two different substances; only that we have different ways of knowing about what goes on in the brain. But there's nothing unusual about that. I take a substance into the chemistry lab, there are lots of ways I can investigate it: testing its specific density, using a spectrograph, examining it under a microscope, studying how it reacts with different chemicals. That doesn't mean that it's several different kinds of substances, just because there are various ways we can examine it."

"Okay, Selina," Sarah said, "but still, there is a difference. Consciousness is not just one more object in the world. I'm not denying that we can study it scientifically: Psychology is a science, true enough. But still, there is something distinctive about consciousness. We know it in a way we don't know anything else. Sometimes imperfectly, I'll grant you that; and you need not go into graphic detail about how I made a fool of myself over David, that worthless snake, to make me acknowledge the imperfections in our knowledge of our own ideas and beliefs. But still, isn't there something special about consciousness, about our minds? We know our own thoughts in a way that we know nothing else. Not that we know them perfectly, or infallibly. Not even Descartes believed that (except for his *cogito, ergo sum*). But still, we do have some immediate access to them, in a way that is special and different. There's this contemporary philosopher, Thomas Nagel. He wrote a little article, 'What Is It Like to Be a Bat?'[2] And his point was a simple one: We *can't* know what it's like to be a bat. Consciousness is special. We can understand a lot about bats, and we can understand how they navigate, and that's all fascinating. But we can't understand what it's like to have the *consciousness* of a bat, because we can never have the special *subjective point of view* of a bat. And that shows that there is something very special about consciousness, about the mind. And this special personal nature of consciousness means that we could never find a way to identify it with something

---

If the facts of experience—facts about what it is like for the experiencing organism—are accessible only from one point of view [the point of view of the experiencing agent], then it is a mystery how the true character of experiences could be revealed in the physical operation of that organism. The latter is a domain of objective facts par excellence—the kind that can be observed and understood from many points of view and by individuals with differing perceptual systems. There are no comparable imaginative obstacles to the acquisition of knowledge about bat neurophysiology by human scientists, and intelligent bats or Martians might learn more about the human brain than we ever will.

Thomas Nagel, "What Is It Like to Be a Bat?" (1974)

---

observable by others and thus no way of even starting on a theory of the *identity* of mind and brain."

Solipsism

Wait a minute, Sarah." Selina did not find that a compelling argument. "Doesn't that prove too much? Wouldn't all knowledge of the consciousness of others be thrown into doubt? We have this special knowledge of our own consciousness, but we can't possibly have any sense of what a bat's consciousness is like, since it is different from our own. But on this view—on which I have special, immediate knowledge only of my *own* consciousness, of my own mind—I could never have any real knowledge of anyone else's consciousness. But that's crazy."

"Actually, Selina, some philosophers think that is not such a crazy idea at all. They believe that there is a genuine problem, a real doubt, about whether we could ever know the minds of others—in fact, a real doubt about whether other minds exist. Not that they deny the existence of other minds, actually; but they deny that we can *know* the existence of other minds. It's not exactly a standard philosophical view, but it is common enough to have its own name. It's called *solipsism*, and people who hold that view are called solipsists."

Ben chimed in. "Somehow I'm not surprised, Sarah. No offense to you or your major, but philosophers seem to come up with rather weird theories."

"Well, maybe not quite as weird as it sounds at first hearing." Both Ben and Sarah stared at Selina. This was not the comment they had expected. She laughed. "Hey, guys, don't look so shocked. It's not like I think solipsism is true. In fact, I don't even find it remotely plausible. But it's not hard to see how some philosophers wound up as solipsists. You have to start with two basic assumptions: first, that the only real knowledge is knowledge that is immediate and certain, and second, that the only thing we really have immediate, certain knowledge of is our minds. After all—if I remember our earlier conversation—those are the assumptions that Descartes was starting from, right? So where does that lead you? I have immediate, certain knowledge of my own mind, but not of anyone else's mind; so I can't be sure that there are any other minds."

"Yeah, that's pretty much how it goes, Selina," said Sarah. "You went right to the core of the argument. Hey, maybe you ought to switch your major to philosophy."

"Thanks for the invitation, Sarah, but I think I'll stick with chemistry. Anyway, it's not so amazing that some philosophers wound up with the solipsism conclusion. What *is* amazing is that, having reached that conclusion, they didn't go back and scrutinize some of their starting assumptions. I mean, after all, I know that my friend Sarah has a mind. I know that it is sometimes troubled, often concerned, always caring, deeply loyal to her friends, sometimes perplexed, always inquiring, always open. And I know that old Ben has a mind, as well: sometimes a bit muddled, but always entertaining and always affectionate. A very nice mind—though frankly, what I'm really crazy about is his body. Now look what you've done, Sarah: You've got me talking this crazy mind–body distinction. I don't mean it literally; it's just a way of speaking. I should have said I like the brain part of his body, but there are other parts I like even more."

Wittgenstein and Privacy

"Anyway," Selina continued, "it's perfectly clear that other people have minds, just as we do. Or better, other people have thinking brains, just as we do. And if a theory leads to doubts about that, then it seems to me that it makes more sense *not* to accept that absurd conclusion as true, but rather to treat it as a *reductio ad absurdum* of the theory and its assumptions. And the underlying assumptions that ought to be examined—and *rejected*—are, first, the assumption that we have special, certain, privileged access to our own thoughts, and second, the assumption that only what we know with immediate certainty counts as real knowledge. In fact, both are wrong. First, this idea that we somehow have special, privileged, indubitable access to the contents of our own thoughts. Suppose Ben loses his faith in God. Maybe he falls in with bad company, falls under the influence of some evil woman, and loses his faith in God. If that happened, it would be very hard for Ben to face, at least in the beginning. After all, his faith gives him a strong sense of security; and besides, it's no small part of his identity. So if that happened, it might well be the case that Ben no longer believed in God, and you and I, Sarah, might know he doesn't believe in God, but he would still not be able to face it directly and still sincerely think that he believes in God. If so, then Ben could be mistaken about his actual thoughts and beliefs—mistaken about the contents of his own 'mind'—and we might know his mind better than he does. And second, even if there were some privileged access to your own mind, that wouldn't really count as the ideal of certain knowledge. In fact, it's not at all clear that it would qualify as knowledge at all. Because you would have nothing to check it against, nothing to confirm it. I have this idea of loving affection, only no one else can have any access to it; it is totally my own immediate idea. In that case, how would I know it was an idea of loving affection? Maybe it's an idea of courage, or a feeling of queasiness, or an intuition of infinity. The point is, if my mind is that isolated and private, I could never know what to name each feeling, since that requires a common language. And I would never know how to identify my private feeling of resentment and distinguish it from my private feeling of gratitude. If all my feelings and ideas were as private as this model suggests, at best I would have a flood of feelings that I could not characterize or classify. And such waves of confusion hardly qualify as *knowledge*, much less absolutely certain knowledge. It's that old Cartesian search for special, privileged knowledge. But that's not a special conception of knowledge: It's a totally misguided way of thinking about knowledge. Knowledge isn't some private privileged preserve, to which only I have special access. It's what we can confirm and repeat—and test and observe."

"Hey, Selina, you sound like Wittgenstein." Sarah was impressed. "If you only know it yourself, you can never really be sure you know at all. Maybe you have totally different ideas every day that you've been calling by the same name, but you have no way of distinguishing them, no independent test to run. If you say 'cat' when it's actually what the rest of us

---

In what sense are my sensations private?—Well, only I can know whether I am really in pain; another person can only surmise it.—In one way this is wrong, and in another nonsense. If we are using the word "to know" as it is normally used (and how else are we to use it?), then other people very often know when I am in pain.—Yes, but all the same not with the certainty with which I know it myself!— It can't be said of me at all (except perhaps as a joke) that I know I am in pain. What is it supposed to mean—except perhaps that I am in pain.

Ludwig Wittgenstein, *Philosophical Investigations*, #246. Trans. by G. E. M. Anscombe

---

call a dog, we can correct your mistake. But if our ideas are perfectly private, they are not subject to such correction. So there's no private language, and there's no private knowledge."

"Oh, yeah, Wittgenstein," said Selina, "I've heard of him. Well, glad to know at least one famous philosopher got this stuff right. I was afraid they were all like Descartes."

"Look, guys, we've gotten off the track. This question about other minds, and can we know that there are other minds, that's interesting." Ben wanted to redirect the discussion. "But can we get back to the basic question? Is the mind distinct from the body, a distinct sort of mental substance that is different from the physical body? I don't doubt the existence of other minds; in fact, I don't doubt that I'm in close contact with two fine and insightful minds in this very conversation. But that's a different issue. What about the relation between mind and body?"

Selina had a quick response. "The stuff about whether other minds exist, about how some people doubt the existence of other minds—what are those people called, Sarah?"

"Solipsists; the view that we cannot be certain that other minds exist is called solipsism."

"Yeah, right, solipsism. That is very relevant to the question of mind–body dualism. Think about it, Ben. How did you learn to recognize and categorize and distinguish your own thoughts and feelings? When your favorite toy got broken and you cried, your mother said, 'Ben, sweetie, I know you're sad, poor baby.' And when your finger was burned, she said, 'Poor Ben, I know that must really hurt.' And when you threw a tantrum, she said, 'Ben, you must learn to control your anger.' They knew your feelings and ideas from observing your body and your bodily behavior—your blistered finger, your crying, your tantrum—so they named them for you, and you learned to recognize and categorize them. But if your mind and your body were totally distinct substances, that would be impossible. Events that happened to your physical body would have no relation to what happened in your mental mind substance; and your mind would have no effect on your body: Your mind might experience anger or disappointment, but those would not be manifested in physical bodily tantrums or tears. But of course, that's not true, so there are not two separate substances: a mental mind and a physical body; there's only one, the body, which includes the brain, which transmits signals to the body through the nerves, and those physical events—the signals—cause physical effects: tantrums, tears, screams, tenseness. And when your finger gets blistered, the nerves carry the message—the physical message—to the brain, which registers pain. And a good thing, too: Otherwise you might leave your hand on the stove until it is severely damaged. If the mind and the body are distinct, none of that makes sense."

Dualistic Interactionism

"Well, actually, Selina, mind–body dualists don't necessarily believe that there is no *connection* between the mind and the body—between the mental substance and the physical substance," Sarah responded. "They believe that the mind and body are distinct, but still connected. In fact, Descartes thought they were very closely and intimately connected. So Descartes was certainly a *dualist:* He believed that the mind and the body were distinct and different substances. But he was also an *interactionist:* He believed that the mind and the body *interact,* that the mind can influence the body, and that bodily events—such as a burned finger—can be swiftly communicated to the mind."

Selina shook her head. "Mystery is added to mystery. This dualism stuff is bad enough: two distinct sorts of substance, a mental and a physical, when really all we need is one, the physical. Now they are supposed to *interact.* How could something purely *non*physical—and that's what this mental mind substance is, right?—have a causal effect on something purely *physical?* The mental stuff, the mind, its ideas: They have no physical force, right? They have no weight, no electrical charge, no magnetic powers, no chemical powers: All of those are *physical* properties, and the mind is totally *non*physical, a separate type of substance. So how could an *idea,* or a *mind*—which has *no* physical powers or properties—cause a physical event, such as the movement of my arm? With my physical monism view. . . . "

"Philosophers call that view 'materialism,' Selina," said Sarah. "The position that there is only one substance, and it is physical substance, is called 'materialism.'"

The view favored by Selina is called "materialism"; however, there is a different meaning of "materialism" that must be distinguished from the view held by Selina. The most common use of "materialist" is to describe someone who is concerned primarily with acquiring material wealth and material goods. Someone obsessed with owning a big car and a big house and expensive clothes and large jewels— and who has little interest in anything other than material wealth—would be considered a materialist, in this sense. But a materialist in the sense that Selina is a materialist is something quite different and is consistent with Selina having little or no interest in material wealth.

"Alright, have it your way, *materialism*—though I think I like 'physical monism' better. Anyway, on my materialist view, all our ideas are really just physical brain states, and those physical nerves stimulate other nerves, which stimulate physical muscles, which pick up physical balls; and there's no problem of interaction, because it's *physical* all the way up and down. On this dualism theory, not only do you get the excessive complication of a second substance, but you also get the mystery of how the two substances interact. Other than providing entertainment for philosophers, I can't see any good in this dualist interactionism."

Sarah nodded. "You've touched a rather sore spot for dualists, Selina. This problem of how the nonphysical mind could interact with the physical body has always been a dilemma for dualists. Descartes proposed his own solution, though he was not very confident of it. Around the time when he was writing, human anatomical studies were being carried out in considerable detail. One of the things that had just been discovered was the pineal gland, located at the base of the skull, suspended near the base of the brain. Of course, by this time they knew a great deal about the nerves, and how nerves from the brain stimulated nerves running throughout the body, and how nerves carried messages from the rest of the body to the brain. They didn't know how it worked, but they knew the nerves were involved in the process. But of course, the nerves and the brain—that was all part of the physical body. The problem was, How could the mind, something nonphysical, communicate messages to and from the nervous system? So far as they could tell, the pineal gland was just hanging there, and it didn't seem to be doing anything. So Descartes suggested—very tentatively—that maybe the pineal gland was where the mental–physical interaction occurred. It seemed just the right place: It was located very close to the brain, and it was suspended, so tiny vibrations could cause it to move, and tiny vibrations from the gland could be transmitted directly to the brain. A creative idea—but of course, it doesn't really work. It doesn't begin to answer the question of how something totally nonphysical can cause a physical event. It doesn't matter whether the physical event is a small vibration or a large tremor: The problem is causing any physical event whatsoever when that event has to be caused by something with *no* physical properties."

"Exactly right, Sarah." Selina nodded her approval. "And that's a problem that sinks mind–body dualism, right?"

"Well, actually, there are some other possibilities. They might sound a bit strange, though."

"A philosophical theory that sounds a bit strange?" Selina smiled. "That's hard to imagine, Sarah."

Ben laughed. "For such a sweet kid, she gives some nasty cuts, doesn't she, Sarah?"

Malebranche and Occasionalism

"Well, Selina won't be the first person to think these theories are strange. But look, keep in mind why they were developed. Like Ben, these philosophers believed that the mind and the body must be distinct substances. And then, as we've seen, they have a very difficult time imagining how they could interact. So they concluded that they *don't* actually interact. They can't; they only *appear* to interact."

Selina was puzzled. "I thought you said dualists believed that the mind and the body, the mental and the physical, *do* interact."

"I said *most* dualists believe that, but not quite all. One philosophical follower of Descartes, Nicolas de Malebranche (1638–1715), developed what is called an *occasionalist* version of dualism. According to Malebranche, neither human minds nor human bodies cause anything, so there is no problem with a human mind causing the movement of the body. God is omnipotent, so God is the cause of *everything* that happens. What appear to be our physical and mental actions are in fact only the *occasions* when God acts through us."

Ben was not pleased. "That solution is worse than the problem. Talk about jumping from the frying pan into the fire! We can't figure out how our minds cause our bodies to act, and the answer is that neither our bodies nor our minds are actually under our control—we perform neither mental nor physical acts. So why are we here, just for decoration?"

Sarah laughed. "Malebranche saw it as a way of truly uniting us to God: We are wholly dependent on God, at every moment, for our existence and our actions. I'm sorry you don't care for Malebranche's solution, Ben; however, I'm sure the theory must have great appeal to Selina."

"Actually, it does have some charm," Selina replied. "When I drink too much, it's actually God causing it; and when I get crazy drunk, it's God's craziness. What's the line from Tom Waits? 'Don't you know there ain't no devil, it's just God when he's drunk.' I always knew Waits was a great blues singer, but now I see he's a great philosopher as well. Works for me. Let's hear it for Malebranche and occasionalism."

Leibniz and Mind–Body Parallelism

Sarah shook her head. "I guess Malebranche's occasionalism has some problems: troubles the saints, and provokes blasphemy from the sinners. Actually, it was never a very popular solution to the mind–body problem.

God is omnipotent, so of course it's no bother for God to constantly intervene on every occasion when we seem to think or move; but even so, the theory seems a bit cumbersome. A more interesting version of noninteractionist dualism was developed by Leibniz. On his view, every mental act is *correlated* with a physical act. Think of a room containing a chiming grandfather clock in one corner and a cuckoo clock in the other. The clocks keep perfect time, so that, hour after hour, the grandfather clock begins to chime, followed immediately by the appearance of the cuckoo. It would be natural to suppose that somehow the two clocks are connected: The chiming of the grandfather clock startles the cuckoo into action. But of course, what actually happens is that the two clocks are running in perfect *parallel* fashion—in *harmony*, though not in any causal interaction. Rather than God constantly intervening to cause mental acts and physical acts, God sets up a wonderful and perfect preestablished harmony, in which the physical and mental realms run perfectly parallel, but without any causal interaction. Instead of God being a constant intervening tinkerer, God is the great designer Who fashions this majestic clockwork, in which minds and bodies keep perfect correlation without any need for intervention or interaction. Quite a marvelous picture, isn't it?"

"It is majestic, I guess. But it's still troubling." Ben did not find this a satisfactory solution. "I don't like it, Sarah. It makes it sound like the mind and the body are preprogrammed. Doesn't leave much room for free will."

"Having everything preprogrammed by an omnipotent and omniscient God wouldn't much bother Leibniz," Sarah replied. "Though he did spend a lot of time worrying about the problem of evil and how to reconcile the existence of suffering with the assumption that the world was created by an omnipotent and omnibenevolent God. But that's an issue we talked about before. Anyway, that's the account offered by Leibniz."

"I still like dualism, but I think I'll stick with interactionism," Ben concluded. "We may not know how the interaction occurs, but it still strikes me as the most plausible view."

"Oh, sure, Ben." Selina was still holding out for monistic materialism. "It's perfectly plausible. All you need is a mysterious miracle-working mind, connected in some mysterious way with the physical body. Compared with that theory, the Easter Bunny is sober scientific truth. In fact, why stop with the Easter Bunny? You can add the tooth fairy and elves and ghosts and goblins and Bigfoot to your theory. Once you've allowed a nice dose of mystery into your theory, you can justify belief in anything."

"Sort of harsh, Selina." Ben felt slightly wounded. "It's true I don't know how to explain the relation between the mental and the physical. But after all, there are some good reasons for thinking that both exist and that there is some connection between them. Just because we don't know *how* they are connected doesn't mean the account is pure fantasy."

Neuroscience and Mind–Body Dualism

Selina-vs.-Ben storm clouds were gathering, and Sarah quickly intervened. "Selina, you make it sound as if dualistic interactionism is the wild raving of some demented philosopher. Okay, it's true, some of the most famous dualistic interactionists of history were philosophers. But it's not only philosophers who are dualistic interactionists. There are also some very distinguished scientists."

"No way, Sarah."

"Yes, way, Selina. For example, John Eccles won the Nobel prize for his work in neuropsychological research, and Eccles was a dualistic interactionist. And among contemporary scientists, there is Benjamin Libet, the physiologist who discovered the readiness potential in his neuropsychological research. And Jeffrey Schwartz, who is on the faculty of the UCLA Department of Psychiatry and incorporates dualistic interactionism principles into his therapeutic practice with obsessive–compulsive sufferers. And Henry Stapp, who is a physicist at the Lawrence Berkeley National Laboratory at the University of California. Admittedly, they hold distinctly minority views in their fields. But the point is, it's not just philosophers who believe in dualism; there are also some scientists among the ranks of dualists."

"But why would any scientist adopt such a strange view, Sarah?" said Selina. "I'm certainly not surprised that the majority of scientists favor monism; but I'm surprised to find any scientists at all favoring this strange dualistic interactionism. What's their justification?"

"Well, for the most part it turns on their belief in free will and their view that free will is incompatible with a purely physical universe. And we said we would leave free will for another day, right? But obviously, we'll have to discuss it eventually. We can't really close the books on the mind–body question until we've talked about free will."

"Exactly right, Sarah. I still think the free-will argument may be the strongest argument for mind–body dualistic interactionism; and I'm delighted to discover that *some* scientists"—Ben rolled his eyes at Selina—"recognize the wisdom and force of that argument."

"But that wasn't actually the point I was going to make, guys." Sarah jumped back in, before Selina could respond to Ben. "What I wanted to say is that some of those scientists have proposed at least a rough theory of how the mind and body could interact. For example, J. C. Eccles suggests that mental events could have neural (physical) effects by causing

It can be stated that it is sufficient for the dualist-interactionist hypothesis to be able to account for the ability of a non-material mental event to effect a changed probability of the vesicular emission from a single bouton on a cortical pyramidal cell. If that can occur for one, it could occur for a multitude of the boutons on that neuron, and all else follows in accord with the neuroscience of motor control.

J. C. Eccles, *How the Self Controls Its Brain* (Berlin: Springer-Verlag, 1994), p. 78

the emission of chemical transmitters into the synapses inside a tiny portion of a cortical pyramidal cell. That would only require a very minute level of energy."

"I don't know, Sarah; sounds pretty doubtful to me." Selina remained skeptical. "Eccles manages to make the force of the interaction much smaller: Instead of wobbling the pineal gland, as Descartes suggested, Eccles operates at the much finer level of vesicular emission from a single bouton on a cortical pyramidal cell. But no matter how minute you make the interaction, the fundamental problem remains: How can something nonphysical (a mental state) activate a physical event? No matter how small the activation, you still have that huge gap to cross between something nonphysical (having no force or weight or charge) and something physical. Large or small or microscopic, that gap remains. And even if you could theoretically show how something totally nonphysical could generate a physical event, you would still have another problem: The addition of the physical energy activated *non*physically would violate the law of conservation of energy."

"Wow, Selina, that's good! Actually, that's exactly what some of Eccles's critics have argued. Anyway, as I noted, it's all rather speculative

---

There appears to be no way that a non-physical mind could act without violating physical laws. Furthermore, there appears to be no obvious way, consistent with our knowledge of neurophysiology and neurochemistry, for such a non-physical mind to bring about volitional acts by altering brain events only at a level within quantum-mechanical uncertainty. . . . Any effective actions by a non-physical entity would produce violations of one or more of the principles or laws of physics. Even were a minimal interference, under the uncertainty principle, shown to be possible, it would not allow a non-physical mind to influence brain without the violation of physical laws because any events occurring within quantum-mechanical uncertainty are required to be random. The patterned firing of action potentials in neurons that appear to be required by volitional actions would be highly non-random.

David L. Wilson, "Mind–Brain Interaction and Violation of Physical Laws," *Journal of Consciousness Studies*, volume 6, numbers 8–9, 1999, p. 195

at this point; and in any case, it's certainly not the view of most scientists, though, of course, as we have already noted, sometimes minority views wind up becoming majority views in future generations. But anyway, I can appreciate your skepticism about interactionism. There's not really any scientific evidence for it; at best, what you get is a rather fanciful account of how such events *might* conceivably happen. But you don't think much of dualism in any form, right, Selina?"

"That's putting it mildly, Sarah. I would rate it somewhere in the vicinity of the Ohio State Buckeyes."

Ben laughed. "About as low as it gets for faithful Wolverines, isn't it?"

Epiphenomenalism

"Selina, there's one version of dualism that might appeal to you," said Sarah. "It's called *epiphenomenalism*. It's an old philosophical theory, and frankly, it never seemed very plausible to me. I guess it seemed implausible to most people. The idea is this: There is the physical body, including the brain; and there are also ideas, the realm of the mental. But the mental doesn't really have any *causal* powers, the mind doesn't *cause* the body to do anything. Instead, the mind and its ideas are *epiphenomena*. That is, there are real ideas, but they don't *do* anything. Our thoughts are a sort of by-product of the brain and the body, and they have no causal influence. They are caused by the physical world, but don't cause things to happen in the physical world. It obviously *seems* as if our ideas cause physical movements: I mentally decide to throw a ball, and sure enough my hand picks up the ball and my arm flings it. But what is actually happening—according to the epiphenomenalists—is that my brain does all the real action, and one 'side effect' of that physical action is that ideas are produced at the same time."

Selina was puzzled. "Sarah, why on earth would you suppose I might find that view plausible? Okay, at least it does dodge one problem: the question of how something nonphysical could cause something physical. And that's a big problem, certainly. But there's still the other direction: How does something physical cause something *non*physical? The only reason that's not such an obvious problem is because the nature of this 'mental stuff' is so obscure—Descartes's claims to the contrary notwithstanding—that it's hard to get any sense of what causation would even look like inside the mental realm. Still, if there were such causation in the mental realm, one might expect it to be ideas changing ideas, not physical events changing ideas. But the main problem with the view is that it smashes itself against the principle of Ockham's razor."

"Whose razor?" Ben looked a bit mystified.

"*Ockham's* Razor, Ben," answered Sarah; "a basic principle of scientific reasoning named for William of Ockham, the illustrious English *philosopher* of the early 14th century. Glad we could help you scientists out, Selina. It's sometimes called 'the principle of parsimony.' The basic idea is that when there are several possible explanatory hypotheses, the *simplest* or most *parsimonious* hypothesis is best. The hypothesis that assumes the least or that posits the fewest entities is more plausible than a more complicated rival. 'What can be done with fewer assumptions is done in vain with more,' as William himself said. 'Entities are not to be multiplied without necessity'—that's a popular way of phrasing it. It's really a commonsense idea, though it's often violated. Just because you find a theory that 'explains' something, that's no reason to suppose you have the *right* explanation. 'What causes lightning flashes?' 'They are hurled down from the clouds by the god Thor.' Well, the Thor theory accounts for lightning flashes, true enough. But no one is likely to adopt that theory as *true* or *justified*, because it is not the *simplest* account available; that is, it posits explanatory entities—the god Thor—beyond necessity. We can explain the lightning flashes more simply in terms of existing electrical charges, without *adding* a god. So the hypothesis of electrical charges is preferred because it is more parsimonious; the Thor hypothesis is rejected because it violates the principle of Ockham's razor."

"And epiphenomenalism violates that principle of Ockham's razor big time." Selina was enjoying this turn in the conversation. "Here's this strange mental stuff that exists, but it does nothing! The physical realm does all the work, causes everything to happen. Now let's see, can we think of a *simpler* theory that explains everything just as well? Physical monism—sorry, *materialism*—sort of leaps forward, doesn't it?"

"Yeah, Selina, you're right. And that's exactly what I always thought about epiphenomenalism. But then I was reading this neuropsychologist, Daniel Wegner. I was surprised, but he sort of made me reconsider. Here's Wegner's view (incidentally, it's held by a number of others as well), which he applies primarily to the concept of *conscious will:* You know, when you will yourself to get up and go to class on a cold Ann Arbor morning when the bed feels snug and warm. Or you consciously will not to eat any more chocolates. It seems that you will to act, and then your willing causes you to act. But it's a strange notion, isn't it? I mean, sometimes you lie there in bed, and you sort of gather your forces of will, and grit your teeth—and nothing happens. You wake up 45 minutes later, missed that 8 o'clock class again. And then what happens when you actually get up? Suddenly you find yourself getting up. And of course you were the one who did it, but you don't actually recall any special act of will that made it happen."

"Sarah, you can't seriously doubt that we have willpower." Ben found this disturbing. "I know that sometimes I am weak willed, and sometimes my will is not as effective as I would like it to be. Sometimes I don't *exercise* my will. But certainly I do will things, and I can make things happen by willing them: I will to pick up my coffee cup, and lo, my coffee cup rises."

"Now that you mention it, Sarah, I've always had some sneaking suspicions about this 'power of will' stuff," Selina said. "Not clear that it explains much. More like a description we add after the fact: If someone succeeds, we say they were strong willed; when someone fails, they must have been weak willed. But that's not much of an explanation is it?"

"Yeah, Selina, I agree. Sorry to disturb you, Ben, but I'm really not sure that will is the mover and shaker we often suppose it to be."

"I'm not at all convinced, Sarah." Ben shook his head. "In the first place, it certainly *seems* as if our wills often causes things to happen. I *will* to pick up my books and study, and then I do it. Okay, not always. But still, I don't see any reason to suppose that my conscious willing is some epiphenomenal side effect. Admittedly, sometimes what *seems* to be the case is wrong: It *seems* that the earth is stationary and the sun moves, and in that case what seems right turns out to be wrong. But you need stronger evidence that this is one of those cases. After all, what seems right sometimes *is* right."

"But Ben," replied Sarah, "there *is* stronger evidence. There was this experiment by Benjamin Libet. He took experimental subjects and attached a device that made it possible to detect an electrical change in a part of their brains. Then he told the experimental subjects to flick their wrists at any time they chose to do so. He also placed a large clock dial with a sweep hand in front of them and had the subjects note the exact location of the sweep hand at the moment they *decided* to flick their wrists. It turned out that there was brain activity just over half a second before the subjects flicked their wrists; and this brain activity was initiated almost one-third of a second *before* the subjects *consciously willed* to flick their wrists! So what does that indicate? The actual choice to flick their wrists started in their brains, *before* the experience of conscious willing."

"Wow! That's a clever experiment." Selina was impressed. "Libet should have been a chemist."

"And there was another experiment that strengthened this view, carried out by Grey Walter.[3] Walter was working with patients who suffered severe episodic neural disorders. One way of trying to control the problem is through inserting an electrode into the motor cortex of the brain and using the electrode to stimulate the brain and prevent the neural problems. Patients with these implanted electrodes were shown slides and were told to advance from one slide to the next at their own pace by pressing a button. The button they pressed actually had no control over the slides. Instead, the slides were advanced when a burst of activity in the neural cortex was transmitted by the implanted electrodes directly to the projector. The patients reported a curious sense that the projector was anticipating their decisions: Just before they would decide to press the button, the projector would advance a slide. Thus again, the actual decision to advance a slide occurs *before* the conscious willing. The conscious willing is a symptom, not a cause. Just as fever doesn't cause infection, but rather indicates the presence of an infection, likewise the conscious willing doesn't cause the act, but is instead a symptom of the causation being initiated nonconsciously by the brain."

Ben was not giving up that easily. "But that makes no sense, Sarah. It's as Selina said: This epiphenomenalist view of the conscious will crashes head on into Ockham's razor. Here's this vivid experience we have of the conscious will, and it does—absolutely nothing. It just gets produced as a useless and powerless by-product. No way."

"Good point, Ben." Sarah turned toward him. "Why would such a vivid experience occur if it has no function? Wegner doesn't think it's totally useless. True, it doesn't *cause* behavior—in that sense, it is epiphenomenal. But it's not useless, either. In fact, it's sort of like taking your temperature: The temperature is a symptom that something is going on inside you. And in a similar way, my experience of conscious will—Wegner maintains—tells me that the act done was done *by* me, that it was not something someone did *to* me. If you pull my hand with a string, the absence of a sense of conscious will tips me off that something outside me is controlling my movements. Actually, if we stimulate your brain in a specific way, we can also make your hand move. But when that is done to experimental subjects, they do *not* experience such movements as their own. So a sense of conscious will is a sort of feedback mechanism, one that tells me when a movement actually originates with my brain. And obviously, that's a valuable bit of information."

"I like that, Sarah," said Selina. "Wegner's form of epiphenomenalism places the causal emphasis precisely where it should be: in the physical brain, not in some strange, separate mental substance. And actually, that's not a dualist theory at all, is it, Selina? For Wegner, at least, the 'epiphenomena' that we experience are not some special mental substance."

"And I hate it." Ben was not at all pleased with this theory. "If this were true, we would be zombies: We move around and do things, but we have no conscious control over our acts. It's like the night of the living dead. It's a horror movie, but I can't close my eyes. I always thought that you materialists wanted to deny our godlike nature and turn us into animals. But it's even worse: You want to reduce us to machines!"

"Get a grip, Ben, it's not as bad as all that." Ben was genuinely disturbed, and Selina was genuinely concerned. "Look, just because your acts aren't guided by your conscious mental processes, that doesn't turn you into a zombie. You've still got feelings, strong wonderful feelings." Selina leaned over and kissed Ben behind the ear. "See? The fact that your body is not controlled by some shadowy nonphysical mind stuff doesn't destroy your emotions, your feelings, your affections, your desires. And you still think, and reason, and plan; it's just that all of that is occurring in your *brain*, not in some ethereal mind substance. But it's still *your* brain, *your* thoughts, *your* acts. Look, you remember a couple of days ago, you were working on your paper on the history of the Iroquois Nation, right? And you were trying to work out why the Iroquois agreed to the Treaty of Lancaster in 1744. You were talking to yourself, rubbing your temples, walking in circles, pondering the question—Selina, that boy is dead sexy when he's thinking hard—and then the next morning at breakfast, just as you were buttering your toast, bam, the answer came to you, when you weren't thinking about it at all. Or rather, you weren't *consciously* thinking of it; but obviously, your brain was still cranking away, and the wheels got into the right alignment, and there was your answer. Actually, there are lots of cases like that. There's the famous story of the great French mathematician, Henri Poincaré. He had worked for many months on a notoriously difficult mathematical problem, a problem no one had been able to solve. Poincaré pondered it day after day, but couldn't quite find the solution. Then one morning as he was stepping onto a bus at Coutances, thinking about something else altogether, the solution came to him in a flash. He wasn't consciously thinking about the problem, but the gears were still grinding. Even better, think of the great 19th century German chemist Friedrich August Kekulé. In 1864, Kekulé had long been trying to discover the chemical structure of the benzene molecule, but without success. One evening, after many hours of study and careful thought, he turned from his desk and dozed by his fireside. As he began to dream, he saw atoms in the form of serpents dancing, long rows twisting in snakelike motion. Then, suddenly, one snake seized its own tail and whirled around. Kekulé awakened with the brilliant idea that the structure of the benzene molecule was a closed ring—an idea he confirmed in his research and that proved enormously important in the development of modern organic chemistry. So you're a brain, not a mystical mind. But that doesn't make you any less rational, nor does it make your thoughts and acts any less your own, nor any less creative. And it doesn't make you any less lovable, for that matter."

"You're sweet, Selina, but it doesn't help. It's not enough that the thoughts happen somewhere inside me. I want to have *conscious* control of my choices, to make choices that totally originated with me."

"Choices that you totally originate with your conscious mind." Sarah smiled. "Sounds to me like you want to be a god, Ben. You want to be an unmoved mover, a first and final and solitary cause, the ultimate power."

Selina laughed. "Yeah, we're glad it's not one of our desires, right, Sarah? Must be a guy thing."

"Maybe so, Selina," Sarah replied, "but I doubt it. Plenty full members of the sisterhood seem to want the same thing. But now we're straying over into the question of free will and ultimate responsibility. Ben keeps pulling us in that direction. It is a fascinating topic, and obviously it's related to the way many people think of the mind. But it's such a huge issue, is it okay if we save it for a leisurely afternoon? Besides, to tell you the truth, I find it a very difficult and confusing issue. I'd like to think about it a little more first."

"It's an easy issue, Sarah." Selina was seldom bothered by indecisiveness. "Free will doesn't exist. Free will belongs in the museum of dead ideas, along with gods and spirits and demons and miracles and mind–body interactionism."

Ben was ready and willing to rise to Selina's challenge. "Free will certainly does exist, and we know its existence perfectly well. It's the cornerstone of rationality, responsibility, and ethics. Without it, nothing makes sense at all."

Sarah waved her hand at them. "You see, it's just possible that you two might have some slight disagreement on this topic. Let's save it for a day when we can thrash it out. I promise we'll come back to it, Ben; I want to talk about it myself. But we haven't quite finished looking at the mind and the body. Selina got excited about epiphenomenalism, and we forgot about another possibility."

"What other possibility, Sarah?" Selina was counting the theories already considered and looking for another alternative. "There's the view that the mind and the body are separate substances: That's one category. And within that category you get interactionism, according to which connections between the mind and the body go back and forth, but no one is sure how it works. And you get those crazy theories like Leibniz's preestablished harmony and Malebranche's occasionalism, where the mind and the body stay separate and the connections only *seem* to occur (but actually everything is operated by independent clocks, or God constantly intervenes, or whatever). And then you have epiphenomenalism, where the real action takes place in the brain, and conscious thought is a sort of useful by-product. And finally you get the view that there is no separate mental substance: There's really just the brain, and our thoughts and 'minds' are identical with the brain and its activities: materialism. My own view, in fact, though I think maybe Wegner's version of epiphenomenalism might be compatible with that position."

"Nice summary, Selina. But really, can't you think of any other possibilities?"

Selina stared at her coffee, and Ben saw his opportunity. "That girl's sexy when she thinks hard." He stroked Selina's eyebrows. "Course, she's also sexy when she doesn't think hard. Just that with Selina, you don't often see her when she isn't thinking hard."

"You're distracting me with all this talk about sexiness." Selina squeezed Ben's hand, took a sip of her coffee, thought some more, turned to Sarah. "No, I can't really think of any other real alternatives for mind–body theories. Maybe since I'm so sure that materialist monism is the right one, it's hard for me to dream up false alternatives."

Idealism

"Hey, I've got one!" Ben was excited; the idea had just popped into his mind. "Okay, some people—rational people, like myself—believe there's a mind *and* a body. And then there are those poor deluded souls—like Selina—who believe there's only *one* substance: the bodily, the physical. But there's another possibility: There's only one substance, but it's *mental.* That avoids all the interactionist problems of how minds could interact with physical substances: They don't! There's only the mental, so all causes and effects remain within the mental realm of thought and ideas."

"Brilliant, Ben. You should have been born a few centuries earlier. You could have been a famous philosopher. Unfortunately, an Irish philosopher—Bishop George Berkeley—beat you to it. Bishop Berkeley (1685–1753) was born in Kilkenny, Ireland, and studied at Trinity College in Dublin, where he later became a fellow. He lived for a few years in the colony of Rhode Island, pursuing his dream of establishing a college in Bermuda, a college that would admit blacks, American Indians, and American colonists; unfortunately, the funding he had been promised from Parliament never materialized. Anyway, as you noted, Berkeley solves the problem of mind–body interaction in one stroke: There is no interaction, because there's nothing physical for minds to interact *with.* This theory is sometimes called immaterialism (that's the term Berkeley himself preferred), but the more common name for it is *idealism.* It probably should be called *ideaism*, because that's what it really is: The world is made up of *ideas* and minds. Calling it idealism is a bit confusing, because it doesn't really have anything to do with the usual concept of idealism, which is concerned with high principles and high ideals and dedication to living by those ideals. But 'ideaism' is hard to say, and it doesn't have a very nice ring to it; so 'idealism' is the name we're stuck with."

"Does philosophy make people crazy, Sarah? Or is it just that crazy people become philosophers?" Selina shook her head. "I thought mind–body dualism was bad, but this takes the prize. And here you are worrying about the *name* of the theory, whether it should be called idealism or ideaism, and worried that the name might be confusing. Sarah, you philosophers strain at a gnat and you swallow a camel. You shouldn't be worried about the name 'idealism'; you should be worried about the mental health of anyone who holds such a theory. It's bad enough to think that there are things in the world that aren't there—like gods and demons and space aliens. But when you think that the whole physical world outside your own little mind doesn't really exist—that's superdelusional. What is it that Cicero once said? 'There is nothing so ridiculous but some philosopher has said it.' Berkeley is surely the proof of that statement."

Sarah laughed. "Steady on, Selina, my friend. Look, is it really so ridiculous? After all, you start from the point that mind and body cannot interact. That's your own view, right? Now the next step may not appeal to you, but it's hardly ridiculous: We do have minds, we have ideas, we have thoughts. So what follows? There are minds and thoughts, and they can never interact with the material world—so there can be no reason whatsoever to believe that some material world of physical objects actually exists. All I ever experience anyway is my own *ideas*, my own mind. It's not such a leap to suppose that there are also other minds and ideas in the world; on the other hand, it's a huge and totally unfounded leap to suppose that there's this physical world out there, so different from our own experience of our ideas, a world that we never actually experience, but that somehow is a match or mirror to our ideas and, in some mysterious manner, causes them. You're a great fan of Ockham's razor, right? So what's the simplest hypothesis here? The world is made up of minds and ideas. And that's all."

"It sounded a bit strange when I first thought of it," Ben said. "But since you put it like that, Sarah, it begins to sound more plausible. Maybe I'll switch my allegiance from dualism to idealism. At least Selina and I would have one thing in common: We would both be monists."

"So what am I, Ben, on your new idealism view? Just a figment of your imagination? Some sort of dream?" Selina still found this incredible.

"And a delightful dream you are, Selina."

"Thanks; or thanks, I guess. I'm not really sure. I'm not sure it's a compliment to be called merely a dream, even if you're regarded as a nice dream."

Sarah intervened. "Well, you aren't just a dream, Selina, on the idealist view. You're also a mind, an independent source of thoughts and ideas."

Selina wasn't buying it. "But we don't really have bodies! Have you thought about all the implications, Ben? Seems to me that would have some distinct disadvantages. Besides, idealism has some other disadvantages. It starts from an assumption of private minds, that operate in their own special space, and have real knowledge only of what goes on in that private space. And there's something else: If there's only our minds and ideas, why is there such continuity in the world? We leave the coffee shop, come back tomorrow morning, we still have the same ideas about it: about the tables, chairs, menu. Why don't we just come up with brand new ideas every time? Seems like doing remodeling would be a breeze. So sometime tonight, none of us are thinking about the chairs and tables in the coffee shop. And of course they're only ideas, right? So when no one is thinking those ideas, the tables and chairs pass out of existence. And then in the morning new tables and chairs appear! Going back to Ockham's razor, idealism doesn't sound like a very economical theory to me: not when it needs a new set of tables and chairs every morning, to replace the ones that slipped out of our minds last night."

Sarah had an answer: "But they don't disappear and get replaced, Selina. Because someone *is* thinking of them."

Idealism as a philosophical system comes in a bewildering variety of forms, and most philosophers who call themselves idealists do not deny the independent existence of material objects. (That is, they are not "idealists" in the sense discussed in this chapter.) If there is a common thread to the many varieties of idealist metaphysics, it is perhaps the belief that common sense and ordinary sense experience are woefully inadequate to grasp the deeper reality and that the deeper reality behind all appearances is some ultimate spiritual reality, a reality that cannot be known through empirical methods. (However, this ultimate spiritual reality is not typically identified with any traditional Judeo–Christian concept of God.) In one form or another, idealism dominated philosophy in England, Europe, and the United States throughout the 19th century. Though it came under intense and increasing attack in the early 20th century—particularly from such influential Cambridge University philosophers as G. E. Moore, Bertrand Russell, and Ludwig Wittgenstein—idealism remained a major philosophical movement during that time, and there are still many philosophers who espouse one form or another of idealism.

Selina sighed. "Don't tell me that they survive as my unconscious thoughts. Not even Freud would buy that sort of expansion of the unconscious mind."

"No, not in the unconscious. Rather, they exist as ideas in the mind of God. And since God is omniscient, it's no problem for God to keep all the ideas in His mind, thus providing the world with all the continuity and coherence you could wish!"

"Forget about it, Sarah." Selina frowned. "Any theory that requires God to step in and save it strikes me as a pretty weak theory on the face of it. I mean, after all, if you can always call on God to miraculously intervene and fill every gap in your theory, then it's easy to construct a theory for anything at all: way too easy."

"Alright, alright, I never expected you to become an idealist. But Ben sort of likes it."

"It does have some charms, I admit. I still prefer dualistic interactionism, its difficulties notwithstanding. But idealism is appealing."

Sarah smiled. "So here we are. Selina is an adamant monist, of the materialist variety. And you, Ben, have made the independent discovery of another form of monism: idealism. Are there any other varieties of monism left to discover?"

Ben puzzled over the question, but came up blank. "I can't see how, Sarah. There are materialist monists and idealist monists. What else could there be? That seems to me to exhaust the possibilities."

"Hang on to your philosophical principles, Ben." Selina regarded Sarah with suspicion. "Sarah is up to her philosophical tricks."

Spinoza and the Dual-Aspect Theory

"No tricks, guys. Just one other monistic perspective you might find interesting. It's a view that goes back at least to Benedict Spinoza (1632–1677), the great Dutch Jewish philosopher of the 17th Century. Well, he was Jewish by birth, anyway. He got kicked out of the temple in Amsterdam: The local Jewish congregation considered his views heretical."

"Oh, yeah, I remember Spinoza. After he got kicked out of the local Jewish community, he lived as a sort of recluse, grinding lenses to earn his bread and writing his secret philosophical works, which became known only after his death."

"Yeah, Ben, that's the story. Not quite accurate, but it's a great story: The isolated philosopher toiling away in solitude and obscurity, whose work is discovered decades later. The popular image of Spinoza is of a lonely philosopher who had been expelled from the Jewish community because of his radical ideas and spent his life as a solitary philosopher, working out an elaborate philosophical theory and earning his bread by grinding lenses. It's a colorful story, the philosophical equivalent of Abraham Lincoln being born in a log cabin. But it's not accurate. Although Spinoza *was* expelled from the Jewish temple, he was a well-known and influential figure in both philosophical and political circles, corresponding with many of the great philosophers and scientists of his era and also being actively involved with the Dutch government. He was a lens grinder; but he was grinding precision scientific lenses, not toiling away in poverty. In fact, he lived rather comfortably—though very simply—and was closely connected with the political powers of the era, who often sought his counsel. And he was hardly isolated: He had many friends, and philosophers throughout Europe knew of his work. Well, his work did become somewhat better known after his death, but the main reason for that was that he refused to let most of his writings be circulated, beyond just a few close friends."

"Why did he get kicked out of the temple, Sarah?"

"A couple of reasons, Ben. First, he rejected the idea of God taking a personal interest in any group or any person; thus, God could not have a 'chosen people.' For Spinoza, that was fundamentally incompatible with his idea of God as a perfect, infinite being: Such a God certainly couldn't play favorites. But even more important were some of the implications that Spinoza drew from his conception of God. He believed that God was infinite in every way: infinitely powerful, omniscient, omnipresent. But— remember, we talked about this a few days ago—if God is infinite and omnipresent, there can be *nothing* outside of God: *Everything* is God. So, of course, there can't be anything other than God; and since anything perfect must be indivisible, there can't be *two* substances; rather, there is only one. We see things only from our limited perspectives: We observe things physically and also from the mental perspective. But those are just different perspectives on the *one* substance. It's sort of like looking at a coin from the side of heads and then tails. It might appear to be two coins; but it is only one, viewed from two different perspectives. The mental and the physical are just different ways of viewing or understanding the same single substance, different aspects of a single substance. So this view has come to be called the *dual-aspect* theory."

"So," asked Selina, "you and Spinoza are dual-aspect theorists?"

"Yes, but we're not the only ones. The distinguished philosopher of science, Herbert Feigl, also held that position. And Daniel Dennett's account of different 'stances' one can take to understanding the mind—the physical stance that examines the brain and its circuitry, or the mental/intentional stance that studies thought and behavior—may also be a variety of dual-aspect theory. In a way, it's really a sort of identity theory: The mind is just identical with the operations of the brain. Except dual-aspect theorists tend to see both aspects as having equal standing, while materialists focus

Consider the case of the chess-playing computer, and the different stances one can choose to adopt in trying to predict and explain its behavior. First there is the design stance. *If one knows exactly how the computer's program has been designed, . . . one can predict the computer's designed response to any move one makes. . . . The essential feature of the design stance is that we make predictions solely from knowledge of or assumptions about the system's design, often without making any examination of the innards of the particular object.*

Second, there is what we may call the physical stance. *From this stance our predictions are based on the actual state of the particular system, and are worked out by applying whatever knowledge we have of the laws of nature. . . . Attempting to give a physical account or prediction of the chess-playing computer would be a pointless and herculean labor, but it would work in principle. One could predict the response it would make in a chess game by tracing out the effects of the input energies all the way through the computer until once more type was pressed against paper and a response was printed.*

There is a third stance one can adopt toward a system, and that is the intentional stance. *This tends to be most appropriate when the system one is dealing with is too complex to be dealt with effectively from the other stances. In the case of the chess-playing computer one adopts this stance when one tries to predict its response to one's move by figuring out what a good or reasonable response would be, given the information the computer has about the situation. Here one assumes not just the absence of malfunction, but the rationality of the design or programming as well.*

Daniel Dennett, "Mechanism and Responsibility," 1973

on the physical brain stuff as having scientific precedence in explaining what is *really* there when we think."

"An interesting and inventive theory, Sarah," said Selina. "You philosophers are full of them. But I still prefer materialism. The only really *accurate* understanding of our thoughts is that they are simply brain processes. The sooner we accept that view, the better off everyone will be."

"Look, Sarah, clearly Selina rejects mental substance—God help her. But it's confusing to call it a *materialist* view. I understand why the term is used: Materialists believe that everything is physical matter—there is no mental substance, only material. But 'materialist' has another meaning in popular usage. A materialist is someone driven by materialist desires: someone who seeks riches and luxuries, diamonds and furs, mansions and limousines—and doesn't much care about anything else. And in that sense, Selina is about the least materialistic person I have ever known. She cares nothing at all for fancy clothes, she finds fur coats repulsive, likes a few simple earth-colored beads and hates expensive jewelry, prefers her bike to a limo. Of course, in Selina's case, she doesn't need cashmere or diamonds to look beautiful; she looks fabulous in old jeans and a work shirt, and diamonds would look shallow and dull compared with the deep brilliant sparkle in Selina's eyes."

"That's why I put up with him, Sarah. He has all these crazy ideas about God and mind, but I just love to hear the boy talk."

"Excuse me a moment while I go gargle. I think I prefer you two when you're fighting—fortunately, that's most of the time. Okay, you're right, Ben, 'materialist' is a bit confusing: When philosophers use the term, they mean something totally different from the popular meaning. Our Selina is philosophically a thorough materialist; but as you say, she is exactly the opposite of a materialist in the popular sense. She may not be much interested in laying up treasure in heaven, but she has no interest in laying up treasure on earth, either."

Eliminative Materialism

Selina nodded. "I'm not much interested in diamonds and pearls. But I *am* interested in seeing the further development of neuropsychology. Some day, the notion of mental substance will be as dead as the notion of ghosts and goblins, and we'll all talk about our brain states instead of our immaterial minds."

"You're really hard core, Selina." Sarah smiled. "There's a name for your view."

"Yeah," Ben intervened, "it's called obnoxious, obstinate materialist arrogance: OOMA, for short."

Selina laughed. "That boy gets off a zinger now and then, doesn't he, Sarah? But what name did you have in mind?"

"Your view is often called *eliminative materialism*. It's a materialist view, of course: There is only one substance, and it is physical or material. And your view is *eliminative*, because you want to eventually *eliminate* mental terms from our vocabulary and replace them with more accurate terms concerning the operations of the brain. Not that eliminative materialists think that that can be accomplished overnight. And in some settings, we might always use mentalistic terms: We might still speak of 'trying to keep body and soul together' when we're talking about just trying to stay alive, just as we still speak of the sun *rise* rather than the Earth *turn*, even though we're all good Copernicans. But eliminative materialists maintain that the terms of our ordinary mentalistic idiom ultimately will not serve us as well as a pure materialist vocabulary that eliminates all mental references to feelings and ideas."

Selina looked skeptical. "I don't know, Sarah. 'Eliminative materialism.' Sounds like the name for a new laxative. That's my position, exactly,

but I think I like Ben's name—OOMA—better. But wouldn't *all* materialists be eliminative materialists? If you reject mental substance, wouldn't
you be eliminating it?"

"True enough, Selina, you would be denying the existence of any special mental substance. But some materialists believe that it may be useful
to go on using mentalistic *language*, even if those terms really refer to
brain states, not separate and distinct mental events. That is, we'll continue to speak of having feelings, and pains, and desires—and find it useful to do so—even after we recognize that they actually are specific brain
states. Or, as Dennett might say, materialists will continue to find the
intentional stance helpful in some contexts."

Ben found this amusing. "Well, let's see, Selina, shall we be eliminative materialists? Which do you prefer? 'I love you, Sweetheart, I think
you are the rising sun and the silver moon, and you make me feel like
springtime.' Or perhaps this: 'Greetings, Selina; upon perceiving you, my
brain registers neurological states B11, D9, and S47.' I'm only a historian,
but it seems to me that maybe something got lost in the translation."

"Okay, Ben, you win on that one." Selina shook her head. "I'm pure
materialist, but maybe it would be okay to keep some of the mental language. After all, if I'm playing chess against the computer, it's convenient
to say that the computer wants to capture my bishop, even though we all
know that the computer is purely material: no one supposes that the computer has some special mental substance hidden away inside. In fact,
that's really the most convenient way of discussing it. Some programmer
might be able to describe it in precise programming language, and perhaps some brilliant hardware engineer could even describe it in terms of
electrical circuits, but that seems almost inconceivable. So what's the
harm in a good materialist using some convenient mental language?"

"No harm at all, Selina," Ben agreed; "though recognizing the distinct
reality of mental substance would be much better."

"No way, Ben." Selina was adamant. "I'll allow mental language, the
language of intentionality, for the sake of convenience. But no mental substance. Let that in, and you open the door to miracles and mysteries and
God knows what else."

"I'm keeping that door open, Selina," replied Ben. " The world seems
much too cold and bleak with that door barred."

"Can't be all that cold and bleak, Ben. I'm part of that material
world, remember? But Sarah, why would eliminative materialists insist on
eliminating all mental terms? They seem useful."

"Actually, eliminative materialists agree that such terms are useful, at
least for the present; but they maintain that when neuropsychology
becomes sufficiently advanced, it will be much more precise and clear to

speak in terms of specific brain states rather than feelings and wishes and thoughts. At one time, when we knew very little about meteorology, it was easier to speak about spirits causing weather patterns; but now we speak of high-pressure systems and movements of the jet stream. It's not quite as colorful, but it increases precision and enhances understanding. Of course, it's still fun to talk about Old Man Winter bringing the snow and Jack Frost painting the autumn leaves, but we all recognize those as poetic images, not explanations. Eliminative materialists look forward to the same thing happening with our mental language; that is, they look forward to replacing what they call the language of "folk psychology" with the language of neuroscience. Just as there is no reason to suppose that our developed meteorological science must match up with our primitive notions of weather (no one would reject contemporary meteorological theory because it has no exact match for Jack Frost), likewise we should not assume that our crude mental ways of speaking can be mapped onto our advanced neuropsychological accounts. Those materialists who are *identity* theorists believe that neuropsychological theories will show us how our ideas and wishes and hopes and beliefs match specific neurological arrangements. The eliminative materialists, who *oppose* identity theorists, believe that advances in neuropsychology will destroy our traditional mental categories and lead to new—and better—ways of speaking about our psychological nature."

"That's an interesting distinction, Sarah." Selina considered it carefully. "I had never really thought about it that way. But I certainly don't think that future neuropsychological science must be bound by our traditional mental way of speaking. Of course, if Ben insists on still talking about how deeply he feels about me and how wonderful he thinks I am, I won't object: I'll just recognize that it's poetic language, not scientific description. But there's nothing in science that would eliminate poetry. I

Both the content and the success of folk psychology have not advanced sensibly in two or three thousand years. The folk psychology of the Greeks is essentially the folk psychology we use today, and we are negligibly better at explaining human behavior in its terms than was Sophocles. This is a very long period of stagnation and infertility for any theory to display, especially when faced with such an enormous backlog of anomalies and mysteries in its own explanatory domain. Perfect theories, perhaps, have no need to evolve. But folk psychology is profoundly imperfect. Its failure to develop its resources and extend its range of success is therefore darkly curious, and one must query the integrity of its basic categories.

Paul M. Churchland, "Eliminative Materialism and the Propositional Attitudes," *The Journal of Philosophy*, vol. 78 (1981)

know, old Willie Wordsworth used to complain that science 'murders to dissect.' But it's been some two hundred years since the scientists did the research he was complaining about, and I haven't seen any shortage of poetry in the last couple of centuries. So maybe I do favor eliminative materialism after all. At least it seems like a possibility. We aren't quite ready to shift over yet, in any case."

"Look, I know it's almost time for class, but I've got a final argument against materialism. I've been saving the best for last. It's simple: Selina is so transcendently glorious and charming that nothing purely material could instantiate her grace, her charm, her infinite variety. So there must be something in Selina beyond the physical; and thus, some form of dualism must be the case."

Selina leaned over and kissed him on the forehead. "Hmm, interesting argument. Could something purely physical contain all the charms and infinite variety of Selina? Got to admit, Sarah, the boy has come up with an intriguing line of thought. Do philosophers have a name for Ben's argument?"

"Certainly we do, Selina," replied Sarah, as she gathered her books and rushed toward her class: "It's called foreplay."

READINGS

In Chapter three, we looked at Descartes's skeptical method and at his conclusion that the first indubitable basic truth he could discover was his own existence. This section is taken from the same work—Descartes's Meditations—*the sixth meditation, in which Descartes develops his account of the relation between mind and body.*

Meditations on First Philosophy

Meditation VI

Of the Existence of Material Things, and of the real distinction between the Soul and Body of Man.

• • •

Now that I begin to know myself better, and to discover more clearly the author of my being, I do not in truth think that I should rashly admit all the matters which the senses seem to teach us, but, on the other hand, I do not think that I should doubt them all universally.

And first of all, because I know that all things which I apprehend clearly and distinctly can be created by God as I apprehend them, it suffices that I am able to apprehend one thing apart from another clearly and distinctly in order to be certain that the one is different from the other, since they may be made to exist in separation at least by the omnipotence of God; and it does not signify by what power this separation is made in order to compel me to judge them to be different: and, therefore, just because I know certainly that I exist, and that meanwhile I do not remark that any other thing necessarily pertains to my nature or essence, excepting that I am a thinking thing, I rightly conclude that my essence consists solely in the fact that I am a thinking thing [or a substance whose whole essence or nature is to think]. And although possibly (or rather certainly, as I shall say in a moment) I possess a body with which I am very intimately conjoined, yet because, on the one side, I have a clear and distinct idea of myself inasmuch as I am only a thinking and unextended thing, and as, on the other, I possess a distinct idea of body, inasmuch as it is only an extended and unthinking thing, it is certain that this I [that is to say, my soul by which I am what I am], is entirely and absolutely distinct from my body, and can exist without it.

I further find in myself faculties employing modes of thinking peculiar to themselves, to wit, the faculties of imagination and feeling, without which I can easily conceive myself clearly and distinctly as a complete being; while, on the other hand, they cannot be so conceived apart from me, that is without an intelligent substance in which they reside, for [in the notion we have of these faculties, or, to use the language of the Schools] in their formal concept, some kind of intellection is comprised, from which I infer that they are distinct from me as its modes are from a thing. I observe also in me some other faculties such as that of change of position, the assumption of different figures and such like, which cannot be conceived, any more than can the preceding, apart from some substance to which they are attached, and consequently cannot exist without it; but it is very clear that these faculties, if it be true that they exist, must be attached to some corporeal or extended substance, and not to an intelligent substance, since in the clear and distinct conception of these there is some sort of extension found to be present, but no intellection at all. There is certainly further in me a certain passive faculty of perception, that is, of receiving and recognising the ideas of sensible things, but this would be useless to me [and I could in no way avail myself of it], if there were not either in me or in some other thing another active faculty capable of forming and producing these ideas. But this active faculty cannot exist in me [inasmuch as I am a thing that thinks] seeing that it does not presuppose thought, and also that those ideas are often produced in me without my contributing in any way to the same, and often even against my will; it is thus necessarily the case that the faculty resides in some substance different from me in which all the reality which is objectively in the ideas that are produced by this faculty is formally or eminently contained, as I remarked before. And this substance is either a body, that is, a corporeal nature in which there is contained formally [and really] all that which is objectively [and by representation] in those ideas, or it is God Himself, or some other creature more noble than body in which that same is contained eminently. But, since God is no deceiver, it is very manifest that He does not communicate to me these ideas immediately and by Himself, nor yet by the intervention of some creature in which their reality is not formally, but only eminently, contained. For since He has given me no faculty to recognise that this is the case, but, on the other hand, a very great inclination to believe [that they are sent to me or] that they are conveyed to me by corporeal objects, I do not see how He could be defended from the accusation of deceit if these ideas were produced by causes other than corporeal objects. Hence we must allow that corporeal things exist. However, they are perhaps not exactly what we perceive by the senses, since this comprehension by the senses is in many instances very obscure and confused; but we must at least admit that all things which I conceive in them clearly and distinctly, that is to say, all things which, speaking generally, are comprehended in the object of pure mathematics, are truly to be recognised as external objects. . . .

There is no doubt that in all things which nature teaches me there is some truth contained; for by nature, considered in general, I now understand no other thing than either God Himself or else the order and disposition which God has established in created things; and by my nature in particular I understand no other thing than the complexus of all the things which God has given me.

But there is nothing which this nature teaches me more expressly [nor more sensibly] than that I have a body which is adversely affected when I feel pain, which has need of food or drink when I experience the feelings of hunger and thirst, and so on; nor can I doubt there being some truth in all this.

Nature also teaches me by these sensations of pain, hunger, thirst, etc., that I am not only lodged in my body as a pilot in a vessel, but that I am very closely united to it, and so to speak so intermingled with it that I seem to compose with it one whole. For if that were not the case, when my body is hurt, I, who am merely a thinking thing, should not feel pain, for I should perceive this wound by the understanding only, just as the sailor perceives by sight when something is damaged in his vessel; and when my body has need of drink or food, I should clearly understand the fact without being warned of it by confused feelings of hunger and thirst. For all these sensations of hunger, thirst, pain, etc. are in truth none other than certain confused modes of thought which are produced by the union and apparent intermingling of mind and body.

Moreover, nature teaches me that many other bodies exist around mine, of which some are to be avoided, and others sought after. And certainly from the fact that I am sensible of different sorts of colours, sounds, scents, tastes, heat, hardness, etc., I very easily conclude that there are in the bodies from which all these diverse sense-perceptions proceed certain variations which answer to them, although possibly these are not really at all similar to them. And also from the fact that amongst these different sense-perceptions some are very agreeable to me and others disagreeable, it is quite certain that my body (or rather myself in my entirety, inasmuch as I am formed of body and soul) may receive different impressions agreeable and disagreeable from the other bodies which surround it.

Gilbert Ryle (1900–1976) was Waynflete Professor of metaphysical philosophy at Oxford, as well as editor of the British philosophy journal Mind. *He was undoubtedly one of the most influential figures in the development of 20th-century Anglo–American philosophy, particularly as regards encouraging the careful use of language analysis in examining philosophical problems. His* Dilemmas *(1954) and* Collected Papers *(1971) offer ample evidence of his own analytic powers; and his* Concept of Mind *(1949)—certainly his best-known work—had a great impact on contemporary thought about the mind–body problem. This reading is from Chapter 1 of Ryle's* Concept of Mind.

Concept of Mind

Descartes' Myth

(1) The Official Doctrine

There is a doctrine about the nature and place of minds which is so prevalent among theorists and even among laymen that it deserves to be described as the official theory. Most philosophers, psychologists and religious teachers subscribe, with minor reservations, to its main articles and, although they admit certain theoretical difficulties in it, they tend to assume that these can be overcome without serious modifications being made to the architecture of the theory. It will be argued here that the central principles of the doctrine are unsound and conflict with the whole body of what we know about minds when we are not speculating about them.

The official doctrine, which hails chiefly from Descartes, is something like this. With the doubtful exceptions of idiots and infants in arms every human being has both a body and a mind. Some would prefer to say that every human being is both a body and a mind. His body and his mind are ordinarily harnessed together, but after the death of the body his mind may continue to exist and function.

Human bodies are in space and are subject to the mechanical laws which govern all other bodies in space. Bodily processes and states can be inspected by external observers. So a man's bodily life is as much a public affair as are the lives of animals and reptiles and even as the careers of trees, crystals and planets.

But minds are not in space, nor are their operations subject to mechanical laws. The workings of one mind are not witnessable by other observers; its career is private. Only I can take direct cognisance of the states and processes of my own mind. A person therefore lives through two collateral histories, one consisting of what happens in and to his body, the other consisting of what happens in and to his mind. The first is public, the second private. The events in the first history are events in the physical world, those in the second are events in the mental world.

It has been disputed whether a person does or can directly monitor all or only some of the episodes of his own private history; but, according to the official doctrine, of at least some of these episodes he has direct and unchallengeable cognisance. In consciousness, self-consciousness and introspection he is directly and authentically apprised of the present states and operations of his mind. He may have great or small uncertainties about concurrent and adjacent episodes in the physical world, but he can have none about at least part of what is momentarily occupying his mind.

It is customary to express this bifurcation of his two lives and of his two worlds by saying that the things and events which belong to the physical world, including his own body, are external, while the workings of his own mind are internal. This antithesis of outer and inner is of course meant to be construed as a metaphor, since minds, not being in space, could not be described as being spatially inside anything else, or as having things going on spatially inside themselves. But relapses from this good intention are common and theorists are found speculating how stimuli, the physical sources of which are yards or miles outside a person's skin, can generate mental responses inside his skull, or how decisions framed inside his cranium can set going movements of his extremities.

Even when 'inner' and 'outer' are construed as metaphors, the problem how a person's mind and body influence one another is notoriously charged with theoretical difficulties. What the mind wills, the legs, arms and the tongue execute; what affects the ear and the eye has something to do with what the mind perceives; grimaces and smiles betray the mind's moods and bodily castigations lead, it is hoped, to moral improvement. But the actual transactions between the episodes of the private history and those of the public history remain mysterious, since by definition they can belong to neither series. They could not be reported among the happenings described in a person's autobiography of his inner life, but nor could they be reported among those described in some one else's biography of that person's overt career. They can be inspected neither by introspection nor by laboratory experiment. They are theoretical shuttlecocks which are forever being bandied from the physiologist back to the psychologist and from the psychologist back to the physiologist.

Underlying this partly metaphorical representation of the bifurcation of a person's two lives there is a seemingly more profound and philosophical assumption. It is assumed that there are two different kinds of existence or status. What exists or happens may have the status of physical existence, or it may have the status of mental existence. Somewhat as the faces of coins are either heads or tails, or somewhat as living creatures are either male or female, so, it is supposed, some existing is physical existing, other existing is mental existing. It is a necessary feature of what has physical existence that it is in space and time. It is a necessary feature of what has mental existence that it is in time but not in space. What has physical existence is composed of matter, or else is a function of matter; what has mental existence consists of consciousness, or else is a function of consciousness.

There is thus a polar opposition between mind and matter, an opposition which is often brought out as follows. Material objects are situated in a common field, known as 'space', and what happens to one body in one part of space is mechanically connected with what happens to other bodies in other parts of space. But mental happenings occur in insulated fields, known as 'minds', and there is, apart maybe from telepathy, no direct causal connection between what happens in one mind and what happens in another. Only through the medium of the public physical world can the mind of one person make a difference to the mind of another. The mind is its own place and in his inner life each of us lives the life of a ghostly Robinson Crusoe. People can see, hear and jolt one another's bodies, but they are irremediably blind and deaf to the workings of one another's minds and inoperative upon them.

What sort of knowledge can be secured of the workings of a mind? On the one side, according to the official theory, a person has direct knowledge of the best imaginable kind of the workings of his own mind. Mental states and processes are (or are normally) conscious states and processes, and the consciousness which irradiates them can engender no illusions and leaves the door open for no doubts. A person's present thinkings, feelings and willings, his perceivings, rememberings and imaginings are intrinsically 'phosphorescent'; their existence and their nature are inevitably betrayed to their owner. The inner life is a stream of consciousness of such a sort that it would be absurd to suggest that the mind whose life is that stream might be unaware of what is passing down it.

True, the evidence adduced recently by Freud seems to show that there exist channels tributary to this stream, which run hidden from their owner. People are actuated by impulses the existence of which they vigorously disavow; some of their thoughts differ from the thoughts which they acknowledge; and some of the actions which they think they will to perform they do not really will. They are thoroughly gulled by some of their own hypocrisies and they successfully ignore facts about their mental lives which on the official theory ought to be patent to them. Holders of the official theory tend, however, to maintain that anyhow in normal circumstances a person must be directly and authentically seized of the present state and workings of his own mind.

Besides being currently supplied with these alleged immediate data of consciousness, a person is also generally supposed to be able to exercise from time to time a special kind of perception, namely inner perception, or introspection. He can take a (non-optical) 'look' at what is passing in his mind. Not only can he view and scrutinize a flower through his sense of sight and listen to and discriminate the notes of a bell through his sense of hearing; he can also reflectively or introspectively watch, without any bodily organ of sense, the current episodes of his inner life. This self-observation is also commonly supposed to be immune from illusion, confusion or doubt. A mind's reports of its own affairs have a certainty superior to the best that is possessed by its reports of matters in the physical world. Sense-perceptions can, but consciousness and introspection cannot, be mistaken or confused.

On the other side, one person has no direct access of any sort to the events of the inner life of another. He cannot do better than make problematic inferences from the observed behaviour of the other person's body to the states of mind which, by analogy from his own conduct, he supposes to be signalised by that behaviour. Direct access to the workings of a mind is the privilege of that mind itself; in default of such privileged access, the workings of one mind are inevitably occult to everyone else. For the supposed arguments from bodily movements similar to their own to mental workings similar to their own would lack any possibility of observational corroboration. Not unnaturally, therefore, an adherent of the official theory finds it difficult to resist this consequence of his premisses, that he has no good reason to believe that there do exist minds other than his own. Even if he prefers to believe that to other human bodies there are harnessed minds not unlike his own, he cannot claim to be able to discover their individual characteristics, or the particular things that they undergo and do. Absolute solitude is on this showing the ineluctable destiny of the soul. Only our bodies can meet.

As a necessary corollary of this general scheme there is implicitly prescribed a special way of construing our ordinary concepts of mental powers and operations. The verbs, nouns and adjectives, with which in ordinary life we describe the wits, characters and higher-grade performances of the people with whom we have do, are required to be construed as signifying special episodes in their secret histories, or else as signifying tendencies for such episodes to occur. When someone is described as knowing, believing or guessing something, as hoping, dreading, intending or shirking something, as designing this or being amused at that, these verbs are supposed to denote the occurrence of specific modifications in his (to us) occult stream of consciousness. Only his own privileged access to this stream in direct awareness and introspection could provide authentic testimony that these mental-conduct verbs were correctly or incorrectly applied. The onlooker, be he teacher, critic, biographer or friend, can never assure himself that his comments have any vestige of truth. Yet it was just because we do in fact all know how to make such comments, make them with general correctness and correct them when they turn out to be confused or mistaken, that philosophers found it necessary to construct their theories of the nature and place of minds. Finding mental-conduct concepts being regularly and effectively used, they properly sought to fix their logical geography. But the logical geography officially recommended would entail that there could be no regular or effective use of these mental-conduct concepts in our descriptions of, and prescriptions for, other people's minds.

(2) The Absurdity of the Official Doctrine

Such in outline is the official theory. I shall often speak of it, with deliberate abusiveness, as 'the dogma of the Ghost in the Machine'. I hope to prove that it is entirely false, and false not in detail but in principle. It is not merely an assemblage of particular mistakes. It is one big mistake and a mistake of a special kind. It is, namely, a category-mistake. It represents the facts of mental life as if they belonged to one logical type or category (or range of types or categories), when they actually belong to another. The dogma is therefore a philosopher's myth. In attempting to explode the myth I shall probably be taken to be denying well-known facts about the mental life of human beings, and my plea that I aim at doing nothing more than rectify the logic of mental-conduct concepts will probably be disallowed as mere subterfuge.

I must first indicate what is meant by the phrase 'Category-mistake'. This I do in a series of illustrations.

A foreigner visiting Oxford or Cambridge for the first time is shown a number of colleges, libraries, playing fields, museums, scientific departments and administrative offices. He then asks 'But where is the University? I have seen where the members of the Colleges live, where the Registrar works, where the scientists experiment and the rest. But I have not yet seen the University in which reside and work the members of your University.' It has then to be explained to him that the University is not another collateral institution, some ulterior counterpart to the colleges, laboratories and offices which he has seen. The University is just the way in which all that he has already seen is organized. When they are seen and when their co-ordination is understood, the University has been seen. His mistake lay in his innocent assumption that it was correct to speak of Christ Church, the Bodleian Library, the Ashmolean Museum *and* the University, to speak, that is, as if 'the University' stood for an extra member of the class of which these other units are members. He was mistakenly allocating the University to the same category as that to which the other institutions belong.

The same mistake would be made by a child witnessing the march-past of a division, who, having had pointed out to him such and such battalions, batteries, squadrons, etc., asked when the division was going to appear. He would be supposing that a division was a counterpart to the units already seen, partly similar to them and partly unlike them. He would be shown his mistake by being told that in watching the battalions, batteries and squadrons marching past he had been watching the division marching past. The march-past was not a parade of battalions, batteries, squadrons *and* a division; it was a parade of the battalions, batteries and squadrons *of* a division.

One more illustration. A foreigner watching his first game of cricket learns what are the functions of the bowlers, the batsmen, the fielders, the umpires and the scorers. He then says 'But there is no one left on the field to contribute the famous element of team-spirit. I see who does the bowling, the batting and the wicket-keeping; but I do not see whose role it is to exercise *esprit de corps*.' Once more, it would have to be explained that he was looking for the wrong type of thing. Team-spirit is not another cricketing-operation supplementary to all of the other special tasks. It is, roughly, the keenness with which each of the special tasks is performed, and performing a task keenly is not performing two tasks. Certainly exhibiting team-spirit is not the same thing as bowling or catching, but nor is it a third thing such that we can say that the bowler first bowls *and* then exhibits team-spirit or that a fielder is at a given moment *either* catching *or* displaying *esprit de corps.*

These illustrations of category-mistakes have a common feature which must be noticed. The mistakes were made by people who did not know how to wield the concepts *University, division* and *team-spirit.* Their puzzles arose from inability to use certain items in the English vocabulary.

The theoretically interesting category-mistakes are those made by people who are perfectly competent to apply concepts, at least in the situations with which they are familiar, but are still liable in their abstract thinking to allocate those concepts to logical types to which they do not belong. An instance of a mistake of this sort would be the following story. A student of politics has learned the main differences between the British, the French and the American Constitutions, and has learned also the differences and connections between the Cabinet, Parliament, the various Ministries, the Judicature and the Church of England. But he still becomes embarrassed when asked questions about the connections between the Church of England, the Home Office and the British Constitution. For while the Church and the Home Office are institutions, the British Constitution is not another institution in the same sense of that noun. So interinstitutional relations which can be asserted or denied to hold between the Church and the Home Office cannot be asserted or denied to hold between either of them and the British Constitution. 'The British Constitution' is not a term of the same logical type as 'the Home Office' and 'the Church of England'. In a partially similar way, John Doe may be a relative, a friend, an enemy or a stranger to Richard Roe; but he cannot be any of these things to the Average Taxpayer. He knows how to talk sense in certain sorts of discussions about the Average Taxpayer, but he is baffled to say why he could not come across him in the street as he can come across Richard Roe.

It is pertinent to our main subject to notice that, so long as the student of politics continues to think of the British Constitution as a counterpart to the other institutions, he will tend to describe it as a mysteriously occult institution; and so long as John Doe continues to think of the Average Taxpayer as a fellow-citizen, he will tend to think of him as an elusive insubstantial man, a ghost who is everywhere yet nowhere.

My destructive purpose is to show that a family of radical categorymistakes is the source of the double-life theory. The representation of a person as a ghost mysteriously ensconced in a machine derives from this argument. Because, as is true, a person's thinking, feeling and purposive doing cannot be described solely in the idioms of physics, chemistry and physiology, therefore they must be described in counterpart idioms. As the human body is a complex organised unit, so the human mind must be another complex organised unit, though one made of a different sort of stuff and with a different sort of structure. Or, again, as the human body, like any other parcel of matter, is a field of causes and effects, so the mind must be another field of causes and effects, though not (Heaven be praised) mechanical causes and effects.

(3) The Origin of the Category-mistake

One of the chief intellectual origins of what I have yet to prove to be the Cartesian category-mistake seems to be this. When Galileo showed that his methods of scientific discovery were competent to provide a mechanical theory which should cover every occupant of space, Descartes found in himself two conflicting motives. As a man of scientific genius he could not but endorse the claims of mechanics, yet as a religious and moral man he could not accept, as Hobbes accepted, the discouraging rider to those claims, namely that human nature differs only in degree of complexity from clockwork. The mental could not be just a variety of the mechanical.

He and subsequent philosophers naturally but erroneously availed themselves of the following escape-route. Since mental-conduct words are not to be construed as signifying the occurrence of mechanical processes, they must be construed as signifying the occurrence of non-mechanical processes; since mechanical laws explain movements in space as the effects of other movements in space, other laws must explain some of the non-spatial workings of minds as the effects of other non-spatial workings of minds. The difference between the human behaviours which we describe as intelligent and those which we describe as unintelligent must be a difference in their causation; so, while some movements of human tongues and limbs are the effects of mechanical causes, others must be the effects of non-mechanical causes, i.e. some issue from movements of particles of matter, others from workings of the mind.

The differences between the physical and the mental were thus represented as differences inside the common framework of the categories of 'thing', 'stuff', 'attribute', 'state', 'process', 'change', 'cause' and 'effect'. Minds are things, but different sorts of things from bodies; mental processes are causes and effects, but different sorts of causes and effects from bodily movements. And so on. Somewhat as the foreigner expected the University to be an extra edifice, rather like a college but also considerably different, so the repudiators of mechanism represented minds as extra centres of causal processes, rather like machines but also considerably different from them. Their theory was a para-mechanical hypothesis.

That this assumption was at the heart of the doctrine is shown by the fact that there was from the beginning felt to be a major theoretical difficulty in explaining how minds can influence and be influenced by bodies. How can a mental process, such as willing, cause spatial movements like the movements of the tongue? How can a physical change in the optic nerve have among its effects a mind's perception of a flash of light? This notorious crux by itself shows the logical mould into which Descartes pressed his theory of the mind. It was the self-same mould into which he and Galileo set their mechanics. Still unwittingly adhering to the grammar of mechanics, he tried to avert disaster by describing minds in what was merely an obverse vocabulary. The workings of minds had to be described by the mere negatives of the specific descriptions given to bodies; they are not in space, they are not motions, they are not modifications of matter, they are not accessible to public observation. Minds are not bits of clockwork, they are just bits of not-clockwork.

As thus represented, minds are not merely ghosts harnessed to machines, they are themselves just spectral machines. Though the human body is an engine, it it not quite an ordinary engine, since some of its workings are governed by another engine inside it—this interior governor-engine being one of a very special sort. It is invisible, inaudible and it has no size or weight. It cannot be taken to bits and the laws it obeys are not those known to ordinary engineers. Nothing is known of how it governs the bodily engine.

A second major crux points [to] the same moral. Since, according to the doctrine, minds belong to the same category as bodies and since bodies are rigidly governed by mechanical laws, it seemed to many theorists to follow that minds must be similarly governed by rigid non-mechanical laws. The physical world is a deterministic system, so the mental world must be a deterministic system. Bodies cannot help the modifications that they undergo, so minds cannot help pursuing the careers fixed for them. *Responsibility, choice, merit* and *demerit* are therefore inapplicable concepts—unless the compromise solution is adopted of saying that the laws governing mental processes, unlike those governing physical processes, have the congenial attribute of being only rather rigid. The problem of the Freedom of the Will was the problem how to reconcile the hypothesis that minds are to be described in terms drawn from the categories of mechanics with the knowledge that higher-grade human conduct is not of a piece with the behaviour of machines.

It is an historical curiosity that it was not noticed that the entire argument was broken-backed. Theorists correctly assumed that any sane man could already recognise the differences between, say, rational and non-rational utterances or between purposive and automatic behaviour. Else there would have been nothing requiring to be salved from mechanism. Yet the explanation given presupposed that one person could in principle never recognise the difference between the rational and the irrational utterances issuing from other human bodies, since he could never get access to the postulated immaterial causes of some of their utterances. Save for the doubtful exception of himself, he could never tell the difference between a man and a Robot. It would have to be conceded, for example, that, for all that we can tell, the inner lives of persons who are classed as idiots or lunatics are as rational as those of anyone else. Perhaps only their overt behaviour is disappointing; that is to say, perhaps 'idiots' are not really idiotic, or 'lunatics' lunatic. Perhaps, too, some of those who are classed as sane are really idiots. According to the theory, external observers could never know how the overt behaviour of others is correlated with their mental powers and processes and so they could never know or even plausibly conjecture whether their applications of mental-conduct concepts to these other people were correct or incorrect. It would then be hazardous or impossible for a man to claim sanity or logical consistency even for himself, since he would be debarred from comparing his own performances with those of others. In short, our characterisations of persons and their performances as intelligent, prudent and virtuous or as stupid, hypocritical and cowardly could never have been made, so the problem of providing a special causal hypothesis to serve as the basis of such diagnoses would never have arisen. The question, 'How do persons differ from machines?' arose just because everyone already knew how to apply mental-conduct concepts before the new causal hypothesis was introduced. This causal hypothesis could not therefore be the source of the criteria used in those applications. Nor, of course, has the causal hypothesis in any degree improved our handling of those criteria. We still distinguish good from bad arithmetic, politic from impolitic conduct and fertile from infertile imaginations in the ways in which Descartes himself distinguished them before and after he speculated how the applicability of these criteria was compatible with the principle of mechanical causation.

He had mistaken the logic of his problem. Instead of asking by what criteria intelligent behaviour is actually distinguished from non-intelligent behaviour, he asked 'Given that the principle of mechanical causation does not tell us the difference, what other causal principle will tell it [to] us?' He realised that the problem was not one of mechanics and assumed that it must therefore be one of some counterpart to mechanics. Not unnaturally psychology is often cast for just this role.

When two terms belong to the same category, it is proper to construct conjunctive propositions embodying them. Thus a purchaser may say that he bought a left-hand glove and a right-hand glove, but not that he bought a left-hand glove, a right-hand glove and a pair of gloves. 'She came home in a flood of tears and a sedan-chair' is a well-known joke based on the absurdity of conjoining terms of different types. It would have been equally ridiculous to construct the disjunction 'She came home either in a flood of tears or else in a sedan-chair'. Now the dogma of the Ghost in the Machine does just this. It maintains that there exist both bodies and minds; that there occur physical processes and mental processes; that there are mechanical causes of corporeal movements and mental causes of corporeal movements. I shall argue that these and other analogous conjunctions are absurd; but, it must be noticed, the argument will not show that either of the illegitimately conjoined propositions is absurd in itself. I am not, for example, denying that there occur mental processes. Doing long division is a mental process and so is making a joke. But I am saying that the phrase 'there occur mental processes' does not mean the same sort of thing as 'there occur physical processes', and, therefore, that it makes no sense to conjoin or disjoin the two.

If my argument is successful, there will follow some interesting consequences. First, the hallowed contrast between Mind and Matter will be dissipated, but dissipated not by either of the equally hallowed absorptions of Mind by Matter or of Matter by Mind, but in quite a different way. For the seeming contrast of the two will be shown to be as illegitimate as would be the contrast of 'she came home in a flood of tears' and 'she came home in a sedan-chair'. The belief that there is a polar opposition between Mind and Matter is the belief that they are terms of the same logical type.

It will also follow that both Idealism and Materialism are answers to an improper question. The 'reduction' of the material world to mental states and processes, as well as the 'reduction' of mental states and processes to physical states and processes, presuppose the legitimacy of the disjunction 'Either there exist minds or there exist bodies (but not both)'. It would be like saying, Either she bought a left-hand and a right-hand glove or she bought a pair of gloves (but not both)'.

It is perfectly proper to say, in one logical tone of voice, that there exist minds and to say, in another logical tone of voice, that there exist bodies. But these expressions do not indicate two different species of existence, for 'existence' is not a generic word like 'coloured' or 'sexed'. They indicate two different senses of 'exist', somewhat as 'rising' has different senses in 'the tide is rising', 'hopes are rising', and 'the average age of death is rising'. A man would be thought to be making a poor joke who said that three things are now rising, namely the tide, hopes and the average age of death. It would be just as good or bad a joke to say that there exist prime numbers and Wednesdays and public opinions and navies; or that there exist both minds and bodies. In the succeeding chapters I try to prove that the official theory does rest on a batch of category-mistakes by showing that logically absurd corollaries follow from it. The exhibition of these absurdities will have the constructive effect of bringing out part of the correct logic of mental-conduct concepts.

(4) Historical Note

It would not be true to say that the official theory derives solely from Descartes's theories, or even from a more widespread anxiety about the implications of seventeenth century mechanics. Scholastic and Reformation theology had schooled the intellects of the scientists as well as of the laymen, philosophers and clerics of that age. Stoic-Augustinian theories of the will were embedded in the Calvinist doctrines of sin and grace; Platonic and Aristotelian theories of the intellect shaped the orthodox doctrines of the immortality of the soul. Descartes was reformulating already prevalent theological doctrines of the soul in the new syntax of Galileo. The theologian's privacy of conscience became the philosopher's privacy of consciousness, and what had been the bogy of Predestination reappeared as the bogy of Determinism.

It would also not be true to say that the two-worlds myth did no theoretical good. Myths often do a lot of theoretical good, while they are still new. One benefit bestowed by the para-mechanical myth was that it partly superannuated the then prevalent para-political myth. Minds and their Faculties had previously been described by analogies with political superiors and political subordinates. The idioms used were those of ruling, obeying, collaborating and rebelling. They survived and still survive in many ethical and some epistemological discussions. As, in physics, the new myth of occult Forces was a scientific improvement on the old myth of Final Causes, so, in anthropological and psychological theory, the new myth of hidden operations, impulses and agencies was an improvement on the old myth of dictations, deferences and disobediences.

Study Questions

1. Describe Descartes's view of the relation between mind and body.
2. What is solipsism, and what basic beliefs led some philosophers to solipsism?
3. What are some of the problems with belief in private knowledge (or a "private language")?
4. What are the key problems for the theory of dualistic interactionism?
5. Not all dualists are interactionists; describe some other alternatives.
6. What is epiphenomenalism?
7. What is the principle of Ockham's razor? Give an example of how it might be applied.
8. What is idealism, and what are the arguments in its favor?
9. Describe the dual-aspect theory of mind and body.
10. What is eliminative materialism?

Exercises

1. Many dualists favor a separation of mind and body because then the mind can be identified with the soul and the soul can survive the death of the physical body. But of course, a mind–body dualist need not believe in a soul or in any sort of survival after death; that is, a dualist might maintain that the mind and body are distinct substances, but that both cease to exist when the body dies. But consider the question from the other direction: Could one consistently believe in an immortal *soul* while rejecting mind–body dualism? In particular, could a monist who takes a materialist view (as opposed to the idealist view) consistently believe in an immortal soul?

2. Descartes's theory of mind separates the mind and body into two distinct substances; and his theory of knowledge (his epistemology) insists on a starting point of fixed and indubitable certainty. If Descartes had adopted a different view of knowledge, do you think that would have resulted in a different mind–body view?

3. With the development of computers have come claims about "artificial intelligence." Some philosophers and artificial-intelligence researchers have put forward a position known as "strong artificial intelligence," or "strong AI." Advocates of this position maintain that the crucial thing about thought is the programming. They hold that if a very powerful computer could be adequately programmed, then, by virtue of that programming, it would actually be thinking—perhaps not thinking in exactly the same way that humans think, since humans have different programming, but nonetheless genuinely thinking, and thinking as well or even better than humans do. John Searle is one of the leading opponents of strong AI: He adamantly opposes the idea that any computer could ever be programmed so that it would actually *think* or *reason.* A computer can sort material admirably well, but it can never really *think,* according to Searle. Some people may suppose that Searle's view is based on dualism: A computer is purely physical, and it cannot really think because only *minds* can think. But Searle insists that he is *not* a dualist, and he is *not* opposed to the idea that material machines can think:

   > My own view is that *only* a machine could think, and indeed only very special kinds of machines, namely brains and machines that had the same causal powers as brains. . . . Whatever else intentionality is, it is a biological phenomenon, and it is likely to be as causally dependent on the specific biochemistry of its origins as lactation, photosynthesis, or any other biological phenomena.

   In fact, Searle attempts to turn the table on his opponents and charges the advocates of strong AI with being mind–body dualists:

   > Strong AI only makes sense given the dualistic assumption that, where the mind is concerned, the brain doesn't matter. In strong AI . . . what matters are programs, and programs are independent of their realization in machines. . . . The single most surprising discovery that I have made in discussing these issues is that many AI workers are quite shocked by my

idea that actual human mental phenomena might be dependent on actual physical–chemical properties of actual human brains. But if you think about it a minute you can see that I should not have been surprised; for unless you accept some form of dualism, the strong AI project hasn't got a chance. The project is to reproduce and explain the mental by designing programs, but unless the mind is not only conceptually but empirically independent of the brain you couldn't carry out the project, for the program is completely independent of any realization. Unless you believe that the mind is separable from the brain both conceptually and empirically— dualism in a strong form—you cannot hope to reproduce the mental by writing and running programs since programs must be independent of brains or any other particular forms of instantiation. If mental operations consist in computational programs on formal symbols, then it follows that they have no interesting connection with the brain; the only connection would be that the brain just happens to be one of the indefinitely many types of machines capable of instantiating the program. This form of dualism is not the traditional Cartesian variety that claims there are two sorts of *substances*, but it is Cartesian in the sense that it insists that what is specifically mental about the mind has no intrinsic connection with the actual properties of the brain. (John R. Searle, "Minds, Brains, and Programs," from *The Behavioral and Brain Sciences*, vol. 3, 1980, p. 423)

This is a continuing controversy between Searle and strong proponents of AI. So if you're interested in artificial intelligence, what's your take on the issue? Is the strong-AI program dualistic as Searle charges? Or is Searle's *opposition* to strong AI actually rooted in dualism, as some charge? How about neither? Both? Or what? *Could* a computer ever be programmed to think?

4. One of the most interesting claims associated with mind–body dualism is that we have special "privileged access" to our own thoughts. Someone else might know my brain better than I (by means of a PET scan, for example), but no one else can know what I am thinking—or at least they cannot know it with the special, immediate knowledge and certainty that I have. Many people believe that claim to be true, and many others think it false; that's not my question. Do mind–body dualists (and, of course, *you* might or might not be included in that group) believe that we have privileged access to our own minds *because* they believe in mind–body dualism? Or do they believe in mind–body dualism because of their more basic belief that we have privileged access to our own minds (and mind–body dualism seems the best way to explain that)? That is, which came first, belief in mind–body dualism or belief in privileged access to one's own mind?

5. Suppose you believe that others can have knowledge of your own mind—your own thoughts—that is at least as good as the knowledge you yourself possess. Would such a belief make it much more difficult to accept mind–body dualism?

6. G. E. Moore was a highly influential British philosopher in the early 20th century. He taught at Cambridge and was a leader in the "common sense" movement, in opposition to the metaphysical idealism that had dominated

Anglo–American philosophy in the century before. Moore's writing was plain and straightforward, as were his arguments. One of his best-known arguments against Berkeley's idealism is the following:

> We *know* that there are and have been in the Universe the two kinds of things—material objects and acts of consciousness. We *know* that there are and have been in the Universe huge numbers of both. We *know* that the vast majority of material objects are unconscious. We *know* that things of both kinds *have* existed in the past, which do not exist now, and things of both kinds do exist now, which did *not* exist in the past. All these things we should, I think, certainly say that we *know*.[4]

What is your evaluation of Moore's argument against idealism?

7. Ludwig Wittgenstein—who was a student and later professor at Cambridge when Moore was one of the senior faculty there—was not convinced by Moore's argument. Not that Wittgenstein was an idealist: He was not. Rather, he simply was not convinced that Moore's example worked against idealism. In *On Certainty*, Wittgenstein raised the following objection:

> When Moore says he *knows* such and such, he is really enumerating a lot of empirical propositions which we affirm without special testing; propositions, that is, which have a peculiar logical role in the system of our empirical propositions. (p. 20) . . . It is not single axioms that strike me as obvious, it is a system in which consequences and premises give one another *mutual* support. (p. 21) . . . I should like to say: Moore does not *know* what he asserts he knows, but it stands fast for him, as also for me; regarding it as absolutely solid is part of our *method* of doubt and certainty. (p. 22) . . . For when Moore says "I know that that's . . ." I want to reply "you don't *know* anything!"—and yet I would not say that to anyone who was speaking without philosophical intention. That is, I feel (rightly?) that these two mean to say something different. (p. 52)[5]

Is Wittgenstein correct that Moore is using "I know that material objects exist" in a way that makes it impossible to use it as a proof against idealism? Wittgenstein seems to be suggesting that Moore's argument commits a fallacy; what fallacy do you think Wittgenstein is charging against Moore? Is it a legitimate charge?

8. In 1734, Berkeley was appointed Anglican bishop of Cloyne, Ireland, a remote and rather poor part of that country. Bishop Berkeley was deeply concerned with the poverty and ill health of his parishioners. In his efforts to improve their health, he became convinced of the positive medicinal quality of tar-water and wrote a book promoting its virtues. Suppose that someone offered the following challenge to Berkeley: "You claim that nothing exists except minds and their ideas; but you are pushing a medicine that is supposed to cure bodily illnesses. Obviously, then, you must really believe that bodies exist if you think you have a way to cure them." Could Berkeley give a satisfactory answer to that challenge?

9. Could an atheist plausibly believe in idealism?

10. Can you imagine replacing the language of "folk psychology" (the language of desires, emotions, attitudes, intentions, beliefs, acts of will, etc.) with the language of neuroscience, as eliminative materialists maintain we must eventually do? Probably not. Is that a legitimate point *against* eliminative materialism?

Glossary

Dual-aspect theory: The view that the mind and body (or mind and brain) make up a single substance, but that that substance can be viewed from either the physical or the mental perspective.

Dualism: Any theory of the mind which claims that the mind and body are distinct and different substances.

Eliminative materialism: A materialist view that favors eventual elimination of the traditional mental vocabulary of "folk psychology" and replacing it with terms drawn from neuropsychological research.

Epiphenomenalism: The view that ideas and thoughts are caused by brain activity, but they do not themselves cause any physical events; rather, they are "side effects" of physical brain activity.

Idealism: The view that everything which exists is mental; there are no physical bodies, no material objects; the world consists entirely of minds and ideas.

Interactionism: A variety of dualist theory which claims that the mind and body, though different substances, can interact and directly influence each other.

Materialism: The view that everything that exists is material (or physical); there is no nonphysical "mind stuff"—no souls or spirits.

Occasionalism: The dualist view that God controls all the acts of both mind and body and keeps them in perfect order and harmony, so that their coordinated acts appear to interact, though they actually do not. Cases in which the mind appears to cause the body to move are merely occasions when God causes both mental ideas and physical movement.

Ockham's razor, principle of: A principle formulated by William of Ockham; specifically, the principle that, all else being equal, the simplest hypothesis is more plausible than a more complicated hypothesis; or, alternatively, the principle that theories should not posit entities beyond necessity. Sometimes called the principle of parsimony (and sometimes spelled "Occam").

Preestablished harmony: A version of mind–body dualism which claims that there is no interaction between mind and body, between the mental and the physical; rather, God establishes a plan and an order that keeps minds and bodies running in perfect harmony.

Reductio ad absurdum: Reduction to absurdity; that is, an argument form that draws out the implications of a position, shows that those implications lead to absurd results, and concludes that, therefore, the position must be false.

Solipsism: The view that I can not be sure that there are any minds other than my own.

Additional Resources

For a good general review of the "mind–body problem," see Keith Campbell's *Body and Mind* (New York: Doubleday–Anchor, 1970); Jerome Shaffer's *The Philosophy of Mind* (Englewood Cliffs, NJ: Prentice Hall, 1968) also examines the issue and the many proposals that have been made to solve the problem. John O' Connor's *Modern Materialism: Readings on Mind–Body Identity* (New York: Harcourt, Brace & World, 1969) is a good collection of contemporary essays; another is David Rosenthal, ed., *Materialism and the Mind–Body Problem* (Englewood Cliffs, N.J.: Prentice-Hall, 1971). The most famous contemporary attack on mind–body dualism is by Gilbert Ryle; his book, *The Concept of Mind* (London: Hutchinson, 1949), has influenced both philosophical and psychological theory.

Two good collections of papers on philosophy of mind, which include historical as well as contemporary writings, are B. Beakley and P. Ludlow, eds., *The Philosophy of Mind: Classical Problems, Contemporary Issues* (Cambridge, MA.: MIT Press, 1992), and G. N. A. Vesey, *Body and Mind: Readings in Philosophy* (London: George Allen & Unwin, 1964). A superb collection (primarily of recent work) is edited by John Heil: *Philosophy of Mind: A Guide and Anthology* (Oxford: Oxford University Press, 2004). Still another good anthology on the philosophy of mind is *The Nature of Mind*, edited by David M. Rosenthal (New York: Oxford University Press, 1991).

Herbert Feigl's version of the dual-aspect theory can be found in his *The "Mental" and the "Physical"* (Minneapolis: University of Minnesota Press, 1967); the essay that forms the heart of the book was originally published in 1958. John Searle's provocative work has stimulated much debate in both philosophy of mind and artificial intelligence. He tackles difficult issues, attacks popular positions, and writes with remarkable clarity. A good introduction to his recent work can be found in John R. Searle, *The Rediscovery of the Mind* (Cambridge, MA: MIT Press, 1992).

A superb collection of essays concerning contemporary neuropsychology and mind–body (as well as free-will) issues is contained in *The Volitional Brain: Towards a Neuroscience of Free Will*, edited by Benjamin Libet, Anthony Freeman, and Keith Sutherland (Exeter, U.K.: Imprint Academic, 1999). Much of this material is very difficult, but the debates among the participants are fascinating, and the essays are generally of very high quality. An excellent and very readable book by a contemporary neuropsychologist defending his own version of epiphenomenalism is Daniel M. Wegner's *The Illusion of Conscious Will* (Cambridge, MA: MIT Press, 2002). Another neuropsychologist who has written interesting and accessible books on issues related to philosophy of mind is Antonio R. Damasio; see *Descartes' Error: Emotion, Reason, and the Human Brain* (New York: G. P. Putnam's Sons, 1994), and *Looking for Spinoza: Joy, Sorrow, and the*

Feeling Brain (Orlando, FL: Harcourt, 2003). Both of Damasio's books are in paperback and are widely available. *Neurophilosophy: Toward a Unified Science of the Mind–Brain*, by Patricia Smith Churchland (Cambridge, MA: MIT Press, 1986) is an insightful examination of the implications of recent work in neuroscience for both philosophy of mind and philosophy of science. A philosophical book that pulls together contemporary work from many disciplines to offer a fresh perspective on the traditional mind–body problem is by Andy Clark: *Being There: Putting Brain, Body, and World Together Again* (Cambridge, MA: MIT Press, 1997).

A wonderful and entertaining collection of essays on philosophy of mind—including work by philosophers, novelists, and cognitive scientists—is edited by Douglas R. Hofstadter and Daniel C. Dennett: *The Mind's I: Fantasies and Reflections on Self and Soul* (New York: Basic Books, 1981); it is also available in a Bantam Books paperback edition (1982).

A particularly clear path into many tricky issues in philosophy of mind is provided by George Graham in *Philosophy of Mind: An Introduction* (Oxford: Blackwell, 1993). Another good and clearly written guide to issues in the philosophy of mind is by Owen Flanagan, *Consciousness Reconsidered* (Cambridge, MA: MIT Press, 1992). Still another excellent introduction is by Paul M. Churchland, *Matter and Consciousness: A Contemporary Introduction to the Philosophy of Mind*, revised edition (Cambridge, MA: MIT Press, 1988).

David Chalmers has compiled a remarkably thorough, beautifully organized, and easily navigated bibliography of recent work on philosophy of mind (back to approximately 1950); many of the entries are annotated. Go to *http://www.uarizona.edu/~chalmers/biblio.html*. His home page also contains a remarkable collection of hundreds of online papers (his own and many others), conveniently arranged by topic and easily available. In addition, there's a section of philosophical humor and of pictures of philosophers taken at various conferences—examine these at your own risk.

"A Field Guide to the Philosophy of Mind" is a very appealing website. Its best feature is an extensive and excellent set of "Guided Tours" to a wide variety of topics in philosophy of mind. The tours are clearly written, and they provide excellent guides to the history of the topic, as well as current research. The guide can be found at *http://host.uniroma3.it/progetti/kant/field/*.

The MIT Encyclopedia of Cognitive Sciences is also a very useful site; go to *http:/cognet.mit.edu/MITECS/login.html*.

The "Wifilosofia" has an excellent and extensive set of weblinks to papers, discussions, and sites related to philosophy of mind. Go to *http://lgxserver.uniba.it/lei/mind/home.htm*.

www.Naturalism.org is an excellent site for papers, articles, and reviews of material on philosophy of mind (as well as on other topics).

Notes

1. Omar Khayyám, The Rubáiyát of Omar Khayyám, trans. Edward Fitzgerald, Stanza 83, second translation.

2. *Philosophical Review*, October 1974, vol. 83 pp. 435–450.

3. This experiment is discussed by Guy Claxton in "Whodunnit? Unpicking the 'Seems' of Free Will," *Journal of Consciousness Studies*, vol. 6, numbers 8–9, 1999, p. 105.

4. G. E. Moore, *Some Main Problems of Philosophy* (New York: Macmillan, 1953).

5. Ludwig Wittgenstein, *On Certainty*, edited by G. E. M. Anscombe and G. H. von Wright (New York: Harper & Row, 1969, 1972).

Chapter *6*

Free Will

in which Selina sees free will from a new perspective

"Hi, Sarah." Ben called to her with enthusiasm, and Selina smiled a warm greeting. "Hey, I'm glad you're here. You promised to join us for a discussion of free will, and that pledge has come due. Good thing you ordered a large coffee: We're going to settle this free-will question once and for all."

"That might require more than one cup of coffee," Sarah replied, as she settled her coffee mug and blueberry muffin on the table and dropped her book bag on the floor. "People have been trying to settle that question for at least twenty-five centuries."

"Well, if we can't settle it for all, maybe we can at least settle it for once. Besides, I still think it's my best argument for mind–body dualism—for the existence of some substance with qualities and powers quite different from those of the material world."

Selina shook her head. "So, Ben, you want to use free will to support mind–body dualism! A false premise leading to a false conclusion. You're trying to explain the obscure by means of the more obscure. This special power of free will is hopeless. The world is a vast and wonderful machine. Its causes are sometimes difficult to fathom, but they are always there. And the world of nature does *not* make a special exception for humans."

Ben was troubled. "It's bad enough that you can believe such craziness, Selina. But you actually seem to *like* the idea, and that I can hardly imagine. If I believed for a moment it were true, it would fill me with despair. Life would be empty, cold, desolate."

"By no means, Ben. For one thing, a determined world would still contain *me*. And no world which holds a Selina can be empty, cold, and desolate."

Ben laughed, but somewhat ruefully. "True, Selina. But you would be my only comfort in such a world: There would be no hope, no freshness, no

Free-will pragmatically means novelties in the world, *the right to expect that in its deepest elements as well as in its surface phenomena, the future may not identically repeat and imitate the past. . . . It holds up improvement as at least possible; whereas determinism assures us that our whole notion of possibility is born of human ignorance, and that necessity and impossibility between them rule the destinies of the world.*

William James,
Pragmatism, Lecture 3
(1907)

It would be very singular that all nature, all the planets, should obey eternal laws, and that there should be a little animal about five foot high, who in contempt of these laws, could act as he pleases, solely according to his caprice.

Voltaire

Napoleon   Bonaparte: "Our hour is marked, and no one can claim a moment of life beyond what fate has predestined."

To Dr. Arnott,
April 1821

open possibilities—instead, a closed, cramped, and tightly constrained existence. Besides, such a determined, closed world could never contain a Selina: You are a woman of infinite variety, fresh ideas, open vistas. No determinist grindings could produce a wonder like Selina."

Selina laughed. "Good try, tiger. You're not going to convince me that determinism is false. But I like the sound of your argument."

"This debate is swiftly degenerating." Sarah took a long drink of coffee. "You guys seem to be talking about two different things."

"Not at all, Sarah." Selina tossed her head. "We're discussing my infinite variety of charms, which is always a delightful topic."

Determinism and Fatalism

"True enough, girl. When the topic is Selina, there is no danger of confusion. For better or worse, there's only one Selina. But your infinite variety of charms notwithstanding, you and Ben seem to be discussing two different things when you talk about *determinism.* Leave aside free will for a minute, and focus on determinism. After all, the question about free will is usually prompted by concerns about determinism. But what Ben describes sounds more like *fatalism* than *determinism.*"

"Wait a minute, now I'm more confused than ever." Ben was shaking his head. "I always thought determinism and fatalism came to the same thing."

"Some certainly would agree with you, Ben. Like "Morning star" and "Evening star," just two names for the same thing: the planet Venus. But perhaps not. Determinism is the view that everything which happens has a definite cause, and given the exact situation and the laws of nature, specific results are *determined* to follow. Given the full set of causal forces operating on the initial conditions, a specific result must

goes; what will be, will be. Don't worry, be happy. And the great stoic philosopher of ancient Rome, Epictetus, taught a fatalistic perspective, too. He compared our lives to that of a dog securely tied to a cart. The cart is on its way to market, drawn by two powerful horses. Now, there's nothing the dog can do about that: He's on his way to the market, that's a settled fact. But either he can be dragged through the dust, fighting and biting every step of the way, miserably and hopelessly resisting, or he can trot along happily beside the cart, enjoying the grass and the flowers and the sunshine. Either way, he arrives at his fate; but if he resists and struggles, he will arrive there miserably, while if he accepts his destination and trots along contentedly, he can enjoy a pleasant trip."

> *Remember that you are an actor in a drama of such sort as the Author chooses—if short, then in a short one; if long, then in a long one. If it be his pleasure that you should enact a poor man, or a cripple, or a ruler, or a private citizen see that you act it well. For this is your business—to act well the given part, but to choose it belongs to another.*
>
> Epictetus, *The Enchiridion*, translated by Thomas W. Higginson

"Still seems spooky to me: I don't want to be destined for market or Samarra." Selina shivered again.

"What are you shivering at, Selina?" Ben saw an opening. "I thought you liked fatalism."

"No way, Ben. I like *determinism*, not fatalism."

Determinism and Choice

"Same difference. If determinism is true, then everything you do is set by determined causes. You're no different from the servant who rides off to Samarra or the soldier who charges the machine gun: Nothing you do makes any difference."

"No, Ben, in determinism what you do *does* make a difference." Sarah was convinced of this distinction. "Look, think about the project you organized last Christmas: 'Unto Us a Child Is Given,' right?"

"Lots of people worked on that. Selina worked just as hard as I did. There were dozens of students, folks from all over Michigan, contributions from all over the country. Wasn't my project."

"Okay, okay, lots of people worked on it. That's true. But I know who set it in motion, who had the idea, who got it moving, who kept it going. Not a lot of people know that—you certainly never wanted any credit for it; maybe that's one of the reasons you made it work. But anyway, it worked; my God, did it ever work. Hundreds of doctors and nurses and dentists pledged thousands of hours to staff the clinics; union groups pledged thousands of volunteer hours to contribute the work of electricians and plumbers and painters and carpenters and masons to fix up free clinics;

What he [humanity] wants to preserve is precisely his noxious fancies and vulgar trivialities, if only to assure himself that men are still men . . . and not piano keys simply responding to the laws of nature. . . .

But even if man was nothing but a piano key, even if this could be demonstrated to him mathematically—even then, he wouldn't come to his senses but would pull some trick out of sheer ingratitude, just to make his point. . . .

Now, you may say that this too can be calculated in advance and entered on the timetable—chaos, swearing, and all—and that the very possibility of such a calculation would prevent it, so that sanity would prevail. Oh no! In that case man would go insane on purpose, just to be immune from reason.

Dostoyevsky, 1864

and there were hours left over to repair homeless shelters and some private residences. Three Detroit shopping malls reduced their holiday decorations and pledged the money to the campaign! It was amazing, wonderful. You had atheists and Christians and Muslims and Jews all working together to provide warm clothes and health care and better housing for the children of Detroit! Michigan students giving up Colorado ski trips and new skis to contribute the time and money to helping inner-city neighborhoods. There are children who are wearing warm coats this winter because of what you started, Ben. And there are children who are getting good health care, and good dental care, and good food, because of what you set in motion. Okay, okay, I know what you're going to say: 'I didn't provide health care for any children; I didn't provide nursing care for any families; I didn't fix the plumbing at any homeless shelter.' But you set it in motion, Ben, you got it rolling, you kept pushing. Without you it would not have happened. I know you don't like to talk about it, and you never claim any credit—never even gave a newspaper interview. Without a tremendous number of other people, it would not have worked: sure, that's true. But I know who got it off the ground, who made it fly, who started that ball rolling. Lots of people were helped. And maybe some of those who were helped the most were the people who gave: They are happier, revitalized."

"Yeah," Selina spoke up, "I remember a tough old union plumber, cursed a blue streak, rough old guy; he said, 'You know, here I am spending my whole Christmas vacation working twelve-hour shifts fixing the pipes in this free clinic; and my grandson, he's been down here handing me tools and working right alongside me; and my daughter has been providing nursing care at the clinic, and my high-and-mighty son-in-law, the distinguished internist, I could never stand him, has come in from his suburban mansion and worked an eighty-hour week providing good, basic medical care. And it's been the best Christmas I can ever remember. I know it's the first Christmas in ten years I haven't had a fight with my daughter and son-in-law. And I'll tell you, it's the best week of plumbing work I've ever done in my life. And these folks who come to the clinic for treatment, they're not deadbeats. They're good folks, had some bad luck. I see this old world a little different now.'"

"Alright," Sarah continued, "without people like that plumber and that doctor and that nurse, nothing good would have happened. But without you starting it rolling, and keeping it rolling over the bumps and problems, it wouldn't have happened at all. Hey, don't get embarrassed. I'm not going to nominate you for a humanitarian award or send a letter to the editor about your selfless sacrifice. But look, here's the only point I wanted to make: You actually did something, you had an effect, what you did made a difference. Now, what's the moral of that long story? Suppose that all your ideas, acts, and projects were completely determined. I know you don't believe that; but just imagine it for a minute. Why did you have the idea of 'Unto Us a Child Is Given'? Why did you launch it? Why did you work so hard on it? Suppose that every part of what you did—the ideas, the planning, the hard work—all of it was *determined* by your past history, your early environment, your genetics, the myriad influences that shaped you. Let's *suppose* it was all determined, caused by previous events. Still, *you* made a difference, *you* made things happen, and without you things would *not* have happened. If you hadn't done what you did, there are children in Detroit who would be shivering in the cold, sick, suffering from toothaches, who are instead snug in their warm coats with their cavities filled and their illnesses treated or prevented. You did it from your *own* desires and commitments and principles, because *you* wanted to do it. That you wanted to, that you had the desire and the commitment and the fortitude, that was determined by your past history and circumstances. Nonetheless, the causal process works through you. *Through* you, not against you. Who you are and what you do is determined, but it's still *you* who are acting and making things happen, by your *own* desires and choices. *Determined* desires and choices, but no less your own."

"I'm not sure, Sarah." Ben shook his head. "I still don't much care for the idea of determinism."

"Okay, now think for a moment of what *fatalism* would look like. If it were your *fate* to launch the 'Unto Us a Child Is Given' program, then you would wind up doing it *no matter what* your own desires and wishes were. You might hate the idea of a program to benefit impoverished children: Maybe you're some vicious Scrooge who takes perverse pleasure in the idea of sick children shivering in the cold. But no matter how you struggle against it—no matter how swiftly you ride toward Samarra—your fate catches up with you, and you wind up launching the program. Maybe your actual plan was to devise a program to destroy all the homeless shelters and free clinics; but instead, the fates conspire to turn your efforts into a successful program that helps poor children. In that case, the program is not really of your own doing; at the very least, it is not your own *purposive* doing, you are not doing what you *wanted* to do, you're just a pawn in the hands of the fates. Many of the ancient Greeks were fatalists. Remember the story of Oedipus? In the Greek drama, Oedipus's fate is foretold: He will slay his father and marry his mother. A terrible fate, a fate that Oedipus resolves to escape. So he goes far away from his home country, far from his mother and father. In this new country he is caught up in a war, and in battle he kills the king. By the custom of that country, a warrior who kills the king is himself crowned king and marries the widowed queen. So Oedipus follows the custom of his adopted country, little suspecting that he had been adopted at birth, and the king he killed in battle was actually his father, and the queen he was marrying was his mother. Certainly not what Oedipus wanted or planned, but that didn't matter: It was his fate, and his own desires and goals and struggles counted for nothing. So under fatalism, you can do whatever you wish, but it will be of no consequence: The fates are pulling your strings, and the important outcome is fixed. You may get to Samarra slowly on foot or swiftly on horseback, but you will meet death in Samarra at the fated hour."

Selina leaned forward. "My favorite line about fate comes from Shakespeare, a line spoken by Cassius, in the play *Julius Caesar*:

> Men at some time are masters of their fates:
> The fault, dear Brutus, is not in our stars,
> But in ourselves.

Sarah clapped her hands. "Exactly, Selina. We are in control of what happens, we are not the pawns of fate. Of course we are shaped by our genetic histories and our environments and our culture, but unless we suppose ourselves self-creating gods, that is not surprising, and it does not make us puppets of our fates. It was determined, Ben, that you would launch 'Unto Us a Child Is Given'; but the determining factors worked through you—through your own values and choices. Your choices are your own, your values are your own, even though there are obviously determining causes of both. But you aren't jerked about by fate; rather, you make your own choices, from your own unique, but determined, character."

Determinism vs. Freedom

Ben was not about to give up. "Yeah, well, 'determined choices' doesn't sound like freedom to me. Fatalism and determinism are just two names for the same thing. If we want genuine free will, we have to reject both."

Ben took a sip of his coffee, leaned back, and continued. "We're not self-creating gods; but we are made in the image of God, and that is the sense in which we are made in God's image: We have the self-creative power of free will, the power to transcend our causal histories. Look, I was just reading some stuff for my Renaissance history seminar." Ben retrieved a book from his backpack and found the right page. "This is by a young nobleman, Giovanni Pico della Mirandola, who comes to Rome to make a name for himself. He was planning to hold a debate, in which he would defend his views against all comers. In preparation, he wrote a summary of his views, and of the position he would defend, and posted it around Rome. He never got to do the debate, since what he wrote was judged by the Church to be dangerous, and he was suspected of heresy—and he found that, for reasons of health, he should take a swift journey out of Rome. But anyway, in part of what he wrote he imagines God speaking to humankind:

> The nature of all other beings is limited and constrained within the bounds of laws prescribed by Us. Thou, constrained by no limits, in accordance with thine own free will, in whose hand We have placed thee, shalt ordain for thyself the limits of thy nature. We have set thee at the world's center that thou mayest from thence more easily observe whatever is in the world. We have made thee neither of heaven nor of earth, neither mortal nor immortal, so that with freedom of choice and with honor, as though the maker and molder of thyself, thou mayest fashion theyself in whatever shape thou shalt prefer. Thou shalt have the power to degenerate into the lower forms of life, which are brutish. Thou shalt have the power, out of thy soul's judgment, to be reborn into the higher forms, which are divine.[1]

"That's very entertaining, Ben. I love all those history cases you come up with, really. But it's not in the least convincing as a reason to believe in free will." Selina continued. "After all, it starts from the notion of God; and appealing to God to explain free will strikes me as a case of trying to explain the doubtful by the utterly implausible. Furthermore, it's a God Who 'set thee at the world's center'; that is, a God who believes that the Earth is the immovable center, and the rest of the world spins around it. A God who is confused about that doesn't strike me as a reliable authority on free will."

"It's not really an argument, Selina. You take it too literally." Ben was rising to the debate. "It just illustrates how we might think of free will: as special and distinctive, a special power, a sort of divine spark. *Not* as a cog in some determinist machine."

God and Determinism

Selina was clearly ready to launch a major assault, and Sarah swiftly intervened to keep the hostilities to a minimum. "But Ben, is that really a view you want to defend? You are a Christian, and your religious views are very important to you, aren't they?"

"Careful, Sarah; don't get him started. A nice Jewish girl like you? He'll be trying to convert you. I think he's about given up on me."

"I'm not trying to convert Sarah: She's a pillar of righteousness. And besides, I have *not* given up on you: Miracles do happen, though I confess I think the conversion of Selina would rank right up there with the parting of the Red Sea. But yes, certainly, I am a Christian, and I take my Christian beliefs very seriously."

"So Ben, do you really think that that view of free will is compatible with Christianity? With all due respect to Mirandola, it seems to me that his view is heretical."

"Why heretical, Sarah? Why couldn't God grant the special power of free will to humans? That sounds to me like the best candidate for how we are made in God's image."

Selina offered a jab. "We aren't made in God's image, Ben. Rather, humans make their gods in their own images. What's the saying? 'If triangles had gods, their gods would have three sides.'"

"Now *that* is heresy," Ben answered. "But I don't see why Mirandola's view of free will should be regarded as Christian heresy."

"Look, Ben, I'm Jewish—and like Spinoza, I don't think my views are always faithful to Jewish doctrine. And this is a question about Christian teachings, so I'm really out of my territory: As Selina's sweet Momma would say, Honey, I don't have a dog in this fight."

Selina laughed heartily. "You be careful, Sarah. Now you're talking like Momma. One more visit down to Birmingham, she'll have you eating ham hocks and chitlings, and I *know* that's not Jewish orthodoxy."

Ben was eager to get back to the question. "Okay, but why isn't Mirandola's free will orthodox Christianity? God gives us the godlike power of free will, which explains how we are made in God's image. What's heretical about that?"

"Well, it's fine with *me*, Ben." Sarah frowned, a look of slight puzzlement. "But I just don't see how it squares with some of the main teachings of Christianity. Part of it goes back to the Christian view of God—or at least the Christian view of God as it developed in modern thought, under the influence of Greek philosophy. God is omniscient and omnipotent, right? And as we talked about it before, that doesn't just mean that God knows a *lot*, or that God has *great* power; it means that God knows *all* and God has *all* power. That raises two immediate problems. First, if God knows everything, then God knows everything in the past, present, and future. But if God already knows what you are going to do, and knew it for all eternity, then how can you be acting freely? It seems as if you would just be following God's script. That bothers a lot of people—how can we act freely if God has foreknowledge of what we are going to do?—but it really isn't the toughest problem. The real problems develop when we think about God's *omnipotence.* If God has *all* power, in what sense can we really *act* at all, much less act *freely.*"

Ben shook his head. "But if God's omnipotence and omniscience undercut human free will, then why do so many Christians place such emphasis on free will? On the *choice* to believe, the *free choice* of salvation?"

Sarah shrugged her shoulders. "You'll have to ask them, Ben. Maybe they haven't thought carefully about it. If you are speaking of the television evangelists, that would probably be the most plausible hypothesis. But I do know that many Christians—some of whom appeared to think a great deal about it—have fiercely *denied* that humans have free will. Martin Luther and John Calvin, for example; and"—Sarah paused while she pulled Ben's Bible from his stack of books and searched for the passage she wanted—"St. Paul, whose position seems clear enough in his letter to the Romans:

> For the children being not yet born, neither having done any good or evil, that the purpose of God according to election might stand, not of works, but of him that calleth; it was said unto her, The elder shall serve the younger. As it is written, Jacob have I loved, but Esau have I hated. . . . For he saith to Moses, I will have mercy on whom I will have mercy, and I will have compassion on whom I will have compassion. So then it is not of him that willeth, nor of him that runneth, but of God that showeth mercy. . . . Therefore hath he mercy on whom he will have mercy, and whom he will he hardeneth. Thou wilt say then unto me, Why does he yet find fault? For who hath resisted his will? Nay but, O man, who are thou that replies against God? Shall the thing formed say to him that formed it, Why has thou made me thus? Hath not the potter power over the clay, of the same lump to make one vessel unto honor, and another unto dishonor?

St. Paul's position is clear: It's not a matter of human will, but of God's choice."

"I don't know. That passage does seem clear. Still, it's very hard for me to believe that we don't have free will—that God would destroy our free will. It doesn't make sense."

"Yeah, Ben," Sarah agreed, "that's exactly what Martin Luther said: It doesn't make sense, it goes against reason. Still, Luther thought it

God foreknows nothing by contingency, but that He foresees, purposes, and does all things according to His immutable, eternal, and infallible will. By this thunderbolt free will is thrown prostrate and utterly dashed to pieces. Those, therefore, who would assert free will must either deny this thunderbolt, or pretend not to see it, or push it from them.

Martin Luther,
The Bondage of the Will,
trans. by Henry Cole

Predestination, by which God adopts some to the hope of life and adjudges others to eternal death, no one, desirous of the credit of piety, dares absolutely to deny. . . . This foreknowledge extends to the whole world and to all the creatures. Predestination we call the eternal decree of God, by which He hath determined in Himself what He would have to become of every individual of mankind. For they are not all created with a similar destiny; but eternal life is foreordained for some, and eternal damnation for others. Every man, therefore, being created for one or the other of these ends, we say, he is predestinated either to life or to death.

John Calvin, from *Institutes of the Christian Religion*, trans. John Allen

---

was true"—as Sarah spoke, she was paging through her textbook, looking for a passage from Luther she remembered highlighting—"and he saw it as one of the main reasons for faith. Yeah, here it is: 'This is the highest degree of faith—to believe that He is merciful, who saves so few and damns so many; to believe Him just, who according to His own will makes us necessarily damnable. . . . If, therefore, I could by any means comprehend how that same God can be merciful and just who carries the appearance of so much wrath and iniquity, there would be no need of faith. But now, since that cannot be comprehended, there is room for exercising faith. . . .' It doesn't make sense, Luther is saying, so faith is required."

Ben shook his head. "I can't go along with Luther on that one. I still believe that we have free will."

"But Ben," Sarah persisted, "how could humans have the power of free choice if God has *all* power, if God is *omni*potent?"

"Maybe God gives humans that power, as Mirandola suggested."

"Well, maybe so." Sarah considered it. "But then God would not be *omni*potent, would not be *all* powerful. Look, suppose Wal-Mart finally drives all the other stores out of business and destroys all the unions, and the Walton family has all the money in the world. Now suppose they give a few dollars away. They would still be *very* rich, but they wouldn't have *all* the wealth."

Ben frowned. "So maybe God is not omnipotent. It's hard for me to believe that God denies us free will."

"Actually," Sarah responded, "William James concluded that God could not be omnipotent for almost that exact reason. Plus James felt that if God were omnipotent, then the ultimate triumph of good over evil was inevitable, and what we do doesn't make much difference. So he believed that God was a strong force for good, but not *all* powerful."

"Careful, guys." Selina offered a warning. "Now you're edging into serious heresy. You know the history. A few hundred years ago, you'd already be tied to the stake and the flames would be roaring."

Oh, Thou, who didst with pitfall and with gin
Beset the Road I was to wander in,
    Thou wilt not with Predestined Evil round
Enmesh, and then impute my Fall to Sin!

Oh, Thou, who Man of baser Earth didst make,
And ev'n with Paradise devise the Snake:
    For all the Sin the Face of wretched Man
Is black with—Man's Forgiveness give—and take!

The Rubáiyát of Omar Khayyám, verses 87–88, translated by Edward Fitzgerald

---

Sarah laughed. "And look who is warning us! You know, materialists and atheists weren't exactly popular back then, either."

Selina was enjoying this. "So we'll all be heretics together! Good for you, Sarah. You may not have rescued Ben from religion, but at least you have led him into heresy. And that's a step in the right direction."

"I'm not a heretic. At least I don't think I am. Look, I still believe that God is omnipotent and omniscient. Anything that's not omnipotent and omniscient is just not God. But I also believe we have free will. I mean, how could it be fair for God to condemn souls to hell if they have no free will? If none of them have free will, how could it be fair for some to be saved and others damned?"

"Ben, those are hard questions. My view of God is somewhat different. I don't think that we can distinguish what is God from what is not, so it makes no sense to think of God standing apart and selecting some for damnation and some for salvation." Sarah paused, then continued. "But there is the traditional answer, given by John Calvin: All are sinners and richly deserve to be eternally damned. But God in His mercy spares a few—which shows the great mercy and generosity of God, which is of course a good thing. So why does God select some for bliss? How does God decide which ones He should choose for salvation? That's a mystery, and we shouldn't ask. After all, who are we to question God?"

Arguing for Determinism

Selina scoffed. "Yeah, that's a great solution: It's all a mystery. Look, Ben, all these religious doctrines are tying you in knots. If you just think about it in terms of the natural world and everyday life, then this whole question of determinism is not so difficult, and it's certainly not scary. Suppose we're all sitting here enjoying our coffee and conversation, and suddenly your coffee cup begins to move across the table. No one touches it. The cup just starts to slowly slide across the table. What would you say happened?"

"It just slid across the table? Well, probably the table wasn't level, and gravity pulled it across."

"No, we check the table carefully: it's dead level."

"Perhaps a tiny tremor, in a small fault line directly below the table, almost undetectable, but just enough to move the cup."

"Nope, no tremors whatsoever."

Ben thought for a moment. "In that case, Sarah probably has a nylon filament attached to the cup, and she is using a trick to prove some exotic philosophical theory."

"No," Selina answered, "we check the cup, there's no nylon filament, no hidden magnet, no magic trick."

"Maybe some folks in the physics department are doing an experiment, they're beaming high-energy gamma rays at the coffee cup from across campus, causing it to move."

Selina laughs. "No gamma rays from the physics department. So why did the cup move?"

"In that case, the cup must have been possessed by a demon. Or maybe it was moved by the ghost of some poor long-dead student troubled by this discussion of determinism, who decided to haunt the coffee shop."

"There, you see!" Selina was triumphant. "You'll consider gravity, tremors, gamma rays, even ghosts—but one thing you will never suggest, one thing that does not seem even remotely possible to you. Ghosts and goblins seem more plausible. The one thing you will never suggest is that it just happened; nothing caused it to move: it just moved. So when something happens in the physical world, you believe there must have been a cause, right?"

"Okay, maybe. So maybe there is a cause for every physical event in the world, maybe determinism applies there. But what does that prove? The real question is about *human* free will, not coffee-cup free will."

Selina's eyes flashed with anger. "Well, forget about it then, Ben, you can believe whatever stupid thing you want! I'm tired of arguing about this, and I'm tired of arguing with you. Just leave me alone."

"Hey, Selina, what's the matter?" Ben was shocked. "That's not like you. You always *love* to argue. And even when we disagree, you never really get angry. You okay? Not feeling well? Is everything okay at home? You worried about your big organic chem test tomorrow? Is it something I did? What's wrong?"

"Nothing's the matter. Just leave me alone."

"Well, something must be wrong. You wouldn't get that angry over nothing. Tell me about it."

Selina patted his hand. "It's okay, Ben, I was just teasing. I wasn't really angry. I was just making a point. I didn't mean to upset you. But look at what happened when I suddenly became angry. You wanted to know why, what had caused it. And you were sweet to be so concerned. You thought it might be bad news, or sickness, or special worries. But one thing you never thought: that my strange behavior had no cause at all, that it just happened. So whether it's human behavior or coffee-cup motion, you *always* believe there's a cause. You may not be able to discover what the cause is, but you always *believe* there's a cause. So for both human behavior and the rest of the world, you believe that *everything* that happens has a specific cause. And that means you believe in *determinism.* You might not like the name, you might not like acknowledging your belief in determinism, but clearly you do believe in it. It's not such a scary doctrine at all, just a common and useful belief."

"Hey, Selina, great argument!" Sarah was delighted. "That's exactly the argument Hume gave for determinism. Yesterday it was Ben speaking for Berkeley, and today you're channeling Hume. Lucky me! Famous philosophers being reincarnated all around me."

"Okay, okay, maybe you guys are right." Ben looked resigned. "Maybe I do believe in determinism after all. Not fatalism, but determinism. Still, it's depressing. I hate the idea that we don't have free will."

"Don't be too hasty, Ben." Sarah smiled at him. "Just because you believe in determinism doesn't mean you can't also believe in free will."

> *All men are born ignorant of the causes of things, that all have the desire to seek for what is useful to them, and that they are conscious of such desire. Herefrom it follows, first, that men think themselves free inasmuch as they are conscious of their volitions and desires, and never even dream, in their ignorance, of the causes which have disposed them so to wish and desire.*
>
> Spinoza, *Ethics*, Part 1, Appendix

Compatibilist Free Will

"Oh, please, Sarah!" Selina couldn't believe what she was hearing. "We finally got Ben to acknowledge determinism. Maybe he's finally getting over this free-will craziness. And now *you* want to save free will, even though you were just celebrating Hume's argument for determinism. I feel like I'm in the house of mirrors. I don't know whether I'm coming or going."

Ben was also confused. "Look, I'm not sure that determinism is true. Maybe it is, but I still have some doubts. And I'm not sure that belief in free will is false. Maybe that's also the case. But one thing *is* sure: If determinism is true, then belief in free will is false. And if free will exists, then determinism does not. You can't have determinism and free will both."

Selina nodded. "He's right, Sarah. The boy gets confused about some things, but he's dead center right on that."

"Alright, alright." Sarah apparently was giving up gracefully. "Enough on free will and determinism for awhile. Are you guys going to the game tomorrow?"

"Watch the Wolverines pound the Wisconsin Badgers? Absolutely right, I'm going. I never miss a Michigan football game, Sarah. You know that. Ben and I are going to a tailgate party for brunch, and then we'll get to the game an hour early to watch the warmups and cheer when the Wolverines take the field. You know, my dad used to play linebacker for Michigan."

Sarah laughed. "Yeah, Selina, I think you've mentioned that once or twice."

Selina tossed her head. "Well, as I was saying, before the philosopher over there interrupted me, my dad loved Michigan football, and we never missed a game when they were on television. Then, once a year, he would bring us all up to Ann Arbor for a game. It was always the highlight of the year, bigger than Christmas! I love Michigan—great classes, great town, great professors—but the main reason I came to Michigan was Wolverine football. Of course, Ben's the same way. He grew up in Michigan, always followed the Wolverines. I mean, I can put up with his weird religious views and his strange tastes in music; but I could never love a man who wasn't a Michigan football fan. If I'm breathing, I'll be at the game."

"So Ben doesn't force you to go?"

Ben laughed. "Nobody forces Selina to do anything, Sarah. But certainly, you don't have to force her to go to a Michigan football game. I mean, *I* love Wolverine football; but *Selina*, it's deep in her soul. Oh, excuse me, Selina, I forgot, you don't have a soul. I mean, it's deep in her body and being. I think her blood must run blue and maize."

"So Selina, you go freely, no coercion by Ben?"

"What are you getting at, Sarah? You know Ben's not the coercive type. Besides, as Ben says, nobody would ever have to force me to go to a Michigan game. I love it, have for years and years. What, is this some kind of sexist stereotyping, Sarah? Girls can't really love football? If girls go to football games, it must be to please guys?"

Sarah laughed. "No, no, Selina, nothing like that. Don't start accusing me of being a sexist. But look, the fact is, you aren't really acting freely when you go to Michigan football games. Sorry to have to tell you."

"What *are* you raving about, Selina? All this philosophy stuff has finally smoked your brain. You know how much I love Michigan football, and you know no one has to force me to go to games. If there's one thing I do freely, it's go to Michigan football games. My Composition Two class, well, that's a different story. But Michigan football, that I do freely and gladly."

"No, sorry, Selina, afraid you're wrong. You remember when you first came to Michigan, every student had to have a physical. They ran a blood test, right? Well, they also checked your DNA. And now with all this human genome research, they have isolated a special gene. Actually, it's easy to spot: It's bright blue and maize in color."

"Get out of here, Sarah! What'd you put in that coffee? You might sell that stuff to old Ben, but this is a chemistry major you're talking to: There are no blue-and-maize genes!"

"I'm surprised you haven't heard about it," Sarah responded. "It was in all the papers. Anyway, as I was saying before I was interrupted by the chemistry major, recent research has revealed a bright-blue-and-maize gene: they call it the UMFF gene, which is an acronym for its full name: the University of Michigan Football Fan gene. It turns out that everyone who has this special gene becomes a rabid fan of the Wolverines. And your DNA tests revealed the UMFF gene quite clearly; you probably inherited it from your father. So it was genetically determined that you would be a University of Michigan football fan, and thus, obviously, you are *not* going to the games freely: Your UMFF gene compels you to go."

Both Selina and Ben were laughing, but Ben managed to stop for a moment. "Look, Sarah, I don't know where this stuff about the UMFF gene is coming from, but gene or no gene, I know for certain that Selina goes to football games because she wants to! Look, you've seen her, right? She paints her face blue; if the temperature is subzero and the wind is blowing and snow is swirling, she doesn't even notice it; and she screams herself hoarse for her beloved Wolverines. I mean, I love Wolverine football, but Selina is at another whole level. Come to think of it, maybe she does have a blue-and-maize gene. But there's no question that she's acting freely when she goes to Michigan Stadium."

"You agree with Ben on that, Selina?"

"Yeah, Ben's right about that. Never freer than when I'm on my way to a Michigan game."

"Exactly! You're both right!" Sarah was delighted. "And even if we suppose that Selina is *genetically determined* to love Wolverine football, that would *not* change the fact that she goes to the games *freely*. Now, obviously, there's no football-fan gene. Why does Selina love Wolverine football? Who knows? But as we talked about before, we do believe there's a *cause* for Selina's avid football-fan behavior. It was probably shaped in her by her early childhood: watching football games with her dad, traveling with the family to Ann Arbor. I'd be willing to wager that her very first stuffed toy was a soft, cuddly blue-and-maize wolverine."

Selina shook her head. "You'd lose your bet, Sarah. My first stuffed toy was a teddy bear. But he was wearing a blue-and-maize Michigan sweater."

Sarah nodded. "Whatever the cause—childhood conditioning, environmental shaping, even genetics—Selina is still *acting freely* when she goes to Wolverine football games. And there is nothing in determinism that prevents her from acting freely. Why does she go to games? Because *she wants to*, because of *her own desires*, from *her own choice*. Her choices and wants and desires are obviously *caused*. As we discussed before, we all *believe*—even though Ben doesn't like saying it—that her choices and desires and behavior are *determined* by past causes. But that doesn't alter the fact that Selina *acts freely*. So determinism is *not* in conflict with free behavior; to the contrary, they are perfectly *compatible*. Incidentally, that's the name philosophers use for those who believe that determinism and free acts can go together: They are *compatibilists*, who believe in *compatibilism* between determinism and free will."

"Wait a minute, Sarah." Selina was looking very puzzled. "You're saying that it's *determined* that I'll go to the football game, but I still go *freely*. No, that just can't be right. It's some sort of philosophical sleight of hand. What's the trick?"

"No trick, Selina. It's not some weird philosophical concoction; it's just plain common sense. The only thing that's confusing is the terminology. People hear 'determinism,' and they get this picture of some powerful force compelling them to do things against their wishes. But that's a totally wrong picture. That might apply to *fatalism*—the fates are these nasty tricksters that thwart your wishes and dash your hopes and disrupt your plans—but *determinism* is not like that at all. Selina goes to the game because *she wants to*, and even if we could specify all the causes that shaped her course, and predict what she is going to do, that doesn't change the fact that *she does it*, from her own desire and choice. What more could you want from freedom than that? So Selina, are you going to the game tomorrow of your own free choice?"

"Well, yes, sure."

"And are there *causes* that determine your desires and character and choices? *Everything* that happens has a cause, right, isn't that what we all agreed? If you were running a study in your chemistry lab, and you combined two chemicals that are supposed to form a stable compound, and this time there was a small explosion, you wouldn't say, 'Oh, that's just the way it goes.' You would be certain that there was some cause: Maybe a test tube was contaminated, or a chemical was mislabeled. And if sweet old Ben suddenly turned nasty and vicious, you wouldn't say, 'Oh, his personality just changed, no cause for it.' You would think somebody drugged him, or he had been brainwashed, or *something*; that is, you would firmly believe there was a *cause* for that change in personality, even if you never discovered what it was. So you believe that *everything* is caused; that is, you believe in determinism, right?"

"Yeah, certainly."

"So what's your problem? You act freely, *and* your acts are determined. Your behavior isn't *forced* against your wishes; instead, you act as *you want* to act, in accordance with your own wishes that were shaped by determined causal forces. Freedom and determinism fit together like—uh, like Selina and Ben."

Libertarian Free Will

Ben laughed. "Selina and I are a good fit, Sarah. Or at least we will be when she finishes pounding me into shape. But freedom and determinism, that's a different story. That freedom–determinism *compatibilism* you were talking about: To use a favorite expression of Selina's daddy, 'That dog won't hunt.'"

Sarah smiled. "Those Alabama folks have a rich range of expressions, don't they? But it seems to me that that dog is a *fine* hunter: Compatibilism is exactly right. What's wrong with it?"

"Just one thing: It leaves out the most important part of freedom. Sure, Selina is doing what she wants to do when she goes to the football game. But that's not nearly enough for genuine free will. The crucial question is this: *Could she have done otherwise?* If she *cannot* do other than she does, then she is *not* acting freely, even if she's doing what she wants

---

Let us imagine a man who, while standing on the street, would say to himself: "It is six o'clock in the evening, the working day is over. Now I can go for a walk, or I can go to the club; I can also climb up the tower to see the sun set; I can go to the theater; I can visit this friend or that one; indeed, I also can run out of the gate, into the wide world, and never return. All of this is strictly up to me, in this I have complete freedom. But still I shall do none of these things now, but with just as free a will I shall go home to my wife." This is exactly as if water spoke to itself: "I can make high waves (yes! in the sea during a storm), I can rush down hill (yes! in the river bed), I can plunge down foaming and gushing (yes! in the waterfall), I can rise freely as a stream of water into the air (yes! in the fountain), I can, finally, boil away and disappear (yes! at a certain temperature); but I am doing none of these things now, and am voluntarily remaining quiet and clear in the reflecting pond."

Arthur Schopenhauer, *Essay on the Freedom of the Will,* 1841;
translated by Konstantine Kolenda

to do. Your 'determined freedom' is a pseudofreedom, a cheap imitation of the real thing. Real freedom means you have genuine *open choices*, that you can really *do otherwise*. And *that* freedom is not compatible with determinism. Determinism takes you down a one-way track, with no options. Maybe you like that track, just as Selina likes going to football games. In that case, it might look like real freedom. But if Selina's behavior is *determined*, and she really could not do otherwise than what she does, then she is not acting freely."

"But Ben, look, no offense, my friend, but that notion of freedom makes no sense." Sarah was intense. "I know lots of people talk about it. In fact, it's been a popular view for many centuries. Philosophers have given it a handy name: the *libertarian* theory of free will."

Ben looked doubtful. "'Libertarian'? I thought that referred to a *political* theory."

Sarah nodded. "Yeah, it does. It's confusing. The libertarian political view is that there should be an absolute minimum of government: no government food or drug inspectors, no firefighters, no government-supported schools. At most, there should be an army to protect us from foreign invasion, but nothing else. You want fire protection, you should join with your neighbors and hire a firefighter. You're free to consult an expert about what foods to buy or drugs to use, but there should be no government restrictions on either. You want to go to school, hire a teacher. But anyway, that's another issue. The libertarian *political* view has nothing to do with the libertarian view of free will. It's unfortunate and confusing that the same word is used for both, but I guess we'll have to live with it. Anyway, the view you favor—free will must involve the power to choose among genuinely open alternatives—is called a *libertarian* view, or *libertarianism*."

"Okay, that's my view. I'm a libertarian. To have genuine free will— genuine *libertarian* free will—you must be capable of *choosing and acting otherwise*. And that seems plain and reasonable to me, Sarah. Why do you say it makes no sense?"

"Look, Ben, sure, Selina could do otherwise. If she *wanted* to go to a concert or a play rather than the football game, she could: No one is forcing her to go to the game. And if circumstances were different—if she had different interests, or different desires, or if her entire future as a chemist depended on her staying in her lab and finishing an experiment instead of going to the game, or if there were a family emergency—then Selina could and would do otherwise. In those cases, there would be a different set of causes, and they would lead to different results. But that's not enough for you, is it? You want Selina to be able to do otherwise under *exactly the same circumstances*, with *exactly the same character and desires* that she now has, being *precisely the same person* she now is. With absolutely everything the same, you want her to be able to choose differently from what she chose, right?"

"Exactly right, Sarah: That would be *real* free will."

"But that's exactly what doesn't make sense, Ben. If everything could be exactly the same, no change in Selina or the conditions, but Selina's choices could go either way, then that's not choice: It's pure randomness. And random events aren't the exercise of free will. Random motions aren't under your control at all: They would be like spasms or seizures. For the act to be of her own free will, then it has to come from her—from her own values and preferences and choices, not from some random event.

"Now I see the problem!" Ben snapped his fingers. "It's the example you're starting with: Does Selina go to a football game? But that's the wrong kind of example. Football isn't that important."

"Bite your tongue, Ben." Selina feigned outrage. "Wolverine football is a matter of life and death."

"Okay, okay, bad choice of words. I didn't mean football wasn't important. You can't spend years in Ann Arbor and doubt the importance of football. I just meant that the choice of going to a football game instead of going to a concert—that doesn't really raise the question of free will. Selina chooses to go to a football game instead of going to a concert. No problem. Maybe that choice is the result of her past history, maybe even her genetic history. Maybe it's completely determined, and in that exact situation she would inevitably go to the football game. Fine. But think of a different situation: Selina wants to go to the football game, but she promised to help one of her friends with his chemistry research. She had thought that Michigan had an off week, got confused about the dates, and *promised* to help her friend with his research. Turns out the only time her friend can do the research is exactly during the time of the football game. Don't ask me why it has to be that time—that's the only time the lab is open, whatever. And no one else can substitute for Selina: After all, she's brilliant at chemistry, and she's obviously irreplaceable. Anyway, this research is very important to her friend, and Selina *promised* to help. Now, there's no question about what Selina *wants* to do, what all her conditioning—and maybe even her genetics—has shaped her to desire: She desperately *wants* to go to the football game. But likewise, she has no doubts about what she *ought* to do: She knows she should keep her promise to her friend. Again, don't worry about how she knows that; she just does, okay? In any case, Selina firmly believes that she is morally obligated to keep her promise and help her friend. Now in *this* situation, where there is *conflict* between her duty and her desire, *that* is where free will gets exercised. That's where *libertarian* free will rules. After all, that's the main place we're concerned about free will, isn't it? In situations where we have a moral choice, situations where we either exert the effort to do our duty or withhold the effort and follow our desire."

"Let me get clear on this, Ben." Sarah had questions. "This special free will you're talking about, I'm not sure I understand it. Here's our lovely Selina, facing a moral quandary. She has to choose whether to keep her promise, which she knows she *should* do; or go to the football game, which she certainly *wants* to do. So now we come to that crucial moment of choice. And Selina chooses to—drum roll, please—*keep her promise.*"

"An amazing exercise of virtue; I really wanted to go to that game."

"Yes, thank you, Selina, you paragon of virtue. But look, Ben, I'm still not clear on this. What happened when Selina made her choice? Did her strong moral character simply overwhelm her desire? Or did her desire somehow weaken? *Why* did she choose duty over desire? What caused her to make that choice?"

"Nothing *caused* her to make that choice, except the making of it. Or if you like, it was *self*-caused, or a choice that *breaks* the whole chain of causality. Don't try those philosopher's tricks on *me*, Sarah; we historians aren't as naive as you imagine. If I start describing what *caused* her choice, you'll just say, 'Oh, then it's all just part of the determined causal sequence.' But it's *not* just part of a long causal sequence: It's a *new* causal sequence, a *break* in the causal chain. This choice wholly originates in Selina's choosing."

"That's very good, Ben. You certainly are *not* philosophically naive. In fact, your view seems very close to the view proposed by a distinguished twentieth-century philosopher: C. A. Campbell. He called this sort of special choice an exercise of *contracausal free will,* and like you, he denied that it had any causal antecedents. And also like you, he insisted that such contracausal free will occurred only in special circumstances: when there was a conflict between duty and desire."

Ben nodded. "That's exactly the right view. This C. A. Campbell was obviously a very bright and insightful philosopher."

"Very modest as well," Selina added. "But I'm like Sarah: I have a hard time understanding what is really going on in this special exercise of—what do you call it?—contracausal free will. It sounds like an almost miraculous sort of power, an inexplicable exception to the causal pattern. I know, you've got all these special nonmaterial mysterious *mental* powers. Is free will one of them?"

"It *does* sound rather special," Sarah agreed. There's another distinguished twentieth-century philosopher who had a similar view." Sarah stopped for a moment until she found a passage in one of her notebooks. "Here it is. Roderick Chisholm acknowledged quite openly the miraculous nature of this free-will power. Chisholm says this:

If we are responsible, and if what I have been trying to say is true, then we have a prerogative which some would attribute only to God: each of us, when we really act, is a prime mover unmoved. In doing what we do, we cause certain events to happen, and nothing and no one, except we ourselves, causes us to cause those events to happen.[2]

Richard Taylor, another late-20th-century American philosopher, embraces a similar view, though not without misgivings. According to Taylor, each deliberative self-determining human is a 'self-moving being' who can 'cause an event to occur—namely, some act of his own—without anything else causing him to do so,' and Taylor admits that this 'conception of men and their powers . . . is strange indeed, if not positively mysterious.'[3] But I take it that miracles hold no terrors for you, right, Ben?"

"I'm not sure that I want to call it miraculous. But the power of free will is quite a remarkable power. It seems to me that it might be the main way that we are 'made in the image of God.'"

"How convenient, Ben." Selina found this very unpalatable. "Anytime you need an 'explanation,' it's easy: It's a *miracle* and thus beyond understanding. Thanks, but I think I'll stick with scientific explanations."

Sarah quickly intervened to minimize the conflict. "I know you're okay with miracles, Ben. But look, don't these disturb you just a bit? After all, as we already noted, many Christians have *denied* that the miraculous power of free will can belong to humans. Furthermore, while humans might be quite special, and God's favorite creation, attributing to humans the power to work miracles is pretty extreme, isn't it? I thought that was a power held exclusively by God."

"Not necessarily," Ben replied. "After all, there are Biblical passages suggesting that believers might also be able to perform miracles—healing the sick, for example."

"Perhaps, but my impression was that such miracles were still performed by God, at the request of the believer. But we're getting a bit off the track here. In any case, under your interpretation of free will, when someone actually performs a contracausal act of free will, her act is a sort of *miracle*, right?"

Ben was not delighted with this outcome, but he stuck to his position. "Yes. That's right. That's my position. I don't see any other possibility. And as you noted, Sarah, there are a number of philosophers—you mentioned Taylor, Chisholm, and Campbell, and I imagine there are others—who agree with me, right? Oh, and don't forget good old Pico della Mirandola!"

"Exactly right," Sarah assured him.

"Then that shows that there are a number of famous philosophers who are just as crazy as you, Ben." Selina was not impressed by contracausal free will. "If I held a view, and the only way I could justify the view was by an appeal to miracles, I think I would see that as good reason to abandon the view altogether. You see it as good reason to stuff every corner of the world with miracles."

Sarah came to Ben's defense. "It's not actually the *only* way to justify the view, Selina. Campbell would say that free will is a special *creative* act, and in order to see free will at work, you must *introspect*, you must *look inside yourself* when you are making a real choice between duty and desire. On those occasions, Campbell would say, you can see clearly that it is *up to you* whether to exert or withhold the effort of will necessary to rise to your duty. And when you sincerely introspect, you cannot doubt that the decision is yours and yours alone and that you can really choose either way. Of course, such introspection doesn't lend itself to empirical testing; but—Campbell argues—acts of free will are special *creative* acts, so they are not available for public observation. But just because the only way you can observe acts of contracausal free will is through special introspective powers, that's no reason to deny the existence of real contracausal free will. Just look, observe: You'll see it for yourself."

Ben nodded. "That makes sense to me, Sarah. For my part, when I am faced with a choice between duty and desire, there is simply no doubt that I could either make the effort of will or not."

"Have I dropped into a time warp? Has the coffee shop suddenly been transported back about seven centuries?" Selina put her hand against her head. "Are you two really sitting here talking about gaining certain knowledge of *causes* by way of *introspection*? Ah, yes, I'm *sure* that black bile causes illness, I just look inside and *know* it. I'm *certain* that demon possession is the cause of madness, I just *know* it intuitively. And I know that the real cause of my virtuous act is a special effort of will, I just *see* it through special introspective powers. Here you are, smack in the middle of this enormous research university, surrounded by physics labs and chemistry labs and psychology labs and biology labs, and you two are discussing how we might *know* about *causes* by way of intuition! If there is anything we have learned from science, it's that you can't just *intuit* causes, whether we are talking about causes of human behavior or causes of droughts or causes of disease."

Ben laughed. "Okay, okay, Selina, you made your point. Look, I agree with you. If we're talking about causes of disease or drought or psychosis, then we have to go to the laboratory. But maybe free will is different! After all, libertarians don't deny that an act of free will is a very special event. Scientific research is great; but isn't there room for a tiny special niche of free will? What's the line from Shakespeare's Hamlet: 'There are more things in heaven and earth, Horatio, than are dreamt of in your philosophy.' You have a rich scientific philosophy, Selina. But are you really so sure it encompasses *everything*?"

"Well, I'm quite sure my philosophy does *not* encompass miracles, either in heaven or on earth. 'Miracle' is just a convenient word for something that's difficult to explain. Actually, *not* such a convenient word: when we designate something a miracle—whether it's a recovery from disease or a human choice—we isolate it from scientific research and make it impossible to understand. Thanks, but I have no use for miracles. Besides, the space available for miracles gets smaller and smaller every day. A few centuries ago, the stars and planets circled the Earth due to God's miraculous powers. Then we found a Newtonian scientific explanation for the motion of the planets. But God was still the great designer; and then we found a Darwinian scientific explanation for apparent design. So the realm of miracles took refuge in the human soul, manifested through human choices. But psychologists and neuropsychologists have relentlessly probed human behavior, and we understand more and more how our environments and genes and brains cause what had appeared to be miraculous free behavior. Psychologists have explained why some people *think* longer than others, why some people have greater *fortitude*, why some *give up* with little effort while others struggle long and hard. They learned it by careful research, not by special intuitive powers; and with every advance in psychological knowledge, 'miraculous free will' retreats farther into its corner. Before long it will be squeezed out altogether."

Autonomous man is a device used to explain what we cannot explain in any other way. He has been constructed from our ignorance and as our understanding increases, the very stuff of which he is composed vanishes. . . . Only by dispossessing him can we turn to the real causes of human behavior. Only then can we turn from the inferred to the observed, from the miraculous to the natural, from the inaccessible to the manipulable.

B. F. Skinner, *Beyond Freedom and Dignity*, 1971, p. 200

"No way, Selina." Ben was ready to take his stand. "True, scientific advances may restrict the area available for free will; but science will never eliminate free will."

"Look, guys, I doubt that we'll settle the question of miracles this morning," Sarah intervened. "Actually, it's a miracle to me that an Alabama atheist and a Michigan Christian ever got together in the first place."

"No miracle at all," Selina smiled. "Pure physical laws of attraction."

"Or two souls finding their true soulmates across vast distances and against all odds," Ben countered. "Though I admit, physical attraction might have had a small part."

"Thanks, but that's really a lot more than I wanted to know. Could we get back to the question of free will?" Sarah sipped her coffee. "Set aside the question of miracles for a moment. Go back to Campbell's account of contracausal free will that Ben so eloquently described: the key choice between duty and desire; or, more precisely, the choice of whether to exert or withhold the effort of will necessary to rise to duty. It's not so much its miraculous nature that disturbs me; it's that I can't quite see how it could be *Ben's choice* at all, miraculous or not. In what sense does this special choice actually come from Ben? It can't come from his character: That, as Campbell acknowledges, is the product of his causal history. And it can't be some random event: In that case, it's not Ben's choice at all. But how can it come from *Ben* if it doesn't come from his *character*—from his desires and values and feelings? If it doesn't come from his character—from *who Ben is*—then how can it be *Ben's* choice?"

"I don't know the answer to that," Ben said, "except to say that I just *know* it's my choice. When I look inside at myself making such a choice, it's not possible to doubt that it's my own choice, and that I really could choose either way."

Existentialist Free Will

Sarah nodded. "Maybe there's another libertarian view that would help. The most famous version of that approach comes from the existentialists, particularly the work of Jean-Paul Sartre. Campbell wants to confine the special powers of free will to the choice between duty and desire, but Sartre has a much more expansive view of free will. We don't just choose between duty and desire; we *choose ourselves*, or rather we *make* ourselves by our own choices. And a radical choice it is, with *no* guidelines." Sarah was looking through her notebook again. "I copied this passage from Sartre, which states his position quite dramatically. Yeah, here it is:

> Everything is indeed permitted if God does not exist, and man is in consequence forlorn, for he cannot find anything to depend upon either within or outside himself. He discovers forthwith, that he is without excuse. For if indeed existence precedes essence, one will never be able to explain one's action by reference to a given and specific human nature, in other words, there is no determinism—man is free, man *is* freedom. Nor, on the other hand, if God does not exist, are we provided with any values or commands that could legitimize our behavior. Thus we have neither behind us, nor before us in a luminous realm of values, any means of justification or excuse. We are left alone, without excuse. That is what I mean when I say that man is condemned to be free. Condemned, because he did not create himself, yet is nevertheless at liberty, and from the moment that he is thrown into this world he is responsible for everything he does.[4]

Jean-Paul Sartre (1905–1980) was a philosopher, political activist, novelist, and dramatist. He fought in the French army in 1939 and was a prisoner of war until the fall of France in 1940. After his release, he returned to Paris, where he taught philosophy and actively participated in the French resistance movement against the Nazis. Regarding free will, he says,

> There are no *accidents* in a life; a community event which suddenly bursts forth and involves me in it does not come from the outside. If I am mobilized in a war, this war is *my* war; it is in my image and I deserve it. I deserve it first because I could always get out of it by my suicide or by desertion; these ultimate possibilities are those which must always be present for us when there is a question of envisaging a situation. For lack of getting out of it, I have *chosen* it.

Being and Nothingness, 1943

So the free will of the existentialists is a miracle-working power of self-creation. There is no essence to define you, no fixed values to guide you, no causal factors to determine you: You have the godlike power to make yourself, and whatever you do with this power, it is completely and inescapably *your* responsibility."

Selina sighed and frowned. "Sarah, how could that possibly help? We were having trouble understanding Campbell's very limited libertarian choice between duty and desire. Or at least *I* was having trouble understanding it: Ben seems to have some sort of special introspective knowledge that I lack. But anyway, how does it help to bring in Sartre's libertarian choice? Campbell's view is at least more modest. Sartre offers us libertarian free choice on steroids."

Sarah laughed. "Well, it's libertarian free choice on a larger scale. I thought it might be easier to see than Campbell's very limited free choice."

"It might be easier to see," Selina agreed, "but it's even harder to believe. However flattering it may be to think that we have godlike powers of self-creation, the idea withers in the harsh light of our actual lives. All of us are well aware—sometimes painfully, sometimes thankfully—of the many forces and influences that shaped us. You have your father's eyes, your mother's hands, your grandmother's fortitude, your grandfather's aptitude for math, your culture's deep values, tastes that were shaped by your friends and by a barrage of advertising, religious beliefs influenced by your parents and priest, prejudices ingrained by your community, knowledge gained by legions of scientists and scholars. There is pitched debate about the relative weight of 'nature' and 'nurture': That is, does our genetic legacy have a greater influence on our lives, or does our social and cultural environment carry greater weight? But there is no debate over whether these factors have a profound influence. You have arms instead of wings, and that was set by your genes, not your godlike choice; and you find cannibalism disgusting, a result of cultural shaping rather than your existential choice of your own values. If we in fact 'create ourselves' uniquely and entirely, then all the empirical studies of human society, psychology, and biology would seem to be impossible. But given the fact that we know a great deal about how our genetic, social, cultural, and family influences shape us, it is difficult to take seriously the notion that we 'make ourselves.'"

"Am I correct in thinking," Sarah smiled, "that you don't much care for Sartre's view?"

Selina replied with a toss of her head and quickly continued. "There's a second problem for the existential notion of self-creation, and it is even more severe. The problem is that it's difficult to get any real sense of what such self-creation could possibly be. Obviously, the choices you make have a profound influence on your life and your character. Your choice to go to college instead of looking for work; your choice to attend a large state university or a small private college; your choice to major in sociology, or secondary education, or civil engineering—all these choices will have a profound and resounding influence on your character, your future, your life, the person you become. So, obviously, we do, to some extent, make ourselves by our choices. And sometimes those choices are pivotal, life-changing choices: the choice to become a musician, rather than joining the wholesale foods company that was founded by your grandfather; the choice to renounce your family's religion and become a Taoist; the choice to leave your unhappy marriage. Such choices are important, and they shape our lives and our characters. But who is making those choices? In Sartre's scheme, we make these self-defining choices *before* we have values, preferences, ideals, characters. We are pure existential points, and the choices we make set the course of how the lines of our character will be drawn. But how is it possible to choose without values, convictions, preferences? It doesn't seem to be *my* choice at all, but instead just a random, capricious event. I can understand making a choice that reflects my own values and deep preferences, and I can understand making a choice to reject some of the values I have previously held (because I have changed and now favor a conflicting value scheme). But I can get no sense at all of what it would be like to make a choice *before* I have any values, direction, or preferences. Who is doing the choosing? If I completely 'make myself' through my choices, then there seems to be no one originally there to set the choices in motion. Saying that I 'make myself through my choices' and that no real self exists prior to those choices (existence precedes essence) leaves a very perplexing question: Who is this 'I' who is doing the choosing?"

"Sartre does have an answer to that question," Sarah ventured.

"I can't wait to hear it."

"Sartre distinguishes two basic categories. Things that do not have the power of free will, that lack the power of genuine self-making, are in the category of 'being-in-itself'; such objects—houses, planets, stones, and hamsters—have their own *given* natures. In contrast, we self-conscious beings who are capable of free self-making choice are in the metaphysical category of 'being-for-itself,' being that defines its *own* character."

"Oh, yeah, that solves the problem: We are 'being-for-itself'; now I understand everything." Selina shook her head. "Just because you give it a fancy name, that doesn't mean you've solved the problem. The question is still there: *How* can we make sense of 'being-for-itself'? How can we make sense of our nonexistent selves (before our chosen selves are created by our choices) making real choices? It won't help to say that these choices are made freely by people who have characters formed by their conditioning and their cultures, but the choices they make are independent of that conditioning. For that leaves us with exactly the same question: If the choice is not a product of my character and my preferences and who I am, then how can 'I' be making the choices at all? Through the power of reason, one might somehow transcend all one's conditioning history and choose the truth; even though it doesn't sound plausible to me, that sort of rationalism might satisfy some people. But that is not the radical choice that Sartre wants. To Sartre, that would be a choice dictated by an objective moral truth, and he denies the existence of any such 'luminous realm of values.' Sartre demands that my choices *create* my own values, my own truth, my own unique self. But for all the fancy categories and brave rhetoric, he never answers the fundamental question: If I am choosing myself, and there is no given self before that self-making choice, then *who* is making the choice; and how could it be *my* choice, and my responsibility? I can't buy it. In the words of Shakespeare, it's a theory that is full of sound and fury, but it signifies nothing."

"Yeah," Ben said. "Frankly, Sarah, I find Campbell more convincing than Sartre. It seems to me that the limited, but special, choice between duty and desire goes to the heart of free will; and the best way to know it is by careful introspection."

Selina frowned. "Neither of them works, Ben. Whether it's Campbell's limited libertarian free will or Sartre's megaversion, they both have the same fundamental flaws."

Free Will and Indeterminacy

Ben and Selina had reached an impasse. When that happened, the next step was sometimes a rather heated argument: Selina would accuse Ben of being soft minded and anti-scientific, and Ben would remark on Selina's dogmatic narrow-mindedness. To avoid conflict, Sarah tried to steer the conversation in a new direction. "You know, guys, there are some free-will accounts that take a very different tack. I mean, after all, there are some very serious scientists who reject determinism, right, Selina?"

"Sure. In at least some interpretations of contemporary quantum mechanics, there is fundamental indeterminacy at the level of subatomic particles. It's very exciting research and fascinating theory. And incidentally, they didn't arrive at it by means of *intuition*." Selina arched her eyebrows at Ben, looking like a beautiful feline whose claws might come out at any moment.

Sarah continued: "So if scientists can propose indeterminacy at the most basic level of the universe, might that leave room for free will?"

"No way, Sarah. In the first place, indeterminacy occurs at the subatomic level, and there is no reason to suppose that it carries over to the macroscopic realm. And there is excellent reason to suppose that it does *not*, namely, the scientific laws we have discovered that describe the regular, lawlike movements of macroscopic phenomena. Planets and people and snowflakes and comets and clouds don't just hop about randomly, whatever subatomic particles may do. And second, that sort of random movement would *not* establish free will. To the contrary, if I'm truly moving about at random, then the acts couldn't be *my* acts at all, free or otherwise."

"Selina, you *are* the reincarnation of David Hume. Of course, Hume didn't know about subatomic particles, but he made exactly the same point about randomness and free will: Random behavior would *not* be free. If you randomly moved in various ways, this would disrupt your plans and thwart your desires, and destroy any freedom you might have. But in one way, you and Hume are very different."

Selina laughed. "You mean Hume's a Scottish man who lived in the 17th century and I'm an African-American woman who lives in the 21st? Yeah, I guess there is some difference."

Sarah smiled. "No, I don't mean trivial differences like that. I mean a *serious* difference: a difference in your *philosophical* views."

"Oh, no, Sarah, that *is* serious. I thought Hume was my soul mate."

"Hey," Ben objected, "I thought I was your soul mate."

"Afraid not." Selina took his hand. "It's Hume. You'll have to settle for being my main squeeze. But Sarah, what philosophical difference is there between Hume and me?"

Hume's Compatibilism

"Okay, you both believe in determinism, and you both reject miracles, and you both favor a strict scientific approach to the world—oh, and you're both serious party animals besides. Or at least you are, and Hume was. But even though Hume was strictly a determinist, he also believed in free will."

"Sarah, you've shattered my world. Isn't that just like a man? You think you know them, they go off and do something absolutely crazy—like believe in free will. How could he do that?"

"Hume didn't believe in the sort of free will that we were discussing before: the sort of contracausal free will that Campbell—and our beloved Ben—believes in. Obviously not, since that sort of free will makes a *break* in determinism, and Hume was a thorough determinist, with no room for exceptions. Instead, Hume interpreted freedom very differently. You remember when we were talking about you going to a Michigan football game? We sort of got sidetracked and plunged into libertarian contra-causal free will. You go to a football game because you want to do so. Then you're acting freely, right? Given your conditioning history and genetic makeup and environmental influences, it was *determined* that you would go to the game, but you still go because you want to go, of your *own* choice. Your own *determined* choice, sure, but still it's *your* choice, it comes from you, you aren't coerced: You act *freely*."

"That still doesn't sound like freedom to me, Sarah," said Ben.

"I know, Ben, I know; but according to Hume, that's the only kind of freedom that makes any sense, and Hume considered it quite enough freedom. It's also a freedom that does *not* conflict with determinism, a freedom we can enjoy even if determinism is true. As Hume put it, in a philosophically famous line, the liberty or freedom to do *as we wish* 'is universally allowed to belong to everyone who is not a prisoner and in chains.' Freedom is acting as *you want* to act, and the *absence* of freedom is when your wishes are thwarted: when you are in chains, for example. Of course Selina doesn't *make herself*—she doesn't preselect her own wishes and desires. That would be nonsense. As Selina said before, *who* would be doing the selecting of your desires and character? It certainly would not be *you* making the decisions about who *you* will be. But she still acts from her own desires and choices, with no outside coercion, and so acts freely."

"Hmmm, Sarah." Selina was considering. "Maybe I could buy into Hume's view of freedom after all. I go to the football game because I want to, I choose to go, no one forces me, I'm following my own wishes. Okay, that's what I call acting freely. But of course, as Hume and I and all *reasonable* people agree"—Selina raised her eyebrows at Ben—"my wishes and choices and desires are all the product of my determined history. So determinism is true, and I still act freely. Okay, makes sense to me. *That* kind of freedom I can buy; in fact, that sort of freedom is a wonderful thing. It's that crazy contracausal, miracle-working, self-creating notion of free will that I reject: *That* notion of free will is contrary to determinism, contrary to reason, and contrary to everything that's good and decent!"

"And that notion of free will," responded Ben, quite undaunted, "is the only notion of free will worthy of the name. Your 'compatibilist' free will is the freedom of a puppet pulled by determinist strings."

Sarah laughed. "I don't think we're going to settle this question today. Maybe tomorrow." She gulped her coffee as she gathered her books. "I gotta get to class. Oh, Selina, Sam and I are cooking dinner tonight at his apartment. Then we're going to study together for our Renaissance philosophy exam. I'll probably be late. Don't wait up for me."

Selina winked. "Yeah, that Renaissance philosophy must be a fascinating subject. This will be the third time this week you and Sam have studied Renaissance philosophy all night."

Sarah called back as she walked toward the door. "Don't go counting up my all night study sessions, Selina; you just be here tomorrow morning. We aren't even close to being done with free will."

READINGS

Lorenzo Valla (1405?–57) was one of the Italian Humanist scholars who favored the teachings of the early Church Fathers (such as Augustine) over the scholasticism of Aquinas. Born in Rome, he lived and worked in many Italian cities, spending the longest period in Naples, living as a distinguished scholar in the court of King Alfonso of Aragon. His dialogue on free will had great influence over the discussion of the subject in later centuries, and it was admired by Erasmus, Luther, Calvin, and Leibniz, all of whom wrote extensively on the question of free will. In the dialogue, Valla's view is represented by "Lor," for Lorenzo. In the course of the dialogue, Valla deals first with the problem of God's foreknowledge and answers that problem to Antonio's satisfaction. But then the discussion turns to God's omnipotence, and that (according to Valla) raises problems that he cannot answer and that (Valla suggests) are unanswerable: To demand an answer to that problem is to demand a dinner (in Valla's playful dialogue) that no mortal can provide.

Dialogue on Free Will

Lor. What do you ask me to explain to you?

Ant. Whether the foreknowledge of God stands in the way of free will and whether Boethius has correctly argued this question.

Lor. I shall attend to Boethius later; but if I satisfy you in this matter, I want you to make a promise.

Ant. What sort of a promise?

Lor. That if I serve you splendidly in this luncheon, you will not want to be entertained again for dinner.

Ant. What do you mean as lunch for me and what as dinner, for I do not understand?

Lor. That contented after discussing this one question, you will not ask for another afterward.

Ant. You say another? As if this one will not be sufficient and more! I freely promise that I will ask no dinner from you.

Lor. Go ahead then and get into the very heart of the question.

Ant. You advise well. If God foresees the future, it cannot happen otherwise than He foresaw. For example, if He sees that Judas will be a traitor, it is impossible for him not to become a traitor, that is, it is necessary for Judas to betray, unless—which should be far from us—we assume God to lack providence. Since He has providence, one must undoubtedly believe that mankind does not have free will in its own power; and I do not speak particularly of evil men, for as it is necessary for these to do evil, so conversely it is necessary for the good to do good, provided those are still to be called good or evil who lack will or that their actions are to be considered right or wrong which are necessary and forced. And what now follows you yourself see: for God either to praise this one for justice or accuse that of injustice and to reward the one and punish the other, to speak freely, seems to be the opposite of justice, since the actions of men follow by necessity the foreknowledge of God. We should therefore abandon religion, piety, sanctity, ceremonies, sacrifices; we may expect nothing from Him, employ no prayers, not call upon his mercy at all, neglect to improve our mind, and, finally, do nothing except what pleases us, since our justice or injustice is foreknown by God. Consequently, it seems that either He does not foresee the future if we are endowed with will or He is not just if we lack free will. There you have what makes me inclined to doubt in this matter.

Lor. You have indeed not only pushed into the middle of the question but have even more widely extended it. You say God foresaw that Judas would be a traitor, but did He on that account induce him to betrayal? I do not see that, for, although God may foreknow some future act to be done by man, this act is not done by necessity because he may do it willingly. Moreover, what is voluntary cannot be necessary.

Ant. Do not expect me to give in to you so easily or to flee without sweat and blood.

Lor. Good luck to you; let us contend closely in hand-to-hand and foot-to-foot conflict. Let the decision be by sword, not spear.

Ant. You say Judas acted voluntarily and on that account not by necessity. Indeed, it would be most shameless to deny that he did it voluntarily. What do I say to that? Certainly this act of will was necessary since God foreknew it; moreover, since it was foreknown by Him, it was necessary for Judas to will and do it lest he should make the foreknowledge in any way false.

Lor. Still I do not see why the necessity for our volitions and actions should derive from God's foreknowledge. For, if foreknowing something *will be* makes it come about, surely knowing something *is* just as easily makes the same thing *be*. Certainly, if I know your genius, you would not say that something *is* because you *know* it is. For example, you know it is now day; because you know it is, is it on that account also day? Or, conversely, because it is day, do you for that reason know it is day?

Ant. Indeed, continue.

Lor. The same reasoning applies to the past. I know it was night eight hours ago, but my knowledge does not make [it] that it was night; rather I know it was night because it was night. Again, that I may come closer to the point, I know in advance that after eight hours it will be night; and will it be on that account? Not at all, but because it will be night, for that reason I foreknew it; now if the foreknowledge of man is not the cause of something occurring, neither is the foreknowledge of God.

Ant. Believe me, that comparison deceives us; it is one thing to know the present and past, another to know the future. For when I know something *is*, it cannot be changed, as that day, which now is, cannot be made not to be. Also the past does not differ from the present, for we did not notice the day when it was past but while it was occurring as the present; I learned it was night not then when it *had passed* but when it was. And so for these times I concede that something *was*, or *is*, not because I know it but that I know it because it *is* or *was*. But a different reasoning applies to the future because it is subject to change. It cannot be known for certain because it is uncertain. And, in order that we may not defraud God of foreknowledge, we must admit that the future is certain and on that account necessary; this is what deprives us of free will. Nor can you say what you said just now that the future is not preordained merely because God foresees it but that God foresees it because the future is preordained; you thus wound God by implying that it is necessary for him to foreknow the future.

Lor. You have come well armed and weaponed for the fight, but let us see who is deceived, you or I. First, however, I would meet this latter point where you say that, if God foresees the future because it is to be, He labors under the necessity to foresee the future. Indeed this should not be attributed to necessity but to nature, to will, to power, unless it is an attribute of weakness perchance that God cannot sin, cannot die, cannot give up His wisdom rather than an attribute of power and of divinity. Thus, when we said He is unable to escape foresight, which is a form of wisdom, we inflicted no wound on Him but did Him honor. So I shall not be afraid to say that God is unable to escape foreseeing what is to be. I come now to your first point: that the present and the past are unalterable and therefore knowable; that the future is alterable and therefore not capable of being foreknown. I ask if it can be changed that at eight hours from now night will arrive, that after summer there will be autumn, after autumn winter, after winter spring, after spring summer?

Ant. Those are natural phenomena always running the same course; I speak, however, of matters of the will.

Lor. What do you say of chance things? Can they be foreseen by God without necessity being imputed to them? Perchance today it may rain or I may find a treasure, would you concede this could be foreknown without any necessity?

Ant. Why should I not concede it? Do you believe I think so ill of God?

Lor. Make sure that you do not think ill when you say you think well. For if you concede in this case, why should you doubt in matters of the will, for both classes of events can happen in two different ways?

Ant. The matter is not that way. For these chance things follow a certain nature of their own, and for this reason doctors, sailors, and farmers are accustomed to foresee much, since they reckon consequences out of antecedents, which cannot happen in affairs of the will. Predict which foot I will move first, and, whichever you have said, you will lie, since I shall move the other.

Lor. I ask you, who was ever found so clever as this Glarea? He thinks he can impose on God like the man in Aesop who consulted Apollo whether the sparrow he held under his coat was dead for the sake of deceiving him. For you have not told me to predict, but God. Indeed, I have not the ability to predict whether there will be a good vintage, such as you ascribe to farmers. But by saying and also believing that God does not know which foot you will move first, you involve yourself in great sin.

Ant. Do you think I affirm something rather than raise the question for the sake of the argument? Again you seem to seek excuses by your speech and, giving ground, decline to fight.

Lor. As if I fought for the sake of victory rather than truth! Witness how I am driven from my ground; do you grant that God now knows your will even better than you yourself do?

Ant. I indeed grant it.

Lor. It is also necessary that you grant that you will do nothing other than the will decides.

Ant. Of course.

Lor. How then can He not know the action if He knows the will which is the source of the action?

Ant. Not at all, for I myself do not know what I shall do even though I know what I have in my will. For I do not will to move this foot or that foot, in any case, but the other than He will have announced. And so, if you compare me with God, just as I do not know what I will do, so He does not know.

Lor. What difficulty is there in meeting this sophism of yours? He knows that you are prepared to reply otherwise than He will say and that you will move the left first if the right is named by Him; whichever one He should say therefore, it is certain to Him what will happen.

Ant. Yet which of the two will He say?

Lor. Do you speak of God? Let me know your will and I will announce what will happen.

Ant. Go ahead, you try to know my will.

Lor. You will move the right one first.

Ant. Behold, the left one.

Lor. How have you shown my foreknowledge to be false, since I knew you would move the left one?

Ant. But why did you say other than you thought?

Lor. In order to deceive you by your own arts and to deceive the man willing to deceive.

Ant. But God Himself would not lie nor deceive in replying, nor did you do rightly in replying for Another as He would not reply.

Lor. Did you not tell me to "predict"? Therefore, I should not speak for God but for myself whom you asked.

Ant. How changeable you are. A little while ago you were saying I told God to "predict," not you; now on the contrary you say the opposite. Let God reply which foot I will move first.

Lor. How ridiculous, as if He would answer you!

Ant. What? Can He not indeed reply truly if He wishes?

Lor. Rather He can lie who is the Truth itself.

Ant. What would He reply then?

Lor. Certainly what you will do, but, you not hearing, He might say to me, He might say to one of those other people, He might say it to many; and, when He has done that, do you not think He will truly have predicted?

Ant. Yea, indeed, He will have truly predicted, but what would you think if He predicted it to me?

Lor. Believe me, you who thus lie in wait to deceive God, if you should hear or certainly know what He said you would do, either out of love or out of fear you would hasten to do what you knew was predicted by

Him. But let us skip this which has nothing to do with foreknowledge. For it is one thing to foreknow and another to predict the future. Say whatever you have in mind about foreknowledge, but leave prediction out of it.

Ant. So be it, for the things that I have said were spoken not so much for me as against you. I return from this digression to where I said it was necessary for Judas to betray, unless we entirely annul providence, because God foresaw it would be thus. So if it was possible for something to happen otherwise than it was foreseen, providence is destroyed; but if it is impossible, free will is destroyed, a thing no less unworthy to God than if we should cancel His providence. I, in what concerns me, would prefer Him to be less wise rather than less good. The latter would injure mankind; the other would not.

Lor. I praise your modesty and wisdom. When you are not able to win, you do not fight on stubbornly but give in and apply yourself to another defense, which seems to be the argument of what you set forth a while back. In reply to this argument, I deny that foreknowledge can be deceived as the consequence of the possibility that something might turn out otherwise than as it has been foreseen. For what prevents it from also being true that something can turn out otherwise than it will immediately happen? Something that can happen and something that will happen are very different. I can be a husband, I can be a soldier or a priest, but will I right away? Not at all. Though I can do otherwise than will happen, nevertheless I shall not do otherwise; and it was in Judas' power not to sin even though it was foreseen that he would, but he preferred to sin, which it was foreseen would happen. Thus foreknowledge is valid and free will abides. This will make a choice between two alternatives, for to do both is not possible, and He foreknows by His own light which will be chosen. . . .

Ant. I will not object further, nor, since I smashed all my weapons, will I fight with tooth and nail as is said; but, if there is any other point through which you can explain it to me more amply and plainly persuade, I wish to hear it.

Lor. You covet the praise of wisdom and modesty again, since you are your true self. And so I will do as you ask because I was doing it anyway of my own will. For what has been said so far is not what I had decided to say but what need of defense itself demanded. Now attend to what persuades me and perhaps it will even persuade you that foreknowledge is no impediment to free will. However, would you prefer me to touch on this subject briefly or to explain it more clearly at greater length?

Ant. It always seems to me, indeed, that those who speak lucidly speak most briefly, while those who speak obscurely, though in the fewest words, are always more lengthy. Besides, fulness of expression has itself a certain appropriateness and aptness for persuasion. Wherefore, since I asked you from the start that this matter be more lucidly stated by you, you should not doubt my wishes; neverthelesss, do whatever is more agreeable to you. For I would never put my judgment ahead of yours.

Lor. Indeed, it is of importance to me to follow your wish, and whatever you think more convenient I do also. Apollo, who was so greatly celebrated among the Greeks, either through his own nature or by concession of the other gods, had foresight and knowledge of all future things, not only those which pertained to men but to the gods as well; thus, if we may believe the tradition, and nothing prevents our accepting it just for the moment, Apollo rendered true and certain prophecies about those consulting him. Sextus Tarquinius consulted him as to what would happen to himself. We may pretend that he replied, as was customary, in verse as follows:

> *An exile and a pauper you will fall,*
> *Killed by the angry city.*

To this Sextus: "What are you saying, Apollo? Have I deserved thus of you that you announce me a fate so cruel, that you assign me such a sad condition of death? Repeal your response, I implore you, predict happier things; you should be better disposed toward me who so royally endowed you." In reply Apollo: "Your gifts, O youth, certainly are agreeable and acceptable to me; in return for which I have rendered a miserable and sad prophecy, I wish it were happier, but it is not in my power to do this. I know the fates, I do not decide them; I am able to announce Fortune, not change her; I am the index of destinies, not the arbiter; I would reveal better things if better things awaited. Certainly this is not my fault who cannot prevent even my own misfortune that I foresee. Accuse Jupiter, if you will, accuse the fates, accuse Fortune whence the course of events descends. The power and decision over the fates are seated with them; with me, mere foreknowledge and prediction. You earnestly besought an oracle; I gave it. You inquired after the truth; I was unable to tell a lie. You have come to my temple from a far-distant region, and I ought not to send you away without a reply. Two things are most alien to me: falsehood and silence." Could Sextus justly reply to this speech: "Yea, indeed, it is your fault, Apollo, who foresee my fate with your wisdom, for, unless you had foreseen it, this would not be about to happen to me"?

Ant. Not only would he speak unjustly but he should never reply thus.

Lor. How then?

Ant. Why do you not say?

Lor. Should he not reply in this way: "Indeed, I give thanks to you, holy Apollo, who have neither deceived me with falsehood nor spurned me in silence. But this also I ask you to tell me: Why is Jupiter so unjust, so cruel, to me that he should assign such a sad fate to me, an undeserving, innocent worshiper of the gods"?

Ant. Certainly I would reply in this way if I were Sextus, but what did Apollo reply to him?

Lor. "You call yourself undeserving and innocent, Sextus? You may be sure that the crimes that you will commit, the adulteries, betrayals, perjuries, the almost hereditary arrogance are to blame." Would Sextus then reply this way: "The fault for my crimes must rather be assigned to you, for it is necessary for me, who you foreknow will sin, to sin"?

Ant. Sextus would be mad as well as unjust if he replied in that way.

Lor. Do you have anything that you might say on his behalf?

Ant. Absolutely nothing.

Lor. If therefore Sextus had nothing which could be argued against the foreknowledge of Apollo, certainly Judas had nothing either which might accuse the foreknowledge of God. And, if that is so, certainly the question by which you said you were confused and disturbed is answered.

Ant. It is indeed answered and, what I scarcely dared to hope, fully solved, for the sake of which I both give you thanks and have, I would say, an almost immortal gift. What Boethius was unable to show me you have shown.

Lor. And now I shall try to say something about him because I know you expect it and I promised to do it.

Ant. What are you saying about Boethius? It will be agreeable and pleasant to me.

Lor. We may follow the line of the fable we started. You think Sextus had nothing to reply to Apollo; I ask you what would you say to a king who refused to offer an office or position to you because he says you would commit a capital offense in that function.

Ant. "I would swear to you, King, by your most strong and faithful right hand that I will commit no crime in this magistracy."

Lor. Likewise perhaps Sextus would say to Apollo, "I swear to you, Apollo, that I will not commit what you say."

Ant. What does Apollo answer?

Lor. Certainly not in the way the king would, for the king has not discovered what the future is, as God has. Apollo therefore might say: "Am I a liar, Sextus? Do I not know what the future is? Do I speak for the sake of warning you, or do I render a prophecy? I say to you again, you will be an adulterer, you will be a traitor, you will be a perjurer, you will be arrogant and evil."

Ant. A worthy speech by Apollo! What was Sextus able to muster against it?

Lor. Does it not occur to you what he could argue in his own defense? Is he with a meek mind to suffer himself to be condemned?

Ant. Why not, if he is guilty?

Lor. He is not guilty but is predicted to be so in the future. Indeed, I believe that if Apollo announced this to you, you would flee to prayer, and pray not to Apollo but to Jupiter that he would give you a better mind and change the fates.

Ant. That I would do, but I would be making Apollo a liar.

Lor. You speak rightly, because if Sextus cannot make him a liar, he employs prayers in vain. What should he do? Would he not be offended, angered, burst forth in complaints? "Thus, Apollo, am I unable to restrain myself from offenses, am I unable to accept virtue, do I not avail to reform the mind from wickedness, am I not endowed with free will?"

Ant. Sextus speaks bravely and truly and justly. What does the god reply?

Lor. "That is the way things are, Sextus. Jupiter as he created the wolf fierce, the hare timid, the lion brave, the ass stupid, the dog savage, the sheep mild, so he fashioned some men hard of heart, others soft, he generated one given to evil, the other to virtue, and, further, he gave a capacity for reform to one and made another incorrigible. To you, indeed, he assigned an evil soul with no resource for reform. And so both you, for your inborn character, will do evil, and Jupiter, on account of your actions and their evil effects, will punish sternly, and thus he has sworn by the Stygian swamp it will be."

Ant. At the same time that Apollo neatly excuses himself, he accuses Jupiter the more, for I am more favorable to Sextus than Jupiter. And so he might best protest justly as follows: "And why is it my crime rather than Jupiter's? When I am not allowed to do anything except evil, why does Jupiter condemn me for his own crime? Why does he punish me without guilt? Whatever I do, I do not do it by free will but of necessity. Am I able to oppose his will and power?"

Lor. This is what I wished to say for my proof. For this is the point of my fable, that, although the wisdom of God cannot be separated from His power and will, I may by this device of Apollo and Jupiter separate them. What cannot be achieved with one god may be achieved with two, each having his own proper nature—the one for creating the character of men, the other for knowing—that it may appear that providence is not the cause of necessity but that all this whatever it is must be referred to the will of God.

Ant. See, you have thrown me back into the same pit whence you dug me; this doubt is like that which I set forth about Judas. There necessity was ascribed to the foreknowledge of God, here to the will; what difference is it how you annul free will? That it is destroyed by foreknowledge, you indeed deny, but you say it is by divine will, by which the question goes back to the same place.

Lor. Do I say that free will is annulled by the will of God?

Ant. Is it not implied unless you solve the ambiguity?

Lor. Pray who will solve it for you?

Ant. Indeed I will not let you go until you solve it.

Lor. But that is to violate the agreement, and not content with luncheon you demand dinner also.

Ant. Is it thus you have defrauded me and coerced me through a deceitful promise? Promises in which deceit enters do not stand, nor do I think I have received luncheon from you if I am forced to vomit up whatever I have eaten, or, to speak more lightly, you send me away no less hungry than you received me.

Lor. Believe me, I didn't want to make you promise in such a way that I would cheat you, for what advantage would there have been to me, since I not even have been allowed to give you luncheon? Since you received it willingly and since you gave me thanks for it, you are ungrateful if you say you were forced by me to vomit it or that I send you away as hungry as you came. That is asking for dinner, not luncheon, and wanting to find fault with luncheon and to demand that I spread before you ambrosia and nectar, the food of the gods, not men. I have put my fish and fowl from my preserves and wine from a suburban hill before you. You should demand ambrosia and nectar from Apollo and Jupiter themselves.

Ant. Are not ambrosia and what you call nectar poetic and fabulous things? Let us leave this emptiness to the empty and fictitious gods, Jupiter and Apollo. You have given luncheon from these preserves and cellars; I ask dinner from the same.

Lor. Do you think I am so rude that I would send away a friend coming to me for dinner? But since I saw how this question was likely to end, I consulted my own interests back there and compelled you to promise that afterward you would not exact from me anything besides the one thing that was asked. Therefore, I proceed with you not so much from right as from equity. Perhaps you will obtain this dinner from others which, if friendship can be trusted, is not entirely in my possession.

Ant. I will give you no further trouble lest I seem ungrateful to a benefactor and distrustful of a friend; but, still, from whom do you suggest I seek this out?

Lor. If I were able, I would not send you away for dinner, but I would go
there for dinner together with you.

Ant. Do you suppose no one has these divine foods, as you call them?

Lor. Why should I not think so. Have you not read the words of Paul
about the two children of Rebecca and Isaac? There he said:

> For the children being not yet born, neither having done any good or evil,
> that the purpose of God according to election might stand, not of works, but
> of him that calleth; it was said unto her, The elder shall serve the younger.
> As it is written, Jacob have I loved, but Esau have I hated. What shall we
> say then? Is there unrighteousness with God? God forbid. For he saith to
> Moses, I will have mercy on whom I will have mercy, and I will have com-
> passion on whom I will have compassion. So then it is not of him that wil-
> leth, nor of him that runneth, but of God that showeth mercy. For the
> scripture saith unto Pharaoh, Even for this same purpose have I raised thee
> up, that I might show my power in thee, and that my name might be
> declared throughout all the earth. Therefore hath he mercy on whom he will
> have mercy, and whom he will he hardeneth. Thou wilt say then unto me,
> Why doth he yet find fault? For who hath resisted his will? Nay but, O man,
> who art thou that repliest against God? Shall the thing formed say to him
> that formed it, Why hast thou made me thus? Hath not the potter power
> over the clay, of the same lump to make one vessel unto honor, and another
> unto dishonor? [Rom. 9:11–21 (King James Version)].

And a little later, as if the excessive splendor of the wisdom of God
darkened his eyes, he proclaimed (Rom. 11:33): "O the depth of the
riches both of the wisdom and knowledge of God! how unsearchable
are his judgments, and his ways past finding out!" For if that vessel of
election who, snatched up even to the third heaven, heard the secret
words which man is not permitted to speak, nevertheless was unable to
say or even to perceive them, who at length would hope that he could
search out and comprehend? Carefully notice, however, free will is not
said to be impeded in the same way by the will of God as by foreknowledge, for the will has an antecedent cause which is seated in the wisdom of God. Indeed the most worthy reason may be adduced as to why
He hardens this one and shows mercy to that, namely, that He is most
wise and good. For it is impious to believe otherwise than that, being
absolutely good, He does rightly.

*David Hume's "Of Liberty and Necessity" is the classic Enlightenment statement of
compatibilist free will. Hume argues first for determinism (or, more precisely, Hume
argues that we all believe in determinism (necessity)) and then attempts to show that*

free will and moral responsibility are not merely compatible *with determinism, but
actually* require *determinism: Without determinism, there is no free will and no moral
responsibility.*

Of Liberty and Necessity

Part I

It might reasonably be expected, in questions which have been canvassed
and disputed with great eagerness since the first origin of science and philosophy, that the meaning of all the terms, at least, should have been
agreed upon among the disputants, and our inquiries, in the course of two
thousand years, been able to pass from words to the true and real subject of
the controversy. For how easy may it seem to give exact definitions of the
terms employed in reasoning, and make these definitions, not the mere
sound of words, the object of future scrutiny and examination? But if we
consider the matter more narrowly, we shall be apt to draw a quite opposite conclusion. From this circumstance alone, that a controversy has been
long kept on foot and remains still undecided, we may presume that there
is some ambiguity in the expression, and that the disputants affix different
ideas to the terms employed in the controversy. For as the faculties of the
mind are supposed to be naturally alike in every individual—otherwise
nothing could be more fruitless than to reason or dispute together—it were
impossible, if men affix the same ideas to their terms, that they could so
long form different opinions of the same subject, especially when they
communicate their views and each party turn themselves on all sides in
search of arguments which may give them the victory over their antagonists. It is true, if men attempt the discussion of questions which lie entirely
beyond the reach of human capacity, such as those concerning the origin of
worlds or the economy of the intellectual system or region of spirits, they
may long beat the air in their fruitless contests and never arrive at any
determinate conclusion. But if the question regard any subject of common
life and experience, nothing, one would think, could preserve the dispute
so long undecided, but some ambiguous expressions which keep the antagonists still at a distance and hinder them from grappling with each other.

   This has been the case in the long-disputed question concerning liberty and necessity, and to so remarkable a degree that, if I be not much
mistaken, we shall find that all mankind, both learned and ignorant, have
always been of the same opinion with regard to this subject, and that a
few intelligible definitions would immediately have put an end to the
whole controversy. I own that this dispute has been so much canvassed on

all hands, and has led philosophers into such a labyrinth of obscure sophistry, that it is no wonder if a sensible reader indulge his ease so far as to turn a deaf ear to the proposal of such a question from which he can expect neither instruction nor entertainment. But the state of the argument here proposed may, perhaps, serve to renew his attention, as it has more novelty, promises at least some decision of the controversy, and will not much disturb his ease by any intricate or obscure reasoning.

I hope, therefore, to make it appear that all men have ever agreed in the doctrine both of necessity and of liberty, according to any reasonable sense which can be put on these terms, and that the whole controversy has hitherto turned merely upon words. We shall begin with examining the doctrine of necessity.

It is universally allowed that matter, in all its operations, is actuated by a necessary force, and that every natural effect is so precisely determined by the energy of its cause that no other effect, in such particular circumstances, could possibly have resulted from it. The degree and direction of every motion is, by the laws of nature, prescribed with such exactness that a living creature may as soon arise from the shock of two bodies, as motion, in any other degree or direction than what is actually produced by it. Would we, therefore, form a just and precise idea of *necessity*, we must consider whence that idea arises when we apply it to the operation of bodies.

It seems evident that, if all the scenes of nature were continually shifted in such a manner that no two events bore any resemblance to each other, but every object was entirely new, without any similitude to whatever had been seen before, we should never, in that case, have attained the least idea of necessity or of a connection among these objects. We might say, upon such a supposition, that one object or event has followed another, not that one was produced by the other. The relation of cause and effect must be utterly unknown to mankind. Inference and reasoning concerning the operations of nature would, from that moment, be at an end; and the memory and senses remain the only canals by which the knowledge of any real existence could possibly have access to the mind. Our idea, therefore, of necessity and causation arises entirely from the uniformity observable in the operations of nature, where similar objects are constantly conjoined together, and the mind is determined by custom to infer the one from the appearance of the other. These two circumstances form the whole of that necessity which we ascribe to matter. Beyond the constant *conjunction* of similar objects and the consequent *inference* from one to the other, we have no notion of any necessity of connection.

If it appears, therefore, that all mankind have ever allowed, without any doubt or hesitation, that these two circumstances take place in the voluntary actions of men and in the operations of mind, it must follow that all mankind have ever agreed in the doctrine of necessity, and that they have hither-to disputed merely for not understanding each other.

As to the first circumstance, the constant and regular conjunction of similar events, we may possibly satisfy ourselves by the following considerations. It is universally acknowledged that there is a great uniformity among the actions of men, in all nations and ages, and that human nature remains still the same in its principles and operations. The same motives always produce the same actions; the same events follow from the same causes. Ambition, avarice, self-love, vanity, friendship, generosity, public spirit—these passions, mixed in various degrees and distributed through society, have been, from the beginning of the world, and still are, the source of all the actions and enterprises which have ever been observed among mankind. Would you know the sentiments, inclinations, and course of life of the Greeks and Romans? Study well the temper and actions of the French and English: you cannot be much mistaken in transferring to the former *most* of the observations which you have made with regard to the latter. Mankind are so much the same, in all times and places, that history informs us of nothing new or strange in this particular. Its chief use is only to discover the constant and universal principles of human nature by showing men in all varieties of circumstances and situations, and furnishing us with materials from which we may form our observations and become acquainted with the regular springs of human action and behavior. These records of wars, intrigues, factions, and revolutions are so many collections of experiments by which the politician or moral philosopher fixes the principles of his science, in the same manner as the physician or natural philosopher becomes acquainted with the nature of plants, minerals, and other external objects, by the experiments which he forms concerning them. Nor are the earth, water, and other elements examined by Aristotle and Hippocrates more like to those which at present lie under our observation than the men described by Polybius and Tacitus are to those who now govern the world.

Should a traveler, returning from a far country, bring us an account of men wholly different from any with whom we were ever acquainted, men who were entirely divested of avarice, ambition, or revenge, who knew no pleasure but friendship, generosity, and public spirit, we should immediately, from these circumstances, detect the falsehood and prove him a liar with the same certainty as if he had stuffed his narration with stories of centaurs and dragons, miracles and prodigies. And if we would explode any forgery in history, we cannot make use of a more convincing argument than to prove that the actions ascribed to any person are directly contrary to the course of nature, and that no human motives, in such circumstances, could ever induce him to such a conduct. The veracity of Quintus Curtius is as much to be suspected when he describes the supernatural courage of Alexander by which he was hurried on singly to attack multitudes, as when he describes his supernatural force and activity by which he was able to resist them. So readily and universally do we acknowledge a uniformity in human motives and actions as well as in the operations of body.

Hence, likewise, the benefit of that experience acquired by long life and a variety of business and company, in order to instruct us in the principles of human nature and regulate our future conduct as well as speculation. By means of this guide we mount up to the knowledge of men's inclinations and motives from their actions, expressions, and even gestures, and again descend to the interpretation of their actions from our knowledge of their motives and inclinations. The general observations, treasured up by a course of experience, give us the clue of human nature and teach us to unravel all its intricacies. Pretexts and appearances no longer deceive us. Public declarations pass for the specious coloring of a cause. And though virtue and honor be allowed their proper weight and authority, that perfect disinterestedness, so often pretended to, is never expected in multitudes and parties, seldom in their leaders, and scarcely even in individuals of any rank or station. But were there no uniformity in human actions, and were every experiment which we could form of this kind irregular and anomalous, it were impossible to collect any general observations concerning mankind, and no experience, however accurately digested by reflection, would ever serve to any purpose. Why is the aged husbandman more skillful in his calling than the young beginner, but because there is a certain uniformity in the operation of the sun, rain, and earth toward the production of vegetables, and experience teaches the old practitioner the rules by which this operation is governed and directed?

We must not, however, expect that this uniformity of human actions should be carried to such a length as that all men, in the same circumstances, will always act precisely in the same manner, without making any allowance for the diversity of characters, prejudices, and opinions. Such a uniformity, in every particular, is found in no part of nature. On the contrary, from observing the variety of conduct in different men we are enabled to form a greater variety of maxims which still suppose a degree of uniformity and regularity.

Are the manners of men different in different ages and countries? We learn thence the great force of custom and education, which mold the human mind from its infancy and form it into a fixed and established character. Is the behavior and conduct of the one sex very unlike that of the other? It is thence we become acquainted with the different characters which nature has impressed upon the sexes, and which she preserves with constancy and regularity. Are the actions of the same person much diversified in the different periods of his life from infancy to old age? This affords room for many general observations concerning the gradual change of our sentiments and inclinations, and the different maxims which prevail in the different ages of human creatures. Even the characters which are peculiar to each individual have a uniformity in their influence, otherwise our acquaintance with the persons, and our observations of their conduct, could never teach us their dispositions or serve to direct our behavior with regard to them.

I grant it possible to find some actions which seem to have no regular connection with any known motives and are exceptions to all the measures of conduct which have ever been established for the government of men. But if we could willingly know what judgment should be formed of such irregular and extraordinary actions, we may consider the sentiments commonly entertained with regard to those irregular events which appear in the course of nature and the operations of external objects. All causes are not conjoined to their usual effects with like uniformity. An artificer who handles only dead matter may be disappointed of his aim, as well as the politician who directs the conduct of sensible and intelligent agents.

The vulgar, who take things according to their first appearance, attribute the uncertainty of events to such an uncertainty in the causes as makes the latter often fail of their usual influence, though they meet with no impediment in their operation. But philosophers, observing that almost in every part of nature there is contained a vast variety of springs and principles which are hid by reason of their minuteness or remoteness, find that it is at least possible the contrariety of events may not proceed from any contingency in the cause but from the secret operation of contrary causes. This possibility is converted into certainty by further observation, when they remark that, upon an exact scrutiny, a contrariety of effects always betrays a contrariety of causes and proceeds from their mutual opposition. A peasant can give no better reason for the stopping of any clock or watch than to say that it does not commonly go right. But an artist easily perceives that the same force in the spring or pendulum has always the same influence on the wheels, but fails of its usual effect perhaps by reason of a grain of dust which puts a stop to the whole movement. From the observation of several parallel instances philosophers form a maxim that the connection between all causes and effects is equally necessary, and that its seeming uncertainty in some instances proceeds from the secret opposition of contrary causes.

Thus, for instance, in the human body, when the usual symptoms of health or sickness disappoint our expectation, when medicines operate not with their wonted powers, when irregular events follow from any particular cause, the philosopher and physician are not surprised at the matter, nor are ever tempted to deny, in general, the necessity and uniformity of those principles by which the animal economy is conducted. They know that a human body is a mighty complicated machine, that many secret powers lurk in it which are altogether beyond our comprehension, that to us it must often appear very uncertain in its operations, and that, therefore, the irregular events which outwardly discover themselves can be no proof that the laws of nature are not observed with the greatest regularity in its internal operations and government.

The philosopher, if he be consistent, must apply the same reasonings to the actions and volitions of intelligent agents. The most irregular and unexpected resolutions of men may frequently be accounted for by those who know every particular circumstance of their character and situation. A person of an obliging disposition gives a peevish answer; but he has the toothache, or has not dined. A stupid fellow discovers an uncommon alacrity in his carriage; but he has met with a sudden piece of good fortune. Or even when an action, as sometimes happens, cannot be particularly accounted for, either by the person himself or by others, we know, in general, that the characters of men are to a certain degree inconstant and irregular. This is, in a manner, the constant character of human nature, though it be applicable, in a more particular manner, to some persons who have no fixed rule for their conduct, but proceed in a continual course of caprice and inconstancy. The internal principles and motives may operate in a uniform manner, notwithstanding these seeming irregularities—in the same manner as the winds, rains, clouds, and other variations of the weather are supposed to be governed by steady principles, though not easily discoverable by human sagacity and inquiry.

Thus it appears not only that the conjunction between motives and voluntary actions is as regular and uniform as that between the cause and effect in any part of nature, but also that this regular conjunction has been universally acknowledged among mankind and has never been the subject of dispute either in philosophy or common life. Now, as it is from past experience that we draw all inferences concerning the future, and as we conclude that objects will always be conjoined together which we find to have always been conjoined, it may seem superfluous to prove that this experienced uniformity in human actions is a source whence we draw *inferences* concerning them. But in order to throw the argument into a greater variety of lights, we shall also insist, though briefly, on this latter topic.

The mutual dependence of men is so great in all societies that scarce any human action is entirely complete in itself or is performed without some reference to the actions of others, which are requisite to make it answer fully the intention of the agent. The poorest artificer who labors alone expects at least the protection of the magistrate to insure him the enjoyment of the fruits of his labor. He also expects that when he carries his goods to market and offers them at a reasonable price, he shall find purchasers and shall be able, by the money he acquires, to engage others to supply him with those commodities which are requisite for his subsistence. In proportion as men extend their dealings and render their intercourse with others more complicated, they always comprehend in their schemes of life a greater variety of voluntary actions which they expect, from the proper motives, to co-operate with their own. In all these conclusions they take their measures from past experience, in the same manner as in their reasonings concerning external objects, and firmly believe that men, as well as all the elements, are to continue in their operations the same that they have ever found them. A manufacturer reckons upon the labor of his servants for the execution of any work as much as upon the tools which he employs, and would be equally surprised were his expectations disappointed. In short, this experimental inference and reasoning concerning the actions of others enters so much into human life that no man, while awake, is ever a moment without employing it. Have we not reason, therefore, to affirm that all mankind have always agreed in the doctrine of necessity, according to the foregoing definition and explication of it?

Nor have philosophers ever entertained a different opinion from the people in this particular. For, not to mention that almost every action of their life supposes that opinion, there are even few of the speculative parts of learning to which it is not essential. What would become of *history* had we not a dependence on the veracity of the historian according to the experience which we have had of mankind? How could *politics* be a science if laws and forms of government had not a uniform influence upon society? Where would be the foundation of *morals* if particular characters had no certain or determinate power to produce particular sentiments, and if these sentiments had no constant operation on actions? And with what pretense could we employ our *criticism* upon any poet or polite author if we could not pronounce the conduct and sentiments of his actors either natural or unnatural to such characters and in such circumstances? It seems almost impossible, therefore, to engage either in science or action of any kind without acknowledging the doctrine of necessity, and this *inference* from motives to voluntary action, from characters to conduct.

And, indeed, when we consider how aptly *natural* and *moral* evidence link together and form only one chain of argument, we shall make no scruple to allow that they are of the same nature and derived from the same principles. A prisoner who has neither money nor interest discovers the impossibility of his escape as well when he considers the obstinacy of the jailer as the walls and bars with which he is surrounded, and in all attempts for his freedom chooses rather to work upon the stone and iron of the one than upon the inflexible nature of the other. The same prisoner, when conducted to the scaffold, foresees his death as certainly from the constancy and fidelity of his guards as from the operation of the ax or wheel. His mind runs along a certain train of ideas: the refusal of the soldiers to consent to his escape; the action of the executioner; the separation of the head and body; bleeding, convulsive motions, and death. Here is a connected chain of natural causes and voluntary actions, but the mind feels no difference between them in passing from one link to another, nor is less certain of the future event than if it were connected with the objects present to the memory or senses by a train of causes cemented together by what we are pleased to call a "physical" necessity. The same experienced union has the same effect on the mind, whether the united objects be motives, volition, and actions, or figure and motion. We may change the names of things, but their nature and their operation on the understanding never change.

Were a man whom I know to be honest and opulent, and with whom I lived in intimate friendship, to come into my house, where I am surrounded with my servants, I rest assured that he is not to stab me before he leaves it in order to rob me of my silver standish; and I no more suspect this event than the falling of the house itself, which is new and solidly built and founded.—*But he may have been seized with a sudden and unknown frenzy.*—So may a sudden earthquake arise, and shake and tumble my house about my ears. I shall, therefore, change the suppositions. I shall say that I know with certainty that he is not to put his hand into the fire and hold it there till it be consumed. And this event I think I can foretell with the same assurance as that, if he throw himself out of the window and meet with no obstruction, he will not remain a moment suspended in the air. No suspicion of an unknown frenzy can give the least possibility to the former event which is so contrary to all the known principles of human nature. A man who at noon leaves his purse full of gold on the pavement at Charing Cross may as well expect that it will fly away like a feather as that he will find it untouched an hour after. Above one-half of human reasonings contain inferences of a similar nature, attended with more or less degrees of certainty, proportioned to our experience of the usual conduct of mankind in such particular situations.

I have frequently considered what could possibly be the reason why all mankind, though they have ever, without hesitation, acknowledged the doctrine of necessity in their whole practice and reasoning, have yet discovered such a reluctance to acknowledge it in words, and have rather shown a propensity, in all ages, to profess the contrary opinion. The matter, I think, may be accounted for after the following manner. If we examine the operations of body and the production of effects from their causes, we shall find that all our faculties can never carry us further in our knowledge of this relation than barely to observe that particular objects are *constantly conjoined* together, and that the mind is carried, by a *customary transition*, from the appearance of the one to the belief of the other. But though this conclusion concerning human ignorance be the result of the strictest scrutiny of this subject, men still entertain a strong propensity to believe that they penetrate further into the powers of nature and perceive something like a necessary connection between the cause and the effect. When, again, they turn their reflections toward the operations of their own minds and *feel* no such connection of the motive and the action, they are thence apt to suppose that there is a difference between the effects which result from material force and those which arise from thought and intelligence. But being once convinced that we know nothing further of causation of any kind than merely the *constant conjunction* of objects and the consequent *inference* of the mind from one to another, and finding that these two circumstances are universally allowed to have place in voluntary actions, we may be more easily led to own the same necessity common to all causes. And though this reasoning may contradict the systems of many philosophers in ascribing necessity to the determinations of the will, we shall find, upon reflection, that they dissent from it in words only, not in their real sentiments. Necessity, according to the sense in which it is here taken, has never yet been rejected, nor can ever, I think, be rejected by any philosopher. It may only, perhaps, be pretended that the mind can perceive in the operations of matter some further connection between the cause and effect, and a connection that has not place in the voluntary actions of intelligent beings. Now, whether it be so or not can only appear upon examination, and it is incumbent on these philosophers to make good their assertion by defining or describing that necessity and pointing it out to us in the operations of material causes.

It would seem, indeed, that men begin at the wrong end of this question concerning liberty and necessity when they enter upon it by examining the faculties of the soul, the influence of the understanding, and the operations of the will. Let them first discuss a more simple question, namely, the question of body and brute unintelligent matter, and try whether they can there form any idea of causation and necessity, except that of a constant conjunction of objects and subsequent inference of the mind from one to another. If these circumstances form, in reality, the whole of that necessity which we conceive in matter, and if these circumstances be also universally acknowledged to take place in the operations of the mind, the dispute is at an end; at least, must be owned to be thenceforth merely verbal. But as long as we will rashly suppose that we have some further idea of necessity and causation in the operations of external objects, at the same time that we can find nothing further in the voluntary actions of the mind, there is no possibility of bringing the question to any determinate issue while we proceed upon so erroneous a supposition. The only method of undeceiving us is to mount up higher, to examine the narrow extent of science when applied to material causes, and to convince ourselves that all we know of them is the constant conjunction and inference above mentioned. We may, perhaps, find that it is with difficulty we are induced to fix such narrow limits to human understanding, but we can afterwards find no difficulty when we come to apply this doctrine to the actions of the will. For as it is evident that these have a regular conjunction with motives and circumstances and character, and as we always draw inferences from one to the other, we must be obliged to acknowledge in words that necessity which we have already avowed in every deliberation of our lives and in every step of our conduct and behavior.

But to proceed in this reconciling project with regard to the question of liberty and necessity—the most contentious question of metaphysics, the most contentious science—it will not require many words to prove that all mankind have ever agreed in the doctrine of liberty as well as in that of necessity, and that the whole dispute, in this respect also, has been hitherto merely verbal. For what is meant by liberty when applied to voluntary actions? We cannot surely mean that actions have so little connection with motives, inclinations, and circumstances that one does not follow with a certain degree of uniformity from the other, and that one affords no inference by which we can conclude the existence of the other. For these are plain and acknowledged matters of fact. By liberty, then, we can only mean *a power of acting or not acting according to the determinations of the will*; that is, if we choose to remain at rest, we may; if we choose to move, we also may. Now this hypothetical liberty is universally allowed to belong to everyone who is not a prisoner and in chains. Here then is no subject of dispute.

Whatever definition we may give of liberty, we should be careful to observe two requisite circumstances: *first*, that it be consistent with plain matter of fact; *secondly*, that it be consistent with itself. If we observe these circumstances and render our definition intelligible, I am persuaded that all mankind will be found of one opinion with regard to it.

It is universally allowed that nothing exists without a cause of its existence, and that chance, when strictly examined, is a mere negative word and means not any real power which has anywhere a being in nature. But it is pretended that some causes are necessary, some not necessary. Here then is the advantage of definitions. Let anyone *define* a cause without comprehending, as a part of the definition, a *necessary connection* with its effect, and let him show distinctly the origin of the idea expressed by the definition, and I shall readily give up the whole controversy. But if the foregoing explication of the matter be received, this must be absolutely impracticable. Had not objects a regular conjunction with each other, we should never have entertained any notion of cause and effect; and this regular conjunction produces that inference of the understanding which is the only connection that we can have any comprehension of. Whoever attempts a definition of cause exclusive of these circumstances will be obliged either to employ unintelligible terms or such as are synonymous to the term which he endeavors to define. And if the definition above mentioned be admitted, liberty, when opposed to necessity, not to constraint, is the same thing with chance, which is universally allowed to have no existence.

Part II

There is no method of reasoning more common, and yet none more blamable, than in philosophical disputes to endeavor the refutation of any hypothesis by a pretense of its dangerous consequences to religion and morality. When any opinion leads to absurdity, it is certainly false; but it is not certain that an opinion is false because it is of dangerous consequence. Such topics, therefore, ought entirely to be forborne as serving nothing to the discovery of truth, but only to make the person of an antagonist odious. This I observe in general, without pretending to draw any advantage from it. I frankly submit to an examination of this kind, and shall venture to affirm that the doctrines both of necessity and liberty, as above explained, are not only consistent with morality, but are absolutely essential to its support.

Necessity may be defined two ways, conformably to the two definitions of *cause* of which it makes an essential part. It consists either in the constant conjunction of like objects or in the inference of the understanding from one object to another. Now necessity, in both these senses (which, indeed, are at bottom the same), has universally, though tacitly, in the schools, in the pulpit, and in common life been allowed to belong to the will of man, and no one has ever pretended to deny that we can draw inferences concerning human actions, and that those inferences are founded on the experienced union of like actions, with like motives, inclinations, and circumstances. The only particular in which anyone can differ is that either perhaps he will refuse to give the name of necessity to this property of human actions—but as long as the meaning is understood I hope the word can do no harm—or that he will maintain it possible to discover something further in the operations of matter. But this, it must be acknowledged, can be of no consequence to morality or religion, whatever it may be to natural philosophy or metaphysics. We may here be mistaken in asserting that there is no idea of any other necessity or connection in the actions of the body, but surely we ascribe nothing to the actions of the mind but what everyone does and must readily allow of. We change no circumstance in the received orthodox system with regard to the will, but only in that with regard to material objects and causes. Nothing, therefore, can be more innocent at least than this doctrine.

All laws being founded on rewards and punishments, it is supposed, as a fundamental principle, that these motives have a regular and uniform influence on the mind and both produce the good and prevent the evil actions. We may give to this influence what name we please; but as it is usually conjoined with the action, it must be esteemed a *cause* and be looked upon as an instance of that necessity which we would here establish.

The only proper object of hatred or vengeance is a person or creature endowed with thought and consciousness; and when any criminal or injurious actions excite that passion, it is only by their relation to the person, or connection with him. Actions are, by their very nature, temporary and perishing; and where they proceed not from some *cause* in the character and disposition of the person who performed them, they can neither redound to his honor if good, nor infamy if evil. The actions themselves may be blamable; they may be contrary to all the rules of morality and religion; but the person is not answerable for them and, as they proceeded from nothing in him that is durable and constant and leave nothing of that nature behind them, it is impossible he can, upon their account, become the object of punishment or vengeance. According to the principle, therefore, which denies necessity and, consequently, causes, a man is as pure and untainted, after having committed the most horrid crime, as at the first moment of his birth, nor is his character anywise concerned in his actions, since they are not derived from it; and the wickedness of the one can never be used as a proof of the depravity of the other.

Men are not blamed for such actions as they perform ignorantly and casually, whatever may be the consequences. Why? But because the principles of these actions are only momentary and terminate in them alone. Men are less blamed for such actions as they perform hastily and unpremeditately than for such as proceed from deliberation. For what reason? But because a hasty temper, though a constant cause or principle in the mind, operates only by intervals and infects not the whole character. Again, repentance wipes off every crime if attended with a reformation of life and manners. How is this to be accounted for? But by asserting that actions render a person criminal merely as they are proofs of criminal principles in the mind; and when, by an alteration of these principles, they cease to be just proofs, they likewise cease to be criminal. But, except upon the doctrine of necessity, they never were just proofs, and consequently never were criminal.

It will be equally easy to prove, and from the same arguments, that *liberty*, according to that definition above mentioned, in which all men agree, is also essential to morality, and that no human actions, where it is wanting, are susceptible of any moral qualities or can be the objects of approbation or dislike. For as actions are objects of our moral sentiment so far only as they are indications of the internal character, passions, and affections, it is impossible that they can give rise either to praise or blame where they proceed not from these principles, but are derived altogether from external violence.

C. A. Campbell (1897–1974) was a Scottish philosopher who taught at the University of Glasgow. In the passage that follows, he develops an uncompromising libertarian view of free will, drawing from his generally Kantian philosophical perspective. This is the view that Ben champions in the dialogue.

Has the Self 'Free Will'?

1. It is something of a truism that in philosophic enquiry the exact formulation of a problem often takes one a long way on the road to its solution. In the case of the Free Will problem I think there is a rather special need of careful formulation. For there are many sorts of human freedom; and it can easily happen that one wastes a great deal of labour in proving or disproving a freedom which has almost nothing to do with the freedom which is at issue in the traditional problem of Free Will. . . .

Fortunately we can at least make a beginning with a certain amount of confidence. It is not seriously disputable that the kind of freedom in question is the freedom which is commonly recognised to be in some sense a precondition of moral responsibility. Clearly, it is on account of this integral connection with moral responsibility that such exceptional importance has always been felt to attach to the Free Will problem. But in what precise sense is free will a precondition of moral responsibility, and thus a postulate of the moral life in general? This is an exceedingly troublesome question; but until we have satisfied ourselves about the answer to it, we are not in a position to state, let alone decide, the question whether 'Free Will' in its traditional, ethical, significance is a reality.

Our first business, then, is to ask, exactly what kind of freedom is it which is required for moral responsibility? And as to method of procedure in this inquiry, there seems to me to be no real choice. I know of only one method that carries with it any hope of success; viz. the critical comparison of those acts for which, on due reflection, we deem it proper to attribute moral praise or blame to the agents, with those acts for which, on due reflection, we deem such judgments to be improper. The ultimate touchstone, as I see it, can only be our moral consciousness as it manifests itself in our more critical and considered moral judgments. . . .

2. The first point to note is that the freedom at issue (as indeed the very name 'Free *Will* Problem' indicates) pertains primarily not to overt acts but to inner acts. The nature of things has decreed that, save in the case of one's self, it is only overt acts which one can directly observe. But a very little reflection serves to show that in our moral judgments upon others their overt acts are regarded as significant only in so far as they are the expression of inner acts. We do not consider the acts of a robot to be morally responsible acts; nor do we consider the acts of a man to be so save in so far as they are distinguishable from those of a robot by reflecting an inner life of choice. Similarly, from the other side, if we are satisfied (as we may on occasion be, at least in the case of ourselves) that a person has definitely elected to follow a course which he believes to be wrong, but has been prevented by external circumstances from translating his inner choice into an overt act, we still regard him as morally blameworthy. Moral freedom, then, pertains to *inner* acts.

The next point seems at first sight equally obvious and uncontroversial; but, as we shall see, it has awkward implications if we are in real earnest with it (as almost nobody is). It is the simple point that the act must be one of which the person judged can be regarded as the *sole* author. It seems plain enough that if there are any *other* determinants of the act, external to the self, to that extent the act is not an act which the *self* determines, and to that extent not an act for which the self can be held morally responsible. The self is only part-author of the act, and his moral responsibility can logically extend only to those elements within the act (assuming for the moment that these can be isolated) of which he is the *sole* author.

The awkward implications of this apparent truism will be readily appreciated. For, if we are mindful of the influences exerted by heredity and environment, we may well feel some doubt whether there is any act of will at all of which one can truly say that the self is sole author, sole determinant. No man has a voice in determining the raw material of impulses and capacities that constitute his hereditary endowment, and no man has more than a very partial control of the material and social environment in which he is destined to live his life. Yet it would be manifestly absurd to deny that these two factors do constantly and profoundly affect the nature of a man's choices. That this is so we all of us recognise in our moral judgments when we 'make allowances', as we say, for a bad heredity or a vicious environment, and acknowledge in the victim of them a diminished moral responsibility for evil courses. Evidently we do *try*, in our moral judgments, however crudely, to praise or blame a man only in respect of that of which we can regard him as *wholly* the author. And evidently we do recognise that, for a man to be the author of an act in the full sense required for moral responsibility, it is not enough merely that he 'wills' or 'chooses' the act: since even the most unfortunate victim of heredity or environment does, as a rule, 'will' what he does. It is significant, however, that the ordinary man, though well enough aware of the influence upon choices of heredity and environment, does not feel obliged thereby to give up his assumption that moral predicates *are* somehow applicable. Plainly he still believes that there is *something* for which a man is morally responsible, something of which we can fairly say that he is the sole author. *What is this something?* To that question common-sense is not ready with an explicit answer—though an answer is, I think, implicit in the line which its moral judgments take. I shall do what I can to give an explicit answer later in this lecture. Meantime it must suffice to observe that, if we are to be true to the deliverances of our moral consciousness, it is very difficult to deny that *sole* authorship is a necessary condition of the morally responsible act.

Thirdly we come to a point over which much recent controversy has raged. We may approach it by raising the following question. Granted an act of which the agent is sole author, does this 'sole authorship' suffice to make the act a morally free act? We may be inclined to think that it does, until we contemplate the possibility that an act of which the agent is sole author might conceivably occur as a necessary expression of the agent's nature; the way in which, e.g. some philosophers have supposed the Divine act of creation to occur. This consideration excites a legitimate doubt; for it is far from easy to see how a person can be regarded as a proper subject for moral praise or blame in respect of an act which he *cannot help* performing—even if it be his own 'nature' which necessitates it. Must we not recognise it as a condition of the morally free act that the agent 'could have acted otherwise' than he in fact did? It is true, indeed, that we sometimes praise or blame a man for an act about which we are prepared to say, in the light of our knowledge of his established character, that he 'could no other'. But I think that a little reflection shows that in such cases we are not praising or blaming the man strictly for what he does *now* (or at any rate we ought not to be), but rather for those past acts of his which have generated the firm habit of mind from which his *present* act follows 'necessarily'. In other words, our praise and blame, so far as justified, are really retrospective, being directed not to the agent *qua* performing *this* act, but to the agent *qua* performing those past acts which have built up his present character, and in respect to which we presume that he *could* have acted otherwise, that there really *were* open possibilities before him. These cases, therefore, seem to me to constitute no valid exception to what I must take to be the rule, viz. that a man can be morally praised or blamed for an act only if he could have acted otherwise. . . .

3. Let me, then, briefly sum up the answer at which we have arrived to our question about the kind of freedom required to justify moral responsibility. It is that a man can be said to exercise free will in a morally significant sense only in so far as his chosen act is one of which he is the sole cause or author, and only if—in the straightforward, categorical sense of the phrase—he 'could have chosen otherwise'.

I confess that this answer is in some ways a disconcerting one. Disconcerting, because most of us, however objective we are in the actual conduct of our thinking, would *like* to be able to believe that moral responsibility is real: whereas the freedom required for moral responsibility, on the analysis we have given, is certainly far more difficult to establish than the freedom required on the analyses we found ourselves obliged to reject. If, e.g. moral freedom entails only that I could have acted otherwise *if* I had chosen otherwise, there is no real 'problem' about it at all. I am 'free' in the normal case where there is no external obstacle to prevent my translating the alternative choice into action, and not free in other cases. Still less is there a problem if all that moral freedom entails is that I could have acted otherwise *if* I had been a differently constituted person, or been in different circumstances. Clearly I am *always* free in *this* sense of freedom. But . . . these so-called 'freedoms' fail to give us the pre-conditions of moral responsibility, and hence leave the freedom of the traditional free-will problem, the freedom that people are really concerned about, precisely where it was. . . .

5. That brings me to the second, and more constructive, part of this lecture. From now on I shall be considering whether it is reasonable to believe that man does in fact possess a free will of the kind specified in the first part of the lecture. If so, just how and where within the complex fabric of the volitional life are we to locate it?—for although free will must presumably belong (if anywhere) to the volitional side of human experience, it is pretty clear from the way in which we have been forced to define it that it does not pertain simply to volition as such; not even to all volitions that are commonly dignified with the name of 'choices'. It has been, I think, one of the more serious impediments to profitable discussion of the Free Will problem that Libertarians and Determinists alike have so often failed to appreciate the comparatively narrow area within which the free will that is necessary to 'save' morality is required to operate. It goes without saying that this failure has been gravely prejudicial to the case for Libertarianism. I attach a good deal of importance, therefore, to the problem of locating free will correctly within the volitional orbit. Its solution forestalls and annuls, I believe, some of the more tiresome clichés of Determinist criticism.

We saw earlier that Common Sense's practice of 'making allowances' in its moral judgments for the influence of heredity and environment indicates Common Sense's conviction, both that a just moral judgment must discount determinants of choice over which the agent has no control, and also (since it still accepts moral judgments as legitimate) that *something* of moral relevance survives which can be regarded as genuinely self-originated. We are now to try to discover what this 'something' is. And I think we may still usefully take Common Sense as our guide. Suppose one asks the ordinary intelligent citizen *why* he deems it proper to make allowances for X, whose heredity and/or environment are unfortunate. He will tend to reply, I think, in some such terms as these: that X has more and stronger temptations to deviate from what is right than Y or Z, who are normally circumstanced, so that he must put forth a *stronger moral effort* if he is to achieve the same level of external conduct. The intended implication seems to be that X is just as morally praiseworthy as Y or Z *if* he exerts an equivalent moral effort, even though he may not thereby achieve an equal success in conforming his will to the 'concrete' demands of duty. And this implies, again, Common Sense's belief that *in moral effort* we have something for which a man is responsible *without qualification*, something that is *not* affected by heredity and environment but depends *solely* upon the self itself.

Now in my opinion Common Sense has here, in principle, hit upon the one and only defensible answer. Here, and here alone, so far as I can see, in the act of deciding whether to put forth or withhold the moral effort required to resist temptation and rise to duty, is to be found an act which is free in the sense required for moral responsibility; an act of which the self is sole author, and of which it is true to say that 'it could be' (or, after the event, 'could have been') 'otherwise'. Such is the thesis which we shall now try to establish.

6. The species of argument appropriate to the establishment of a thesis of this sort should fall, I think, into two phases. First, there should be a consideration of the evidence of the moral agent's own inner experience. What *is* the act of moral decision, and what does it imply, from the standpoint of the actual participant? Since there is no way of knowing the act of moral decision—or for that matter any other form of activity—except by actual participation in it, the evidence of the subject, or agent, is on an issue of this kind of palmary importance. It can hardly, however, be taken as in itself conclusive. For even if that evidence should be overwhelmingly to the effect that moral decision does have the characteristics required by moral freedom, the question is bound to be raised—and in view of considerations from other quarters pointing in a contrary direction is *rightly* raised—Can we *trust* the evidence of inner experience? That brings us to what will be the second phase of the argument. We shall have to go on to show, if we are to make good our case, that the extraneous considerations so often supposed to be fatal to the belief in moral freedom are in fact innocuous to it.

In the light of what was said in the last lecture about the self's experience of moral decision as a *creative* activity, we may perhaps be absolved from developing the first phase of the argument at any great length. The appeal is throughout to one's own experience in the actual taking of the moral decision in the situation of moral temptation. 'Is it possible', we must ask, 'for anyone so circumstanced to *dis*believe that he could be deciding otherwise?' The answer is surely not in doubt. When we decide to exert moral effort to resist a temptation, we feel quite certain that we *could* withhold the effort; just as, if we decide to withhold the effort and yield to our desires, we feel quite certain that we *could* exert it—otherwise we should not blame ourselves afterwards for having succumbed. It may be, indeed, that this conviction is mere self-delusion. But that is not at the moment our concern. It is enough at present to establish that the act of deciding to exert or to withhold moral effort, as we know it from the inside in actual moral living, belongs to the category of acts which 'could have been otherwise'.

Mutatis mutandis, the same reply is forthcoming if we ask, 'Is it possible for the moral agent in the taking of his decision to *dis*believe that he is the *sole* author of that decision?' Clearly he cannot disbelieve that it is *he* who takes the decision. That, however, is not in itself sufficient to enable him, on reflection, to regard himself as *solely* responsible for the act. For his 'character' as so far formed might conceivably be a factor in determining it, and no one can suppose that the constitution of his 'character' is uninfluenced by circumstances of heredity and environment with which *he* has nothing to do. But as we pointed out in the last lecture, the very essence of the moral decision as it is experienced is that it is a decision whether or not to *combat* our strongest desire, and our strongest desire *is* the expression in the situation of our character as so far formed. Now clearly our character cannot be a factor in determining the decision whether or not to *oppose* our character. I think we are entitled to say, therefore, that the act of moral decision is one in which the self is for itself not merely 'author' but 'sole author'.

7. We may pass on, then, to the second phase of our constructive argument; and this will demand more elaborate treatment. Even if a moral agent *qua* making a moral decision in the situation of 'temptation' cannot help believing that he has free will in the sense at issue—a moral freedom between real alternatives, between genuinely open possibilities— are there, nevertheless, objections to a freedom of this kind so cogent that we are bound to distrust the evidence of 'inner experience'?

I begin by drawing attention to a simple point whose significance tends, I think, to be under-estimated. If the phenomenological analysis we have offered is substantially correct, no one while functioning as a moral agent can help believing that he enjoys free will. Theoretically he may be completely convinced by Determinist arguments, but when actually confronted with a personal situation of conflict between duty and desire he is quite certain that it lies with him here and now whether or not he will rise to duty. It follows that if Determinists could produce convincing theoretical arguments against a free will of this kind, the awkward predicament would ensue that man has to deny as a theoretical being what he has to assert as a practical being. Now I think the Determinist ought to be a good deal more worried about this than he usually is. He seems to imagine that a strong case on general theoretical grounds is enough to prove that the 'practical' belief in free will, even if inescapable for us as practical beings, is mere illusion. But in fact it proves nothing of the sort. There is no reason whatever why a belief that we find ourselves obliged to hold *qua* practical beings should be required to give way before a belief which we find ourselves obliged to hold *qua* theoretical beings; or, for that matter, *vice versa*. All that the theoretical arguments of Determinism can prove, unless they are reinforced by a refutation of the phenomenological analysis that supports Libertarianism, is that there is a radical conflict between the theoretical and the practical sides of man's nature, an antinomy at the very heart of the self. And this is a state of affairs with which no one can easily rest satisfied. I think therefore that the Determinist ought to concern himself a great deal more than he does with phenomenological analysis, in order to show, if he can, that the assurance of free will is not really an inexpugnable element in man's practical consciousness. There is just as much obligation upon him, convinced though he may be of the soundness of his theoretical arguments, to expose the errors of the Libertarian's phenomenological analysis, as there is upon us, convinced though we may be of the soundness of the Libertarian's phenomenological analysis, to expose the errors of the Determinist's theoretical arguments.

8. However, we must at once begin the discharge of our own obligation. The rest of this lecture will be devoted to trying to show that the arguments which seem to carry most weight with Determinists are, to say the least of it, very far from compulsive. . . .

These arguments can, I think, be reduced in principle to no more than two: first, the argument from 'predictability'; second, the argument from the alleged meaninglessness of an act supposed to be the self's act and yet not an expression of the self's character. Contemporary criticism of free will seems to me to consist almost exclusively of variations on these two themes. I shall deal with each in turn.

9. On the first we touched in passing at an earlier stage. Surely it is beyond question (the critic urges) that when we know a person intimately we can foretell with a high degree of accuracy how he will respond to at least a large number of practical situations. One feels safe in predicting that one's dog-loving friend will not use his boot to repel the little mongrel that comes yapping at his heels; or again that one's wife will not pass with incurious eyes (or indeed pass at all) the new hat-shop in the city. So to

behave would not be (as we say) 'in character'. But, so the criticism runs, you with your doctrine of 'genuinely open possibilities', of a free will by which the self can diverge from its own character, remove all rational basis from such prediction. You require us to make the absurd supposition that the success of countless predictions of the sort in the past has been mere matter of chance. If you *really* believed in your theory, you would not be surprised if tomorrow your friend with the notorious horror of strong drink should suddenly exhibit a passion for whisky and soda, or if your friend whose taste for reading has hitherto been satisfied with the sporting columns of the newspapers should be discovered on a fine Saturday afternoon poring over the works of Hegel. But of course you *would* be surprised. Social life would be sheer chaos if there were not well-grounded social expectations; and social life is not sheer chaos. Your theory is hopelessly wrecked upon obvious facts.

Now whether or not this criticism holds good against some versions of Libertarian theory I need not here discuss. It is sufficient if I can make it clear that against the version advanced in this lecture, according to which free will is localised in a relatively narrow field of operation, the criticism has no relevance whatsoever.

Let us remind ourselves briefly of the setting within which, on our view, free will functions. There is X, the course which we believe we ought to follow, and Y, the course towards which we feel our desire is strongest. The freedom which we ascribe to the agent is the freedom to put forth or refrain from putting forth the moral effort required to resist the pressure of desire and do what he thinks he ought to do.

But then there is surely an immense range of practical situations—covering by far the greater part of life—in which there is no question of a conflict within the self between what he most desires to do and what he thinks he ought to do? Indeed such conflict is a comparatively rare phenomenon for the majority of men. Yet over that whole vast range there is nothing whatever in our version of Libertarianism to prevent our agreeing that character determines conduct. In the absence, real or supposed, of any 'moral' issue, what a man chooses will be simply that course which, after such reflection as seems called for, he deems most likely to bring him what he most strongly desires; and that is the same as to say the course to which his present character inclines him.

Over by far the greater area of human choices, then, our theory offers no more barrier to successful prediction on the basis of character than any other theory. For where there is no clash of strongest desire with duty, the free will we are defending has no business. There is just nothing for it to do.

But what about the situations—rare enough though they may be—in which there *is* this clash and in which free will does therefore operate?

Does our theory entail that there at any rate, as the critic seems to suppose, 'anything may happen'?

Not by any manner of means. In the first place, and by the very nature of the case, the range of the agent's possible choices is bounded by what he thinks he ought to do on the one hand, and what he most strongly desires on the other. The freedom claimed for him is a freedom of decision to make or withhold the effort required to do what he thinks he ought to do. There is no question of a freedom to act in some 'wild' fashion, out of all relation to his characteristic beliefs and desires. This so-called 'freedom of caprice', so often charged against the Libertarian, is, to put it bluntly, a sheer figment of the critic's imagination, with no *habitat* in serious Libertarian theory. Even in situations where free will does come into play it is perfectly possible, on a view like ours, given the appropriate knowledge of a man's character, to predict within certain limits how he will respond.

But 'probable' prediction in such situations can, I think, go further than this. It is obvious that where desire and duty are at odds, the felt 'gap' (as it were) between the two may vary enormously in breadth in different cases. The moderate drinker and the chronic tippler may each want another glass, and each deem it his duty to abstain, but the felt gap between desire and duty in the case of the former is trivial beside the great gulf which is felt to separate them in the case of the latter. Hence it will take a far harder moral effort for the tippler than for the moderate drinker to achieve the same external result of abstention. So much is matter of common agreement. And we are entitled, I think, to take it into account in prediction, on the simple principle that the harder the moral effort required to resist desire the less likely it is to occur. Thus in the example taken, most people would predict that the tippler will very probably succumb to his desires, whereas there is a reasonable likelihood that the moderate drinker will make the comparatively slight effort needed to resist them. So long as the prediction does not pretend to more than a measure of probability, there is nothing in our theory which would disallow it.

I claim, therefore, that the view of free will I have been putting forward is consistent with predictability of conduct on the basis of character over a very wide field indeed. And I make the further claim that that field will cover all the situations in life concerning which there is any empirical evidence that successful prediction is possible.

10. Let us pass on to consider the second main line of criticism. This is, I think, much the more illuminating of the two, if only because it compels the Libertarian to make explicit certain concepts which are indispensable to him, but which, being desperately hard to state clearly, are apt not to be stated at all. The critic's fundamental point might be stated somewhat as follows:

'Free will as you describe it is completely unintelligible. On your own showing no *reason* can be given, because there just *is* no reason, why a man decides to exert rather than to withhold moral effort, or *vice versa*. But such an act—or more properly, such an "occurrence"—it is nonsense to speak of as an act of a *self*. If there is nothing in the self's character to which it is, even in principle, in any way traceable, the self has nothing to do with it. Your so-called "freedom", therefore, so far from supporting the self's moral responsibility, destroys it as surely as the crudest Determinism could do.'

If we are to discuss this criticism usefully, it is important, I think, to begin by getting clear about two different senses of the word 'intelligible'.

If, in the first place, we mean by an 'intelligible' act one whose occurrence is in principle capable of being inferred, since it follows necessarily from something (though we may not know in fact from what), then it is certainly true that the Libertarian's free will is unintelligible. But that is only saying, is it not, that the Libertarian's 'free' act is not an act which follows necessarily from something! This can hardly rank as a *criticism* of Libertarianism. It is just a description of it. That there can be nothing unintelligible in *this* sense is precisely what the Determinist has got to *prove*.

Yet it is surprising how often the critic of Libertarianism involves himself in this circular mode of argument. Repeatedly it is urged against the Libertarian, with a great air of triumph, that on his view he can't say *why* I now decide to rise to duty, or now decide to follow my strongest desire in defiance of duty. Of course he can't. If he could he wouldn't *be* a Libertarian. To 'account for' a 'free' act is a contradiction in terms. A free will is *ex hypothesi* the sort of thing of which the request for an *explanation* is absurd. The assumption that an explanation must be in principle possible for the act of moral decision deserves to rank as a classic example of the ancient fallacy of 'begging the question'.

But the critic usually has in mind another sense of the word 'unintelligible'. He is apt to take it for granted that an act which is unintelligible in the *above* sense (as the morally free act of the Libertarian undoubtedly is) is unintelligible in the *further* sense that we can attach no meaning to it. And this is an altogether more serious matter. If it could really be shown that the Libertarian's 'free will' were unintelligible in this sense of being meaningless, that, for myself at any rate, would be the end of the affair. Libertarianism would have been conclusively refuted.

But it seems to me manifest that this can *not* be shown. The critic has allowed himself, I submit, to become the victim of a widely accepted but fundamentally vicious assumption. He has assumed that whatever is meaningful must exhibit its meaningfulness to those who view it from the standpoint of external observation. Now if one chooses thus to limit one's self to the rôle of external observer, it is, I think, perfectly true that one can attach no meaning to an act which is the act of something we call a 'self' and yet follows from nothing in that self's character. But then *why should we* so limit ourselves, when what is under consideration is a subjective activity? For the apprehension of subjective acts there is *another* standpoint available, that of *inner experience*, of the practical consciousness in its actual functioning. If our free will should turn out to be something to which we can attach a meaning from *this* standpoint, no more is required. And no more ought to be expected. For I must repeat that only from the inner standpoint of living experience *could* anything of the nature of 'activity' be directly grasped. Observation from without is in the nature of the case impotent to apprehend the active *qua* active. We can from without observe sequences of states. If into these we read activity (as we sometimes do), this can only be on the basis of what we discern in ourselves from the inner standpoint. It follows that if anyone insists upon taking his criterion of the meaningful simply from the standpoint of external observation, he is really deciding in advance of the evidence that the notion of activity, and *a fortiori* the notion of a free will, is 'meaningless'. He looks for the free act through a medium which is in the nature of the case incapable of revealing it, and then, because inevitably he doesn't find it, he declares that it doesn't exist!

But if, as we surely ought in this context, we adopt the inner standpoint, then (I am suggesting) things appear in a totally different light. From the inner standpoint, it seems to me plain, there is no difficulty whatever in attaching meaning to an act which is the self's act and which nevertheless does not follow from the self's character. So much I claim has been established by the phenomenological analysis, in this and the previous lecture, of the act of moral decision in face of moral temptation. It is thrown into particularly clear relief where the moral decision is to make the moral effort required to rise to duty. For the very function of moral effort, as it appears to the agent engaged in the act, is to enable the self to act against the line of least resistance, against the line to which his character as so far formed most strongly inclines him. But if the self is thus conscious here of *combating* his formed character, he surely cannot possibly suppose that the act, although his own act, *issues from* his formed character? I submit, therefore, that the self knows very well indeed—from the inner standpoint—what is meant by an act which is the *self's* act and which nevertheless does not follow from the self's *character.*

What this implies—and it seems to me to be an implication of cardinal importance for any theory of the self that aims at being more than superficial—is that the nature of the self is for itself something more than just its character as so far formed. The 'nature' of the self and what we commonly call the 'character' of the self are by no means the same thing, and it is utterly vital that they should not be confused. The 'nature' of the self comprehends, but is not without remainder reducible to, its 'character';

it must, if we are to be true to the testimony of our experience of it, be taken as including *also* the authentic creative power of fashioning and re-fashioning 'character'.

The misguided, and as a rule quite uncritical, belittlement, of the evidence offered by inner experience has, I am convinced, been responsible for more bad argument by the opponents of Free Will than has any other single factor. How often, for example, do we find the Determinist critic saying, in effect, '*Either* the act follows necessarily upon precedent states, *or* it is a mere matter of chance and accordingly of no moral significance'. The disjunction is invalid, for it does not exhaust the possible alternatives. It seems to the critic to do so only because he *will* limit himself to the standpoint which is proper, and indeed alone possible, in dealing with the physical world, the standpoint of the external observer. If only he would allow himself to assume the standpoint which is not merely proper for, but necessary to, the apprehension of subjective activity, the inner standpoint of the practical consciousness in its actual functioning, he would find himself obliged to recognise the falsity of his disjunction. Reflection upon the act of moral decision as apprehended from the inner standpoint would force him to recognise a *third* possibility, as remote from chance as from necessity, that, namely, of *creative activity*, in which (as I have ventured to express it) nothing determines the act save the agent's doing of it.

11. There we must leave the matter. But as this lecture has been, I know, somewhat densely packed, it may be helpful if I conclude by reminding you, in bald summary, of the main things I have been trying to say. Let me set them out in so many successive theses.

1. The freedom which is at issue in the traditional Free Will problem is the freedom which is presupposed in moral responsibility.

2. Critical reflection upon carefully considered attributions of moral responsibility reveals that the only freedom that will do is a freedom which pertains to inner acts of choice, and that these acts must be acts (*a*) of which the self is *sole* author, and (*b*) which the self could have performed otherwise.

3. From phenomenological analysis of the situation of moral temptation we find that the self as engaged in this situation is inescapably convinced that it possesses a freedom of precisely the specified kind, located in the decision to exert or withhold the moral effort needed to rise to duty where the pressure of its desiring nature is felt to urge it in a contrary direction.

Passing to the question of the *reality* of this moral freedom which the moral agent believes himself to possess, we argued:

4. Of the two types of Determinist criticism which seem to have most influence today, that based on the predictability of much

human behaviour fails to touch a Libertarianism which confines the area of free will as above indicated. Libertarianism so understood is compatible with all the predictability that the empirical facts warrant. And:

5. The second main type of criticism, which alleges the 'meaninglessness' of an act which is the self's act and which is yet not determined by the self's character, is based on a failure to appreciate that the standpoint of inner experience is not only legitimate but indispensable where what is at issue is the reality and nature of a subjective activity. The creative act of moral decision is inevitably meaningless to the mere external observer; but from the inner standpoint it is as real, and as significant, as anything in human experience.

Study Questions

1. What is the difference between fatalism and determinism (according to those who believe there *is* a difference)?
2. What standard characteristics of God (as represented by the Jewish, Christian, and Muslim faiths) cause problems for the view that humans have free will?
3. What basic argument does Selina give (on behalf of David Hume) to show that we all actually believe in determinism?
4. What is the argument in favor of *compatibilist* free will?
5. Describe the *libertarian* view of free will.
6. Name some philosophers who have held the libertarian view of free will.
7. Discuss some of the major objections to libertarian free will.
8. Compare Campbell's version of libertarian free will with Sartre's existentialist version of free will.
9. What is the significance of the term "existentialist"? That is, why do existentialists use that name for their position?
10. Lorenzo Valla claims that God's omniscience—God's foreknowledge—poses no problem for human free will. What is his argument for that claim?
11. What does Lorenzo Valla regard as the main problem for the possibility of human free will?

Exercises

1. Sarah's friend Joe is a fellow philosophy major. Sarah and Joe have had several classes together, they have often studied together, and they are close friends. Joe is gay and lives openly with his lover, Sal. He has made no secret of the fact that he and Sal are lovers. At departmental functions when majors are invited and allowed to bring a guest—such as the annual departmental picnic and the annual undergraduate awards dinner—Joe typically invites Sal as his guest. Faculty and students in the department are aware of the relation between Joe and Sal, and everyone thinks it's fine—everyone, that is, with the notable exception of Professor Slago, who finds their relationship disgusting.

Knowing Professor Slago's dislike of homosexuals, Joe has avoided taking a class from him; but ancient philosophy is a required course for majors, and Professor Slago is the only person who teaches it, so this semester Joe is enrolled in Professor Slago's course. Professor Slago makes no secret of his hostility to Joe and has several times openly ridiculed him in front of the class. Joe has suffered such treatment silently and gracefully, but that has not lessened Professor Slago's hostility; if anything, it has grown more intense.

The grade for the course is determined by a midsemester exam, a final exam, and a term paper, each of which count for one-third of the course grade. Joe and Sarah study intensely for the midsemester exam, and both are confident they did well. When their papers are returned, Sarah receives an A; Joe gets an F. In comparing their essays, Sarah is convinced that Joe's is at least as good as her own—if anything, just a little better. Joe goes to Professor Slago to ask about the grade, but Professor Slago refuses to discuss it. The next step in the grievance procedure is to file a formal complaint with the department chair. Joe prepares his complaint, but it is obvious that he is very worried; furthermore, he has never had a class with the chairperson, whom Joe finds somewhat intimidating. Sarah has had two classes with the department chair, made top scores in both, and knows that the chair respects her as a philosophy student and as a person. Knowing that Joe is very nervous, Sarah insists on going with him to meet with the chairperson and support Joe's complaint. "No, Sarah, you mustn't do that," Joe responds. "It's very kind of you, but you know what will happen. The chairperson will call a meeting with Professor Slago and two other faculty members to discuss my complaint; and when Professor Slago sees that you are supporting my claim of bias, he will hate you as much as he hates me—maybe more! And you know how vindictive he is. He'll probably try to flunk you, too. At the very least, he'll do everything he can to harm you—probably try to block you from going to graduate school. And Professor Slago is a very powerful person in the philosophical realm, with lots of friends. After all, he can be quite charming when he wishes to be. No, Sarah, I appreciate it, but you should keep out of this; you've got too much to lose."

"No way, Joe," Sarah answers. "I can't stay out of it. It's not like I'm some moral saint or something, but I just can't stand aside on this. What Slago did was wrong, dead wrong; in fact, his treatment of you this entire semester has been abominable, and I can't just sit on the sideline and watch: I could never live with myself if I did that. No, Joe, I'm going with you, and I'm going to tell the committee exactly what Professor Slago did and what kind of sleazy homophobic bigot he really is, consequences be damned. I'm going with you, Joe; I have to go."

Of course, Sarah could do something else if she were someone else or had different values. But *suppose* that what she is saying is true: Given who she is and the values she holds, she cannot act otherwise than to stand beside Joe in his complaint. If so, is Sarah acting freely?

2. Your friend Lynn never gets things done until the last minute; in fact, he often doesn't get them done until somewhat *after* the last minute and frequently

hands in late papers with weak excuses. ("I'm so sorry, Dr. Stone, I had my paper finished and ready to print, and then my hard drive completely froze; is it okay if I turn it in tomorrow?") He often makes plans to finish work early, but those plans never quite work out. Semester after semester, you find Lynn pounding away at his keyboard at 4 A.M., trying to finish a term paper due at 8. Sure enough, his history term paper is due in two weeks, and here is Lynn, making big plans to work hard all weekend and finish the paper two weeks ahead of schedule. You smile knowingly, wish him luck, and leave for your weekend ski trip, confident that two weeks from now Lynn will be scrambling to finish his paper. When you return late Sunday night, there is Lynn, collecting the pages of his term paper from the printer and doing one more proofread on his final draft. You are astonished. "Lynn," you say, "what happened? You finished your paper this weekend, and it's not due for two more weeks."

"Yep," Lynn says, stapling the pages together, "all done."

"But you've *never* finished a paper two weeks early! I don't think you've ever finished a paper two *hours* early. What happened? Did Professor Slotkin read you the riot act after you turned in that last paper late?"

"No, Professor Slotkin didn't say anything."

"I bet your parents threatened to cut off your funds if you didn't pull up your grade point average."

"No, nothing like that."

"I know: Teresa laid down the law—said you had to clean up your act or she was going to dump you. Nothing like the love of a good woman to straighten a man out."

"No, Teresa never said a thing about it."

"Well, what happened? Have you been in some psych experiment, where they feed you motivation drugs or something?"

"No, nothing at all happened. Nothing changed. Always in the past when I needed to get work done, I just failed to make the effort to resist temptation. You know, there are always temptations: a party down the hall, going out with Teresa, watching a movie, playing a video game. Always something I would rather be doing than writing a paper. But this time I just exerted the effort, and overcame all temptations, and did my duty. That's the whole explanation; there was nothing else different."

This story about Lynn is exactly what Campbell says happens in the exercise of libertarian, contracausal free will. Those who reject Campbell's account will believe that something else must have happened to cause such a dramatic change: Perhaps even Lynn is not aware of what that something was, but it had to be present to produce the different outcome. So, how plausible does Lynn's explanation seem to you? That is, how plausible do you find the libertarian account in this case?

3. You have an old and dear friend who has known you for years. In fact, this friend knows you better, perhaps, than you know yourself. She can often tell exactly what you are going to do before you do it—indeed, even before you have *decided* to do it. You go to a restaurant, you are looking through the menu deciding on your dinner selection, and she has already written down

what you will select! And it's not as if you get the same thing every night: You like a wide variety of foods, and there are perhaps a dozen entrees you like. Still, she invariably gets it right. One night you decide to cross her up and order something you never order, something you don't even like, just to make her prediction wrong. But no, she had predicted you would do exactly that! One night you become angry with your lover, and you end the relationship: You learn that your friend had predicted it two weeks earlier, right down to the hour when the breakup would occur (and two weeks ago, *you* were certain that this was the love of your life). You go to the racetrack and spend hours pondering which horses to bet on; your friend has already figured out which horses you would choose and placed the bets you would have made. *If* you had a friend who could predict with such uncanny accuracy exactly what you were going to do, well before you did it or even decided to do it, would that show that you are *not* acting freely, that you do *not* have free will?

4. William James regards determinism as a *pessimistic* view, a view that stifles hope and blocks genuine reform; in contrast, many determinists regard determinism from an *optimistic* perspective (the psychologist B. F. Skinner, for example, and also the French social reformers of the 18th century, such as Diderot and D'Holbach), as a belief that promotes progress. *Why* would the opposing views see determinism in such different lights? Do *you* find the idea of determinism depressing or hopeful? Why?

5. Margaret and Christine both play the violin, and both are superb violinists. They love to play, they play in string quartets and the university orchestra, they play for weddings and parties, and both want to make a career playing the violin. Whenever they have any spare time, you will find them in the practice rooms, happily playing their violins. They play with equal enthusiasm, dedication, passion, and skill. However, they came to their love of the violin by very different paths. Margaret never wanted to play the violin when she was a child: She didn't like music very much; instead she loved sports. But Margaret's mother and father were frustrated musicians, who had always loved music, especially the violin, but were never quite good enough to play professionally. They desperately wanted Margaret to succeed in music and to have the musical career they had always wanted for themselves. So they strongly discouraged her interest in sports and pushed her hard to play the violin. They provided excellent violin teachers, rewarded her for practicing, expressed great delight when she played well, and grounded her when she neglected her violin practice. After several years, Margaret became an excellent violinist, and gradually she came to enjoy playing the violin more and more, and at the same time she began to lose all interest in sports. Finally, she developed into a very enthusiastic and talented violinist, and now she loves playing the violin. Christina, on the other hand, loved the violin from the moment she first heard one played. Her parents, however, did not think music a good career path: They wanted her to study biology and chemistry and eventually go to medical school. They bought Christina a chemistry set, but refused to buy her a violin and refused to provide her with violin lessons.

Christina begged the loan of an old violin from her music teacher, and for
years she mowed her teacher's lawn and shoveled the snow from his driveway
in exchange for private violin lessons. Her parents were always disappointed
that she had chosen music over medicine, but Christina prevailed and followed her love of the violin. Although Margaret and Christina arrived at this
point in very different ways, they are now equally passionate about playing
the violin, equally skilled, and equally dedicated. Set aside the question of
how free they were in their *childhoods*, when they were learning to play the
violin. Does the difference in their childhood experiences have any bearing on
whether they are *now* acting freely when they play the violin? Would those
childhood differences lead you to conclude than one is *now* freer than the
other, though both now equally love playing the violin?

Glossary

Compatibilism: The view that determinism is compatible with free will; we can
have free will even if determinism is true.

Contracausal free will: A special power claimed by those who believe in libertarian free will—the power to make a choice that is not fixed by its causal
antecedents. Some libertarians describe it as the power of being a first cause
or the power of being an uncaused cause.

Determinism: The view that, given the state of the universe at any point, all
future events are fixed by causal laws, and only one future course is genuinely possible.

Existentialism: The philosophical position based on the claim that "existence
precedes essence"—that is, the view that we make and define ourselves by
our own choices, rather than being determined or limited by our given characters or histories or natures.

Fatalism: The view that the most significant events in our lives (such as our key
successes or failures, as well as our deaths) are fixed by fate, and we can do
nothing to alter our fates. We may be able to make some choices of details,
but our larger fate is set and inescapable.

Heresy: A thesis or claim that is in conflict with the accepted or orthodox views
of a religion; such a thesis is characterized as being heretical, and those who
hold them are heretics.

Libertarianism: The position that we have a special power of free will (usually a
form of contracausal free will) that is strictly incompatible with determinism.

Predestination: A religious view, favored by such theologians as Luther and
Calvin (and perhaps Valla), which holds that God selects (predestines) each
person for either salvation or damnation. Those selected for salvation receive
the gift of God's grace, while those who do not receive that gift are damned;
the choice is entirely up to God, God's choice is made before the individual

humans are even born, and God's decision has nothing to do with the choices, works, or worth of the individuals.

Additional Resources

There are many excellent anthologies on free will. Perhaps the best small collection is edited by Gary Watson: *Free Will* (Oxford, U.K.: Oxford University Press, 1982). A recent anthology of the same caliber is edited by Laura Waddell Ekstrom: *Agency and Responsibility* (Boulder, CO.: Westview Press, 2001), and another is *Philosophical Perspectives 14, Action and Freedom, 2000*, edited by James E. Tomberlin (Oxford, U.K.: Blackwell, 2000).

A number of books consider the question of free will in light of recent research in biology and psychology. John M. Doris, in *Lack of Character: Personality and Moral Behavior* (Cambridge, U.K.: Cambridge University Press, 2002), organizes and reviews several decades of psychological research (particularly social psychology research) and draws out, in detail and depth, its philosophical implications in the areas of free will and moral responsibility. One of the most interesting and important books written on free will is by the neuropsychologist Daniel M. Wegner: *The Illusion of Conscious Will* (Cambridge, MA: Bradford Books, 2002) is a very readable book that draws out the implications of decades of neuropsychological research and its often-surprising results. A superb collection of essays—and commentary—on the implications of contemporary neuroscience for questions of free will can be found in *The Volitional Brain: Towards a Neuroscience of Free Will*, edited by Benjamin Libet, Anthony Freeman, and Keith Sutherland (Thorverton, Exeter, U.K.: Imprint Academic, 1999). Bruce N. Waller, *The Natural Selection of Autonomy* (Albany, NY: SUNY Press, 1998) uses recent research in biology and psychology in an attempt to uncover some of the motives common to both libertarian and compatibilist views of free will and to attack traditional justifications for moral responsibility.

For the best, clearest, and most evenhanded guide to the issues surrounding the free-will debate (and also for a very creative addition to that debate), see two books by Richard Double: *The Non-Reality of Free Will* (New York: Oxford University Press, 1991), and *Metaphilosophy and Free Will* (New York: Oxford University Press, 1996).

For a fascinating libertarian account of free will from the Italian Renaissance, see Giovanni Pico della Mirandola, "The Dignity of Man" (sometimes titled "Oration on the Dignity of Man"), available in several Renaissance anthologies. C. A. Campbell's *On Selfhood and Godhood* (London: George Allen & Unwin, 1957) is the classic modern source. Peter van Inwagen's *An Essay on Free Will* (Oxford, U.K.: Clarendon Press, 1983) is a very influential contemporary defense of libertarian free will. Robert Kane has developed what is undoubtedly the most sophisticated and interesting contemporary defense of libertarian free will, in *Free Will and Values* (Albany, NY: SUNY Press, 1985) and *The Significance of Free Will* (Oxford, U.K.: Oxford University Press, 1996). Kane's edited work, *The Oxford Handbook of Free Will* (Oxford, U.K.: Oxford University Press, 2002) is a wonderful guide to contemporary thought concerning free will. Two other influential sources for incompatibilist views of free will are William James, "The Dilemma of Determinism" (1884, available in a number of anthologies), and Jean-Paul Sartre, *Being and Nothingness* (New York: Philosophical Library, 1956). A thorough and subtle treatment of libertarian free will that sorts out a variety of libertarian positions is Randolph Clarke's *Libertarian Accounts of Free Will* (New York: Oxford University Press, 2003).

The classic presentation of both determinism and compatibilism is David Hume, *An Inquiry Concerning Human Understanding*, Section 8, and in his *Treatise of Human Nature*, Book II, Part III. Thomas Hobbes developed an earlier, similar account (1651) in *Leviathan*, Chapter 2. A more recent argument for compatibilism can be found in A. J. Ayer, "Freedom and Necessity," in his *Philosophical Essays* (London: Macmillan, 1954). For a delightful critique of compatibilism, presented in a spirited dialogue by an Italian Humanist philosopher of the 15th century, see Lorenzo Valla, "Dialogue on Free Will," which can be found in *The Renaissance Philosophy of Man*, edited by Ernst Cassirer, Paul Oskar Kristeller, and John Herman Randall (Chicago: The University of Chicago Press, 1948). The book also contains an excellent translation of Pico della Mirandola's "The Dignity of Man."

Philosophers who deny the existence of free will altogether (generally because they favor determinism and believe that determinism and free will are incompatible) include Baron D'Holbach (1770) and Arthur Schopenhauer, whose *Essay on the Freedom of the Will* was first published in 1841 and reissued in 1960 (New York: Liberal Arts Press). More recently, John Hospers has denied free will (making extensive use of Freudian psychology in his arguments); see "What Means This Freedom," in Sidney Hook, ed., *Determinism and Freedom in the Age of Modern Science* (New York: New York University Press, 1958). B. F. Skinner, in *Beyond Freedom and Dignity* (New York: Alfred A. Knopf, 1971), as well as in his utopian novel *Walden Two* [first published in 1948; available in paperback (New York: Macmillan, 1976)], is often thought to be rejecting free will altogether. In fact, his writings reject *libertarian* free will (and moral responsibility), but he strongly champions compatibilist free will.

A superb website on free will, determinism, fatalism, and moral responsibility that contains a number of excellent links and is beautifully organized is the Determinism and Freedom Philosophy Website, at *www.ucl.ac.uk/~uctytho/ dfwIntroIndex.htm*. A very nice collection of online papers on free will has been compiled by David Chalmers and is available at his home page: *jamaica.u.arizona .edu/~chalmers/online2.html#freewill*. Naturalism.org, at *www.naturalism.org/ freewill.htm*, offers a number of excellent papers and reviews on issues related to free will. Another very good site, with good disscussion boards and lots of papers, is the Garden of Forking Paths: A Free Will/Moral Responsibility Blog, at *gfp.typepad.com*.

For an interesting account of the relation of God's will and God's foreknowledge to human moral responsibility from a Sunni perspective, go to *www.sunnipath.com/resources/Questions/qa00000130.aspx*. An attempt to reconcile moral responsibility with Christianity can be examined at *www.thirdmill.org/ files/english/html/th/TH.h.Frame.FreeWill.MoralResp.html*.

Notes

1. Giovanni Pico della Mirandola, "Oration on the Dignity of Man," trans. Paul O. Kristeller, in *The Renaissance Philosophy of Man*, ed. Ernst Cassirer, Paul O. Kristeller, and John H. Randall (Chicago: University of Chicago Press, 1948), 224–225.
2. Roderick Chisholm, "Human Freedom and the Self," in *Free Will*, ed. Gary Watson (Oxford, U.K.: Oxford University Press, 1982), p. 32.
3. Richard Taylor, *Metaphysics* (Englewood Cliffs, NJ: Prentice-Hall, Inc., 1963), p. 52.
4. Jean-Paul Sartre, "Existentialism is a Humanism," in W. Kaufmann, editor, *Existentialism from Dostoyevsky to Sartre* (New York: New Arena Library, 1975), p. 352. First published in 1946.

Chapter 7

Further Adventures with Free Will

in which Sarah takes responsibility, but avoids blame

"Look, Ben, forget for a minute what shaped you to be the delightful person you are, where your desires originated from, your genetic and environmental history. Leave all that aside. Today you are here drinking coffee and discussing philosophy with Selina and me, and enjoying it, and doing it because it's what *you want to do*, and no one is forcing you to do it. Isn't that enough? You're acting freely, and nothing in your causal history could alter that simple fact. Your behavior and your desires are *determined*; but that determinism is quite *compatible* with freedom."

Frankfurt's Hierarchical Compatibilism

"Sarah, this is certainly a delightful way to pass the morning, with charming company, delicious coffee, and fascinating conversation. And I don't deny that I'm acting freely at the moment. But I'm not at all convinced that whenever we act from our own desires and we are 'not in chains,' that's enough to show that we are acting freely. Maybe it's necessary; but it's *not* sufficient for freedom. Here's an example: I certainly desire to play video games; but sometimes I'm afraid they're becoming a bit of an obsession and taking me away from things that I would *really* prefer: like when I play a video game rather than read a history book that I *know* is really more interesting and worthwhile. Of course, when I follow my immediate, strong desire and play the video game, no one *coerces* me; I'm not in chains. But I'm not sure I count it as a real exercise of freedom."

"The boy has a point, Sarah. Remember when your grandmother sent you that box of chocolate chip cookies? Your grandmother makes the best chocolate chip cookies in the entire cosmos, girl: so soft, with big gooey bits of creamy chocolate, fresh crunchy nuts, moist, wonderful. Anyway, we were both on a diet, trying to avoid sweets, right? And you opened that box of cookies, and we wolfed down just about the whole box. Well, obviously, we *wanted* to eat those cookies: Nobody held a gun to our heads, no one locked us in chains and force-fed us chocolate chip cookies. But in another sense—maybe a *deeper* sense—we did *not* want to eat those cookies. You know what I mean?"

Sarah nodded. "Yeah, I know exactly what you mean. I certainly desired the cookies; but I didn't *desire* to desire the cookies. I *wish* that I had strong cravings for carrot sticks and celery, instead of chocolate chip cookies and dark chocolate caramels. I do have a strong desire for chocolate chip cookies, and no doubt it's my desire. But that's not a desire I favor, or even identify with, though it is my own. When I give in to that desire, it seems more like giving in to a weakness than an exercise of freedom."

"Exactly!" There was a triumphant note in Ben's voice. "You are following your own desire, but you are *not* acting freely. So what follows? Following your own desires, being loosed from shackles, is *not* enough for real freedom, *not* enough for genuine free will, whatever Hume might say to the contrary."

"Very nice point, Ben. You put your finger on a sore spot in Hume's view, a real problem for the claim that determinism is compatible with freedom. But," Sarah continued, "it's a sore spot that more recent compatibilists have tried to heal."

"Compatibilism needs a priest, not a doctor." Ben was ready to drive the stake through the heart of compatibilism. "Read compatibilism its last rites and lay it to rest."

"Don't be too hasty, Ben." Sarah smiled. "I don't think compatibilism has suffered a fatal injury, though I agree that your example causes problems for the view. Here's the therapy prescribed by a twentieth-century philosopher, Harry Frankfurt. Frankfurt raised exactly the points you and Selina brought up: You want to play video games, but at a deeper level you *prefer* to read a history book; Selina wants to eat chocolate chip cookies, but she wishes she desired celery instead. The desire to read history and eat celery: those are deeper desires that you two reflectively approve, right?"

"Okay," Ben agreed, "but I don't see how that helps compatibilism."

"Well, Frankfurt used the same sort of example: His favorite one was of a drug addict. Easy to imagine. I toy with drugs, think I'm completely in control. But one day I wake up and realize that I have a raging drug addiction and I don't have the resources to fight it. I hate my addiction. I certainly love and desire drugs, but it is decidedly *not* a desire I identify with, not a desire I reflectively approve. I desire drugs, and I take drugs because of my own desire, no one forces me; but I'm *not free*."

Ben registered his approval. "Frankfurt is exactly on the money."

"Then Frankfurt takes the next step," Sarah continued. "The drug addict who despises her addiction is not free. But suppose we move to a higher level of willing—or if you like, suppose we look *deeper* into motives and preferences. That is, consider *levels* of willing, a *hierarchical* model of compatibilist free will (as distinguished from Hume's *simple* compatibilism). Imagine a different addict: one who *likes* being addicted, who reflectively *approves* her addiction, who *wants* to be addicted to drugs. Frankfurt says she is a *willing* addict. She has the will she wants, the will she reflectively approves, and thus she has free will. As Frankfurt puts it, she may not have everything she could possibly want; but she has everything she could wish for in the way of free will. Now notice: The willing addict's behavior is fixed. She is an addict, and she will definitely take drugs; that's set, and she *cannot do otherwise*. But she is free, nonetheless, because she has the desires and will that *she approves*. Thus, Frankfurt concludes, it is not necessary to be able to do otherwise in order to have free will. Rather, what is required is that you reflectively approve—at a higher level—of your own desires."

"Wait a minute, Sarah." Ben's head was spinning. "Frankfurt says that someone addicted to drugs can be free, even though she cannot break her addiction and cannot avoid taking drugs? Something seems wrong here."

"Maybe the drug-addict example is throwing you. Let's take a more pleasant one. Selina, you love studying chemistry, right?"

"Yeah, it's fascinating. There are all these wonderful puzzles to solve, and they're fun to think about, and you get a clear, definite answer when you solve them correctly. And there's no end to new puzzles. Plus, I want to use my chemistry background to do pharmacological research: find new drugs and vaccines to help people live longer and healthier and happier. That would be deeply satisfying, doing what I love and helping others in the process."

"Do you ever wish you were less interested in chemistry? I mean, you're not going to get rich doing chemistry research, Selina. You ever wish you were more interested in some area that would be more likely to make you wealthy? Philosophy, for example?"

"No, I'll leave the big bucks for you philosophers. I've thought about being wealthy, even fantasized about it. I guess everyone has. But it doesn't strike me as a very worthwhile goal. On the other hand, becoming an excellent chemical researcher, maybe discovering a cure for Alzheimer's, or a vaccination against a deadly disease—that's something I have thought about carefully, and it's a goal I deeply approve of. I love chemistry, and I'm very glad that I love chemistry."

"Alright, Ben, now consider Selina's love of chemistry. Suppose that we could trace her fascination with chemistry to the junior chemistry set her uncle gave her and maybe even to summer afternoons when she would play with her chemistry set at her grandmother's house. Then, immediately afterward, her grandmother would give her cookies and praise her experiments, so Selina was gradually shaped to love chemistry. Or maybe her fascination with chemistry is rooted in her genetic history (though I certainly doubt it). None of that history matters. What matters is that Selina studies chemistry because *she loves* chemistry, and she deeply and reflectively *approves* of her fascination with chemistry, and she *wants* to be the sort of person who loves chemistry. Selina is acting freely: She has full *hierarchical* free will. Of course, if Selina had different interests, she could pursue those. But given the interests she has—and of which she deeply approves—she will work on chemistry. No one forces her to; rather, she does it from her own wishes. Her own wishes and interests were shaped by her history, of course, and given the way she was shaped and her own desires, it is *determined* that she will do chemistry research. But that doesn't make her interests any less her own, nor does it make her any less free when she pursues those interests."

Ben shook his head. "I could almost be tempted to agree that Selina is free when she pursues her *determined* interests. But it doesn't work. And if you get away from Selina's pleasant hours in the chemistry laboratory and return to Frankfurt's own example—the example you mentioned of the willing addict—then it's easy to see why it doesn't work. A drug addict who desires drugs, but hates her addiction and longs to escape it, is not

---

It is said that even though behavior is completely determined, it is better that a man "feel free" or "believe that he is free." If this means that it is better to be controlled in ways which have no aversive consequences, we may agree, but if it means that it is better to be controlled in ways against which no one revolts, it fails to take account of the possibility of deferred aversive consequences. A second comment seems more appropriate: "It is better to be a conscious slave than a happy one." The word "slave" clarifies the nature of the ultimate consequences being considered: they are exploitative and hence aversive. What the slave is to be conscious of is his misery; and a system of slavery so well designed that it does not breed revolt is the real threat. The literature of freedom has been designed to make men "conscious" of aversive control, but in its choice of methods it has failed to rescue the happy slave.

B. F. Skinner, *Beyond Freedom and Dignity*, 1971

free. On that point I agree with Frankfurt. But a drug addict who desires drugs and approves her addiction and embraces her addiction to drugs—she does not suddenly become free. She may have 'the will she wants to have,' but what she wants is enslavement to addiction, and enslavement is not freedom, whether one embraces one's enslavement or not."

Selina nodded. "He's right, Sarah, I can't buy Frankfurt's account of freedom. Suppose you were born into a culture that regarded women as properly subordinate, as people who should take their orders from men and not think for themselves. You hate it: You want to be independent, make your own choices, have the recognition of your own equal status. You struggle against it, but you are kept in a subordinate, dependent role. You're obviously not free, and Frankfurt agrees that you are not free. Your entire culture, your family, your friends, all are against you: They regard your desire for independence as willful and evil. Gradually, you feel your desire for independence weakening. Your insistence on thinking for yourself as a full equal is slipping away, eroded by the heavy pressure to conform to your cultural role of subordination. You now want to be dependent and subordinate, but you hate the change that is taking place: You don't reflectively approve of your desire to be an unthinking subordinate, though you recognize you now have that desire. But the pressures continue, and finally you fully embrace this culture that subordinates women, you regard your youthful views as wicked wilfulness, you deeply and reflectively approve your acquiescent subordination, and you endeavor to raise your daughters to be dutiful and subservient. Now, according to Frankfurt, you have gained real freedom! But that's absurd. The slave who struggles unsuccessfully to escape is not free; but the slave who gives up and embraces her enslavement is even *less* free. The contented subservient wife, the defeated 'willing addict,' the 'happy slave,' and all who have been so profoundly worn down that they have lost even the dream of freedom—they are *not* free, and their having given up the struggle only makes them more deeply enslaved."

Sarah frowned. "I see your point, but not everyone would agree with you. I recently read a book by Gerald Dworkin—a philosopher whose position on freedom runs along the same hierarchical lines as Frankfurt's—who firmly believes that the willing addict and happy slave have genuine freedom." Sarah reached into her backpack, pulled out a book and turned to the first of several pages she had marked, then continued. "As Dworkin says,

> a person who wants to be restricted in various ways . . . is not, on that account alone, less autonomous. . . . In my conception, the autonomous person can be a tyrant or a slave. . . . [1]

So suppose some people *embrace* slavery; they *want* to be slaves. Does that mean they aren't free?"

"That's exactly what it means," Ben said, and Selina nodded.

Rationalist Compatibilism

"Alright, I see we aren't going to resolve that conflict: I guess you two are unlikely to adopt the hierarchical compatibilism that Frankfurt and Dworkin favor. And in fact, lots of people have been disturbed by some of the implications of their position, particularly that the happy slave and willing addict are really free. Some compatibilists have tried to find a way to circumvent that problem. Susan Wolf agrees with Frankfurt that 'freedom to do otherwise' is not necessary for freedom, but Wolf would not count Frankfurt's willing addict—who approves of his addictive desire—as free. Wolf sets a stronger condition for freedom."

"We're not headed back toward miracle-working contracausal free will, are we?" Selina frowned. "Not another version of Campbell's libertarian mysteries, I hope."

"No," Sarah replied, "not Campbell's contracausal free will. Susan Wolf does not believe that freedom requires open alternatives, a break from determinism; after all, she's a compatibilist, who believes that freedom is *compatible* with determinism. No, what Susan Wolf requires for real freedom is that one's acts and choices be fully *rational* and that they be aimed at what is genuinely right and good. To distinguish Wolf's compatibilism from Hume's *simple* compatibilism and Frankfurt's *hierarchical* compatibilism, we might call Wolf's version *rationalist* compatibilism. Susan Wolf"—Sarah had her notebook open and was looking for a quotation she had written down—"says that, on the open-alternatives model of free will (Campbell's libertarian model), we 'want not only the ability to act rationally but also the ability to act *ir*rationally—but the latter is a very strange ability to want, if it is an ability at all.'[2] Wolf's position is developed out of a long and illustrious rationalist tradition in ethics that stretches back to Plato. If you do something wrong, you are acting in ignorance. As Plato insisted, to know the good is to do it. When you genuinely understand what is good and virtuous, you are immediately attracted to it. So if someone acts viciously, it is because he or she doesn't *really* know what is good. Wolf draws out an interesting implication of this position: If you do something wrong, it's because you were deceived, you were acting in ignorance; but of course, if you were acting in ignorance, then you can't really be *morally responsible* for your act. So while it may be possible to deserve reward for your wise and virtuous behavior, no one can be held responsible—no one can deserve blame or punishment—for her bad acts. But the whole ques-

David Hume, Harry Frankfurt, and Susan Wolf are all compatibilists; *that is, they all agree that determinism is* compatible *with free will. But they diverge on what they think is required for genuine free will. On Hume's simple* compatibilist view, *you are free when you are "not in chains"; that is, you are free when you are not being coerced—when you are following your own desires. Frankfurt considers that criterion inadequate. After all, your own desires—such as your addictive desire for drugs—may be experienced as alien and coercive. Thus, Frankfurt's hierarchical compatibilism goes deeper: The exercise of free will requires that you be able to follow your own wishes and desires, but you must also (at a higher level)* approve *of your desires and acknowledge them as your own. Susan Wolf's rationalist compatibilism sets still stronger requirements for genuine free will. According to Wolf, to have genuine free will, you must reflectively choose the* right *path for the* right *reason.*

tion of just deserts and moral responsibility—that's really another issue. Wolf's key point is that genuine freedom consists in following the narrow path of the True and Good. So open alternatives are an *impediment* to true freedom. Here's a line from Wolf that I love: 'Why would one want the ability to pass up the apple when to do so would be merely unpleasant or arbitrary?'[3] It would be like judging a train superior because of its ability to occasionally jump the tracks. Krishnamurti asserts that 'a truly intelligent [enlightened] mind simply cannot have choice,' since it must always 'choose the path of truth.'[4] On Wolf's view, to be genuinely enlightened—and genuinely free—means following a narrow, fixed path."

"Look, Sarah," said Selina, "I like reason, especially when I'm in the laboratory. And there's certainly a place for careful thought in our everyday lives. But reason isn't everything. I'm not sure I want to be locked into always doing the rational thing."

"Yeah, I understand what you're getting at, Selina. What's that line from e e cummings?

Wholly to be a fool when spring is in the world my blood approves;
Kisses are a better fate than wisdom. . . ."

Ben nodded. "Agreed. Kisses are wonderful, no doubt of that: Selina's are like cool strawberry wine on a dry summer day."

Selina leaned over and kissed him. "No one sweeter than my Ben, is there, Sarah?"

Sarah shook her head. "I'm sorry I brought up kisses. Like you two need any special encouragement."

"In any case," Ben continued, "if we're talking about real freedom, I'm not sure that reason is enough. You also have to have genuine open alternatives to reason about."

Selina laughed. "I can certainly see some advantages to Susan Wolf's view, especially the part about you are responsible only for your good behavior. When I act virtuously, I deserve a reward; when I'm bad, I do not deserve blame. That really would be the best of all possible worlds. Still, Wolf's position, for all its charms, seems like a severely rationalist view of free behavior. Reason and scientific method and careful deliberation unclouded by passion—that's the way to go; I'm all for science and reason and cool deliberation. But there are times when hot, irrational passion is also rather nice." Selina nudged Ben. "Besides, Sarah, as you were pointing out a couple of days ago, some of the most insightful scientific research started with a scientist taking a chance, playing a hunch, believing what initially appeared to be an implausible hypothesis. Of course, a lot of those hunches turn out to be wrong, and careful rational scientific research is what shows them to be wrong, and it's also what is required to prove a hunch right. Still, there's room for spontaneity."

"Oh, yeah, listen to the determinist here." Ben saw his opening.

"Hey, look, I never said I was against spontaneity. I love it. Like last Tuesday afternoon, remember, I was working late in the chemistry lab, you stopped by to see if I wanted to take a break for dinner, no one else was there, it was quiet, the snow was falling outside, and. . . ."

"Selina! Can't we keep a few secrets?"

Determinism and Spontaneity

"Don't get upset, Ben. I was just making a philosophical point. Spontaneity is great. Even for hardheaded scientists and adamant determinists. You don't have to reject determinism to accept the value of spontaneity; you just have to recognize that spontaneity also has its determining causes. Last semester, Sarah, remember our class on behavioral psychology? Professor DeMaio was telling us about this experiment done by J. Lee Kavanau. Kavanau was teaching feral white-footed mice to run a maze, with a food reward at the end of the maze. After several trials, the mice had apparently mastered the swiftest path to their reward and could fly through the maze. But the mice still did not consistently run the 'correct' path through the maze, instead occasionally taking wrong turns and slower routes. Kavanau wondered why these mice were such bad learners, still making mistakes. But finally he realized that their behavior was not flawed at all: It was highly adaptive behavior for animals that live in changing environments. The path that currently offers the most reliable food source is traveled most often, but exploring alternative paths (paths that the white-footed mouse has successfully learned are not now the most promising) is valuable, because it keeps options open. If the current food source dries up or is blocked, then the white-footed mouse will have other

paths to pursue; and if a new food source develops, the mouse's deep preference for exploring alternatives makes its discovery more likely. So there
is nothing mysterious or miraculous about our commitment to spontaneous behavior and open alternatives, whether we are humans or chimps
or white-footed mice.[5] Such preferences do not involve contracausal free
will or any other special metaphysical or super-rational powers. In fact, it
is not difficult to find the causal basis for valuing spontaneity and open
alternatives. We evolved in a world filled with changes. That doesn't mean
we can't successfully follow the same path to food or safety or the laboratory. But still, our environment does change. Productive food sources
wither, formerly barren berry patches become fruitful, and favorite paths
are blocked by predators and floods and highway construction. Animals
that keep their options open enhance their survival chances. There are
advantages to open escape alternatives, whether you are a deer exploring
the forest, a rabbit visiting Mr. McGregor's garden, or a student trying to
avoid the professor whose class you just cut."

Ben shook his head. "Selina, I don't see how you can compare human
free will with the behavior of rabbits and deer and white-footed mice."

"But they *are* comparable," Selina replied. "Spontaneous variations
help us avoid starvation, predators, and traffic jams, and it is not surprising that we value such spontaneity and the avoidance of dull routine.
Humans may be able to create more alternatives and, through the
resources of language and higher cognitive abilities—and novels and
movies and paintings—explore paths without physically trudging down
them. But the value of our more elaborate alternatives is rooted in the
same survival advantages that lead mice and rabbits and chimpanzees to
also value open options and spontaneous forays. It's only when we seek
ways in which humans are somehow special and distinct and different in
kind from the rest of the animal world that this common and valuable element of free behavior gets transformed into something mysterious and
complex—the exclusive property of godlike humans. I don't see any conflict between open, spontaneous behavior and determinism or between
open alternatives and determinism. I'm a naturalist, through and through.
But deterministic naturalism does not eliminate spontaneity. It *does* eliminate the sort of contracausal free will that Campbell and Sartre—and old
Ben—like. Whether it eliminates *all* free will: Well, I guess, that depends
on your definition of free will."

Ben was ready in defense of special powers of free will. "I like a
world that contains mysteries and miracles, even if Selina doesn't. But
I'm glad to know that Selina's determinist philosophy leaves room for
spontaneity. I never doubted that Selina loves spontaneity; it's nice to
know that her life and her philosophy are in harmony. And I agree with
Selina's view of Susan Wolf: Her version of rationalist free will doesn't

---

The goal, to put it bluntly, is the True and the Good. The freedom we want is the freedom to find it. But such a freedom requires not only that we, as agents, have the right sorts of abilities—the abilities, that is, to direct and govern our actions by our most fundamental selves. It requires as well that the world cooperate in such a way that our most fundamental selves have the opportunity to develop into the selves they ought to be.

Susan Wolf, "Asymmetrical Freedom," 1980

---

look very free to me. Enslavement to rationality still seems like enslavement, not freedom."

"Just listen to yourself, Ben!" Sarah laughed. "'Enslavement to reason!' Susan Wolf isn't talking about being a *slave* to reason. Reason is what *frees* you from enslavement to prejudice and irrationality and tradition and passion. You don't follow the rational path because reason holds a gun to your head and coerces you or locks you in shackles. You follow reason because it reveals the best path, the right road, the correct solution. And reason doesn't *keep* you from exploring and discovering. To the contrary, it *opens up* paths of discovery and innovation by freeing you from irrational beliefs—false beliefs that are held in place by bias and illegitimate authority and the dead weight of tradition. So, you want the freedom to make stupid mistakes, follow mindless prejudices, enslave yourself to unexamined tradition, and be the pawn of irrational fancies. Be my guest. Doesn't sound like real freedom to me."

"Wow, Sarah, that was quite a speech!" Selina was impressed. "Look, I'm all for reason; you're preaching to the choir, girl, as far as I'm concerned. A lot better than prejudice and irrationality and blind tradition, amen. Let's hear it for reason! But it's that *single-minded* reason that gives me pause. It's as Karl Popper says: It's our boldly *mistaken* theories that are likely to be of greatest benefit. It's not that I deny that there is a truth about the world: I think there is, but it basically functions as an ideal which prompts further scientific inquiry. We aren't anywhere near any such final truth, and the path we have to take is one of twists and turns—including wrong turns, which may wind up being beneficial, like the 'wrong turns' of the white-footed mice that increase their options. The idea of a single, fixed truth, an *absolute* truth—*the* True and *the* Good—such a straight and narrow path strikes me as too narrow and precise, too purely rationalistic for the grubby, confusing world we live in and study. Let a hundred flowers blossom, Chairman Mao used to say. Let theories and ideas compete, and better explanations will emerge. Okay, the mistaken theories were wrong, even if they were still useful and provocative; but it is something else entirely to suppose that those bold thinkers who championed flawed theories were therefore not really acting freely. You know, Sarah, Susan Wolf's theory of freedom sounds too much like my Momma's old trick: 'You are free to eat your candy any time you choose, Sweetheart, so long as you choose wisely and save it for after dinner.' Freedom to follow a prescribed track: That's not what I call freedom."

"Okay, Selina, I knew you were going to balk at any reference to *the* True and Good. Sounds too rationalistic for an old empiricist like you. But Ben, I thought that, given your Christian views, you might find Wolf's account of genuine freedom more appealing. After all, don't at least some Christians claim that the only *true* freedom is perfect obedience to God's commands, and the only *truly* free act is walking the straight and *narrow* path of righteousness? And in Heaven, the elect will be in God's immediate presence, and then it will be *impossible* to stray from God's glorious Goodness—and that will be the highest form of freedom. Perfect freedom is found in perfect obedience to God."

"Alright, there is that element of Christianity. But real freedom still requires the ability to do otherwise. You are *really* free when you follow the right path, but choosing the wrong path has to also be a genuine open possibility."

Sarah smiled. "Look, Ben, I'm just a New York Jewish kid, I'm not interested in enforcing Christian orthodoxy. But that's *not* what Christians like Luther and Calvin thought. They believed that God's grace is irresistible, and those to whom God gives His grace—those whom God elects for salvation—*cannot* do otherwise than follow God in all His glory. They simply *cannot* resist God's grace. Or as some of my fellow New Yorkers might say, 'When God offers you grace, He's making you an offer you can't refuse.' So although no other option is really open, they believe that, by God's irresistible grace, you find perfect freedom in following God."

"Maybe so, Sarah. But if that's the orthodox position," Ben continued, "I'm afraid I must not be perfectly orthodox. It still seems to me that a choice has to be among genuinely open alternatives in order to be a free choice, and it must be genuinely possible to freely choose among the alternatives."

"And *that* sort of free will does not exist," Selina added. "In fact, it's such an impossibly confused notion—a choice that's my choice, but doesn't come from my character—that I'm not even sure what it could look like."

Moral Responsibility

"Okay, let's not start back down that road; we never seem to reach the end. Anyway, we've hardly mentioned the issue that drives most discussions of free will." Sarah plunged back into her notebook, in search of yet another favorite passage. "C. A. Campbell—Ben's ally in the battle for libertarian, contracausal free will—perhaps said it best:

> It is not seriously disputable that the kind of freedom in question is the freedom which is commonly recognised to be in some sense a precondition of moral responsibility. Clearly, it is on account of this integral connection with moral responsibility that such exceptional importance has always been felt to attach to the Free Will problem. But in what precise sense is free will a precondition of moral responsibility, and thus a postulate of the moral life in general?[6]

And of course, for Campbell, the only sort of free will that can support claims of moral responsibility is contracausal free will. Perhaps that's why Ben is so insistent on this strong contracausal, miracle-working free will: Ben believes that God rewards and punishes in the afterlife—rewards generously, but punishes rather harshly, as I understand it—and how could God justly reward and punish if we could not genuinely have chosen otherwise than we did? If God marches us down a predestined path, then it hardly seems fair to punish us for following a path we could not avoid. God punishes and rewards, and God must be just, and just punishment requires that we genuinely could have done otherwise; that is, it requires contracausal free will. Right, Ben?"

"Look, guys." Ben was clearly a bit uncomfortable. "I'm not sure I believe quite all of that—not literally. I mean the stuff about lakes of fire and eternal damnation. No matter how many bad things someone has done, it's still a *finite* number, right? And to be burned for *infinity*; well, that seems out of line with what a just and loving God would do. Just punishment is one thing; eternal torture is something else entirely."

Selina laughed. "Oh, ye of little faith! Come on, Ben, you're straining at a gnat and swallowing a camel. You buy all this stuff about God making the world, and about God being omnipotent but we still have some sort of mysterious free will, and about God being infinite but still there are things outside of God. You can believe all that, and then you strain on the belief that God could burn me for all eternity in a lake of fire just because I find His existence implausible?"

Practical Punishment

"Look, I believe that God changeth not. But maybe our understanding of God changes. At one time, people thought of God as this supervengeful God, a harsh and punitive God; but now we understand God better—as a God of love. Okay, a just God, as well. I believe in just punishments and just rewards. And I don't believe it's fair and just to punish people for what they can't help doing. That's one reason I believe God gives us free will, to make our own free choices: choices that are really open, that could genuinely go either way. Otherwise, it wouldn't be *fair* to hold us morally responsible, to blame and punish and reward. That's not the *only* reason I believe in free will. As Campbell says, we do observe, in ourselves, that we can make free choices. Still, free choices are essential for real responsibility and just deserts; and I certainly believe that we have moral responsibility."

"Ben, I actually agree with you about something!" Selina was smiling. "I believe in punishment and reward, too. But Ben, you don't need all that stuff about just Gods and contracausal free will to justify punishment and reward. Punishment and reward are useful parts of our nonmiraculous natural world. Who deserves punishment? The person who did wrong— and who did wrong from his or her own wishes. Did the person act with some miraculous contracausal free will? Of course not. Does the person 'justly deserve' punishment in some ultimate cosmic justice sense? Maybe yes, maybe no. Who cares? The only relevant question is whether punishing the person will prevent her from doing wrong in future and perhaps deter others from doing wrong. If the person is demented, then we don't punish her: Punishing her won't change her behavior. If someone held a gun to her head and forced her to commit a crime, we don't punish her: Punishment is designed to change character and behavior, and we don't need to change her character, since the act didn't come from her character. It's the same with reward: You do something right, we want to encourage you to keep doing it; we want to entrench that character trait, so we reward you. Who deserves punishment? The person whose behavior will be changed by it. That's why we don't punish the innocent, the coerced, the insane. That's why we punish those who willingly choose to do wrong. It doesn't matter what *ultimately* caused their behavior: their early childhood conditioning or genes or whatever. It's way too late to have any effect on those. What we *can* change is the person who willingly did wrong; and that's where the punishment is *deserved*. Punishment and reward are simple and practical matters, and we don't need mysteries of contracausal free will to make them work."

"Ah, Selina," Sarah said, "you are once again the voice of Hume. That's exactly the justification he would give for punishment. In fact, that's the justification most empiricists would offer: Moritz Schlick is a noteworthy example."

"And exactly the right justification it is. Punishment and reward are justified when they *work*. What *other* justification could one offer?"

Ben shook his head. "I can think of one other justification, Selina. They're justified because they are *justly deserved*. If they happen to work, that's fine; but that's not the *justification* for punishment. Look, suppose

Punishment is concerned only with the institution of causes, of motives of conduct, and this alone is its meaning. Punishment is an educative measure, and as such is a means to the formation of motives, which are in part to prevent the wrongdoer from repeating the act (reformation) and in part to prevent others from committing a similar act (intimidation). Analogously, in the case of reward we are concerned with an incentive.

Hence the question regarding responsibility is the question: Who, in a given case, is to be punished? Who is to be considered the true wrongdoer? This problem is not identical with that regarding the original instigator of the act; for the great-grandparents of the man, from whom he inherited his character, might in the end be the cause, or the statesmen who are responsible for his social milieu, and so forth. But the "doer" is the one upon whom the motive must have acted in order, with certainty, to have prevented the act (or called it forth, as the case might be). Consideration of remote causes is of no help here, for in the first place their actual contribution cannot be determined, and in the second place they are generally out of reach. Rather, we must find the person in whom the decisive junction of cause lies. The question of who is responsible is the question concerning the correct application of the motive. . . . It is a matter only of knowing who is to be punished or rewarded, in order that punishment and reward function as such—be able to achieve their goal.

Moritz Schlick, "When Is a Man Responsible?" 1939

we have a crime wave, and people start thinking they can get away with criminal acts. So we frame this poor recluse, and we punish him severely, and that reduces the crime rate. Would that mean the punishment was *justified*—that he *deserved* punishment?"

Selina shook her head. "That would be a bad use of punishment, Ben. Because it's likely the facts would be revealed, and that would cause even less confidence that people who actually commit crimes will be punished."

"Oh, I see: So long as we can keep this miscarriage of justice hidden, it's justified. No way, Selina. It's *wrong*, because no matter whether it ultimately prevents crime or not, it's *unjust* to punish this man. Now think of another case. Here's a little girl, she puts her hand on a hot stove and gets a bad burn. She learns her lesson: She won't put her hand on a stove again. It worked! So, did she *justly deserve* her burn?"

"There's another problem, Selina, with trying to justify punishment and reward in terms of their good effects," Sarah weighed in. "Punishment and reward—at least punishment and reward as we traditionally assign them—don't work very well. That's no surprise to you, is it? After all, you've taken some courses in psychology. Look, suppose we want to improve the behavior of Selina and Sarah. Selina is incredibly industrious, hardworking, disciplined, brilliant, creative. Sarah, in contrast, is lazy, slow, undisciplined, dull witted, plodding. Selina and Sarah both have a project due, and Selina gives it less effort than usual, devotes minimum thought and little creativity, yet still produces a moderately good result. Sarah manages more than her usual effort and works to the best of her modest abilities—yet her work is still significantly inferior to Selina's below-average effort. Who *deserves* reward? Selina's work is better, and she gave more thought and effort to the project than Sarah did, though, given her great store of fortitude, well below her usual standards. Sarah's work is not very good, but her small efforts and meager result are a significant advance over how she usually does. Still, Selina produced a better result and gave more effort: She *deserves* a greater reward—if we reward on the traditional basis of 'just deserts.' But such a reward system is likely to encourage a weakening of Selina's fortitude and efforts and abilities by rewarding her for less than her usual efforts; and our failure to reward Sarah will extinguish her small start at doing better work and exerting more effort. Or take it from another angle: Sarah hardly ever does anything, she is profoundly lethargic. If we want her to develop more drive and energy, we'll reward her when she makes even a slight effort, and we'll continue to do so when she makes slightly greater efforts. By contrast, energetic Selina will develop even greater fortitude if we 'stretch the interval' between rewards: Instead of rewarding her for every effort, we reward her only after every third, then after every fifth, and so on. Selina will learn to continue her efforts through many failures: She will become a scientist who endures dozens of failed experiments in her search for a successful solution. But to make that work, we shall have to give *more* rewards to lethargic Sarah for doing less work and exerting initially less effort than is put forth by hardworking Selina. The point is an obvious one, long confirmed by psychological research, and well known to every introductory psychology student: Rewarding and punishing on the basis of traditional 'just deserts' is not the best way to shape good behavior. If you want to complain that such a pattern of rewarding is not *fair*—it's not fair and just to reward Selina less when she does more work than Sarah— then, fine; but notice, you have now given up the idea that rewards and just deserts can be based on their usefulness and practicality, and you've gone back to a notion of fairness and justice. So if you want to justify 'just deserts,' you'll have to do it on the basis of justice or rightness or fairness or something of that sort; you cannot justify it on the basis of its practical usefulness. Giving out 'just deserts' doesn't work very well, if at all."

Denying Moral Responsibility

"Okay," Selina responded, "you've made your point. But what's your conclusion? Do you want to eliminate rewards altogether? That doesn't seem like a good idea."

"No, of course not." Sarah was emphatic. "You couldn't if you tried, and there's no reason to try. After all, when you work long and hard to solve a scientific puzzle, and finally you find the solution, that's very rewarding, right? Or you write an essay, and you put a lot of effort into it, and when you're done, you read it over and you say to yourself, 'Way to go, Selina, you did a great job on that': that's inherently satisfying, you find it deeply rewarding. Right? And it's important that you feel that sense of satisfaction; it helps to keep you working hard. So inherent rewards are very nice. You keep your head down, pivot smoothly, swing easily, and the ball goes flying far down the fairway, with perhaps a slight fade to the right. Wow, that's very nice! And experiencing that sort of reward keeps you going and helps you improve. No one wants to eliminate those. And external rewards can also be helpful. When you've spent weeks in your lab, tracking down dead ends but still not finding the answer, and you're feeling a bit frustrated, it's nice when Professor Sykes stops by the lab and brings you coffee and praises you for all the hard work you've put in and the fortitude you've shown. So, rewards are great. But useful rewards have nothing to do with *just deserts* and *moral responsibility*. Those are notions that get in the way of trying to understand and improve behavior. Frankly, all the stuff about just deserts and moral responsibility belongs with miracles and mysteries, Selina, and it has no place in your worldview."

"Wait a minute, Sarah." Selina was not entirely convinced. "That seems hasty. *No* place for just deserts and moral responsibility? Okay, I agree that sometimes the idea of just deserts seems unfair. Some people really do have better opportunities than others. I remember in high school, I was on the track team, ran the 1600. I was decent; in fact, by the time I was a junior, I was pretty good. I worked hard at it. When it rained, I ran. When it got cold, I ran. When it got hot and muggy—and believe me, it gets hot and muggy in Alabama—Selina was still out there running. Trained hard, watched what I ate, worked at it, day after day and month after month. By the time I was a junior, I was the best 1600 runner on the team. But there was this girl at Western High, our crosstown rivals, she was the same year I was. Man, I wanted to beat her. I *worked* at beating her, trained hard, ran my heart out. But I never could. Never even got close. She could run like a gazelle. Her feet hardly seemed to touch the track, she was that smooth. Oh, she worked at it. You don't get to be a good distance runner without working at it. But I know she didn't train as hard as I did. She would skip training days, eat candy, skip a week when it got really hot. But she always won the district trophy for the 1600. She won it fair and square. She wasn't using steroids or anything. But still, it wasn't really fair: She just had more talent than I, she had the right genes for running. She was lucky."

Sarah nodded. "Yeah, Selina, exactly right. She was lucky. In one sense, of course, she justly deserved to win the trophy. But in another, clear sense, it wasn't fair: You never had a chance, because you weren't as lucky as she. And luck can't be a good basis for just deserts."

Selina frowned. "Yeah, but that still bothers me. Look, she was lucky at running. I was lucky at math. I had friends in high school who worked just as hard as I did at mathematics—even harder—and could never get it. So maybe it all evens out: We're all lucky in some ways, unlucky in others, but unless we have some disastrous misfortune, such as severe brain damage or something terrible like that, we can all use our wits and efforts to succeed. Luck averages out. Sure, the ball takes a bad hop sometimes, but that happens to everybody. That doesn't mean luck cancels out just deserts. I'm never going to be an Olympic distance runner, no matter how hard I train. Tough luck. But there are successes I can achieve by my own efforts and for which I deserve my just rewards. Everybody has their own abilities, everybody gets their share of luck." Selina turned toward Ben. "What are your lucky areas, Ben? An aptitude for history, right?"

"I'm lucky to have you, Selina. That's enough luck for any man."

Selina put her hand on Ben's, kissed his fingers, and turned back toward Sarah. "Isn't he the sweetest thing? What's your luck, Sarah?"

"I'm lucky to have a strong stomach. You guys would make a soap opera blush. But look, Selina, you don't really believe that stuff about 'luck averages out,' do you? I mean, it's nice for fairy tales and children's inspirational books, but it's not true. Look, here's my friend Selina. Let's compare her with one of her friends back home—call her Sandra. Selina starts out with a little luck: She's a little brighter than Sandra, slightly more inquisitive. But not by that much, they're fairly close. Selina goes to school, her teachers notice that she's particularly bright and inquisitive, and they give her special attention. Maybe they don't really plan to, they try to treat everyone the same; but Selina is more rewarding to work with, so they give her extra time. And so Selina continues to get better, and then she gets selected for some special summer science programs—Sandra was not that far behind, but only one kid was selected, and Selina was a little better—and those special summer science programs gave Selina special training and great encouragement and clearer goals, so she continued to get better and better. And don't say Sandra could have tried harder and evened things out. The capacity to try hard is also shaped by our successes. Selina and Sandra both tried hard, but Selina's efforts were more regularly rewarded, and Sandra's were more often ignored, so Selina's capacity for hard work and sustained effort grew stronger while Sandra's weakened. This continued through high school, and Selina's initial small advantage continued to accumulate further benefits. Eventually, she wound up with a full scholarship to the University of Michigan, while Sandra—who didn't win a scholarship—couldn't afford college. So Selina's initial luck is *not* balanced by Sandra's subsequent good luck; rather, the initial advantage tends to grow larger."

"Yeah, Sarah, I know how that works!" Ben had another example to add. "I used to play baseball, loved it. Had a friend, John, and we were both decent players, but John was a little better; not that much, just a little better. So what happened? John got to play a little more than I did, and the coaches gave him a little more attention. Then, at the end of the season, they picked the all-star teams, to play additional games in the tournaments. John made it, and I just missed. So he played several more games, got some special coaching. Then the next year, because he had been on an all-star team, he was picked for a better league, and I got left in the recreational league. John played more games, against better competition, better coaching. By the time we got to high school, he was significantly better than I. We both tried out for the varsity: He made it, I didn't. We both kept playing baseball, but he got professional coaching from the high school coach, and I played only in recreational leagues. Since he was on the high school varsity, he played in much better summer leagues, played more games, still had better coaching. They had special facilities, could practice all winter in indoor batting cages; and without an indoor facility, you don't play much baseball in the Michigan winter. I kept trying hard, but I finally got discouraged; John tried hard, and his efforts were rewarded. So by the end of high school, I had quit playing baseball, and John is now playing college ball. There wasn't much difference when we started, but those small differences got amplified, not reduced. 'Luck' is cumulative, not even."

"You were lucky after all, Sugar." Selina patted his hand. "If you had become a better baseball player, you'd probably be playing shortstop for the Wolverines, and then you might not have met me."

Sarah laughed. "Yeah, sometimes even a country boy from Michigan draws the winning ticket. But the point is simple: Luck and opportunities simply do *not* balance out. The story of the plodding tortoise with great fortitude beating the swift hare is a wonderful children's story, but it's not realistic. Of course, sometimes a player with greater drive and fortitude beats a player with more talent, and a shrewd player may edge a more talented one. But stories of greater fortitude edging superior talent are more often the stuff of fantasy. The more talented player gets more playing time and develops more confidence as well as greater fortitude, and because she plays more, she also has more court savvy."

"You're right, Sarah; but still, I *like* the story of the hare and the tortoise," Ben protested. "I liked it as a kid, and I think it's good for children to hear such stories."

Unable to fully understand how and why some individuals are able to demonstrate self-control in the face of very trying circumstances, we have attributed such behavior to willpower, to some supernatural entity, or to an underlying personality trait. These ways of thinking about the problem have unfortunately retarded understanding and discouraged research. A vicious tautology or circularity has been created. The person who succeeds in demonstrating self-control by resisting a major temptation—for example, the heavy smoker who quits cold turkey—is often described as having willpower. How do we know that he has willpower? Well, he quit smoking, didn't he? This circular route of observing a self-regulative behavior, inferring willpower, and then using the latter to "explain" the former is an all too frequent journey in self-control discussions. We have not gotten beyond the behavior to be explained. Moreover, this tautology discourages further inquiries into the factors affecting self-control.

Michael Mahoney and Carl Thoresen, *Self-Control: Power to the Person*
(Monterey, CA: Brooks/Cole, 1974), pp. 20–21

"I agree with you, Ben." Sarah nodded. "I'm not suggesting that we ban the story of the hare and the tortoise. In fact, I think it's valuable. Children should learn that, with diligence and effort and fortitude, they can succeed. Perhaps hearing such stories will increase their diligence—though when it comes to developing fortitude, stories are no substitute for the experience of success in tasks that are neither impossibly difficult nor overly easy. Skill and fortitude and shrewdness are important; it's not just a matter of luck that those having such capacities meet with success. But having those capacities in the first place *is* ultimately a matter of luck, and luck is no foundation for moral responsibility and just deserts."

Ben frowned. "Doesn't that go too far, Sarah? Do you really want to deny the existence of moral responsibility and just deserts? Deny that anyone *ever* justly deserves reward or punishment?"

"That's exactly what I want to deny, Ben. I think we can make good sense of freedom and free will. Not the contracausal free will you favor, sorry, but still a substantial freedom: the freedom to follow our own desires and to carefully consider our deepest motives, and the freedom to make things happen, and the freedom to make a difference. And the freedom to explore new paths, just as the white-footed mice did. That's plenty of freedom for me: I don't need to make miraculous choices. But it's not enough for moral responsibility. Whether you try to base moral responsibility on effort, or choice, or character, or accomplishments, or whatever, soon you run aground on the fact that those powers and characteristics stem from circumstances that were just a matter of good or bad luck, not something over which you had control—no more than over the color of your eyes. You have beautiful dark-brown eyes, Ben; I'm sure Selina could give a fonder description than I. But though they are certainly *yours*, you don't deserve special praise or reward for them. Likewise, you are a man of great patience; after all, only a man of great patience could put up with Selina."

Selina laughed. "Careful, girl, let's not get personal."

Ben nodded. "The patience of Job, Sarah, the patience of Job."

"And it is certainly a virtue, Ben," Sarah continued, "and it is your virtue, and I admire you for it. Perhaps Selina even loves you for it. But it does *not* follow that you deserve any special credit or reward for your genuine virtue. And you have other characteristics that are your own. You are not, as you noted, a wonderful baseball player. But as you also noted, there are perfectly clear causes for your weaknesses in that respect. I don't regard being a mediocre athlete as a vice; if it is, then I am irreparably flawed. But even if it were, you would not deserve *blame* for it, no more than your friend, who is a better player, deserves special credit. He was luckier. That's not to say he didn't work hard at becoming a good player, just as Selina worked hard to become a good scientist. But neither deserves any special credit or reward."

Ben shook his head. "Maybe not for baseball ability, or scientific talents, either. Maybe not for patience. But I can't buy your assertion that there are *no* areas for just deserts, and justified reward and punishment, and *moral responsibility*. Some things are the result of good luck, and fortunate backgrounds, and desirable genetic legacies. But *some* things are the result of *free choice*, and *there* is the basis for moral responsibility and just deserts. When you *choose* to exert or withhold the effort of will: *that's* what you're responsible for."

"Okay, we're back to that miraculous power of contracausal free will." Sarah sighed. "To be brutally honest, I still don't think it makes a lick of sense, Ben. But I do agree with you on one thing: If we are going to have moral responsibility, that sort of miraculous power of contracausal free will would be required for it."

"Wait a minute, guys." Selina was frowning. "I don't agree with either of you. I don't think we have miraculous powers of contracausal free will, but I'm not at all sure I want to reject moral responsibility. Look, suppose Sarah is right that punishing and rewarding in accordance with traditional notions of just deserts is not all that *useful*, not really very effective in shaping good behavior or discouraging bad behavior. Alright, agreed. But still, that doesn't mean we have to give up moral responsibility, it doesn't mean we have to give up the idea that sometimes we *deserve* reward or punishment. Sarah, you said you believed in free will. Not Ben's miraculous contracausal free will, but still, you believe that free will is compatible with determinism, and that we often *do* act freely, and that freedom is very important. So how can you believe in free will, but not moral responsibility? They go together like Bonnie and Clyde."

"Yeah, I know, lots of people think that." Sarah shook her head. "But lots of people are wrong. You're in good company, Selina. Willard Gaylin, the distinguished bioethicist and psychiatrist, sums up his view of the question thus:

> Freedom demands responsibility; autonomy demands culpability.[7]

That is all Gaylin has to say on the subject. He takes it that the connection between freedom or autonomy and moral responsibility or culpability is so obvious that it need only be stated. And the philosopher Walter Glannon confidently asserts, 'Autonomy and responsibility are mutually entailing notions.'[8] In fact, most philosophers seem to take it as perfectly obvious."

"Hey, Sarah, I thought you said I was in good company. If my view agrees with what most philosophers think, then maybe I ought to rethink my position."

Sarah smiled. "Okay, good shot, Selina. But yeah, I think you ought to rethink your position, whether it is one held by most philosophers or not."

"But why, Sarah? Look, here's old Ben. He really is a very patient man. Why is he so patient? I don't know. Maybe he has the patience gene; it's on the same strand as that Michigan football-fan gene you were talking about before. Or maybe it's because his parents raised him well. Or maybe it's because God blessed him with the virtue of patience. Who cares? He's still a wonderfully patient man. And here's Sarah, my very kind friend. And you really are, Sarah, you're one of the most unfailingly and genuinely kind people I have ever known. I'm *sometimes* kind: like after Michigan has just beaten the Buckeyes, or after I've aced an organic chem exam, or after a night—well, I won't go into details. But you're *always* kind, no matter how tired or unhappy or discouraged you are, your kindness to others is a constant. When I'm kind—well, that might be an accident; depends on the circumstances. When you are kind, and Ben is patient, those aren't just accidental behaviors; they are deep parts of your character, and your acts of kindness and patience are settled and deliberate. So it seems perfectly legitimate to say that Ben and Sarah *deserve praise*, they are *morally responsible*, for their virtues and for the behavior that flows from them. And the same point cuts the other way. If someone is deeply vicious, brutal, callous, greedy, selfish, then those are enduring traits of that person. When a greedy and dishonest person cheats some elderly widow out of her home and her life savings, that person is not doing so by accident and is not pushed by special circumstances to do something out of character; rather, the vile act comes from deep in her character, a deliberate act that is *characteristic* of that greedy person. Such a heartless cheat *deserves* condemnation and is *morally responsible* for her vicious conduct."

Sarah nodded. "There's a contemporary philosopher, Daniel Dennett, who agrees with you, Selina. I remember a line from one of his books on free will: 'Who more deserves to be despised than someone utterly despicable?'"[9]

"And Dennett was exactly right," Selina said. "If you're utterly despicable, you obviously *deserve* to be despised."

"Yes, Selina, a very interesting passage." Sarah was not backing down. "It goes to the root of the whole problem. 'Despicable' is ambiguous; it has two very different meanings. It can be used as a term of evaluation: She is despicable, meaning that she is vile, vicious, mean. But Dennett is then switching to the other meaning: She is despicable, meaning that she *deserves* to be despised. But you can be despicable in the first sense without being despicable in the second. Your vicious cheat really is a nasty, vile person. But the question of whether she *deserves blame* for her nasty character and conduct is a very different question. In my British novels class, we just finished reading Charles Dickens' 'Christmas Carol.'" Sarah pulled her paperback copy from her book bag and opened it on the table. Like most of Sarah's books, it had lived a rough life: Pages were dog eared and liberally smeared with yellow highlighter, and the cover was torn. "I thought I knew the story. I mean, I've seen it on television several times. But reading the book is different. Dickens is really good. Read the novel, you get a different perspective on Scrooge. Clearly, Ebenezer Scrooge—before meeting the ghosts—is a thoroughly mean-spirited person who is 'utterly despicable.' Furthermore, Scrooge is a man of sharp intelligence who can weigh alternatives and make his own choices; and he resolutely follows miserliness and greed. Scrooge is utterly despicable, and his miserly character is thoroughly his own. But it does not follow that he 'deserves to be despised,' for it is something quite different to say that Scrooge is morally responsible, that he deserves blame." Sarah was turning to favorite passages she had marked. "Dickens shows us how Scrooge's early poverty marked him with a terrible fear of the cruel treatment the world metes out to the impoverished— 'there is nothing on which it [the world] is so hard as poverty,' he asserts—and his early love, Belle, describes his resulting character accurately: 'You fear the world too much. . . . All your other hopes have merged into the hope of being beyond the chance of its sordid reproach. I have seen your nobler aspirations fall off one by one, until the master passion, Gain, engrosses you.' But miserliness is a characteristic Scrooge considers and approves: 'What then? Even if I have grown so much wiser, what then?' Scrooge is a thoroughly sordid and greedy character. But when Dickens shows us the grinding poverty that shaped him, we feel less confident that he *deserves blame*—that he is morally responsible. Certainly, Scrooge has moral faults that are his *own* moral flaws; and those flaws are deep, steady character traits, like Ben's patience. But it does not follow that he is morally responsible for his moral faults. It's one thing to consider a person bad, mean spirited, greedy, wicked; it's quite another to suppose that the individual deserves blame for that character."

Selina was doubtful. "Alright, I see the distinction, Sarah. But I'm still not convinced that we should eliminate moral responsibility. Scrooge may have had a bad childhood; but he's still a nasty miser, and I'm not so sure he doesn't deserve blame."

Sarah took a sip of coffee, leaned toward Selina. "Look, let's simplify it. Here's good old Ben, sweet character, wonderfully patient, kind and warmhearted. Lousy baseball player, but otherwise exemplary, right?"

"A perfect sugar bear." Selina smiled.

"Perhaps not the phrase I had in mind, but it will do. Okay, suppose that this afternoon a nefarious crew of neuropsychologists kidnap our beloved Ben, and they completely rearrange his gray matter: Instead of generous, he is now selfish; vicious, rather than kind; abrupt and rude rather than patient. As I recall, you believe that the mind is just the brain, right? So there's no reason, in principle, that they couldn't carry out such a dastardly transformation, is there?"

"I don't like this story, Sarah. I like Ben just the way he is."

"Just stay with me for a moment more, Selina. So now Ben is transformed, and all his virtues have become vices. And the change is deep and thorough and lasting: Ben is now thoroughly and profoundly vicious and vile. And he does vicious, vile, selfish things. Would you blame him for those acts? Would you hold him morally responsible for his vile character?"

"No, of course not, Sarah." Selina shook her head. "The kidnappers made him like that. He doesn't deserve to be blamed; he deserves to be rescued."

"Exactly, Selina, exactly. But what difference does it make whether the transformation occurred over one day, or—as in Scrooge's case—many years? Unless you think you somehow make yourself—as Sartre believes, but *you* don't—then the time frame is irrelevant. The only difference is that in the former case you can see the causes more easily, and it's easier to see why it's basically *unfair* to hold people morally responsible for their behavior and their characters."

Selina thought for a minute, finished her coffee. "Alright, Sarah, good example. But I'm still not sure I want to do away with moral responsibility

One is absolutely sickened, not by the crimes that the wicked have committed, but by the punishments that the good have inflicted; a community is infinitely more brutalized by the habitual employment of punishment than it is by the occasional occurrence of the crime.

Oscar Wilde, "The Soul of Man Under Socialism," in *Fortnightly Review*, London, February 1891

and just deserts and blame and punishment. All these people who pull the stock scams and enrich themselves while cheating working people out of their savings and their pensions—you think we should just wish them well and send them on their way?"

"Certainly not, Selina. They should have to give back the money they stole, and we want to make sure they aren't in a position to steal more. And anyone who can enrich themselves by stealing money from the savings and pension funds of thousands of hardworking people and leave them destitute—that sort of person really is vile and greedy and callous, and we need to work very hard at changing his character, as well as studying what *caused* the person to be that way, so we can prevent others from becoming like him. But blaming the person, holding him morally responsible—that doesn't accomplish anything. In fact, it distracts us from what needs to be done: changing bad characters and keeping people from developing bad characters."

Varieties of Responsibility

"But Sarah, surely that is *not* the best way to develop better character!" Ben found Sarah's position profoundly painful. "People have to *take responsibility* for their acts and their own moral development and their own characters! If people come to believe that they are never really responsible, that they can never do anything or control anything, that they can never *take responsibility* for their own lives and acts, that will make them weak and helpless and destroy any hope of self-control or moral improvement."

"Gotta agree with the boy on this one, Sarah. It's like my dear old Grandmother always taught me: 'Selina, take responsibility for yourself. Take responsibility, and don't ever try to duck your responsibilities.' I thought that was good advice. Still think so."

Sarah nodded. "Your grandmother was exactly right, Selina. That was excellent advice. It's very important to take responsibility, especially to take responsibility for yourself."

Selina looked amazed. "I don't understand you at all, Sarah. First you say there's no responsibility, that no one is ever responsible, that we ought to get rid of the whole idea of responsibility. And now you tell me that responsibility is great, that it's very important to take responsibility! Make up your mind!"

"Not at all. We're just talking about two different notions of responsibility. Your grandmother was right: It's very important to take responsibility, especially to take responsibility for yourself. It's psychologically healthy, and as Ben pointed out, it's an important part of making your character better and stronger. But *moral* responsibility, the responsibility of blame and punishment and reward, the responsibility of *just deserts:* that's a different sort of responsibility altogether."

"I don't think I follow you, Sarah." Ben also looked puzzled.

Sarah laughed. "I know it sounds confusing, but it's really not. Moral responsibility is the stuff of just deserts and retribution and right rewards; in contrast, taken responsibility is the responsibility we claim for our roles or offices, our acts, or even ourselves. Taken responsibility is vitally important. If we could never take and exercise responsibility, then our lives would be impoverished: We might be slaves, or infants, or incompetents, but not moral agents. However, the responsibility we *take* is not the moral responsibility of just deserts. When Selina *takes* responsibility for setting up a chemistry experiment for the lab, then it's her responsibility. If someone else tries to take over the project, she will be resentful: It would imply that she is incompetent to carry out the responsibilities she claimed and would undercut her opportunity to make choices and exercise control. If Selina's opportunities to take responsibility are consistently blocked, then she cannot function as a moral agent who exercises effective control. But this vitally important *taken* responsibility is not *moral* responsibility. For if Selina totally botches the laboratory setup, we might reasonably and consistently say that she had complete (taken) responsibility for the lab, but she is not (morally) responsible for failing at the task, since she was under severe stress: Her grandmother was very ill. (Of course, someone might still want to hold Selina morally responsible for her failure, but the point is that such a judgment is clearly a separate and distinct issue from the question of whether she has *taken* responsibility.) Or again, suppose Selina *takes* responsibility for the lab setup, and the results are wonderful. She now claims that she *justly deserves* a special reward—that is, that she is *morally* responsible for the splendid outcome. Nonsense, we might reply; it was your (taken) responsibility, true enough, but you don't deserve any special credit, because your industrious assistant did all the work, or because you are just lucky to have been blessed with the laboratory setup gene, or because you had the fortunate upbringing that shaped you to be an effective and industrious and intelligent worker. Selina might dispute that assessment of her lack of moral responsibility and might claim that she still justly deserves a special reward. But it will not help her case to insist that she *took* responsibility for the project. Everyone agrees that she has *taken* responsibility; the issue is whether she has *moral* responsibility."

"Okay," Selina replied, "that works for lab experiments. But important as those experiments are, they aren't my whole life. The distinction between taken responsibility and moral responsibility makes sense when we're talking about something as specific as setting up a lab experiment. But when we push deeper, and we talk about responsibility for my life and my basic values, then the line between taken responsibility and moral responsibility gets blurred."

Sarah shook her head. "No, the distinction between *taken* responsibility and *moral* responsibility remains and becomes even more important when the focus moves from taking responsibility for lab setups to taking responsibility for our own moral lives. If I cannot make my own moral decisions, follow my own drummer, and exercise control over my plans and purposes—in short, *take* responsibility for my own moral life—then I cannot be a full moral being. If you make all my moral decisions for me, usurp my authority, and prevent me from taking responsibility, then I am a puppet rather than a moral agent. I must be able to take responsibility for my own moral life if I am to have a moral life at all. But though I take responsibility for my own moral life, it is a very different matter to judge that I am *morally responsible*. Selina makes her own decisions, she takes responsibility for them, and she rightly resents interference; but one might acknowledge that Selina takes full responsibility for her life while still questioning whether she *justly deserves* credit or blame (whether she is *morally* responsible). After all, it is quite legitimate to say that Selina has taken full responsibility for her moral life; but when we understand how vilely she was treated as a child, and how few psychological resources she has for living a virtuous life, we should not blame her for exercising her taken responsibility so miserably. And the same issues arise if Selina lives a life of great moral worth: Selina takes responsibility for her own life and decisions; but is she really morally responsible for her virtuous life, or is she instead lucky to have the early environment and moral fortitude and generous sympathies that enabled her to choose and follow a virtuous life course? Of course, some might maintain—implausibly, in my judgment— that Selina really is *morally* responsible. But that will be a second and *different* issue from judging that she has *taken* responsibility. So, agreed, it is important that we take responsibility; that's a vital element of a satisfying life, and taking and exercising responsibility often makes us better at it. But we can have a full measure of the genuinely valuable *taken* responsibility without requiring any *moral* responsibility—any just deserts and justified punishment—whatsoever."

"That's good enough for me, Sarah." Selina liked the distinction. "I definitely want responsibility for my own life, my own decisions; but to tell you the truth, I never really cared much for the notion of just deserts anyway. Has an air of self-righteousness and sleazy sanctimony about it."

The Right to Be Punished

"For some people, maybe." Ben was not buying it. "But don't be too quick to cast aside moral responsibility. You may be throwing away something of very great value: the power that makes us distinctly human."

"That's fine with me, Ben." Selina was ready for battle. "I don't particularly wish to be 'distinctly human'; that 'distinctly human' stuff is used to set us apart from the world, to set us outside scientific study, to grant us a place of transcendent privilege. I'd rather study and understand humans than deify or mystify them."

Ben frowned. "So what will you do with those 'human specimens' in your scientific studies, the ones who don't quite measure up? The ones who commit crimes or fail to contribute—who don't make the grade? Suppose I rob a bank; you can't punish me, I'm not morally responsible, I don't *justly deserve* punishment. No, I'm just *flawed*, I have to be *treated* and *cured*. You will 'recondition' me, like a used car that needs some bodywork. Maybe I don't want to be cured or reconditioned. Doesn't matter: I'm flawed, damaged goods; what use is my opinion? So you can *treat* me, *rehabilitate* me, *modify* me. All with the best intentions, of course: You're doing it for my own good, you're not *blaming* me or *punishing* me. Well, God preserve me from such a brave new world. I would not like being sent to prison, but it sounds way better than falling into the hands of a bunch of people who are out to 'rehabilitate' me. In prison, I at least have a set sentence. In rehabilitation, you've got me for as long as it takes. In prison, I still have some rights: You can't brainwash me. In 'rehabilitation,' there are no limits: After all, you're doing it for my own good. And in prison, I'm still a *person* who has responsibility for his own life and choices and destiny; but in your 'rehabilitation' center, I'm just an object for *treatment*, with no rights at all. Prison is looking better and better. Thanks, but I'll stick with moral responsibility and just deserts."

Sarah smiled. "Sort of harsh, Ben. Do you really think I want to deprive people of all their rights and turn them over to a bunch of sadistic doctors and psychiatrists who remake them as they wish?"

Ben shook his head. "No, I don't think that's what you want. But that's exactly the danger of denying moral responsibility. Sounds good: no blame, no punishment, sweet mercy rolling down for everyone. But that

A man has the right to be punished rather than treated if he is guilty of some offense. And, indeed, one can imagine a case in which, even in the face of an offer of a pardon, a man claims and ought to have acknowledged his right to be punished. The primary reason for preferring the system of punishment as against the system of therapy might have been expressed in terms of the one system treating one as a person and the other not. . . . When we talk of not treating a human being as a person or "showing no respect for one as a person" what we imply by our words is a contrast between the manner in which one acceptably responds to human beings and the manner in which one acceptably responds to animals and inanimate objects. When we treat a human being merely as an animal or some inanimate object our responses to the human being are determined, not by his choices, but ours in disregard of or with indifference to his. And when we "look upon" a person as less than person or not a person, we consider the person as incapable of a rational choice. In cases of not treating a human being as a person we interfere with a person in such a way that what is done, even if the person is involved in the doing, is done not by the person but by the user of the person.

Herbert Morris, "Persons and Punishment," 1968

merciful rose has a very sharp thorn: Instead of justice and individual rights, you get 'therapy' doled out 'for your own good,' with no limits or restrictions. Besides, the whole thing is demeaning. If I do something wrong, it's because *I did it*, not because I'm sick or incompetent or helpless. Hegel spoke of having a 'right' to be punished. That sounds strange, of course; it hardly seems like a right anyone would want to claim. But the right to be punished is an essential element of the right to be treated like a real autonomous person, with free will, who makes his or her own choices and claims the consequences of those choices. Give up that right, and you give up the right to your own freedom and autonomy. You surrender them to the 'benevolent despotism' of 'therapists' who 'treat' you for 'your own good,' with no regard to whether you freely agree with that good or not."

Sarah nodded. "Look, Ben, I agree with you, that would be awful. But you don't need moral responsibility and 'the right to be punished' to establish protections against such things. Besides, moral responsibility is certainly not some magic talisman that protects against that sort of abuse. To the contrary, it's under a system of moral responsibility and just deserts that the worst abuses occur—*not* under the denial of moral responsibility. Look at what we do in our society: Someone commits a crime, we lock them in some hellhole of a prison, and we do nothing to change the conditions and problems that caused the person to make a mistake, and nothing to prevent others living in the same environment from making the same

mistake and winding up in the same place. What
do we do if we *reject* moral responsibility and
'just deserts'? Obviously, we can't just ignore
bank robbers or murderers or financial swindlers
and let them repeat their crimes. But we don't
just lock them away or execute them and pretend
we've solved the problem. Because we haven't:
We've left in place the same conditions that will
produce more criminals. If we want to prevent
crime, we have to look at its *causes*, not focus so
narrowly on punishing the criminals. And that's
exactly what moral responsibility keeps us from
doing: Wayne robbed the bank, he deserves punishment because he acted from his own contracausal free will, and it was his totally free choice,
so his past history *doesn't matter*, and we
shouldn't worry about it."

Ben agreed. "Okay, Sarah, that's a good
point. True enough, too often we just lock criminals away and ignore the conditions that caused
them to become criminals. And too often we
suppose we've solved the problem if we 'crack down on crime.' Even if
'getting tough on crime' were a good way of reforming criminals—and
everyone admits that it's not—that would still make about as much sense
as supposing that we have dealt effectively with the *causes* of cancer if we
find better cancer *treatments.* So I agree, we have to look at the causes of
crime and try to change them. But what do we do with the criminals
themselves, the ones who have committed crimes? I still think it's wrong
to suppose that we can just 'treat' them, as if they were sick and we are
allowed to take whatever drastic 'treatment measures' we choose, for
'their own good.'"

"Maybe we're closer to agreement than it might seem," Sarah replied.
"Should we treat criminals as sick and deranged individuals to whom we
can do anything at all in the name of 'curing' them? Of course not. That's
wrong in two basic ways. First, it supposes that the only ground for denying moral responsibility is that someone is hopelessly flawed. That's usually our reason for denying that someone is morally responsible: The
person is sick, or insane, and therefore should be *excused* as a special
case. But I believe that *no one* is *ever* morally responsible. People who
commit crimes do not deserve punishment, because they are not morally
responsible; but that doesn't make them any different from the rest of us.
The *universal* denial of moral responsibility doesn't place criminals in a

special subhuman category, as 'nonpersons'; rather, it encourages us to recognize that they are just *like* the rest of us, except with a different causal history. It seems to me that that would encourage more humane and respectful treatment of prisoners, rather than the dehumanizing brutality meted out by our current system of just deserts and moral responsibility. Second, you can't really reform someone by that sort of *Clockwork Orange* brutality. Instead, we need to develop real powers of free choice and personal responsibility and help people freely choose other options. In any case, we aren't likely to treat them in a more dehumanizing way than does the current system of moral responsibility. After all, the most brutal treatment—whether by the Roman Catholic Inquisition or the prisons of the French Reign of Terror or the United States high-security prisons—is handed out under the justification of just deserts. If we regard those who break the law as persons shaped by causal forces—and there but for the grace of God and fortunate circumstances go I—we are not likely to treat them *worse.*"

Ben was unmoved. "No, Sarah, I just can't agree with you. Even if denying moral responsibility meant that prisoners would be treated better, that reform measures would be more effective, and that the causes of crime would be reduced, I *still* would not give up moral responsibility. It would still be too high a price to pay. Being morally responsible, *ultimately* responsible, for our acts and our characters—that's the pearl of great price, that's what makes us human, makes us special. If I don't have ultimate moral responsibility, then I'm just one more item of worldly furniture, whirled around in my fixed orbit. But I'm *not* just one more step in the causal process. I'm an *originator.* The buck stops—and *starts*—here, and I'm the only one who deserves credit or blame for my acts. *I* am the captain of my soul; without moral responsibility, I'm just a foot soldier following orders."

Selina patted Ben's cheek. "I think the boy has strong convictions on this point, Sarah. He may look like just another pretty face, but he's stubborn. I think you two are just gonna have to agree to disagree. Not the first time, I guess."

"Nor the last," Ben added. "But tomorrow, let's talk about ethics. And I think then we'll be allies, Sarah. Selina claims there is no real objective ethical truth. We'll join forces and show Selina the error of her ways."

Selina laughed. "That should be easy, Ben: Just show me solid scientific proof of an ethical principle, and I'll be a believer. Until then, I see no reason to believe in the objectivity of ethics."

"Come on, Selina. Do you think *everything* has to be based in science?"

"Course not." Selina kissed him lightly as she gathered her books and headed for class. "Just everything we *know.*"

READINGS

Charles Taylor (born 1931) taught at McGill University in Montreal from 1961 until his retirement in 1997. He is well known in Canada for his advocacy of cultural respect, and he is philosophically famous for his work on Hegel, the philosophy of language, political philosophy, and moral theory. His major books include Hegel *(Cambridge, U.K.: Cambridge University Press, 1975);* Human Agency and Language *(Cambridge, U.K.: Cambridge University Press, 1985);* Sources of the Self: The Making of the Modern Identity *(Cambridge, MA: Harvard University Press, 1989);* The Ethics of Authenticity *(Cambridge, MA: Harvard University Press, 1991); and* Philosophical Arguments *(Cambridge, MA: Harvard University Press, 1995). The selection here is taken from "Responsibility for Self," in* The Identities of Persons, *ed. Amélie Oksenberg Rorty (Berkeley, CA: University of California Press, 1976), pp. 281–99. Copyright 1976 by The Regents of the University of California.*

In this essay, Charles Taylor focuses on the importance of deep self-evaluations for our sense of responsibility, concluding that, because carrying out such radical evaluations is "always up to us to do it, even when we don't," there are good grounds for moral responsibility. In reading Taylor's essay, you might consider how his position compares with Campbell's.

Responsibility for Self

III

What then is the sense we can give to the responsibility of the agent, if we are not to understand it in terms of radical choice? There is in fact another sense in which we are radically responsible. Our evaluations are not chosen. On the contrary they are articulations of our sense of what is worthy, or higher, or more integrated, or more fulfilling, and so forth. But this sense can never be fully or satisfactorily articulated. And moreover it touches on matters where there is so much room for self-deception, for distortion, for blindness and insensitivity, that the question can always arise whether one is sure, and the injunction is always in place to look again.

We touch here on a crucial feature of our evaluations—one which has given some of its plausibility to the theory of radical choice. They are not simply descriptions, if we mean by this characterizations of a fully independent object, that is, an object which is neither altered in what it is, nor in the degree or manner of its evidence to us by the description. In this way my characterization of this table as brown, or this line of mountains as jagged, is a simple description.

Our strong evaluations may be called by contrast articulations, that is, they are attempts to formulate what is initially inchoate, or confused, or badly formulated. But this kind of formulation or reformulation doesn't leave its object unchanged. To give a certain articulation is to shape our sense of what we desire or what we hold important in a certain way.

Let us take the case . . . of the man who is fighting obesity and who is talked into seeing it as a merely quantitative question of more satisfaction, rather than as a matter of dignity and degradation. As a result of this change, his inner struggle itself becomes transformed, it is now quite a different experience. The opposed motivations—the craving for cream cake and his dissatisfaction with himself at such indulgence—which are the 'objects' undergoing redescription here, are not independent in the sense outlined above. When he comes to accept the new interpretation of his desire to control himself, this desire itself has altered. True, it may be said on one level to have the same goal, that he stop eating cream cake, but since it is no longer understood as a seeking for dignity and self-respect it has become quite a different kind of motivation.

Of course, even here we often try to preserve the identity of the objects undergoing redescription—so deeply rooted is the ordinary descriptive model. We might think of the change, say, in terms of some immature sense of shame and degradation being detached from our desire to resist over-indulgence, which has now simply the rational goal of increasing over-all satisfaction. In this way we might maintain the impression that the elements are just rearranged while remaining the same. But on a closer look we see that on this reading, too, the sense of shame doesn't remain self-identical through the change. It dissipates altogether, or becomes something quite different.

Thus our descriptions of our motivations, and our attempts to formulate what we hold important, are not simple descriptions, in that their objects are not fully independent. And yet they are not simply arbitrary either, such that anything goes. There are more or less adequate, more or less truthful, more self-clairvoyant or self-deluding interpretations. Because of this double fact, because an articulation can be *wrong*, and yet it shapes what it is wrong about, we sometimes see erroneous articulations as involving a distortion of the reality concerned. We don't just speak of error but frequently also of illusion or delusion.

We could put the point this way. Our attempts to formulate what we hold important must, like descriptions, strive to be faithful to something. But what they strive to be faithful to is not an independent object with a fixed degree and manner of evidence, but rather a largely inarticulated sense of what is of decisive importance. An articulation of this 'object' tends to make it something different from what it was before. And by the same token a new articulation doesn't leave its 'object' evident or obscure to us in the same manner or degree as before. In the act of shaping it, it makes it accessible and/or inaccessible in new ways. Because articulations partly shape their objects in these two ways, they are intrinsically open to challenge in a way that simple descriptions are not. Evaluation is such that there is always room for re-evaluation. But our evaluations are the more open to challenge precisely in virtue of the very character of depth which we see in the self. For it is precisely the deepest evaluations which are least clear, least articulated, most easily subject to illusion and distortion. It is those which are closest to what I am as a subject, in the sense that shorn of them I would break down as a person, which are among the hardest for me to be clear about.

The question can always be posed: ought I to re-evaluate my most basic evaluations? Have I really understood what is essential to my identity? Have I truly determined what I sense to be the highest mode of life? This kind of re-evaluation will be radical, not in the sense of radical choice, however, that we choose without criteria, but rather in the sense that our looking again can be so undertaken that in principle no formulations are considered unrevisable.

What is of fundamental importance for us will already have an articulation, some notion of a certain mode of life as higher than others, or the belief that some cause is the worthiest that can be served; or the sense that belonging to this community is essential to my identity. A radical re-evaluation will call these formulations into question. But a re-evaluation of this kind, once embarked on, is of a peculiar sort. It is unlike a less than radical evaluation which is carried on within the terms of some fundamental evaluation, when I ask myself whether it would be honest to take advantage of this income-tax loophole, or smuggle something through customs. These latter can be carried on in a language which is out of dispute. In answering the questions just mentioned the term 'honest' is taken as beyond challenge. But in radical re-evaluations the most basic terms, those in which other evaluations are carried on, are precisely what is in question. It is just because all formulations are potentially under suspicion of distorting their objects that we have to see them all as revisable, that we are forced back, as it were, to the inarticulate limit from which they originate.

How then can such re-evaluations be carried on? There is certainly no metalanguage available in which I can assess rival self-interpretations. If there were, this would not be a radical re-evaluation. On the contrary the re-evaluation is carried on in the formulae available, but with a stance of attention, as it were, to what these formulae are meant to articulate and with a readiness to receive any *Gestalt* shift in our view of the situation, any quite innovative set of categories in which to see our predicament, that might come our way in inspiration.

Anyone who has struggled with a philosophical problem knows what this kind of enquiry is like. In philosophy typically we start off with a question, which we know to be badly formed at the outset. We hope that in struggling with it, we shall find that its terms are transformed, so that in the end we will answer a question which we couldn't properly conceive at the beginning. We are striving for conceptual innovation which will allow us to illuminate some matter, say an area of human experience, which would otherwise remain dark and confused. The alternative is to stick to certain fixed terms (are these propositions synthetic or analytic, is this a psychological question or a philosophical question, is this view monist or dualist?).

The same contrast can exist in our evaluations. We can attempt a radical re-evaluation, in which case we may hope that our terms will be transformed in the course of it; or we may stick to certain favoured terms, insist that all evaluations can be made in their ambit, and refuse any radical questioning. To take an extreme case, someone can adopt the utilitarian criterion and then claim to settle all further issues about action by some calculation.

The point has been made again and again by non-naturalists, existentialists and others that those who take this kind of line are ducking a major question, should I really decide on the utilitarian principle? But this doesn't mean that the alternative to this stance is a radical choice. Rather it is to look again at our most fundamental formulations, and at what they were meant to articulate, in a stance of openness, where we are ready to accept any categorical change, however radical, which might emerge. Of course we will actually start thinking of particular cases, e.g. where our present evaluations recommend things which worry us, and try to puzzle further. In doing this we will be like the philosopher with his initially ill-formed question. But we may get through to something deeper.

In fact this stance of openness is very difficult. It may take discipline and time. It is difficult because this form of evaluation is deep in a sense, and total in a sense that the other less than radical ones are not. If I am questioning whether smuggling a radio into the country is honest, or I am judging everything by the utilitarian criterion, then I have a yardstick, a definite yardstick. But if I go to the radical questioning, then it is not exactly that I have no yardstick, in the sense that anything goes, but rather that what takes the place of the yardstick is my deepest unstructured sense of what is important, which is as yet inchoate and which I am trying to bring to definition. I am trying to see reality afresh and form more adequate categories to describe it. To do this I am trying to open myself, use all of my deepest, unstructured sense of things in order to come to a new clarity.

Now this engages me at a depth that using a fixed yardstick does not. I am in a sense questioning the inchoate sense that led me to use the yardstick. And at the same time it engages my whole self in a way that judging by a yardstick does not. This is what makes it uncommonly difficult to reflect on our fundamental evaluations. It is much easier to take up the formulations that come most readily to hand, generally those which are going the rounds of our milieu or society, and live within them without too much probing. The obstacles in the way of going deeper are legion. There is not only the difficulty of such concentration, and the pain of uncertainty, but also all the distortions and repressions which make us want to turn away from this examination; and which make us resist change even when we do re-examine ourselves. Some of our evaluations may in fact become fixed and compulsive, so that we cannot help feeling guilty about X, or despising people like Y, even though we judge with the greatest degree of openness and depth at our command that X is perfectly all right, and that Y is a very admirable person. This casts light on another aspect of the term 'deep', as applied to people. We consider people deep to the extent, *inter alia*, that they are capable of this kind of radical self-reflection.

This radical evaluation is a deep reflection, and a self-reflection in a special sense: it is a reflection about the self, its most fundamental issues, and a reflection which engages the self most wholly and deeply. Because it engages the whole self without a fixed yardstick it can be called a personal reflection . . . ; and what emerges from it is a self-resolution in a strong sense, for in this reflection the self is in question; what is at stake is the definition of those inchoate evaluations which are sensed to be essential to our identity.

Because this self-resolution is something we do, when we do it, we can be called responsible for ourselves; and because it is within limits always up to us to do it, even when we don't—indeed, the nature of our deepest evaluations constantly raises the question whether we have them right—we can be called responsible in another sense for ourselves whether we undertake this radical evaluation or not. . . . And it is this kind of responsibility for oneself, I would maintain, not that of radical choice, but the responsibility for radical evaluation implicit in the nature of a strong evaluator, which is essential to our notion of a person.

Elizabeth Lane Beardsley (born 1914) taught at Swarthmore College until her retirement. She edited, with Monroe Beardsley, the Prentice-Hall Foundations of Philosophy Series; and she coauthored, again with Monroe Beardsley, a widely used introductory text, Invitation to Philosophical Thinking. *She was the author of a number of important articles in philosophy of language as well as in ethics. The essay reprinted here is "Determinism and Moral Perspectives," which originally appeared in* Philosophy and Phenomenological Research, *Volume 21 (1960), pp. 1–20.*

Elizabeth Beardsley presents a very sophisticated account of moral responsibility that requires considering and distinguishing three different moral perspectives. Beardsley maintains that all three perspectives are possible, that all three are important, and each perspective is incomplete in itself. The challenge, Beardsley believes, is in recognizing which perspective is appropriate for various contexts and questions.

Determinism and Moral Perspectives

Can determinists find a satisfactory rationale for moral praise and blame? On this question, determinists themselves have long been divided. Although the affirmative answer has enjoyed the status of a majority opinion, the negative answer has at times found very effective support. . . .

The negative answer to the question posed here is unsatisfactory, I think; but in some ways it is preferable to the affirmative answer as the latter is usually given and supported. In this paper, I shall argue that judgments of moral praise and blame, affirmative as well as negative, can be made within the frame-work of determinism, provided that we accept a more complex account of these judgments and their foundations than is ordinarily supplied or assumed. I shall maintain that judgments concerning the presence or absence of moral praiseworthiness and blameworthiness are made from several different standpoints, which I shall call "moral perspectives." My primary purpose is to show how an understanding of these perspectives and their relations can contribute substantially toward relieving the tension widely felt (even by some who are reluctant to admit it) to exist between determinism and certain of our basic ethical concepts.

• • •

Determinist Views of Praise and Blame

Before discussing judgments of praise and blame, it will be helpful to consider briefly certain moral judgments of a different kind. The standpoint from which we affirm or deny that acts are objectively right or wrong I shall call the "perspective of objective rightness or wrongness." A judgment of objective rightness or wrongness is a judgment made about an act, not an agent; and it does not carry with it any implication about the praiseworthiness or blameworthiness of an agent. Statements like "Smith's act was objectively right, but he deserves no praise for it" not only are self-consistent, but are often true; objectively right acts can be committed inadvertently, or from reprehensible motives.

The judgment that an act is objectively right furnishes insufficient evidence for a judgment that its agent is praiseworthy, because certain key facts concerning the causal antecedents of the right act remain to be supplied. The objective rightness or wrongness of an act does not depend in any way on its causal antecedents, but on other considerations, such as its consequences (for teleologists), or its harmony with the will of God, moral rules, or the like (for formalists). It is therefore appropriate to call this perspective a "noncausal" one, for it takes no account of whether an act had causal antecedents of one kind rather than another, or indeed had completely determining causal antecedents at all. . . .

Among leading determinists who believe that valid affirmative judgments of praise and blame can be made, a fairly clear account of the criteria for praiseworthiness and blameworthiness seems to have emerged. I shall call those who subscribe to this account "Group I determinists." Details of the account vary, but a substantial area of agreement remains. It is commonly held that if an agent has acted wrongly, without external constraint ("voluntarily"), without ignorance of relevant facts, and from a motive or because of a trait that is undesirable, then, and only then, the agent deserves blame for his act. Similar conditions are held to govern praiseworthiness.

Group I determinists deny that there is anything here to conflict with the truth of determinism. They point out that those who make judgments of praise and blame must indeed attend to several key factors among the causal conditions that produced the acts whose agents are judged. But any *other* causal conditions that may have been present and, in particular, antecedents of antecedents, are to be completely disregarded. Moral praisers and blamers, on this view, are simply not concerned with the nature, or even the existence, of such additional factors. Determinism is thus fully compatible with attributions of praiseworthiness and blameworthiness.

To determinists of a second group—"Group II determinists"—this account seems seriously over-simplified. They contend that the same reasoning which leads us to withhold praise and blame from agents whose acts were committed involuntarily will, when combined with the thesis of determinism, lead on inexorably to the conclusion that no one ever deserves praise or blame for anything. They are haunted by the knowledge that many of the causal antecedents of acts have not been investigated by those who mete out praise and blame on the grounds specified above; and most particularly they are haunted by the knowledge that not all of the causal antecedents of voluntary acts are voluntary acts. Thus they come to believe that no distinction between "voluntary" and "involuntary" acts that a determinist can consistently make can sustain the moral weight that it must bear if we are to judge men praiseworthy or blameworthy. How, they ask, could we ever be justified in blaming or praising someone for a voluntary act and not an involuntary one, when we know full well that even the voluntary act can be traced back to causes—environmental or hereditary—belonging to a world the agent never made?

I believe that there are elements of truth in each of these brands of determinism, and I shall try to show that this is the case.

The Perspective of Moral Worth

Surely there is no doubt that the conditions for praiseworthiness and blameworthiness set forth in the Group I determinists' account do in fact constitute one important and familiar standard according to which we make judgments of praise and blame. It is highly convenient to introduce a special term for the characteristic of moral value that may be said to belong to an agent who has performed an act that meets the conditions specified. I shall say that an agent has "positive moral worth" if and only if he has acted rightly, voluntarily, with knowledge of relevant facts, and from a desire that is good in its situation. . . .

I shall call the standpoint from which we make judgments of moral worth the "perspective of moral worth." This is plainly not a wholly non-causal perspective, as is the perspective of objective rightness or wrongness. Because *some* (a strictly limited set) of the circumstances causally relevant to the performance of an act are taken into account when the moral worth of its agent is being judged, this perspective may accurately be called a "causally limited" perspective. . . .

Group II determinists are likely to feel that the introduction of the term "moral worth" is unobjectionable, and perhaps even useful, provided that judgments of moral worth are not held to imply judgments of praise or blame. Thinkers of this group may be disposed to admit that human beings do indeed have a strong psychological tendency to experience positive feelings when confronted by the gestalt agent-performing-act-under-conditions-for-positive-moral-worth, and to experience negative feelings when confronted by the corresponding negative gestalt. . . . In any case, the important point, for the Group II determinist, is that we should avoid the confusion of believing that persons who happen to form part of the pleasant or unpleasant gestalts just mentioned deserve praise or blame for what they do. Because the crucial distinction between voluntary and involuntary acts is bound to collapse in the end, no one ever deserves praise or blame. Perhaps judgments of praise and blame *are* made from the perspective of moral worth, but they *should* not be.

To this the Group I determinist will reply that, since the conditions for "moral worth" were originally taken directly from an analysis of conditions for praiseworthiness and blameworthiness, it is highly arbitrary, to say the very least, to attempt to purge judgments of moral worth of all association with judgments of praise and blame. Moreover, he will continue, the assertion that human beings have "feelings" which are merely "positive" or "negative," when they encounter persons exhibiting positive or negative moral worth, is decidedly misleading. The "feelings" referred to consist of definite reactions of a specific sort, to which are added, for most moral judges, quite explicit reflective convictions. Human beings feel—and reserve—a very special kind of approval and disapproval for those members of their species who perform acts that have certain salient features. Furthermore, the majority of those who have reflected on the matter seem to have been convinced that approval and disapproval of this special kind are reactions to which the persons in question have a morally justified claim. It is this claim which is put forth in affirmative judgments of praise and blame. In view of these considerations, a heavy burden of proof rests on the Group II determinist, who proposes to eliminate from moral discourse all affirmative judgments of praise and blame. This burden, the Group I determinist charges, has not been effectively sustained.

The Group I determinist will go on to admit readily that, among those features which an act must have if its agent is to merit praise or blame, the requirement that it be voluntary is indeed crucial. But, he will say, to establish voluntariness we need examine only certain of the immediate causal ancestors of an act. Considerations about more remote causal forebears are as irrelevant here as information about a man's grandparents would be if proffered in reply to a query about his parents. Therefore it is the case, not only that we *do* make judgments of praise and blame from the perspective of moral worth, but that this procedure is entirely legitimate, and is not threatened by determinism. Thus, concludes the Group I determinist, the problem of praise and blame has been solved.

The Group I determinist may seem, on the face of it, to have had the better of the argument in the exchange just described. He is right, I think, in maintaining that judgments of praise and blame, affirmative as well as negative, have an extremely strong claim to be retained in moral discourse. He is right, also, in insisting that the distinction between voluntary and involuntary acts which is needed for affirmative judgments of praise and blame can be made by determinists. Finally, he is right in holding that what has been called here the "standard of moral worth" is the standard on which many affirmative and negative judgments of praise and blame are based.

Where the Group I determinist is wrong is in his tacit assumption that *all* judgments of moral praise and blame are made from the perspective of moral worth, and that when a man has been judged praiseworthy or blameworthy from this perspective there is nothing more to say about his moral claim to be praised or blamed for the act under consideration. The truth, as I shall go on to try to show, is much less simple than this. There is indeed a network of causes stretching out in all directions, far beyond the worth-determining factors on which the Group I determinists so resolutely fix their minds. Moreover, these other causal factors are by no means without moral significance. We cannot hope to set up a genuinely effective defense against the Group II determinist's harsh view of what that significance is, unless some other way of doing justice to these additional causal factors can be found.

The Perspective of Moral Credit

I want now to examine a second moral perspective from which we appraise agents. . . . When we examine our affirmative and negative judgments of praise and blame, we find that many are made by the standard of moral worth; but we also find, I think, that many are not. A second standard of appraisal often comes into operation after a judgment based on moral worth has been made, when we go on to ask further questions about the individual situation of an agent who has performed an act for which he is judged morally worthy or unworthy. Here individual circumstances which facilitated or hampered the performance of the act are taken into account. What we do, that is, is to investigate factors which made the performance of a certain act by a certain agent particularly "easy" or "difficult" for *him*. On the basis of this information, a further judgment of praise or blame is made.

How do we ascertain that the performance of act A by agent X was "easy" or "difficult?" Not by endeavoring to estimate the intensity of his subjective feelings of effort. What is needed here is an objective correlate; and this, I think, is provided by the concept of circumstances *favorable* or *unfavorable* to the performance of a certain act, i.e., circumstances in whose presence the performance of such an act is either more or less likely to occur than it is in their absence. Given that an act is one for which its agent has positive or negative moral worth, a judgment is made to the effect that the balance of known circumstances causally relevant to the performance of that act was favorable or unfavorable. We try to decide, that is, whether, in view of all the things we know about him, it was antecedently probable that a certain act should have been performed by its agent. If an agent has performed an act for which he has positive moral worth, and if it was antecedently improbable that he should have performed this act, then he is praiseworthy by our new standard as well as by the standard of moral worth. We say that such an act was performed "in spite of obstacles" or "against odds." Similar remarks, of course, could be made regarding blameworthiness as judged by this new standard; and it is convenient at times, though somewhat unidiomatic, to speak of an act for which an agent is morally unworthy and which was antecedently improbable as having also been performed "against odds."

To those who deny that the performance against odds of an act for which the agent is morally worthy or unworthy earns for that agent special praise or blame the only answer can be an invitation to look again, more closely, at the moral appraisals we all make. Evidence confirming the view defended here can be found on all sides. For example, it was maintained not long ago by Auxiliary Bishop Joseph M. Marling of the Roman Catholic Church that the presence of severe neurosis in certain Catholic saints could be admitted, since it not only did not detract from their saintliness, but actually contributed to it, in that a neurosis constitutes a serious obstacle to the achievement of spiritual perfection.

There are strong reasons, I think, for maintaining that the criteria for moral appraisals now being examined constitute a standard separate and distinct from the standard of moral worth. The alternative "single-standard" view (the belief that both sets of criteria can be combined into one complex standard) appears to be widely, though casually, held; but I think it is mistaken. . . .

By our second standard, then, an agent X is praiseworthy for his act A to some degree if and only if: (1) X has positive moral worth to some degree for A, and (2) X's situation at the time of performing A included among the known circumstances a preponderance or balance of circumstances (other than the amount of "effort" put forth by the agent) which are reasonably judged to be unfavorable to the performance of the act. Similar conditions govern the presence of blameworthiness as judged by this second standard. Agents who perform acts under the conditions for praiseworthiness just specified will be said to have "positive moral credit" for their acts. Like moral worth, moral credit may be present in either a positive or a negative form. . . .

The moral perspective from which judgments of moral credit are made may be called the "perspective of moral credit," and judgments of praise and blame based on the moral credits standard may also be said to be made from this perspective. In order to judge from the perspective of moral credit, we investigate the causal antecedents of an act more extensively than is done for judgments made from the perspective of moral worth. Any instance of any kind of factor which can reasonably be judged to be an unfavorable or favorable circumstance for a given kind of act is potentially a "credit-determining" factor for any agent performing an act of that kind, even though in common practice, to be sure, not all potential credit-determining factors are investigated before assigments are made. The perspective of moral credit, accordingly, may be called a "causally extended" perspective, as compared with our causally limited perspective of moral worth, and our noncausal perspective of objective rightness or wrongness.

Judgments made from the perspective of moral credit supplement judgments made from the perspective of moral worth. They do not supplant them, any more than judgments about the objective rightness or wrongness of acts are supplanted by judgments about the moral worth of their agents. The latter are self-contained judgments, perfectly satisfactory and significant in their own right. Nevertheless, the perspective of moral credit does set limits to the perspective of moral worth, in that it is important for those who make judgments by the moral worth standard to remember that such judgments do not give us the whole moral truth about an agent. Even when we do not actually go on to ascertain the moral credit-rating of an agent to whom we ascribe positive or negative moral worth, we must bear in mind that further questions along such lines *could* be asked. Judgments of praise and blame made from the perspective of moral worth will be made less dogmatically, with less show of finality, by those who understand that there is another moral perspective from which an individual can be judged. But those who make judgments from the perspective of moral credit must not forget the importance of the perspective of moral worth. Judges who constantly focus their attention on the "ease" or "difficulty" with which something was accomplished need to be reminded at times, to look at the quality of the moral accomplishment itself. Neither of these two moral perspectives can be said to be superior to the other.

It seems clear that the use of the perspective of moral credit is fully compatible with determinism. And the identification of the new standpoint of moral appraisal as a separate moral perspective lends needed strength to the philosophical position of determinism, principally by revealing it to be less dogmatic and impersonal than it is often taken to be. . . .

In the end, however, the convinced Group II determinist will always reply that the effort to set up a perspective of moral credit cannot salvage judgments of praise and blame. He will maintain that judgments of praise and blame based on moral credit are ultimately no more compatible with determinism than are judgments of praise and blame based on moral worth. As before, he may look tolerantly, or even benevolently, on the procedure of setting up a "perspective of moral credit," just so long as judgments of praise and blame are kept out of the picture. Again his reaction springs from his awareness of additional causal factors, this time of causal factors lying behind those taken into account from the perspective of moral credit. The Group II determinists will say that, although those who make judgments based on moral credit may make extensive inquiries into the factors causally relevant to human acts, sooner or later, because of the limits of time or energy or human knowledge, they must bring their investigations to a close. And when they do, they will not have told the whole causal story; and the part that will remain untold will invalidate judgments of praise and blame made from this moral perspective.

I believe that this charge can be answered, but I want to show first how it might be supported. Let us consider a comparison between two individuals, Jones and Smith. Jones has performed an act having a high degree of positive moral worth in spite of very unfavorable circumstances, whereas Smith, confronted by essentially the same kind of circumstances and placed in a very similar situation, has performed an act having a much lower degree of positive moral worth. It is clear that Jones possesses a higher degree of positive moral credit for his act than does Smith for his, since the circumstances and situation constitute greater obstacles for Jones' act than for Smith's.

Now, no matter how strong our psychological tendency to feel a greater admiration for the achievement of Jones, such an attitude, the Group II determinist would claim, is not justifiable. For moral credit is ascribed on the basis of finding that a preponderance of the *known* circumstances in an agent's situation was unfavorable to the performance of a given act. Judgments of moral credit deal with acts whose performance was improbable; nevertheless, they deal with acts that *were* performed, events that *happened*. If determinism is true, these happenings were caused. Therefore for each act for which an agent possesses moral credit there must exist also a cluster of one or more unknown circumstances causally relevant to the performance of the act, and a preponderance of *these* circumstances must have been favorable, rather than unfavorable. It is all very well, then, to judge that Jones performed under great odds an act for which he is morally worthy; but such a judgment is superficial and unstable. For, if determinism is true, these vaunted "odds" disappear upon examination; and Jones is seen to have done only what the causal factors in his situation, unknown as well as known, brought forth. So did Smith, and so do we all. How then can praise and blame by the standard of moral credit be justified?

It is evident that this reasoning is too cogent to be set aside. At the close of the preceding section, it was asserted that the causal factors not dealt with in judgments of moral worth were nevertheless morally significant, and would have to be taken care of in some other way. Many of these "left-over" causal factors have now been shown to provide a basis for judgments of praise and blame made from a second moral perspective, the perspective of moral credit. But the Group II determinist now reminds us that behind even the credit-determining factors lie still others, and that these too have a moral significance that cannot be lightly dismissed. His interpretation of the moral significance of this most distant range of causal factors is, as we have seen, simply that they invalidate all affirmative judgments of praise and blame. In the remainder of this paper, I shall try to show that another interpretation is possible, and that it is to be preferred.

The Perspective of Ultimate Moral Equality

In the course of our discussion, we have now sorted out three groups of factors causally relevant to human behavior: worth-determining factors, credit-determining factors, and what may be called "ultimate" causal factors, which are simply those factors that are left out of account when we make judgments based on moral worth and moral credit. If determinism is true, we may be said to know, for any given act, *that* there are ultimate causal factors. But we do not know *what* they are: if we did know they would take their place among the potential credit-determining factors for the act in question. It is strange that this shadowy group of unknown circumstances should be morally so significant; but I think that there is no doubt that their moral significance is real.

When we are mindful of the existence of the ultimate causal factors, we look at human beings and their acts in a special way. This was brought out by the example of Jones and Smith. When we look at persons in this special way, they are seen to be equals, as far as their claims to moral praise and blame are concerned, or, rather, they are seen to have passed beyond any point at which discriminations of praiseworthiness or blameworthiness are applicable. Seen in this way, all men are members of a moral or spiritual democracy. This is a realm lying behind our distinctions of moral worth and moral credit, a realm in which each is simply the person he is. When we take into account the full range of factors causally relevant to human acts, we must regard human beings as a flock without goats and without sheep.

I propose to say that this special way of looking at persons, in the light of the existence of ultimate causal factors for their behavior, constitutes another moral perspective. This I shall call the "perspective of ultimate moral equality." From this perspective we look at persons and their acts in the widest possible causal contexts, contexts without limits of any kind. Therefore we may call this a "causally unlimited" perspective. As a moral perspective it is, of course, strikingly different in some respects from the others that we have examined. Judgments made from the perspective of moral worth and the perspective of moral credit are judgments of discrimination. This is obvious in the case of comparative judgments, but it is also true of noncomparative ones. Our interest in knowing that X possesses positive moral worth for his honest act, and Y negative moral credit for his cowardly one, stems in large part from the fact that there are honest acts whose agents do not possess positive moral worth, and cowardly acts whose agents earn no negative moral credit. Judgments of praise and blame based on moral worth and moral credit are answers to questions which can in principle be answered either affirmatively or negatively.

This is not true of judgments made from the perspective of ultimate moral equality. Here all are on the same moral footing: none has any ultimate claim to praise or blame, and the judgments made from this perspective are all negative. No matter what acts a person has performed, all that we can say of him from this final moral perspective is that he deserves no praise for what he has done, or that he deserves no blame. . . .

If determinism is true, we know of any event that it has ultimate causes, and we know this without any specific investigation. The behavior of all men is causally determined, and the nature of what we have called the "ultimate" causes is equally unknown in each case. This eradication of all distinctions in the causal status of acts erases all distinctions in the moral status of their agents. Therefore in one way it can never be news that Brown does not ultimately deserve praise for his kind deed, or that Robinson does not ultimately deserve blame for his unkind one.

In another way, however, these assertions *are* news, and important news. The fact that Brown and Robinson are ultimately moral equals is a vital part of the whole moral truth about them. Compare the situation for a factual account. In factual descriptions of human beings we are interested in the qualities in which they differ, to be sure; but we are also interested in the qualities in which they are alike. For some purposes, and in some contexts, the similarities may be legitimately disregarded; but this does not mean that they can always be left out of account. Sometimes they are more significant than the differences, and they are never more significant than they become when we are in danger of assuming that the differences tell the whole factual story. So it is with moral appraisals of human beings. For the whole moral story, judgments of praise and blame based on moral worth and moral credit need to be supplemented by judgments made from the perspective of ultimate moral equality.

Because this is true, we are justified in regarding the perspective of ultimate moral equality as a genuinely "moral" perspective, even though it eradicates moral discriminations. The knowledge that when persons are viewed in relation to the ultimate causal factors of their behavior moral discriminations no longer apply to them is a piece of moral knowledge, at least in being knowledge about moral matters. It is curious that as we go from a causally limited perspective to a causally extended one we increase our power to make moral discriminations, whereas when we come to a causally unlimited perspective these moral discriminations stop altogether. But the knowledge that this is so is moral knowledge, and it has important bearings on the rest of our moral knowledge.

The relation that holds between the perspective of ultimate moral equality and the other moral perspectives from which judgments of praise and blame are made is analogous in certain ways to the relation between the perspective of moral credit and that of moral worth. Judgments based on moral credit, as we have seen, set limits to judgments based on moral worth. Similarly, the knowledge that human beings can be viewed from a perspective which will show them to be morally equal will remind those who make judgments based on moral worth and moral credit that these judgments of moral inequality do not tell the whole story about the individuals being judged. This knowledge, in turn, will affect the attitudes of those who have it: they will regard themselves and each other with more tolerance than before. Feelings of admiration, contempt, guilt, and pride, will all be experienced more moderately by those who know that no man is ever the *first* cause of good or evil deeds, or *finally* responsible for winning or losing when confronted by moral odds. But this is not to say that such feelings will not be experienced at all, or that they should not be.

For the perspective of ultimate moral equality cannot give us the whole truth about the praiseworthiness and blameworthiness of human beings either. The fact that X has negative moral worth for his act, or that Y has positive moral credit for his, is not cancelled by saying that X does not ultimately deserve blame, or that Y does not ultimately deserve praise. We value in a special way those whose acts meet the standards of moral worth and moral credit, and this is something that we cannot change. As Spinoza saw, it is true—even in a determined universe—that "we desire to form for ourselves an idea of man upon which we may look as a model of human nature." The idea of a man who performs a right act voluntarily, knowingly, and from a good desire, and the idea of a man who, when confronted by odds, can still do these things—these *are* the models we have formed. Conformity to these patterns is what we regard as worthy of praise, and deviation from them in certain ways is what we regard as worthy of blame. We cannot feel about persons who thus conform or deviate as we do about animals or inanimate objects which measure up or fail to measure up to certain other standards. All this being so, judgments of praise and blame based on moral worth and moral credit are not only legitimate but vitally necessary parts of moral discourse. They are answers to questions that we cannot help asking.

The full moral truth about a man and his act, then, might run as follows: that he deserves a low degree of praise for it by the standard of moral worth, a high degree of praise for it by the standard of moral credit, and ultimately no praise for it when he is judged from the perspective of ultimate moral equality. There is no reason why the three statements cannot be true simultaneously. Also, these perspectives seem to be genuinely coordinate, and complementary: we need them all. . . .

The acquiring of moral wisdom, at least as far as moral appraisals are concerned, does not consist only in learning how to make sound judgments from each moral perspective. It consists also in learning under what circumstances each of the moral perspectives should be used. . . . Here let us note only that most of the questions about the praiseworthiness and blameworthiness of human beings that are actually asked are questions to which the appropriate answer is a judgment based on moral worth or one based on moral credit. Writers on ethics have pointed out that we feel something peculiarly objectionable in an attempt by a wrongdoer to exculpate himself on the ground that all his acts were caused and therefore he deserves no blame. Here an inquiry into his blameworthiness is launched from one moral perspective and a reply is made from another. But moral perspectives, however coordinate, are certainly not interchangeable. Questions about praiseworthiness or blameworthiness should be answered from the perspective from which they are asked, whenever it is possible to tell what this is. Sometimes it will be appropriate, and even very desirable, to add to this answer a judgment made from another moral perspective; but often it will not be. Particular caution must be exercised in advancing judgments made from the perspective of ultimate moral equality. These are illuminating, and even inspiring, when made in the right context, and by those who know how to make accurate discriminations by the standards of moral worth and moral credit. Otherwise they are apt to seem shallow, and somehow sentimental, or cheap.

• • •

In this paper, I have been arguing that the question with which we began, "Can determinists find a rationale for moral praise and blame?" can be answered affirmatively. I have tried to show, however, that the unrecognized assumption behind the typical and influential affirmative answers that have been given—the assumption that judgments of praise and blame are made from a single moral perspective—is mistaken. I have maintained that those determinists who give a negative answer to our original question have caught sight of some important truths that the others have missed. In the end, however, with their attempts to set up the perspective of ultimate moral equality as the sole valid perspective for judgments of praise and blame, they have fallen into the same fundamental error as the others. One group eternally confronts the other with the question "How can you deny that human beings can be said to be praiseworthy and blameworthy, in view of the fact that they commit acts that are right or wrong, and at the same time done voluntarily, knowingly, and from good or bad desires?" To which the second group incessantly hurls back a question of its own: "How can you assert that human beings can be said to be praiseworthy or blameworthy, in view of the fact that their acts, like all other events, are wholly subject to causal laws, and must be traced back, in the end, to factors wholly beyond the agents' control?" The account given here, which may be called the "theory of multiple moral perspectives," is designed to help put an end to this durable impasse. I have tried to show that the first group is speaking from the perspective of moral worth, while the second replies from the perspective of ultimate moral equality. Both perspectives are valid; but each perspective is incomplete.

Three moral perspectives are necessary, I have contended, if we are to tell the whole about the praiseworthiness and blameworthiness of human beings. One of these, the perspective of ultimate moral equality, takes form as a consequence of assuming determinism to be true; but its adoption is not without moral and spiritual benefits. The other perspectives can be exhibited in an examination of judgments of praise and blame conducted quite independently of any determinist assumptions; and we can then see that determinism is—at the very least—fully compatible with the use of these moral perspectives. It seems to me that considerable work remains to be done in clarifying and refining these concepts and principles, and in exploring their implications in many directions but if the claims made here are in essentials justified, it follows that determinists need not feel that old familiar uneasiness when confronted by the concepts of moral praise and blame. On the contrary, it may be that we stand here on solid ground.

Study Questions

1. Describe Frankfurt's hierarchical compatibilism, and compare it with Hume's simpler version.
2. What is rationalist compatibilism?
3. Susan Wolf—who is a rationalist compatibilist—claims that we can be morally responsible for our good behavior, but not for what we do wrong. How does she reach that conclusion?
4. Selina gives the classic compatibilist justification for punishment and reward, a justification which does not require contracausal free will (which does not require that we be able to do otherwise)—the justification offered by David Hume. What is that justification?
5. What are the main objections to the compatibilist justification for punishment and reward?

6. Some claim that luck undercuts moral responsibility and just deserts, while others argue that it does not. What are the arguments on both sides?
7. What is the distinction between *moral* responsibility and *taken* responsibility?
8. Some philosophers—such as Hegel and, yes, Ben—favor a "right to be punished." What is their reason for claiming that right?
9. What grounds does Charles Taylor offer for holding people responsible?
10. According to Elizabeth Beardsley, what are the key perspectives one can take on the question of moral responsibility?

Exercises

1. According to most Christian theologians, God is an absolutely perfect being and God *could not* commit a morally bad act. If so, does that imply that God does not have complete free will (or, for that matter, that God is not omnipotent)?
2. Suppose that Selina had convinced Ben that his dualist view on mind and body is *wrong*, and Ben has now become a strict materialist, like Selina. Would Ben also have to give up his libertarian view of free will?
3. Suppose we discovered that Sartre's account of free will is *correct*. (I have no idea how we could discover that; use your imagination.) Would that destroy the possibility of a *science* of psychology?
4. The distinguished historian Arnold Toynbee was fiercely opposed to determinism. He expressed his opposition to determinism rather eloquently:

> I do not think that either heredity or environment, or these two forces together, fully account for the behavior of Hosea, Zarathustra, Jeremiah, the Buddha, Socrates, Jesus, Muhammad, and Saint Francis of Assisi. I believe that these "great souls" did have the freedom to take spiritual action that has no traceable source. I also believe that there is a spark of this creative spiritual power in every human being. "Great Expectations," in Harvey Wheeler, ed., *Beyond the Punitive Society* (San Francisco: W. H. Freeman and Company, 1973).

Suppose that Ben made that statement to Selina. How would Selina answer? (Okay, obviously, she would say he is *wrong*; but what reasons might she give?)

5. In *The Metaphysical Elements of Justice*, Immanuel Kant makes a very strong claim concerning the obligation to punish:

> Even if a civil society were to dissolve itself by common agreement of all its members (for example, if the people inhabiting an island decided to separate and disperse themselves around the world), the last murderer remaining in prison must first be executed, so that everyone will duly receive what his actions are worth and so that the bloodguilt thereof will not be fixed on the people because they failed to insist on carrying out the punishment; for if they fail to do so, they may be regarded as accomplices in this public violation of legal justice.

So we cannot just sail away from the island and leave the last murderer there, to live like a shipwrecked Robinson Crusoe; in fact, Kant thinks that would be wrong even if we were certain that the abandoned prisoner would live out his life in isolation and never again encounter a human being.

Why do you suppose Kant holds this view? Do you find his position plausible? Do you think any of the participants in the dialogue agree with Kant's position?

6. Of the perspectives on moral responsibility developed by Elizabeth Beardsley, which one do you think Kant would favor? What about Hume? Would they agree with Beardsley that *all* the perspectives are important, but for different contexts?

What would Sarah think of Beardsley's position?

Glossary

Compatibilism: The view that determinism is compatible with free will; we can have free will even if determinism is true.

Hierarchical compatibilism: A compatibilist view that requires a higher reflective level for freedom: To act freely, we must be able to do as we wish, and we must also have a higher order will of which we reflectively approve. For hierarchical compatibilists, a drug addict may be acting freely when he takes drugs, but that will require not only that he can obtain the drugs he desires, but also that he gives higher order approval to his strong desire for drugs.

Moral responsibility: A condition in which one justly deserves punishment or reward, praise or blame; one has moral responsibility in circumstances when it is appropriate that one receive "just deserts" for one's acts.

Rationalist compatibilism: A version of compatibilism which maintains that the only genuine freedom consists in doing the right act for the right reason: One is free only when one is dedicated to following the single true path.

Simple compatibilism: The compatibilist view which holds that we are free so long as we are not acting under coercion; that is, we are free if we are "not in chains."

Taken responsibility: A type of responsibility that is distinguished from moral responsibility; the responsibility one takes or claims for a project or act or even for one's own character and life (sometimes called role responsibility).

Additional Resources

The "Additional Resources" section of Chapter six is obviously relevant to this chapter as well. Some very good anthologies that cover issues raised in this chapter (and in Chapter six) include John Martin Fischer, ed., *Moral Responsibility* (Ithaca, NY: Cornell University Press, 1986); Ferdinand Schoeman, ed., *Responsibility, Character, and the Emotions: New Essays in Moral Psychology* (Cambridge, U.K.: Cambridge University Press, 1987); and John Christman, ed., *The Inner Citadel: Essays on Individual Autonomy* (New York: Oxford University Press, 1989). For an anthology that collects the key historical writings on free will and responsibility, as well as many important legal essays on the subject, see Herbert Morris, ed., *Freedom and Responsibility* (Stanford, CA: Stanford University Press, 1961).

The position we called hierarchical compatibilism is championed by Harry G. Frankfurt, who developed his views in a number of essays, all of them collected in *The Importance of What We Care About* (Cambridge, U.K.: Cambridge University Press, 1988). Another excellent hierarchical compatibilist source is Gerald Dworkin's *The Theory and Practice of Autonomy* (Cambridge, U.K.: Cambridge University Press, 1988).

Rationalist compatibilism is presented most effectively by Susan Wolf, in *Freedom within Reason* (New York: Oxford University Press, 1990).

An excellent anthology containing original essays on the issue of alternative possibilities (and whether alternative possibilities are required for free will and moral responsibility) is David Widerker and Michael McKenna, *Moral Responsibility and Alternative Possibilities* (Burlington, VT: Ashgate, 2003).

An attempt to find some common ground between libertarian and compatibilist views is made by Bruce N. Waller in "A Metacompatibilist Account of Free Will: Making Compatibilists and Incompatibilists More Compatible," *Philosophical Studies*, Volume 112, Number 2/3 (2003), pp. 209–224.

Daniel Dennett has written two very entertaining and readable books that take a compatibilist view on free will: *Elbow Room: The Varieties of Free Will Worth Wanting* (Cambridge, MA: MIT Press, 1984); and *Freedom Evolves* (New York: Viking, 2003). P. F. Strawson's "Freedom and Resentment" was originally published in 1962; it is now widely anthologized, including in the excellent Gary Watson anthology, *Free Will* (Oxford, U.K.: Oxford University Press, 1982). Strawson's essay has been a very influential compatibilist view, arguing that we simply can't get along without our basic concepts of freedom and responsibility, whatever scientists might discover about determinism.

H. L. A. Hart draws a very important distinction between role responsibility and moral responsibility (which is the foundation for the distinction between taken responsibility and moral responsibility) in *Punishment and Responsibility: Essays in the Philosophy of Law* (London: Oxford University Press, 1968).

A superb collection of essays on the issues surrounding punishment and just deserts is edited by Jeffrie G. Murphy, *Punishment and Rehabilitation*, 2d ed. (Belmont, CA: Wadsworth, 1985). Among other excellent articles, Murphy's anthology contains the definitive contemporary defense of "the right to be punished": Herbert Morris, "Persons and Punishment," originally published in 1968. A more recent article in favor of the right to be punished is by Andrew Oldenquist, "An Explanation of Retribution," in *The Journal of Philosophy*, volume 85, pages 464–478. For a more popular presentation of that view, see an article by C. S. Lewis, "The Humanitarian Theory of Punishment," in *Undeceptions* (London: Curtis Brown, 1970).

For an excellent debate between two outstanding philosophers who examine these questions carefully, give fair and honest consideration to their opponents' views, and offer their own conclusions with style and strength, see Jeffrie G. Murphy and Jean Hampton, *Forgiveness and Mercy* (Cambridge, U.K.: Cambridge University Press, 1988).

Notes

1. Gerald Dworkin, *The Theory and Practice of Autonomy* (Cambridge, U.K.: Cambridge University Press, 1988), pp. 18, 29.
2. Susan Wolf, *Freedom within Reason* (New York: Oxford University Press, 1990), p. 54.
3. *Ibid.*, p. 55.
4. Jiddu Krishnamurti, *Total Freedom: The Essential Krishnamurti* (New York: HarperCollins, 1996).
5. Recent research on sensation seeking establishes strong links between the human preference for open alternatives and comparable preferences in other animals—links that include common psychophysiological phenomena in the sensation seeking (alternative pursuing) of humans and other species. J. Lee Kavanau ("Behavior of captive white-footed mice," *Science* 155: 1623–1639) was among the first to recognize the importance of alternatives for species different from humans, and his insights have been confirmed by other studies. For example, while studying sensation seeking in rats, G. D. Ellison ("Animal Models of Psychopathology: The Low-norepinephrine and Low-serotonin Rats," *American Psychologist* 32: 1036–1045) found levels of serotonin and norepinephrine that were correlated with the levels in sensation-seeking humans. In addition, research by D. Redmond, D. Murphy, and J. Baulu ("Platelet Monoamine Oxidase Activity Correlates with Social Affiliative and Agonistic Behaviors in Normal Rhesus Monkeys," *Psychosomatic Medicine* 41: 87–100) found corresponding variations in levels of platelet monoamine oxidase in rhesus monkeys and humans that were high in sensation seeking, and W. Shekim, D. Bylund, F. Frankel, J. Alexson, S. Jones, L. Blue, J. Kirby, and C. Cochoran ("Platelet MAO Activity and Personality Variations in Normals," *Psychiatry Research* 27: 81–88) found similar results in human personality studies. (See also M. Zuckerman, "A Biological Theory of Sensation Seeking," in M. Zuckerman (ed.), *Biological Bases of Sensation Seeking, Impulsivity, and Anxiety* (Hillsdale, NJ: Lawrence Erlbaum, 1983); and M. Zuckerman, *Behavioral Expressions and Biosocial Bases of Sensation Seeking* (Cambridge, U.K.: Cambridge University Press, 1994).)
6. C. A. Campbell, *On Selfhood and Godhood* (London: George Allen & Unwin, 1957), p. 59.
7. Willard Gaylin, *The Killing of Bonnie Garland* (New York: Simon and Schuster, 1982), p. 338.
8. Walter Glannon, "Responsibility, Alcoholism, and Liver Transplantation," *Journal of Medicine and Philosophy*, Vol. 23(1): 1998, p. 45.
9. Daniel Dennett, *Elbow Room: The Varieties of Free Will Worth Wanting* (Cambridge, MA: MIT Press, 1984), p. 167.

Chapter 8

Ethics

in which Selina considers a pleasure machine

Sarah placed her coffee and her cinnamon scone on the table and dropped her book bag on the floor. Ben closed the book he had been reading, leaned back in his chair, and smiled a greeting. Selina moved her organic chemistry book over to give Sarah room: "Rest yourself, Sarah. You look like you could make good use of that coffee."

"Yeah, just finished Dr. Thomson's exam on Spinoza and Leibniz." Sarah shook her head. "I like Spinoza. But Leibniz is tough. His monadology blows my mind. Any room for another chemistry major, Selina? I think this history of modern philosophy may be the death of me."

Selina laughed. "No offense, Sarah, but you philosophy people are so weird. Here you are taking a class in *modern* philosophy, and the modern philosophers you're talking about are from the 17th Century! Correct me if I'm wrong, but didn't you say Leibniz was born in 1646? We're talking about a man who was living a century *before* the American Revolution! Somehow that doesn't strike me as *modern*."

Sarah smiled. "Well, Selina, that's what happens when your subject is the queen of the sciences. Philosophy has been around for at least twenty-five hundred years. We have a longer view of the world: To philosophers, a few centuries seems like yesterday."

"Now that you mention it," Selina answered, "I have noticed you seem to get confused about time. Punctuality isn't a philosophical virtue, is it?"

"Well, I'm here at last. And today we were going to discuss ethics, right? An excellent idea. I dare say, you could both use some ethical instruction."

Peter van Inwagen is one philosopher who agrees with Ben that the denial of moral responsibility entails the denial of all moral judgments: "I have listened to philosophers who deny the existence of moral responsibility. I cannot take them seriously. I know a philosopher who has written a paper in which he denies the reality of moral responsibility. And yet this same philosopher, when certain of his books were stolen, said, 'That was a shoddy thing to do.' But no one can consistently say that a certain act was a shoddy thing to do and say that its agent was not morally responsible when he performed it."

Peter van Inwagen, *An Essay on Free Will*
(Oxford, U.K.: Clarendon Press, 1983), p. 207

Ethics and Moral Responsibility

Ben was ready. "Actually, I've been thinking about that. If we discuss ethics, it will have to be a monologue. Selina doesn't believe in objective ethics, so she can't have anything to say. And you, Sarah, you deny the existence of moral responsibility. And without moral responsibility, there certainly can't be any ethics. So it looks like I'm the only one who can legitimately talk about ethics: The two of you can just drink your coffee, munch your scones, and benefit from my wisdom."

Sarah rose to the challenge. "Always delighted to benefit from your wisdom, Ben. But why would you suppose that just because I deny moral responsibility, I can't legitimately talk about ethics?"

"It's perfectly obvious, isn't it? If you can't hold people morally responsible, then all moral claims and evaluations lose their purpose."

Sarah shook her head, picked up a notebook, starting flipping through the pages. "Lots of philosophers agree with you, Ben. For example, your hero in the battle for contracausal free will, C. A. Campbell, asserts that the denial of justly deserved praise and blame would destroy 'the reality of the moral life.'[1] But this conclusion is hardly confined to Campbell. You remember Susan Wolf, for whom genuine freedom consists in rationally following the True and the Good. She concurs with Campbell that if we deny moral responsibility, then we must

> . . . stop thinking in terms of what ought and ought not to be. We would have to stop thinking in terms that would allow the possibility that some lives and projects are better than others.[2]

The Catholic philosopher F. C. Copleston insists that, without moral responsibility, 'there would be no objective moral distinction between the emperor Nero and St. Francis of Assisi.' And Jeffrie Murphy—who shares little common ground with Copleston—agrees, cautioning that denial of moral responsibility would destroy 'the moral significance of human beings that is founded upon such responsibility—would, indeed, spell the end of one's own moral significance.'"[3] Sarah came to the end of her favorite quotes and put aside her notebook. "They all agree with you, Ben. Like you, to them it's obvious that denying moral responsibility means denying all morality and ethics and moral evaluations and moral claims. But you must forgive me, I'm rather dull witted, and what is obvious to others is often obscure to me. True, I deny all moral responsibility; that is, I deny that anyone ever deserves blame or reward. I deny that there is ever such a thing as *just deserts*. But I can't see why that should keep me from making moral claims. In fact, it seems to me that my very *denial* of moral responsibility is based on a moral claim: I claim that blame and punishment are *unfair* and *unjust*, because one's behavior and character are ultimately based on good or bad luck in 'the natural lottery' of genetics, early conditioning, and environmental contingencies. Maybe I'm wrong. Lots of people think I am. But it doesn't seem to me to be *incoherent* to make such a moral claim as the very *basis* for denying moral responsibility."

"Well, maybe not incoherent." Ben was giving ground grudgingly. "But even if you can still *make* moral judgments, I don't see what *use* you could make of them. What good does it do to judge an act morally bad or a character morally virtuous if there is no question of punishment or reward, if no just deserts or consequences can attach to your moral judgments? Your moral judgments wouldn't be the basis for *doing* anything, so what use would they have? None. Without moral responsibility, moral judgments are 'like a tale told by a mad man: full of sound and fury, but signifying nothing.'"

Selina laughed and raised her coffee cup in a toast to Ben. "Nice shot, Ben. I think he scored a point with that one, Sarah."

"Certainly, he gets full credit for style," Sarah smiled, "but no points for substance."

Selina laughed and patted Ben's hand. "Be careful, Ben. I should have warned you. My roommate may be small, but she's quick. She throws a wicked counterpunch. But look, Sarah, I gotta go with Ben on this one. What use would there be for ethics without moral responsibility?"

"Plenty of use, guys. Look, do you really think that ethics consists entirely of blaming and praising, rewarding and punishing? Take my good friend Ben. He has a terribly mistaken moral viewpoint that involves belief in just deserts and blame and punishment. It's misguided, wrongheaded, morally bankrupt, and fundamentally unsound. It causes enormous harm and brings terrible suffering upon the world."

Sarah paused, and Selina lifted her cup in a salute: "You go, girl!"

"*But*," Sarah continued, "Ben should not be *blamed* for his profoundly mistaken and harmful views: Given his flawed history, it was inevitable that he would make such mistakes. Still, it's very important to note that his views *are* morally appalling. It's important, because then we can try to *change* his views and correct and reform him. *Not* by punishing him, of course; that would *not be just.* But people can change without being punished. One way is by reasoning with him, helping him to understand his egregious errors and profound flaws, and showing him how to reform his views. And it's also important to note that his views are *morally wrong*, so we can study the causes that led him down such a path of moral depravity and prevent others from making such mistakes. For example, we might want to make some changes in the environment that shaped him. If you have young people in urban ghettoes joining violent street gangs and committing acts of callous cruelty, then it is useless—and on my view, morally *wrong*—to blame them; but that doesn't mean that it is useless to note that their violent behavior is itself morally wrong, so we can try to take *effective* steps in reforming them and in preventing their younger brothers and sisters from following in their footsteps. We need to learn what *caused* their violent behavior and *change* that causal environment. And we can do that while *denying* that they are *morally responsible* for their morally bad behavior; in fact, we are likely to do a much better job of making effective changes if we *reject* such useless notions as moral responsibility and just deserts."

Ben threw up his hands. "Alright, alright, you can talk about ethics. I still think you're dead wrong about denying moral responsibility. Looking at environmental causes is fine, but if you really want to understand *free human actions*, you have to look internally, at the individual will. On that point, however, I doubt that we'll ever agree. But enough of moral responsibility, at least for today. Let's look at some other ethical issues."

"Sounds good, Ben." Sarah smiled. "Nothing better than hot coffee, warm scones, good friends, and intense ethical discussion."

"Exactly, Sarah. But I'm afraid Selina will be left out of our discussion. She doesn't believe that we can know anything about ethics."

"Come now, Ben. Do you really suppose that Selina is going to sit quietly? I rather doubt it."

"Well," Ben replied, "this would be a good time for her to learn her place. Women should learn to speak only when they are spoken to and generally keep silent when men are present."

"What's gotten into you, Ben?" Selina had fire in her eyes. "Where did all this stupid sexist ranting come from? I've never heard you say anything so vile; I'd better never hear you say anything like it again!"

"Steady on, Selina." Ben laughed. "What right do you have to call *anything* vile, whether it's sexism or racism or even genocide? You don't believe there is any objective right or wrong, remember?"

"Very clever, Ben. But just because I don't think there's any objective fact of the matter in ethics, that doesn't mean that I have no ethical views, no moral convictions. I certainly do, and I feel very strongly about them."

"Yes, Selina." Ben smiled. "We're aware you are a person of great spirit. But if you deny that there is any objective right or wrong, you can't call sexism *vile*. You might regard it as distasteful—maybe like putting a melted cheese sauce on sushi. But you can't really call it *wrong*. On your view, there are no ethical facts to be right or wrong about. You may not like sexism, but you can't call it wrong."

"The devil I can't. You make another sexist crack, and you'll see."

Emotivism

Sarah laughed. "Look, Selina, maybe you *can* still say that sexism is wrong, even though you reject ethical objectivity. You could adopt a view called *emotivism*. It was very popular among scientifically oriented philosophers of the early to mid-twentieth century, a group of empiricists who were following in the tradition of David Hume. The emotivists claimed that any meaningful statement had to be *verifiable*; that is, if a statement is meaningful, there must be some clear, concrete way that the statement could be proved right or wrong. Not that we must be able to carry out the test *now*. For example, do the planets of stars other than our Sun also have moons, just as Earth and Jupiter have moons? We don't know; but we certainly know *how* we could go about testing that claim; we know what would *count* as proving it true or proving it false. Build a much stronger telescope, and take a look. Or send a spacecraft on an incredibly

---

The presence of an ethical symbol in a proposition adds nothing to its content. Thus if I say to someone, 'You acted wrongly in stealing that money,' I am not stating anything more than if I had simply said, 'You stole that money.' In adding that this action is wrong I am not making any further statement about it. I am simply evincing my moral disapproval of it. . . . If now I generalise my previous statement and say, 'Stealing money is wrong,' I produce a sentence which has no factual meaning—that is, expresses no proposition which can be either true or false. . . . Another man may disagree with me about the wrongness of stealing, in the sense that he may not have the same feelings about stealing as I have, and he may quarrel with me on account of my moral sentiments. But he cannot, strictly speaking, contradict me. For in saying that a certain type of action is right or wrong, I am not making any factual statement, not even a statement about my own state of mind.

A. J. Ayer, *Language, Truth and Logic* (London: V. Gollancz, 1946), p. 106

long journey, and land on one of those moons. But what about a meta-physical statement, such as 'This is the best of all possible worlds,' or 'The dominant monad of a plant is in a state of slumber,' or 'All people who are courageous participate in the essence of courage'? What would *count* as proving such a statement false or true? If nothing could count as falsifying or verifying the statement, then the statement must be *meaningless*. But then people started asking about *ethical* statements: What would *prove* the truth or falsity of 'stealing is wrong' or 'benevolence is a virtue'? There seems no clear way of *testing* such ethical assertions; but they seem to be perfectly legitimate statements that are *not* meaningless. So the claim put forward by the empiricists that all meaningful, genuine statements must be verifiable or falsifiable doesn't work: Ethical statements are real statements, but they are not verifiable. The emotivists proposed this answer: Ethical statements are *not* real statements of fact; instead, they are *expressions of emotion*. When I say 'stealing is wrong,' it might look as if I am making a factual assertion; but actually, I'm only expressing my disgust and my opposition to stealing. I may feel very strongly about it, and I may use such emotive expressions in an attempt to get others to share my feelings. 'Stealing is wrong' is like saying 'Go, Michigan!' Both express emotion, and they may arouse emotion in others, but they don't state facts. So it's perfectly legitimate for Selina to say 'Sexism is wrong,' since that expresses her disgust with sexism."

"I like that, Sarah!" Selina was smiling. "What did you say it was called?"

"Emotivism."

"Emotivism. Okay, I'm an emotivist. And you, Ben, are a sexist pig, and your views are vile and despicable. Hey, this is fun. Could I buy an emotivist T-shirt?"

"Or maybe an emotivist bumper sticker: 'Warning, beware of emotivist.'" Ben shook his head. "No offense to any of your philosophical heroes, Sarah, but I don't think emotivism works. When I yell 'Go, Michigan, stomp Ohio State,' and across the way all the people in red are screaming 'Go, Buckeyes,' well, fine, I'm a Michigan fan, they're Ohio State fans, go in peace. But when I say that racism is bad, I mean a lot more than that. I do express my dislike for racism, but that's certainly not all. I also claim that racism is morally wrong and that if you approve of racism, you are *wrong*. Besides, when I say 'Racism is wrong,' I want to *convince* people that racism is wrong. If it were just an expression of emotion, how could it serve that function? I yell myself hoarse on Saturday screaming my deep emotional support of the Wolverines, but that never convinces a single Ohio State Buckeye to join the Michigan cause; it's not even *intended* to do that."

"Are you so sure," Selina said softly, "that expressions of emotion are never convincing, Ben my darling, sugar bear, sweetheart?"

"Alright, Selina, point for you. Still, when you said sexism was wrong, you were certainly expressing emotion; but it didn't *stop* with that. It wasn't like 'Go, Michigan' or 'Ooh, sunset.' You felt emotional about it *because* you think it is wrong. If I were really a sexist, you wouldn't just express an emotion of disgust; you would try to convince me that sexism is wrong and that I *ought* to be disgusted by it. On this emotivist view, once you've expressed your disgust, that's it; there's nothing more to say."

"Well, I'm not sure there's *nothing* more to say," Sarah responded. "Still, I see your point. If I know Selina, she wouldn't stop with just expressing her disgust; she would want to *argue* that sexism is wrong. And according to the emotivist view, that's impossible. In fact, A. J. Ayer, one of the leading emotivists, explicitly claimed that it is *impossible* to argue about ethics."

Selina frowned. "Alright, maybe I'm not an orthodox emotivist after all: I do like to argue, and ethics is one of my favorite things to argue about. But how could Ayer claim that we don't argue about ethics? I've argued with people about sexism, and affirmative action, and abortion, and animal rights, and capital punishment, and euthanasia—and all those seem to be *ethical* issues. Isn't it obvious that we argue about ethics? How could Ayer suggest otherwise, Sarah?"

"Ayer said that if you look closely at those arguments, they weren't really arguments about *ethics* or about *values;* instead, they were arguments about other issues. For example, think back to one of your arguments over capital punishment. You certainly did *argue,* but did you actually argue about *values?* You argued about whether capital punishment deters crime, sure; but that's a question of sociology. Maybe you argued about whether murderers were insane, or whether they were the products of terrible environments, or whether persons who commit vicious crimes are capable of reform; but those are questions of psychology. Or whether the death penalty is administered in an evenhanded manner, rather than discriminating against the poor and minorities; but that's a question of political science and sociology. Or maybe you argued about whether society could be protected by a sentence of life imprisonment; but that's a question of criminology. But suppose you actually got all the way down to a genuine conflict over *values*—to a basic ethical question: You say it's *wrong* to execute people, it's treating a human like an *object,* it's wrong because it is an act of cruelty; and your opponent insists that such executions are *just*—that when someone has committed a terrible crime, it is fair and right to make them pay the ultimate penalty. At *that* level of disagreement you might have called each other names—knee-jerk liberal, callous killer, whatever—but genuine argument was no longer possible. That's what Ayer claims."

"But can't the argument still continue, even then?" Ben wore a look of puzzlement. "Actually, Selina and I have had this argument. Not that we ever *really* argue, of course." Selina laughed, Sarah shook her head, and Ben continued. "And our argument doesn't stop at that point. And we don't start calling each other names—that comes later. I argue that unless this person is truly insane, justice requires that the most vicious and heinous crimes be punished by the ultimate penalty; and Selina says that such penalties are simply unfair, when you consider carefully what forces shaped people to become murderers, and that genuine justice does *not* require blood sacrifice—she sometimes goes on to say some rather harsh things about religious traditions, but I won't repeat those in pleasant company."

Sarah nodded. "Exactly. And that's where the argument ends. There's nowhere else for it to go. When you get to that level—that fundamental level of ethical conflict—argument is no longer possible. Or so Ayer insists."

Selina was not quite convinced. "But I'm not quite sure the argument does end there, Sarah. There are still things we can do. I might take Ben to see a movie like *Dead Man Walking*, or tell him the detailed life story of some prisoner awaiting execution who suffered a brutal childhood, and ask him to put himself in that person's shoes: murderer, yes, but also victim."

"And I might take Selina to meet the family—the mother and father, the husband, the children—of some innocent woman who was brutally raped and murdered by a vicious man now awaiting execution—a family that now longs for the closure that an execution would bring."

"Yes, precisely," Sarah agreed. "But though that might modify someone's views, it is not argument. When you reach that point, argument ends, and other forms of persuasion begin. That's what Ayer thinks ethical language really does: It uses emotive force to persuade others to change their views. Such persuasion may be effective, and there is nothing wrong with using such emotive language to persuade. Likewise, art or music or drama or a novel may also be very persuasive and perfectly legitimate, though it does not use *reason* or *argument* to persuade. Goya's paintings can be persuasive testimony of the horrors of war, *Uncle Tom's Cabin* persuaded many of the terrible brutality of slavery, and the novels of Dickens and Steinbeck awakened sympathies for the plight of the poor and displaced. All are nonrational means of persuasion, just as—according to Ayer—the use of ethical language is a form of nonrational persuasion. But not everything has to be rational, does it? Certainly, *some* forms of nonrational persuasion are repulsive: brainwashing, torture, deceit. But as the saying goes, 'Music hath charms to soothe the savage breast'; and if music and movies and novels and emotive language can soothe savagery and make people kinder and better, that seems perfectly fine to me."

"Sounds good. Emotivism forever. But," Selina continued, with a nod at Ben, who was frowning deeply, "I don't think it will do much to soothe old Ben's savage breast."

"Sarah, that is the most appalling view of ethics I have ever heard. It's not ethics at all: It's antiethics. Emotivism is an ethical theory the way atheism is a religion: Both are the denial of everything good and true. Besides, it's thoroughly ridiculous and even self-contradictory. What were you saying about different forms of 'nonrational persuasion'? Music and poetry and novels are okay; but—you said—brainwashing and torture are repulsive. Well, of course they are repulsive; but when an *emotivist* says torture is morally repulsive, all she is saying is something like 'Ooh, torture, yucky.' But that reduces ethics to something trivial and stupid. 'Ooh, brussels sprouts, yucky,' that's okay; but when I say that *torture is wrong*, I mean something a lot stronger than that."

"But look, Ben," Sarah replied, "some of our emotions and commitments are stronger than others. They aren't all trivial, like your distaste for brussels sprouts or Selina's fondness for chocolate chip cookies."

Selina laughed. "Hey, girl, there's nothing trivial about my affection for chocolate chip cookies."

"Okay, bad example. But you get the idea: There are some things you care about, but not profoundly, and it doesn't matter so much if others don't agree with you. You like popcorn, I prefer pretzels, so what. It's like, 'You say to*may*to, I say to*mah*to,' who cares. But if someone feels strongly that women should always be subservient and submissive, or if someone thinks that torturing children is a pleasant hobby, then that's a different matter altogether. Even if I don't think that there is ultimately any truth or falsity in our different views—there are no objective moral *facts* to prove that sexism or torture are wrong—that doesn't lessen my strong convictions about those issues: convictions I'm willing to fight for. And I'm not about to quietly tolerate our differences on those issues: If you want to adopt sexist policies, then you've got a battle on your hands."

Ben shook his head. "That's still not enough, guys. Sexism, torture, racism, rape, murder—those aren't just things I happen to feel strongly about. They are *wrong*. Part of the reason I *feel* so strongly about sexism is that I believe that it is *morally wrong*. Besides, ethical statements are *logically different* from mere expressions of emotion—even deep and strongly held emotions. When our beloved Wolverines take the field, we yell 'Yea' while Buckeye fans yell 'Boo,' and though our sentiments are certainly different, there is no contradiction between them. But when I say that sexism is morally *wrong*, and someone else says that sexism is morally *right*, our views are contradictory. If Joe loves Michelangelo's paintings, but hates his sculptures, we might be surprised, but we would not say that his tastes are *contradictory*. But if Joe says he thinks it is wrong to treat women as less than equals, but it's fine to deny women admission to medical school or law school, then Joe is contradicting himself. He's contradicting himself because he is making statements of *fact*— not expressions of emotion."

Ethical Nonobjectivism

"Ben," replied Sarah, "as usual, you've gone to the heart of the issue. That's one of the major criticisms made against emotivism. In fact, it led most emotivists, including Ayer, to revise their account and give up the claim that ethical claims are just expressions of emotion. So now they don't really consider themselves *emotivists*. But they stand by their position that, at the most basic level of value commitments, there is *no* fact of the matter in ethics. We may have strongly held principles, principles we cherish and are willing to fight for. But we can't know them to be true, because, at that most basic level, there simply are no *facts* available. It is not a fact that torture is wrong, much as we may despise torture. We feel profoundly upset by torture, we vigorously oppose its use, we don't regard opposition to torture as merely a matter of taste, but instead we view it as one of our most basic values—a value of great and enduring importance. But we can offer no scientific or logical proof that torture is morally wrong: There is no moral *fact* that shows the wrongness of torture. It is nonetheless one of our basic moral principles. You might think of it as a moral *postulate*, an ethical axiom. Of course, from a more immediate per-

---

The supreme norms of a given ethical system provide the ultimate ground for the validation of moral judgments. No matter how long or short the chain of validating inferences, the final court of appeal will consist in one or the other type of justifying principles. Rational argument presupposes reference to a set of such principles at least implicitly agreed upon. Disagreement with respect to basic principle can only be removed if the very frame of validation is changed. This can occur either through the disclosure and explication of a hitherto unrecognized common set of standards, i.e. still more fundamental validating principles to which implicit appeal is made in argument, or it can be achieved through the pragmatic justification of the adoption of an alternative frame, or finally, through sheer persuasion by means of emotive appeals.

Herbert Feigl, "Validation and Vindication: An Analysis of the Nature and the Limits of Ethical Arguments," 1952

---

spective, we might well say that torture is *wrong*. For example, suppose we are discussing the interrogation of prisoners, and someone suggests that we should force them to stay awake for many hours and keep them naked in cold, wet, dark dungeons, keep them hooded and helpless and chained in awkward positions, pretend that we are about to kill them and then grant them a reprieve, and again drag them in front of a firing squad, only to throw them back in their dungeons. Someone might well say that that would be wrong—that would be a form of psychological and physical torture, and torture is wrong. So we can certainly reason *from* the basic postulate that torture is wrong; and in that context, when we are reasoning about the implications of that postulate, even those who deny the *objective* truth of our basic values might say that it is therefore *true* that the psychological and physical abuse of prisoners is wrong. But if we get down to questions about those basic principles, then argument is not possible: The basic ethical principles are based, not on facts, or reason, or observation, but rather on our strong feelings and preferences and commitments. At that level, there is no objectivity."

Ben looked disappointed. "Sarah, I never thought you would deny the objective reality of basic moral principles. Selina, okay, I'm not surprised: If she can't measure it in a test tube, she doesn't think it exists. But can you really believe that there are ultimately no moral facts? That slavery is not *really* wrong, that it is not *objectively* true that torture is morally wrong, that Mother Teresa was *actually* no better than Hitler?"

Sarah patted his hand. "Don't despair, Ben. I didn't say I was a nonobjectivist. I was just talking about the position I thought Selina might hold."

"Frankly, that nonobjectivist view sounds good to me," Selina said. "Ben's right: If I can't measure it in a test tube, or at least find some clear objective test or measurement, then I tend to be skeptical. And I don't see how basic ethical claims meet that requirement. Of course, if we agree on some basic moral principles—we agree that all persons should be treated with respect, for example—we can argue about what that implies and what policies are consistent or inconsistent with that basic principle. But if we really get down to the level of basic principles—for example, you favor elitist principles, and I'm more egalitarian—then, at that level, there's no room for argument; we must rely on emotive persuasion, because there are no objective facts to argue about."

"You and David Hume," Sarah added. "There have been lots of moral nonobjectivists, but Hume gave perhaps the boldest statement of the position for modern philosophy."

"Ah, yes, David Hume. Hey, I'm not surprised I'm on Hume's side; from what I've heard of his views, I think he's my favorite philosopher—

present company excluded, of course. And I'm not surprised that he made a bold statement of nonobjectivism. We empiricists tend to be bold!"

"Well, Hume won't disappoint you. Hume believed there are only two ways to know objective truths: through mathematics or through empirical science. Since Hume believed—like his soulmate, Selina—that ethical beliefs are ultimately based on *feelings*, that means there can be no objective truths of ethics. That doesn't imply, however, that we don't have strong ethical convictions. We can and do have strong *feelings* about ethical issues. But feelings are not reasons, and ethics is not a sphere of reason or objectivity. As Hume states it (rather dramatically),

> 'Tis not contrary to reason to prefer the destruction of the whole world to the scratching of my finger.[4]

If that preference is based on a false judgment—such as the belief that I would die from a scratch on my finger, but survive the destruction of the world—then reason might correct it; if not, then strange as that preference may be, it cannot be refuted by reason. If you believe that smoking contributes to good health and improves your athletic performance, then reason might alter your views. But if you prefer the pleasures of smoking over avoiding the significantly increased risk of cancer and emphysema, and if you prefer to have everything you eat or drink taste like stale tobacco and your breath smell like a sewer, then reason cannot touch your preferences. Our basic preferences, values, and desires are not based on reason; rather, they *use* reason to find means of gaining satisfaction. There's another philosophically famous line from Hume:

> Reason is, and ought only to be the slave of the passions, and can never pretend to any other office than to serve and obey them.[5]

Given your basic feelings and preferences, reason can guide you effectively on what path you should take. But when it comes to *basic ethical views*, those are based on our feelings, and feelings are not sources of objective truth."

"Well done, David Hume!" Selina clapped her hands. "Now there's a philosopher who knows the difference between feelings and facts, and knows the genuine importance of both."

Ben shook his head. "Selina was already in favor of moral nonobjectivism; now that she has David Hume on her side, she'll be absolutely incorrigible."

"Yeah," Sarah agreed, "I don't think you're going to convert Selina to moral objectivism any time soon. She's a fervent nonobjectivist; and as you may have noted, Selina is a trifle stubborn."

"It's one of my many charms," Selina retorted.

God and Ethics

"Your charms are like the stars on a summer night, Selina," said Ben, "but ethical nonobjectivism is not one of them. Really, though, I shouldn't have been surprised that Selina is a nonobjectivist. When you think about it, Selina *has* to be a nonobjectivist. After all, she's an atheist. And without God, there can be no objective ethics. What is it that Dostoyevsky says? 'In the absence of God, everything is permitted.' And he's right. Without God, there can be no objective ethics."

"That's a bold statement," said Sarah, "and a very controversial one. Think about it from another angle. Ben, tell me, you believe that murder is wrong, correct?"

"Absolutely, Sarah. It's one of God's basic commandments: Thou shalt not kill."

"Okay, let's agree that God commands us not to murder. Here's my question. Is murder wrong *because* God commands it? Or does God command us not to murder because murder is *wrong?*"

Ben frowned, thought hard for a moment. "Run that by me again, would you, Sarah?"

"Alright, think about it this way. God would never command us to do anything wrong; you believe that, right?"

"Of course."

"So *why* would God never command what is wrong? Is it because whatever God commands is automatically good? Or is it because God, being perfect, has perfect knowledge of what is good and thus invariably gives the right commandments? On the former view, if God commands us to torture babies, then torturing babies becomes an act of virtue: God commands it, so it is automatically right, since God's commandment is what *makes* it right. But on the latter view, God does not order us to torture babies because God *knows*—in God's perfect knowledge—that torturing babies is *wrong.*"

"Okay, I see what you mean. I guess I never really thought about it before. Alright, God commands us not to murder because God knows that murder is wrong, not the other way around. God commands us to honor our parents because honoring our parents *is good*, as God perfectly

The option that Ben rejects is called theological voluntarism. It is so named because it makes ethical principles dependent on what God wills, on God's voluntary choice. Something is good because God wills that it be so, not because God recognizes it to be good. It is also called the divine command *theory of ethics: Good is whatever God commands, and only what God commands is good. On this view, God's will or God's command is the whole of ethics. A law or principle is right if and only if it is willed (commanded) by God.*

"A man's ethical be-havior should be based effectually on sympathy, education, and social ties and needs; no religious basis is necessary. Man would indeed be in a poor way if he had to be restrained by fear of punishment and hope of reward after death."

Albert Einstein, in *New York Times Magazine*, Sept. 11, 1930

understands; it doesn't *become* good just because God ordered it. Otherwise, God's commandments would just be arbitrary."

"But if that's the case," Sarah said, "then there must be some independent standard for good and bad; and that standard would exist even *without* God. Thus, the objectivity of ethics does not depend on the existence of God."

"Okay," Ben agreed. "Still, it seems to me that the only reliable way for humans to *know* what is right or wrong is by following God's rules, since they are based on God's perfect wisdom. Other than by God's instruction, how could we have reliable knowledge of what is objectively right and wrong?"

Ethical Intuitionism

"Maybe you've been looking too hard," Sarah said, "looking too far in the distance. Try looking closer to home."

"I'm not following you, Sarah. What do you mean, 'look closer to home'?"

"It shouldn't be hard for you to follow, Ben. You like Campbell's view of free will, right? So how," Sarah asked, "does Campbell say we *know* about contracausal free will?"

"You have to introspect, look inside yourself when you are choosing between duty and desire. Oh, I get it." Ben smiled. "We *introspect* certain ethical truths."

"Exactly. After all, aren't there some ethical truths you just immediately *know*, as soon as you think clearly about them? For example," Sarah continued, "you *know* that you should keep your promises. Perhaps you could also figure that out by some reasoning process; but you already *know* that you should keep your promise. You have a special *intuitive* knowledge that it is right to keep promises, that it's wrong to torture, that it's right to help others. *Some* people may try to cast doubts on our intu-itions of right and wrong"—Sarah arched her eyebrows and nodded toward Selina—"but if you introspect honestly, you cannot really doubt the truth of your ethical intuitions."

Selina frowned. "Look, Sarah, everybody has those feelings—except maybe for some real sociopaths, who lack any capacity of concern for others. But that's exactly what they are: *feelings*, not intuitive sources of deep truth."

The following proposition seems to me in a high degree probable—namely, that any animal whatever, endowed with well-marked social instincts, the parental and filial affections being here included, would inevitably acquire a moral sense or conscience, as soon as its intellectual powers had become as well, or nearly as well developed, as in man. . . .

It may be well first to premise that I do not wish to maintain that any strictly social animal, if its intellectual faculties were to become as active and as highly developed as in man, would acquire exactly the same moral sense as ours. In the same manner as various animals have some sense of beauty, though they admire widely different objects, so they might have a sense of right and wrong, though led by it to follow widely different lines of conduct. If, for instance, to take an extreme case, men were reared under precisely the same conditions as hive-bees, there can be no doubt that our unmarried females would, like the worker-bees, think it a sacred duty to kill their brothers, and mothers would strive to kill their fertile daughters; and no one would think of interfering. Nevertheless, the bee, or any other social animal, would gain in our supposed case, as it appears to me, some feeling of right or wrong, or a conscience.

Charles Darwin, *The Descent of Man*, 2d ed., 1875

Ben was looking reflective. "I think there's something to this intuitionism, Selina. Something more than just feelings. Feelings come and go, and they're not very reliable. Not that I'm knocking feelings"—Ben patted Selina's hand—"but we can all think of feelings that are less than constant and less than trustworthy. Like my roommate my freshman year: He had very strong feelings of eternal undying love for Cindy; and then next week he had absolutely true feelings of love for Nania; and two weeks later his till-death-do-us-part-and-maybe-after love was fixed on Tamara. And then there's my friend David: He has these tremendously certain feelings that he has the winning lottery ticket, or that he knows the winner of the Super Bowl. He's never right, but the next day he's back with a new feeling that just can't be wrong. But our intuitions of right and wrong aren't just *feelings*; they're something very different. To recognize the difference, you must honestly consult your *own* intuitions of what is right and wrong."

"Sorry, guys, I can't buy it," Selina answered. "Maybe I'm not very good at this introspection business, but when I look hard, I don't find any deep intuitive truths. I find strong *feelings*, certainly, such as the feeling that sexism is wrong. But some people report having strong and indubitable *intuitions* that it is simply wrong for women to work outside the home or think for themselves or even go to college. Frankly, I don't think there are any objective truths of ethics; but if I *were* in search of objective ethical truths, I'd want a more reliable source than intuitions, no matter how strongly I *felt* about them."

"Okay, Selina," Sarah said. "To tell you the truth, I'm a bit skeptical about intuitive ethical truths myself. But don't let that bother you, Ben. Intuitionism is an ethical theory favored by many very respectable philosophers."

Selina laughed. "Isn't that an oxymoron, Sarah? 'Respectable philosopher'?"

"I'm going to let that pass, Selina." Sarah smiled. "You can't really expect anything better from a nonobjectivist. But if you don't like intuitionism, maybe we should look at a philosopher who based ethical truths on pure reason. Immanuel Kant developed a method for discovering objective ethical truths using reason alone—analogous to the way we discover truths in geometry or mathematics."

Kantian Objectivism

"Oh, yeah, we talked about Kant before, when we were discussing theories of knowledge," Selina said. "Did Kant have something to say about ethics also?"

"He had a *lot* to say about ethics. In fact, Kant's ethics is a landmark that dominates the ethical horizon. Many people think Kant was terribly wrong, and many others believe he was fundamentally right, but almost everyone agrees that he developed a very important ethical theory. Kant did believe in God; but he also believed that we can prove the existence of objective ethical principles—absolute and universal ethical principles—without appealing to belief in God or revelation. For Kant, ethical principles must be absolute and universal, and such truths can be known only by pure *reason.*"

"Objective ethical truths, based purely on reason, no appeal to emotion." Selina was skeptical. "Sounds like an ambitious project to me."

"Ambitious indeed," Sarah agreed. "But for Kant, ethical principles must be *absolute*—they must be universal and *categorical*. Not like, 'Eat your broccoli *if* you want to be healthy.' Rather, an ethical principle can have no 'ifs' about it: 'Tell the truth,' period; not 'Tell the truth *if* you want to be respected.' And such absolute universal categorical principles cannot be discovered through observation or experiment; they can be discovered only by pure *reason*, like the universal truths of mathematics or geometry. They are true for everyone, everywhere. Like mathematical truths, the truths of ethics are equally true in Ann Arbor and Cairo and Paris and Bangkok; and they are true whether anyone recognizes them or not, and their truth has nothing to do with how we *feel* about them. The square root of 16 is 4, and whether that makes me happy or sad is irrelevant."

"That's my kind of ethical truth!" Ben was delighted. "No wishy-washiness about old Kant, was there? But how could you establish such truths through pure reason?"

"It's not really that hard," Sarah said. "Look, suppose I'm trying to sell my old car. I know that it burns oil like a furnace, the frame is badly bent, and the transmission is living on borrowed time. But I find some naive kid who is desperate for a car. If I tell him that the car looks a little rough, but it runs great, and it should give him trouble-free transportation for several years, then he'll believe me; and by the time the car breaks down completely—which will no doubt be soon—I'll be long gone. Is it okay for me to deceive and cheat this person? *Think* about it, Kant would say. Would you approve if someone cheated you like that, *used* you in that manner? No, of course not. *You* don't want to be cheated, and you do *not* want to live in a world where people cheat one another and no one can be trusted. You want people to deal honestly with *you:* You cannot truthfully say that you think it is alright for others to cheat you. But there is *no morally relevant difference* between you and the person you are cheating. So you *cannot* rationally and consistently say that it is *right* for you to cheat him, but *wrong* for others to cheat you. All of us have our own plans and hopes, all of us are vulnerable, and all of us are rational, autonomous persons. So *rational consistency* requires that all of us be treated alike. It would be *irrational* to treat basically similar cases by fundamentally different principles. That would be like saying that *this* angle is a right angle, but another, *identical* angle is not."

Sarah paused for a sip of coffee, then continued. "So through pure rational deliberation, we reach a basic ethical principle—the principle that Kant called *the categorical imperative:* Always act in such a way that you could will that your act should be a universal law."

"Sounds a lot like the Golden Rule," Ben said: "Do unto others as you would have them do unto you."

"Right, Ben," Sarah continued, "or as it's stated in the Jewish tradition, 'That which is hateful to you, do not unto others.' But Kant insists that the rule can be discovered purely by reason, without requiring religious revelations. Nor does it require emotions or feelings. In fact, Kant regards feelings as an *impediment* to genuine ethical conduct, because they distract us

". . . as to moral feeling, this supposed special sense, the appeal to it is indeed superficial when those who cannot think believe that feeling will help them out, even in what concerns general laws: and besides, feelings which naturally differ infinitely in degree cannot furnish a uniform standard of good and evil, nor has any one a right to form judgments for others by his own feelings . . ."

Immanuel Kant,
*Fundamental Principles
of the Metaphysics
of Ethics*

from *duty*. For Kant, acting morally requires following the rules of duty purely because we rationally recognize it to be our *duty*, and *not* because it is pleasant or agreeable. So there you have it: a robust, categorical ethical principle, absolute and universal, based purely on reason, without any taint of emotion."

"Impressive, Sarah." Ben nodded. "Frankly, I was skeptical about the possibility of establishing moral principles through rationality. But Kant makes a strong case for ethics based on reason."

Selina shook her head. "No way. Kant has everything turned upside down. If you take feelings out of ethics, you take away the heart and core of ethical behavior. Take away the *feelings* of affection and pity and sympathy, and you've destroyed the roots of ethics: Ethical behavior would dry up and blow away. That's not philosophical speculation; it's solid empirical fact. When people suffer brain injuries that destroy their emotions, they don't become rationally devoted to duty; rather, they become sociopaths, with no concern for ethics at all."[6]

"I'm not sure Kant would count that as disproof of his position," Sarah said. "After all, he would agree that *most* people are guided by emotions, so if you destroy their feelings of affection, they will behave badly. But he would still claim that those whose *rationality* remains intact *could* follow ethical principles. If they don't, it doesn't show that there are no pure rational principles to follow, any more than the fact that most people can't follow mathematical reasoning undercuts the truth of mathematics."

Selina frowned. "It seems to me that Kant has set up this system of rational ethics in a way that sets it sublimely apart from all empirical considerations whatsoever. Some people may see that as a virtue of his system." Selina rolled her eyes at Ben. "But I certainly do not."

Ben rose to the challenge. "Okay, there *is* something sublime about Kant's ethics of rational duty. And certainly, Kant sets a high standard for genuine ethical behavior. Yeah, I guess I count that as a virtue of his system."

"On that point, children," Sarah intervened, "I think you'll have to agree to disagree. But look, Selina, what do you think of Kant's categorical imperative? Does he manage to establish it through objective, rational argument?"

"It's not that I disagree with the principle," Selina replied. "But I don't think we *can* establish it on rational grounds. There are some elitists who don't think that everyone should be treated as ends in themselves. They think that special traits—such as strength, or intelligence, or whatever—entitles people to treat others as considerably *less* than ends in themselves. And while some of those people (in fact, I think the great majority of them) may just be shortsighted, there are also some who would insist that it is right, even if they themselves were in the inferior position. I'm not saying they wouldn't change their minds if they actually *were* in such a situation, but there is nothing rationally *inconsistent* in holding such a view."

"It seems to me," Ben replied, "that such people are simply refusing to *consider* reasons, refusing to think carefully; and if that's the case, it's hardly surprising that reasons cannot convince them."

"No," Selina said, "they aren't refusing to reason. They're just starting from a basically different ethical perspective. And when that happens, reason cannot establish one over the other. Kant builds an impressive looking rational ethical structure, but the foundation is weak. No, I can't see it: Reason is good for lots of things, but no way it gives us fixed, absolute ethical truths."

Ben held up his hands. "Hopeless, Sarah. Selina just won't budge off this vile nonobjectivism."

Utilitarian Ethics

Sarah laughed. "Don't despair, Ben. There's an objectivist ethical theory that empiricists often find appealing. Maybe Selina will favor a utilitarian ethical system. It's not the pure rational ethics of Kant, but at least it makes objective ethical claims."

"'Utilitarian.' Yeah, I've heard of utilitarian ethics," said Ben. "It was popular during the 19th century in England. Some of the British reformers favored utilitarianism: people like Jeremy Bentham and John Stuart Mill. Are there still utilitarians around?"

"The philosophical woods are full of 'em, Ben. Ever heard of Peter Singer, the guy who champions animal rights? He's a utilitarian—a very dedicated utilitarian, in fact."

This caught Selina's attention. "Alright, so what's this utilitarian theory you think I might like? I do like Peter Singer's work on animal rights. Maybe I'll convert to utilitarianism. So what are the distinguishing marks of the utilitarian species?"

"It's basically a simple theory, Selina. The utilitarians start from one simple premise. What is it we desire? Pleasure. And what do we seek to avoid? Suffering. Lying, theft, torture, and bias are all bad because they produce greater suffering; benevolence and honesty and generosity are good because they produce pleasure and reduce suffering. So what is the right act to do, what is the *objectively good* act? Whatever act produces the *greatest balance of pleasure over suffering* for everyone involved. Calculate the results, and your calculation yields the right act."

Selina nodded. "It does sound simple, clean, straightforward: Do the calculations, get the result."

The creed which accepts as the foundation of morals "utility" or the "greatest happiness principle" holds that actions are right in proportion as they tend to promote happiness; wrong as they tend to produce the reverse of happiness. By happiness is intended pleasure and the absence of pain; by unhappiness, pain and the privation of pleasure. To give a clear view of the moral standard set up by the theory, much more requires to be said; in particular, what things it includes in the ideas of pain and pleasure, and to what extent this is left an open question. But these supplementary explanations do not affect the theory of life on which this theory of morality is grounded—namely, that pleasure and freedom from pain are the only things desirable as ends; and that all desirable things (which are as numerous in the utilitarian as in any other scheme) are desirable either for pleasure inherent in themselves or as means to the promotion of pleasure and the prevention of pain.

John Stuart Mill, *Utilitarianism*, 1863

"The basic idea is simple," Sarah agreed, "but—as utilitarians are quick to note—practicing utilitarian ethics is not such an easy task. First off, calculating the right act is a formidable enterprise. It makes calculating the orbit of Halley's comet look trivial. Think about it: The act that will produce the greatest balance of pleasure over pain, taking into account the pleasure and pain of *everyone*; and not just for the moment, but including remote consequences. I mean, staying up all night with your friends polishing off a bottle of good Irish whiskey and chasing it with dark lager is certainly a pleasure; but tomorrow's consequences, not to mention the long-term effects, certainly call into question the utilitarian wisdom of such a party."

Selina shook her head. "Brings back some painful memories of my freshman year. The utilitarians have a good point: The pleasure-pain calculations have to be done carefully."

"And they get even tougher," Sarah continued. "Suppose you promised to give me a ride to the airport, so I can catch my flight for a long, warm, sunny weekend in Miami. But the time comes for you to pick me up, and you are deeply immersed in an exciting research project at the chemistry lab. This looks like it might be a real scientific breakthrough, an important scientific advance; and if you stop now, the entire project will be lost."

"I'd call Ben and ask him to drive you."

"Ben is visiting his parents."

"I would call you and tell you to catch the shuttle to the airport."

"Too late; the only shuttle that would get there on time already left."

"I'd tell you to take the extra set of car keys out of my desk, take my car, and just leave it at the airport parking lot until you return."

"I don't know how to drive. Give me a break, Selina, would you just deal with the case, for pity's sake? You have a choice: You can either keep your promise and drive me to the airport and abandon your research project, or break your promise and finish your research. So what's it going to be?"

"I wouldn't be very happy about it, girlfriend, but I'd close the lab and drive you to the airport."

"I know you would, Selina; you're a true friend. But what I'm really asking is this: From the utilitarian perspective, what *should* you do? It's not easy to decide. Utilitarians insist that you must consider my pleasure and pain in making your calculation, but you must consider your own, as well. Your pleasure and pain don't count for more than mine, but everyone counts. If you continue your research, you'll gain the pleasure of working on your project and avoid the pain of losing all the work you have invested. But I'll suffer deep frustration from losing my weekend in Miami and miss the pleasure I could have had sipping rum coolers on those sugary beaches. And those calculations are wrapped in uncertainty: Maybe your research project would have discovered amazing results that eventually led to a cure for cancer; or maybe it would have reached a profoundly depressing dead end. And maybe I would have found the love of my life in the south Florida sand; or maybe I would have returned with a nasty sunburn and unhappy memories."

"It's hopeless, Sarah," Selina said; "these utilitarian calculations are starting to look impossible."

"And there are still more problems to consider. When you break your promise to me, not only will that cause tension between us, but it would also lead me to have less trust in you, and that would be a painful loss. And Ben would hear about it, and he might then have less confidence in promises and promise keeping, and that would cause problems. In fact, the whole thing about promise keeping is so complicated that it has divided utilitarians into two camps: *Act* utilitarians and *rule* utilitarians. Act utilitarians insist that all acts should be judged entirely on their overall effects. But rule utilitarians maintain that for acts involving *practices* or *institutions* or *rules*—such as promise keeping—we should evaluate the overall *practice* by utilitarian standards, but if we conclude that the practice is a good one, then we must consider the specific act in terms of how it fits under that practice, and not on its individual consequences. Because after all, you really can't have a *practice* of promise keeping if you break promises every time it becomes slightly more advantageous to do so. 'I promise to take you to the airport' means 'I *will* take you to the airport, unless some serious emergency prevents it.' It does *not* mean 'I'll take you to the airport, unless something better comes along.' Of course,

---

It is indisputable that the being whose capacities of enjoyment are low has the greatest chance of having them fully satisfied; and a highly endowed being will always feel that any happiness which he can look for, as the world is constituted, is imperfect. But he can learn to bear its imperfections, if they are at all bearable; and they will not make him envy the being who is indeed unconscious of the imperfections, but only because he feels not at all the good which those imperfections qualify. It is better to be a human being dissatisfied than a pig satisfied; better to be Socrates dissatisfied than a fool satisfied. And if the fool, or the pig, are of a different opinion, it is because they only know their own side of the question.

John Stuart Mill, *Utilitarianism*, 1863

---

if an act doesn't fit under any practice, then we just do a straight utilitarian calculation."

"That makes sense; and actually," Selina said, "it makes the utilitarian calculations somewhat easier: Trying to run a utilitarian calculation on whether I should keep my promise to you was making my head spin; figuring out how my promise fits under the promise-keeping practice will still be challenging (I'll have to decide whether my *excuse* is a legitimate part of the practice), but at least its manageable."

"There's another consideration, however, that greatly complicates utilitarian calculations—and incidentally, it's a source of deep disagreement among utilitarians themselves: Should our utilitarian calculations be confined to the overall *quantity* of pleasure, or should the *quality* of pleasure also be a factor? Jeremy Bentham maintained that 'push-pin is as good as poetry,' or, to put it in contemporary terms, video games are as good as poetry. For Bentham, the only relevant consideration was the overall balance of pleasure over pain. If people get as much pleasure from playing video games as they would from a poetry reading, then playing video games is just as good as poetry. John Stuart Mill, a leading utilitarian of the next generation, strongly disagreed. Mill thought that utilitarians should also factor in the *quality* of pleasure: Reading poetry is a much *higher quality* pleasure than playing video games. On Mill's view, if six people want the lounge for a poetry reading, and twelve people want to use the lounge for a video game tournament, the difference in the *quality* of each of these pleasures might lead a utilitarian to favor the smaller number of poetry lovers. But as I noted, that's controversial. In the first place, it's very difficult to decide how we could judge and measure *qualities* of pleasure; and second, many utilitarians fear that allowing *qualities* of pleasure opens the door to the sort of elitism and special privilege that utilitarian ethics was originally designed to combat."

"I'm not sure about utilitarianism," Selina said. "I can see how it might be useful in setting social policies and for thinking hard about all the consequences of our behavior. I'm not ready to renounce nonobjectivism and become a utilitarian, but utilitarianism has its charms. At least it keeps its feet planted firmly in our grubby real world of pleasures and pains."

"This is ridiculous!" Ben was genuinely disturbed. "Utilitarianism is *not* ethics. It's like a paint-by-numbers copy of a Rembrandt portrait. Selina denies ethical objectivity, but at least she's still talking about ethics. But utilitarians trash ethics and turn it into hedonistic bookkeeping. 'Let's see, will I be happier if I keep my promise?' You call that an ethical consideration?"

> *Morality is not properly the doctrine of how we may make ourselves happy, but how we may make ourselves worthy of happiness.*
>
> Kant, *Critique of Practical Reason*, 1788

Sarah spoke softly. "I know it's not a system of fixed ethical principles, Ben, but couldn't it still offer helpful ethical guidelines? After all, utilitarianism is not a narrow or selfish view. Utilitarians insist that, in deciding what is right, we must take careful account of the pleasure and pain of *everyone* and adopt policies and perform acts that yield the greatest balance of benefit for all concerned. Is that really such a terrible ethical system?"

Ben was not placated. "Look, suppose someone shows up on campus and offers to throw a magnificent party for all the students at Michigan: greatest party in the history of Ann Arbor, and Ann Arbor has seen some great parties. This will be like Mardi Gras and spring break and beating Ohio State, all rolled into one. Fabulous fun. Just one condition: First we

---

Many moral theories . . . employ the assumption that to increase the utility of individuals is a good thing to do. But if asked why *it is a good thing to increase utility, or satisfy desire, or produce pleasure, or* why *doing so counts as a good reason for something, it is very difficult to answer. The claim is taken as a kind of starting assumption for which* no *further reason can be given. It seems to rest on a view that people seek pleasure, or that we can recognize pleasure as having more intrinsic value. But if women recognize quite different assumptions as more likely to be valid, that would certainly be of importance to ethics. We might then take it as one of our starting assumptions that creating good relations of care and concern and trust between ourselves and our children, and creating social arrangements in which children will be valued and well cared for, are more important than maximizing individual utilities. And the moral theories that might be compatible with such assumptions might be very different from those with which we are familiar.*

Virginia Held, "Feminism and Moral Theory,"
in Eva Feder Kittay and Diana T. Meyers, eds., *Women and Moral Theory*
(Totowa, NJ: Rowman & Littlefield, 1987), p. 126.

must severely flog a small child. The child is a friendless orphan, so no one else will be disturbed by it. And the child won't be killed, or even permanently damaged—maybe a few lasting scars, but no permanent disability. But what's one small child's misery compared to the ecstatic pleasure of tens of thousands? So obviously, by utilitarian lights, we ought to flog the kid and throw the party, right? But that is obviously *wrong*. And anyone who thinks for a minute that it's right is not a shrewd moral calculator, but a vicious moral beast. Oh, I've no doubt that a clever utilitarian can deal with this example: If we flog this child, we might discover that we rather like torturing children, and that would cause tremendous harm to future children. Or flogging the child might make us callous toward children, and we would be cold to our own future children. Or maybe the party would actually cause great suffering: Tens of thousands of Michigan students nursing tens of thousands of severe hangovers is not a cheerful thought. But the point is, it would be morally *disgraceful* even to consider such calculations. Suppose Selina receives such an offer, and she answers, 'Well, let me run some calculations, and I'll get back to you.' You wouldn't say, 'Oh, good job, Selina, calculate carefully and let us know what we should do.' You'd say, 'My God, Selina, how could you even *consider* such an offer?' You can talk all you like about rules of practices and qualities of pleasure and long-term consequences, but it doesn't change the basic flaw at the heart of utilitarian theory: Ethics is *not* a matter of maximizing pleasure. Doing the right thing doesn't always produce the greatest happiness."

Sarah laughed. "Well, one good thing you can say about utilitarianism: It certainly stirs the antiutilitarians to heights of eloquence! Well argued, Ben. Still, for those who deny the absolute values of rationalist ethics and reject the brilliant ethical light of intuition, might utilitarianism at least offer some ethical guidance? Isn't it an improvement over ethical nonobjectivism?

"I guess utilitarianism is an improvement over nonobjectivism; but it's not much of an improvement. It may be a form of ethical objectivism, but it's surely the mildest possible form." Ben shook his head. "In fact, now that I think about it, utilitarianism may be even *worse* than nonobjectivism. Nonobjectivists deny that there are ethical truths; but utilitarians try to transform the wonderful and inspiring truths of ethics into something calculating and cheap. It's the difference between an honest opponent and a traitor."

Sarah nodded. "Utilitarianism can look a bit squalid in some lights. But think of it from a wider perspective. Ben, you remember what you first said about utilitarian ethics? It was developed by 19th century social reformers, people who were dedicated to reforming British society—establishing equal rights for women, providing universal education, stopping the terrible abuses of children in the workplace, providing decent pay and housing for everyone. The utilitarians who struggled to carry out such reforms were not moral monsters who wanted to justify the torture of children; to the contrary, they were struggling to establish *better* conditions for the oppressed. So their motives were good, right?"

"The road to hell is paved with good intentions, Sarah."

Selina laughed. "The boy is really riled up about this utilitarian business, Sarah. I don't think you're going to persuade him that it contains any good whatsoever."

"You may be right, Selina. But look, Ben, suppose we're trying to decide what reforms are needed. Utilitarianism is a powerful weapon for reform, whether we're talking about 19th-century Britain or 21st-century United States. Some people live in great luxury, with mansions and summer estates—today I guess it would be several BMW's and a Lear jet; in 19th-century Britain it might have been several coaches and a yacht—and luxurious clothes and extravagant meals. Others live in poverty, without decent health care, not even enough clothes to stay warm, no place to sleep. Obviously, such an arrangement does *not* maximize pleasure and minimize suffering for everyone. Sure, adding another classy designer suit to the dozens that are hanging in your closet is pleasurable; but if you weigh it against the increase in pleasure and reduction in suffering that a good, thick winter coat would provide for an impoverished child in a Michigan winter, it's obvious that the warm winter coat would be a morally better choice. If you live in a twenty-thousand-square-foot mansion, then adding another wing of a thousand feet—maybe a spacious new billiard room—increases your pleasure; but it's a poor comparison with providing a snug little cottage for a homeless family. Starting your luxurious seven-course dinner with an appetizer of caviar and champagne is surely delightful; but how does that additional gluttonous pleasure compare with the increased pleasure and decreased suffering of a good, simple wholesome meal for a hungry child? By utilitarian principles, the conclusion is painfully clear. And of course, the utilitarian calculations go far beyond that. Utilitarians are concerned with *all* suffering and pleasure, not just that within one's own society. No doubt it is pleasant to drive gargantuan gas-guzzling SUV's, but is it morally legitimate when we consider the waste of resources that could be used to relieve the suffering of impoverished people in other countries, not to mention the suffering caused by the increase in pollution? And the delicacies provided by imports of tropical fruits is certainly pleasurable; but if such pleasures are purchased at the price of political corruption in third-world countries, and the destruction of the small farms that provided food and comfort for farmers and their families, then is the price too high? Of course, there's also the question of whether those who are wrapped up in a frenzy of shopping and consumer goods and fashion are *really* increasing their happiness; but that's another issue. Even if they were gaining a marginal increase in happiness, it comes at an enormous price in suffering. So utilitarian calculation is a favorite tool for reformers. Peter Singer is a utilitarian who campaigns for reform of our treatment of animals. No doubt, many people find significant pleasure in a char-grilled beefsteak. But even if we leave aside the increased dangers in heart disease and mad cow disease, is it really worth it? After all, eating a beefsteak is clearly a luxury: We could all survive without eating beef; in fact, we would probably be a good deal healthier if we dropped it entirely from out diets. And can the enjoyment of such a luxury compare with the suffering of cattle that are castrated, raised in confined quarters on factory farms, crowded onto packed trucks, and shipped off to slaughterhouses? There is no doubt that the cattle suffer to provide us with an increase in dining pleasure; and even if you count the suffering of a calf as less important than the suffering of a human—and from a utilitarian perspective, it's hard to justify such a distinction—it's still clear that the suffering far outweighs the gain in dining pleasure. Thus, utilitarian ethics forces us to look closely at the social structure of our societies, as well as our own individual behavior: Am *I* morally justified in spending so much on my own luxury when there are others who suffer from want of bare necessities? So even if you don't see utilitarianism as the best system of ethics, it might still have some uses in making us aware of unfairness and inequity—unfairness that can easily become so commonplace that we fail to see it clearly."

"I know Ben hates it, but I see some advantages to utilitarianism," Selina said. "It does seem useful in pointing out the clear need for some basic reforms."

"Look, Selina, I agree with you on the need for reform." Ben spoke softly, but with deep conviction. "Any society that has millions of children living in poverty, without even decent health care or adequate housing, while millions of others live in wasteful, glittering luxury, is a society that obviously needs some fundamental reforms. But you don't need utilitarianism to recognize such wrongs. I know utilitarian theory has its charms for a tough-minded scientist like you: Study all the consequences, make the calculations, get your answer. But as a tough-minded scientist, you should consider the empirical psychological adequacy—or inadequacy—of utilitarian ethics. Is it really true that what we seek is pleasure and the avoidance of suffering? There's no doubt that we are *shaped* by experiences of suffering and pleasure; the behavioral psychologists have demonstrated that quite thoroughly. Reward a mouse for running down a maze or a pigeon for pressing a bar, it tends to repeat the behavior. Stretch out or vary the interval between reinforcements, and the mouse and pigeon become dedicated to maze running and bar pressing. Same thing for humans: Give them a reward when they pull a lever, they tend to pull the lever again. Vary the intervals between rewards—sometimes after the second pull on the lever, then after the ninth, then following the fifth—and they will stand in casinos pulling on levers for an entire night. But though our behavior may be shaped by pleasant rewards, it is something very different to suggest that our only real goal is the seeking of pleasure and the avoidance of pain. Look, Selina, you love chemistry, right?"

"Absolutely. Working out hypotheses, running experiments, figuring out puzzles, making discoveries: that's what I want to do my whole life. Graduate school, then some position doing research—maybe at a university, teach chemistry and do research on chemistry. Maybe I'll discover a new compound with amazing new properties. I've loved chemistry ever since I got my first chemistry set, when I was ten years old."

"I'll make you a deal, Selina. You can have all the pleasure you get from doing chemistry research—we'll stream it into the pleasure center of your brain, or give you a drug, or whatever—but you can't actually *do* any of the research. You'll have all the pleasure, but no chemistry research. Okay?"

"What are you raving about, Ben? I don't just want the *pleasure* that I get from doing chemistry research: I want to actually *do the research*. If I didn't get pleasure from it, I might not do it. And I can imagine that if, year after year, all my experiments failed, then I might finally lose my joy in doing chemistry. But that's not the point. I do chemistry because I love doing chemistry, not in order to gain pleasure. I mean, after all, chemistry is a lot of hard work: I've spent a lot of long, lonely nights in that chemistry lab. If I just wanted pleasure, there are plenty of ways to get pleasure that are a lot easier than studying chemistry. Sure, chemistry is reinforcing for me, I find pleasure in it; but I don't do it for the pleasure."

"Exactly, Selina." Ben was delighted. "So utilitarianism is false at its very roots. It's just not true that what everyone wants is to maximize pleasure and minimize pain. And adding 'high-quality' pleasures to the mix doesn't change that. Utilitarians may have some useful points to

---

Think of someone—yourself, if you can—facing an important self-defining decision. If you are a woman with a chance to begin a demanding career that intrigues you, but only by sacrificing time with your young children, which choice do you make? Or, if you are a law-school graduate with an offer from an established firm, do you reject it for a less challenging offer that is more likely—but by no means certain—to lead to a political career later? Or, if you are a Jew, should you abandon your comfortable life in Los Angeles and emigrate to Israel to identify yourself firmly with that nation's fate? People do not make momentous decisions like these by trying to predict how much pleasure each choice might bring.

Ronald Dworkin, *Life's Dominion: An Argument about Abortion, Euthanasia, and Individual Freedom* (New York: Knopf, 1993), p. 205.

make about public policy. But as a personal ethics, utilitarianism is a failure. Remember the famous hedonist paradox: Those who seek after pleasure are the least likely to find it."

"Your argument against utilitarian ethics sounds a lot like an argument that was developed by Robert Nozick, a philosopher who taught at Harvard during the late 20th Century." Sarah sipped her coffee and continued. "Nozick imagined the existence of a pleasure machine: You enter the machine, and you lose all knowledge that you are in a machine, any memory that you ever entered the machine. It's like a super trip through cyberspace, with complete belief that you are living in the real world. The pleasure machine gives you a steady diet of pleasures, very intense pleasures: You quarterback Michigan to four consecutive national championships, your book on colonial history wins the Pulitzer prize, a couple of years later you win the Nobel prize, and you spend wild nights of abandoned pleasure in the warm breezes of an isolated Hawaiian Beach. And there are just enough frustrations to keep things fascinating: You fumble in the fourth quarter of the Rose Bowl, and Southern Cal takes the lead, but then you lead the Wolverines in a brilliant final-seconds comeback. None of this will actually be happening, of course. But you will *believe* it's happening, and you will gain all the pleasure that you would experience if it were actually happening. And to make the example work, you have to assume that your family and friends are not distressed by your disappearance into the pleasure machine and that the operator of the machine is not some nefarious monster who has trapped you there in order to ultimately perform gruesome experiments on you. Oh, and of course you have to assume that God is not going to punish you for your choice. Okay, Nozick asks: Would you enter the machine, *on this condition:* Once you enter, you must remain there. You can't go in for a couple of hours or a long weekend; you are there permanently. Few of us would enter, and the moral of Nozick's story is obvious: What we seek is *not* the maximizing of pleasure. If it were, we would be eager to live out our lives in Nozick's pleasure machine, which will yield pleasure in a steady, reliable stream. Someone profoundly depressed, despairing, and hopeless might enter the machine; but most of us would not. So maximizing pleasure is *not* our basic goal."

Ben raised his cup. "I drink to Robert Nozick and to the total defeat of utilitarian ethics. May its armies be destroyed, its walls beaten down, and its fields sown with salt, amen."

Selina laughed. "I think he means he doesn't much like utilitarianism, Sarah. I confess, I think there may be more to it than Ben allows. But Ben will hear nothing good of utilitarian ethics, even though it *is* an objectivist view. Maybe I'll just stick with nonobjectivism."

"Maybe so," Sarah answered, "or maybe not. We haven't covered all the possibilities yet: Nonobjectivism and utilitarianism are hardly the only options. For example, you might be a do-it-yourselfer when it comes to ethics, Selina: You might like to build your own ethical system. But that will have to wait for tomorrow. Duty calls, in the form of a Renaissance philosophy seminar."

"Yeah," Selina replied, "isn't that the seminar you have with Sam? Is that duty calling you, Sarah, or pleasure?"

"Maybe it's both," Sarah said. "What's that line from Ogden Nash? 'O Duty, why hast thou not the visage of a sweetie or a cutie?' In this case, duty does seem sweet. Might not work for Kant, but it's fine for me. Ciao, Sister."

READINGS

David Hume is eloquent in defense of the empiricist position, and his writings often establish the classic version of that position on various issues. Ethics is no exception. Though many empiricists have views on ethics very different from the one developed by Hume, his ethical theory—and his insistence that, in ethical issues, "reason is, and ought only to be the slave of the passions"—has inspired, challenged, and infuriated philosophers in the centuries since he wrote.

A Treatise of Human Nature

Of the Influencing Motives of the Will

Nothing is more usual in philosophy, and even in common life, than to talk of the combat of passion and reason, to give the preference to reason, and to assert that men are only so far virtuous as they conform themselves to its dictates. Every rational creature, 'tis said, is oblig'd to regulate his actions by reason; and if any other motive or principle challenge the direction of his conduct, he ought to oppose it, 'till it be entirely subdu'd, or at least brought to a conformity with that superior principle. On this method of thinking the greatest part of moral philosophy, ancient and modern, seems to be founded; nor is there an ampler field, as well for metaphysical arguments, as popular declamations, than this suppos'd pre-eminence of reason above passion. The eternity, invariableness, and divine origin of the former have been display'd to the best advantage: The blindness, unconstancy, and deceitfulness of the latter have been as strongly insisted on. In order to shew the fallacy of all this philosophy, I shall endeavour to prove *first*, that reason alone can never be a motive to any action of the will; and *secondly*, that it can never oppose passion in the direction of the will.

The understanding exerts itself after two different ways, as it judges from demonstration or probability; as it regards the abstract relations of our ideas, or those relations of objects, of which experience only gives us information. I believe it scarce will be asserted, that the first species of reasoning alone is ever the cause of any action. As its proper province is the world of ideas, and as the will always places us in that of realities, demonstration and volition seem, upon that account, to be totally remov'd, from each other. Mathematics, indeed, are useful in all mechanical operations, and arithmetic in almost every art and profession: But 'tis not of themselves they have any influence. Mechanics are the art of regulating the motions of bodies *to some design'd end or purpose;* and the reason why we employ arithmetic in fixing the proportions of numbers, is only that we may discover the proportions of their influence and operation. A merchant is desirous of knowing the sum total of his accounts with any person: Why? but that he may learn what sum will have the same *effects* in paying his debt, and going to market, as all the particular articles taken together. Abstract or demonstrative reasoning, therefore, never influences any of our actions, but only as it directs our judgment concerning causes and effects; which leads us to the second operation of the understanding.

'Tis obvious, that when we have the prospect of pain or pleasure from any object, we feel a consequent emotion of aversion or propensity, and are carry'd to avoid or embrace what will give us this uneasiness or satisfaction. 'Tis also obvious, that this emotion rests not here, but making us cast our view on every side, comprehends whatever objects are connected with its original one by the relation of cause and effect. Here then reasoning takes place to discover this relation; and according as our reasoning varies, our actions receive a subsequent variation. But 'tis evident in this case, that the impulse arises not from reason, but is only directed by it. 'Tis from the prospect of pain or pleasure that the aversion or propensity arises towards any object: And these emotions extend themselves to the causes and effects of that object, as they are pointed out to us by reason and experience. It can never in the least concern us to know, that such objects are causes, and such others effects, if both the causes and effects be indifferent to us. Where the objects themselves do not affect us, their connexion can never give them any influence; and 'tis plain, that as reason is nothing but the discovery of this connexion, it cannot be by its means that the objects are able to affect us.

Since reason alone can never produce any action, or give rise to volition, I infer, that the same faculty is as incapable of preventing volition, or of disputing the preference with any passion or emotion. This consequence is necessary. 'Tis impossible reason cou'd have the latter effect of preventing volition, but by giving an impulse in a contrary direction to our passion; and that impulse, had it operated alone, wou'd have been able to produce volition. Nothing can oppose or retard the impulse of passion, but a contrary impulse; and if this contrary impulse ever arises from reason, that latter faculty must have an original influence on the will, and must be able to cause, as well as hinder any act of volition. But if reason has no original influence, 'tis impossible it can withstand any principle, which has such an efficacy, or ever keep the mind in suspense a moment. Thus it appears, that the principle, which opposes our passion, cannot be the same with reason, and is only call'd so in an improper sense. We speak not strictly and philosophically when we talk of the combat of passion and of reason. Reason is, and ought only to be the slave of the passions, and can never pretend to any other office than to serve and obey them. As this opinion may appear somewhat extraordinary, it may not be improper to confirm it by some other considerations.

A passion is an original existence, or, if you will, modification of existence, and contains not any representative quality, which renders it a copy of any other existence or modification. When I am angry, I am actually possest with the passion, and in that emotion have no more a reference to any other object, than when I am thirsty, or sick, or more than five foot high. 'Tis impossible, therefore, that this passion can be oppos'd by, or be contradictory to truth and reason; since this contradiction consists in the disagreement of ideas, consider'd as copies, with those objects, which they represent.

What may at first occur on this head, is, that as nothing can be contrary to truth or reason, except what has a reference to it, and as the judgments of our understanding only have this reference, it must follow, that passions can be contrary to reason only so far as they are *accompany'd* with some judgment or opinion. According to this principle, which is so obvious and natural, 'tis only in two senses, that any affection can be call'd unreasonable. First, When a passion, such as hope or fear, grief or joy, despair or security, is founded on the supposition of the existence of objects, which really do not exist. Secondly, When in exerting any passion in action, we chuse means insufficient for the design'd end, and deceive ourselves in our judgment of causes and effects. Where a passion is neither founded on false suppositions, nor chuses means insufficient for the end, the understanding can neither justify nor condemn it. 'Tis not contrary to reason to prefer the destruction of the whole world to the scratching of my finger. 'Tis not contrary to reason for me to chuse my total ruin, to prevent the least uneasiness of an *Indian* or person wholly unknown to me. 'Tis as little contrary to reason to prefer even my own acknowledg'd lesser good to my greater, and have a more ardent affection for the former than the latter. A trivial good may, from certain circumstances, produce a desire superior to what arises from the greatest and most valuable enjoyment; nor is there any thing more extraordinary in this, than in mechanics to see one pound weight raise up a hundred by the advantage of its situation. In short, a passion must be accompany'd with some false judgment, in order to its being unreasonable; and even then 'tis not the passion, properly speaking, which is unreasonable, but the judgment.

The consequences are evident. Since a passion can never, in any sense, be call'd unreasonable, but when founded on a false supposition, or when it chuses means insufficient for the design'd end, 'tis impossible, that reason and passion can ever oppose each other, or dispute for the government of the will and actions. The moment we perceive the falshood of any supposition, or the insufficiency of any means our passions yield to our reason without any opposition. I may desire any fruit as of an excellent relish; but whenever you convince me of my mistake, my longing ceases. I may will the performance of certain actions as means of obtaining any desir'd good; but as my willing of these actions is only secondary, and founded on the supposition, that they are causes of the propos'd effect; as soon as I discover the falshood of that supposition, they must become indifferent to me. . . .

Those who affirm that virtue is nothing but a conformity to reason; that there are eternal fitnesses and unfitnesses of things, which are the same to every rational being that considers them; that the immutable measures of right and wrong impose an obligation, not only on human creatures, but also on the Deity himself: All these systems concur in the opinion, that morality, like truth, is discern'd merely by ideas, and by their juxta-position and comparison. In order, therefore, to judge of these systems, we need only consider, whether it be possible, from reason alone, to distinguish betwixt moral good and evil, or whether there must concur some other principles to enable us to make that distinction.

If morality had naturally no influence on human passions and actions, 'twere in vain to take such pains to inculcate it; and nothing would be more fruitless than that multitude of rules and precepts with which all moralists abound. Philosophy is commonly divided into *speculative* and *practical*; and as morality is always comprehended under the latter division, 'tis supposed to influence our passions and actions, and to go beyond the calm and indolent judgments of the understanding. And this is confirm'd by common experience, which informs us, that men are often govern'd by their duties, and are deter'd from some actions by the opinion of injustice, and impell'd to others by that of obligation.

Since morals, therefore, have an influence on the actions and affections, it follows, that they cannot be deriv'd from reason; and that because reason alone, as we have already prov'd, can never have any such influence. Morals excite passions, and produce or prevent actions. Reason of itself is utterly impotent in this particular. The rules of morality, therefore, are not conclusions of our reason. . . .

But can there be any difficulty in proving, that vice and virtue are not matters of fact, whose existence we can infer by reason? Take any action allow'd to be vicious: Wilful murder, for instance. Examine it in all lights, and see if you can find that matter of fact, or real existence, which you call *vice*. In which-ever way you take it, you find only certain passions, motives, volitions and thoughts. There is no other matter of fact in the case. The vice entirely escapes you, as long as you consider the object. You never can find it, till you turn your reflexion into your own breast, and find a sentiment of disapprobation, which arises in you, towards this action. Here is a matter of fact; but 'tis the object of feeling, not of reason. It lies in yourself, not in the object. So that when you pronounce any action or character to be vicious, you mean nothing, but that from the constitution of your nature you have a feeling or sentiment of blame from the contemplation of it. Vice and virtue, therefore, may be compar'd to sounds, colours, heat and cold, which, according to modern philosophy, are not qualities in objects, but perceptions in the mind: And this discovery in morals, like that other in physics, is to be regarded as a considerable advancement of the speculative sciences; tho', like that too, it has little or no influence on practice. Nothing can be more real, or concern us more, than our own sentiments of pleasure and uneasiness; and if these be favourable to virtue, and unfavourable to vice, no more can be requisite to the regulation of our conduct and behaviour.

I cannot forbear adding to these reasonings an observation, which may, perhaps, be found of some importance. In every system of morality, which I have hitherto met with, I have always remark'd, that the author proceeds for some time in the ordinary way of reasoning, and establishes the being of a God, or makes observations concerning human affairs; when of a sudden I am surpriz'd to find, that instead of the usual copulations of propositions, *is*, and *is not*, I meet with no proposition that is not connected with an *ought*, or an *ought not*. This change is imperceptible; but is, however, of the last consequence. For as this *ought*, or *ought not*, expresses some new relation or affirmation, 'tis necessary that it shou'd be observ'd and explain'd; and at the same time that a reason should be given, for what seems altogether inconceivable, how this new relation can be a deduction from others, which are entirely different from it. But as authors do not commonly use this precaution, I shall presume to recommend it to the readers; and am persuaded, that this small attention wou'd subvert all the vulgar systems of morality, and let us see, that the distinction of vice and virtue is not founded merely on the relations of objects, nor is perceiv'd by reason.

Immanuel Kant's ethical system is an uncompromising rationalism, and occupies the opposite pole from David Hume. Kant (1724–1804) insists that genuine ethical principles must be universal and absolute, and that they must be based purely on reason. Feelings contribute nothing whatsoever to Kantian ethics; to the contrary, Kant regards emotions as distractions from our impersonal obligation to follow duty for duty's sake.

The reading below is drawn primarily from Kant's Fundamental Principles of the Metaphysics of Morals, *1785; the concluding paragraph is from* The Critique of Practical Reason, *1788; both are translated by Thomas K. Abbott.*

Fundamental Principles of the Metaphysic of Morals

Transition from the Common Rational Knowledge of Morality to the Philosophical

Nothing can possibly be conceived in the world, or even out of it, which can be called good, without qualification, except a good will. Intelligence, wit, judgement, and the other talents of the mind, however they may be named, or courage, resolution, perseverance, as qualities of temperament, are undoubtedly good and desirable in many respects; but these gifts of nature may also become extremely bad and mischievous if the will which is to make use of them, and which, therefore, constitutes what is called character, is not good. It is the same with the gifts of fortune. Power, riches, honour, even health, and the general well-being and contentment with one's condition which is called happiness, inspire pride, and often presumption, if there is not a good will to correct the influence of these on the mind, and with this also to rectify the whole principle of acting and adapt it to its end. The sight of a being who is not adorned with a single feature of a pure and good will, enjoying unbroken prosperity, can never give pleasure to an impartial rational spectator. Thus a good will appears to constitute the indispensable condition even of being worthy of happiness.

A good will is good not because of what it performs or effects, not by its aptness for the attainment of some proposed end, but simply by virtue of the volition; that is, it is good in itself, and considered by itself is to be esteemed much higher than all that can be brought about by it in favour of any inclination, nay even of the sum total of all inclinations. Even if it should happen that, owing to special disfavour of fortune, or the niggardly provision of a step-motherly nature, this will should wholly lack power to accomplish its purpose, if with its greatest efforts it should yet achieve nothing, and there should remain only the good will (not, to be sure, a mere wish, but the summoning of all means in our power), then, like a jewel, it would still shine by its own light, as a thing which has its whole value in itself. Its usefulness or fruitfulness can neither add nor take away anything from this value. It would be, as it were, only the setting to enable us to handle it the more conveniently in common commerce, or to attract to it the attention of those who are not yet connoisseurs, but not to recommend it to true connoisseurs, or to determine its value.

There is, however, something so strange in this idea of the absolute value of the mere will, in which no account is taken of its utility, that notwithstanding the thorough assent of even common reason to the idea, yet a suspicion must arise that it may perhaps really be the product of mere high-flown fancy, and that we may have misunderstood the purpose of nature in assigning reason as the governor of our will. Therefore we will examine this idea from this point of view.

In the physical constitution of an organized being, that is, a being adapted suitably to the purposes of life, we assume it as a fundamental principle that no organ for any purpose will be found but what is also the fittest and best adapted for that purpose. Now in a being which has reason and a will, if the proper object of nature were its conservation, its welfare, in a word, its happiness, then nature would have hit upon a very bad arrangement in selecting the reason of the creature to carry out this purpose. For all the actions which the creature has to perform with a view to this purpose, and the whole rule of its conduct, would be far more surely prescribed to it by instinct, and that end would have been attained thereby much more certainly than it ever can be by reason. Should reason have been communicated to this favoured creature over and above, it must only have served it to contemplate the happy constitution of its nature, to admire it, to congratulate itself thereon, and to feel thankful for it to the beneficent cause, but not that it should subject its desires to that weak and delusive guidance and meddle bunglingly with the purpose of nature. In a word, nature would have taken care that reason should not break forth into practical exercise, nor have the presumption, with its weak insight, to think out for itself the plan of happiness, and of the means of attaining it. Nature would not only have taken on herself the choice of the ends, but also of the means, and with wise foresight would have entrusted both to instinct.

And, in fact, we find that the more a cultivated reason applies itself with deliberate purpose to the enjoyment of life and happiness, so much the more does the man fail of true satisfaction. And from this circumstance there arises in many, if they are candid enough to confess it, a certain degree of misology, that is, hatred of reason, especially in the case of those who are most experienced in the use of it, because after calculating all the advantages they derive, I do not say from the invention of all the arts of common luxury, but even from the sciences (which seem to them to be after all only a luxury of the understanding), they find that they have, in fact, only brought more trouble on their shoulders, rather than gained in happiness; and they end by envying, rather than despising, the more common stamp of men who keep closer to the guidance of mere instinct and do not allow their reason much influence on their conduct. And this we must admit, that the judgement of those who would very much lower the lofty eulogies of the advantages which reason gives us in regard to the happiness and satisfaction of life, or who would even reduce them below zero, is by no means morose or ungrateful to the goodness with which the world is governed, but that there lies at the root of these judgements the idea that our existence has a different and far nobler end, for which, and not for happiness, reason is properly intended, and which must, therefore, be regarded as the supreme condition to which the private ends of man must, for the most part, be postponed.

For as reason is not competent to guide the will with certainty in regard to its objects and the satisfaction of all our wants (which it to some extent even multiplies), this being an end to which an implanted instinct would have led with much greater certainty; and since, nevertheless, reason is imparted to us as a practical faculty, i.e., as one which is to have influence on the will, therefore, admitting that nature generally in the distribution of her capacities has adapted the means to the end, its true destination must be to produce a will, not merely good as a means to something else, but good in itself, for which reason was absolutely necessary. This will then, though not indeed the sole and complete good, must be the supreme good and the condition of every other, even of the desire of happiness. Under these circumstances, there is nothing inconsistent with the wisdom of nature in the fact that the cultivation of the reason, which is requisite for the first and unconditional purpose, does in many ways interfere, at least in this life, with the attainment of the second, which is always conditional, namely, happiness. Nay, it may even reduce it to nothing, without nature thereby failing of her purpose. For reason recognizes the establishment of a good will as its highest practical destination, and in attaining this purpose is capable only of a satisfaction of its own proper kind, namely that from the attainment of an end, which end again is determined by reason only, notwithstanding that this may involve many a disappointment to the ends of inclination.

We have then to develop the notion of a will which deserves to be highly esteemed for itself and is good without a view to anything further, a notion which exists already in the sound natural understanding, requiring rather to be cleared up than to be taught, and which in estimating the value of our actions always takes the first place and constitutes the condition of all the rest. In order to do this, we will take the notion of duty, which includes that of a good will, although implying certain subjective restrictions and hindrances. These, however, far from concealing it, or rendering it unrecognizable, rather bring it out by contrast and make it shine forth so much the brighter.

To be beneficent when we can is a duty; and besides this, there are many minds so sympathetically constituted that, without any other motive of vanity or self-interest, they find a pleasure in spreading joy around them and can take delight in the satisfaction of others so far as it is their own work. But I maintain that in such a case an action of this kind, however proper, however amiable it may be, has nevertheless no true moral worth, but is on a level with other inclinations, e.g., the inclination to honour, which, if it is happily directed to that which is in fact of public utility and accordant with duty and consequently honourable, deserves praise and encouragement, but not esteem. For the maxim lacks the moral import, namely, that such actions be done from duty, not from inclination. Put the case that the mind of that philanthropist were clouded by sorrow of his own, extinguishing all sympathy with the lot of others, and that, while he still has the power to benefit others in distress, he is not touched by their trouble because he is absorbed with his own; and now suppose that he tears himself out of this dead insensibility, and performs the action without any inclination to it, but simply from duty, then first has his action its genuine moral worth. Further still; if nature has put little sympathy in the heart of this or that man; if he, supposed to be an upright man, is by temperament cold and indifferent to the sufferings of others, perhaps because in respect of his own he is provided with the special gift of patience and fortitude and supposes, or even requires, that others should have the same—and such a man would certainly not be the meanest product of nature—but if nature had not specially framed him for a philanthropist, would he not still find in himself a source from whence to give himself a far higher worth than that of a good-natured temperament could be? Unquestionably. It is just in this that the moral worth of the character is brought out which is incomparably the highest of all, namely, that he is beneficent, not from inclination, but from duty.

It is in this manner, undoubtedly, that we are to understand those passages of Scripture also in which we are commanded to love our neighbour, even our enemy. For love, as an affection, cannot be commanded, but beneficence for duty's sake may; even though we are not impelled to it by any inclination—nay, are even repelled by a natural and unconquerable aversion. This is practical love and not pathological—a love which is seated in the will, and not in the propensions of sense—in principles of action and not of tender sympathy; and it is this love alone which can be commanded.

The second proposition is: That an action done from duty derives its moral worth, not from the purpose which is to be attained by it, but from the maxim by which it is determined, and therefore does not depend on the realization of the object of the action, but merely on the principle of volition by which the action has taken place, without regard to any object of desire. It is clear from what precedes that the purposes which we may have in view in our actions, or their effects regarded as ends and springs of the will, cannot give to actions any unconditional or moral worth. In what, then, can their worth lie, if it is not to consist in the will and in reference to its expected effect? It cannot lie anywhere but in the principle of the will without regard to the ends which can be attained by the action. For the will stands between its a priori principle, which is formal, and its a posteriori spring, which is material, as between two roads, and as it must be determined by something, in that it must be determined by the formal principle of volition when an action is done from duty, in which case every material principle has been withdrawn from it.

The third proposition, which is a consequence of the two preceding, I would express thus: Duty is the necessity of acting from respect for the law. I may have inclination for an object as the effect of my proposed action, but I cannot have respect for it, just for this reason, that it is an effect and not an energy of will. Similarly I cannot have respect for inclination, whether my own or another's; I can at most, if my own, approve it; if another's, sometimes even love it; i.e., look on it as favourable to my own interest. It is only what is connected with my will as a principle, by no means as an effect—what does not subserve my inclination, but overpowers it, or at least in case of choice excludes it from its calculation—in other words, simply the law of itself, which can be an object of respect, and hence a command. Now an action done from duty must wholly exclude the influence of inclination and with it every object of the will, so that nothing remains which can determine the will except objectively the law, and subjectively pure respect for this practical law, and consequently the maxim that I should follow this law even to the thwarting of all my inclinations.

Thus the moral worth of an action does not lie in the effect expected from it, nor in any principle of action which requires to borrow its motive from this expected effect. For all these effects-agreeableness of one's condition and even the promotion of the happiness of others—could have been also brought about by other causes, so that for this there would have been no need of the will of a rational being; whereas it is in this alone that the supreme and unconditional good can be found. The pre-eminent good which we call moral can therefore consist in nothing else than the conception of law in itself, which certainly is only possible in a rational being, in so far as this conception, and not the expected effect, determines the will. This is a good which is already present in the person who acts accordingly, and we have not to wait for it to appear first in the result.

But what sort of law can that be, the conception of which must determine the will, even without paying any regard to the effect expected from it, in order that this will may be called good absolutely and without qualification? As I have deprived the will of every impulse which could arise to it from obedience to any law, there remains nothing but the universal conformity of its actions to law in general, which alone is to serve the will as a principle, i.e., I am never to act otherwise than so that I could also will that my maxim should become a universal law. Here, now, it is the simple conformity to law in general, without assuming any particular law applicable to certain actions, that serves the will as its principle and must so serve it, if duty is not to be a vain delusion and a chimerical notion. The common reason of men in its practical judgements perfectly coincides with this and always has in view the principle here suggested. Let the question be, for example: May I when in distress make a promise with the intention not to keep it? I readily distinguish here between the two significations which the question may have: Whether it is prudent, or whether it is right, to make a false promise? The former may undoubtedly be the case. I see clearly indeed that it is not enough to extricate myself from a present difficulty by means of this subterfuge, but it must be well considered whether there may not hereafter spring from this lie much greater inconvenience than that from which I now free myself, and as, with all my supposed cunning, the consequences cannot be so easily foreseen but that credit once lost may be much more injurious to me than any mischief which I seek to avoid at present, it should be considered whether it would not be more prudent to act herein according to a universal maxim and to make it a habit to promise nothing except with the intention of keeping it. But it is soon clear to me that such a maxim will still only be based on the fear of consequences. Now it is a wholly different thing to be truthful from duty and to be so from apprehension of injurious consequences. In the first case, the very notion of the action already implies a law for me; in the second case, I must first look about elsewhere to see what results may be combined with it which would affect myself. For to deviate from the principle of duty is beyond all doubt wicked; but to be unfaithful to my maxim of prudence may often be very advantageous to me, although to abide by it is certainly safer. The shortest way, however, and an unerring one, to discover the answer to this question whether a lying promise is consistent with duty, is to ask myself, "Should I be content that my maxim (to extricate myself from difficulty by a false promise) should hold good as a universal law, for myself as well as for others? and should I be able to say to myself, "Every one may make a deceitful promise when he finds himself in a difficulty from which he cannot otherwise extricate himself?" Then I presently become aware that while I can will the lie, I can by no means will that lying should be a universal law. For with such a law there would be no promises at all, since it would be in vain to allege my intention in regard to my future actions to those who would not believe this allegation, or if they over hastily did so would pay me back in my own coin. Hence my maxim, as soon as it should be made a universal law, would necessarily destroy itself.

I do not, therefore, need any far-reaching penetration to discern what I have to do in order that my will may be morally good. Inexperienced in the course of the world, incapable of being prepared for all its contingencies, I only ask myself: Canst thou also will that thy maxim should be a universal law? If not, then it must be rejected, and that not because of a disadvantage accruing from it to myself or even to others, but because it cannot enter as a principle into a possible universal legislation, and reason extorts from me immediate respect for such legislation. I do not indeed as yet discern on what this respect is based (this the philosopher may inquire), but at least I understand this, that it is an estimation of the worth which far outweighs all worth of what is recommended by inclination, and that the necessity of acting from pure respect for the practical law is what constitutes duty, to which every other motive must give place, because it is the condition of a will being good in itself, and the worth of such a will is above everything.

Conclusion

Two things fill the mind with ever new and increasing admiration and awe, the oftener and the more steadily we reflect on them: the starry heavens above and the moral law within. I have not to search for them and conjecture them as though they were veiled in darkness or were in the transcendent region beyond my horizon; I see them before me and connect them directly with the consciousness of my existence. The former begins from the place I occupy in the external world of sense, and enlarges my connection therein to an unbounded extent with worlds upon worlds and systems of systems, and moreover into limitless times of their periodic motion, its beginning and continuance. The second begins from my invisible self, my personality, and exhibits me in a world which has true infinity, but which is traceable only by the understanding, and with which I discern that I am not in a merely contingent but in a universal and necessary connection, as I am also thereby with all those visible worlds. The former view of a countless multitude of worlds annihilates as it were my importance as an animal creature, which after it has been for a short time provided with vital power, one knows not how, must again give back the matter of which it was formed to the planet it inhabits (a mere speck in the universe). The second, on the contrary, infinitely elevates my worth as an intelligence by my personality, in which the moral law reveals to me a life independent of animality and even of the whole sensible world, at least so far as may be inferred from the destination assigned to my existence by this law, a destination not restricted to conditions and limits of this life, but reaching into the infinite.

Study Questions

1. Does the denial of moral responsibility make ethics impossible? What are the main arguments on both sides of that issue?
2. What is emotivism? What considerations led some philosophers to adopt the emotivist theory?
3. What are the major objections to emotivism?
4. What is theological voluntarism, and what are the objections to that view?
5. Describe the intuitionist view of ethics and some challenges to intuitionism.
6. According to Kant, what is the appropriate role of emotions in ethics? Why?

7. What is Kant's categorical imperative? What argument does he give for its objective truth?
8. What is utilitarian ethics?
9. Describe the difference between how act utilitarians and rule utilitarians would decide what is right.
10. A key difference between Bentham and Mill is over *qualities* of pleasure. Describe their differences on that issue.
11. Describe and discuss some of the major objections to utilitarian ethics.

Exercises

1. Suppose that two students, Adam and Ivana, both devote their spring breaks to working as math and reading tutors in an underfunded and isolated rural elementary school. At the end of the week, they are driving back to the university, having spent six straight fourteen-hour days tutoring inside the school and then at the homes of children needing special help. "I'm exhausted," Adam says, "but that was the best spring break I've ever had. It was so much fun, working with these kids, taking kids who thought they could never do math and helping them realize they really can do it! Their eyes literally light up! I've never gotten more satisfaction, more real joy, out of anything I've ever done."

   "Boy, Adam," answered Ivana, "we really had different experiences! That was not *my* idea of a great spring break. Oh, it was satisfying, that's certainly true. But I wouldn't call it a 'joyous' experience, not by a long shot. A joyous spring break involves white sand, dancing all night, and margaritas for breakfast, lunch, and dinner. It certainly does *not* involve rural poverty and exhausting days. Still, I know it was my duty to help those kids: I'm a good tutor, and they really need help, and my work will make a big difference for a number of kids. It was the right thing to do, I have no doubts about that. But if someone else would have done it for me and let me spend my week at the beach, that would have brought *me* a lot more happiness."

   Suppose—a supposition you may find very doubtful, in fact—that Adam and Ivana are equally good at their tutoring and they helped an equal number of children and with equal effectiveness. Which of the two—if either—is *morally* superior?

2. You enjoy a good meal, and you like going out with your friends to nice restaurants. Not that you're a gourmet, but you enjoy good food. One summer, one of your friends, Jacques, invites you to spend a couple of weeks with his family at their home in Paris. Well, a couple of weeks in Paris certainly sounds appealing, right? And that's not all. It turns out that Jacques's family runs one of the best small restaurants in all of Paris, and his parents love to introduce people to the finer points of French cuisine. "You won't believe it," Jacques tells you. "By the time you've lived with my family for two weeks, you will have tasted some of the finest culinary treats ever created! Food like you've never even imagined."

   It happens that the two of you have a mutual friend, Joe, who visited Jacques for two weeks last summer. Before accepting Jacques's invitation, you call Joe and ask how his visit went. "It was fabulous," Joe says; "Jacques's family was wonderful, very kind. And the food! Mon Dieu! It was magnifique! Just one problem: You'll learn a lot about food and cuisine and fine wines, and you'll learn to appreciate the artistry of great chefs. But when you come back and eat what beforehand you would have considered a superb meal, you will recognize all the flaws in the preparation, and it won't taste nearly so good to you. In fact, you will hardly ever have a meal that really measures up to your new standards. Still, on those rare occasions when you *do* get a really exquisite dish, you'll be able to appreciate all its nuances and artistry." Would this enhanced and heightened appreciation be an *advantage* or a *disadvantage* of the trip to Paris?

3. Look at the boxed quotation from Charles Darwin that occurs in the section on intuitionism. Would you regard Darwin as a *supporter* or an *opponent* of intuitionism?

4. Neruopsychologist Antonio Damasio claims that it is impossible to separate reason from the emotions:

> . . . emotions and feelings may not be intruders in the bastion of reason at all: they may be enmeshed in its networks, for worse *and* for better. The strategies of human reason probably did not develop, in either evolution or any single individual, without the guiding force of the mechanisms of biological regulation, of which emotion and feeling are notable expressions. Moreover, even after reasoning strategies become established in the formative years, their effective deployment probably depends, to a considerable extent, on a continued ability to experience feelings.[7]

> This is a controversial position; but suppose that Damasio is right. Then, if someone favoring a Kantian ethical system became convinced of the truth of Damasio's claim, what would the Kantian regard as the implications for ethics? Is there any way to save the fundamentals of Kantian ethics while agreeing with Damasio?

Glossary

Act utilitarianism: A version of utilitarian ethics in which the rightness or wrongness of all acts are judged by whether they maximize pleasure and minimize suffering.

Divine command theory: The view that all values and ethical commandments are established by God's command or by God's will; also known as theological voluntarism.

Emotivism: A form of ethical nonobjectivism according to which all value assertions are actually disguised commands or expressions of emotion; value assertions and ethical assertions do not make real statements and are neither true nor false. Sometimes called noncognitivism.

Intuitionism, ethical: The view that ethical truths are known by special powers of intuition.

Nonobjectivism: The view that in ethics there is no truth and no objective facts.

Objectivism: The view that there are genuine objective ethical facts; ethical claims are factually true or false.

Rule utilitarianism: A version of utilitarian ethics according to which rules and institutions are judged by utilitarian standards (do they maximize pleasure and minimize suffering) and the rightness or wrongness of individual acts is determined by whether they fit under the rules of beneficial institutions and practices.

Utilitarian ethics: The ethical theory that judges the rightness or wrongness of an act in terms of its consequences—in particular, whether it produces the greatest possible balance of pleasure over suffering for everyone involved.

Verifiability standard, or verifiability criterion: The principle that all meaningful statements must be verifiable in principle; that is, for a statement to be meaningful, it must be possible to state what would count as proving it true or false.

Additional Resources

Among general works on ethics, Peter Singer's edited work *A Companion to Ethics* (Oxford, U.K.: Blackwell Publishers, 1991) is a superb guide to many topics in ethical theory as well as in applied ethics. An excellent collection of readings is edited by Hugh LaFollette: *The Blackwell Guide to Ethical Theory* (Oxford, U.K.: Blackwell Publishers, 2000). Another collection of outstanding contemporary articles is Stephen Darwall, Allan Gibbard, and Peter Railton, eds., *Moral Discourse and Practice* (Oxford, U.K.: Oxford University Press, 1997).

A number of contemporary philosophers have argued against moral objectivity. Among the emotivists are A. J. Ayer, *Language, Truth and Logic* (London: V. Gollancz, 1946), and C. L. Stevenson, who wrote *Ethics and Language* (New Haven, CT: Yale University Press, 1944) and *Facts and Values* (New Haven, CT: Yale University Press, 1963). Another influential contemporary nonobjectivist is Gilbert Harman, *The Nature of Morality* (Oxford, U.K.: Oxford University Press, 1977). A particularly strong case for nonobjectivism is made by John Mackie in *Ethics: Inventing Right and Wrong* (Hammondsworth, U.K.: Penguin, 1977). One of the strongest nonobjectivist writers is Herbert Feigl. See his "Validation and Vindication," in Wilfrid Sellars and John Hospers, eds., *Readings in Ethical Theory* (New York: Appleton-Century-Crofts, 1952), and *"'De Principiis non Disputandum . . . ?'* On the Meaning and the Limits of Justification," in Max Black, ed., *Philosophical Analysis* (Ithaca, NY: Cornell University Press, 1950). An interesting recent version of nonobjectivism has been proposed by Simon Blackburn; see his *Essays on Quasi-Realism* (Oxford, U.K.: Oxford University Press, 1993).

Plato's *Euthyphro* (available in a number of translations and editions) remains the classic source for the argument against theological voluntarism. Kai Nielsen, *Ethics without God* (London: Pemberton Press; and Buffalo: Prometheus Books, 1973), is perhaps the best and clearest contemporary argument against basing ethics on religion. A very sophisticated and interesting opposing view that argues for the importance of religious considerations in ethics can be found in George N.

Schlesinger, *New Perspectives on Old-Time Religion* (Oxford, U.K.: Clarendon Press, 1988). A brief argument for how ethics might be based on religion is given by Jonathan Berg, "How Could Ethics Depend on Religion?" in Peter Singer, ed., *A Companion to Ethics* (Oxford, U.K.: Blackwell, 1991). Philip L. Quinn develops a detailed and sophisticated defense of theological voluntarism in "Divine Command Theory," in Hugh LaFollette, ed., *The Blackwell Guide to Ethical Theory* (Oxford, U.K.: Blackwell Publishers, 2000). There are two excellent anthologies on the subject: P. Helm, ed., *Divine Commands and Morality* (Oxford, U.K.: Oxford University Press, 1981); and G. Outka and J. P. Reeder, Jr., eds., *Religion and Morality: A Collection of Essays* (Garden City, NY: Anchor/Doubleday, 1973).

David Hume has two classic works on ethics and emotions (though both also contain much more). The first is *A Treatise of Human Nature*, originally published in 1738. A good edition is by L. A. Selby-Bigge (Oxford, U.K.: Clarendon Press, 1978). The second is *An Inquiry Concerning Human Understanding*, originally published in 1751. A good edition is L. A. Selby-Bigge's *Hume's Enquiries*, 2d ed. (Oxford, U.K.: Clarendon Press, 1902). Kai Nielsen, *Why Be Moral?* (Buffalo: Prometheus Books,1989) is a very readable defense of nonobjectivist ethics based in emotions.

Among the most important and influential intuitionist writings are G. E. Moore, *Principia Ethica* (New York: Cambridge, 1959); H. A. Prichard, *Moral Obligation* (Oxford, U.K.: Clarendon Press, 1949); W. D. Ross, *The Right and the Good* (Oxford, U.K.: Clarendon Press, 1930); W. D. Ross, *Foundations of Ethics* (Oxford, U.K.: Clarendon Press, 1939); and D. D. Raphael, *The Moral Sense* (London: Oxford University Press, 1957).

Among Kant's classic works on ethics are *Groundwork of the Metaphysic of Morals*, trans. H. J. Paton as *The Moral Law* (London: Hutchinson, 1953); *Critique of Practical Reason*, trans. L. W. Beck (Indianapolis: Bobbs-Merrill, 1977); and *Religion within the Limits of Reason Alone*, trans. T. M. Greene and H. H. Hudson (New York: Harper and Row, 1960). Excellent works on Kant's ethics include Lewis White Beck's *A Commentary on Kant's Critique of Practical Reason* (Chicago: University of Chicago Press, 1960) and Onora O'Neill, *Constructions of Reason: Explorations of Kant's Practical Philosophy* (Cambridge, U.K.: Cambridge University Press, 1989). A fascinating brief challenge to Kant's ethical system is Rae Langton's "Maria von Herbert's Challenge to Kant," which can be found in Peter Singer, ed., *Ethics* (Oxford, U.K.: Oxford University Press, 1994).

Many outstanding contemporary philosophers follow—to at least some degree—the Kantian tradition in ethics. A small sample would include Kurt Baier, *The Moral Point of View* (Ithaca, NY: Cornell University Press, 1958); Stephen Darwall, *Impartial Reason* (Ithaca, NY: Cornell University Press, 1983); Alan Donagan, *The Theory of Morality* (Chicago: University of Chicago Press, 1977); and Thomas Nagel, *The View from Nowhere* (New York: Oxford University Press, 1986).

Kantian ethics can seem cold and austere. For a more engaging experience of it, try some essays by Thomas E. Hill, Jr., who is clearly a Kantian, but writes with grace, charm and clarity on a variety of ethical issues. See his essays in *Respect, Pluralism, and Justice: Kantian Perspectives* (Oxford, U.K.: Oxford University

Press, 2000) and *Human Welfare and Moral Worth: Kantian Perspectives* (Oxford, U.K.: Oxford University Press, 2002).

The classic utilitarian writings are Jeremy Bentham, *An Introduction to the Principles of Morals and Legislation* (London: 1823) and John Stuart Mill, *Utilitarianism* (London: 1863). Perhaps the most influential contemporary utilitarian, and certainly one of the most readable, is Peter Singer. His *Writings on an Ethical Life* (New York: HarperCollins, 2000) is the work of a philosopher thinking carefully about ethical obligations and also striving to live his life by the right ethical standards. Whatever one thinks of Singer's views—he holds very controversial positions on abortion, animal rights, the obligations of the affluent toward those who are less fortunate, and euthanasia, and has been the target of more protests than any other contemporary philosopher—not even his fiercest critics deny that Singer is an outstanding example of someone who takes ethical issues and living ethically very seriously. Singer's *Writings on an Ethical Life* shows a dedicated utilitarian wrestling honestly with serious ethical issues. See also Singer's *Practical Ethics* (Cambridge, U.K.: Cambridge University Press, 1979) for Singer's views on a variety of ethical issues.

For a critique of utilitarian ethics, see Samuel Scheffler, *The Rejection of Consequentialism* (Oxford, U.K.: Clarendon Press, 1982). An excellent debate on utilitarian ethics can be found in J. J. C. Smart and Bernard Williams, *Utilitarianism: For and Against* (Cambridge U.K.: Cambridge University Press, 1973).

The best website I've found that is specifically on ethics is Ethics Update, run by Lawrence M. Hinman, professor of philosophy at the University of San Diego. It is a very comprehensive and easily navigated site, with excellent links. It also offers a wide range of very good case studies, a nice collection of video lectures on ethics, and a great variety of papers on ethics (including a number of classic sources that are available online at the site). For almost any topic on ethics (especially applied ethics), this is a great place to start your Internet inquiries. Go to *www.ethics.acusd.edu.*

Stephen Darwall, professor of philosophy at the University of Michigan, has made the lecture notes for several of his classes available at his home page: *www.personal.umich.edu/~sdarwall.* There is excellent material on Hobbes, Hume, Kant, Bentham, and Mill. Ty's David Hume Homepage at *www.geocities.com/Athens/3067/hume/h_index.html,* is well organized, and contains extensive links.

A lengthy, but readable and interesting, essay by Michael Shermer on "the riddle of ethics without religion" is available at *www.skeptic.com/04.2.Shermer-sphinx.html.*

Jan Garrett's guide to W. D. Ross is an excellent resource on this leading intuitionist. You can find it at *www.wku.edu/~jan.garrett/ethics/rossethc.htm.*

An excellent site for material on Immanuel Kant is "Kant on the Web," at *www.hkbu.edu.hk/~ppp/Kant.html.* This site has very good links, including links to valuable information on teaching Kant's ethics.

For more information on utilitarianism, there are several interesting sites. *www.la.utexas.edu/cuws/index.html* is the Classical Utilitarianism Web Site. It offers a variety of classic utilitarian writings, as well as some more recent papers.

www.utilitarian.org/one.html is a site that promotes the practical application of utilitarian principles. *www.utilitarianism.com* has a good collection of links to websites related to utilitarian ethics.

Notes

1. C. A. Campbell, *On Selfhood and Godhood* (London: George Allen & Unwin, 1957).
2. Susan Wolf, "The Importance of Free Will," *Mind*, Vol. 90, 1981; pp. 386–405.
3. Jeffrie G. Murphy, in Jeffrie G. Murphy and Jean Hampton, *Forgiveness and Mercy* (Cambridge, U.K.: Cambridge University Press, 1988), p. 102. Additional examples of the assumption that the denial of moral responsibility entails the denial of genuine morality can be found in John Hospers, "What Means This Freedom?" in Sidney Hook, ed., *Determinism and Freedom in the Age of Modern Science* (New York: Collier Books, 1961), pp. 126–142; Howard Hintz, "Some Further Reflections on Moral Responsibility," also in the Hook anthology, pp. 176–179; and Joseph F. Rychlak, *Discovering Free Will and Personal Responsibility* (New York: Oxford University Press, 1979).

   The view that morality requires moral responsibility does not command universal philosophical agreement. A noteworthy dissenter was John Stuart Mill:

   . . . the highest and strongest sense of the worth of goodness, and the odiousness of its opposite, is perfectly compatible with even the most exaggerated form of fatalism. *An Examination of Sir William Hamilton's Philosophy*, 1865.

   And since Mill clearly holds that fatalism destroys moral responsibility, he is maintaining that "the strongest sense" of morality is "perfectly compatible" with the absence of moral responsibility.

   More recent among those sharing Mill's view on this issue are Lawrence A. Blum, in *Friendship, Altruism, and Morality* (London: Routledge & Kegan Paul, 1980), p. 189; Jonathan Bennett, "Accountability," in Zak van Straaten, editor, *Philosophical Subjects* (Oxford, U.K.: Oxford University Press, 1980), p. 31; Judith Andre, "Nagel, Williams, and Moral Luck," *Analysis*, volume 43, 1983, pp. 202–207; Bruce N. Waller, *Freedom without Responsibility* (Philadelphia: Temple University Press, 1990); Michael Slote, "Ethics without Free Will," *Social Theory and Practice* 16 (1990), pp. 369–383; Saul Smilansky, "The Ethical Advantages of Hard Determinism," *Philosophy and Phenomenological Research* 54 (1994), pp. 355–363; and Michael Otsuka, "Incompatibilism and the Avoidability of Blame," *Ethics* 108 (1998), pp. 685–701.
4. David Hume, *A Treatise on Human Nature*, ed. L. A. Selby-Bigge (Oxford, U.K.: Clarendon Press, 1988), p. 416. First published in 1738.
5. *Ibid.*, p. 414.
6. Support for Selina's claim can be found in Antonio R. Damasio, *Descartes' Error: Emotion, Reason, and the Human Brain* (New York: Putnam, 1994).
7. Damasio, *op. cit.*, p. xii.

Chapter 9

Further Reflections on Ethics

in which Selina faces a moral quandary

"Sarah!" Selina called to her roommate above the steady buzz of conversation and clinking coffee cups. "Come sit down! I already got your coffee and muffin for you. Thought you would need it after that all night study session on Renaissance philosophy."

"Thanks, Selina. You're right: My caffeine level has sunk to a dangerous low." Sarah sat down and immediately drained about half the coffee in her large mug.

"You look a bit tired, Sarah," Ben said. "Studying Renaissance philosophy all night takes its toll on a person. Did you and Sam discuss my philosophical hero, Pico della Mirandola?"

"Ben," Sarah smiled, "we hardly talked about anything else. Selina, it's very kind of you to buy me coffee, especially after I left you all alone last night. I'm afraid you must have been terribly lonely."

"Think nothing of it," Selina answered. "I wasn't too lonely: Ben stopped by for a few minutes."

"That was nice of you, Ben, to keep my lonesome roommate company."

"Glad to do it, Sarah," Ben answered. "I guess virtue just comes naturally to me."

"If you've recovered from your labors with Renaissance philosophy, you said there were other ethical alternatives: You were raving about some sort of do-it-yourself ethical system."

"There *are* some other alternatives, Selina," said Sarah. "We've been looking at whether we could *find* ethical principles. Some people think we should make them ourselves: Ethics does not occur naturally, but it can be created."

"Maybe by God," Ben interjected. "But no, we've already considered the theological voluntarist position, and it has too many problems. You mean *we* could devise an ethical system? Well, I suppose we could; but I don't see why anyone would pay attention to it. It reminds me of that line from Shakespeare's *King Henry IV*:

Glendower: I can call spirits from the vasty deep.
Hotspur: Why, so can I, or so can any man. But will they come when you do call for them?

Sure, we could *contrive* an ethical system; but why should anyone accept it as legitimate, unless its legitimacy comes from reason; and if it comes from reason, then we don't make it, we *discover* it."

"Perhaps it could gain legitimacy *because* everyone accepts it. It's legitimate because we agree to it, accept it, and enforce it."

"No good, Sarah." Selina shook her head. "That sounds like another version of 'Might makes right.' With enough force, you might compel people to follow a set of rules, but that doesn't make them legitimate."

"Well said, Selina!" Ben nodded, took Selina's hand and kissed it. "Thou art as wise as thou art beautiful."

"You inspired me, Ben."

Sarah put her hand to her head. "Come on, guys, I'm still on my first cup of coffee. Can we get back to the question? There's more to this than just 'Might makes right,' though might does have something to do with it. But social-contract theory isn't just a glorification of brute force."

Social-Contract Theory

"Social-contract theory!" Ben looked excited. "Why didn't you say so, Sarah? That's an interesting theory. False, but interesting."

Sarah laughed. "This man has strong opinions, doesn't he?"

"Yes, and he's stubborn about them, too," Selina agreed.

Ben smiled. "And Selina, of course, is always happy to change her mind. Be careful where you throw those rocks, Sweetheart. Your house has its share of glass windows."

"Well, at least I'm open minded about social-contract theory, and you're not. But I thought it was more of a political theory: The United States was founded on a social contract. Not for my ancestors, of course; nobody asking any slaves about signing contracts. But that's another issue. Anyway, what does social contract theory have to do with ethics?"

"Social-contract theory has been a major part of ethics for centuries. Here's the basic idea, as it was developed by Thomas Hobbes, way back in the early 17th century. Hobbes believed that the 'state of nature,' in which there was no law and no government, was a state of constant war, with 'every man against every man.' In that condition"—Sarah found the right passage in her history of modern philosophy textbook—"there are

> No arts; no letters; no society; and which is worst of all, continual fear and danger of violent death; and the life of man, solitary, poor, nasty, brutish, and short."[1]

"And probably the life of women was even worse, right, Sister?"

"No doubt, Selina. Anyway, in this state of nature there are no rules, no rights, no protection. Even the strong could not be secure—because the strongest is vulnerable when asleep. So suppose we get tired of living in such nasty circumstances. We might all agree to a set of rules for our mutual benefit. I agree not to steal or kill if others agree to follow the same rules. The rules will be enforced by our common power: If I break the rules, everyone will join together to punish me. And that's fair, because I agreed to the rules and receive the benefit of them. So we don't need some special transcendent source of moral rules, or any special intuitions or powers of reason. The moral rules are simply those we all accept. Of course, no one supposes we *literally* drew up a social contract: that one day we all put down our clubs and sat down by the fire and signed a contract. Instead, the idea of the social contract is that the legitimate rules are the rules we *would* agree to under those circumstances: those rules we could all accept as legitimate and mutually advantageous. Obviously, I might prefer a rule which stipulates that I am allowed to steal and cheat and lie, but no one can do the same to me. But you would never agree to such a rule. In order to protect your own goods, you might well agree to a rule that *no one* is allowed to steal. Under social contract ethics, that would therefore be a legitimate rule."

It is manifest, that during the time men live without a common power to keep them all in awe, they are in that condition which is called war; and such a war, as is of every man, against every other man. For WAR, consisteth not in battle only, or the act of fighting; but in a tract of time, wherein the will to contend by battle is sufficiently known; and therefore the notion of time, *is to be considered in the nature of war; as it is in the nature of weather. For as the nature of foul weather, lieth not in a shower or two of rain; but in an inclination thereto of many days together: so the nature of war, consisteth not in actual fighting; but in the known disposition thereto, during all the time there is no assurance to the contrary. . . .*

To this war of every man against every man, this also is consequent; that nothing can be unjust. The notions of right and wrong, justice and injustice have there no place. Where there is no common power, there is no law: where no law, no injustice. Force, and fraud, are in war the two cardinal virtues.

Thomas Hobbes, *Leviathan*, Part 1, Chapter 13 (1651)

Ben shook his head. "That's not bad, as far as it goes; but it doesn't go very far, does it? I want more from ethics than merely a general agreement that we won't kill or assault one another."

"Yeah," Selina smiled, "Ben likes his ethics brought down from heaven, not built here on Earth."

"That's a bit strong, Selina," Ben laughed. "But I do like my ethics based on absolute reason, rather than on what a bunch of folks happen to accept at the moment. And I also think that ethics involves more than just agreeing not to kill or maim one another."

Rawls and the Veil of Ignorance

"There's a more recent version of social-contract ethics you might find more appealing, Ben. It was developed by John Rawls, who taught at Harvard along with Robert Nozick. Rawls and Nozick were colleagues for many years, but there was not much agreement between them on philosophical issues. Anyway, Rawls used social-contract theory to develop his ethical system, a system that goes way beyond what Hobbes envisioned. Instead of starting from a 'state of nature,' Rawls starts from behind a 'veil of ignorance.'

"I understand about the 'state of nature,'" Selina said, "though I'm not sure any humans ever lived in such a state. We're much too social a species to have evolved in a war of all against all. A war of group against group, that's more believable. But anyway, what is this 'veil of ignorance' that Rawls is talking about?"

"The veil of ignorance is a philosophical myth, but a useful one. It's designed to stimulate your imagination—though, frankly, I'm not sure that the two of you need any more imaginative stimulation than you already have. But here's the idea: Suppose you are living in a sort of ethereal state, as a disembodied soul. This may be easier for Ben to imagine than for you, Selina, but give it a try. Anyway, there you are, a bunch of disembodied souls, about to be embodied and placed in the world. You know that you will be humans, that you will have the general desires and needs and vulnerabilities of humans, but you know nothing else about what sort of person you will be. You may be short or tall, male or female, athletically gifted or physically disabled, energetic and industrious or tired and lethargic. You don't know what your ethnic group will be, your religious convictions—if any—your political views, your tastes. Perhaps you will be a physically disabled black man who loves classical music and is brilliant at mathematics. Or maybe you'll be a devout orthodox Jewish woman who is born into an impoverished family. Maybe you'll be lucky and be born into wealth, or unlucky and born into poverty. Lucky and brilliant, or unlucky and dull. While all of you are behind the veil of ignorance—Rawls calls this 'the original position'—you must draw up rules for your society: Will you have free speech or censorship, roughly equal distribution of wealth or enormous disparities of wealth, excellent public educational facilities for everyone or only for the wealthy elite? Will everyone be equally eligible for public office and desirable positions, or will such positions go only to males, or only to whites? I might be tempted to suggest that philosophy majors should receive a large proportion of the wealth and that only philosophers should be allowed to hold positions of authority. Or Ben might be tempted to allow only men to vote in our new society. Perhaps Selina would like to have all religious practices banned. But we would be stupid to favor such rules. After all, we don't know anything about who we'll be. Ben might be a woman, and I might hate philosophy, and Selina might be a fervent Roman Catholic. Sure, I might like the idea of imposing my religious views on everyone in the society, but *not* when I realize that I might be the "imposee" instead of the imposer. So the rules we'll choose will be rules that will be *fair to everyone*, since everyone will have to live within the system and no one will have advance knowledge of his or her particular characteristics. Think of what rules we would select if we didn't know who we would be or what abilities or disabilities we would have. The result is rules that are free of bias and special interests, rules that are *fair* for everyone. We might have some doubts about the laws passed by the United States Senate, since the great majority of the Senators are wealthy white males with powerful self-interests. But if all the Senators knew that tomorrow they *might* be impoverished inner-city children or migrant farm laborers, then we would get a very different set of laws being passed—and they would be a lot fairer than the laws we have now. If every Senator knew that he might wake up tomorrow as an impoverished sick child in Appalachia, with no access to health care services or medication, then Senators would swiftly pass legislation establishing universal health care. From behind the veil of ignorance, stripped of our prejudices and special interests, we can get a clearer view of what rules are *fair* and what aspects of our own society are *unfair*."

"You're right, Sarah," Ben said, "I do like that form of the social-contract theory. It gives us a very nice way of thinking about rules and fairness and about the fairness of our own behavior. If I didn't know my own position—whether I would be the liar or the person lied to, the perpetrator or the victim of discrimination—then I would take a much closer and clearer look at my own acts, without the distortions imposed by biased self-interest. But as much as I like Rawls's system of 'justice as fairness' from behind the veil of ignorance, it's really not surprising that I like it. After all, isn't it really a clearer picture of Kantian ethics? It seems to me that the veil of ignorance is just an imaginative way of pushing us to consider ethics from the perspective of Kant's Categorical Imperative: Always act in such a way that you could will your act to become a universal law."

"Yeah, exactly, Ben," Sarah agreed. "Except it's Kant without the absolutism. Don't look to special powers of reason to deliver perfect rational rules. Instead, simply think *impartially* about everyone, and from this perspective of *impartiality*, you can reach legitimate conclusions about what is fair and just."

"Maybe even Selina would like it," Ben said hopefully. "Forget about absolute moral rules and special powers of reason; set aside biases and prejudices and special interests; consider everyone *impartially*, and that tells you what is fair and just. Isn't that a form of ethical objectivism you could agree with, Selina? After all, that's what you scientists try to do, right? If you develop a new drug, you test it by means of a *double-blind* experiment, in which the experimental subjects don't know whether they are taking the drug or a placebo and even the researchers themselves don't know who is getting which. The double-blind experiment is a sort of 'veil of ignorance' designed to keep your special interests and strong biases and fervent hopes from corrupting your observations and calculations. When you reason impartially about ethics, you get the same objective truths. Of course, some people refuse to practice the scientific method, and they get different results, but that doesn't show that there is no objective scientific truth. And some people refuse to step behind the veil of ignorance and reason impartially about ethics, but that doesn't show that there are no reasonable truths about what is fair and just."

Selina nodded, but also frowned. "Look, guys, I like what I hear about Rawls. And I like the veil of ignorance. Heaven knows, anything that will get us to put aside our biases and treat others with greater fairness is a wonderful thing. I think we ought to adopt some of it tomorrow: take the president and the Cabinet and all members of the House of Representatives and the Senate and make them into a large crew of migrant farmworkers for about six months, harvesting grapes in California and apples in Washington and wheat in Nebraska. They would probably do a lousy job of harvesting the crops, but when they got back to the capitol, they would do a much better job of governing. Still, as much as I like Rawls's ideas, I'm not ready to agree that his method gives us objective ethical truths that are analogous to scientific objectivity."

"But Selina," Ben persisted, "even if you aren't willing to say that the truths of ethics are like the truths of science, don't you agree that, from a standpoint of impartiality, we *can* reach some legitimate and reasonable and *true* ethical conclusions? From behind the veil of ignorance, we would reach the objectively true principle that it is wrong for anyone to be mistreated or subjected to less than equal opportunity on the basis of race or gender."

"Obviously I think that's a wonderful principle, Ben, and it has my wholehearted endorsement. Still, I suspect the endorsement comes from my heart—my feelings—rather than my reason. And I don't think feelings are a source of objective truth."

"Why do you say it's based on feelings, Selina?" Ben had not given up. "If you think about it coolly and impartially and free of bias and special interest—and what more could you ask of a definition of *rational* thinking?—then you conclude that discrimination on the basis of race or gender is *unfair*, that it's *wrong*. That sounds reasonable and objective and *true* to me."

"Okay, Ben, what do you say if someone goes behind the veil of ignorance and still says that women should always be subordinate and subservient, and if I step out from the behind the veil of ignorance and find that I am a woman, I should be subordinate and subservient to men?"

"Nobody would say that, not if they were genuinely behind the veil of ignorance. The only way one could say that is to carry their sexist prejudices behind the veil with them."

"But that begs the question, doesn't it?" Selina continued. "You say it would be eliminated, because it's just a prejudice. People who favor such sexist views claim they would maintain their views even behind the veil of ignorance, because those views are morally sound. Remember the old slogan: 'If men could get pregnant, abortion would be a sacrament.' And if we put everyone behind the veil of ignorance, I'm confident that a lot of the men who now oppose abortion would suddenly see the value in women having control of their own bodies. But not all. After all, some of the most adamant opponents of abortion are women. Think about some of the people who despise homosexuals as evil and condemn homosexuality as morally wrong. Sometimes, when their sons or daughters turn out to be homosexuals, they change their minds. But sometimes they don't. In fact, sometimes when they recognize that they themselves are homosexuals, they continue to condemn homosexuality as wrong and try to repress their own homosexual desires. Strikes me as very sad, the unfortunate result of stupid religious biases. Just because several thousand years ago a bunch of savage desert nomads—a bloodthirsty crew that gloried in genocidal wars and had to promote heterosexuality and polygamy in order to produce enough children to replace those who were killed in their constant battles— just because they opposed homosexuality, we should now think it's 'God's law' that homosexuality is wrong?"

"Careful there, Selina," interrupted Sarah. "Those are my ancestors you're talking about."

"Oops, sorry, Sister. But don't worry about it. We've all got a few skeletons in the ancestral closet."

"Not me," said Ben. "All my ancestral skeletons are out of the closet."

Sarah laughed. "Selina, can't you control that boy?"

"I do my best, Sarah, but you know how hard it is to train a man. You got some rolled up newspaper I could hit him with? Anyway, as I was saying before all our ancestors got into the story, I hate these appeals to the moral codes of Sarah's savage nomadic forefathers. (Sarah, I'm sure your foremothers were a much nicer lot; unfortunately, we hardly ever hear about them.) But of course, not everyone who believes that homosexuality is wrong bases it on religious biases. If someone adamantly asserts that homosexuality is wrong and that, if she were homosexual, she would believe that her own sexual desires were wrong, then I don't know what I could say to such a person, other than to try reshaping the way she *feels*—through emotional appeals or by having them be around happy and pleasant homosexual couples. But that's very different from giving them *reasons*. Of course, if they believe stupid things, such as the belief that homosexuals *choose* their sexual orientation, we can rationally refute that: When did you *choose* to have heterosexual desires? Or if they believe that homosexuals are pedophiles, we can give them solid facts showing that most child sexual abuse is committed by heterosexuals and that homosexuals are no more likely to be child abusers than are heterosexuals. But if they know all that and still insist that homosexuality is morally wrong, then it seems to me we have reached the limits of what reason can do."

"True enough, Selina," Ben responded. "But that just shows that reason can't convince people who refuse to listen to reason."

Selina laughed. "True, Ben, reason can't convince people who refuse to listen to reason; but reason also can't convince people when there are no reasons left to assert. And at that level, I think reason has reached its limits and emotions prevail. I certainly don't like the emotions of people who stubbornly assert that, even if they were women, they would think it right that women be treated as subordinate, and of people who think that they should be condemned as evil if they themselves are homosexual. And I'm perfectly happy to make emotional appeals that might change their views. Not torture or brainwashing, of course, but emotional persuasion is not confined to such brutal forms: There are also movies and friendships and novels that can broaden our horizons and expand our sympathies."

Ben shook his head. "It still seems to me that if people actually put aside their biases and thought impartially—if they genuinely stepped behind the veil of ignorance and left their prejudices on the other side of the veil—then we could agree on reasonable and fair principles of ethics."

I have been arguing against the view that value depends entirely on my own subjective desires. Yet I am not defending the objectivity of ethics in the traditional sense. Ethical truths are not written into the fabric of the universe: to that extent the subjectivist is correct. If there were no beings with desires or preferences of any kind, nothing would be of value and ethics would lack all content. On the other hand, once there are beings with desires, there are values that are not only the subjective values of each individual being. The possibility of being led, by reasoning, to the point of view of the universe provides as much "objectivity" as there can be. When my ability to reason shows me that the suffering of another being is very similar to my own suffering and (in an appropriate case) matters just as much to that other being as my own suffering matters to me, then my reason is showing me something that is undeniably true. I can still choose to ignore it, but then I can no longer deny that my perspective is a narrower and more limited one than it could be. This may not be enough to yield an objectively true ethical position. (One can always ask: what is so good about having a broader and more all-encompassing perspective?) But it is as close to an objective basis for ethics as there is to find.

Peter Singer, Writings on an Ethical Life, p. 269

"And it seems to me," Selina responded, "that even if we could eliminate bias, there would still be basic value differences that cannot be rationally resolved."

Cultural Relativism

"So what are you saying, Selina? That whatever value system any culture adopts is right for that culture? War and aggression were right for my ancestors, the savage desert nomads, but wrong for our society? That legitimate morality is whatever your society agrees on?" Sarah looked puzzled.

"Of course not." Selina shook her head briskly. "Think of what that would mean. Slavery is now wrong in Michigan, but it was morally legitimate in Alabama in 1840? Definitely not. That would mean that Frederick Douglass was wrong when he tried to abolish slavery; but then, when slavery was finally abolished, suddenly his abolitionist message was correct. If cultural relativism is right, then cultural reformers are always wrong. No way. Slavery was wrong in Alabama in 1840. If it was culturally acceptable then, then the culture was profoundly wrong. I despise discrimination in all its ugly forms, whether against gays or women or blacks or Jews or Hispanics or Irish. But I can't appeal to any objective moral fact to prove the truth of my moral views, because—at the most basic level of values—there are simply no objective facts there. If you ask me what I think of discrimination, I'll answer that it's *unfair* and that it's morally wrong, everywhere, in all cultures. That deep moral conviction is not based on reason or objective facts, but that doesn't change my passionate commitment to the moral *wrongness* of discrimination. And it certainly doesn't make me a cultural relativist. Cultural relativists believe there are *many* true ethical systems—as many as there are cultures. I don't think we can ever say that an ethical system is objectively true. But I certainly don't give my moral blessing to a culture that subjugates women; to the contrary, I deplore it."

Ben smiled. "Alright, Selina, at least we can agree on that much." He looked at his watch, stood up, and slung his backpack over his shoulder. "I have to go get this paper printed out before my seminar. Shouldn't take too long. If I have time, I'll come back here before class. You guys will have to put the finishing touches on ethical theory without me."

An Ethical Quandary

Selina reached out and touched his hand. "Okay, Ben. If you don't get back before class, I'll be in the lab all afternoon. Stop by if you want to grab some dinner." Selina smiled, watched as Ben walked out of the coffee shop, then turned quickly to Sarah. "Sarah, while Ben's gone, I need to talk with you, I need some advice. Girl to girl, woman to woman, sister to sister. I know I can trust you."

"Sure, Selina. It will be our secret, always. What's troubling you? This doesn't sound like a dispute over rationalism and empiricism."

"No, this isn't philosophical speculation, this is real, girl. Well, you know I love Ben. I don't know why—that man drives me crazy sometimes. But then, he also drives me crazy sometimes, you know what I mean?"

"No, I don't have a clue, Selina, but I'll try to guess. Anyway, what's the problem?"

"Well, the chamber orchestra is leaving tomorrow for our spring tour. Flying down to New Orleans, then a charter bus, we'll play in New Orleans, Mobile, Tampa Bay, Atlanta, then fly home. Great trip, great music, great time—get out of this Michigan cold and soak up some rays, hallelujah."

"Sounds great; I wish *I* had such problems."

"That's not it, Sarah. Here's the thing: You know Donnell, he's principal viola. He plays fine, he looks fine. Well, we've known each other for years now. There's always been a bit of chemistry, a spark. It's not like I feel about Ben. But still, it's there, this attraction. And I know he has the same feeling; I can see it in his eyes, it's there, girl. Well, we're going to be down South, sitting in the sunshine, drinking margaritas, I've got that deadly little yellow bikini for the beach. And it's a whole week, far from

Michigan, far from Ben. And Donnell, well, that's just a physical thing, really. I mean, I like him, and I love the way he plays the viola, but we're not soul mates or anything. But a week with that man in the southern sunshine—well, that would be a very nice spring break. And Donnell is discreet, he's wise. Besides, he's got a good thing going with Rhonda, and he'd be coming home to her, and he knows about Ben and me, he knows the score. Some warm nights, with that Gulf breeze blowing in through the windows; well, Donnell and I could have a really nice spring break. And we'll be careful, of course: all the precautions. Nobody will get hurt. What is it that the French say? 'Infidelity, if discovered, is but a small thing; if not discovered, 'tis nothing at all.' What do you think, Sarah?"

"In this case, if discovered, it might not be such a small thing: Ben might feel badly betrayed. And the trust in your relationship could be damaged, maybe destroyed."

"Yeah, maybe. But it would *not* be discovered. Like I said, Donnell is very discreet; and believe me, Ben will never suspect a thing."

"Well, in that case, it sounds like a great idea, Selina. You and Donnell have a passionate spring fling down in the sunny South. Course, old Ben, he'll be up here in the cold Michigan March. But don't worry about him. You know, Ben's a really sexy guy, and, well, you probably noticed, there's been a little spark between us. And you know how the winter is up here: You need somebody to snuggle with, to get you through those long winter nights. Some hot café mocha with Ben one afternoon, then a warm dinner at a cozy restaurant, sparks fly, one thing leads to another. Yeah, you have your fling with Donnell; I'm sure Ben and I can figure out some way to stay warm."

"Hey, watch it, Sarah! I mean, I love you like a sister, you know that. But you lay a hand on my man, I'll claw your eyes out."

Sarah laughed. "Claw *my* eyes out? What about Ben's eyes?"

"Nah, Ben's an innocent. If you two had an affair, I'd know you seduced him, you witch."

"Aw, come on, Selina. What were you saying? 'Infidelity, if discovered, is but a small thing. If not discovered, 'tis nothing at all.'"

"I meant *my* infidelity, not Ben's. If I have a fling, it's just an innocent fling. But Ben is so serious, he'd have to put his whole heart into it."

"But look, if you have a purely bodily thing, then you put your whole being into it. After all, you're a materialist: The body is all there is. But Ben has a body *and* a soul: If he has a purely physical fling, his soul is untouched. So nobody gets hurt. We'll take all the precautions. Just good, clean physical fun. I mean, I know I'm not going to replace Selina in Ben's affections, but I'm sure Ben and I could have a very pleasant week in your absence. The Gulf breeze is romantic, no doubt of that; but the howling north wind also has its charms when you're snuggled under a blanket with someone warm."

"Alright, alright, very cute, Sarah. I get your point. As my grandmother used to say, what's sauce for the goose is sauce for the gander, right? But look, it's really not the same. You might get away with it: You've got a devious streak in you, girl. But Ben? If that boy held hands with another woman, the guilt would be all over his face. I'd know, and it would make me angry, and we'd fight, so people really would get hurt. Starting with whoever curled under that blanket with my Ben. But I could spend a wild and wonderful week with Donnell, and Ben would never be the wiser. So where's the harm?"

Virtue Ethics

"Okay, Selina, you've convinced me. Have your fling. You probably could get away with it. After all, you're a superb liar, and you can pluck old Ben's heartstrings like a harp: A smile here, a kiss there, poor old Ben plays just about any tune you like. When it comes to deceit, you're a pro. Ben calls your room late one night, you're snuggled under the covers with Donnell, you could still coo to old Ben like a turtle dove, whisper sweet things to that boy while you run your fingers through Donnell's hair. Yeah, when it comes to lying and deceiving, you are the master, girl. And after you spend a week with Donnell, lying to old Ben every day, and then come back and lie to him about it all the rest of the spring semester—well, that's like a graduate seminar in deceit. You'll be a polished liar, a real artist. You'll get so good at it that lies won't bother you at all, lying will come natural and easy. You're right, Selina: With a talent like that, you don't want to waste it."

"Wait just a minute here, Sarah. Alright, I tell a lie now and then. What, do I look like George Washington? If I chopped down my daddy's cherry tree, I'd probably try to convince him the damage was done by a colony of industrious beavers. But I'm not some all-star liar! Besides, this is not that big a deal: I'm not committing stock fraud or something like that. It's just a little lie. Okay, maybe a medium-sized lie. But it's not like I'm a habitual liar!"

"Mm hm, you tell lies, but you're not really a liar. Is that sort of like if you eat chocolate chip cookies during finals, they don't count against your diet?"

"We are what we repeatedly do. Excellence, then, is not an act, but a habit."

Aristotle,
Nicomachean Ethics

"But Sarah, I'm not going to make a practice of lying to Ben. I'm not going to make a practice of lying, period."

"Selina, I don't want to exaggerate this. I'm not laying down some absolute Kantian moral principle that forbids lying under any circumstances. Look, if the Nazis come to the door looking for Jews, you tell 'em I'm a Gentile, okay? But lying to Ben is not like lying to the Nazis. It isn't a one-time thing. You start by telling Ben how much you're going to miss him when you kiss him goodbye; you tell him how lonesome you are when he calls you; he wants to hear all about your trip, and that will involve telling more lies. But the main point is, you have to decide the sort of person you want to be. If you want to be a practiced liar, then practice lying. Your moral character isn't something hidden away, securely isolated from your behavior. You become what you practice; character is shaped by what you do. And that shaping doesn't start when you graduate and take your first job. Why do so many people get caught up in these huge financial swindles and stock manipulation deals? Suppose you asked them in college, What sort of person do you want to be? None of them would say, 'Oh, I think I'd like to be a swindler who steals money from pension funds and robs the life savings of old folks.' But what happens is that they start with some misrepresentations, some exaggerations, occasional deceptions; and what they practice is what they become. 'Oh, I tell lies, sure, but deep down I'm really a very honest person. Sure, I hoard my wealth and never provide any help for the poor, but still I'm actually profoundly generous.' Doesn't work. If you want to be a generous person, practice generosity. If you want to be an honest person, tell the truth. The seed you sow in practice is the character you reap—the character you develop. If you practice telling lies, you become a practiced liar. I'm not saying that if you tell one lie your character is permanently stamped as a liar. But the more you tell lies, the easier it becomes, and the harder it is to reverse your formed character. Our daily practice makes us what we are: We shape our characters by our daily choices. Look, Selina, what sort of character you want to have, that's up to you. But your character is not something locked away, a fixed point independent of your acts; it's what you yourself practice."

"And so I'll be sleeping alone, and Donnell will be sleeping alone, and we'll both be frustrated, and we could have been so happy. Oh well, I guess you're right: I really don't want to become a good liar. Besides, it probably wouldn't really be fair to Ben. But I'll tell you one thing, Girl: Next time I need advice when I'm thinking about a spring fling, I'm going to find a nice utilitarian."

Sarah laughed. "A utilitarian would certainly appreciate the pleasures of a week of Gulf Coast passion. But I'm not sure a utilitarian would give her blessings to the sort of deceptions that would follow in its wake."

"Alright, I admit, the stuff you say about developing good habits makes sense. But maybe I should follow St. Augustine; wasn't it

St. Augustine who prayed that God would 'make me virtuous, but not just yet'? I'm perfectly willing to be an honest and virtuous person; but couldn't I wait a few years?"

"Sure you can, Selina. If you believe that God is going to just suddenly swoop down and transform your deceitful character into one of glowing integrity, then no problem. But if you think that your character is shaped by your daily life and your own activities, then you have to think more carefully about what kind of character you're shaping."

Ben entered the coffee shop, shook off some snow, removed his gloves, and walked toward their table. Selina put a finger to her lips and looked at Sarah. "There's Ben. Not a word about our conversation, remember?"

"Don't worry, Selina. I promised never to tell. And I'm not the sort of person who breaks her promises."

Selina rolled her eyes. "Give it a rest, Sarah."

"Hi, guys. My paper is printed, and I have time to finish my coffee. So, did you two settle all the questions of ethics?"

"Actually, we've just been discussing virtue theory," Sarah replied. "Virtue theorists believe that we have overemphasized rules of behavior and what acts are right; instead, we should look more at character: What character traits are virtuous, and how are virtuous characters formed? Instead of thinking exclusively about whether it is right or wrong to provide help to those in need, we might consider the sort of *character* we think is worthwhile. Do you want to be the sort of person who hoards every penny and thinks only of himself and his interests? Or would you prefer to be someone who helps others, someone who is considerate of the less fortunate, someone of a generous character?"

"I like virtue theory; it's a good way to think about lots of moral issues." Selina smiled, a bit ruefully, at Sarah. "But it's not a way to prove that there are objective moral values. In the first place, what do you say to someone who does *not* wish to be virtuous? I like generosity, and you like generosity, and we want to have that virtue. But suppose someone sincerely says, 'No, I've thought about it, and I don't want to be generous. Generosity is for suckers. I want to get ahead. The race is fast and furious, there's no time to stop and help those who falter, and that's the way I like it.'"

"In that case, Selina, maybe there's not much you could say to such a person," Sarah replied. "But after all, what kind of reason would you *expect* to give such a person? You can't give a moral reason, because this person has no moral concerns. Still, there may be an answer that works for most people. Suppose someone sincerely asks, 'Why should I be moral?' Perhaps the best answer is to say, look, do you really want to be a liar, a cheat, greedy, callous about the needs of others, totally self-absorbed? If you can seriously consider such a character worthwhile, then perhaps there is no moral reason that could convince you of the worth of morality. But fortunately, very few people really find the character and life of an Ebenezer Scrooge particularly attractive."

"Okay, granted, it's useful to think about what sort of character I reflectively approve," Ben said, "and how my acts contribute to or block the development of that character. But virtue theory does have some limits. After all, people have held a wide variety of virtue ideals. Like Nietzsche, who was grateful for having a 'hard and stony heart.' For Aristotle, a key virtue was pride; for the Christian Church, Pride is a deadly sin, and humility is a virtue. For the Nazis, the ability to inflict great suffering without flinching was a high virtue. For some, feeling warm and sympathetic is a virtue; for others, it goes against the virtue of 'manliness.' For men, the virtue was aggressiveness; for women, meekness and submissiveness. Who would have been considered the most virtuous person in Georgia in 1850? Some man who owned a large plantation with many slaves and punished any slave's attempted escape severely, who passed his leisure time enjoying cockfights or dogfights, who acted as a stern head of his household and kept his wife submissive and obedient, and who was ready to kill with pistol or sword at the most trivial affronts to his 'honor.' So before we sing the praises of virtue, we should be very sure about what notion of virtue we are praising."

"Point well taken, Ben," Selina replied. "I think virtue theory can offer a useful perspective on ethical issues, but it has some problems of its own. Still, there are some contexts where it seems particularly useful. Think of medicine. If you wish to be a good physician, there are clearly some virtues you must develop. You have to be able to keep confidences: When you visit your physician, you tell her things that are private, perhaps about your sex life, or your drug problem, or your sense of depression. If your physician entertains her golfing friends with details about your problems, then your physician has failed to develop a key virtue that is essential in her profession. And we can also think of the ideals of the profession in terms of virtues. When the AIDS epidemic was new and spreading rapidly, we were less certain about how contagious the disease really was. Many physicians, especially surgeons, refused to treat AIDS patients. In doing so, they failed to live up to the ideals of the medical profession: Medical caregivers must have the courage to treat their patients, even though they place themselves at risk. They need not be foolhardy, of course. They should take reasonable precautions, such as wearing masks and gloves. But they cannot legitimately refuse to treat a patient because the patient poses a risk, any more than a police officer can opt out of pursuing dangerous criminals: Courage is an essential virtue for both professions. And of course, such physicians also failed to live up to the principle of placing the patient's interest ahead of their own. Perhaps those physicians needed to think more about their own ideal of a virtuous physician and how far their own behavior fell short of that standard. They might have asked themselves, Do I really want to be a physician who shirks her duty when the duty is dangerous or difficult? So, in some contexts—particularly where there is a strong accepted ideal of virtue—the virtue approach to ethics can be very valuable.

"Yeah, virtue theory has its advantages," Selina concluded. Then she arched an eyebrow at Sarah: "But it also has some distinct disadvantages."

Moral Realism

Ben put his coffee down, leaned forward. "Yesterday, after our disputes about ethical objectivity, I was in the library looking up some stuff for my history seminar. But I was still thinking about some of our arguments about ethical truth, so I decided to check out what philosophers had recently written about moral objectivity."

Sarah raised her coffee cup in a salute. "Wow, Ben, you're looking up philosophy articles in the library? I'm impressed!"

"Yeah," Ben answered, "You see what happens when you fall in with bad company. Even an upstanding historian can get corrupted. Anyway, I was scouting around, and I came across several references to 'moral realism'. Sounded like just the ticket. So I started looking up contemporary work on moral realism."

Selina looked skeptical. "Moral realism. What was it classified under? 'Philosophical fantasies'?"

"Don't prejudge it, Selina. There are some parts of contemporary moral realism I think you might like." Ben continued. "Anyway, I think I figured out the crux of it—or at least the basic idea of some versions of moral realism. As with everything else in philosophy, there seem to be almost as many versions of moral realism as there are philosophers who write about the topic."

"We can be a rather contentious lot," Sarah agreed. "But anyway, tell me what you learned about moral realism."

"Well, in the first place," Ben continued, "This is not the moral realism of Plato or even Kant. It's not your grandmother's moral realism, Selina. And it's not the moral realism of your ancestors, Sarah: Moral realists don't expect to find moral laws written on stone tablets. In fact, most contemporary moral realists are not even sure that moral realism is true."

"You're right, Ben," Selina smiled, "I do like some parts of moral realism. Especially that part about it not being true."

"I didn't say they didn't think it was true," Ben said. "I said that some moral realists do not claim to *know* that moral realism is true. Instead, they believe that moral realism is a plausible hypothesis and that we might eventually have good grounds for believing it true. Moral realists don't think the issue can be settled by digging up a 'real moral fact' and putting it on display. Do electrons exist? I can't catch one in my hand and then place it on a napkin for everyone to see, and say, 'See, there's an electron; that settles it.' We believe that electrons exist because a theory that includes electrons among its objects gives us better explanations than do theories that deny the existence of electrons. And ultimately, that will be the test of moral realism: Does a theory that posits the existence of real moral facts give us better explanations and guidance than we get from theories that deny moral facts."

Selina was still skeptical. "Alright, I'll bite. Exactly what is it that this moral realist theory is supposed to explain better?"

"I'm glad you asked that question, Selina," Ben smiled. "One key thing that moral realism predicts and explains is emerging moral consensus: broader agreement on ethical issues and basic values is best explained by the existence of *objective moral facts* that guide disputants toward agreement."

"Oh, right." Selina shook her head. "We do need something to account for the emerging moral consensus. Tell me, Ben, are you speaking of the emerging moral consensus on the issue of abortion? Or on capital punishment? Or the just distribution of wealth? Or on when war is morally justified? Exactly what 'moral consensus' are the moral realists planning to explain?"

"Okay, I get your point, Selina." Ben laughed. "There doesn't appear to be a lot of sweet harmony on ethical questions at the moment. But maybe the prospects for moral consensus aren't quite as bleak as they appear at first glance. Take the abortion debate. Certainly, the exchanges are heated, and the opposing sides seem absolutely intransigent—no chance of any common ground. But if we can get people to calm down for just a minute, maybe there's a lot more agreement than there appears to be when people are screaming at each other."

"You know, Ben, I think you might be right about that." Sarah leaned forward. "Last week, I was reading some of the articles about the abortion debate for my social ethics class, and I came across this passage from Daniel Callahan that I really liked." Sarah was looking through her notebook, searching for the right place. "Here it is. Listen to what Callahan writes:

> Although the contending sides in the abortion debate commonly ignore, or systematically deride, the essentially positive impulses lying behind their

opponents' positions, the conflict is nonetheless best seen as the pitting of essentially valuable impulses against one another. The possibility of a society which did allow women the right and the freedom to control their own lives is a lofty goal. No less lofty is that of a society which, with no exceptions, treated all forms of human life as equally valuable. In the best of all possible worlds, it might be possible to reconcile these goals. In the real world, however, the first goal requires the right of abortion, and the second goal excludes that right. This, I believe, is a genuine and deep dilemma. That so few are willing to recognize the dilemma, or even to admit that any choice must be less than perfect, is the most disturbing element of the whole debate.[2]

That's something all of us could probably agree on, right? We all believe that it is very important that women have the right to control their own lives; and we all agree that all humans should receive equal treatment. Obviously, there are differences; for example, there are disputes about whether the fetus is a full human life—whether it is really a person—and about which rights take precedence if there's a conflict. But what's interesting is that even on a subject where there appears to be nothing in common between the opposing sides, where the conflicts are most heated and the debates most acrimonious, still we can look more deeply and find some very important elements of moral consensus."

"Maybe not as much moral consensus as you suppose, Sarah." Selina was still skeptical. "Certainly, *we* all agree that it is morally good for women to have the right and freedom to control their own lives. But is there really consensus on that moral ideal? Many religions would find that a vile and hateful principle. And anyone who believes that there is general agreement on the other principle—all human lives are equally valuable—is not very observant. Perhaps we mouth the principle, but any society that allows millions of its children to live in poverty without health care, with inadequate nutrition, in terrible housing, and receiving clearly inferior educational opportunities obviously does not really believe that all humans lives are equally valuable."

"That's true, Selina." Sarah conceded. "Depressing, but true. Still, contemporary moral realists aren't ready to give up. It's true that often people reject such principles, and certainly they often reject them in practice even when they claim to support them. But suppose that we eliminate the biases and distortions imposed by religious dogma, and we put aside the heated rhetoric and name-calling, and instead we look at moral questions from a calmer, cooler, quieter perspective. Stripped of our prejudices and biases and dogmas and narrow self-interests—maybe imagining ourselves behind Rawls's veil of ignorance—very few people would favor treating women as second-class citizens, and most people would agree that in an affluent society it is morally wrong for millions of children to live in poverty. So maybe if we approach these issues from a calm, cool, reflective perspective, we'll find substantial consensus. And that fits the approach you would favor in science, right? When we look at the heated contests between those who favor teaching Darwinian evolution in our public schools and those who want to teach 'creationism' or some other religious doctrine, it seems unlikely that any consensus can be found. But if we remove the religious dogmas and look at the issue calmly and reflectively and with full information, then we soon find that there is broad consensus that Darwinian evolution is a well-confirmed and central principle of contemporary biological science. If we do the same in the abortion controversy, we may still not reach agreement on whether abortion should be legal or illegal, but we may find more elements of agreement than appear on the surface."

"Or we may not," Selina replied.

"True, we may not," Ben took up the argument. "But that remains an open question. And if it turns out that there *is* significant moral consensus, then what is the best and most productive *explanation* for that consensus? Maybe the best explanation will have nothing to do with real objective moral values, but will instead come from a study of biology or neuropsychology or anthropology. But *maybe* the best overall explanatory account will involve the positing of real moral values, just as the best contemporary account of astronomical phenomena involves the positing of neutralinos. We believe in neutralinos, not because we can kick them or taste them or stack them in a pile; rather, we believe there are neutralinos because a theory that encompasses neutralinos works better than any theory that does not. And the moral realists claim that *if* moral realism proves true—and they do *not* claim to know that it will prove true, only that it's a viable hypothesis—then it will be proved true in a way that is analogous to the way scientific theories are proved true."

Of course, it must be agreed on all sides that moral argument has not yet produced the sort of convergence in our desires that would make the idea of a moral fact . . . look plausible. But neither has moral argument had much of a history in times in which we have been able to engage in free reflection unhampered by a false biology (the Aristotelian tradition) or a false belief in God (the Judeo-Christian tradition). It remains to be seen whether sustained moral argument can elicit the requisite convergence in our moral beliefs, and corresponding desires, to make the idea of a moral fact look plausible. The kind of moral realism described here holds out the hope that it will. Only time will tell.

Michael Smith, "Realism," in Peter Singer, ed., *A Companion to Ethics* (Oxford, U.K., and Cambridge, MA: Blackwell Reference, 1991), p. 409

"*If* we reach consensus on basic value questions, and *if* moral realism proves the simplest and best explanation for that hoped-for consensus, then moral realism will be plausible." Selina shook her head. "Some awfully big 'ifs' there. Still, I admit it's about the least arrogant claim I have ever heard by a philosopher, so at least it has that in its favor. But even if we reached some consensus, even if there were some movement toward *convergence* of ethical theories, that still would not establish the existence of objective moral truths. We would have to ask whether there is a *simpler* explanation available for that convergence, one that didn't require the positing of such exotic entities as 'objective moral facts.' The moral-facts hypothesis violates the principle of Ockham's razor, because simpler explanations are available. And that's the basic problem with moral realism. Suppose we do get some convergence of moral beliefs. What would be the best hypothesis to explain that convergence? Perhaps it's because the Western industrialized nations have gained such enormous economic power over the world that their culture and ideas and ethical principles have become more influential. That may or may not be the best explanation of moral convergence; but in any case, it's a *simpler* explanation than the moral-facts hypothesis. And there are other possible explanations for such hypothetical agreement: Perhaps there is agreement because of the common evolutionary history of our species. When I took that biology seminar last semester, we read Michael Ruse, the contemporary philosopher *and* biologist. Ruse had this great line. I liked it so much I copied it in my notebook. Here it is. Ruse put it this way: 'We are what we are because we are recently evolved from savannah-dwelling primates. Suppose that we had evolved from cave-dwellers, or some such thing. We might have as our highest principle of moral obligation the imperative to eat each others' faeces. Not simply the desire, but the obligation.[3]'"

> *If there were objective values, then they would be entities or qualities or relations of a very strange sort, utterly different from anything else in the universe. Correspondingly, if we were aware of them, it would have to be by some very special faculty of moral perception or intuition, utterly different from our ordinary ways of knowing anything else.*
>
> J. L. Mackie, *Ethics: Inventing Right and Wrong*, 1977, p. 38

"Yecch," Sarah grimaced. "Thanks a lot, Selina. Anyone want the rest of this muffin?"

"Sorry, Sister," Selina laughed. "Anyway, the point is that even if moral convergence occurs, there are simpler explanations available that don't involve the positing of a special category of objective moral facts. Think about Hobbes's version of the social contract: We put down our weapons, call a truce in our war of all against all, and try to find some agreement about a few ethical principles. Most of us would say, okay, let's start with an agreement that we will live at peace with one another: I won't attack you if you won't attack me. That sounds like a good start, right? But not everyone would actually agree, even with that basic starting point of ethical cooperation. For example, King David—pardon me for bringing up another of your warlike ancestors, Sarah—sings verses of praise (Psalm 18) to the 'God that girdeth me with strength' and 'teacheth my hands to war.' And Sarah's family isn't the only one with a few warlike members: One of Ezra Pound's poems celebrates 'the battle's rejoicing, when our elbows and swords drip the crimson' and pronounces this curse: 'May God damn for ever all who cry "Peace!"' Of course, some people who glorify war have no idea what it's really like: They put on a flight suit and land on an aircraft carrier filled with military bands and a rifled salute and imagine themselves valiant warriors. But if they saw the maimed bodies and the dead children and the weeping loved ones, they might have a different perspective. And others might value war because they suppose that war is essential for progress: They have a crude notion of social Darwinism and believe that only bloody struggle advances us toward some "higher form." But even if you put aside all those who have basic misconceptions of what war is and of its enormous destructive effects, you may still have some who find war exhilarating and thrilling and who genuinely prefer war to peace. If we point out that in war many innocent people are maimed and slaughtered and that societies at war tend to become brutal and repressive, this person judges that a small price to pay for the glories of war. And if the person considers that he himself may well be one of those killed, he responds that a short warlike life is better than a long peaceful one. We may well despise such a person and call him a moral monster. But that's a label, not an argument. And there are no 'moral facts' to settle the issue."

"But Selina," Ben said, "that sort of person would surely be very rare. Most of us would agree that peace is better."

"Of course," Selina replied. "But that doesn't show that we have reached agreement on the basis of reason, or by recognizing *moral facts*. If most of us did not prefer to cooperate rather than kill one another, our species would have died out long ago. We're rather weak, and we aren't very swift, and we don't have bony exoskeletons to protect us. Those of our species who preferred to band together and cooperate and defend the group from predators rather than killing one another were more likely to survive and pass on their cooperative genes. That doesn't show that peaceful cooperation is an objective moral truth. Among mountain gorillas, when a male ascends to a position of dominance, he immediately kills all infants in the colony. That tendency makes these powerful and rather solitary males more likely to pass on their own genes—it's a successful evolutionary strategy—but it does not make it morally sound. So, in short, we have a simpler explanation for our tendency to agree on cooperation than the supposition of objective ethical facts. If you insist, you can say that this agreement that we should not attack one another is based on special intuitions, or that it comes from recognizing objective facts. But if we can explain it more simply by appealing to our evolutionary history, then is anything really gained by positing an additional set of 'objective moral facts'?"

"I think the jury is still out on moral realism," Sarah said. "Ockham's razor is important, certainly; but simplicity isn't the *only* standard for the best explanation, in science or in ethics."

"True," Selina agreed, "but it's difficult for me to imagine how objective moral facts could wind up being part of the best explanation for our moral beliefs."

"Maybe that's just a measure of the poverty of your imagination." Ben winked, and poked Selina's arm.

Selina smiled. "The boy's got a wicked left hook, Sarah. You let down your guard for just a moment, he gets you with a nasty shot."

"Sorry," Ben said, "just trying to score a point for the embattled moral objectivists. But frankly, Sarah, moral realism seems too tentative for me. When it comes right down to it, I agree with Kant: Reason guides us to objective, absolute, universal moral truths. If you want moral facts, reason is the right path. It's a steep and narrow path, but then, virtue isn't supposed to be easy. What is it that Montaigne said? 'The easy, gentle, and sloping path . . . is not the path of true virtue. It demands a rough and thorny road.'[4] If you want an easy, gentle path, you can follow Selina down the broad thoroughfare of nonobjectivism. For real objective ethics, you need absolute universal principles derived through reason."

Care Ethics

"Look, Ben, let's set aside the question of whether ethics is objective and whether there are any real moral facts and, if so, how we could know them. I doubt that we'll reach agreement on that." Sarah leaned forward and looked at Ben intensely. "But whatever you think about moral objectivity, do you really believe that everything of moral importance must be governed by universal rules and rational principles? Affection and friendship and love are also important, and it's difficult to capture them in general rules, whether those rules are Kantian or utilitarian or social-contract rules. In fact, relations of friendship and affection tend to be *undermined* by rules: If I am in the hospital, and you visit me with flowers and books, that will certainly cheer me up. But if I suspect that your visit is motivated by *duty*—poor old Sarah is in the hospital, I have to go visit her, I hate to do it, but I know it's my duty—rather than simple affection, then much of the joy I have in your visit will be lost. If your mother read you a bedtime story and tucked you in bed because she felt that it was her duty, that may be better than nothing, but not nearly as good as if she reads you a bedtime story and tucks you in bed simply because she loves you and takes joy in making you feel comfortable and secure and loved. Suppose that you need to make a quick trip to the airport—there's an emergency and you must fly home—and you ask Selina for a ride. Selina thinks about it carefully and decides that it is her duty to take you, because she must reciprocate a past kindness you did for her. Or maybe she calculates precisely and determines that taking you to the airport will produce a greater balance of pleasure over suffering for everyone, so she drives you there. If that happens, then something very important has been lost from your relationship. What is lost is the special relation of *caring* and affection that operates in personal relationships. It cannot be captured adequately by impersonal utilitarian calculations and universal Kantian rules, precisely because those rules *are* faceless and impersonal and universal: Maximize pleasure and minimize suffering for *everyone* affected, without regard to who those individuals are; act so that you could will your act to be a *universal* impersonal law. Those universal impersonal rules omit the personal affections that are a vital element of our moral lives. That doesn't mean that there is no place in ethics for general rules, no place for calculations of pleasure and suffering, no place for careful impersonal rational deliberation. But it *does* mean that there is *more* to ethics—*much* more—than such impersonal rational principles."

Ben shook his head. "Feelings are fine; I like them, okay? Caring for others is important. Special affection among family members, friends, sweethearts—that's a wonderful part of life. But when it comes to *ethics*, we're better off with reason. Sure, it's nice to visit your sick friend out of friendship and sympathy and affection. But feelings of sympathy are not sufficient. After all, we also owe moral duties to people who are *not* particularly appealing and for whom we have little sympathy or affection. I love my mother, and I would visit her in the hospital out of affection. But she can also be a bit trying: She tends to be very controlling, and we have some deep differences in viewpoint. My *affection* for her is sometimes weakened by those differences; but my *duty* to her doesn't waver."

Selina raised her hand. "You're looking at one of the differences. Ben's Mom was sort of hoping he might bring a nice blonde Christian Midwestern corn-fed farm girl, ready to devote her life to teaching Sunday School and having babies. Mom was, uh, a bit shocked."

"Alright, my mother has her limits. We don't see eye to eye on a lot of things. The fact is, she can be a pain. I still love her, of course. But suppose the differences are such that I eventually lose all affection for her. I would still have a duty toward her. If you make ethics depend on affections, you are resting ethics on a shaky and unstable foundation. Affections aren't under our control. I love Selina; can't help it; wouldn't have it any other way. Not rational. What am I doing with this atheist, who doesn't even believe in objective values? I can't help loving Selina; and if I really thought it a bad idea, that wouldn't matter: My affections aren't under my rational control. But ethics, that's another matter. Reason tells me what is right and wrong, and I make the decision to follow my duty. That's what following duty is: doing it whether you like it or not, whether you happen to be moved by affection or you are left cold. Affection and friendship and love are wonderful, but they are in a different category from ethics."

"Come on, Ben," Sarah said, "do you really want to leave emotions and caring outside of ethics? Emotions are important in motivating us to do the right thing. Back in the early 19th century, lots of people believed that slavery was wrong. But the emotions aroused by books like Harriet Beecher Stowe's *Uncle Tom's Cabin* helped push those beliefs into action. Impassive reason may be fine for mathematics, but you need more than that for ethics."

Ben would not budge. "Emotions might have been used to push for the destruction of slavery, sure; but don't forget, emotions were used to hold slavery in place, too. And to hold racism in place, long after slavery was officially ended. What about the film *The Birth of a Nation?* It roused strong feelings: The Klan sometimes used it in recruiting rallies. Not to mention the aroused emotions that lead to 'just wars' and the burning of witches. Sure, emotions can lead to opposing slavery, but also to preserving slavery. Careful reasoning shows the wrongness of slavery, and cool, careful *reasoning* is not subject to abuse. Reason is steadier: Through reason and consideration of principle, I can recognize my duty to my mother when my affections are worn away."

"But it's not just emotional persuasion that I'm thinking of, Ben. It's the importance of caring itself. Utilitarianism turns ethics into an impersonal system of adding up pleasures and pains; and Kant's system is even worse: Feelings get in the way of following duty for duty's sake. But affection among friends, love of your children and siblings and parents, concern for a neighbor—those are *not* impersonal relations, and any attempt to reduce such relations to rules or calculations ignores or even denies the special personal and intimate nature of such *caring* relationships. Where affection and care have been lost, duty may be of some use: If my friendship with Selina were destroyed beyond repair, I might still feel an obligation to do her a favor, to reciprocate kindnesses she has done to me—or just because she is a person in need of help. But that is very different from doing her a kindness out of the personal affection I feel for my dear friend Selina. If you make ethics purely a process of calculated rule following, then you undervalue or ignore a vital part of our ethical lives, and you wind up with a distorted ethical perspective. It makes ethics look like a set of rules to govern commerce with strangers, and it marginalizes the caring relationships that many consider the heart and soul of ethics."

Ben shook his head. "Caring is wonderful, and feelings are delightful. But they have no more place in ethics than they do in physics. Maybe less."

Sarah sighed. "On this one, Ben, we'll probably never agree. Well, we can at least say this for the value of friendship: It must have special powers to survive *our* differences. Here we've discussed ethics for hours, and we wind up with views that could not be further apart: a pure rationalist who absolutely excludes feelings from ethics; a care theorist, who believes affections and caring form the essential ethical core; and a nonobjectivist, who believes that neither feelings nor reason can lead to ethical truth, because such truth is nonexistent."

"I may not know any moral facts," Selina said, "but I do know one specific fact: I've got to run to my lab. Come with me," Selina turned to Ben, "and I'll show you more facts than Sarah has had coffees."

"I'm off to my history seminar, Selina. We have our share of facts there as well. Real facts—though, like real moral facts, you can't put them in a test tube and see how they react when they're heated. But that doesn't make them any less real."

READINGS

Virginia Held is Distinguished Professor of Philosophy at the City University Graduate Center of the City University of New York and a well-known ethicist whose beautifully written work is solidly grounded in our real-life experiences. Her books include Feminist Morality: Transforming Culture, Society, and Politics *(Chicago: University of Chicago Press, 1993); and* Rights and Goods: Justifying Social Action *(New York: The Free Press, 1984).*

Feminist Transformations of Moral Theory

The history of philosophy, including the history of ethics, has been constructed from male points of view, and has been built on assumptions and concepts that are by no means gender-neutral.

• • •

The split between reason and emotion is one of the most familiar of philosophical conceptions. And the advocacy of reason "controlling" unruly emotion, of rationality guiding responsible human action against the blindness of passion, has a long and highly influential history, almost as familiar to non-philosophers as to philosophers. We should certainly now be alert to the ways in which reason has been associated with male endeavor, emotion with female weakness, and the ways in which this is of course not an accidental association. As Lloyd writes, "From the beginnings of philosophical thought, femaleness was symbolically associated with what Reason supposedly left behind—the dark powers of the earth goddesses, immersion in unknown forces associated with mysterious female powers. The early Greeks saw women's capacity to conceive as connecting them with the fertility of Nature. As Plato later expressed the thought, women 'imitate the earth.'"

Reason, in asserting its claims and winning its status in human history, was thought to have to conquer the female forces of Unreason. Reason and clarity of thought were early associated with maleness, and as Lloyd notes, "what had to be shed in developing culturally prized rationality was, from the start, symbolically associated with femaleness." In later Greek philosophical thought, the form/matter distinction was articulated, and with a similar hierarchical and gendered association. Maleness was aligned with active, determinate, and defining form; femaleness with mere passive, indeterminate, and inferior matter. . . .

The associations, between Reason, form, knowledge, and maleness, have persisted in various guises, and have permeated what has been thought to be moral knowledge as well as what has been thought to be scientific knowledge, and what has been thought to be the practice of morality. . . . Ethics, thus, has not been a search for universal, or truly human guidance, but a gender-biased enterprise.

Other distinctions and associations have supplemented and reinforced the identification of reason with maleness, and of the irrational with the female; on this and other grounds "man" has been associated with the human, "woman" with the natural. Prominent among distinctions reinforcing the latter view has been that between the public and the private, because of the way they have been interpreted. Again, these provide as familiar and entrenched a framework as do reason and emotion, and they have been as influential for non-philosophers as for philosophers. It has been supposed that in the public realm, man transcends his animal nature and creates human history. As citizen, he creates government and law; as warrior, he protects society by his willingness to risk death; and as artist or philosopher, he overcomes his human mortality. Here, in the public realm, morality should guide human decision. In the household, in contrast, it has been supposed that women merely "reproduce" life as natural, biological matter. Within the household, the "natural" needs of man for food and shelter are served, and new instances of the biological creature that man is are brought into being. But what is distinctively human, and what transcends any given level of development to create human progress, are thought to occur elsewhere.

This contrast was made highly explicit in Aristotle's conceptions of polis and household; it has continued to affect the basic assumptions of a remarkably broad swath of thought ever since. In ancient Athens, women were confined to the household; the public sphere was literally a male domain. In more recent history, though women have been permitted to venture into public space, the associations of the public, historically male sphere with the distinctively human, and of the household, historically a female sphere, with the merely natural and repetitious, have persisted. These associations have deeply affected moral theory, which has often supposed the transcendent, public domain to be relevant to the foundations of morality in ways that the natural behavior of women in the household could not be. To take some recent and representative examples, David Heyd, in his discussion of supererogation, dismisses a mother's sacrifice for her child as an example of the supererogatory because it belongs, in his view, to "the sphere of natural relationships and instinctive feelings (which lie outside morality)." J. O. Urmson had earlier taken a similar position. In his discussion of supererogation, Urmson said, "Let us be clear that we are not now considering cases of natural affection, such as the sacrifice made by a mother for her child; such cases may be said with some justice not to fall under the concept of morality. . . ." Without feminist insistence on the relevance for morality of the experience in mothering, this context is largely ignored by moral theorists. And yet, from a gender-neutral point of view, how can this vast and fundamental domain of human experience possibly be imagined to lie "outside morality"?

The result of the public/private distinction, as usually formulated, has been to privilege the points of view of men in the public domains of state and law, and later in the marketplace, and to discount the experience of women. Mothering has been conceptualized as a primarily biological activity, even when performed by humans, and virtually no moral theory in the history of ethics has taken mothering, as experienced by women, seriously as a source of moral insight, until feminists in recent years have begun to. Women have been seen as emotional rather than as rational beings, and thus as incapable of full moral personhood. Women's behavior has been interpreted as either "natural" and driven by instinct, and thus as irrelevant to morality and to the construction of moral principles, or it has been interpreted as, at best, in need of instruction and supervision by males better able to know what morality requires and better able to live up to its demands.

The Hobbesian conception of reason is very different from the Platonic or Aristotelian conceptions before it, and from the conceptions of Rousseau or Kant or Hegel later; all have in common that they ignore and disparage the experience and reality of women. Consider Hobbes' account of man in the state of nature contracting with other men to establish society. These men hypothetically come into existence fully formed and independent of one another, and decide on entering or staying outside of civil society. As Christine Di Stefano writes, "What we find in Hobbes's account of human nature and political order is a vital concern with the survival of a self conceived in masculine terms. . . . This masculine dimension of Hobbes's atomistic egoism is powerfully underscored in his state of nature, which is effectively built on the foundation of denied maternity." In *The Citizen*, where Hobbes gave his first systematic exposition of the state of nature, he asks us to "consider men as if but even now sprung out of the earth, and suddenly, like mushrooms, come to full maturity, without all kind of engagement with each other." As Di Stefano says, it is a most incredible and problematic feature of Hobbes's state of nature that the men in it "are not born of, much less nurtured by, women, or anyone else." To abstract from the complex web of human reality an abstract man for rational perusal, Hobbes has, Di Stefano continues, "expunged human reproduction and early nurturance, two of the most basic and typically female-identified features of distinctively human life, from his account of basic human nature. Such a strategy ensures that he can present a thoroughly atomistic subject. . . ." From the point of view of women's experience, such a subject or self is unbelievable and misleading, even as a theoretical construct. The Leviathan, Di Stefano writes, "is effectively comprised of a body politic of orphans who have reared themselves, whose desires are situated within and reflect nothing but independently generated movement. . . . These essential elements are natural human beings conceived along masculine lines."

Rousseau, and Kant, and Hegel, paid homage to the emotional power, the aesthetic sensibility, and the familial concerns, respectively, of women. But since in their views morality must be based on rational principle, and women were incapable of full rationality, or a degree or kind of rationality comparable to that of men, women were deemed, in the view of these moralists, to be inherently wanting in morality. For Rousseau, women must be trained from childhood to submit to the will of men lest their sexual power lead both men and women to disaster. For Kant, women were thought incapable of achieving full moral personhood, and women lose all charm if they try to behave like men by engaging in rational pursuits. For

Hegel, women's moral concern for their families could be admirable in its proper place, but is a threat to the more universal aims to which men, as members of the state, should aspire.

These images, of the feminine as what must be overcome if knowledge and morality are to be achieved, of female experience as naturally irrelevant to morality, and of women as inherently deficient moral creatures, are built into the history of ethics. Feminists examine these images, and see that they are not the incidental or merely idiosyncratic suppositions of a few philosophers whose views on many topics depart far from the ordinary anyway. Such views are the nearly uniform reflection in philosophical and ethical theory of patriarchal attitudes pervasive throughout human history. Or they are exaggerations even of ordinary male experience, which exaggerations then reinforce rather than temper other patriarchal conceptions and institutions. They distort the actual experience and aspirations of many men as well as of women. Annette Baier recently speculated about why it is that moral philosophy has so seriously overlooked the trust between human beings that in her view is an utterly central aspect of moral life. She noted that "the great moral theorists in our tradition not only are all men, they are mostly men who had minimal adult dealings with (and so were then minimally influenced by) women." They were for the most part "clerics, misogynists, and puritan bachelors," and thus it is not surprising that they focus their philosophical attention "so single-mindedly on cool, distanced relations between more or less free and equal adult strangers. . . ."

As feminists, we deplore the patriarchal attitudes that so much of philosophy and moral theory reflect. But we recognize that the problem is more serious even than changing those attitudes. For moral theory as so far developed is incapable of correcting itself without an almost total transformation. It cannot simply absorb the gender that has been "left behind," even if both genders would want it to. To continue to build morality on rational principles opposed to the emotions and to include women among the rational will leave no one to reflect the promptings of the heart, which promptings can be moral rather than merely instinctive. To simply bring women into the public and male domain of the polis will leave no one to speak for the household. Its values have been hitherto unrecognized, but they are often moral values. Or to continue to seek contractual restraints on the pursuits of self-interest by atomistic individuals, and to have women join men in devotion to these pursuits, will leave no one involved in the nurturance of children and cultivation of social relations, which nurturance and cultivation can be of greatest moral import.

There are very good reasons for women not to want simply to be accorded entry as equals into the enterprise of morality as so far developed.

In a recent survey of types of feminist moral theory, Kathryn Morgan notes that "many women who engage in philosophical reflection are acutely aware of the masculine nature of the profession and tradition, and feel their own moral concerns as women silenced or trivialized in virtually all the official settings that define the practice." Women should clearly not agree, as the price of admission to the masculine realm of traditional morality, to abandon our own moral concerns as women. . . .

Not all feminists, by any means, agree that there are distinctive feminist virtues or values. Some are especially skeptical of the attempt to give positive value to such traditional "feminine virtues" as a willingness to nurture, or an affinity with caring, or reluctance to seek independence. They see this approach as playing into the hands of those who would confine women to traditional roles. Other feminists are skeptical of all claims about women as such, emphasizing that women are divided by class and race and sexual orientation in ways that make any conclusions drawn from "women's experience" dubious.

Still, it is possible, I think, to discern various important focal points evident in current feminist attempts to transform ethics into a theoretical and practical activity that could be acceptable from a feminist point of view. In the glimpse I have presented of bias in the history of ethics, I focused on what, from a feminist point of view, are three of its most questionable aspects: 1) the split between reason and emotion and the devaluation of emotion; 2) the public/private distinction and the relegation of the private to the natural; and 3) the concept of the self as constructed from a male point of view. In the remainder of this article, I shall consider further how some feminists are exploring these topics.

• • •

I. Reason and Emotion

In the area of moral theory in the modern era, the priority accorded to reason has taken two major forms. A) On the one hand has been the Kantian, or Kantian-inspired search for very general, abstract, deontological, universal moral principles by which rational beings should be guided. Kant's Categorical Imperative is a foremost example: it suggests that all moral problems can be handled by applying an impartial, pure, rational principle to particular cases. It requires that we try to see what the general features of the problem before us are, and that we apply an abstract principle, or rules derivable from it, to this problem. On this view, this procedure should be adequate for all moral decisions. We should thus be able to act as reason recommends, and resist yielding to emotional inclinations and desires in conflict with our rational wills.

B) On the other hand, the priority accorded to reason in the modern era has taken a Utilitarian form. The Utilitarian approach, reflected in rational choice theory, recognizes that persons have desires and interests, and suggests rules of rational choice for maximizing the satisfaction of these. While some philosophers in this tradition espouse egoism, especially of an intelligent and long-term kind, many do not. They begin, however, with assumptions that what are morally relevant are gains and losses of utility to theoretically isolatable individuals, and that the outcome at which morality should aim is the maximization of the utility of individuals. Rational calculation about such an outcome will, in this view, provide moral recommendations to guide all our choices. As with the Kantian approach, the Utilitarian approach relies on abstract general principles or rules to be applied to particular cases. And it holds that although emotion is, in fact, the source of our desires for certain objectives, the task of morality should be to instruct us on how to pursue those objectives most rationally. Emotional attitudes toward moral issues themselves interfere with rationality and should be disregarded. Among the questions Utilitarians can ask can be questions about which emotions to cultivate, and which desires to try to change, but these questions are to be handled in the terms of rational calculation, not of what our feelings suggest.

Although the conceptions of what the judgments of morality should be based on, and of how reason should guide moral decision, are different in Kantian and in Utilitarian approaches, both share a reliance on a highly abstract, universal principle as the appropriate source of moral guidance, and both share the view that moral problems are to be solved by the application of such an abstract principle to particular cases. Both share an admiration for the rules of reason to be appealed to in moral contexts, and both denigrate emotional responses to moral issues.

Many feminist philosophers have questioned whether the reliance on abstract rules, rather than the adoption of more context-respectful approaches, can possibly be adequate for dealing with moral problems, especially as women experience them. Though Kantians may hold that complex rules can be elaborated for specific contexts, there is nevertheless an assumption in this approach that the more abstract the reasoning applied to a moral problem, the more satisfactory. And Utilitarians suppose that one highly abstract principle, The Principle of Utility, can be applied to every moral problem no matter what the context.

A genuinely universal or gender-neutral moral theory would be one which would take account of the experience and concerns of women as fully as it would take account of the experience and concerns of men. When we focus on the experience of women, however, we seem to be able to see a set of moral concerns becoming salient that differs from those of traditional or standard moral theory. Women's experience of moral problems seems to lead us to be especially concerned with actual relationships between embodied persons, and with what these relationships seem to require. Women are often inclined to attend to rather than to dismiss the particularities of the context in which a moral problem arises. And we often pay attention to feelings of empathy and caring to suggest what we ought to do rather than relying as fully as possible on abstract rules of reason. . . .

The work of psychologists such as Carol Gilligan and others has led to a clarification of what may be thought of as tendencies among women to approach moral issues differently. Rather than interpreting moral problems in terms of what could be handled by applying abstract rules of justice to particular cases, many of the women studied by Gilligan tended to be more concerned with preserving actual human relationships, and with expressing care for those for whom they felt responsible. Their moral reasoning was typically more embedded in a context of particular others than was the reasoning of a comparable group of men. . . . Many feminists see our own consciously considered experience as lending confirmation to the view that what has come to be called "an ethic of care" needs to be developed. Some think it should supersede "the ethic of justice" of traditional or standard moral theory. Others think it should be integrated with the ethic of justice and rules.

In any case, feminist philosophers are in the process of reevaluating the place of emotion in morality in at least two respects. First, many think morality requires the development of the moral emotions, in contrast to moral theories emphasizing the primacy of reason. As Annette Baier notes, the rationalism typical of traditional moral theory will be challenged when we pay attention to the role of parent. "It might be important," she writes, "for father figures to have rational control over their violent urges to beat to death the children whose screams enrage them, but more than control of such nasty passions seems needed in the mother or primary parent, or parent-substitute, by most psychological theories. They need to love their children, not just to control their irritation." So the emphasis in many traditional theories on rational control over the emotions, "rather than on cultivating desirable forms of emotion," is challenged by feminist approaches to ethics.

Secondly, emotion will be respected rather than dismissed by many feminist moral philosophers in the process of gaining moral understanding. The experience and practice out of which feminist moral theory can be expected to be developed will include embodied feeling as well as thought. In a recent overview of a vast amount of writing, Kathryn Morgan states that "feminist theorists begin ethical theorizing with embodied, gendered subjects who have particular histories, particular communities, particular allegiances, and particular visions of human flourishing. The starting point involves valorizing what has frequently been most mistrusted and despised in the western philosophical tradition. . . ." Among the elements being reevaluated are feminine emotions. The "care" of the alternative feminist approach to morality appreciates rather than rejects emotion. The caring relationships important to feminist morality cannot be understood in terms of abstract rules or moral reasoning. And the "weighing" so often needed between the conflicting claims of some relationships and others cannot be settled by deduction or rational calculation. A feminist ethic will not just acknowledge emotion, as do Utilitarians, as giving us the objectives toward which moral rationality can direct us. It will embrace emotion as providing at least a partial basis for morality itself, and for moral understanding.

Annette Baier stresses the centrality of trust for an adequate morality. Achieving and maintaining trusting, caring relationships is quite different from acting in accord with rational principles, or satisfying the individual desires of either self or other. Caring, empathy, feeling with others, being sensitive to each other's feelings, all may be better guides to what morality requires in actual contexts than may abstract rules of reason, or rational calculation, or at least they may be necessary components of an adequate morality.

• • •

II. The Public and the Private

The second questionable aspect of the history of ethics on which I focused was its conception of the distinction between the public and the private. As with the split between reason and emotion, feminists are showing how gender-bias has distorted previous conceptions of these spheres, and we are trying to offer more appropriate understandings of "private" morality and "public" life.

Part of what feminists have criticized has been the way the distinction has been accompanied by a supposition that what occurs in the household occurs as if on an island beyond politics, whereas the personal is highly affected by the political power beyond, from legislation about abortion to the greater earning power of men, to the interconnected division of labor by gender both within and beyond the household, to the lack of adequate social protection for women against domestic violence. Of course we recognize that the family is not identical to the state, and we need concepts for thinking about the private or personal, and the public or political. But they will have to be very different from the traditional concepts.

Feminists have also criticized deeper assumptions about what is distinctively human and what is "natural" in the public and private aspects of human life, and what is meant by "natural" in connection with women. Consider the associations that have traditionally been built up: the public realm is seen as the distinctively human realm in which man transcends his animal nature, while the private realm of the household is seen as the natural region in which women merely reproduce the species. These associations are extraordinarily pervasive in standard concepts and theories, in art and thought and cultural ideals, and especially in politics.

Dominant patterns of thought have seen women as primarily mothers, and mothering as the performance of a primarily biological function. Then it has been supposed that while engaging in political life is a specifically human activity, women are engaged in an activity which is not specifically human. Women accordingly have been thought to be closer to nature than men, to be enmeshed in a biological function involving processes more like those in which other animals are involved than like the rational discussion of the citizen in the polis, or the glorious battles of noble soldiers, or the trading and rational contracting of "economic man." The total or relative exclusion of women from the domain of public life has then been seen as either inevitable or appropriate.

The view that women are more determined by biology than are men is still extraordinarily prevalent. It is as questionable from a feminist perspective as many other traditional misinterpretations of women's experience. Human mothering is an extremely different activity from the mothering engaged in by other animals. The work and speech of men is recognized as very different from what might be thought of as the "work" and "speech" of other animals. Human mothering is fully as different from animal mothering. Of course all human beings are animal as well as human. But to whatever extent it is appropriate to recognize a difference between "man" and other animals, so would it be appropriate to recognize a comparable difference between "woman" and other animals, and between the activities—including mothering—engaged in by women and the behavior of other animals.

Human mothering shapes language and culture, it forms human social personhood, it develops morality. Animal behavior can be highly impressive and complex, but it does not have built into it any of the consciously chosen aims of morality. In creating human social persons, human mothering is different in kind from merely propagating a species. And human mothering can be fully as creative an activity as those activities traditionally thought of as distinctively human, because to create *new* persons, and new types of *persons*, can surely be as creative as to make new objects, products, or institutions. *Human* mothering is no more "natural" or "primarily biological" than is any other human activity.

• • •

III. The Concept of Self

Let me turn now to the third aspect of the history of ethics which I discussed and which feminists are re-envisioning: the concept of self. One of the most important emphases in a feminist approach to morality is the recognition that more attention must be paid to the domain between, on the one hand, the self as ego, as self-interested individual, and, on the other hand, the universal, everyone, others in general. Traditionally, ethics has dealt with these poles of individual self and universal all. Usually, it has called for impartiality against the partiality of the egoistic self; sometimes it has defended egoism against claims for a universal perspective. But most standard moral theory has hardly noticed as morally significant the intermediate realm of family relations and relations of friendship, of group ties and neighborhood concerns, especially from the point of view of women. When it has noticed this intermediate realm it has often seen its attachments as threatening to the aspirations of the Man of Reason, or as subversive of "true" morality. In seeing the problems of ethics as problems of reconciling the interests of the self with what would be right or best for "everyone," standard ethics has neglected the moral aspects of the concern and sympathy which people actually feel for particular others, and what moral experience in this intermediate realm suggests for an adequate morality.

The region of "particular others" is a distinct domain, where what can be seen to be artificial and problematic are the very egoistic "self" and the universal "all others" of standard moral theory. In the domain of particular others, the self is already constituted to an important degree by relations with others, and these relations may be much more salient and significant than the interests of any individual self in isolation. The "others" in the picture, however, are not the "all others," or "everyone," of traditional moral theory; they are not what a universal point of view or a view from nowhere could provide. They are, characteristically, actual flesh and blood other human beings for whom we have actual feelings and with whom we have real ties.

From the point of view of much feminist theory, the individualistic assumptions of liberal theory and of most standard moral theory are suspect. Even if we would be freed from the debilitating aspects of dominating male power to "be ourselves" and to pursue our own interests, we would, as persons, still have ties to other persons, and we would at least in part be constituted by such ties. Such ties would be part of what we inherently are. We are, for instance, the daughter or son of given parents, or the mother or father of given children, and we carry with us at least some ties to the racial or ethnic or national group within which we developed into the persons we are.

If we look, for instance, at the realities of the relation between mothering person (who can be female or male) and child, we can see that what we value in the relation cannot be broken down into individual gains and losses for the individual members in the relation. Nor can it be understood in universalistic terms. Self-development apart from the relation may be much less important than the satisfactory development of the relation. What matters may often be the health and growth of and the development of the relation-and-its-members in ways that cannot be understood in the individualistic terms of standard moral theories designed to maximize the satisfaction of self-interest. The universalistic terms of moral theories grounded in what would be right for "all rational beings" or "everyone" cannot handle, either, what has moral value in the relation between mothering person and child. . . .

Relationships can be evaluated as trusting or mistrustful, mutually considerate or selfish, harmonious or stressful, and so forth. Where trust and consideration are appropriate, which is not always, we can find ways to foster them. But understanding and evaluating relationships, and encouraging them to be what they can be at their best, require us to look at relationships between actual persons, and to see what both standard moral theories and their nonfeminist critics often miss. To be adequate, moral theories must pay attention to the neglected realm of particular others in the actual relationships and actual contexts of women's experience. In doing so, problems of individual self-interest vs. universal rules may recede to a region more like background, out-of-focus insolubility or relative unimportance. The salient problems may then be seen to be how we ought best to guide or to maintain or to reshape the relationships, both close and more distant, that we have, or might have, with actual other human beings. Particular others can be actual children in need in distant continents, or the anticipated children of generations not yet even close to being born. But they are not "all rational beings" or "the greatest number," and the self that is in relationships with particular others and is composed to a significant degree by such relations is not a self whose ego must be pitted against abstract, universal claims. Developing the needed guidance for maintaining and reshaping relationships presents enormous problems, but a first step is to recognize how traditional and nonfeminist moral theory of both an individualistic and communitarian kind falls short in providing it. . . .

I have examined three topics on which feminist philosophers and feminists in other fields are thinking anew about where we should start and how we should focus our attention in ethics. Feminist reconceptualizations and recommendations concerning the relation between reason and emotion, the distinction between public and private, and the concept of the self, are providing insights deeply challenging to standard moral theory. The implications of this work are that we need an almost total reconstruction of social and political and economic and legal theory in all their traditional forms as well as a reconstruction of moral theory and practice at more comprehensive, or fundamental, levels.

Jonathan Bennett (born 1930) taught philosophy at the University of Cambridge, the University of British Columbia, and Syracuse University. He has written important philosophical works in a wide variety of areas, including history of philosophy, logic, philosophy of language, and ethics. Among his books are A Study of Spinoza's Ethics *(Indianapolis: Hackett, 1984);* Events and Their Names *(Indianapolis: Hackett, 1989);* Rationality: An Essay towards an Analysis *(Indianapolis: Hackett, 1989);* Learning from Six Philosophers *(Oxford, U.K.: Oxford University Press, 2001); and* A Philosophical Guide to Conditionals *(Oxford, U.K.: Oxford University Press, 2003). The paper included here, "The Conscience of Huckleberry Finn," was originally published in* Philosophy 49 (1974): 123–134.

The Conscience of Huckleberry Finn

I

In this paper, I shall present not just the conscience of Huckleberry Finn but two others as well. One of them is the conscience of Heinrich Himmler. He became a Nazi in 1923; he served drably and quietly, but well, and was rewarded with increasing responsibility and power. At the peak of his career he held many offices and commands, of which the most powerful was that of leader of the S.S.—the principal police force of the Nazi regime. In this capacity, Himmler commanded the whole concentration-camp system, and was responsible for the execution of the so-called "final solution of the Jewish problem." It is important for my purposes that this piece of social engineering should be thought of not abstractly but in concrete terms of Jewish families being marched to what they think are bathhouses, to the accompaniment of loud-speaker renditions of extracts from *The Merry Widow* and *Tales of Hoffmann*, there to be choked to death by poisonous gases. Altogether, Himmler succeeded in murdering about four and a half million of them, as well as several million gentiles, mainly Poles and Russians.

The other conscience to be discussed is that of the Calvinist theologian and philosopher Jonathan Edwards. He lived in the first half of the eighteenth century, and has a good claim to be considered America's first serious and considerable philosophical thinker. He was for many years a widely renowned preacher and Congregationalist minister in New England; in 1748 a dispute with his congregation led him to resign (he couldn't accept their view that unbelievers should be admitted to the Lord's Supper in the hope that it would convert them); for some years after that he worked as a missionary, preaching to Indians through an interpreter; then in 1758 he accepted the presidency of what is now Princeton University, and within two months died from a smallpox inoculation. Along the way he wrote some first-rate philosophy; his book attacking the notion of free will is still sometimes read. Why I should be interested in Edwards' *conscience* will be explained in due course.

I shall use Heinrich Himmler, Jonathan Edwards, and Huckleberry Finn to illustrate different aspects of a single theme, namely the relationship between *sympathy* on the one hand and *bad morality* on the other.

II

All that I can mean by a "bad morality" is a morality whose principles I deeply disapprove of. When I call a morality bad, I cannot prove that mine is better; but when I here call any morality bad, I think you will agree with me that it is bad; and that is all I need.

There could be dispute as to whether the springs of someone's actions constitute a *morality*. I think, though, that we must admit that someone who acts in ways which conflict grossly with our morality may nevertheless have a morality of his own—a set of principles of action which he sincerely assents to, so that for him the problem of acting well or rightly or in obedience to conscience is the problem of conforming to *those* principles. The problem of conscientiousness can arise as acutely for a bad morality as for any other: Rotten principles may be as difficult to keep as decent ones.

As for "sympathy" I use this term to cover every sort of fellow-feeling, as when one feels pity over someone's loneliness, or horrified compassion over his pain, or when one feels a shrinking reluctance to act in a way which will bring misfortune to someone else. These *feelings* must not be confused with *moral judgments*. My sympathy for someone in distress may lead me to help him, or even to think that I ought to help him; but in itself it is not a judgment about what I ought to do but just a *feeling* for him in his plight. We shall get some light on the difference between feelings and moral judgments when we consider Huckleberry Finn.

Obviously, feelings can impel one to action, and so can moral judgments; and in a particular case sympathy and morality may pull in opposite directions. This can happen not just with bad moralities, but also with good ones like yours and mine. For example, a small child, sick and miserable, clings tightly to his mother and screams in terror when she tries to pass him over to the doctor to be examined. If the mother gave way to her sympathy, that is to her feeling for the child's misery and fright, she would hold it close and not let the doctor come near; but don't we agree that it might be wrong for her to act on such a feeling? Quite generally, then, anyone's moral principles may apply to a particular situation in a way which runs contrary to the particular thrusts of fellow-feeling that he has in that situation. My immediate concern is with sympathy in relation to bad morality, but not because such conflicts occur only when the morality is bad.

Now, suppose that someone who accepts a bad morality is struggling to make himself act in accordance with it in a particular situation where his sympathies pull him another way. He sees the struggle as one between doing the right, conscientious thing, and acting wrongly and weakly, like the mother who won't let the doctor come near her sick, frightened baby. Since we don't accept this person's morality, we may see the situation very differently, thoroughly disapproving of the action he regards as the right one, and endorsing the action which from his point of view constitutes weakness and backsliding.

Conflicts between sympathy and bad morality won't always be like this, for we won't disagree with every single dictate of a bad morality. Still, it can happen in the way I have described, with the agent's right action being our wrong one, and and vice versa. That is just what happens in a certain episode in Chapter 16 of *The Adventures of Huckleberry Finn*, an episode which brilliantly illustrates how fiction can be instructive about real life.

III

Huck Finn has been helping his slave friend Jim to run away from Miss Watson, who is Jim's owner. In their raft-journey down the Mississippi river, they are near to the place at which Jim will become legally free. Now let Huck take over the story:

> Jim said it made him all over trembly and feverish to be so close to freedom. Well I can tell you it made me all over trembly and feverish, too, to hear him, because I begun to get it through my head that he *was* most free—and

who was to blame for it? Why, *me*. I couldn't get that out of my conscience, no how nor no way. . . . It hadn't ever come home to me, before, what this thing was that I was doing. But now it did; and it stayed with me, and scorched me more and more. I tried to make out to myself that *I* warn't to blame, because *I* didn't run Jim off from his rightful owner; but it warn't no use, conscience up and say, every time: "But you knowed he was running for his freedom, and you could a paddled ashore and told somebody." That was so—I couldn't get around that, no way. That was where it pinched. Conscience says to me: "What had poor Miss Watson done to you, that you could see her nigger go off right under your eyes and never say one single word? What did that poor old woman do to you, that you could treat her so mean? . . ." I got to feeling so mean and miserable I most wished I was dead.

Jim speaks of his plan to save up to buy his wife, and then his children, out of slavery; and he adds that if the children cannot be bought he will arrange to steal them. Huck is horrified:

Thinks I, this is what comes of my not thinking. Here was this nigger which I had as good as helped to run away, coming right out flat-footed and saying he would steal his children—children that belonged to a man I didn't even know; a man that hadn't ever done me no harm.

I was sorry to hear Jim say that, it was such a lowering of him. My conscience got to stirring me up hotter than ever, until at last I says to it: "Let up on me—it ain't too late, yet—I'll paddle ashore at first light, and tell." I felt easy, and happy, and light as a feather, right off. All my troubles was gone.

This is bad morality all right. In his earliest years Huck wasn't taught any principles, and the only one he has encountered since then are those of rural Missouri, in which slave-owning is just one kind of ownership and is not subject to critical pressure. It hasn't occurred to Huck to question those principles. So the action, to us abhorrent, of turning Jim in to the authorities presents itself *clearly* to Huck as the right thing to do.

For us, morality and sympathy would both dictate helping Jim to escape. If we felt any conflict, it would have both these on one side and something else on the other—greed for a reward, or fear of punishment. But Huck's morality conflicts with his sympathy, that is, with his unargued, natural feeling for his friend. The conflict starts when Huck sets off in the canoe towards the shore, pretending that he is going to reconnoiter, but really planning to turn Jim in:

As I shoved off, [Jim] says: "Pooty soon I'll be a-shout'n for joy, en I'll say, it's all on accounts o' Huck I's a free man . . . Jim won't ever forgit you, Huck; you's de bes' fren' Jim's ever had; en you's de *only* fren' old Jim's got now."

I was paddling off, all in a sweat to tell on him; but when he says this, it seemed to kind of take the tuck all out of me. I went along slow then, and I warn't right down certain whether I was glad I started or whether I warn't. When I was fifty yards off, Jim says:

> "Dah you goes, de ole true Huck; de on'y white genlman dat ever kep'
> his promise to ole Jim." Well, I just felt sick. But I says, I *got* to do it—I can't
> get *out* of it.

In the upshot, sympathy wins over morality. Huck hasn't the strength of
will to do what he sincerely thinks he ought to do. Two men hunting for
runaway slaves ask him whether the man on his raft is black or white:

> I didn't answer up prompt. I tried to, but the words wouldn't come. I tried,
> for a second or two, to brace up and out with it, but I warn't man enough—
> hadn't the spunk of a rabbit. I see I was weakening; so I just give up trying,
> and up and says: "He's white."

So Huck enables Jim to escape, thus acting weakly and wickedly—he
thinks. In this conflict between sympathy and morality, sympathy wins.

One critic has cited this episode in support of the statement that Huck
suffers "excruciating moments of wavering between honesty and respectability." That is hopelessly wrong, and I agree with the perceptive comment on it by another critic, who says:

> The conflict waged in Huck is much more serious: He scarcely cares for
> respectability and never hesitates to relinquish it, but he does care for hon-
> esty and gratitude—and both honesty and gratitude require that he should
> give Jim up. It is not, in Huck, honesty at war with respectability but love
> and compassion for Jim struggling against his conscience. His decision is for
> Jim and hell: a right decision made in the mental chains that Huck never
> breaks. His concern for Jim is and remains *irrational*. Huck finds many rea-
> sons for giving Jim up and none for stealing him. To the end Huck sees his
> compassion for Jim as a weak, ignorant, and wicked felony.

That is precisely correct—and it can have that virtue only because Mark
Twain wrote the episode with such unerring precision. The crucial point
concerns *reasons*, which all occur on one side of the conflict. On the side
of conscience we have principles, arguments, considerations, ways of
looking at things:

> "It hadn't ever come home to me before what I was doing"
> "I tried to make out that I warn't to blame"
> "Conscience said 'But you knowed . . .'—I couldn't get around that"
> "What had poor Miss Watson done to you?"
> "This is what comes of my not thinking"
> ". . . children that belonged to a man I didn't even know."

On the other side, the side of feeling, we get nothing like that. When Jim
rejoices in Huck, as his only friend, Huck doesn't consider the claims of
friendship or have the situation "come home" to him in a different light.
All that happens is: "When he says this, it seemed to kind of take the tuck

all out of me. I went along slow then, and I warn't right down certain whether I was glad I started or whether I warn't." Again, Jim's words about Huck's "promise" to him don't give Huck any *reason* for changing his plan: In his morality promises to slaves probably don't count. Their effect on him is of a different kind: "Well, I just felt sick." And when the moment for final decision come, Huck doesn't weigh up pros and cons: he simply *fails* to do what he believes to be right—he isn't strong enough, hasn't "the spunk of a rabbit." This passage in the novel is notable not just for its finely wrought irony, with Huck's weakness of will leading him to do the right thing, but also for its masterly handling of the difference between general moral principles and particular unreasoned emotional pulls.

IV

Consider now another case of bad morality in conflict with human sympathy: the case of the odious Himmler. Here, from a speech he made to some S.S. generals, is an indication of the content of his morality:

> What happens to a Russian, to a Czech, does not interest me in the slightest. What the nations can offer in the way of good blood of our type, we will take, if necessary by kidnapping their children and raising them here with us. Whether nations live in prosperity or starve to death like cattle interests me only in so far as we need them as slaves to our *Kultur*; otherwise it is of no interest to me. Whether 10,000 Russian females fall down from exhaustion while digging an antitank ditch interests me only in so far as the antitank ditch for Germany is finished.

But has this a moral basis at all? And if it has, was there in Himmler's own mind any conflict between morality and sympathy? Yes there was. Here is more from the same speech:

> I also want to talk to you quite frankly on a very grave matter . . . I mean . . . the extermination of the Jewish race. . . . Most of you must know what it means when 100 corpses are lying side by side, or 500, or 1,000. To have stuck it out and at the same time—apart from exceptions caused by human weakness—to have remained decent fellows, that is what has made us hard. This is a page of glory in our history which has never been written and is never to be written.

Himmler saw his policies as being hard to implement while still retaining one's human sympathies—while still remaining a "decent fellow." He is saying that only the weak take the easy way out and just squelch their sympathies, and is praising the stronger and more glorious course of retaining one's sympathies while acting in violation of them. In the same spirit, he ordered that when executions were carried out in concentration camps, those responsible "are to be influenced in such a way as to suffer no ill effect in their character and mental attitude." A year later he boasted that the S.S. had wiped out the Jews

> without our leaders and their men suffering any damage in their minds and souls. The danger was considerable, for there was only a narrow path between the Scylla of their becoming heartless ruffians unable any longer to treasure life, and the Charybdis of their becoming soft and suffering nervous breakdowns.

And there really can't be any doubt that the basis of Himmler's policies was a set of principles which constituted his morality—a sick, bad, wicked *morality*. He described himself as caught in "the old tragic conflict between will and obligation." And when his physician Kersten protested at the intention to destroy the Jews, saying that the suffering involved was "not to be contemplated," Kersten reports that Himmler replied:

> He knew that it would mean much suffering for the Jews. . . . "It is the curse of greatness that it must step over dead bodies to create new life. Yet we must . . . cleanse the soil or it will never bear fruit. It will be a great burden for me to bear."

This, I submit, is the language of morality.

So in this case, tragically, bad morality won out over sympathy. I am sure that many of Himmler's killers did extinguish their sympathies, becoming "heartless ruffians" rather than "decent fellows"; but not Himmler himself. Although his policies ran against the human grain to a horrible degree, he did not sandpaper down his emotional surfaces so that there was no grain there, allowing his actions to slide along smoothly and easily. He did, after all, bear his hideous burden, and even paid a price for it. He suffered a variety of nervous and physical disabilities, including nausea and stomach-convulsions, and Kersten was doubtless right in saying that these were "the expression of a psychic division which extended over his whole life."

This same division must have been present in some of those officials of the Church who ordered heretics to be tortured so as to change their theological opinions. Along with the brutes and the cold careerists, there must have been some who cared, and who suffered from the conflict between their sympathies and their bad morality.

V

In the conflict between sympathy and bad morality, then, the victory may go to sympathy as in the case of Huck Finn, or to morality as in the case of Himmler.

Another possibility is that the conflict may be avoided by giving up, or not ever having, those sympathies which might interfere with one's principles. That seems to have been the case with Jonathan Edwards. I am afraid that I shall be doing an injustice to Edwards' many virtues, and to his great intellectual energy and inventiveness; for my concern is only with the worst thing about him—namely his morality, which was worse than Himmler's.

According to Edwards, God condemns some men to an eternity of unimaginably awful pain, though he arbitrarily spares others—"arbitrarily" because none deserve to be spared:

> Natural men are held in the hand of God over the pit of hell; they have deserved the fiery pit, and are already sentenced to it; and God is dreadfully provoked, his anger is as great toward them as to those that are actually suffering the executions of the fierceness of his wrath in hell . . . ; the devil is waiting for them, hell is gaping for them, the flames gather and flash about them, and would fain lay hold on them . . . ; and . . . there are no means within reach that can be any security to them. . . . All that preserves them is the mere arbitrary will, and uncovenanted unobliged forebearance of an incensed God.

Notice that he says "they have deserved the fiery pit." Edwards insists that men *ought* to be condemned to eternal pain; and his position isn't that this is right because God wants it, but rather that God wants it because it is right. For him, moral standards exist independently of God, and God can be assessed in the light of them (and of course found to be perfect). For example, he says:

> They deserve to be cast into hell; so that . . . justice never stands in the way, it makes no objection against God's using his power at any moment to destroy them. Yea, on the contrary, justice calls aloud for an infinite punishment of their sins.

Elsewhere, he gives elaborate arguments to show that God is acting justly in damning sinners. For example, he argues that a punishment should be exactly as bad as the crime being punished; God is infinitely excellent; so any crime against him is infinitely bad; and so eternal damnation is exactly right as a punishment—it is infinite, but, as Edwards is careful also to say, it is "no more than infinite."

Of course, Edwards himself didn't torment the damned; but the question still arises of whether his sympathies didn't conflict with his *approval* of eternal torment. Didn't he find it painful to contemplate any fellow-human's being tortured for ever? Apparently not:

> The God that holds you over the pit of hell, much as one holds a spider or some loathsome insect over the fire, abhors you, and is dreadfully provoked; . . . he is of purer eyes than to bear to have you in his sight; you are

ten thousand times so abominable in his eyes as the most hateful venomous serpent is in ours.

When God is presented as being as misanthropic as that, one suspects misanthropy in the theologian. This suspicion is increased when Edwards claims that "the saints in glory will . . . understand how terrible the sufferings of the damned are; yet . . . will not be sorry for [them]." He bases this partly on a view of human nature whose ugliness he seems not to notice:

> The seeing of the calamities of others tends to heighten the sense of our own enjoyments. When the saints in glory, therefore, shall see the doleful state of the damned, how will this heighten their sense of the blessedness of their own state. . . . When they shall see how miserable others of their fellow-creatures are . . . ; when they shall see the smoke of their torment, . . . and hear their dolorous shrieks and cries, and consider that they in the mean time are in the most blissful state, and shall surely be in it to all eternity; how they will rejoice!

I hope this is less than the whole truth! His other main point about why the saints will rejoice to see the torments of the damned is that it is *right* that they should do so:

> The heavenly inhabitants . . . will have no love nor pity to the damned. . . . [This will not show] a want of spirit of love in them . . . ; for the heavenly inhabitants will know that it is not fit that they should love [the damned] because they will know then, that God has no love to them, nor pity for them.

The implication that *of course* one can adjust one's feelings of pity so that they conform to the dictates of some authority—doesn't this suggest that ordinary human sympathies played only a small part in Edwards' life?

VI

Huck Finn, whose sympathies are wide and deep, could never avoid the conflict in that way; but he is determined to avoid it, and so he opts for the only other alternative he can see—to give up morality altogether. After he has tricked the slave-hunters, he returns to the raft and undergoes a peculiar crisis:

> I got aboard the raft, feeling bad and low, because I knowed very well I had done wrong, and I see it warn't no use for me to try to learn to do right; a body that don't get *started* right when he's little, ain't got no show—when the pinch comes there ain't nothing to back him up and keep him to his work, and so he gets beat. Then I thought a minute, and says to myself, hold on—s'pose you'd a done right and give Jim up; would you feel better than what you do now? No, says I, I'd feel bad—I'd feel just the same way I do now. Well, then, says I, what's the use you learning to do right, when it's

troublesome to do right and ain't no trouble to do wrong, and the wages is just the same? I was stuck. I couldn't answer that. So I reckoned I wouldn't bother no more about it, but after this always do whichever come handiest at the time.

Huck clearly cannot conceive of having any morality except the one he has learned—too late, he thinks—from his society. He is not entirely a prisoner of that morality, because he does after all reject it; but for him that is a decision to relinquish morality as such; he cannot envisage revising his morality, altering its content in face of the various pressures to which it is subject, including pressures from his sympathies. For example, he does not begin to approach the thought that slavery should be rejected on moral grounds, or the thought that what he is doing is not theft because a person cannot be owned and therefore cannot be stolen.

The basic trouble is that he cannot or will not engage in abstract intellectual operations of any sort. In chapter 33 he finds himself "feeling to blame, somehow" for something he knows he had no hand in; he assumes that this feeling is a deliverance of conscience; and this confirms him in his belief that conscience shouldn't be listened to:

> It don't make no difference whether you do right or wrong, a person's conscience ain't got no sense, and just goes for him *anyway*. If I had a yaller dog that didn't know no more than a person's conscience does, I would poison him. It takes up more than all of a person's insides, and yet ain't no good, nohow.

That brisk, incurious dismissiveness fits well with the comprehensive rejection of morality back on the raft. But this is a digression.

On the raft, Huck decides not to live by principles, but just to do whatever "comes handiest at the time"—always acting according to the mood of the moment. Since the morality he is rejecting is narrow and cruel, and his sympathies are broad and kind, the results will be good. But moral principles are good to have, because they help to protect one from acting badly at moments when one's sympathies happen to be in abeyance. On the highest possible estimate of the role one's sympathies should have, one can still allow for principles as embodiments of one's best feelings, one's broadest and keenest sympathies. On that view, principles can help one across intervals when one's feelings are at less than their best, i.e. through periods of misanthropy or meanness or self-centeredness or depression or anger.

What Huck didn't see is that one can live by principles and yet have ultimate control over their content. And one way such control can be exercised is by checking of one's principles in the light of one's sympathies. This is sometimes a pretty straightforward matter. It can happen that a certain moral principle becomes untenable—meaning literally that one cannot hold it any longer—because it conflicts intolerably with the pity or revulsion or whatever that one feels when one sees what the principle leads to. One's experience may play a large part here: Experiences evoke feelings, and feelings force one to modify principles. Something like this happened to the English poet Wilfred Owen, whose experiences in the First World War transformed him from an enthusiastic soldier into a virtual pacifist. I can't document his change of conscience in detail; but I want to present something which he wrote about the way experience can put pressure on morality.

The Latin poet Horace wrote that it is sweet and fitting (or right) to die for one's country—*dulce et decorum est pro patria mori*—and Owen wrote a fine poem about how experience could lead one to relinquish that particular moral principle. He describes a man who is too slow donning his gas mask during a gas attack—"As under a green sea I saw him drowning," Owen says. The poem ends like this:

> *In all my dreams before my helpless sight*
> *He plunges at me, guttering, choking, drowning.*
> *If in some smothering dreams, you too could pace*
> *Behind the wagon that we flung him in,*
> *And watch the white eyes writhing in his face,*
> *His hanging face, like a devil's sick of sin;*
> *If you could hear, at every jolt, the blood*
> *Come gargling from the froth-corrupted lungs,*
> *Bitter as the cud*
> *Of vile, incurable sores on innocent tongues,—*
> *My friend, you would not tell with such high zest*
> *To children ardent for some desperate glory,*
> *The old Lie: Dulce et decorum est*
> *Pro patria mori.*

There is a difficulty about drawing from all this a moral for ourselves. I imagine that we agree in our rejection of slavery, eternal damnation, genocide, and uncritical patriotic self-abnegation; so we shall agree that Huck Finn, Jonathan Edwards, Heinrich Himmler, and the poet Horace would all have done well to bring certain of their principles under severe pressure from ordinary human sympathies. But then we can say this because we can say that all those are bad moralities, whereas we cannot look at our own moralities and declare them bad. This is not arrogance: It is obviously incoherent for someone to declare the system of moral principles that he *accepts* to be *bad*, just as one cannot coherently say of anything that one *believes* it but it is *false*.

Still, although I can't point to any of my beliefs and say "That is false," I don't doubt that some of my beliefs *are* false; and so I should try to remain open to correction. Similarly, I accept every single item in my morality—that is inevitable—but I am sure that my morality could be improved, which is to say that it could undergo changes which I should be glad of once I had made them. So I must try to keep my morality open to revision, exposing it to whatever valid pressures there are—including pressures from my sympathies.

I don't give my sympathies a blank check in advance. In a conflict between principle and sympathy, principles ought sometimes to win. For example, I think it was right to take part in the Second World War on the allied side; there were many ghastly individual incidents which might have led someone to doubt the rightness of his participation in that war; and I think it would have been right for such a person to keep his sympathies in a subordinate place on those occasions, not allowing them to modify his principles in such a way as to make a pacifist of him.

Still, one's sympathies should be kept as sharp and sensitive and aware as possible, and not only because they can sometimes affect one's principles or one's conduct or both. Owen, at any rate, says that feelings and sympathies are vital even when they can do nothing but bring pain and distress. In another poem he speaks of the blessings of being numb in one's feelings: "Happy are the men who yet before they are killed/Can let their veins run cold," he says. These are the ones who do not suffer from any compassion which, as Owen puts it, "makes their feet/Sore on the alleys cobbled with their brothers." He contrasts these "happy" ones, who "lose all imagination," with himself and others "who with a thought besmirch/Blood over all our soul." Yet the poem's verdict goes against the "happy" ones. Owen does not say that they will act worse than the others whose souls are besmirched with blood because of their keen awareness of human suffering. He merely says that they are the losers because they have cut themselves off from the human condition:

> By choice they made themselves immune
> To pity and whatever moans in man
> Before the last sea and the hapless stars;
> Whatever mourns when many leave these shores;
> Whatever shares
> The eternal reciprocity of tears.

Study Questions

1. Describe Hobbes's version of social contract theory.
2. According to Hobbes, what sort of life would we have without a social contract?

3. In Rawls's version of social contract theory, what is the "veil of ignorance"?
4. What is cultural relativism? What are the main objections to cultural relativism?
5. What is distinctive about virtue ethics, compared with most other contemporary ethical theories?
6. According to virtue ethics, how does my character develop?
7. Describe some of the key challenges to virtue theory.
8. What is contemporary moral realism? How does it compare with traditional moral realism?
9. Compare and contrast care ethics with more traditional ethical theories, such as Kantian or utilitarian theories.

Exercises

1. You do biological research at a major university, with a joint appointment at the medical school and in the department of biology. You have carried out many valuable research projects, and your work is well respected in the research community. You're not in line for a Nobel prize, but your research is certainly of high quality. Unfortunately, budgets are very tight: The state has made substantial cuts in funding for both the university and the medical school, there are fewer research grants available from the government and private institutions, and, as a result, your research budget has been badly squeezed. You have several excellent graduate students you would like to fund as research assistants next year, but unless more funds are made available soon, you will not be able to fund them. Then, to the delight of you and your research colleagues, you get a visit from a representative of a major pharmaceutical company that is in the final stages of developing a new drug for the treatment of rheumatoid arthritis. The company wants your department to do a major research study on the effectiveness of the drug. The study will take a couple of years, you will need to hire a number of research assistants, and the funding is *very* generous: You and your colleagues and your graduate students will be well paid, and the laboratory will be able to purchase some valuable new equipment. Everything sounds fine, until the pharmaceutical representative hands over the research contract. There's a clause in the contract that gives the pharmaceutical company control over the publication of your research on the project. If everything goes well, and the results are positive, they will allow the results to be published. But if your research indicates that the drug doesn't work or that the side effects are worse than the benefits—well, in that case, the company could decide just to file your study and never allow it to be released. You balk at that clause: "Look, we are a university research team. We believe in openness of scientific research. The results, whether good, bad, or indifferent, should be available to the entire research community. The honest sharing of research results is one of the basic values of scientific research."

"Look, Professor," the pharmaceutical representative replies, "we will fund this research very generously. But we *must* have the right to veto the publication of any negative results from your research. It's a standard part of the contract, and there are plenty of universities conducting medical research under exactly these conditions. Besides, it's unlikely to be an issue: We think this is an excellent drug and our preliminary tests have all been positive, so it's very probable that your team will find positive results and they will be published openly and everyone will be happy. But we cannot work with you without this veto clause. If you can't agree to it, we'll have to take our research funding to some other university. Think it over."

When the pharmaceutical representative leaves, the research team gathers together to discuss the proposal. Your colleague, Professor Bryant, is strongly in favor of accepting the veto, signing the contract, taking the much-needed research money, and carrying out the research. "Look," your colleague says, "I don't like this veto clause any more than you do. It's wrong, and it violates the ethics of science. But here's the deal: If we turn this down, we all know that there are plenty of other excellent university research facilities that will be delighted to accept this grant, sign the veto contract, and do the research. So taking a principled stand on this issue won't change a thing —except that many of our graduate students won't have research funding for next year. The point is, if we don't do it, someone else will. So I say we should sign the contract."

How would a Kantian respond to that argument? A utilitarian? A virtue theorist? How would *you* respond?

2. Chapter One contains a discussion of the fallacy of appeal to ignorance and of how the burden of proof should be placed. In the controversy between moral objectivists and moral *non*objectivists, who bears the burden of proof? "It's the *objectivist* who bears the burden of proof; after all, the objectivist is claiming the existence of objective moral truths, so it is up to him or her to prove the assertion." "No, the burden of proof should be on the *non*objectivist, for it's the nonobjectivist who is making a very special claim: Contrary to all our traditions, basic beliefs, and long-term common sense, the nonobjectivist is claiming that there is *no* objective basis to our many moral and value assertions." Which side is right? Where should the burden of proof rest?

3. The years go by. Selina and Ben are now married, with children. But of course, they are still arguing with each other, and now one of their arguments is over the best way to raise their children. They basically *agree* on what sorts of values they want their children to develop: They want them to be courageous, inquisitive, kind to others, committed to making the world a better place, patient, and hardworking. But they have some basic disagreements about *how* they go about promoting such values in their children. Give some specifics as to how they might disagree on raising their kids.

4. You are a nephrologist—a kidney specialist—and you often help your patients who need kidney transplants. You do not perform transplant surgery, but you determine whether patients are appropriate candidates for kidney transplants, and you carefully check to make sure that a proposed transplant organ is a good match. Unfortunately, there is a great shortage of kidneys available for transplant, and many people who need transplants die on the waiting list. Your patient, Barbara, age 25, has been on dialysis for several years. While

she is not in immediate danger of dying, her quality of life would be greatly improved by a kidney transplant, and in your professional judgment, a kidney transplant would restore her to excellent health, with the full expectation of a long and healthy life. Even though Barbara is on the waiting list for a transplant, her chance of receiving a kidney during the next two years is no more than one in three. Barbara's father, Edward, asks if he can be tested as a possible kidney donor for his daughter. Edward knows that close relatives are more likely to be good tissue matches, and Edward, who is 45, is in good health, and both of his kidneys are in good condition. Many people donate one of their kidneys to a relative while still alive and continue in perfect health for the rest of their natural lives. Of course, some time is required for recovery from the transplant surgery, but no lasting effects on Edward are likely. You have participated in a number of living-donor kidney transplants, with great success, and you think that Edward's decision to be tested as a possible living donor for his daughter is an excellent idea. Edward has asked that no one else be told that he is having the tests done—he doesn't want to get his daughter's hopes up, in case he is not a good match—and you agree to honor his confidentiality.

The day comes, and you run the tests on Edward. Edward and Barbara are not a good tissue match, and Edward cannot be a kidney donor for Barbara; sadly, you inform Edward of that result. However, there is something else that you have discovered from the tissue tests: Edward is not Barbara's biological father. Should you inform Edward of that result as well? Does he have a right to know? A right not to know?

Next, think back to *how* you proceeded in reaching your answer to the preceding questions. Was there a particular approach to ethics that you made use of? Utilitarian? Kantian? Virtue theory? Humean? Or what?

What ethical decision do you think a *utilitarian* would make on this issue? A *Kantian?* If you were the doctor, how would you answer if you applied a *virtue* theory approach? (Obviously, there may be room for disagreement on these questions.)

5. The great British dramatist George Bernard Shaw once said that "Virtue consists, not in abstaining from vice, but in not desiring it." Would you agree or disagree? Of the ethical theories considered in this chapter and the previous one, which theory do you think would come closest to agreeing with Shaw? Which one would most likely disagree?

Glossary

Cultural relativism: The ethical theory which asserts that ethical principles are relative to cultures; what is right or wrong is determined by the individual culture and practices and will differ from culture to culture.

Moral realism: In its contemporary form, the view that objective moral facts will prove to be the best possible explanation for our experiences of moral phenomena.

Social-contract theory: A type of ethical or political theory that starts from the perspective of what system of rules or ethical principles would be favored by those drawing up a mutual agreement for governing themselves.

State of nature: In social-contract theory, the mythical situation prior to any social contract; in Hobbes's theory, a state of war of all against all, with no rights or rules.

Veil of ignorance: In John Rawls's social-contract theory, what prevents those drawing up the agreement from devising rules designed to favor their own situation; those behind the veil of ignorance are referred to as being in the "original position."

Virtue theory: An approach to ethics that focuses on the character of the ethical actor and how good character develops, rather than on duties, rules, and determination of the right act in a specific situation.

Additional Resources

The classic sources for social-contract theory are Thomas Hobbes's *Leviathan,* John Locke's *Second Treatise on Government,* and Jean-Jacques Rousseau's *Social Contract (Du Contrat Social). Leviathan* is available from Bobbs-Merrill (Indianapolis: 1958); it was originally published in 1651. The *Second Treatise on Government* was originally published in 1690; an accessible edition is, again, Bobbs-Merrill's (Indianapolis: Library of Liberal Arts, 1952). The *Social Contract* was originally published in 1762; it can be found in an edition edited by R. Masters (New York: St. Martin's Press, 1978).

Discussions of social-contract-theory tradition include Jean Hampton, *Hobbes and the Social Contract Tradition* (Cambridge, U.K.: Cambridge University Press, 1986); and P. Riley, *Will and Political Legitimacy: A Critical Exposition of Social Contract Theory in Hobbes, Locke, Rousseau, Kant, and Hegel* (Cambridge, MA: Harvard University Press, 1982).

Probably the best-known philosophical book of the late 20th century presented an updated version of social-contract theory: John Rawls, *A Theory of Justice* (London: Oxford University Press, 1971). For comments on the book, see *Rawls: A Theory of Justice and Its Critics,* edited by Chandran Kukathas and Philip Pettit (Stanford, CA: Stanford University Press, 1990), as well as *The Idea of a Political Liberalism,* edited by Victoria Davion and Clark Wolf (Lanham, MD: Rowman and Littlefield, 2000). David Gauthier's version of contractarian theory can be found in *Morals by Agreement* (Oxford, U.K.: Oxford University Press, 1986) and *Moral Dealing* (Ithaca, NY: Cornell University Press, 1990). For discussions and critiques of Gauthier's theory, see Peter Vallentyne, ed., *Contractarianism and Rational Choice* (New York: Cambridge University Press, 1991).

The classic source for virtue ethics is Aristotle's *Nicomachean Ethics.* Perhaps the most influential contemporary book on virtue theory is by Alasdair MacIntyre, *After Virtue* (Notre Dame, IN: University of Notre Dame Press, 1981). An excellent exposition of contemporary virtue theory is found in Edmund Pincoffs, *Quandaries and Virtues* (Lawrence, KS: University of Kansas Press, 1986).

An intriguing brief case for virtue theory is presented by novelist and philosopher Iris Murdoch in *The Sovereignty of Good* (New York: Schocken Books, 1971), though Murdoch's work encompasses a great deal more than just a defense of virtue theory. Other influential accounts of virtue theory include Philippa Foot, *Virtues and Vices* (Berkeley, CA: University of California, 1978) and Michael Slote, *Goods and Virtues* (New York: Oxford University Press, 1984), and *From Morality to Virtue* (New York: Oxford University Press, 1992). Major recent works in the virtue theory tradition are Philippa Foot, *Natural Goodness* (Oxford, U.K.: Oxford University Press, 2001); Rosalind Hursthouse, *On Virtue Ethics* (Oxford, U.K.: Oxford University Press, 1999); and Michael Slote, *Morals from Motives* (Oxford, U.K.: Oxford University Press, 2000).

Carol Gilligan, *In a Different Voice: Psychological Theory and Women's Development* (Cambridge, MA: Harvard University Press, 1982), had a powerful impact on the contemporary development of care ethics. Nel Noddings's work has been influential in both philosophy and education; see her *Caring: A Feminine Approach to Ethics and Moral Education* (Berkeley, CA: University of California Press, 1984) and *Educating Moral People: A Caring Alternative to Character Education* (New York: Teachers College Press, 2002). Annette C. Baier is a clear and cogent writer on this topic, who is particularly insightful in placing care ethics in a larger philosophical perspective. See her *Moral Prejudices* (Cambridge, MA: Harvard University Press, 1994). Among the best advocates of care ethics is Lawrence A. Blum, *Friendship, Altruism and Morality* (London: Routledge & Kegan Paul, 1980). Virginia Held's edited collection *Justice and Care* (Boulder, CO: Westview Press, 1995) is an excellent collection of essays on the subject. A very good and wide-ranging anthology is Eva Feder Kittay and Diana T. Meyers, eds., *Women and Moral Theory* (Totowa, NJ: Rowman & Littlefield, 1987).

Geoff Sayre-McCord, *Essays on Moral Realism* (Ithaca, NY: Cornell University Press, 1988) is a superb anthology, bringing together many of the best papers on moral realism. Another excellent anthology—that discusses moral realism and a great deal more—is David Copp and David Zimmerman, eds., *Morality, Reason and Truth: New Essays on the Foundations of Ethics* (Totowa, NJ: Rowman & Allanheld, 1984). One of the best and clearest accounts of moral realism is a paper by Peter Railton in *The Philosophical Review* (volume 95, 1986: 163–207). An excellent book-length study of moral realism is David O. Brink's *Moral Realism and the Foundations of Ethics* (Cambridge, U.K.: Cambridge University Press, 1989).

For social-contract theory and other topics, visit Paul Leighton's website at *www.paulsjusticepage.com*. Professor Leighton is a criminologist and sociologist at Eastern Michigan University, and his interests are wide ranging. A good resource for more information on John Rawls can be found at Policy Library, at *www.policylibrary.com/rawls*.

Helpful discussions and lectures on virtue theory can be found at Jan Garrett's home page at *www.wku.edu/~jan.garrett/ethics/virtthry.htm* and at the Paideia Project On-Line at *www.bu.edu/wcp/Papers/TEth/TEthcafa.htm*.

Among the excellent sites on care ethics and feminist ethics are the Feminist Theory Website at *www.cddc.vt.edu/feminism/eth.html* and Feminist Ethics Links at *www.unf.edu/~mgillis/femeth.htm*.

An interesting survey of moral realist views in a paper by M. Y. Chew is available at *www.bu.edu/wcp/Papers/TEth/TEthChew.htm.* For a brief biography of Michael Smith (a leading writer on moral realism), an extensive list of his publications, and an excellent selection of recent papers and works in progress that are available online, go to *philrsss.anu.edu.au/~msmith.*

Notes

1. Thomas Hobbes, *Leviathan*, 1651, part 1, chapter 13.
2. Daniel Callahan, in "The Abortion Debate," in *Abortion: Understanding Differences*, edited by Sidney Callahan and Daniel Callahan (New York: Plenum Press, 1984), p. 294.
3. Michael Ruse, *Taking Darwin Seriously* (Oxford, U.K.: Basil Blackwell, 1986), p. 263.
4. Michel de Montaigne, *Essays*, book 2, Chapter 11 (1580).

Chapter *10*

Political Philosophy

in which three friends distribute the wealth

"Ben, how can you possibly *say* that? Health care isn't just something nice: Without decent health care, people suffer. Conditions that could have been treated early and effectively become chronic and untreatable, and the result is complete debilitation. Without decent health care, people *die*—little *children* die from diseases that should have been prevented."

Selina's voice was genuinely outraged. This wasn't the playful enthusiasm heard in most of her disputes with Ben, but the sound of Selina truly upset. Sarah slid into a seat next to the two of them, in hopes of averting a major conflict. Selina immediately turned to her. "Can you believe this? You think you *know* a man; you don't know him. Ben actually opposes universal health care! What other enlightened political views do you hold, Ben? Should we repeal the voting rights act? Maybe reverse the emancipation proclamation?"

Individual Freedom

"Wait a minute, Selina, that's not fair," said Ben. "I don't believe the government should provide universal health care, that's true. But that doesn't mean I want to deny basic rights. Exactly the contrary: Basic individual rights are the very heart of my belief. Of course I don't support slavery: It was abominable, a terrible wrong, a profound evil, the most fundamental violation of basic human rights. And I think any form of discrimination is wrong: Women should have the same rights to run for office and vote and run corporations as men do; and so should African-Americans, of course—and homosexuals as well. Don't start accusing me of some stupid prejudice that I'm not guilty of. I have enough real faults without you adding imaginary ones. I believe in basic individual rights. There should be absolutely no difference between the rights of men and women, gays and straights, blacks and whites. I don't care if you're white or black or yellow or red or blue or green, you should have the right to live your life as you wish, so long as you don't harm others. And the same applies to homosexuals. If homosexuals wish to marry, that's their business, and it's wrong to deny homosexuals the rights held by heterosexuals. What homosexuals do is their own business. What heterosexuals do is *their* own business. It's as my grandfather used to say: I don't care what you do, so long as you don't do it in the streets and frighten the horses. Whether I happen to like homosexual marriage doesn't matter: If it doesn't harm anyone else, then people should be free to do as they wish. I don't like Selina's atheism, but so long as she doesn't try to force me to follow her beliefs, she's free to believe as she wishes. I think Sarah is probably corrupting her mind and perhaps endangering her soul through the study of philosophy; but any harm she does is to herself, not to others, so she should be free to hold and preach any views she favors. I believe in freedom— maximum freedom for everyone—so long as it does not infringe upon the rights and freedoms of others, so long as it causes no harm to others. If I claim the freedom to exclude blacks or Jews or homosexuals from my public restaurant, then that 'freedom' *does* harm others and it is not a legitimate exercise of freedom. But no harm, no foul: Play on, brothers and sisters, play on."

"Whoa, I think you touched a nerve there, Selina." Sarah smiled. "Old Ben got downright eloquent!"

"Alright, I apologize. I was guilty of a straw-man fallacy, right, Sarah? I distorted Ben's position: He's opposed to universal health care, not to individual liberty. But it's not entirely my fault! I was in shock. Ben, I still can't believe you don't support health care for everyone. How can you believe it's okay for people to be without health care? What about your Christian principles, Ben? What was it Jesus said? 'Come, ye blessed of my Father, For I was an hungred, and ye gave me meat: I was thirsty, and ye gave me drink: I was a stranger, and ye took me in: Naked, and ye clothed me: I was sick, and ye visited me.' Isn't that the teaching, Ben? That's the way I heard it back in the Birmingham Solid Rock Holiness Church. Maybe you should read that Bible you carry around. I'm not a Christian, as you well know; but I agree with Jesus on that: We have an obligation to take care of the sick and hungry and homeless. It's just wrong not to care for the sick; and it's especially wrong for a country as rich as the United States to leave people without health care. It's a national disgrace and a moral shame."

"Look, Selina," Ben replied, "I believe in helping the poor—providing clothing and shelter and medical care to the poor. But that is my free *choice*, and the government should not impose it on me. That's the point where we differ. But it's an important point: It's the difference between my helping freely, of my own free and responsible choice, and my being compelled to contribute to the welfare of others. I believe no one should be prevented by law from doing something, so long as they don't harm others. Obviously, I can be constrained from driving a hundred miles an hour through downtown, since that poses great risks to others; but if I want to drive a race car on a private track and risk my neck doing so, it's no one's business but my own. Same thing for smoking cigarettes—or marijuana, for that matter—so long as I don't inflict my secondhand smoke on others or place others at risk by driving while I'm impaired. And no one should be compelled to do things except when they have agreed by a mutually beneficial contract. If I wish to help others who are in no position to help me—and I strongly believe that that *is* a morally *good* thing to do—then that's another matter altogether. But no one should be able to *impose* their moral standards of what is good on me, except insofar as they can show that not following those standards will harm others."

"A classic statement of John Stuart Mill's position on liberty," said Sarah. "You express it well, Ben."

"Yeah, it's a beautiful statement of a repulsive position," Selina responded. "No obligation to anyone other than yourself. If you help others, it's a bonus, not an obligation: Give a crust of bread to a beggar or medicine to a sick child, you deserve a medal. No thanks: That seems a narrow and selfish view of obligation to me."

"You're among friends, Selina; you can tell us what you really feel about Ben's view. Don't mince words." Sarah laughed, then shook her

---

The temporal goods which God grants us, are ours as to the ownership, but as to the use of them, they belong not to us alone but also to such others as we are able to succor out of what we have over and above our needs. Hence Basil says "If you acknowledge them [your temporal goods] as coming from God, is He unjust because He apportions them unequally? Why are you rich while another is poor, unless it be that you may have the merit of good stewardship, and he the reward of patience? It is the hungry man's bread that you withhold, the naked man's cloak that you have stored away, the shoe of the barefoot that you have left to rot, the money of the needy that you have buried underground: and so you injure as many as you might help."

St. Thomas Aquinas, *Summa Theologica*, II-II, Question 32, article 5

---

head. "I'm not sure I can find much common ground on this one. You two are at opposite poles of a very old debate. Why am I not surprised? Still, I enjoy tilting at windmills and pursuing hopeless quests: Why else would I be a philosophy major? So look, Ben, what is it you really value about this position that you champion? What's the basic value at its foundation?"

"Pure selfishness and self-congratulation and greed, obviously," Selina interjected.

"Not at all," Ben shook his head. "This isn't a selfish view. It's a view that maximizes freedom—not just for me, obviously, but for everyone. And it doesn't spurn generosity. To the contrary, it allows generosity to flower and flourish, in the only way it can: when it is freely given, rather than compelled."

"It's a view that tells the haves that they have no obligation to the have-nots; and if they hand out a few crumbs, they are being kind and generous and going beyond what duty demands," Selina answered. "Sounds like selfishness to me."

"You're casting Ben's position in an awfully harsh light, Selina," Sarah was still trying to be a peacemaker. "Try to see it from the most positive perspective. After all, Ben is not a selfish person. Some people who advocate this view may well be; but Ben is not, and you know it. So what is the positive perspective on Ben's view?"

"Okay," Selina answered, still reluctantly; "It's a celebration of individual freedom. Still seems to me a distorted perspective on freedom, a gross exaggeration of freedom. It's freedom from obligation, freedom to take what you want, and everyone else be damned. We have some obligations we never chose: You don't choose to be obligated to your parents and your family, but you do have such obligations."

"Alright, alright," Sarah said, "I gather you don't like the view. But focus on the positive for just a moment. Ben wants individual freedom; that's one of his basic values, that's what motivates this position. And individual freedom is a good thing, right? You would agree with that, wouldn't you?"

"Yeah, sure, let freedom ring," Selina answered. "I believe in free speech and freedom of religion—or freedom *from* religion if that's your choice. And I think marijuana should be legal, along with tobacco and alcohol and skydiving. I find smoking cigarettes repulsive, but people should be free to smoke—so long as I don't have to breathe it. But there's more to life than just the freedom to do what you want. That's an awfully narrow and depressing and selfish outlook."

"Of course there's more to life than just freedom to do what you want," Ben answered; "lots more. Probably the most important things in life. But we're not talking personal ethics here; this is a question of political structure, of the *rules* that govern a society. And at that level, maximum liberty and minimum obligation is the best policy."

Negative Liberty

"Okay, Ben," Sarah said, "you favor a political philosophy that maximizes individual *liberty*. But what you want is a specific sort of liberty: *negative* liberty, rather than positive liberty."[1]

Ben frowned. "What do you mean, 'negative liberty'? I favor maximizing liberty for everyone; what's negative about that?"

"I didn't mean that your view is negative, Ben," said Sarah. "I was just making a distinction that political philosophers often draw between *negative* liberty and *positive* liberty. Negative liberty is basically the liberty to be left alone and to do as one wishes with one's own resources. It's a liberty of *noninterference*, so is called negative liberty. If you have negative liberty, then no one will interfere with your acts and choices, so long as you cause no harm to others. If you want to go hang gliding and risk injury to yourself, you are free to do so. If you want to blow ten grand in a casino, and it's your money, then roll the dice. If you want to blow a hundred grand on cosmetic surgery and a luxurious spa, then spend your money as you wish. No one will stand in your way. Use your time, energy, and resources as you see fit."

"And," Ben added, "if you want to spend your money feeding the poor or building a medical clinic for those with no medical care, you are also free to do that."

"Exactly right," Sarah agreed, "you are free to do as you wish, pursue the goals you choose. Freedom reigns for everyone. And that's surely a good thing: We like to be free from the interference of others, free to choose our own paths and set our own goals and worship as we please and study what we wish and pursue our own chosen ends."

"Hear, hear! Three cheers for negative freedom! Down with coercion and interference!" Ben lifted his coffee cup in salute.

"Oh, yeah, it's great," replied Selina. "Let's follow our own choices, enjoy our freedom, no interference. Where shall we stay this weekend? How wonderful to have free choices! Perhaps our apartment in Manhattan? Or our summer place at the lake? Maybe skiing at our chalet in

> *"It does me no injury for my neighbor to say that there are twenty gods or no god. It neither picks my pocket nor breaks my leg."*
>
> Thomas Jefferson

> *The law, in its majestic equality, forbids the rich as well as the poor to sleep under bridges, to beg in the streets, and to steal bread.*
>
> Anatole France, *The Red Lily* (1894)

Aspen? Or would you just prefer to stay home in our mansion? And to which prep school shall we send Buffy and Trevor? And where shall we dine? At our club or one of our favorite expensive restaurants? Or shall we just have our chef whip up something at home? And where shall I have my cosmetic surgery done? San Francisco? London? Or that lovely surgeon in Miami whom Sandra just adored? Such fun, such freedom. Except most people don't have the opportunity to make such choices. In fact, lots of people don't get many choices at all. They can't choose which college to attend, because they can't afford any of them. They can't choose what doctor to see, because they are minimum-wage workers with no insurance, and no doctor will see them. They can't choose a school for their children, because the only one available is a failing, crime-ridden school where most of the children drop out before graduating and most of the teachers have long since quit trying. No health care, no educational opportunities, no choices, no hope. But don't worry, no one will interfere with them: They can use their resources however they wish. Except they have no resources, they have no choices, and their 'freedom' is a sham."

> *There is no such thing as freedom in the abstract. . . . Whatever else the conception may imply, it involves a power of choice between alternatives, a choice which is real, not merely nominal, between alternatives which exist in fact, not only on paper.*
>
> R. H. Tawney, *Equality* (London: Allen & Unwin, 1931)

Positive Liberty

"Ah, yes," Sarah said, "and now we hear from the *positive* liberty perspective. Some people—such as Selina—argue that yes, freedom is great, but benign neglect is not the best means of promoting freedom. Suppose we tell the thousands of orphaned and impoverished slum children in Mexico

---

Not only is one's freedom extended by education, it is also restricted by 'mis-education'—by the inculcation of ideas and attitudes which reconcile one to existing circumstances or channel one's choices in certain specific directions. This will be partly a matter of direct and conscious manipulation, as in the form of political propaganda or commercial advertising, but partly a matter also of the unconscious acceptance of the prejudices and thought-patterns of one's own community. Consequently one's ability to make choices will require an ability to question and criticize the dominant attitudes; and that too is an ability which has to be fostered by the right kind of education.

Richard Norman, *Free and Equal*
(Oxford, U.K.: Oxford University Press, 1987), 48–49

The American people may be mistaken as to men and measures, but we are confident that in principle, they will all assent to the doctrine of equality. We feel confident of their unanimous support, when we say that all the members of the community should have, so far as society is concerned, equal chances. But equal chances imply equal starting points. Nobody, it would seem, could pretend that where the points of departure were unequal the chances could be equal. Do the young man inheriting ten thousand pounds, and the one whose inheritance is merely the gutter, start even? Have they equal chances? It may be said both are free to rise as high as they can,—one starting with ten thousand pounds in advance, and the other starting with the gutter. But it might as well be said the chances of the eldest son of the Duke of Newcastle, and those of the eldest son of one of the lowest of the Duke's tenants, are equal, since both unquestionably are free to rise as high as they can,—one starting with a dukedom in advance, and the other with nothing. But to pretend this is mere jesting.

Orestes Brownson, *Boston Quarterly Review* (October 1840)

City or Rio de Janeiro—or one of the impoverished children of Chicago or rural Mississippi, for that matter—that they are free to do as they wish, no one will interfere so long as they do not harm anyone, they can pursue whatever course they choose. Without decent health care and a good education and at least minimal resources, these children don't have any freedom open to them. If we value freedom, then negative freedom is often not enough: We must be sure that people have the resources and the opportunities to genuinely exercise freedom—the health care, the education, the encouragement, the confidence, the genuine opportunity to choose among open paths. Negative liberty is important; but without a commitment to positive liberty, the negative liberty will be of no use to many people."

"Alright, good point," Ben admitted. "But isn't there a danger that too much emphasis on *positive* liberty will wind up destroying *negative* liberty? After all, how do we obtain the resources to provide support for positive liberty? They have to come from the people who own those resources. And you've already said that just voluntarily donating such resources isn't enough: Since everyone should have the resources necessary to exercise liberty, the society has an obligation to make those resources available if possible. So those who have the resources will be *required*—by taxation, for example—to provide resources (education, health care, whatever) that can be transferred to others who need them when those resources are essential for the genuine exercise of liberty. But one very important *negative* liberty is the liberty to use your own resources as you wish, without interference, so long as you cause no harm to others. Promoting *positive* liberty seems to compromise the negative liberty to use my resources as I choose."

We are so accustomed to great social and economic inequalities that it is easy to become dulled to them. But if everyone matters just as much as everyone else, it is appalling that the most effective social systems we have been able to devise permit so many people to be born into conditions of harsh deprivation which crush their prospects for leading a decent life, while many others are well provided for from birth, come to control substantial resources, and are free to enjoy advantages vastly beyond the conditions of mere decency. The mutual perception of these material inequalities is part of a broader inequality of social status, personal freedom, and self-respect. Those with high income, extensive education, inherited wealth, family connections, and genteel employment are served and in many cultures treated deferentially by those who have none of these things. One cannot ignore the difficulties of escaping from this situation, but that is no reason not to dislike it.

Thomas Nagel, *Equality and Partiality*
(New York: Oxford University Press, 1991), p. 64

Selina was ready for battle. "Yeah, it does. So what? Suppose that a rich person is taxed to obtain resources to positively enhance the liberty of those who have no access to health care and education. That means the rich person's liberty suffers some interference: She is required to give up some of her resources, so she can't buy another diamond necklace; or he loses some of his wealth, so he can't afford to buy another BMW. Their liberty—their ability to do what they want with their resources, without any interference—is then compromised. But look carefully at that compromise: How do we most effectively *maximize* liberty? By letting the rich person make an additional free choice of a diamond necklace, or by providing an education and decent health care for a poor person? Without the new diamond necklace, the rich person still has *lots* of free choices: She can wear one of her old diamond necklaces, or wear her emeralds or her pearls. An additional bauble does not add much to her freedom. But the difference between having good educational opportunities and *not* having such opportunities makes an enormous difference in the scope of your free choice and opportunity. And the difference between having decent health care and no health care is a difference that may well keep a person healthy and fit, rather than chronically diseased and disabled; and that is a difference that makes a vast difference in personal freedom and opportunity. Anyone who promotes negative liberty out of a love of liberty (and negative liberty *is* worth promoting) should also favor a strong commitment to positive liberty, even if that involves some minor compromise of negative liberty."

Ben wasn't quite ready to retreat. "But if the state has the power to take some of my resources in order to promote positive liberty for others, isn't that a deeper threat to negative liberty than you might realize? After all, if the state has the power to take some of my resources, then what's to stop it from taking *all* my resources? So I could never be secure in my property, never be sure that I have the right to use my resources as I wish; and that would pose a major threat to my negative liberty."

Selina waved her hand and shook her head. "Come on, Ben, that's a bogus argument. Just because the state has the power to take some of your resources and use them to enhance the liberty of others doesn't mean that the state will then be likely to take *all* your resources. Look, the State now has the power to deprive you of liberty altogether, by locking you up in prison. But because the state uses that power in some limited circumstances doesn't mean that you must live in fear that any moment the state might arbitrarily confine you to prison. There's always the danger of governments becoming oppressive; that's why citizens must be vigilant. If we allow our government to lock up people without trials or access to a lawyer or even the right to have the charges against them made public, that endangers the liberty of us all. Of course, some people get so obsessed with hoarding wealth that being required to give up just a small portion of it for the benefit of others seems a terrible threat to their liberty. But those people are so enslaved to greed and their possessions that it seems unlikely that they have much freedom in any case."

"Still," Ben persisted, "doesn't this policy of promoting positive liberty deprive me of another important exercise of liberty? If society requires that I give up some of my wealth to enhance the liberty and opportunity and well-being of others, doesn't that deprive me of the opportunity to freely *choose* to share my goods with others who have greater needs?"

"Not at all," Selina answered. "You can still freely donate resources to help others. From the fact that society *requires* you to provide some of your resources to enhance the opportunities of others, it doesn't follow that you could not also freely choose to donate additional resources to those in need."

"Okay, suppose we agree there's a need for positive liberty in addition to negative liberty," Ben said. "How do we decide what distribution of resources is fair?"

Just Distribution of Resources

Sarah laughed. "Nice simple question, Ben. I'm sure we can resolve it while we finish our coffee."

"Maybe not a simple question, but it has a simple answer," Selina said. "The only fair system of distribution is egalitarian. Everyone's share should be roughly equal."

"Are you serious, Selina?" Ben shook his head. "It's always easy for me to know where I stand on any issue: Just figure out your view, and mine will be the precise opposite."

"My view is easy to locate, Ben," Selina said. "I just follow the teachings of Jesus: 'Sell all that you have, and give it to the poor.' Wasn't that his instruction? I know the television evangelists seem to get it confused— sell all that you have, and send the money to *me*—but the position of Jesus seems simple and clear: Share with others, don't hoard wealth, care for the poor and hungry and homeless, don't worry about the morrow. I'm not claiming that I live up to those principles, but they do seem to me a good policy. Perhaps you should read the teachings of Jesus, Ben; you might like them."

Ben rolled his eyes. "Thanks very much, Selina. Always nice to hear from the atheistic apostle."

Sarah intervened. "Look, we're back to that old distinction between what individuals *should* do, voluntarily, and what states should *require*. Selina, do you really believe that the government should enforce strict equality of resources among its citizens?"

"Well, no, not *exact* equality." Selina smiled. "Actually, I mainly wanted to take a shot at Ben; he's such a nice sexy target. But I do believe that at least *rough* equality of resources is a reasonably good guide to fair distribution."

"Once again, Selina, we line up on opposite sides," Ben responded. "Look, suppose I concede the point about opportunity: It's important that everyone have the goods that are basic for decent opportunity, for acting freely, for making their own choices."

"Merciful Heaven!" Selina raised her hands. "Did you hear that, Sarah? Ben actually changed his mind! It's a miracle. I'll admit *I* was wrong, too: There must be a God, miracles do happen!"

"Alright, alright, so I changed my mind. That's one more time than you've ever changed *your* mind, Selina."

"Well," Selina replied, "when you've discovered the truth, there's no virtue in pursuing error."

Sarah laughed. "And I thought *philosophers* were arrogant! We're not even in the same league with you chemistry majors."

"We historians are rational people," Ben said. "When we discover an inconsistency in our views, we alter them. You guys should try it some-time. Anyway, think about your own view, Selina, and *why* you believe in universal health care and universal education. Because those are essential to genuine opportunity and because they enhance freedom and opportunity, right?"

"Exactly so," Selina nodded.

Robert Nozick

"Well," Ben continued, "property rights also enhance freedom and opportunity. After all, private property gives us options and choices and freedoms we could not have otherwise. You have a home, and that gives you the freedom to enjoy privacy, not to mention a sense of security. You have books, and that makes it possible for you to carry out your studies and make plans for further studies. If those books could be taken away at any moment, you couldn't plan your research. Besides, through private property, you can carry out projects and plans and pursue goals that wouldn't otherwise be available. I want to write a fabulous history of colonial Latin America. I want to invest myself and my energies into that project, and I want it to be *my* accomplishment. Without respect for private property—including copyrights—that goal would make no sense. I could still write the book, but I couldn't keep my accomplishment. Suppose I want to build a larger house, or construct a beautiful garden, for myself and my family. Unless the property is my own, and I can have some security in that property, then that goal can't even get started, and that option is not open to me. Oh, sure, I can still plant a beautiful flower bed in a public park, and that's fine—that's a worthwhile project. But, without secure private property, some legitimate and valuable options and goals are closed off. If you value liberty, and the maximizing of open options and liberties, then you must also value private property. But if you insist on everyone having equal resources, then such goals become impossible. Suppose we all start with a small house and a shabby garden, and then Sarah—by the sweat of her brow and through her own ingenuity and effort—turns her garden into a beautiful oasis of serenity and transforms her house into a charming and comfortable multistory dwelling. Wait, we're no longer equal! Sarah has to give up one story of her addition to me and half her garden to you. But that's not fair: Sarah's labor is taken away from her, and her personal goals—in which she has invested so much of herself—are thwarted, and she is deprived of a very important part of her liberty. So fine, let's have universal health care and universal education: Those are essential for genuine opportunity. And I'll even go further: Let's have universal housing and make sure everyone is well fed and well housed. But not general equality of resources: That destroys freedom, rather than enhancing it."

Sarah raised her cup in salute. "That was well argued, Ben. In fact, it sounded a lot like an argument given by Robert Nozick, a famous political philosopher of the late 20th century. He believed that private property was essential to liberty and that, even if you started everyone off equal, there would soon be significant differences. Your example of making improvements to a house or garden—and thus upsetting equality—is good. Here's one from Nozick: Suppose everyone starts equal, with equal property and equal financial resources. But there's one person in our group who is particularly talented at something. Nozick's example is a famous basketball player, Wilt Chamberlain, whom many people enjoyed watching play. But you could make it a wonderful violinist, or dancer, or skater—whatever."

"How about a famous philosopher, someone people love to hear philosophize?" Selina smiled.

"That's the best example yet, Selina!" Sarah clapped. "Suppose there's this great philosopher, and we all want to hear her philosophize. So we each pay the philosopher a dollar, each out of our own legitimate property that we can freely use as we individually wish, to watch this wonderful philosophical display. That's perfectly fair, right? No one is forced to pay, and, of course, the philosopher isn't compelled to philosophize. And allowing such transactions surely enhances liberty: Those who freely *choose* to pay a dollar for the philosophical performance can do so, and those who have no taste for philosophy can follow their own preferences. In fact—as Nozick points out—*denying* us the opportunity to spend our resources in this manner would be a basic *violation* of our liberty—what he calls the forbidding of 'capitalist acts between consenting adults.' But now notice what happens: We all act freely, both the brilliant philosopher and her audience; but as a result of this free liberty-enhancing transaction, the philosopher will wind up with considerably more than others. Suppose everyone starts with a thousand dollars, a situation of perfect equality, and a thousand people now freely give one dollar to the performing philosopher. Well, the philosopher suddenly has *two* thousand dollars, twice as much as anyone else. So *freedom* upsets equality, and the only way to maintain equality would be by a repressive system of denying free acts and free choices."

"Exactly!" Ben agreed, "You don't have to be some sort of coldhearted, greedy Scrooge to have respect for property. Property rights are important protections for our basic liberties."

Selina shook her head. "Sarah, you're on Ben's side on this issue?"

I know of no country, indeed, where the love of money has taken stronger hold on the affections of men and where a profounder contempt is expressed for the theory of the permanent equality of property.

Alexis de Tocqueville [speaking of the U.S.A.], *Democracy in America,* Part 1, Chapter 3 (1835)

"Actually, I was just presenting Nozick's view." Sarah frowned. "I think it's a complicated question. I'm not a strict egalitarian: It seems to me that trying to enforce even a close approximation of equal resources would involve a lot more interference in our lives than we want. But on the other hand, I don't see property rights as some sort of sacred highest principle. Private property is useful, as Ben notes. But there are other values that are also important. Freedom, for example. And while it's true that private property rights can help protect some of our liberties and choices, it is also important to ensure that—at least in an affluent society like our own—everyone has sufficient resources to secure housing and health care and education and at least a decent standard of life: If we really believe that freedom is important, then we should be sure that everyone has the resources to pursue their choices and opportunities. That's a point Ben already accepted. And of course, in order to do that, it will be necessary to redistribute at least some resources from the wealthy to those who have little or nothing, probably through some sort of tax system."

Encouraging Effort

"Okay," Ben agreed, "that sounds good. But one thing worries me: If we provide everyone with the basic necessities, won't that undercut any motivation to work? After all, if you're guaranteed decent housing, food, clothing, medical care, and education, then why work? Won't it encourage people not to work, not to exert any real effort?"

"That's an empirical question, Ben," Selina replied. "It can't be answered just by reasoning. But there is some strong psychological evidence available. In the first place, people generally don't avoid work. Under the right conditions, people usually enjoy working, they find it satisfying. Look, suppose someone offers to support you all your life, on the condition that you never do any productive work: You'll spend the rest of your life just sitting around. Would you accept that offer? Not many people would. Think about when you are putting in hard hours, completing a project you find worthwhile. You may be tired, but you also find it very satisfying. In fact, one of the best signs of severe depression is lethargy. You don't feel like doing anything: you just want to sit around, and it doesn't seem worth it to exert any effort. But that's not a *desirable* state; it's associated with great misery."

"Selina's right," agreed Sarah, "we know a lot about when and why people work. And when and why they do *not* want to work—typically, when they become hopeless and severely depressed. Placing people in desperate poverty is not the best way to encourage strong effort. To the contrary, such situations tend to promote a sense of helplessness, a sense that

---

It may be laid down as a general rule, with but few exceptions, that men are rewarded in an inverse ratio to the amount of actual service they perform. Under every government on earth the largest salaries are annexed to those offices which demand of their incumbents the least amount of actual labor either mental or manual. And this is in perfect harmony with the whole system of repartition of the fruits of industry, which obtains in every department of society. Now here is the system which prevails, and here is its result. The whole class of simple laborers are poor, and in general unable to procure anything beyond the bare necessities of life.

Orestes Brownson, 1840

---

things are outside one's effective control, a fatalistic resignation to one's unfortunate situation. Most persons who live in poverty *have* made efforts to escape their miserable situations, but their efforts have failed. In that situation, the lesson learned is that effort is useless: There's no escape and no hope, and there's nothing one can do about it. Poverty breeds hopelessness, not industry and fortitude."

"There's no deep mystery about what causes people to work hard," added Selina. "When work is rewarded effectively—with decent pay and benefits, and a satisfying work environment, and appropriate encouragement and opportunity for development and advancement—people eagerly work hard. Obviously, you can't set it up the way we do, in which working means sacrificing your health care and continuing to live in poverty, in a dead end job with no challenges or satisfaction. When decent jobs are offered, people wait in the cold for hours in hopes of getting one. If we want people to work—and take pleasure and pride in their work, which is a vital part of a satisfying life—then we must have environments that *reward* efforts. Dead-end jobs don't do that. Working long hours at exhausting jobs—as many impoverished persons do—while never getting decent health care or better living conditions and without any chance of advancing is exactly the environment to foster hopelessness and lethargy."

Unequal Wealth

"Alright," Ben agreed, "you've convinced me of the importance of good jobs, with living wages and decent benefits and opportunities for advancement and development. But that still leaves open some basic questions of the just distribution of resources. Let's agree that, in a wealthy society like our own, everyone should have a decent job with good pay and benefits, and everyone should be able to live comfortably with good health care and educational opportunities and retirement plans. But once a very decent basic standard of living is guaranteed for all, it still seems to me that it is legitimate for the society to have considerable differences in wealth. So long as everyone lives in a comfortable cottage, what's wrong with some people living in luxurious mansions? If my family can afford a vacation at the Jersey shore, what's wrong if some other family can afford to cruise the Riviera? So long as my kids and I can get afford to eat hot dogs in the bleachers, what's wrong with someone else eating caviar in a luxury box?"

"If you want to eat caviar and drink champagne in one of those luxury boxes," Selina said, "you'll have to watch the game without me. I'm a beer-and-bleachers sort of girl; anyway, that's where the real baseball fans sit."

"It was just an example, Selina," replied Ben. "Actually, I have no desire to sit in a luxury box at a baseball game: If you want to watch the game from inside, stay home and turn on your television. But I admit, sometimes I'd like seats on the third-base line, rather than high up in right field. But the point is, if everyone's basic needs are met, what's wrong with some people being significantly wealthier than others? For example, some people might want to work longer hours and accumulate greater wealth, and invest their wealth and become still wealthier; others might prefer to spend their leisure time discussing philosophy in coffee shops or going to baseball games, and are not so interested in becoming wealthy. Or some people might have special talents—a musician or an athlete or a surgeon or an inventor, for example—that enable them to accumulate significant wealth. If they make that sort of investment of their time and energy and talents, why shouldn't they receive special rewards? Rewards like that would encourage hard work and stimulate the economy, and no one is harmed. Taking away the fruits of their extra labor to enforce some arbitrary equality rule seems to me a serious violation of individual liberties."

Democracy and Wealth

Sarah shook her head. "Look, Ben, I agree with you that it would be silly—and very intrusive, as well—to enforce a universal standard of strict economic equality. But when you approve of vast differences in wealth and resources, I become uneasy. You say no one is harmed when some people become very wealthy—much wealthier than everyone else. I'm not sure that's true. A concentration of wealth is practically equivalent to a concentration of power. And that causes lots of problems. The most obvious is that when some people have a vastly disproportionate share of wealth, they can exert effective control over the media, over elections, and, ultimately, over government."

> *We can have a democratic society or we can have great concentrated wealth in the hands of a few. We cannot have both.*
>
> U.S. Supreme Court
> Justice Louis Brandeis

"Okay, Sarah," Ben answered, "concentrating wealth may cause problems, but let's not exaggerate them. Our government is elected by all our citizens, and the poorest laborer gets one vote, just like the richest CEO. That's the great advantage of democracy, which has thrived in American for well over two centuries."

Selina shook her head. "Ben, what's a democracy?"

Ben frowned. "Come on, Selina, you know perfectly well what a democracy is. You learned that in the first grade. America was founded on democratic principles: Every citizen gets the same equal vote, the same voice in choosing our government and our legislators."

Sarah smiled. "Sounds good to me. So when this country was founded, it was a democracy. Suppose it's 1790, and we have an election. You, Selina, and I would all get an equal vote, right?"

"Of course," Ben answered. "That's what democracy *means.*"

"But Ben," Sarah said gently, "perhaps you never noticed, but Selina and I are *girls.*"

"Okay, I see your point," Ben frowned. "Alright, that's true, women couldn't originally vote. In fact, they couldn't vote until 1920."

"Sorry to bother you with details," Sarah said, "but if half the citizens are not allowed to vote, that is *not* a democracy. Actually, it was well over half."

"Exactly so," Selina agreed. "Blacks couldn't vote, no matter what our gender. In fact, blacks were systematically—and brutally—excluded from voting booths in this country until late in the 20th century. And we haven't even mentioned all the obstacles that were set up to keep *poor* white males from voting—poll taxes, which weren't abolished until 1960, and property requirements, for example."

"Okay, you guys are right, of course," Ben replied. "You grow up hearing, from first grade on, how America was founded as a great democracy. Maybe in theory. But it certainly was not in practice. Still, hasn't it finally *become* a democracy?"

"Abraham Lincoln, in his Gettysburg Address, spoke of his fervent hope 'that government of the people, by the people, for the people, shall not perish from the earth.' But," Sarah continued, "when hundreds of millions of dollars are spent in presidential election campaigns, and tens of millions in Senate contests, it is clear that those with disproportionate wealth will have disproportionate control over the election process and thus over the government. In order to be a serious candidate for national office, you must have access to enormous sums of money. Thus, only those who receive the approval of the holders of wealth are eligible for office. Those who hold office need not be wealthy themselves—though, of course, most of our senators and presidents have been quite wealthy—but they must have the support and approval of the wealthy. That is not a democracy of the people, but rather an oligarchy run by and for a comparatively small wealthy elite. When that happens, you get the sort of government you might expect: Tax codes leave large loopholes that are tailored to let the very wealthy pay only a small amount in taxes or, in many cases, nothing at all. And the taxation burden falls more heavily on the middle class, which has little political power. Obviously, there are many more poor people in our country than wealthy; if this were really a democracy, run by and for the people, wouldn't there be more laws helping the poor and many fewer laws giving special benefits to the rich? The loss of self-government seems to me a very substantial harm, and it is a harm that follows from the concentration of wealth and power in the hands of the few. And that's not just a theoretical problem: In the United States, one-third of the wealth is held by the wealthiest one percent of the population, while the poorest forty percent altogether hold less than *one-third of one percent* of the wealth. Democracy is wonderful. I hope someday America becomes one. But if wealth continues to be more and more concentrated in the hands of an elite few, I fear that that day will never come."

"Okay," Ben answered, "I agree that concentration of wealth poses a threat to democracy, to government 'by the people.' But while it may pose a threat, it hasn't taken away our freedoms. After all, we still have our basic freedoms: freedom of speech, for example. I'm free to criticize the president and the Senate, and I'm free to advocate any law I favor or political candidate I support. I can freely say that I think the president is doing a lousy job and that his policies are fundamentally unfair, and I can take part in a demonstration against administration policies, without having to worry about the secret police coming for me in the night."

"That's basically true, Ben, and it's very important," Sarah agreed. "Being able to say what you wish, and speak freely, and protest against the actions of your government: that's a profoundly important freedom. I'm not quite as confident as you that those basic liberties are really safe and secure, though. There *are* some significant threats to your freedom of speech. For example, suppose you give a speech or write a letter to the editor of a newspaper raising questions about the safety of nuclear power plants, or the health effects of eating beef, or the risks from pesticide contamination of fruits and vegetables. That would seem to be a legitimate exercise of free speech, right? But be careful: If what you say offends those with money to throw around, they can file a libel suit against you and make you pay quite severely for your exercise of 'free speech.' For example, the wealthy can hammer you with libel and slander suits that effectively silence criticism. Remember when Oprah Winfrey talked on her show about the health problems that could result from eating beef? A bunch of Texas ranchers and meatpackers filed a lawsuit against her, sued her for damaging their business. When these wealthy ranchers and meatpackers attacked Oprah, she had the resources to fight back. Oprah has the wealth to hire a whole team of excellent lawyers, and she has the media power to make her views known. By the time the trial was over—and Oprah won—the Texas cattlemen were wishing they had never tangled with Oprah Winfrey. But if they had attacked you or me, they would have easily bankrupted us long before we got our day in court. That has a sobering effect on free speech and also on freedom of the press: Many publishers are afraid to publish anything critical of large corporations, for fear that they will be hit with an enormous and expensive and lengthy libel suit that—even if the publisher eventually wins—will drive the publisher into bankruptcy."

Ben frowned. "But Sarah, libel laws are not always bad things. If someone makes a vicious and unjustified attack on you and damages your reputation or your business or your employment prospects, surely you should have the right to fight back with a libel suit, shouldn't you? Suppose you're applying to graduate school in philosophy, and I write a letter to the graduate schools accusing you of plagiarizing all your papers, cheating on your GRE exam, stealing funds from the Fund for the Homeless, and forging your letters of reference. In that case, you would suffer severe damage: Your reputation would be trashed, graduate schools would reject you, and your career prospects would gutter out. Shouldn't you be able to bring libel charges against me and sue me for damages to your reputation and your career?"

"If you did something like that, Ben, I'd just turn those letters over to my friend Selina," replied Sarah. "She would do you a lot more damage than even the meanest libel lawyer I could possibly hire. But seriously, Ben, in that kind of case the use of libel laws is legitimate. I do have a right to protect my reputation and defend myself from your reckless and scurrilous charges. I scrape together my savings and hire a lawyer, and you do the same, and the contest is basically even. But when one side is enormously wealthy and the other is poor or even solidly middle class, the wealthy side can use that wealth like a hammer: not just to fight back, but to silence its critics, no matter what the merits of those critics' position. And when wealthy interests can get special laws passed—like the Texas 'veggie libel law' that was used in the suit against Oprah Winfrey—it has a very chilling effect on free speech. Go ahead and criticize, but it may cost you dearly, and the cards will be stacked against you when you go to court. If you're Oprah Winfrey, you may still win, but if you don't have enormous

Though the earth and all inferior creatures be common to all men, yet every man has a property in his own person; this nobody has any right to but himself. The labour of his body and the work of his hands we may say are properly his. Whatsoever, then, he removes out of the state that nature hath provided and left it in, he hath mixed his labour with, and joined to it something that is his own, and thereby makes it his property. It being by him removed from the common state nature placed it in, it hath by this labour something annexed to it that excludes the common right of other men. For this labour being the unquestionable property of the laborer, no man but he can have a right to what that is once joined to, at least where there is enough, and as good left in common for others.

John Locke, *Second Treatise of Civil Government*, paragraph 27

wealth and a nationwide television show on which to make your views known, then you might want to think twice about exercising your 'right of free speech,' since exercising that right may ruin you. So what's the moral of that story? When the distribution of wealth and resources in a society are grossly disproportionate, those with less may suffer bad consequences, even if their basic needs of housing and health care and food and transportation are met, and even if they have decent satisfying jobs. They may suffer bad consequences when the wealthier and more powerful groups use their massive resources to threaten the actual liberties of the less wealthy and to effectively exclude them from an equal voice in their government. Look, Ben, I'm not saying anything you don't already know. Do you suppose that you have as much voice in how your government is run as do the CEO of Halliburton and the head of Exxon and the president of General Motors?"

Property Rights

"Sadly not, Sarah," replied Ben. "Alright, it's obvious enough that great disparities of wealth can and do corrupt the political system. Still, property rights are not insignificant. There are dangers of abuse, certainly; but let's not throw out the baby with the bathwater."

"I'm not trying to throw out all property rights, Ben. I agree, they're valuable. And I don't buy the idea that we can just abolish private property and live in a peaceful, cooperative harmony of perfect sharing. I think one of the first

Many causes have ". . . divided mankind into parties, inflamed them with mutual animosity, and rendered them much more disposed to vex and oppress each other than to cooperate for their common good. . . . But the most common and durable source of factions has been the various and unequal distribution of property."

James Madison,
The Federalist, no. 10
(1787)

words I learned in play school was 'Mine!' And I still remember that great kick I gave Bobby Silvers when he tried to take away my bright-blue shiny police car with the flashing light and the wonderful siren. I scored three goals during my years of playing wing for the Jefferson Wildcats—I don't like to brag about my athletic accomplishments, but it's true—and none of those kicks gave me anything like the pleasure I derived from that great shot to Bobby Silvers's left shin. I got in trouble and had to sit in time-out, and my mother gave me a stern lecture; but nobody else tried to take away my shiny blue police car, not for the entire year. So okay, I believe in property rights. But they're not absolute rights, they're not sacred rights proclaimed by God, and there are times when we need limits on property rights. And one of those times is when one group begins to accumulate so much that they gain the power to corrupt the government and establish a very uneven playing field that is unfair for everyone else. For example, suppose that—by some legitimate means—you could get control of all the petroleum in the country. In that case, you could exert monopoly powers over the oil industry: All the people who need heating oil for their homes or gasoline for their cars or trucks would have to pay whatever price you named, and you would hold an enormous and unfair advantage. So even if you could gain control of the oil legally, it would be important—for the benefit of all the rest of us—that your monopoly power over oil be eliminated. And that's why we have laws against monopolies: That's why we place restrictions on private ownership. Private property rights are important, but they can be trumped by other rights and other goods. Opening the possibility for genuine democratic self-government is one such good that justifies limits on private property.

"Besides," Sarah added, "the whole notion of 'private property' is sort of tricky. We tend to start from the assumption that it makes perfectly good sense and that we all agree on what justifies the concept of private property; but when we actually try to figure out what it's based on, our notion of private property is not nearly so obvious. The legitimacy of property has always been a tricky question. The traditional answer was given by Locke: Something becomes your property when you 'mix your labor with it.' But even in Locke's day, that was problematic. Many nobles 'owned' enormous estates, though they certainly never mixed any of their labor with their land: That part was done by the peasants. When people—such as the Diggers—tried to take Locke's views literally, they soon learned that whatever theory might say, practice was quite different.

Ben's face brightened. "Yeah, the Diggers! They were an interesting group!"

*Gerrard Winstanley was a leader of the "Diggers" or "True Levellers," a group
who advocated land reform during the time of the English Revolution. In 1650,
Winstanley wrote these lines in one of his pamphlets, addressed to the lords of the
manors:*

> The power of enclosing land and owning property was brought into the
> creation by your ancestors by the sword; which first did murder their fellow
> creatures, men, and after plunder or steal away their land, and left this land
> successively to you, their children. And therefore, though you did not kill or
> thieve, yet you hold that cursed thing in your hand by the power of the sword;
> and so you justify the wicked deeds of your fathers.

From G. H. Sabine, editor, *The Works of Gerrard Winstanley*
(Ithaca, NY: Cornell University Press, 1941), pp. 251–2, 269

"Are you two talking some private language?" Selina was temporarily
lost. What are you talking about, the 'Diggers.' Sounds like some weird
philosophical movement."

"Well, in a way, I guess they were," Sarah answered. "A sort of
religious–philosophical–populist–agrarian movement that developed in
17th-century England. Philosophers don't talk about them much—though
I think we should. Anyway, Ben knows more about them than I do. Tell
Selina about the Diggers. And tell me, too, for that matter."

"Around the time of the English civil war, there were many peasants
who were starving. Much of the land was controlled by a few 'noble'
families, and there wasn't enough left for the poor people to grow food
for themselves and their families. They couldn't even go into the forests
and hunt, for those lands were also controlled by the nobility. Anyone
caught hunting would be arrested for poaching, and the penalties were
severe. Many people were roaming the countryside, looking for food
or work. They would come upon these huge
empty lands, where fields were lying barren,
not being farmed or used in any way. So the
'Diggers' would stake a claim to the land by
digging in it, cultivating it, improving it. They
argued that just because some Duke held a title
to land, that didn't give him the right to land
that he had no real use for, especially when others desperately needed the land to grow food.
Of course, they were beaten down and defeated,
but their movement left its mark on British
history."[2]

*Whenever there are in
any country unculti-
vated lands and unem-
ployed poor, it is clear
that the laws of property
have been so far ex-
tended as to violate nat-
ural right.*

Thomas Jefferson,
1785, Letter to
James Madison

"That whole idea of claiming property because one works it, improves it, 'mixes one's labor' with it: That goes way back," Sarah said. "And it has some plausibility. But if your great grandfather 'mixed his labor' with the land, and your grandparents and parents never cultivated the land or even lived on it, does it make sense that they can somehow now give this land to you? What right do you have to that land? We might make sense of claiming land by working on it, so long as there is always more land to be cultivated. And one could move west and start a homestead, though there was a real question about whether land that native American peoples had lived on and hunted and buried their dead in, but without drawing 'property lines' in the European sense, was simply available for the taking. If people are living on land and gaining their livelihood from it, but not 'improving' it, can it be claimed by others? Suppose this land has been our hunting grounds for many generations, but we have never 'improved' it: We like it the way it is and are glad to live in harmony with it. If you arrive with a plow or a roll of barbed wire, is it suddenly yours by right of your labor? Still, if there is land *no one* is using, and I cultivate it and build a house on it and mix my labor with it, then I have some claim to it. But if my great-grandfather cultivated it, and it has

> "... it's our land. We measured it and broke it up. We were born on it, and we got killed on it, died on it. Even if it's no good, it's still ours. That's what makes it ours—being born on it, working it, dying on it. That makes ownership, not a paper with numbers on it."
>
> John Steinbeck, *The Grapes of Wrath*, 1939

been handed down for several generations to people who have done nothing with the land— or perhaps rented it out to others, never again 'mixing their labor' with it—in what sense does the present 'owner' hold legitimate title to that land? People get around the problem by trying to trace ownership back to legitimate bequeathing or willing of the property from one person to another. But that's a rather silly myth. We all know that the process by which people acquired wealth in the past—the wealth that has been handed down to others—was perhaps in some measure by honest labor and ingenuity, but with a very substantial element of theft, chicanery, violence, bribery, corruption, and fraud—and sometimes, indeed, by wars of conquest, enslavement, and brutal mistreatment of victims of prejudice."

"Yeah, good point," Ben agreed. "Shall I tell you one of the dark secrets of my family? Goes back a few generations, to the Civil War, my great-great-great grandfather Ben. I was indirectly named after the old gentleman, since I was named after my grandfather, and he was named after the original Ben, my ancestor, the subject of this story. Anyway, this great patriarch of the Slater family was a Civil War hero who fought in

The assumptions Locke makes concerning the justifiable acquisition of property are almost never met in the contemporary world. The unowned wilderness waiting to be appropriated, so central to Locke's argument, no longer exists. Rarely do we simply mix our labor with nature. Nearly always we mix our labor with an economic system and an already developed industrial economy, and it makes little sense to think of the result as the outcome of our labor. A person cannot distinguish his or her labor from the other labor it is mixed with in producing a product or contributing to production. Furthermore, the service sector of the economy does not fit the depiction, nor does the labor involved in raising the next generation of workers.

Virginia Held, "Property and Economic Activity," *Rights and Goods*
(Chicago: University of Chicago Press, 1989), p. 173

several battles, was wounded twice, and came back to the warm reception of his hometown. That's the myth, and that's the way we record it in the Slater genealogy. Well, in fact, he did come back to a warm reception from his hometown: a very warm reception. Turns out that my distinguished old ancestor was a bounty jumper during the Civil War. The Union was having trouble recruiting soldiers, so they started paying a rather substantial bonus to new recruits. That sounded good to great-granddaddy Ben, so he signed up, went off to war. He discovered he didn't much care for war. Didn't mind sitting around the campfire singing songs and playing cards, but he did not like the part where you lined up and marched across a field and people shot at you. When he got wounded in the leg, he was sent home to recuperate. Come time to return, he just sort of disappeared: had his wife send a letter to the captain saying that he had developed an infection in his leg and had died from his wound. Well, that was fine, Ben sort of laid low for awhile—he wasn't the first soldier who failed to go back, and nobody in town thought much about it—but then he started missing the good times around the campfire and decided he would return. But he couldn't go back under his old name, so he just went to another town and signed up under a new name—and collected another handsome bonus. After a few months, about the time Ben's unit was marching in the general direction of some very loud and frightening cannon fire, Ben recollected why it was he had not enjoyed the army that much; so as they marched through a wooded area, he slipped away to the side, through the trees, left his rifle and discarded his uniform, and headed home. But with the war still going on, times were hard and money was short. Great Granddaddy Ben soon figured out—he was a rather bright fellow, my old ancestor, if not entirely scrupulous—that the easiest way to collect a nice payday was to sign up for the army. So he headed to another town, joined another volunteer unit, and received another bonus. Fact is, he apparently signed up for five units, collected five bonuses, and deserted five times. But word finally got around what was going on—he had run into a couple of boys from his earlier units when he was marching with his new units, and they didn't buy his story about getting wounded and then attached to a new unit to help train the raw recruits—and when he came back home after the war, some of the veterans wanted to hang him as a deserter. Turns out old Ben's brother, my uncle from many generations back, had been a genuine war hero, and he was highly respected, and he managed to rescue his brother Ben just before they got the noose around his neck. But anyway, the point of that sordid story is this: The money that my ancestor Ben got from all those bonuses was used to buy a very nice farm; and that farm supported our family quite decently for many generations and provided the funds for my father to go to law school, and his legal practice now pays my college tuition. But the origins of our family fortune—such as it is—lie in ill-gotten gains. So, is all the money from my father's law practice (which he would not have had if the income from the farm had not financed his law school education) illegitimate? And when I get my history degree, also paid for from the very same source, will the megabucks I make as a history professor be tainted and not genuinely mine?"

"My family history offers a different twist on Ben's story," Selina said. "Go back all those generations to Ben's great-grandfather and then several generations beyond that. My ancestors were working in the cotton fields of Alabama and the sugarcane fields of south Louisiana and the cornfields of Mississippi: they built those plantations, and they grew the crops, and they created the wealth. But their labor was stolen from them, coerced from them with whips and guns. All the people who derived their fortunes from that stolen labor, and all their ancestors who continue to derive the benefits of that accumulated wealth—are their holdings now legitimate? If the roots of the property are rotten, is the fruit that it bears several generations later still corrupted?"

"It's a sad story, isn't it, Selina?" Sarah continued. "My family have been merchants in New York for many generations. The dark family secrets stay hidden away, and they don't get passed on to the next generation; but the profits do. Still, I'm confident that you wouldn't have to trace our history back too far before you would find some marks in the family financial books that we're not too proud of: an official paid off for a sweetheart insurance contract, a brother cheated out of his inheritance, a shipment of overpriced and underquality uniforms that Ben's great-grandfather might have worn. The money trails and the property accumulation are not as sweet and pure as the private-property myth suggests.

And everybody knows it—but that doesn't prevent people from pretending otherwise to make the story about property work." Sarah stopped to look through a book she had fished out of her book bag, found the right passage, then continued. "Robert Nozick, the philosopher we were discussing before; this is from one of his most influential books, *Anarchy, State, and Utopia:*

> A distribution is just if it arises from another just distribution by legitimate means. The legitimate means of moving from one distribution to another are specified by the principle of justice in transfer. The legitimate first "moves" are specified by the principle of justice in acquisition. Whatever arises from a just situation by just steps is itself just.

Fine so far, but there's a glaring problem in using this as a model of any actual distribution of goods, as Nozick recognizes:

> Some people steal from others, or defraud them, or enslave them, seizing their product and preventing them from living as they choose, or forcibly exclude others from competing in exchanges. None of these are permissible modes of transition from one situation to another. And some persons acquire holdings by means not sanctioned by the principle of justice in transfer.

A major problem for his proposed model of just distribution, when it is applied to the actual world, right? So what's the solution? Nozick candidly admits: "I do not know of a thorough or theoretically sophisticated treatment of such issues." But he suggests that we might formulate one, though he admits that his suggestion involves 'idealizing greatly.' And that's an understatement: Nozick suggests that what we should do is consider what the situation would have been had the injustice not occurred and then go on from there, making our best estimate of what would have happened in the absence of that initial injustice (and without any subsequent injustices), and see what sort of situation we would be in now, based on that initial revised scenario. If the likely result that would have followed without the injustice is different from our actual situation, then justice requires shifting resources to match the revised outcome."

"Oh, I get it, it's simple, really." Selina laughed. "All we have to do is figure out what sort of distribution of goods would have resulted if blacks had not been enslaved, if they had not been subject to beatings and lynchings in the years following, if their labor and their goods had not been stolen from them, if they had not been denied the right to vote, had not been forced into segregated ghettoes, had not been denied admission to colleges and graduate schools, had never been refused jobs or denied advancement because of racism; now project that over the years, and bingo, you wind up with a model of just distribution of resources. Give me a minute, I'll draw up the calculations now."

Sarah shook her head. "Okay, philosophers sometimes do have some rather implausible notions, I confess. You're right, of course: There's no way on Earth to make any such calculation, not even roughly. Take a much simpler case: the ill-gotten gains of Ben's old bounty-jumping great-grandfather. If we assume that the money he used to buy the farm was unjustly obtained, how could we possibly calculate the consequences of that over a period of generations? And that calculation is child's play compared with the one Selina is discussing: It doesn't involve prejudice, or violent intimidation by organized hate groups, or laws that institutionalized discrimination. But the point is, this goes to the very heart of the traditional account of just distribution of goods. At the core of the theory, the theory simply doesn't work: There's no way to plausibly suppose that either the initial acquisition of goods or their transfer met any plausible standard of justice. In some ideal world, such a model might make sense; but in a world of theft, slavery, fraud, bribery, violence, and prejudice, the traditional model of just distribution is hopeless."

Selina nodded. "Even the original idea of appropriating wealth—mixing your labor with some unimproved object to enhance its value—doesn't work very well—at least, not now. I mean, where do you see all these natural resources ready to be claimed, these tracts of land awaiting improvement by the first industrious person who decides to labor on them? And there's something else that bothers me about the traditional notion of individual property and the just distribution of goods."

Ben put up his hands in an appeal for mercy. "Come on, guys, you've just ripped the heart out of the traditional account of property. Can't you let it lie? Do you have to desecrate the corpse?"

Sarah laughed. "Selina, I'm afraid we've upset one of Ben's cherished beliefs. He'll spend the whole weekend worrying about whether his beat-up old Honda, with 190 thousand miles and a crumpled fender and rusted out back floorboard, is legitimately his own. Don't worry, Ben: No matter how unjustly your great-grandfather acted in launching the family fortune, we aren't going to take your beloved old car from you. I don't think much justice is required in order to establish your right to that pile of junk."

"Pile of junk?" Ben leaped to his car's defense. "My car runs smooth as silk, never burns an ounce of oil."

"Now look what you've done, Sarah. It's not bad enough you destroy his cherished beliefs about private property, but you also insult the man's car." Selina and Sarah were now laughing together. "Look, Ben, we're sorry, really. Peace offering. We'll get the refills on coffee. Come on, Sarah."

"How about a scone with your coffee, Ben?" Selina asked.

"No, just the coffee, thanks. I don't think I'm justly entitled to a scone."

Individuals and Community

When they had resettled coffee cups, Ben leaned forward. "Okay, Selina, I'm fortified with Colombia's finest mountain roast. What's this other objection you have to the traditional account of property and just distribution?"

"It's the same objection I would make to social-contract theory: It's too individualistic, and it ignores the importance of community and society, as well as the importance of common contributions to our welfare. I want to study chemistry, go to graduate school, and, ultimately, do pharmacological research at a university, in connection with university hospitals. Maybe here at the University of Michigan, that would be great. Or almost any university with a medical school and a good research program. Except Ohio State, of course."

Ben nodded. "Sounds good, Selina. Glad to see you have your priorities straight."

Selina continued. "So suppose I'm doing drug research at some non-Buckeye University. And one day, voilà, there it is, I make the great discovery I've been working for—a cure for Alzheimer's disease, suppose. Okay, I did the work, and now I spin off into a nice little biotech company, Selina Pharmaceuticals, and I complete the research on this fabulous new drug, and Selina Pharmaceuticals stock soars, and I've got megabucks. Well, I deserve it, don't I? I did the research, I discovered the cure. To the victor belong the spoils. But something's wrong with that scenario. Sure, I did a tremendous amount of work, and I made a wonderful discovery. But do I, individually, justly deserve all the profits—and the glory, for that matter—from this new drug? I took the material that was available and 'mixed my labor with it,' true enough. But there's a lot more mixed into that result. Isaac Newton's discovery of the laws of motion was one of the greatest scientific accomplishments; and Newton was proud of what he had discovered. But he also gave an honest and insightful assessment of what he had done, when he said: 'If I have seen further it is by standing on the shoulders of Giants.' For without the earlier research of Copernicus and Kepler and Galileo, Newton would have been in no position to work his calculations and make his discoveries. And had he not lived in a culture that offered a good education (at least to Newton, if certainly not to all) and had institutions for preserving records of scientific research and allowing free scientific inquiry, he could not have developed his theory. So while Newton's accomplishment was great, it was hardly the work of a solitary individual. And should I manage to make my own contribution to medical science, likewise the contribution will not be mine alone. It was supported by the efforts of my high school chemistry teacher who nurtured my interest in chemistry, my uncle who bought me my first chemistry set, my mother who never complained when I made malodorous messes in her

I have no doubt that the fact that the old men of America still insist on being so busy and active can be directly traced to individualism carried to a foolish extent. It is their pride and their love of independence and their shame of being dependent upon their children. But among the many human rights the American people have provided for in their Constitution, they have strangely forgotten about the right to be fed by their children, for it is a right and an obligation growing out of service. How can any one deny that parents who have toiled for their children in their youth, have lost many a good night's sleep when they were ill, have washed their diapers long before they could talk and have spent about a quarter of a century bringing them up and fitting them for life, have the right to be fed by them and loved and respected when they are old. Can one not forget the individual and his pride of self in a general scheme of home life in which men are justly taken care of by their parents and, having in turn taken care of their children, are also justly taken care of by the latter? The Chinese have not got the sense of individual independence because the whole conception of life is based upon mutual help within the home, hence there is no shame attached to the circumstance of one's being served by his children in the sunset of one's life. Rather it is considered good luck to have children who can take care of one. One lives for nothing else in China.

Lin Yutang; from *The Importance of Living*, by Lin Yutang, p. 199.
Copyright (c) 1995 by Lin Tai Yi and Hsiang Ju Lin

kitchen with my chemicals, my community that paid for my public school education, my first-grade teacher who taught me how to read; and also by the efforts of people who struggled to make it possible for a black woman to be admitted to a prestigious university, and by the citizens of Michigan who built and funded the university, and by my professors, and by all the thousands of people who built up the body of scientific knowledge that was the essential foundation for my own research. Sure, I made the discovery; but lots of other people had an essential hand in it, even if they never set foot in my laboratory. So is it really fair to say that the discovery is 'my property,' and I justly deserve the profits from its sale? It seems rather arbitrary to assign all the benefits to the person who happens to be the final link in a long essential chain."

"Alright, I grant you there are problems with giving a traditional justification for private property," Ben said, "and I'll also grant that the notion of 'rugged individuals' who single-handedly do great deeds looks better in John Wayne westerns than under careful scrutiny. Still, I think it's important that we save the notion of private property. It's an important part of our security and our sense of accomplishment; and it may be important for stimulating sustained goal-oriented effort. Granted, for those purposes you don't need huge and disproportionate masses of private property, but you may need some. There's a line by Hegel that I like:

'A person must translate his freedom into an external sphere in order that he may achieve his ideal existence.'[3] That is, it's not enough to just dream of goals; it's also important to actually put flesh on them. And without private property, accomplishing your goals—'translat[ing] your freedom into an external sphere'—becomes all but impossible. Private property helps us turn our dreams into reality, whether that dream is a great painting or a scientific discovery or a productive farm or a thriving business."

"Yeah, I see the direction you're going," Selina responded. "Private property is the cornerstone of freedom and independence, and everyone ought to pursue his or her own interests. If my goal is to accumulate a vast fortune, then it's not fair to stop me from 'translating my dreams into the external sphere' and stashing away great treasure and rattling around in a vast mansion. If others are hungry or homeless, well, that's their tough luck. But if everyone just pursues their own selfish interests, then, ultimately, it will all work out for the best."

"Not fair, Selina. That's a straw-man attack. You can believe in the good of private property without believing the 'rugged individual' nonsense. There seems to me altogether enough selfishness in the world without someone promoting it as a virtue. If you think for a moment of what your life would be like without community support—brief and desperate, for a species as individually weak as ours—then there is less inclination to see social obligations as a burden. That is not to deny," Ben continued, "that it is acceptable for people to pursue their own ends. It is legitimate for people to pursue their own goals, and it is important that we have a sphere of private activity. Suppose Selina wants to devote her chemistry talents to developing a better tasting lime soda. That's hardly as noble or socially valuable a goal as finding a cure for pancreatic cancer, but she should be able to follow her own lights, march to her own drummer. It works better if people can choose their own pursuits. Centrally controlled societies concentrate too much power, and power leads to corruption. But that's true also when you concentrate enormous power in the hands of a few very wealthy private individuals. Such concentrated wealth does not magically lead to good results; it leads instead to monopolies, corruption of the political process, and the exploitation of weaker groups. But the point is, if there's a private sphere, then we need private goods and private resources. Okay, you've convinced me: The notion of private property as some absolute God-given right or some fixed natural right—that's absurd. There's just no way to make sense of it. Maybe in some primitive world, where I can pick up a stick that no one else wants, fashion it into a spear by my own labor, and thus claim it as my own exclusive creation. But that primitive model doesn't work in *our* world, where raw materials are not free for the taking, all the land is claimed, our material wealth has been passed down (with varying degrees of legitimacy) for generations, and all production is dependent on knowledge and skills and institutions that are our common social legacy. Still, we do need a notion of private property, to support our interest in a private sphere of life and choice."

"It sounds," said Sarah, "as if you have arrived at a view of property similar to David Hume's. Private property is useful because it encourages 'useful habits and accomplishments'; but its justification is its usefulness, not some natural or absolute law. We find it useful and agreeable to respect individual private property, but the rights of private property reach only so far as they are generally beneficial. If a massive concentration of property causes great harm, then such accumulation should be restricted for the common good."

"Exactly right," Selina agreed. "And above all, we should remember the first principle of private property and self-preservation: Hands *off* Sarah's shiny blue police car. It belongs to Sarah, and she need not share it with anyone unless *she chooses* to do so. But that doesn't mean she has a right to control the entire toy chest."

"Alright," Ben said, "the blue police car is Sarah's. And it's her choice what to do with it. So maybe there's room for agreement. Private property is important: It can enhance our freedom, enlarge our options. But that's exactly why it's valuable, and when private property becomes too concentrated, it can wind up closing off opportunities for others. And by looking at what is required to enhance genuine opportunities, we can get some idea of what benefits and resources and services should be available to *everyone* in an affluent society."

"That almost sounds like Ben and Selina singing in harmony," said Sarah, as she swung her backpack over her shoulder and picked up her empty coffee cup. "And lifted on that rare harmonious note, I must fly to my seminar. Happy trails, campers."

READINGS

John Stuart Mill (1806–1873) was born in London and was certainly the best known English philosopher of the 19th century. His work on economics, political philosophy, ethics, logic, and the rights of women were widely read during the 19th century and— particularly his writings on ethics and political philosophy—are still very influential. Mill's major works include A System of Logic *(London, 1843);* Principles of Political Economy *(London, 1848);* On Liberty *(London, 1859);* Utilitarianism *(London, 1863);* An Examination of Sir William Hamilton's Philosophy *(London, 1865); and* The Subjection of Women *(London, 1869). His development and refinement of utilitarian ethical theory ensures his place in the history of ethics, and his small treatise* On Liberty—*which Mill himself thought the most likely of his books to endure and from which the reading that follows is excerpted—is a perennially popular defense of freedom of thought.*

On Liberty

Introductory

• • •

The struggle between Liberty and Authority is the most conspicuous feature in the portions of history with which we are earliest familiar, particularly in that of Greece, Rome, and England. But in old times this contest was between subjects, or some classes of subjects, and the Government. By liberty, was meant protection against the tyranny of the political rulers. The rulers were conceived (except in some of the popular governments of Greece) as in a necessarily antagonistic position to the people whom they ruled. They consisted of a governing One, or a governing tribe or caste, who derived their authority from inheritance or conquest, who, at all events, did not hold it at the pleasure of the governed, and whose supremacy men did not venture, perhaps did not desire, to contest, whatever precautions might be taken against its oppressive exercise. Their power was regarded as necessary, but also as highly dangerous; as a weapon which they would attempt to use against their subjects, no less than against external enemies. To prevent the weaker members of the community from being preyed upon by innumerable vultures, it was needful that there should be an animal of prey stronger than the rest, commissioned to keep them down. But as the king of the vultures would be no less bent upon preying on the flock than any of the minor harpies, it was indispensable to be in a perpetual attitude of defense against his beak and claws. The aim, therefore, of patriots was to set limits to the power which the ruler should be suffered to exercise over the community; and this limitation was what they meant by liberty. It was attempted in two ways. First, by obtaining a recognition of certain immunities, called political liberties or rights, which it was to be regarded as a breach of duty in the ruler to infringe, and which, if he did infringe, specific resistance, or general rebellion, was held to be justifiable. A second, and generally a later expedient, was the establishment of constitutional checks, by which the consent of the community, or of a body of some sort, supposed to represent its interests, was made a necessary condition to some of the more important acts of the governing power. To the first of these modes of limitation, the ruling power, in most European countries, was compelled, more or less, to submit. It was not so with the second; and, to attain this, or when already in some degree possessed, to attain it more completely, became everywhere the principal object of the lovers of liberty. And so long as mankind were content to combat one enemy by another, and to be ruled by a master, on condition of being guaranteed more or less efficaciously against his tyranny, they did not carry their aspirations beyond this point.

A time, however, came, in the progress of human affairs, when men ceased to think it a necessity of nature that their governors should be an independent power, opposed in interest to themselves. It appeared to them much better that the various magistrates of the State should be their tenants or delegates, revocable at their pleasure. In that way alone, it seemed, could they have complete security that the powers of government would never be abused to their disadvantage. By degrees this new demand for elective and temporary rulers became the prominent object of the exertions of the popular party, wherever any such party existed; and superseded, to a considerable extent, the previous efforts to limit the power of rulers. As the struggle proceeded for making the ruling power emanate from the periodical choice of the ruled, some persons began to think that too much importance had been attached to the limitation of the power itself. *That* (it might seem) was a resource against rulers whose interests were habitually opposed to those of the people. What was now wanted was, that the rulers should be identified with the people; that their interest and will should be the interest and will of the nation. The nation did not need to be protected against its own will. There was no fear of its tyrannizing over itself. Let the rulers be effectually responsible to it, promptly removable by it, and it could afford to trust them with power of which it could itself dictate the use to be made. Their power was but the nation's own power, concentrated, and in a form convenient for exercise. This mode of thought, or rather perhaps of feeling, was common among the last generation of European liberalism, in the Continental section of which it still apparently predominates. Those who admit any limit to what a government may do, except in the case of such governments as they think ought not to exist, stand out as brilliant exceptions among the political thinkers of the Continent. A similar tone of sentiment might by this time have been prevalent in our own country, if the circumstances which for a time encouraged it, had continued unaltered.

But, in political and philosophical theories, as well as in persons, success discloses faults and infirmities which failure might have concealed from observation. The notion, that the people have no need to limit their power over themselves, might seem axiomatic, when popular government was a thing only dreamed about, or read of as having existed at some distant period of the past. Neither was that notion necessarily disturbed by such temporary aberrations as those of the French Revolution, the worst of which were the work of an usurping few, and which, in any case, belonged, not to the permanent working of popular institutions, but to a sudden and convulsive outbreak against monarchical and aristocratic despotism. In time, however, a democratic republic came to occupy a large portion of the earth's surface, and made itself felt as one of the most powerful members of the community of nations; and elective and responsible government became subject to the observations and criticisms which wait upon a great existing fact. It was now perceived that such phrases as "self-government," and "the power of the people over themselves," do not express the true state of the case. The "people" who exercise the power are not always the same people with those over whom it is exercised; and the "self-government" spoken of is not the government of each by himself, but of each by all the rest. The will of the people, moreover, practically means the will of the most numerous or the most active *part* of the people; the majority, or those who succeed in making themselves accepted as the majority; the people, consequently, *may* desire to oppress a part of their number; and precautions are as much needed against this as against any other abuse of power. The limitation, therefore, of the power of government over individuals loses none of its importance when the holders of power are regularly accountable to the community, that is, to the strongest party therein. This view of things, recommending itself equally to the intelligence of thinkers and to the inclination of those important classes in European society to whose real or supposed interests democracy is adverse, has had no difficulty in establishing itself; and in political speculations "the tyranny of the majority" is now generally included among the evils against which society requires to be on its guard.

Like other tyrannies, the tyranny of the majority was at first, and is still vulgarly, held in dread, chiefly as operating through the acts of the public authorities. But reflecting persons perceived that when society is itself the tyrant—society collectively, over the separate individuals who compose it—its means of tyrannizing are not restricted to the acts which it may do by the hands of its political functionaries. Society can and does execute its own mandates: and if it issues wrong mandates instead of right, or any mandates at all in things with which it ought not to meddle, it practices a social tyranny more formidable than many kinds of political oppression, since, though not usually upheld by such extreme penalties, it leaves fewer means of escape, penetrating much more deeply into the details of life, and enslaving the soul itself. Protection, therefore, against the tyranny of the magistrate is not enough: there needs protection also against the tyranny of the prevailing opinion and feeling; against the tendency of society to impose, by other means than civil penalties, its own ideas and practices as rules of conduct on those who dissent from them; to fetter the development, and, if possible, prevent the formation, of any individuality not in harmony with its ways, and compel all characters to fashion themselves upon the model of its own. There is a limit to the legitimate interference of collective opinion with individual independence: and to find that limit, and maintain it against encroachment, is as indispensable to a good condition of human affairs, as protection against political despotism.

But though this proposition is not likely to be contested in general terms, the practical question, where to place the limit—how to make the fitting adjustment between individual independence and social control—is a subject on which nearly everything remains to be done. All that makes existence valuable to any one, depends on the enforcement of restraints upon the actions of other people. Some rules of conduct, therefore, must be imposed, by law in the first place, and by opinion on many things which are not fit subjects for the operation of law. What these rules should be, is the principal question in human affairs; but if we except a few of the most obvious cases, it is one of those which least progress has been made in resolving. No two ages, and scarcely any two countries, have decided it alike; and the decision of one age or country is a wonder to another. Yet the people of any given age and country no more suspect any difficulty in it, than if it were a subject on which mankind had always been agreed. The rules which obtain among themselves appear to them self-evident and self-justifying. This all but universal illusion is one of the examples of the magical influence of custom, which is not only, as the proverb says, a second nature, but is continually mistaken for the first. The effect of custom, in preventing any misgiving respecting the rules of conduct which mankind impose on one another, is all the more complete because the subject is one on which it is not generally considered necessary that reasons should be given, either by one person to others, or by each to himself. People are accustomed to believe, and have been encouraged in the belief by some who aspire to the character of philosophers, that their feelings, on subjects of this nature, are better than reasons, and render reasons unnecessary. The practical principle which guides them to their opinions on the regulation of human conduct, is the feeling in each person's mind that everybody should be required to act as he, and those with whom he sympathizes, would like them to act. No one, indeed, acknowledges to himself that his standard of judgment is his own liking; but an opinion on a point of conduct, not supported by reasons, can only count as one person's preference; and if the reasons, when given are a mere appeal to a similar preference felt by other people, it is still only many people's liking instead of one. To an ordinary man, however, his own preference, thus supported, is not only a perfectly satisfactory reason, but the only one he generally has for any of his notions of morality, taste, or propriety, which are not expressly written in his religious creed; and his chief guide in the interpretation even of that. Men's opinions, accordingly, on what is laudable or blameable, are affected by all the multifarious causes which influence their wishes in regard to the conduct of others, and which are as numerous as those which determine their wishes on any other subject. Sometimes their reason—at other times their prejudices or superstitions: often their social affections, not seldom their antisocial ones, their envy or jealousy, their arrogance or contemptuousness: but most commonly, their desires or fears for themselves—their legitimate or illegitimate self-interest. Wherever there is an ascendant class, a large portion of the morality of the country emanates from its class interests, and its feelings of class superiority. The morality between Spartans and Helots, between planters and negroes, between princes and subjects, between nobles and roturiers, between men and women, has been for the most part the creation of these class interests and feelings: and the sentiments thus generated, react in turn upon the moral feelings of the members of the ascendant class, in their relations among themselves. Where, on the other hand, a class, formerly ascendant, has lost its ascendancy, or where its ascendancy is unpopular, the prevailing moral sentiments frequently bear the impress of an impatient dislike of superiority. Another grand determining principle of the rules of conduct, both in act and forbearance, which have been enforced by law or opinion, has been the servility of mankind towards the supposed preferences or aversions of their temporal masters, or of their gods. This servility, though essentially selfish, is not hypocrisy; it gives rise to perfectly genuine sentiments of abhorrence; it made men burn magicians and heretics. Among so many baser influences, the general and obvious interests of society have of course had a share, and a large one, in the direction of the moral sentiments: less, however, as a matter of reason, and on their own account, than as a consequence of the sympathies and antipathies which grew out of them: and sympathies and antipathies which had little or nothing to do with the interests of society, have made themselves felt in the establishment of moralities with quite as great force.

The likings and dislikings of society, or of some powerful portion of it, are thus the main thing which has practically determined the rules laid down for general observance, under the penalties of law or opinion. And in general, those who have been in advance of society in thought and feeling, have left this condition of things unassailed in principle, however they may have come into conflict with it in some of its details. They have occupied themselves rather in inquiring what things society ought to like or dislike, than in questioning whether its likings or dislikings should be a law to individuals. They preferred endeavoring to alter the feelings of mankind on the particular points on which they were themselves heretical, rather than make common cause in defense of freedom, with heretics generally. The only case in which the higher ground has been taken on principle and maintained with consistency, by any but an individual here and there, is that of religious belief: a case instructive in many ways, and not least so as forming a most striking instance of the fallibility of what is called the moral sense: for the *odium theologicum*, in a sincere bigot, is one of the most unequivocal cases of moral feeling. Those who first broke the yoke of what called itself the Universal Church, were in general as little willing to permit difference of religious opinion as that church itself. But when the heat of the conflict was over, without giving a complete victory to any party, and each church or sect was reduced to limit its hopes to retaining possession of the ground it already occupied; minorities, seeing that they had no chance of becoming majorities, were under the necessity of pleading to those whom they could not convert, for permission to differ. It is accordingly on this battle-field, almost solely, that the rights of the individual against society have been asserted on broad grounds of principle, and the claim of society to exercise authority over dissentients, openly controverted. The great writers to whom the world owes what religious liberty it possesses, have mostly asserted freedom of conscience as an indefeasible right, and denied absolutely that a human being is accountable to others for his religious belief. Yet so natural to mankind is intolerance in whatever they really care about, that religious freedom has hardly anywhere been practically realized, except where religious indifference, which dislikes to have its peace disturbed by theological quarrels, has added its weight to the scale. In the minds of almost all religious persons, even in the most tolerant countries, the duty of toleration is admitted with tacit reserves. One person will bear with dissent in matters of church government, but not of dogma; another can tolerate everybody, short of a Papist or a Unitarian; another, every one who believes in revealed religion; a few extend their charity a little further, but stop at the belief in a God and in a future state. Wherever the sentiment of the majority is still genuine and intense, it is found to have abated little of its claim to be obeyed.

In England, from the peculiar circumstances of our political history, though the yoke of opinion is perhaps heavier, that of law is lighter, than in most other countries of Europe; and there is considerable jealousy of direct interference, by the legislative or the executive power, with private conduct; not so much from any just regard for the independence of the individual, as from the still subsisting habit of looking on the government as representing an opposite interest to the public. The majority have not yet learnt to feel the power of the government their power, or its opinions their opinions.

When they do so, individual liberty will probably be as much exposed to invasion from the government, as it already is from public opinion. But, as yet, there is a considerable amount of feeling ready to be called forth against any attempt of the law to control individuals in things in which they have not hitherto been accustomed to be controlled by it; and this with very little discrimination as to whether the matter is, or is not, within the legitimate sphere of legal control; insomuch that the feeling, highly salutary on the whole, is perhaps quite as often misplaced as well grounded in the particular instances of its application. There is, in fact, no recognized principle by which the propriety or impropriety of government interference is customarily tested. People decide according to their personal preferences. Some, whenever they see any good to be done, or evil to be remedied, would willingly instigate the government to undertake the business; while others prefer to bear almost any amount of social evil, rather than add one to the departments of human interests amenable to governmental control. And men range themselves on one or the other side in any particular case, according to this general direction of their sentiments; or according to the degree of interest which they feel in the particular thing which it is proposed that the government should do, or according to the belief they entertain that the government would, or would not, do it in the manner they prefer; but very rarely on account of any opinion to which they consistently adhere, as to what things are fit to be done by a government. And it seems to me that in consequence of this absence of rule or principle, one side is at present as often wrong as the other; the interference of government is, with about equal frequency, improperly invoked and improperly condemned.

The object of this Essay is to assert one very simple principle, as entitled to govern absolutely the dealings of society with the individual in the way of compulsion and control, whether the means used be physical force in the form of legal penalties, or the moral coercion of public opinion. That principle is, that the sole end for which mankind are warranted, individually or collectively, in interfering with the liberty of action of any of their number, is self-protection. That the only purpose for which power can be rightfully exercised over any member of a civilized community, against his will, is to prevent harm to others. His own good, either physical or moral, is not a sufficient warrant. He cannot rightfully be compelled to do or forbear because it will be better for him to do so, because it will make him happier, because, in the opinions of others, to do so would be wise, or even right. These are good reasons for remonstrating with him, or reasoning with him, or persuading him, or entreating him, but not for compelling him, or visiting him with any evil in case he do otherwise. To justify that, the conduct from which it is desired to deter him, must be calculated to produce evil to some one else. The only part of the conduct of any one, for which he is amenable to society, is that which concerns others. In the part which merely concerns himself, his independence is, of right, absolute. Over himself, over his own body and mind, the individual is sovereign. . . .

But there is a sphere of action in which society, as distinguished from the individual, has, if any, only an indirect interest; comprehending all that portion of a person's life and conduct which affects only himself, or if it also affects others, only with their free, voluntary, and undeceived consent and participation. When I say only himself, I mean directly, and in the first instance: for whatever affects himself, may affect others through himself; and the objection which may be grounded on this contingency will receive consideration in the sequel. This, then, is the appropriate region of human liberty. It comprises, first, the inward domain of consciousness; demanding liberty of conscience, in the most comprehensive sense; liberty of thought and feeling; absolute freedom of opinion and sentiment on all subjects, practical or speculative, scientific, moral, or theological. The liberty of expressing and publishing opinions may seem to fall under a different principle, since it belongs to that part of the conduct of an individual which concerns other people; but, being almost of as much importance as the liberty of thought itself, and resting in great part on the same reasons, is practically inseparable from it. Secondly, the principle requires liberty of tastes and pursuits; of framing the plan of our life to suit our own character; of doing as we like, subject to such consequences as may follow: without impediment from our fellow creatures, so long as what we do does not harm them, even though they should think our conduct foolish, perverse, or wrong. Thirdly, from this liberty of each individual, follows the liberty, within the same limits, of combination among individuals; freedom to unite, for any purpose not involving harm to others: the persons combining being supposed to be of full age, and not forced or deceived.

No society in which these liberties are not, on the whole, respected, is free, whatever may be its form of government; and none is completely free in which they do not exist absolute and unqualified. The only freedom which deserves the name, is that of pursuing our own good in our own way, so long as we do not attempt to deprive others of theirs, or impede their efforts to obtain it. Each is the proper guardian of his own health, whether bodily, or mental and spiritual. Mankind are greater gainers by suffering each other to live as seems good to themselves, than by compelling each to live as seems good to the rest.

Lani Guinier, Bennett Boskey Professor of Law at Harvard Law School, joined the Harvard Law faculty in 1998. In addition to penning many law review articles, Guinier has written Becoming Gentlemen: Women, Law Schools, and Institutional

Change *(1995) and a personal memoir,* Lift Every Voice: Turning a Civil Rights Setback into a New Vision of Social Justice *(1998). In 1993, after she was nominated to be assistant attorney general for civil rights, Guinier was subjected to strident attacks from critics who represented her views as extreme and even antidemocratic. The attacks became so severe that her nomination was eventually withdrawn. In fact, her work grapples with issues that are at the heart of democratic theory, and she deals with problems that writers on political philosophy and democracy (such as Alexander de Tocqueville and John Stuart Mill) have discussed for centuries. As societies, including the United States, become increasingly stratified, and hostility among various groups intensifies, Guinier's work gains even greater importance. You will have to decide for yourself about her proposals to deal with these problems, but perhaps the greatest strength of her work is in making manifest some serious problems that remain all but invisible to many Americans. The article included here, "The Tyranny of the Majority," is excerpted from her book* The Tyranny of the Majority: Fundamental Fairness in Representative Democracy *(New York: The Free Press, 1994).*

The Tyranny of the Majority

I have always wanted to be a civil rights lawyer. This lifelong ambition is based on a deep-seated commitment to democratic fair play—to playing by the rules as long as the rules are fair. When the rules seem unfair, I have worked to change them, not subvert them. When I was eight years old, I was a Brownie. I was especially proud of my uniform, which represented a commitment to good citizenship and good deeds. But one day, when my Brownie group staged a hatmaking contest, I realized that uniforms are only as honorable as the people who wear them. The contest was rigged. The winner was assisted by her milliner mother, who actually made the winning entry in full view of all the participants. At the time, I was too young to be able to change the rules, but I was old enough to resign, which I promptly did.

To me, fair play means that the rules encourage everyone to play. They should reward those who win, but they must be acceptable to those who lose. The central theme of my academic writing is that not all rules lead to elemental fair play. Some even commonplace rules work against it.

The professional milliner competing with amateur Brownies stands as an example of rules that are patently rigged or patently subverted. Yet, sometimes, even when rules are perfectly fair in form, they serve in practice to exclude particular groups from meaningful participation. When they do not encourage everyone to play, or when, over the long haul, they do not make the losers feel as good about the outcomes as the winners, they can seem as unfair as the milliner who makes the winning hat for her daughter.

Sometimes, too, we construct rules that force us to be divided into winners and losers when we might have otherwise joined together. This idea was cogently expressed by my son, Nikolas, when he was four years old, far exceeding the thoughtfulness of his mother when she was an eight-year-old Brownie. While I was writing one of my law journal articles, Nikolas and I had a conversation about voting prompted by a *Sesame Street Magazine* exercise. The magazine pictured six children: four children had raised their hands because they wanted to play tag; two had their hands down because they wanted to play hide-and-seek. The magazine asked its readers to count the number of children whose hands were raised and then decide what game the children would play.

Nikolas quite realistically replied, "They will play both. First they will play tag. Then they will play hide-and-seek." Despite the magazine's "rules," he was right. To children, it is natural to take turns. The winner may get to play first or more often, but even the "loser" gets something. His was a positive-sum solution that many adult rule-makers ignore.

The traditional answer to the magazine's problem would have been a zero-sum solution: "The children—all the children—will play tag, and only tag." As a zero-sum solution, everything is seen in terms of "I win; you lose." The conventional answer relies on winner-take-all majority rule, in which the tag players, as the majority, win the right to decide for all the children what game to play. The hide-and-seek preference becomes irrelevant. The numerically more powerful majority choice simply subsumes minority preferences.

In the conventional case, the majority that rules gains all the power and the minority that loses gets none. For example, two years ago Brother Rice High School in Chicago held two senior proms. It was not planned that way. The prom committee at Brother Rice, a boys' Catholic high school, expected just one prom when it hired a disc jockey, picked a rock band, and selected music for the prom by consulting student preferences. Each senior was asked to list his three favorite songs, and the band would play the songs that appeared most frequently on the lists.

Seems attractively democratic. But Brother Rice is predominantly white, and the prom committee was all white. That's how they got two proms. The black seniors at Brother Rice felt so shut out by the "democratic process" that they organized their own prom. As one black student put it: "For every vote we had, there were eight votes for what they wanted. . . . [W]ith us being in the minority we're always outvoted. It's as if we don't count."

Some embittered white seniors saw things differently. They complained that the black students should have gone along with the majority: "The majority makes a decision. That's the way it works."

In a way, both groups were right. From the white students' perspective, this was ordinary decisionmaking. To the black students, majority rule sent the message: "we don't count" is the "way it works" for minorities. In a racially divided society, majority rule may be perceived as majority tyranny.

That is a large claim, and I do not rest my case for it solely on the actions of the prom committee in one Chicago high school. To expand the range of the argument, I first consider the ideal of majority rule itself, particularly as reflected in the writings of James Madison and other founding members of our Republic. These early democrats explored the relationship between majority rule and democracy. James Madison warned, "If a majority be united by a common interest, the rights of the minority will be insecure." The tyranny of the majority, according to Madison, requires safeguards to protect "one part of the society against the injustice of the other part."

For Madison, majority tyranny represented the great danger to our early constitutional democracy. Although the American revolution was fought against the tyranny of the British monarch, it soon became clear that there was another tyranny to be avoided. The accumulations of all powers in the same hands, Madison warned, "whether of one, a few, or many, and whether hereditary, self-appointed, or elective, may justly be pronounced the very definition of tyranny."

As another colonist suggested in papers published in Philadelphia, "We have been so long habituated to a jealousy of tyranny from monarchy and aristocracy, that we have yet to learn the dangers of it from democracy." Despotism had to be opposed "whether it came from Kings, Lords or the people."

The debate about majority tyranny reflected Madison's concern that the majority may not represent the whole. In a homogeneous society, the interest of the majority would likely be that of the minority also. But in a heterogeneous community, the majority may not represent all competing interests. The majority is likely to be self-interested and ignorant or indifferent to the concerns of the minority. In such case, Madison observed, the assumption that the majority represents the minority is "altogether fictitious."

Yet even a self-interested majority can govern fairly if it cooperates with the minority. One reason for such cooperation is that the self-interested majority values the principle of reciprocity. The self-interested majority worries that the minority may attract defectors from the majority and become the next governing majority. The Golden Rule principle of reciprocity functions to check the tendency of a self-interested majority to act tyrannically.

So the argument for the majority principle connects it with the value of reciprocity: You cooperate when you lose in part because members of the current majority will cooperate when they lose. The conventional case for the fairness of majority rule is that it is not really the rule of a fixed group—The Majority—on all issues; instead it is the rule of shifting majorities, as the losers at one time or on one issue join with others and become part of the governing coalition at another time or on another issue. The result will be a fair system of mutually beneficial cooperation. I call a majority that rules but does not dominate a Madisonian Majority.

The problem of majority tyranny arises, however, when the self-interested majority does not need to worry about defectors. When the majority is fixed and permanent, there are no checks on its ability to be overbearing. A majority that does not worry about defectors is a majority with total power.

In such a case, Madison's concern about majority tyranny arises. In a heterogeneous community, any faction with total power might subject "the minority to the caprice and arbitrary decisions of the majority, who instead of consulting the interest of the whole community collectively, attend sometimes to partial and local advantages."

"What remedy can be found in a republican Government, where the majority must ultimately decide," argued Madison, but to ensure "that no one common interest or passion will be likely to unite a majority of the whole number in an unjust pursuit." The answer was to disaggregate the majority to ensure checks and balances or fluid, rotating interests. The minority needed protection against an overbearing majority, so that "a common sentiment is less likely to be felt, and the requisite concert less likely to be formed, by a majority of the whole."

Political struggles would not be simply a contest between rulers and people; the political struggles would be among the people themselves. The work of government was not to transcend different interests but to reconcile them. In an ideal democracy, the people would rule, but the minorities would also be protected against the power of majorities. Again, where the rules of decisionmaking protect the minority, the Madisonian Majority rules without dominating.

But if a group is unfairly treated, for example, when it forms a racial minority, *and* if the problems of unfairness are not cured by conventional assumptions about majority rule, then what is to be done? The answer is that we may need an *alternative* to winner-take-all majoritarianism. In this book, a collection of my law review articles, I describe the alternative, which, with Nikolas's help, I now call the "principle of taking turns." In a racially divided society, this principle does better than simple majority rule if it accommodates the values of self-government, fairness, deliberation, compromise, and consensus that lie at the heart of the democratic ideal.

In my legal writing, I follow the caveat of James Madison and other early American democrats. I explore decisionmaking rules that might work in a multi-racial society to ensure that majority rule does not become majority tyranny. I pursue voting systems that might disaggregate The Majority so that it does not exercise power unfairly or tyrannically. I aspire to a more cooperative political style of decisionmaking to enable all of the students at Brother Rice to feel comfortable attending the same prom. In looking to create Madisonian Majorities, I pursue a positive-sum, taking-turns solution.

Structuring decisionmaking to allow the minority "a turn" may be necessary to restore the reciprocity ideal when a fixed majority refuses to co-operate with the minority. If the fixed majority loses its incentive to follow the Golden Rule principle of shifting majorities, the minority never gets to take a turn. Giving the minority a turn does not mean the minority gets to rule; what it does mean is that the minority gets to influence decisionmaking and the majority rules more legitimately.

Instead of automatically rewarding the preferences of the monolithic majority, a taking-turns approach anticipates that the majority rules, but is not overbearing. Because those with 51 percent of the votes are not assured 100 percent of the power, the majority cooperates with, or at least does not tyrannize, the minority.

The sports analogy of "I win; you lose" competition within a political hierarchy makes sense when only one team can win; Nikolas's intuition that it is often possible to take turns suggests an alternative approach. Take family decisionmaking, for example. It utilizes a taking-turns approach. When parents sit around the kitchen table deciding on a vacation destination or activities for a rainy day, often they do not simply rely on a show of hands, especially if that means that the older children always prevail or if affinity groups among the children (those who prefer movies to video games, or those who prefer baseball to playing cards) never get to play their activity of choice. Instead of allowing the majority simply to rule, the parents may propose that everyone take turns, going to the movies one night and playing video games the next. Or as Nikolas proposes, they might do both on a given night.

Taking turns attempts to build consensus while recognizing political or social differences, and it encourages everyone to play. The taking-turns approach gives those with the most support more turns, but it also legitimates the outcome from each individual's perspective, including those whose views are shared only by a minority.

In the end, I do not believe that democracy should encourage rule by the powerful—even a powerful majority. Instead, the ideal of democracy promises a fair discussion among self-defined equals about how to achieve our common aspirations. To redeem that promise, we need to put the idea of taking turns and disaggregating the majority at the center of our conception of representation. Particularly as we move into the twenty-first century as a more highly diversified citizenry, it is essential that we consider the ways in which voting and representational systems succeed or fail at encouraging Madisonian Majorities.

To use Nikolas's terminology, "it is no fair" if a fixed, tyrannical majority excludes or alienates the minority. It is no fair if a fixed, tyrannical majority monopolizes all the power all the time. It is no fair if we engage in the periodic ritual of elections, but only the permanent majority gets to choose who is elected. Where we have tyranny by The Majority, we do not have genuine democracy.

My life's work, with the essential assistance of people like Nikolas, has been to try to find the rules that can best bring us together as a democratic society. Some of my ideas about democratic fair play were grossly mischaracterized in the controversy over my nomination to be Assistant Attorney General for Civil Rights. Trying to find rules to encourage fundamental fairness inevitably raises the question posed by Harvard Professor Randall Kennedy in a summary of this controversy: "What is required to create political institutions that address the needs and aspirations of all Americans, not simply whites, who have long enjoyed racial privilege, but people of color who have long suffered racial exclusion from policymaking forums?" My answer, as Professor Kennedy suggests, varies by situation. But I have a predisposition, reflected in my son's yearning for a positive-sum solution, to seek an integrated body politic in which all perspectives are represented and in which all people work together to find common ground. I advocate empowering voters and their representatives in ways that give even minority voters a chance to influence legislative outcomes.

But those in the majority do not lose; they simply learn to take turns. This is a positive-sum solution that allows all voters to feel that they participate meaningfully in the decisionmaking process. This is a positive-sum solution that makes legislative outcomes more legitimate.

My work did not arise in a vacuum. Lost in the controversy over my nomination was the long history of those before me who have sought to change the rules in order to improve the system. There have been three generations of attempts to curb tyrannical majorities. The first generation focused directly on access to the ballot on the assumption that the right to vote by itself is "preservative of all other rights." During the civil rights movement, aggrieved citizens asserted that "tyrannical majorities" in various locales were ganging up to deny black voters access to the voting booth.

The 1965 Voting Rights Act and its amendments forcefully addressed this problem. The act outlawed literacy tests, brought federal registrars to troubled districts to ensure safe access to polls, and targeted for federal administrative review many local registration procedures. Success under the act was immediate and impressive. The number of blacks registered to vote rose dramatically within five years after passage.

The second generation of voting rights litigation and legislation focused on the Southern response to increased black registration. Southern states and local subdivisions responded to blacks in the electorate by switching the way elections were conducted to ensure that newly voting blacks could not wield any influence. By changing, for example, from neighborhood-based districts to jurisdiction-wide at-large representatives, those in power ensured that although blacks could vote, and even run for office, they could not win. At-large elections allowed a unified white bloc to control all the elected positions. As little as 51 percent of the population could decide 100 percent of the elections, and the black minority was permanently excluded from meaningful participation.

In response, the second generation of civil rights activism focused on "qualitative vote dilution." Although everyone had a vote, it was apparent, that some people's votes were qualitatively less important than others'. The concerns raised by the second generation of civil rights activists led Congress to amend the Voting Rights Act. In 1982, congressional concern openly shifted from simply getting blacks the ability to register and vote to providing blacks a realistic opportunity to elect candidates of their choice. Thus, the new focus was on electing more black officials, primarily through the elimination of at-large districts, and their replacement by majority-black single-member districts. Even if whites continued to refuse to vote for blacks, there would be a few districts in which whites were in the minority and powerless to veto black candidates. The distinctive group interests of the black community, which Congress found had been ignored in the at-large racially polarized elections, were thus given a voice within decisionmaking councils.

The second generation sought to integrate physically the body politic. It was assumed that disaggregating the winner-take-all at-large majority would create political access for black voters, who would use that access to elect black representatives.

In many places, second-generation fights continue today. A number of redistricting schemes have been challenged in court, and not all courts agree on the outcomes, let alone the enterprise itself. Nevertheless, few disagree that blacks continue to be underrepresented in federal, state, and local government.

Even in governments in which minority legislators have increased, the marginalization of minority group interests has often stubbornly remained. Third-generation cases have now begun to respond. Third-generation cases recognize that it is sometimes not enough simply to ensure that minorities have a fair opportunity to elect someone to a legislative body. Under some unusual circumstances, it may be necessary to police the legislative voting rules whereby a majority consistently rigs the process to exclude a minority.

The Supreme Court's recent decision in *Presley v. Etowah County* heralds the arrival of this concern. Although black representatives for the first time since Reconstruction enjoyed a seat on the local county commission in Etowah and Russell counties in Alabama, they did not enjoy much else. Because of second-generation redistricting, black county commissioners were elected to county governing bodies in the two counties. Immediately upon their election, however, the white incumbents changed the rules for allocating decisionmaking authority. Just like the grandfather clauses, the literacy tests, the white primary, and other ingenious strategies devised to enforce white supremacy in the past, rules were changed to evade the reach of the earlier federal court decree.

In one county the newly integrated commission's duties were shifted to an appointed administrator. In the other county, its duties were shifted from individual commissioners to the entire commission voting by majority rule. Because voting on the commission, like voting in the county electorate, followed racial lines, "majority rule" meant that whites controlled the outcome of every legislative decision. The incumbents defended this power grab as simply the decision of a bona-fide majority.

This happened as well in Texas when the first Latino was elected to a local school board. The white majority suddenly decided that two votes were henceforth necessary to get an item on the agenda. In Louisiana, the legislature enacted a districting plan drawn up by a group of whites in a secret meeting in the subbasement of the state capitol, a meeting from which all black legislators were excluded.

Through these three generations of problems and remedies, a long trail of activists has preceded me. In 1964, ballot access was defended eloquently by Dr. Martin Luther King, Jr., and Fannie Lou Hamer. In 1982, redistricting was the consensus solution to electoral exclusion championed by the NAACP, the League of Women Voters, the Mexican-American Legal Defense Fund, and many others.

My ideas follow in this tradition. They are not undemocratic or out of the mainstream. Between 1969 and 1993, the Justice Department under both Democratic and Republican presidents disapproved as discriminatory over one hundred sets of voting rules involving changes to majority voting. None of these rules was unfair in the abstract, but all were exclusionary in practice. President Bush's chief civil rights enforcer declared some of them to be "electoral steroids for white candidates" because they manipulated the election system to ensure that only white candidates won.

This history of struggle against tyrannical majorities enlightens us to the dangers of winner-take-all collective decisionmaking. Majority rule, which presents an efficient opportunity for determining the public good, suffers when it is not constrained by the need to bargain with minority interests. When majorities are fixed, the minority lacks any mechanism for holding the majority to account or even to listen. Nor does such majority rule promote deliberation or consensus. The permanent majority simply has its way, without reaching out to or convincing anyone else.

Any form of less-than-unanimous voting introduces the danger that some group will be in the minority and the larger group will exploit the numerically smaller group. This is especially problematic to defeated groups that do not possess a veto over proposals and acts that directly affect them or implicate concerns they value intensely. Thus, the potential for instability exists when any significant group of people ends up as permanent losers.

The fundamentally important question of political stability is how to induce losers to continue to play the game. Political stability depends on the perception that the system is fair to induce losers to continue to work within the system rather than to try to overthrow it. When the minority experiences the alienation of complete and consistent defeat, they lack incentive to respect laws passed by the majority over their opposition.

As Tocqueville recognized, "[T]he power to do everything, which I should refuse to one of my equals, I will never grant to any number of them." Or as Hamilton put it, when the many are given all the power, "they will oppress the few." The problem is that majoritarian systems do not necessarily create winners who share in power. Politics becomes a battle for total victory rather than a method of governing open to all significant groups.

This is what happened in Phillips County, Arkansas, where a majority-vote runoff requirement unfairly rewarded the preferences of a white bloc-voting majority and, for more than half a century, excluded a permanent voting minority. Predominantly rural and poor, Phillips County has a history of extremely polarized voting: Whites vote exclusively for white candidates and blacks vote for black candidates whenever they can. In many elections, no white person ever publicly supports or endorses a black candidate. Although qualified, highly regarded black candidates compete, local election rules and the manipulation of those rules by a white bloc have meant that no black person in over a century had been elected to any countywide office when I brought a lawsuit in 1987. Yet blacks were just less than half of the voting-age population.

Reverend Julious McGruder, a black political candidate and a former school board member, testified on the basis of fifteen years of working in elections that "no white candidate or white person has come out and supported [a] black." Black attorney Sam Whitfield won a primary and requested support in the runoff from Kenneth Stoner, a white candidate he had defeated in the first round. In a private conversation, Stoner told Whitfield that he personally thought Whitfield was the better remaining candidate but that he could not support him. As Whitfield recounted the conversation at trial, Stoner said, "He could not support a black man. He lives in this town. He is a farmer. His wife teaches school here and that there is just no way that he could support a black candidate."

Racially polarized voting is only one of the political disadvantages for blacks in Phillips County. Blacks, whose median income is less than three thousand dollars annually, also suffer disproportionately from poverty, which works to impede their effective participation in the political process. For example, 42 percent of blacks have no car or truck, while only 9 percent of the white population are similarly encumbered; and 30 percent of blacks, compared to 11 percent of whites, have no telephone. Thus isolated by poverty, black voters are less able to maneuver around such obstacles as frequent, last-minute changes in polling places. County officials have moved polling places ten times in as many elections, often without prior notice and sometimes to locations up to twelve to fifteen miles away, over dirt and gravel roads. Moreover, because of the relative scarcity of cars, the lack of public transportation in the county, and the expense of taxis, the election campaigns of black candidates must include a get-out-and-vote kind of funding effort that a poor black community simply cannot afford.

Black candidates who win the first round come up against one particular local election rule—the majority vote runoff law—that doubles the access problem, by requiring people to get to the polls two times within a two-week period. Because this rule combines with local racism, almost half the voters for over a century never enjoyed any opportunity to choose who represents them. As a numerical, stigmatized, and racially isolated minority, blacks regarded the majority vote requirement as simply a tool to "steal the election"—a tool that had the effect of demobilizing black political participation, enhancing polarization rather than fostering debate, and in general excluding black interests from the political process. As Rev. McGruder testified, running twice to win once "*just kill[s] all the momentum, all of the hope, all of the faith, the belief in the system.*" Many voters "really can't understand the situation where you say 'You know, Brother Whitfield won last night' and then come up to a grandma or my uncle, auntie and say 'Hey, you know, we're going to have to run again in the next 10 days and—because we've got a runoff.'"

In fact, between the first and second elections, turnout drops precipitously, so that the so-called majority winner in the runoff may receive fewer votes than the plurality winner in the first primary. In fact, in all three black-white runoff contests in 1986, the white runoff victor's majority occurred only because the number of people who came out to vote in the second primary went down.

Indeed, the district court that heard the challenge in 1988 to the Arkansas law did not dispute the facts: that no black candidate had ever been elected to countywide or state legislative office from Phillips County and that "race has frequently dominated over qualifications and issues" in elections. The court, nonetheless, preferred to stick with this obviously unfair electoral scheme, reasoning that The Majority should prevail even when The Majority is the product of a completely artificial and racially exclusionary runoff system. It is decisions like this one that continue to inspire me to work for a better way.

The court failed to see that the unfairness wrought by winner-take-all majority rule was inconsistent with democratic fair play in this county. At first blush, the unfairness of 51 percent of the people winning 100 percent of the power may not seem obvious. It certainly seems to be much less than the unfairness of a professional hatmaker's competing against kids. But in some ways it is worse. For example, when voters are drawn into participation by seemingly fair rules, only to discover that the rules systematically work against their interests, they are likely to feel seduced and abandoned. Moreover, those Brownies who made their own hats could at least be assured that others would sympathize with their having been taken advantage of. People who have been systematically victimized by winner-take-all majority rules usually get little sympathy from a society that wrongfully equates majority tyranny with democracy.

As the plaintiffs' evidence demonstrated, this was precisely the situation in Phillips County, where the fairness of the majority requirement was destroyed by extreme racial polarization, the absence of reciprocity, and the artificial majorities created in the runoffs. Judge Richard Arnold put it simply in a related case: Implementation of the majority vote requirement in eastern Arkansas represented a pattern of actions in which "a systematic and deliberate attempt" was made to "close off" avenues of opportunity to blacks in the affected jurisdictions.

In other words, my project has been to return the inquiry to its most authoritative source—the voters themselves. For example, Milagros

Robledo, a Latino voter in Philadelphia, is one of many voters who say they are angry, confused and more cynical than ever about the political process. After a recent scandal involving the solicitation of absentee ballots in a hotly contested local election, Mr. Robledo lamented, "After going through this whole thing, I now really know the value of my vote. It means nothing to me, and it means a lot to the politicians." For Mr. Robledo, his community has continuously been shortchanged by elected officials who are more interested in getting elected than in representing the people.

I take my cue from people like Milagros Robledo. I seek to keep their faith that votes should not count more than voters. I struggle to conceptualize the representatives' relationship with voters to make that relationship more dynamic and interactive.

It is in the course of this struggle that I made my much maligned references to "the authenticity assumption." Authenticity is a concept I describe within my general criticism of conventional empowerment strategies. The Voting Rights Act expressly provides that black and Latino voters must be afforded an equal opportunity "to participate in the political process and to elect representatives of their choice." The question is: which candidates are the representatives of choice of black or Latino voters?

Authenticity subsumes two related but competing views to answer that question. The first version of authenticity seeks information from election results to learn how the voters perceive elected officials. In this view, voting behavior is key. Authentic representatives are simply those truly chosen by the people. The second authenticity assumption is that voters trust elected officials who "look like" or act like the voters themselves. In this view, authenticity refers to a candidate who shares common physical or cultural traits with constituents. In this aspect of authenticity, the nominally cultural becomes political.

Despite the importance of voter choice in assessing minority preferred or minority sponsored candidates, those who support the second authenticity assumption substitute the concept of presumptive or descriptive representativeness in which candidates who look like their constituents are on that basis alone presumed to be representative. In the name of authenticity, these observers have argued that the current voting rights litigation model is effective because it provides blacks or Latinos an opportunity to elect physically black or culturally Latino representatives. This is an understandable position, and I present it as such, but it is not *my* position. Indeed, I term it "a limited empowerment concept."

My preference is for the first view of authenticity, the one that focuses on the voter, not the candidate. In *Thornburg v. Gingles*, a 1986 Supreme Court opinion, Justice William Brennan stressed that it is the "status of the candidate as the chosen representative of a particular racial group, not the race of the candidate, that is important."

This leads to two complementary conclusions that are firmly embedded in the caselaw and the literature. First, white candidates can legitimately represent nonwhite voters if those voters elected them. . . . And second, the election of a black or Latino candidate or two will not defeat a voting rights lawsuit, especially if those black or Latino elected officials did not receive electoral support from their community. Just because a candidate is black does not mean that he or she is the candidate of choice of the black community.

Borrowing from the language of the statute, I say voters, not politicians, should count. And voters count most when voters can exercise a real choice based on what the candidates think and do rather than what the candidates look like.

As I wrote these law review articles, my thinking evolved. New ideas emerged and old ones were rejected as I struggled to understand the tyranny of different majorities. But one idea remained constant: I am a democratic idealist, committed to making American politics open to genuine participation by all voters. It is as part of this life-long commitment to democratic fair play that I explore the many dimensions of majority tyranny.

Concern over majority tyranny has typically focused on the need to monitor and constrain the substantive policy outputs of the decisionmaking process. In my articles, however, I look at the *procedural* rules by which preferences are identified and counted. Procedural rules govern the process by which outcomes are decided. They are the rules by which the game is played.

I have been roundly, and falsely, criticized for focusing on outcomes. Outcomes are indeed relevant, but *not* because I seek to advance particular ends, such as whether the children play tag or hide-and-seek, or whether the band at Brother Rice plays rock music or rap. Rather, I look to outcomes as *evidence* of whether all the children—or all the high school seniors—feel that their choice is represented and considered. The purpose is not to guarantee "equal legislative outcomes"; equal opportunity to *influence* legislative outcomes regardless of race is more like it.

For these reasons, I sometimes explore alternatives to simple, winner-take-all majority rule. I do not advocate any one procedural rule as a universal panacea for unfairness. Nor do I propose these remedies primarily as judicial solutions. They can be adopted only in the context of litigation after the court first finds a legal violation.

Outside of litigation, I propose these approaches as political solutions if, depending on the local context, they better approximate the goals of democratic fair play. One such decisionmaking alternative is called cumulative voting, which could give all the students at Brother Rice multiple votes and allow them to distribute their votes in any combination of their choice. If each student could vote for ten songs, the students could plump or aggregate their votes to reflect the intensity of their preferences. They could put ten votes on one song; they could put five votes on two songs. If a tenth of the students opted to "cumulate" or plump all their votes for one song, they would be able to select one of every ten or so songs played at the prom. The black seniors could have done this if they chose to, but so could any other cohesive group of sufficient size. In this way, the songs preferred by a majority would be played most often, but the songs the minority enjoyed would also show up on the play list.

Under cumulative voting, voters get the same number of votes as there are seats or options to vote for, and they can then distribute their votes in any combination to reflect their preferences. Like-minded voters can vote as a solid bloc or, instead, form strategic, cross-racial coalitions to gain mutual benefits. This system is emphatically not racially based; it allows voters to organize themselves on whatever basis they wish.

Corporations use this system to ensure representation of minority shareholders on corporate boards of directors. Similarly, some local municipal and county governments have adopted cumulative voting to ensure representation of minority voters. Instead of awarding political power to geographic units called districts, cumulative voting allows voters to cast ballots based on what they think rather than where they live.

Cumulative voting is based on the principle of one person—one vote because each voter gets the same total number of votes. Everyone's preferences are counted equally. It is not a particularly radical idea; thirty states either require or permit corporations to use this election system. Cumulative voting is certainly not antidemocratic because it emphasizes the importance of voter choice in selecting public or social policy. And it is neither liberal nor conservative. Both the Reagan and Bush administrations approved cumulative voting schemes pursuant to the Voting Rights Act to protect the rights of racial- and language-minority voters.

But, as in Chilton County, Alabama, which now uses cumulative voting to elect both the school board and the county commission, any politically cohesive group can vote strategically to win representation. Groups of voters win representation depending on the exclusion threshold, meaning the percentage of votes needed to win one seat or have the band play one song. That threshold can be set case by case, jurisdiction by jurisdiction, based on the size of minority groups that make compelling claims for representation.

Normally the exclusion threshold in a head-to-head contest is 50 percent, which means that only groups that can organize a majority can get elected. But if multiple seats (or multiple songs) are considered simultaneously, the exclusion threshold is considerably reduced. For example, in Chilton County, with seven seats elected simultaneously on each governing body, the threshold of exclusion is now one-eighth. Any group with the solid support of one-eighth the voting population cannot be denied representation. This is because any self-identified minority can plump or cumulate all its votes for one candidate. Again, minorities are not defined solely in racial terms.

As it turned out in Chilton County, both blacks and Republicans benefited from this new system. The school board and commission now each have three white Democrats, three white Republicans, and one black Democrat. Previously, when each seat was decided in a head-to-head contest, the majority not only ruled but monopolized. Only white Democrats were elected at every prior election during this century.

Similarly, if the black and white students at Brother Rice have very different musical taste, cumulative voting permits a positive-sum solution to enable both groups to enjoy one prom. The majority's preferences would be respected in that their songs would be played most often, but the black students could express the intensity of their preferences too. If the black students chose to plump all their votes on a few songs, their minority preferences would be recognized and played. Essentially, cumulative voting structures the band's repertoire to enable the students to take turns.

As a solution that permits voters to self-select their identities, cumulative voting also encourages cross-racial coalition building. No one is locked into a minority identity. Nor is anyone necessarily isolated by the identity they choose. Voters can strengthen their influence by forming coalitions to elect more than one representative or to select a range of music more compatible with the entire student body's preferences.

Women too can use cumulative voting to gain greater representation. Indeed, in other countries with similar, alternative voting systems, women are more likely to be represented in the national legislature. For example, in some Western European democracies, the national legislatures have as many as 37 percent female members compared to a little more than 5 percent in our Congress.

There is a final benefit from cumulative voting. It eliminates gerrymandering. By denying protected incumbents safe seats in gerrymandered districts, cumulative voting might encourage more voter participation. With greater interest-based electoral competition, cumulative voting could promote the political turnover sought by advocates of term limits. In this way, cumulative voting serves many of the same ends as periodic elections or rotation in office, a solution that Madison and others advocated as a means of protecting against permanent majority factions. . . .

I hope that we can learn three positive lessons from my experience. The first lesson is that those who stand for principles may lose in the short run, but they cannot be suppressed in the long run. The second lesson is that public dialogue is critical to represent all perspectives; no one viewpoint should be permitted to monopolize, distort, caricature, or shape public debate. The tyranny of The Majority is just as much a problem of silencing minority viewpoints as it is of excluding minority representatives or preferences. We cannot all talk at once, but that does not mean only one group should get to speak. We can take turns. Third, we need consensus and positive-sum solutions. We need a broad public conversation about issues of racial justice in which we seek win-win solutions to real-life problems. If we include blacks and whites, and women and men, and Republicans and Democrats, and even people with new ideas, we will all be better off. . . .

Most of all, I hope we begin to consider the principle of taking turns as a means to bring us closer to the ideal of democratic fair play. Justice Potter Stewart wrote in 1964 that our form of representative self-government reflects "the strongly felt American tradition that the public interest is composed of many diverse interests, [which] . . . in the long run . . . can better be expressed by a medley of component voices than by the majority's monolithic command." In that "strongly felt American tradition," I hope more of us aspire to govern like Madisonian Majorities through "a medley of component voices." In that "strongly felt American tradition," I hope more of us come to reject the "monolithic command" of The fixed Majority.

After all, government is a public experiment. Let us not forget Justice Louis Brandeis's advice at the beginning of this century: "If we guide by the light of reason, we must let our minds be bold." At the close of the same century, I hope we rediscover the bold solution to the tyranny of The Majority, which has always been more democracy, not less.

Study Questions

1. What is the distinction between negative liberty and positive liberty? What are the main arguments for each?
2. What is Nozick's argument for property rights?
3. Discuss some of the arguments, both pro and con, on the issue of limiting the concentration of wealth.
4. What is the traditional justification for property rights (as given by John Locke)? What are some traditional objections to that account?
5. Some people claim that even if the traditional Lockean account of property rights was once plausible, it does not work in contemporary society. What reasons do they give?
6. According to Mill, what limits can legitimately be placed on one's freedom of action?
7. Guinier is a strong advocate of democracy, but she sees some problems in the system, particularly in some types of societies. What problems does she discuss?

Exercises

1. One of the great American slogans is that the United States is a land of "equal opportunity." What changes would be required in American society in order to make that slogan true?

2. What would count as a "fair distribution of wealth"? John Rawls claims that the best way to answer that question is to step behind his "veil of ignorance" (in which you are about to enter a society, but you have no idea of what your gender, race, inheritance, talent, and goals will be) and reach your answer free from special interests. From behind the veil of ignorance, what distribution of wealth would *you* favor?

   Rawls believes that, from behind the veil of ignorance, we would choose a strategy that "maximizes the minimum." That is, we would favor a system that provided the *worst off* in the society with the largest possible share. That would probably *not* be a strictly egalitarian system, according to Rawls; instead, by allowing some unequal distribution of goods, we might provide incentives for people to work harder and thus increase the overall wealth of the society; and because the overall wealth would then be greater (the pie would be larger), those getting the smallest slices would still get *larger* slices than they would if they received an exactly equal portion of a smaller pie. Does Rawls's distribution model match the one you selected? If not, do you now think that Rawls's model is preferable to the one you selected? Why?

3. Thomas Jefferson believed that the essential foundation of democratic government is in private businesses: the shopkeeper who owns and operates her own shop, the farmer who owns his own land and runs his own farm. According to Jefferson, this independent management of a business—making your own decisions, reaping the benefits of your own labor and ingenuity—gives you a stake in the future of the country, as well as experience in making your own decisions, and both are vital to the democratic process. In our contemporary economic system, Jefferson's values seem rather quaint: Small family farms cannot compete with huge agribusinesses and so have largely disappeared, small businesses typically either fail or get bought out by huge corporations, and local shopkeepers have been displaced by gargantuan retail chains. We now live in an economy of concentrated wealth, enormous and powerful corporations, and a top-down management style in which most workers have few opportunities for significant independent decision making. In this economy, is there any workable substitute for the practice of independent decision making and individual responsibility that ownership of small businesses and farms provided to past generations?

4. Describe in detail the essential conditions for a country to be a genuine democracy.

5. In the United States, it is illegal to buy and sell transplant organs (such as hearts and kidneys). Should that ban be lifted and organs be made available to the highest bidder? For example, if you wish to sell one of your extra kidneys on E-bay, should you be allowed to do so?

In the United States, it is legal to sell blood, and commercial blood banks advertise for donors and sell the blood they collect (although, of course, most blood is collected through free donations). In Great Britain, it is illegal to buy blood from donors: All blood comes from the gift of donors. Which system do you think is best?

6. In the previous two chapters, Ben favors a *libertarian* view of free will: Free will involves a special power to act as a "self-moved mover," to act in ways that are *not* determined by one's past environment. In this chapter, Ben is the strongest advocate of *negative* liberty. Of course, there is no perfect match between those two views: Obviously, some libertarians will be zealous advocates of positive liberty and consider negative liberty inadequate. But do you think there is likely to be a *positive correlation* between libertarians and those who favor negative liberties? That is, do you think there is something about the libertarian view of free will that leads one toward a negative-liberty view, or (from the other direction) do you think that there is something about favoring the negative-liberty perspective that would lead one toward libertarian free will? Or are the two issues basically unrelated?

Glossary

Negative liberty: The liberty to be left alone; that is, the liberty of noninterference.

Positive liberty: The liberty of opportunity; that is, the liberty of having adequate resources for the pursuit of one's choices and goals.

Additional Resources

The additional resources for Chapter Nine—especially those related to social-contract theory—are also relevant here.

Isaiah Berlin is the main source for the distinction between positive and negative liberty; see *Four Essays on Liberty* (New York: Oxford University Press, 1969). An excellent biography of Berlin is by Michael Ignatieff: *Isaiah Berlin: A Life* (New York: Vintage, 2000).

The position that some inequality is acceptable so long as the basic needs of everyone are met is championed by Joel Feinberg in *Social Philosophy* (Englewood Cliffs, NJ: Prentice-Hall, 1973).

The position that freedom and equality are in conflict can be found in F. A. Hayek, *The Constitution of Liberty* (Chicago: University of Chicago Press, 1960); in Milton Friedman, *Capitalism and Freedom* (Chicago: University of Chicago Press, 1962); and in Robert Nozick, *Anarchy, State, and Utopia* (New York: Basic Books, 1974). The opposing view is presented by Michael Walzer, *Spheres of Justice* (New York: Basic Books, 1983); Kai Nielsen, *Equality and Liberty* (Totowa, NJ: Rowman and in Allanheld, 1985); Virginia Held, "Rights to Equal Liberty," in *Rights and Goods* (New York: Free Press, 1984); and Richard Norman, *Free and Equal* (Oxford, U.K.: Oxford University Press, 1987).

For a history of political thought, there are many choices. Among the best resources are Iain Hampsher-Monk, *A History of Political Thought: Major Political Thinkers from Hobbes to Marx* (Oxford, U.K.: Blackwell, 1992); and a two-volume study by Janet Coleman: *A History of Political Thought: From Ancient Greece to Early Christianity* (Oxford, U.K.: Blackwell, 2000) and *A History of Political Thought: From the Middle Ages to the Renaissance* (Oxford, U.K.: Blackwell, 2000).

One of the great contrasts in modern political thought is between liberalism and conservatism. Immanuel Kant is a classical source for modern liberalism. His political writings can be found in *Political Writings*, edited by Hans Reiss (Cambridge, U.K.: Cambridge University Press, 1996). John Stuart Mill's *On Liberty*—discussed by Ben—is a major work in this tradition, and many good editions are widely available. Perhaps the best-known contemporary philosopher in the liberal tradition is John Rawls; see the suggestions for additional resources at the end of Chapter Nine and also his *Political Liberalism* (New York: Cambridge University Press, 1993). Ronald Dworkin is another major figure in contemporary liberal philosophy; see his *Taking Rights Seriously* (London: Duckworth, 1977). The classic source for conservative thought is Edmund Burke: Among his vast output of writings, one of the most readable is *Reflections on the Revolution in France*, available in many editions. More recent conservative writers include Michael Oakeshott, *Rationalism in Politics and Other Essays* (London: Methuen, 1962), and Milton Friedman's aforementioned *Capitalism and Freedom*.

For the contrast between liberal individualism and communitarian views, see *The Communitarian Challenge to Liberalism*, edited by F. D. Miller, Jr., and J. Paul (Cambridge, U.K.: Cambridge University Press, 1996). Alasdair MacIntyre's *After Virtue* (London: Duckworth, 1981) is a widely read philosophical essay that champions the communitarian view. Among the many excellent books on feminist political theory are J. B. Landes, ed., *Feminism, the Public and the Private* (Oxford, U.K.: Oxford University Press, 1998), and G. Bock and S. James, eds., *Beyond Equality and Difference: Citizenship, Feminist Politics and Female Subjectivity* (London: Routledge, 1992).

Among the important views of property are those by John Locke in *Two Treatises of Government* (originally published in 1690), David Hume in *Treatise of Human Nature* (1640), and John Stuart Mill, *Principles of Political Economy*, 7th ed. (1871). For the views of Karl Marx, see "Economic and Philosophic Manuscripts," in *Karl Marx: Early Writings*, translated by T. B. Bottomore (New York: McGraw-Hill, 1964). An interesting critique of the traditional justification of property rights is offered by the sociologist Emile Durkheim in *Professional Ethics and Civic Morals*, trans. by Cornelia Brookfield (London: Routledge & Paul, 1957). An excellent anthology, that includes a number of essays on the question of property written from a variety of perspectives is *Justice and Economic Distribution*, edited by John Arthur and William H. Shaw (Englewood Cliffs, NJ: Prentice-Hall, 1978). A very distinctive perspective on property was developed by Thorstein Veblen in *The Theory of the Leisure Class* (New York: The Macmillan Company, 1899). A particularly clear and well-written book (and one in dialogue form) that devotes considerable attention to concepts of property is Frances Moore Lappé, *Redis-covering America's Values* (New York: Ballantine Books, 1989).

There are some superb Internet resources for political philosophy. One of my favorites—which contains a particularly good set of links—is maintained by the University of British Columbia Library and can be found at *http://www.library .ubc.ca/poli/theory.html*. Another very good site—organized very effectively and with extensive links—is maintained by the Department of Political Science at the University of Pisa; go to *http://lgxserver.uniba.it/lei/filpol/filpole/homepage.htm*. The online *Stanford Encyclopedia of Philosophy* is an excellent site for almost any topic in philosophy in general, practically any topic in political philosophy, or virtually any influential political philosopher, from ancient to contemporary; go to *http://plato.stanford.edu/*. The *Internet Encyclopedia of Philosophy* at *http:// www.utm.edu/research/iep/Wikipedia*, is also very good, and "the free *encyclopedia*," at *http://en.wikipedia.org/wiki*, is a good source for biographies, especially of contemporary philosophers.

A much-debated contemporary issue in the United States—one that brings into focus many of the issues discussed in this chapter—is whether there should be a repeal of the inheritance tax (the estate tax—those who favor repealing the tax sometimes call it the death tax). An overview of the issue can be found at *http:// www.pbs.org/now/politics/inheritance.html*. An argument in favor of repealing the tax can be found at *http://www.capitalism.net/articles/Inhertax.html*. The web-site, which features the work of George Reisman, who teaches economics at Pep-perdine, represents itself as being "The Intellectual Voice of Capitalism on the Internet." The case in favor of keeping the inheritance tax can be found at the website for "Responsible Wealth," at *http://www.responsiblewealth.org*.

Notes

1. This distinction was drawn by Isaiah Berlin in "Two Concepts of Liberty," in *Four Essays on Liberty* (New York: Oxford University Press, 1969).
2. For more on the Diggers and Levellers, see a superb work by Christopher Hill: *The World Turned Upside Down: Radical Ideas during the English Revolution* (Hammondsworth, U.K.: Penguin Books, 1972, 1975).
3. Hegel, *Philosophy of Right*, Section 41.

Chapter *11*

Personal Identity

in which Sarah wonders who she is

"Hi, Sarah. You look deep in thought."

"Oh, hi, Selina. Yeah, I was. Just puzzling about something. Sit down, I need your help."

"Oh, no, I know that look. This is another of those deep philosophical quandaries, isn't it? I just got out of organic. I'm not sure I can stand any more quandaries."

"But this one's child's play, Selina. I was remembering back when I was very small, and my mother used to read some book to me, and then we'd play this silly game. I loved it, and I wanted to play it every night. She'd tuck me into bed and tell me that she loved me more than anything in the world, more than the Sun and the stars. And I'd say something like, if I turned into a duck, would you still love me? And she'd say yes, I would still love you. If I turned into a big hairy spider, would you still love me? Yes, I'd still love you. If somehow they had mixed up the babies at the hospital and I wasn't really your baby, would you still love me? Yes, I'd still love you, and you'd still be my special baby, no matter what. If you found out I was really a creature from Mars, would you still love me? Yes, Sugar, I'd still love you; now go to sleep, and dream about little bunny rabbits hopping through the clover."

Selina laughed. "Yeah, my Momma used to play a game like that with me. She'd say, Selina, Honey, I love you, love you, love you. And I'd say, would you love me if I turned into a turnip, and she'd say, why, you'd be the cutest turnip I ever saw, and I would love you just as much. But I don't remember anything about little bunnies hopping through the clover. I think it was little lambs playing in the tall green grass. But that part's a little fuzzy."

"Well, it was that stuff about still loving you if you turned into a turnip, or still loving you if you turned into a big hairy spider. That's what

505

I was thinking about. It was great, and I loved to hear it every night. And when I have kids, I'm going to tell them exactly the same thing. Unconditional love, no exceptions, no changes possible: That's what kids need. It's psychologically sound. But the problem is, it's philosophically perplexing."

"Why perplexing? Still sounds good to me."

"But how can you still love someone when she turns into a turnip? I mean, maybe you could love a turnip: People love diamonds, why not turnips? Though, actually, I'm not sure that when they say they love diamonds, they mean it in quite the same way. Not being that fond of diamonds, I really couldn't say. But I do know that no *turnip* would be the same as Selina. Turnips don't have Selina's wicked wit, or her devilish charm, or her sparkling eyes. I'm not sure what the essential features of being Selina are; but whatever they are, no turnip could have them."

"What if the turnip had all my memories?"

"Get out of here, Selina. You've been watching too many cartoons. Hi, kids, here's *Selina*, the chemistry-loving turnip. No way. You should have paid closer attention in your biology class: Turnips don't have central nervous systems. Without a central nervous system, you don't major in chemistry, you don't discuss philosophy, and you *don't* have memories."

"Aw, Sarah, you've destroyed one of my fondest dreams: I always wanted to be reincarnated as a bright orange carrot."

"Find another dream, Selina. There may be carrots of all sorts and sizes, but none of them will be the reincarnation of Selina. What characteristics must you still have to be Selina? Hard to say, but a carrot couldn't have them."

"Actually, I agree with you, Sarah. Suppose a malevolent demon transforms me into a frog, with a taste for flies and no reasoning ability and no memory of my past life as a human; then perhaps it would be more reasonable to say that the demon destroyed me and created a new frog, rather than saying 'I became a frog.' After all, how could my identity carry over into the frog? Someone might say that I still have the same soul, but that shows how empty the notion of a soul really is."

"So are there any qualities that are essential for you to remain Selina? Any clear criteria for your own personal identity?"

"It's an interesting question, Sarah: What qualities must I have to remain Selina? Obviously, some of them aren't essential. I remember my Momma marking the kitchen wall, the day I reached four feet tall. I was so proud! Now I'm five two, but I'm still Selina. So it can't be height. In eighth grade I was in love with Jimmy Lavelle, and a year later I couldn't stand him, but I was still Selina. And Selina used to believe every single doctrine taught by the Solid Rock Holiness Church, and now I don't; but I'm still Selina. So exactly what is it that makes me who I am?"

"Hi guys." Ben placed his books and coffee cup on the table.

"Ben, who am I?" Selina tried the direct approach.

"You're the most amazing, infinitely wonderful, stunningly beautiful, fabulously sexy creature on the face of the Earth."

"Well, I guess that settles that question." Selina laughed, leaned up toward Ben as he sat down, and kissed him intensely.

"Maybe not, Selina." Sarah had another question. "Ben, you said that Selina is stunningly beautiful—as, indeed, she is—and you identified her with that characteristic. Suppose she lost her beauty and became an ugly old hag. Would she still be Selina?"

"Wait a minute, Sarah. I haven't even had a sip of coffee, and you're asking me a question that's likely to land me in a world of trouble."

Selina smiled at him. "Yes, Ben, watch your step. This personal identity business is packed with perils. Sarah, why did you lead us into these treacherous philosophical waters?"

Problems of Personal Identity

"It is a tough philosophical issue, true enough. But it can also be a very practical issue. Suppose I committed a terrible murder when I was eighteen, but there was not enough evidence to bring charges against me. There's no statute of limitations on murder, however. Now, seventy years later, investigators analyze some DNA from the murder scene, and they discover that I committed the murder. But am I the same person? Is it right to punish an old woman of eighty-eight years for something done by an impetuous eighteen-year-old kid? I mean, even if you believe in just deserts and retribution and all that, are you sure you're punishing the *right person*?"

"Yeah, a similar question came up in my bioethics class," Selina said, "when we were discussing living wills. Sarah, you're a philosopher: You place great value on careful thought and rational deliberation. Suppose you decide that, if you lost your capacity for deep rational deliberation, you would not want to go on living. So you draw up a living will clearly stating your wishes: In case you are permanently mentally incapacitated, you want no medical measures taken to extend your life. You leave explicit orders: no resuscitation if you have a heart attack, no medication if you develop a fatal disease. Sure enough, what you dread actually happens, and you develop a brain disease that causes severe dementia, and you have permanently lost your rational faculties. But you are now—at least to all appearances—a very happy individual: You go around with a big smile on your face, and you seem to take delight in simple, bright-colored objects. When you are given several brightly colored plastic blocks, you sit on the floor for hours, just moving them around and laughing with delight. Friends who visit say that Sarah is happier than she has ever been. She always seemed worried, driven, tightly wound, troubled by philosophical quandaries to which she could find no answer. Now she is happy, content, delighted for hour after hour."

"I don't know, Selina. If I had lost my ability to think rationally, to contemplate philosophical questions, then that wouldn't really be me. Whoever that happy individual is who is contentedly playing with the brightly colored blocks, she's not Sarah: I'm not that person."

"Exactly right!" Selina was delighted. "Now suppose this happy individual, whoever she is, develops an infection. The infection is easily treatable with antibiotics, and with the right treatment she will be well within a few days. But remember the living will you wrote? It says *no* lifesaving treatment. But if the Sarah who wrote the living will is a different person from the brain-damaged Sarah now happily playing with the blocks, why should the first Sarah have any say over what happens to this new Sarah? *You* might not wish to live if you lost your rationality; but this new individual seems to like it fine."

"There's another important place where the question of personal identity comes up," said Ben. "What about continued existence in the afterlife? It's not an issue for Selina, since she plans to turn into dust when she drops off the twig. But for some of us, the question of how we could survive as specific identifiable individuals after our bodily deaths is a very serious question indeed."

"Don't worry, Ben," Sarah smiled, "it's a miracle, right? God will take care of everything. We'll understand it better in the sweet by-and-by."

"I know you're just teasing, Selina, but you're probably right. Now we see through a glass darkly, and then we'll see more clearly. Still, I would like to understand it better in the sweet here and now."

"Actually, I do think the question of personal identity is important," Selina said, "though not because I want to keep my identity after St. Peter fits me with wings and a halo. Frankly, if there is someone named Selina who is absolutely pure of heart and singing soprano in the Heavenly choir, then whoever that devout angel is, it would not be me. But a cranky old woman wearing a bright-purple warm-up suit and mixing manhattans at the old-folks' home: Well, maybe that *would* be me. Not if she votes Republican, though—and not if she speaks a kind word about Ohio State. But anyway, what *would* make that old woman identical with *me?*"

Bodies and Brains

"One answer," said Sarah, "is bodily continuity. Major idea in the Jewish and Christian traditions, right, Ben? What happens on judgment day? The sea shall give up its dead, the graves will open, the dead shall be resurrected. That's a neat and easy solution."

"Neat and easy," Selina replied, "but not very plausible. After all, our bodies are constantly remade. Besides, there are too many exceptions. You lose your arm or your leg, or you donate one of your kidneys; you haven't lost a piece of your self. If my leg were amputated, I wouldn't be only ninety percent of Selina. If we had a major operation, and some mad surgeons exchanged our arms and legs and hearts and kidneys and lungs, you would still be one hundred percent Sarah and I'd be one hundred percent Selina."

"Yeah," agreed Sarah. "This philosopher, Sydney Shoemaker, came up with a weird example—weird, but effective. Suppose that surgeons have developed a new way to deal with brain tumors. They remove the entire brain, perform the operation, and then insert the brain back into the body. It seems to work fine. One day they have two operations at the same time, on Mr. Brown and Mr. Robinson. Unfortunately, there's a mixup and the brains get reversed, with Brown's brain going into Robinson's body and Robinson's brain into Brown's body. The individual who has Brown's body and Robinson's brain doesn't recover, but the fellow with Brown's brain and Robinson's body does. The surviving individual—call him Brownson— recognizes Brown's wife and family and friends (though he had never met them before), describes Brown's life in detail, and has all the likes and dislikes, mannerisms and quirks, personality traits and values that characterized Brown; and he acts and thinks very differently from the old Robinson. In that case, we would likely conclude that Brownson is really Brown, and though Robinson's body is still functioning, Robinson is dead."

"Nice story," Ben said, "but we don't really need science fiction to make that point. After all, if someone is in a permanent vegetative state— where almost all the brain has stopped functioning and the individual has no consciousness—we may keep the individual breathing and the heart pumping and the body functioning, but that person is essentially dead."

"So what establishes your personal identity is your *brain*," Selina said triumphantly. "There's no mind, no spirit, distinct from the brain. Materialism is vindicated!"

"Maybe so, Selina," Sarah replied, "but maybe not. Suppose we were taking some old car apart, and replacing it piece by piece. Some people have suggested that a similar process might happen to the brain. In fact, at least one distinguished researcher on artificial intelligence—Hans Moravec—seems to consider it likely that such a process will actually occur within a few decades. Anyway, here's our dear Ben. Unfortunately, Ben suffers a disease that will soon cause damage to part of his brain. Just a tiny section in the frontal lobes, but it causes serious cognitive difficulties."

"No problem," said Selina. "Ben's blessed with an immaterial soul, remember? His soul could take over; he doesn't need a brain. He could be like the scarecrow in the *Wizard of Oz*!"

The story of Brownson is thought provoking, but the idea of Brownson being Brown, even though Brown's brain now inhabits Robinson's body, may be more difficult than such thought examples make it seem. Consider the following passage from Bernard Williams:

> Suppose a magician is hired to perform the old trick of making the emperor and the peasant become each other. He gets the emperor and the peasant in one room, with the emperor on his throne and the peasant in the corner. What will count as success? Clearly not that after the smoke has cleared the old emperor should be in the corner and the old peasant on the throne. That would be a rather boring trick. The requirement is presumably that the emperor's body, with the peasant's personality, should be on the throne, and the peasant's body with the emperor's personality, in the corner. What does this mean? In particular, what has happened to the voices? The voice presumably ought to count as a bodily function; yet how would the peasant's gruff blasphemies be uttered in the emperor's cultivated tones, or the emperor's witticisms in the peasant's growl? A similar point holds for the features; the emperor's body might include the sort of face that just *could not* express the peasant's morose suspiciousness, the peasant's a face no expression of which could be taken for one of fastidious arrogance. These 'could's are not just empirical—such expressions on these features might be unthinkable.

Bernard Williams, *Problems of the Self*
(Cambridge, U.K.: Cambridge University Press, 1973), pp.11–12

"Thanks a lot, Selina. Here I am suffering brain damage, and you're cracking jokes about the scarecrow."

"Yeah, the scarecrow," Sarah laughed, "'If I only had a brain!' Well, instead of going to the wizard for a brain, Ben goes to a surgeon who implants a tiny computer chip that takes over the functions of Ben's damaged frontal lobes. And everything is fine: Ben remains the charming, brilliant, cuddly old Ben we all know and love. No one—not even Selina—can tell any difference."

"Could you ask the surgeon to make a slight change, so that I'm no longer a fan of the Chicago Cubs? I think that would make my life a lot happier."

"Nope, no modifications allowed, Ben. You're still the same long-suffering Cubs fan you were before the operation. Okay, the story continues. The disease spreads. Ben doesn't actually suffer any brain damage, but unless something is done, he soon will. So another brain part is replaced by a computer chip—the disease destroys only brain tissue, so it does no damage to the chip—and again, there is no change. This continues until the entire brain is replaced, bit by bit, and Ben's 'brain' is now a computer, rather than nerves; but neither Ben nor anyone else can detect the slightest difference. It would still be Ben, right? So it's not the brain that establishes identity, because the entire brain might be replaced while Ben's identity remains. He's still the same old Ben who argues with us over coffee, the same old Ben whom Selina loves."

Ben frowned. "But look, I'm not so sure that this computer-driven Ben is still me."

"Why not?" Sarah asked. "He walks like Ben, talks like Ben, thinks like Ben. So at what point would you stop being Ben? Surely not when just a tiny portion of your brain was replaced by a computer. When your computer parts totaled more than half? When the very last section of brain was replaced?"

Ben shook his head. "I'm not sure, Sarah. Taking it in small steps like that, it's hard to say. But still, anyone whose thoughts and ideas are all computer generated does not seem to me to be identical with me."

Continuity

"Hey, I think I've got this personal-identity stuff figured out!" Selina was excited. "It's *continuity* that establishes identity. Selina at twenty is very different from the ten-year old girl who was living in Birmingham: different beliefs, interests, friends, goals, tastes, not to mention that I'm stronger, taller, and even better looking now. If you just put them down side by side, you might say that they are two different people. But young Selina changed into older Selina bit by bit, and the same basic biological organization remained intact. I changed bit by bit, but there was still a distinct person changing throughout, even if the ultimate result was radically different. So long as there is *continuity*, identity remains."

"So continuity establishes identity, is that your view, Selina?" Sarah smiled and held up an imaginary object. "See this axe I'm holding? This axe is very special; it's been in the family for many generations. In fact, this is the axe that my great-great-great-great grandfather used when he cleared a farm in Pennsylvania, a few years before the American Revolution. The very same axe. Of course, the handle has been replaced six times, and the head of the axe has been replaced twice; still, it's the same axe that has been in the family all these years. Sometimes we replace the head, sometimes the handle, but never both at once. So there was always continuity, so it's the same axe."

Selina laughed. "You philosophy majors are so obnoxious! Always the clever counterexamples. No, it's not the same axe, Ms. Clever Socrates. But that's because the axe is too simple to really have any systematic continuity. Take my old Chevy. Needs a new set of tires. Fine, still the same car, right? Then I replace the shocks, the next day the brakes, then it needs a new carburetor. I get into a fender bender on this slick Michigan ice, have to replace a fender and a door. Then it needs a new piston, there's rust in another fender, and I replace it from the junkyard. And my dad had the car for ten years before I did, and he replaced lots of parts, especially after a couple of small accidents. Well, over the years, I finally realize that we've replaced every single part in the car, from the front bumper to the taillights, piece by piece. But it's still my dad's old car, right? And why? Because the continuity was maintained. None of the original parts are left, but it's still the same car. If we take the car, melt it down, and use the material to build a picnic table, it would be silly to point to the picnic table and say, 'There's my old '92 Chevy.' It's the same physical stuff, but it doesn't have the same identity. But my car—which has none of its original parts—does retain its identity. The sapling that was planted by my great grandfather is now the enormous oak tree where I had my tire swing. But it's still the same oak tree my great grandfather planted. Of course, it must have sufficient internal complexity to make identity possible. Doesn't work with an axe. But for cars, oak trees, and humans, continuity is the key factor. Personal identity is determined by continuity."

Ben was skeptical. "Maybe for oak trees and chevy sedans, Selina. But not for persons. Physical continuity isn't enough. What counts is mental continuity. For me, what is essential is the continued existence of the spirit, the soul."

"So, lacking a soul," Selina replied, "I guess I've never existed at all."

"You have a wonderful soul, Selina. You just refuse to acknowledge it."

"I've got soul, Ben, no question of that. But not *a* soul. But I have all the existence I need."

"Let's get back to Selina's continuity idea, okay, guys?" Sarah wanted to head off what looked like the start of a long dispute. "Think of another case, a philosophical favorite: Scientists have devised a new way to travel. When you wish to take a long trip, you step inside this cubicle that makes a complete record of you molecule by molecule. That record is then transmitted electronically to another machine at your destination—in Japan, Australia, or even Mars. Your old body is destroyed—vaporized, disintegrated, whatever; it's painless and instantaneous—and then you are reconstructed, molecule by molecule, according to the recorded data, in whatever location you chose. People report no problems or distress when they step out of the distant cubicle, their friends can tell no difference whatsoever, they have all their old memories and beliefs and desires. It's like taking a brief nap and waking up in a new place. Alright, it's science fiction, sure. But you're a materialist, Selina. You shouldn't have any trouble accepting the idea. Selina steps into a "transporter cubicle" in Ann Arbor, and a few seconds later she steps out of a transporter cubicle in Tokyo, still the same delightful Selina, right?"

Selina looked suspicious. "Okay, I'll play. That's still Selina who is walking around in Tokyo. What's your point?"

"Suppose there's a delay. You step into the cubicle at Ann Arbor, they make a record of Selina and send it to Japan, and then your old body is destroyed. But the cubicle in Tokyo is under repair, and they have to wait a couple of days to 'reconstitute' you in Tokyo. So for a couple of days, there's no Selina. There's a record of Selina; but it is certainly not Selina: The record doesn't laugh, or talk, or love, or reason. It's a detailed record of Selina, but it's not Selina. Until the cubicle is fixed and Selina is 'reembodied,' there's no Selina. Finally, the Tokyo cubicle is ready, and out steps Selina, in all her glory. But what happened to the continuity? Of course, she still has the same memories and ideas and beliefs she had when she was in Ann Arbor. She is still Selina. But it isn't *continuity* that is the key to her identity. There can't be continuity between the Ann Arbor Selina and the Tokyo Selina, since, for two days in between, Selina did not exist. So there's no bridge between them, no continuity."

"Alright," Selina said. "It's not physical continuity. It's continuity of ideas and beliefs and memories. That doesn't mean I'm not a materialist: The ideas and beliefs and memories are the product of physical stuff, namely, my brain. After all, when the transporter made a record, it recorded *physical molecules* and then made a copy based on that tape of physical features. Even if there's a gap in time, the continuity of memory and belief established continued personal identity."

"But not *continued memory*, of course," Sarah said. "There was no continued memory during the time you didn't exist. There was a tape, but the tape wasn't remembering anything."

"Right," Selina agreed. "There was continuity of memory in the sense that the memories fit together in an ordered pattern. That's the source of my identity: my memories, beliefs, ideas, affections, goals. If those got totally muddled—I have memories, but they're in no order; and I have values, but they totally shift from minute to minute; and I have beliefs, but they have no rhyme or reason, they're just a stock of unrelated beliefs that come and go—then I would no longer have any real identity. It doesn't mean they can't change, of course: I'm adding new ones constantly, and I forget things, and my beliefs and values are sometimes altered. But there's a coherence and continuity among them that makes them mine, and that establishes my personal identity. And they don't have to be there constantly. Suppose I fall into a deep sleep or am comatose for a period; there may be a time when I'm not thinking or remembering, but such gaps do not destroy my individual identity, so long as they don't rob me of my general set of beliefs and values and memories."

"I think you're right, Selina." Ben recorded his agreement. "Not about the materialism, of course. On that, you're hopeless. But on the memory and belief: That's what makes us who we are."

Duplicate Persons

"Well, it's nice to see you two actually agree on something." Sarah continued. "Look, go back to the molecular transporter for a moment. Turns out the one in Tokyo was working fine: Selina steps out of the cubicle and immediately starts out in search of some great sushi. But back in Ann Arbor, there was a power outage just after the tape was transmitted to Tokyo, so the original Selina was not destroyed. Instead, the door opened, and out she walked. She just assumed that the transporter had malfunctioned. In fact, she has no idea that she's currently munching on sushi in Tokyo. She thinks she is drinking coffee with her friends in Ann Arbor."

"Wait a minute, Sarah; you're making my head spin." Ben frowned. "Which one is Selina?"

"Well, Selina said she was the person in Tokyo, right? So I guess the Ann Arbor Selina must be an impostor. Careful, Ben. You get cozy with this beautiful woman sitting beside you, you're cheating on Selina."

Selina laughed. "No way, Sarah. I'm still Selina. And don't you tell my main squeeze anything different."

"Then who," Sarah asked, "is the person eating sushi in Tokyo? A minute ago, she was Selina, no problem: She's got the right memories, beliefs, continuity. Now suddenly, just because you're still here, she's lost her identity?"

Selina paused, took a long sip of coffee, toyed with her scone. "Okay, I know I'm Selina. They made a duplicate: That can't change the fact that I'm Selina. Now, what about this person over in Tokyo who has the same thoughts and ideas and beliefs? Well, she has to be Selina, also."

"So there will now be two of you?" Sarah leaned forward. "There are now two persons, both of whom are you?"

"Well, two of us who are identical; we both have the same right to use the name Selina."

"Who gets the balance in your checking account?"

"She can have it," Selina replied. "I think it's overdrawn, so it's all hers."

"But now there will be two persons, both of whom are Selina?" Sarah asked.

"Not for long," Selina replied. "We'll soon have separate identities. After all, she's over in Tokyo eating delicious fresh sushi, while I'm eating a stale scone and puzzling about personal identity with this crazy philosophy major."

"Well," Sarah said, "I guess you're the lucky one, right?"

"Lucky or not," replied Selina, "I'm certainly now a different person from the Tokyo Selina. We now have different memories, different experiences."

"Actually," Sarah said, "the idea of duplicate persons isn't really that strange. Suppose we reproduced simply by dividing, just as the paramecium does."

"Wouldn't be nearly as much fun," Selina said.

"Thank you, Selina, for sharing that with us. Anyway, imagine yourself dividing into two identical Selinas, each sharing all the memories and beliefs and tastes and affections of the other. The two of you will have common memories, beliefs, feelings—up to the point that you divide. And then you'll start to diverge. To avoid confusion, you might take different names. Of course, you'll keep a common store of memories—even more so than identical twin sisters. After all, there's a difference between remembering falling off my bike and breaking my arm, and remembering when my sister fell off her bike and broke her arm. Still, though you will retain some identical memories, you will soon become different people with different experiences."

"That's probably true," said Ben, "but it seems a bit strange. Selina and her 'other half' are identical persons now, yet in a couple of hours they will definitely be different persons. But we wouldn't say that if there were only one Selina. Selina will be somewhat different tomorrow than she is today, but she'll still be the *same person*, her identity will not have changed—unless she undergoes some amazing transformation. But if she has a duplicate, and they start off as identical persons, then even very mundane experiences will soon result in their being *different* persons. If those same experiences don't make Selina herself a different person, why should they differentiate between two persons who were originally identical to Selina?"

New Strains on the Concept of Personal Identity

"Good point, Ben. Maybe that indicates that we're using the standards of identity for different purposes. In the case of the initially identical persons, we'll treat any difference at all as significant. After all, we need a way to separate the two. But in normal circumstances, when there is only one Selina—and after all, we know there is no one like our Selina, right?—we don't much need to distinguish different 'Selina stages' or 'Selina revised versions.' Indeed, it takes quite a lot to convince us that Selina has become 'a different person.'"

"Determining personal identity is usually easy," said Ben. "I think of my grandfather, who has changed considerably over the years I've known him. His hair is now gray, and there are deep lines in his face, he's gained several pounds, and he walks a little slower. And his personality has changed: He is often in pain from arthritis, so he's not as easily cheerful as he once was, and he's somewhat quieter; perhaps he's also a little less adventurous than he was when I was a child. But he's still wonderfully patient and gentle, and he still loves bluegrass music, and he's still a dedicated union man. The changes have been significant, but there's no doubt that he's still the same person. I have several reliable indicators of who he is: I know him by his face, by his smile, by his personality and his character. But if it were different, I might not be so certain. If people's minds—or brains if Selina prefers—occasionally got switched into other bodies, then being sure that the person was the same would be more challenging."

"Yeah," Selina agreed, "philosophers have a way of making things difficult. But these are interesting issues, nonetheless. When Sarah places strains on some of our standards of personal identity, we have to think harder about what elements really are decisive."

"They are fun questions," Sarah said, "but sometimes they seem to stretch our concepts of personal identity almost beyond the breaking point. As Ben notes, our standards of personal identity were designed to do duty under less difficult circumstances. By playing around with concepts like duplicate persons or duplicate bodies, you can easily reach questions to which there doesn't seem to be any clear answer. For example, suppose I commit a terrible crime. Then I rig the transporter and have myself sent to Tokyo, Sidney, Rio, and Rome, all at the same time. If I am now caught here in Ann Arbor, and tried and convicted and sentenced to prison, will all those others have to be extradited and locked up also? Or do they get to party in Rio and Rome while I do hard time? Would they have a right to be tried separately? Or think of another case: Someone goes into the transporter, and a duplicate is created in Helsinki. But instead of destroying the original immediately—as is supposed to happen—the transporter operator keeps the original alive for a couple of hours and then kills him. Is that a case of murder? Or is it only assault?"

"You get some serious difficulties about identity even without science fiction," Selina said. "Think of 'multiple-personality disorder'; I think psychologists now refer to it as 'dissociative disorder.' I'm a bit skeptical of it, but suppose it really exists. Imagine that Jeff commits a crime. Is it fair that Will and Jim and Fred—who had nothing to do with the crime and may not even know that it was committed—also get locked up, just because they had the misfortune to share a body with the violent Jeff?"

"And what about reincarnation?" Ben asked. "I don't believe it actually occurs, but the whole concept raises some perplexing questions. Memory of past lives is, I suppose, the best evidence for reincarnation—and when some pirate captain is reincarnated and leads me to his buried treasure, then I'll take reincarnation seriously. But even then, how would you know the difference between being the reincarnated soul of Abraham Lincoln and having clairvoyant knowledge of the details of Lincoln's life?[1] Of course, we generally think we know when we are *remembering* things we did, but the very common phenomenon of false and implanted memories is enough to undermine any confidence about that. Besides, what if I happen to be the reincarnation of a soul with a very poor memory? Maybe I'm currently the reincarnation of half a dozen souls, all of whom have little or no memory of their past lives. Our notion of personal identity doesn't seem well suited for the concept of reincarnation—though maybe the problem is that reincarnation itself is basically incoherent, rather than our concept of personal identity being inadequate."

Sarah shook her head. "Or maybe the problem is deeper: Perhaps we don't have an adequate standard of identity at all. We muddle along by identifying people in terms of bodily continuity, but in fact there is no clear principle of identity, so troublesome cases quickly plunge us into quandaries. Actually"—Sarah paused to turn a page in her notebook—"that was David Hume's view on the subject: 'All the nice and subtle questions concerning personal identity can never possibly be decided, and are to be regarded rather as grammatical than as philosophical difficulties.' Hume believed that our sense of identity developed from the easy transition among ideas; but the ease of the transition is a matter of degree, and 'we have no just standard by which we can decide any dispute concerning the time when they acquire or lose a title to the name of identity.' So maybe our problem is that we're looking for a standard of personal identity that doesn't exist. We can *decide* on what we will count as personal identity and as continuity of identity, but—as Hume states—that will just be a decision about what we shall count as the proper use of language, *not* the discovery of genuine personal identity."

Ben frowned. "That's giving up on the problem of identity, not solving it."

"But Hume thought there is no solution," Sarah replied. "What counts as a smile? Well, obviously, when you see Selina approaching, that silly grin on your face qualifies as a smile. And when Michigan loses to Ohio State, the expressions on our faces are *not* smiles. But what about an expression of pleased triumph over a fallen foe? Or the sickly effort at warmth when greeting someone you despise? Or that thing on your face when you were ten and your mother forced you to stand there in that stupid bunny costume and have your picture taken? Or the insincere rigid white-teeth flashing mask that Miss America contestants constantly wear? We can *decide* that these are smiles or that they are not, but we can't *discover* an objective standard for what counts as a smile and what does not. And saying that is not giving up on the question; instead, it's recognizing that it's the wrong sort of question and that it doesn't have an answer."

"No," Ben disagreed, "I still think there's a standard. It may be difficult to find, but there must be an objectively right answer to the question of whether the kid who sat in the front row of Ms. Kravnak's first grade class at West Elementary is the same as the person now drinking coffee with Sarah and Selina. I know that Hume is one of the philosophical gods, but on this point he's wrong."

"Hume is not the only philosopher to raise that question," Sarah said. "A contemporary British philosopher, Derek Parfit, maintains that personal identity is a matter of degree. According to Parfit, if you ask whether the six-year-old Ben in West Elementary School is the same person as the Ben who studies history at the University of Michigan, then the answer might be 'More or less.' They are the same to a greater degree than the Ben of present company and the newborn Ben, and to a lesser degree than the Ben who is drinking coffee with us today and the Ben who was sharing coffee with us yesterday. Is the Michigan football team that will play in the Rose Bowl the same as the team that opened the season against Illinois? Not exactly: Some players are injured and are no longer playing; others have recovered from injuries and are now on the team; the later team has considerably more experience. Is the team that played Illinois the same team that played Ohio State two years ago? Well, it's still the University of Michigan football team, of course; and it's the same team to a much greater degree than the University of Michigan team of 1930. God may be the same yesterday, today, and tomorrow. But the Michigan football team, and Ben, and the city of Birmingham are *more or less* the same as the entities that went by the same names ten years ago."

"Works for me," Selina said. "Maybe with souls it's all or nothing. But with living, changing humans, it seems reasonable to say that I am more or less the same as that kid named Selina who attended Ridgewood Middle School several years ago."

Ben shook his head and drank his coffee reflectively. "Well, you guys can raise problems about souls all you like. At least with souls you know where you stand. If my identity depends on my soul, then it's all or nothing. I'm not more or less Ben; I'm totally, permanently, and certainly Ben. And you're Selina, and 'Age cannot wither her, nor custom stale her infinite variety,' and fifty years from now you will still be the same fascinating and beautiful and delightful Selina."

"You know," Selina smiled and put her hand on Ben's, "now that I think about it, maybe the boy is right about this personal-identity business."

Sarah laughed. "Glad to see you are so firm in your philosophical convictions, Selina."

Life Narratives and Personal Identity

"Actually," Selina said, "when I think of personal identity—not that I think about it as much as you philosophers do, but when I do consider it—I think of it somewhat differently. Leaving aside reincarnation and transporters and duplicate persons—and all the other flights of philosophical fantasy—I think of my identity in terms of what is really important to me." Selina thought for a moment and continued: "Look, I love to have grits for breakfast. I know you guys think they're awful, but grits with sweet melted butter and fresh scrambled eggs—that's a special breakfast. And don't you make faces, Sarah; I'll put my grits up against your bagel and lox any day of the week. But suppose that after a few years of grits deprivation in Michigan, I discovered I had lost my taste for grits: just didn't care for them anymore. I might feel like I'd lost a little piece of my culture, my history. But it wouldn't be that big a deal. I wouldn't feel as if some essential part of me had been lost. But if tomorrow morning I woke up and had no interest in chemistry—that would be another matter. I love chemistry, and I think of myself as a scientist: that's who I am. If I were no longer interested in chemistry and chemistry research, and instead I wanted to read economics and found myself putting aside the chemistry journals in favor of *The Wall Street Journal*, then I would feel that the old Selina—or at least a key element of her identity—had died."

"That's interesting, Selina," Sarah responded. "Some people prefer to think of their own personal identity in terms of a 'life narrative,' and that approach has some points in common with the view you were just describing."

"What's a life narrative?" asked Ben. "What, your autobiography?"

"I am the subject of a history that is my own and no one else's, that has its own peculiar meaning. When someone complains—as do some of those who attempt or commit suicide—that his or her life is meaningless, he or she is often and perhaps characteristically complaining that the narrative of their life has become unintelligible to them, that it lacks any point, any movement towards a climax or a telos. Hence the point of doing any one thing rather than another at crucial junctures in their lives seems to such a person to have been lost."

Alasdair MacIntyre, *After Virtue: A Study in Moral Theory*
(Notre Dame, IN: University of Notre Dame Press, 1981), p. 202

"Not exactly, though that's close." Sarah thought for a moment. "It's more like the story you tell in trying to make sense of your life—in trying to fashion the significance of your own life. But it's not just a past history. It also involves your hopes and aspirations. It doesn't have to be a story of success. For example, someone might shape the narrative of her life around a dedicated, but failed, struggle to secure a Palestinian homeland. It's a narrative of how you see yourself, how you weave the various strands of your own life into a coherent and meaningful story. That story need not be happy or even satisfying. T. S. Eliot writes haunting lines about characters, such as J. Alfred Prufrock, whose self-narratives are perhaps disappointing to themselves:

> *I have seen the eternal Footman hold my coat, and snicker,*
> *And in short, I was afraid.*

Still, that narrative gives definition—perhaps even integrity—to one's life; and it gives a strong sense of continuing personal identity."

"That's interesting, Sarah," Ben nodded. "We've been looking for personal identity, but perhaps that's the wrong approach. We make our own identity by our own narratives of our lives. Personal identity is constructed, not discovered. Of course, you can't just make it up as you go: The narrative of my life does not include Ben scoring four touchdowns in Michigan's spectacular comeback victory over Ohio State, no matter how much I wish it did. Still, it does make sense to think of one's identity in terms of purposes and values and one's own narrative flow."

"Yeah, Ben, your narrative has a great story line: 'Kid from rural Michigan meets fascinating dark-skinned beauty from Birmingham and lives happily ever after.'"

"Selina, you turned my life's narrative from dull to delightful." Ben squeezed her hand. "A fascinating narrative, though certainly not a peaceful one."

"If it's peace you want, you got the wrong girl. Life's for living. What does old Omar Khayyám say?

> *Come, fill the cup, and in the fire of Spring*
> *Your Winter-garment of Repentance fling:*
> > *The Bird of Time has but a little way*
> *To flutter—and the Bird is on the Wing.*"

Sarah turned to Selina. "I don't think you ever owned a 'winter garment of repentance,' Selina; but if you did, you surely burned it in the fire of Spring. There is certainly a clear thread to Selina's narrative: Live life fully, enjoy every moment, don't look back."

"Well," Ben said, "that's Selina's narrative line up to this point. But doesn't that raise a question about using narratives to establish identity?

Suppose that Selina undergoes a profound religious experience, and she renounces her worldly life, gives up chemistry, becomes a Carmelite nun devoted to prayer and silence and celibacy. She would still be Selina, though she would probably get a new name: perhaps Sister Chastity. But that would completely disrupt the narrative flow of Selina's life, wouldn't it? So how could a narrative work as an account of Sister Chastity's—or rather, Selina's—personal identity?"

"Forget about it, Ben. You'll become a Satan worshipper long before I become a nun. I've got my narrative figured out: Chemistry is included in every chapter and chastity in none. So the Selina narrative *does* have continuity and consistency, and don't you forget it."

"Yeah," Ben replied, "but just imagine you changed radically. People do, you know. My life changed when I met you. Completely for the better, but still a radical change. But my personal identity remains; after all, *I'm* the one who changed. So what about it, Sarah? Can the narrative theory of identity work as an account of personal identity for people who undergo radical, script-altering changes?"

"It seems to me that it works fine," Sarah replied. "Part of your life narrative consists in the changes in your life: how you have grown and developed and changed. Of course, most of the changes will likely be narrated as positive development—after all, *you're* constructing the narrative. And in most cases, if you didn't like the change, you wouldn't make it. In fact, narrative may be one of the better ways to integrate various elements of our lives into a coherent personal identity. Think of an alcoholic who stops drinking, or a Ku Klux Klan member who has an insight into the ugly wrongness of racism and becomes a champion of civil rights. Is that still the same person? The narrative account offers a natural way of making sense of continued identity through such dramatic alterations. Among the key elements of my life narrative are the *changes* in my life. For example, I'm the person who grew up in a life of wealth and privilege, and renounced that way of life and the values associated with it to become a union organizer; or I'm a person who grew up in a Christian family, with Christian beliefs, but became a Buddhist; or I'm the person who one day gave all my Brooks Brothers suits to Goodwill, resigned my position in the family Wall Street investment firm, and hitchhiked to New Orleans to play the blues. Those changes—including *my* own *past* values and goals and life—are an important chapter in the single narrative story of my life."

"At least the narrative has a single person—the narrator, the subject—who remains the same individual throughout the story," Ben said. "My narrative is about *me*, not *more or less* about me."

Sarah nodded. "And there is one important context in which the narrative model seems particularly valuable. And it's not a case of philosophical science fiction, but instead of depressing reality. Medical science does wonderful things, keeps us alive longer, and often keeps us healthy into advanced old age. But there are also problems. Because people now live much longer, more people suffer the ravages of diseases that plague the elderly: diseases such as Alzheimer's, for example, which, in advanced form, results in severe dementia, leaving the individual bereft of memory, reason—and perhaps identity, as well. Others are kept alive by medical technology, but often they become totally dependent and helpless, and enter a permanent vegetative state in which they lack even basic consciousness. Some people value the struggle to continue existence even in such circumstances. Helga Wanglie was a famous case: an eighty-five-year-old woman in a permanent vegetative state, who would never regain consciousness, who was fed by means of a tube, and who required a respirator to continue breathing. Her family insisted that all efforts be made to keep her body functioning, and they refused to consider turning off the respirator; and there was some reason to think that Helga Wanglie would have wanted such treatments continued—that fighting for life until the bitter end was the way she would have wanted her narrative to close."

"More power to you, Helga Wanglie," said Selina, "but that's certainly not the way I want my final chapter to read. I would hate the idea of ending my life tethered to a machine, in a coma or so demented that I couldn't even recognize my friends, much less read or reason. It's not the way I want to live my life, and it's not the way I want to die my death."

"Exactly so," replied Sarah. "Even if you were comatose, with no suffering whatsoever, that's not the final chapter that you would want in Selina's life narrative. Sometimes it seems difficult to say *why* that should matter to us; after all, we're suffering no pain, we're not even conscious of existing, so why should it matter whether we are hooked up to a respirator and fed with tubes for a couple of months? But it does matter: It's not the way we want our stories to end. Perhaps some people, like Helga Wanglie, do see this as a fitting close to their narratives; but for others, it would be a very bad ending indeed." Sarah was once again paging through her notebook. "Yeah, here it is. Listen to what Ronald Dworkin says about it: 'There is no doubt that most people treat the manner of their deaths as of special, symbolic importance: they want their deaths, if possible, to express and in that way vividly to confirm the values they believe most important to their lives.'[2] If we think of our lives as narratives, we can make better sense of why that's important to us."

"I like the narrative model," Selina said. "I'm not sure it solves all the problems about personal identity; but then, I'm not sure those problems *can* be solved by philosophical reflection. If our brave new world produces brain transplants, and artificial computer-driven brains become as common as artificial legs, then we'll have to work out—by practice—a serviceable revised sense of personal identity. But in any case, the narrative model does make sense of why I would feel deeply disturbed by the prospect of being in a coma for six months, even if I experienced no suffering whatsoever: It's not the way I want the final chapter of my life's narrative to read. In fact, it also helps make sense of why we regard the moment of our deaths as of such significance: why 'last words' and a 'dignified death' take on such importance. Why should those final moments of our lives have any greater significance than a comparable length of time somewhere in the middle? It's because it wraps up our life narratives, brings the story to a close; and a bad ending can ruin an otherwise excellent story. Of course, for Ben, it's only the close of a chapter; but even for those who believe in immortality or reincarnation or whatever, it's still the close of a very important phase."

Ben glanced at his watch, drained his coffee, and quickly gathered his books. "Sorry, guys, I've got to close this narrative chapter and go. I wouldn't want my life narrative to contain a section noting that I was late for my history seminar because I was discussing philosophical quandaries of personal identity."

READINGS

John Locke's account of personal identity centers on memory and consciousness. He maintains that a single person might take on several different substances (bodies) while remaining the same person, so long as the individual consciousness—of which each person is immediately aware—remains the same. Locke regards the question of individual identity as essential for determining who justly deserves punishment and reward. The passage that follows is from Book II of Locke's Essay Concerning Human Understanding.

Essay Concerning Human Understanding

Personal identity.—To find wherein personal identity consists, we must consider what *person* stands for; which, I think, is a thinking intelligent being, that has reason and reflection, and can consider itself as itself, the same thinking thing, in different times and places; which it does only by that consciousness which is inseparable from thinking, and as it seems to me essential to it; it being impossible for any one to perceive without perceiving that he does perceive. When we see, hear, smell, taste, feel, meditate, or will anything, we know that we do so. Thus it is always as to our present sensations and perceptions: and by this every one is to himself that which he calls *self*; it not being considered, in this case, whether the same self be continued in the same or diverse substances. For since consciousness always accompanies thinking and it is that that makes every one to be what he calls self, and thereby distinguishes himself from all other thinking things; in this alone consists personal identity, i.e., the sameness of a rational being: and as far as this consciousness can be extended backwards to any past action or thought, so far reaches the identity of that person; it is the same self now it was then; and it is by the same self with this present one that now reflects on it, that that action was done.

Consciousness makes personal identity:—But it is farther enquired, whether it be the same identical substance. This few would think they had reason to doubt of, if these perceptions, with their consciousness, always remained present in the mind, whereby the same thinking thing would be always consciously present, and, as would be thought, evidently the same to itself. But that which seems to make the difficulty is this, that this consciousness being interrupted always by forgetfulness, there being no moment of our lives wherein we have the whole train of all our past actions before our eyes in one view; but even the best memories losing the sight of one part whilst they are viewing another; and we sometimes, and that the greatest part of our lives, not reflecting on our past selves, being intent on our present thoughts, and in sound sleep having no thoughts at all, or, at least, none with that consciousness which remarks our waking thoughts: I say, in all these cases, our consciousness being interrupted, and we losing the sight of our past selves, doubts are raised whether we are the same thinking thing, i.e., the same substance, or no. Which, however reasonable or unreasonable, concerns not *personal identity* at all: the question being what makes the same person, and not, whether it be the same identical substance which always thinks in the same person, which in this case matters not at all: different substances, by the same consciousness (where they do partake in it), being united into one person, as well as different bodies by the same life are united into one animal, whose identity is preserved, in that change of substances, by the unity of one continued life. For it being the same consciousness that makes a man be himself to himself, personal identity depends on that only, whether it be annexed only to one individual substance, or can be continued in a succession of several substances. For as far as any intelligent being can repeat the idea of any past action with the same consciousness it had of it at first, and with the same consciousness it has of any present action; so far it is the same personal self. For it is by the consciousness it has of its present thoughts and actions that it is *self to itself* now, and so will be the same self, as far as the same consciousness can extend to actions past or to come; and would be by distance of time, or change of substance, no more two persons, than a man be two men by wearing other clothes to-day than he did yesterday, with a long or short sleep between: the same consciousness uniting those distant actions into the same person, whatever substances contributed to their production.

Personal identity in change of substances.—That this is so, we have some kind of evidence in our very bodies, all whose particles, whilst vitally united to this same thinking conscious self, so that we feel when they are touched, and are affected by and conscious of good or harm that happens to them, are a part of ourselves, i. e., of our thinking conscious self. Thus the limbs of his body are to every one a part of himself: he sympathizes and is concerned for them. Cut off a hand and thereby separate it from that consciousness we had of its heat, cold, and other affections, and it is then no longer a part of that which is himself, any more than the remotest part of matter. Thus we see the substance, whereof personal self consisted at one time, may be varied at another, without the change of personal identity; there being no question about the same person, though the limbs which but now were a part of it, be cut off.

Whether in the change of thinking substances.—But the question is, whether, if the same substance which thinks be changed, it can be the same person, or remaining the same, it can be different persons. As to the first part of the question, whether, if the same thinking substance (supposing immaterial substances only to think) be changed, it can be the same person, I answer, That cannot be resolved but by those who know what kind of substances they are that do think; and whether the consciousness of past actions can be transferred from one thinking substance to another. I grant, were the same consciousness the same individual action, it could not; but it being but a present representation of a past action, why it may not be possible that that may be represented to the mind to have been, which really never was, will remain to be shown. And therefore, how far the consciousness of past actions is annexed to any individual agent, so that another cannot possibly have it, will be hard for us to determine, till we know what kind of action it is, that cannot be done without a reflex act of perception accompanying it, and how performed by thinking substances, who cannot think without being conscious of it. But that which we call the same consciousness, not being the same individual act, why one intellectual substance may not have represented to it as done by itself what it never did, and was perhaps done by some other agent; why, I say, such a representation may not possibly be without reality of matter of fact, as well as several representations in dreams are, which yet whilst dreaming we take for true, will be difficult to conclude from the nature of things. And that it never is so, will by us, till we have clearer views of the nature of thinking substances, be best resolved into the goodness of God, who, as far as the happiness or misery of any of his sensible creatures is concerned in it, will not by a fatal error of theirs transfer from one to another that consciousness which draws reward or punishment with it. How far this may be an argument against those who would place thinking in a system of fleeting animal spirits, I leave to be considered. But yet, to return to the question before us, it must be allowed that if the same consciousness (which, as has been shown, is quite a different thing from the same numerical figure or motion in body) can be transferred from one thinking substance to another, it will be possible that two thinking substances may make but one person. For the same consciousness being preserved, whether in the same or different substances, the personal identity is preserved.

As to the second part of the question, whether the same immaterial substance remaining, there may be two distinct persons; which question seems to me to be built on this, whether the same immaterial being, being conscious of the actions of its past duration, may be wholly stripped of all the consciousness of its past existence, and lose it beyond the power of ever retrieving again: and so, as it were, beginning a new account from a new period, have a consciousness that cannot reach beyond this new state. All those who hold pre-existence are evidently of this mind, since they allow the soul to have no remaining consciousness of what it did in that pre-existent state, either wholly separate from body, or informing any other body. So that personal identity reaching no farther than consciousness reaches, a pre-existent spirit not having continued so many ages in a state of silence, must needs make different persons. Suppose a Christian Platonist or Pythagorean should, upon God's having ended all his works of creation the seventh day, think his soul hath existed ever since, and should imagine it has revolved in several human bodies; as I once met with one who was persuaded his had been the soul of Socrates (how reasonably I will not dispute: this I know, that in the post he filled, which was no inconsiderable one, he passed for a very rational man; and the press has shown that he wanted not parts or learning)—would any one say that he, being not conscious of any of Socrates' actions or thoughts, could be the same person with Socrates? Let any one reflect upon himself, and conclude, that he has in himself an immaterial spirit, which is that which thinks in him, and, in the constant change of his body, keeps him the same, and is that which he calls himself: let him also suppose it to be the same soul that was in Nestor or Thersites, at the siege of Troy (for souls being, as far as we know anything of them, in their nature indifferent to any parcel of matter, the supposition has no apparent absurdity in it), but he now having no consciousness of any of the actions either of Nestor or Thersites, does or can he conceive himself the same person with either of them? Can he be concerned in either of their actions, attribute them to himself, or think them his own, more than the actions of any other man that ever existed? So that this consciousness not reaching to any of the actions of either of those men, he is no more one *self* with either of them, than if the soul or immaterial spirit that now informs him had been created and began to exist when it began to inform his present body, though it were never so true that the same spirit that informed Nestor's or Thersites' body were numerically the same that now informs his. For this would no more make him the same person with Nestor, than if some of the particles of matter that were once a part of Nestor were now a part of this man; the same immaterial substance, without the same consciousness, no more making the same person by being united to any body, than the same particle of matter, without consciousness, united to any body, makes the same person. But let him once find himself conscious of any of the actions of Nestor, he then finds himself the same person with Nestor.

And thus we may be able, without any difficulty, to conceive the same person at the resurrection, though in a body not exactly in make or parts the same which he had here, the same consciousness going along with the soul that inhabits it. But yet the soul alone, in the change of bodies, would scarce to any one but to him that makes the soul the man, be enough to make the same man. For should the soul of a prince, carrying with it the consciousness of the prince's past life, enter and inform the body of a cobbler, as soon as deserted by his own soul, every one sees he would be the same person with the prince, accountable only for the prince's actions: but who would say it was the same man? The body too goes to the making of the man, and would, I guess, to everybody determine the man in this case, wherein the soul, with all its princely thoughts about it, would not make another man; but he would be the same cobbler to every one besides himself. I know that, in the ordinary way of speaking, the same person, and the same man, stand for one and the same thing. And indeed every one will always have a liberty to speak as he pleases, and to apply what articulate sounds to what ideas he thinks fit, and change them as often as he pleases. But yet, when we will enquire what makes the same *spirit, man,* or *person,* we must fix the ideas of spirit, man, or person, in our minds; and having resolved with ourselves what we mean by them, it will not be hard to determine in either of them, or the like, when it is the same, and when not.

Consciousness makes the same person.—But though the same immaterial substance or soul does not alone, wherever it be, and in whatsoever state, make the same man; yet it is plain, consciousness, as far as ever it can be extended, should it be to ages past, unites existences and actions, very remote in time, into the same person, as well as it does the existence and actions of the immediately preceding moment: so that whatever has the consciousness of present and past actions is the same person to whom they both belong. Had I the same consciousness that I saw the ark and Noah's flood, as that I saw an overflowing of the Thames last winter, or as that I write now, I could no more doubt that I that write this now, that saw the Thames overflowed last winter, and that viewed the flood at the general deluge, was the same *self*, place that self in what substance you please, than that I that write this am the same *myself* now whilst I write (whether I consist of all the same substance, material or immaterial, or no) that I was yesterday. For as to this point of being the same self, it matters not whether this present self be made up of the same or other substances, I being as much concerned and as justly accountable for any action was done a thousand years since, appropriated to me now by this self-consciousness, as I am for what I did the last moment.

Self depends on consciousness.—Self is that conscious thinking thing (whatever substance made up of, whether spiritual or material, simple or compounded, it matters not) which is sensible, or conscious of pleasure and pain, capable of happiness or misery, and so is concerned for itself, as far as that consciousness extends. Thus every one finds, that whilst comprehended under that consciousness, the little finger is as much a part of itself as what is most so. Upon separation of this little finger, should this consciousness go along with the little finger, and leave the rest of the body, it is evident the little finger would be the person, the same person; and self then would have nothing to do with the rest of the body. As in this case it is the consciousness that goes along with the substance, when one part is separate from another, which makes the same person, and constitutes this inseparable self: so it is in reference to substances remote in time. That with which the consciousness of this present thinking thing can join itself makes the same person, and is one self with it, and with nothing else; and so attributes to itself and owns all the actions of that thing as its own, as far as that consciousness reaches, and no farther; as every one who reflects will perceive.

Object of reward and punishment.—In this personal identity is founded all the right and justice of reward and punishment, happiness and misery being that for which every one is concerned for himself, not mattering what becomes of any substance not joined to or affected with that consciousness. For as is evident in the instance I gave but now, if the consciousness went along with the little finger when it was cut off, that would be the same self which was concerned for the whole body yesterday, as making a part of itself, whose actions then it cannot but admit as its own now. Though if the same body should still live, and immediately from the separation of the little finger have its own peculiar consciousness, whereof the little finger knew nothing, it would not at all be concerned for it, as a part of itself, or could own any of its actions, or have any of them imputed to him.

This may show us wherein personal identity consists, not in the identity of substance, but, as I have said, in the identity of consciousness, wherein if Socrates and the present mayor of Queenborough agree, they are the same person. If the same Socrates waking and sleeping do not partake of the same consciousness, Socrates waking and sleeping is not the same person; and to punish Socrates waking for what sleeping Socrates thought, and waking Socrates was never conscious of, would be no more of right than to punish one twin for what his brother-twin did, whereof he knew nothing, because their outsides were so like that they could not be distinguished.

But yet possibly it will still be objected, Suppose I wholly lose the memory of some parts of my life, beyond the possibility of retrieving them, so that perhaps I shall never be conscious of them again; yet am I not the same person that did those actions, had those thoughts, that I was once conscious of, though I have now forgot them? To which I answer, That we must here take notice what the word *I* is applied to; which in this case, is the man only. And the same man being presumed to be the same person, *I* is easily here supposed to stand also for the same person. But if it be possible for the same man to have distinct incommunicable consciousness at different times, it is past doubt the same man would at different times make different persons; which, we see, is the sense of mankind in the solemnest declaration of their opinions, human laws not punishing the mad man for the sober man's actions, nor the sober man for what the mad man did, thereby making them two persons; which is somewhat explained by our way of speaking in English, when we say, such an one is 'not himself', or is 'beside himself,' in which phrases it is insinuated as if those who now or, at least, first used them, thought that self was changed, the selfsame person was no longer in that man.

Consciousness alone makes self.—Nothing but consciousness can unite remote existences into the same person; the identity of substance will not do it. For whatever substance there is, however framed, without consciousness there is no person: and a carcase may be a person, as well as any sort of substance be so without consciousness.

Could we suppose two distinct incommunicable consciousnesses acting the same body, the one constantly by day, the other by night; and, on the other side, the same consciousness acting by intervals two distinct bodies: I ask, in the first case, whether the day and the night man would not be two as distinct persons as Socrates and Plato; and whether, in the second case, there would not be one person in two distinct bodies, as much as one man is the same in two distinct clothings. Nor is it at all material to say, that this same and this distinct consciousness, in the cases above mentioned, is owing to the same and distinct immaterial substances, bringing it with them to those bodies. For granting that the thinking substance in man must be necessarily supposed immaterial, it is evident that immaterial thinking thing may sometimes part with its past consciousness, and be restored to it again, as appears in the forgetfulness men often have of their past actions; and the mind many times recovers the memory of a past consciousness which it had lost for twenty years together. Make these intervals of memory and forgetfulness to take their turns regularly by day and night, and you have two persons with the same immaterial spirit, as much as in the former instance two persons with the same body. So that self is not determined by identity or diversity of substance, which it cannot be sure of, but only by identity of consciousness.

Indeed it may conceive the substance whereof it is now made up to have existed formerly, united in the same conscious being: but, consciousness removed, that substance is no more itself, or makes no more a part of it, than any other substance; as is evident in the instance we have already given of a limb cut off, of whose heat or cold or other affections having no longer any consciousness, it is no more of a man's self than any other matter of the universe. In like manner it will be in reference to any immaterial substance, which is void of that consciousness whereby I am myself to myself: if there be any part of its existence which I cannot upon recollection join with that present consciousness whereby I am now myself, it is in that part of its existence no more *myself* than any other immaterial being. For whatsoever any substance has thought or done, which I cannot recollect, and by my consciousness make my own thought and action, it will no more belong to me, whether a part of me thought or did it, than if it had been thought or done by any other immaterial being anywhere existing.

I agree, the more probable opinion is, that this consciousness is annexed to, and the affection of, one individual immaterial substance.

But let men, according to their diverse hypotheses, resolve of that as they please. This every intelligent being, sensible of happiness or misery, must grant—that there is something that is *himself* that he is concerned for, and would have happy; that this self has existed in a continued duration more than one instant, and therefore it is possible may exist, as it has done, months and years to come, without any certain bounds to be set to its duration; and may be the same self, by the same consciousness, continued on for the future. And thus, by this consciousness, he finds himself to be the same self which did such or such an action some years since, by which he comes to be happy or miserable now. In all which account of self, the same numerical substance is not considered as making the same self: but the same continued consciousness, in which several substances may have been united, and again separated from it, which, whilst they continued in a vital union with that wherein this consciousness then resided, made a part of that same self. Thus any part of our bodies vitally united to that which is conscious in us, makes a part of ourselves; but upon separation from the vital union by which that consciousness is communicated, that which a moment since was part of ourselves, is now no more so than a part of another man's self is a part of me; and it is not impossible, but in a little time may become a real part of another person. And so we have the same numerical substance become a part of two different persons; and the same person preserved under the change of various substances. Could we suppose any spirit wholly stripped of all its memory or consciousness of past actions, as we find our minds always are of a great part of ours, and sometimes of them all; the union or separation of such a spiritual substance would make no variation of personal identity, any more that that of any particle of matter does. Any substance vitally united to the present thinking being is a part of that very same self which now is: anything united to it by a consciousness of former actions makes also a part of the same self, which is the same both then and now.

Person, a forensic term.—Person, as I take it, is the name for this self. Wherever a man finds what he calls *himself*, there, I think, another may say is the same person. It is a forensic term appropriating actions and their merit; and so belongs only to intelligent agents capable of a law, and happiness and misery. This personality extends itself beyond present existence to what is past, only by consciousness; whereby it becomes concerned and accountable, owns and imputes to itself past actions, just upon the same ground and for the same reason that it does the present. All which is founded in a concern for happiness, the unavoidable concomitant of consciousness; that which is conscious of pleasure and pain desiring that that self that is conscious should be happy. And therefore whatever past actions it cannot reconcile or appropriate to that present self by consciousness, it can be no more concerned in, than if they had never been done: and to receive pleasure or pain, i.e., reward or punishment, on the account of any such action, is all one as to be made happy or miserable in its first being without any demerit at all. And therefore, conformable to this, the apostle tells us, that at the great day, when every one shall 'receive according to his doings, the secrets of all hearts shall be laid open', The sentence shall be justified by the consciousness all persons shall have that they *themselves*, in what bodies soever they appear, or what substances soever that consciousness adheres to, are the *same* that committed those actions, and deserve that punishment for them.

David Hume rejects any notion of an underlying "soul substance" that marks personal identity. Instead, Hume maintains that the self is "a bundle or collection of different perceptions," with no unified substance to hold it together. For Hume, the search for a definitive standard of personal identity is a futile quest prompted by verbal confusions. The passage that follows is from A Treatise of Human Nature.

A Treatise of Human Nature

Of personal identity

There are some philosophers, who imagine we are every moment intimately conscious of what we call our SELF; that we feel its existence and its continuance in existence; and are certain, beyond the evidence of a demonstration, both of its perfect identity and simplicity. The strongest sensation, the most violent passion, say they, instead of distracting us from this view, only fix it the more intensely, and make us consider their influence on *self* either by their pain or pleasure. To attempt a farther proof of this were to weaken its evidence; since no proof can be deriv'd from any fact, of which we are so intimately conscious; nor is there any thing, of which we can be certain, if we doubt of this.

Unluckily all these positive assertions are contrary to that very experience, which is pleaded for them, nor have we any idea of *self*, after the manner it is here explain'd. For from what impression cou'd this idea be deriv'd? This question 'tis impossible to answer without a manifest contradiction and absurdity; and yet 'tis a question, which must necessarily be answer'd, if we wou'd have the idea of self pass for clear and intelligible. It must be some one impression, that gives rise to every real idea. But self or person is not any one impression, but that to which our several impressions and ideas are suppos'd to have a reference. If any impression gives rise to the idea of self, that impression must continue invariably the same, thro' the whole course of our lives; since self is suppos'd to exist after that manner. But there is no impression constant and invariable. Pain and pleasure, grief and joy, passions and sensations succeed each other, and never all exist at the same time. It cannot, therefore, be from any of these impressions, or from any other, that the idea of self is deriv'd; and consequently there is no such idea.

But farther, what must become of all our particular perceptions upon this hypothesis? All these are different, and distinguishable, and separable from each other, and may be separately consider'd, and may exist separately, and have no need of any thing to support their existence. After what manner, therefore, do they belong to self; and how are they connected with it? For my part, when I enter most intimately into what I call *myself*, I always stumble on some particular perception or other, of heat or cold, light or shade, love or hatred, pain or pleasure. I never can catch *myself* at any time without a perception, and never can observe any thing but the perception. When my perceptions are remov'd for any time, as by sound sleep; so long am I insensible of *myself*, and may truly be said not to exist. And were all my perceptions remov'd by death, and cou'd I neither think, nor feel, nor see, nor love, nor hate after the dissolution of my body, I shou'd be entirely annihilated, nor do I conceive what is farther requisite to make me a perfect non-entity. If any one upon serious and unprejudic'd reflexion, thinks he has a different notion of *himself*, I must confess I can reason no longer with him. All I can allow him is, that he may be in the right as well as I, and that we are essentially different in this particular. He may, perhaps, perceive something simple and continu'd, which he calls *himself*; tho' I am certain there is no such principle in me.

But setting aside some metaphysicians of this kind, I may venture to affirm of the rest of mankind, that they are nothing but a bundle or collection of different perceptions, which succeed each other with an inconceivable rapidity, and are in a perpetual flux and movement. Our eyes cannot turn in their sockets without varying our perceptions. Our thought is still more variable than our sight; and all our other senses and faculties contribute to this change; nor is there any single power of the soul, which remains unalterably the same, perhaps for one moment. The mind is a kind of theatre, where several perceptions successively make their appearance; pass, re-pass, glide away, and mingle in an infinite variety of postures and situations. There is properly no *simplicity* in it at one time, nor *identity* in different; whatever natural propension we may have to imagine that simplicity and identity. The comparison of the theatre must not mislead us. They are the successive perceptions only, that constitute the mind; nor have we the most distant notion of the place, where these scenes are represented, or of the materials, of which it is compos'd.

What then gives us so great a propension to ascribe an identity to these successive perceptions, and to suppose ourselves possest of an invariable and uninterrupted existence thro' the whole course of our lives? In order to answer this question, we must distinguish betwixt personal identity, as it regards our thought or imagination, and as it regards our passions or the concern we take in ourselves. The first is our present subject; and to explain it perfectly we must take the matter pretty deep, and account for that identity, which we attribute to plants and animals; there being a great analogy betwixt it, and the identity of a self or person.

We have a distinct idea of an object, that remains invariable and uninterrupted thro' a suppos'd variation of time; and this idea we call that of *identity* or *sameness*. We have also a distinct idea of several different objects existing in succession, and connected together by a close relation; and this to an accurate view affords as perfect a notion of *diversity*, as if there was no manner of relation among the objects. But tho' these two ideas of identity, and a succession of related objects be in themselves perfectly distinct, and even contrary, yet 'tis certain, that in our common way of thinking they are generally confounded with each other. That action of the imagination, by which we consider the uninterrupted and invariable object, and that by which we reflect on the succession of related objects, are almost the same to the feeling, nor is there much more effort of thought requir'd in the latter case than in the former. The relation facilitates the transition of the mind from one object to another, and renders its passage as smooth as if it contemplated one continu'd object. This resemblance is the cause of the confusion and mistake, and makes us substitute the notion of identity, instead of that of related objects. However at one instant we may consider the related succession as variable or interrupted, we are sure the next to ascribe to it a perfect identity, and regard it as invariable and uninterrupted. Our propensity to this mistake is so great from the resemblance above-mention'd, that we fall into it before we are aware; and tho' we incessantly correct ourselves by reflexion, and return to a more accurate method of thinking, yet we cannot long sustain our philosophy, or take off this biass from the imagination. Our last resource is to yield to it, and boldly assert that these different related objects are in effect the same, however interrupted and variable. In order to justify to ourselves this absurdity, we often feign some new and unintelligible principle, that connects the objects together, and prevents their interruption or variation. Thus we feign the continu'd existence of the perceptions of our senses, to remove the interruption; and run into the notion of a *soul*, and *self*, and *substance*, to disguise the variation. But we may farther observe, that where we do not give rise to such a fiction, our propension to confound identity with relation is so great, that we are apt to imagine something unknown and mysterious, connecting the parts, beside their relation; and this I take to be the case with regard to the identity we ascribe to plants and vegetables. And even when this does not take place, we still feel a propensity to confound these ideas, tho' we are not able fully to satisfy ourselves in that particular, nor find any thing invariable and uninterrupted to justify our notion of identity.

Thus the controversy concerning identity is not merely a dispute of words. For when we attribute identity, in an improper sense, to variable or interrupted objects, our mistake is not confin'd to the expression, but is commonly attended with a fiction, either of something invariable and uninterrupted, or of something mysterious and inexplicable, or at least with a propensity to such fictions. What will suffice to prove this hypothesis to the satisfaction of every fair enquirer, is to shew from daily experience and observation, that the objects, which are variable or interrupted, and yet are suppos'd to continue the same, are such only as consist of a succession of parts, connected together by resemblance, contiguity, or causation. For as such a succession answers evidently to our notion of diversity, it can only be by mistake we ascribe to it an identity; and as the relation of parts, which leads us into this mistake, is really nothing but a quality, which produces an association of ideas, and an easy transition of the imagination from one to another, it can only be from the resemblance, which this act of the mind bears to that, by which we contemplate one continu'd object, that the error arises. Our chief business, then, must be to prove, that all objects, to which we ascribe identity, without observing their invariableness and uninterruptedness, are such as consist of a succession of related objects.

In order to this, suppose any mass of matter, of which the parts are contiguous and connected, to be plac'd before us; 'tis plain we must attribute a perfect identity to this mass, provided all the parts continue uninterruptedly and invariably the same, whatever motion or change of place we may observe either in the whole or in any of the parts. But supposing some very *small* or *inconsiderable* part to be added to the mass, or substracted from it; tho' this absolutely destroys the identity of the whole, strictly speaking; yet as we seldom think so accurately, we scruple not to pronounce a mass of matter the same, where we find so trivial an alteration. The passage of the thought from the object before the change to the object after it, is so smooth and easy, that we scarce perceive the transition, and are apt to imagine, that 'tis nothing but a continu'd survey of the same object.

There is a very remarkable circumstance, that attends this experiment; which is, that tho' the change of any considerable part in a mass of matter destroys the identity of the whole, yet we must measure the greatness of the part, not absolutely, but by its *proportion* to the whole. The addition or diminution of a mountain wou'd not be sufficient to produce a diversity in a planet; tho' the change of a very few inches wou'd be able to destroy the identity of some bodies. 'Twill be impossible to account for this, but by reflecting that objects operate upon the mind, and break or interrupt the continuity of its actions not according to their real greatness, but according to their proportion to each other: And therefore, since this interruption makes an object cease to appear the same, it must be the uninterrupted progress of the thought, which constitutes the identity.

This may be confirm'd by another phænomenon. A change in any considerable part of a body destroys its identity; but 'tis remarkable, that where the change is produc'd *gradually* and *insensibly* we are less apt to ascribe to it the same effect. The reason can plainly be no other, than that the mind, in following the successive changes of the body, feels an easy passage from the surveying its condition in one moment to the viewing of it in another, and at no particular time perceives any interruption in its actions. From which continu'd perception, it ascribes a continu'd existence and identity to the object.

But whatever precaution we may use in introducing the changes gradually, and making them proportionable to the whole, 'tis certain, that where the changes are at last observ'd to become considerable, we make a scruple of ascribing identity to such different objects. There is, however, another artifice, by which we may induce the imagination to advance a step farther; and that is, by producing a reference of the parts to each other, and a combination to some *common end* or purpose. A ship, of which a considerable part has been chang'd by frequent reparations, is still consider'd as the same; nor does the difference of the materials hinder us from ascribing an identity to it. The common end, in which the parts conspire, is the same under all their variations, and affords an easy transition of the imagination from one situation of the body to another.

But this is still more remarkable, when we add a *sympathy* of parts to their *common end*, and suppose that they bear to each other, the reciprocal relation of cause and effect in all their actions and operations. This is the case with all animals and vegetables; where not only the several parts have a reference to some general purpose, but also a mutual dependance on, and connexion with each other. The effect of so strong a relation is, that tho' every one must allow, that in a very few years both vegetables and animals endure a *total* change, yet we still attribute identity to them, while their form, size, and substance are entirely alter'd. An oak, that grows from a small plant to a large tree, is still the same oak; tho' there be not one particle of matter, or figure of its parts the same. An infant becomes a man, and is sometimes fat, sometimes lean, without any change in his identity.

We may also consider the two following phænomenona, which are remarkable in their kind. The first is, that tho' we commonly be able to distinguish pretty exactly betwixt numerical and specific identity, yet it sometimes happens, that we confound them, and in our thinking and reasoning employ the one for the other. Thus a man, who hears a noise, that is frequently interrupted and renew'd, says, it is still the same noise; tho' 'tis evident the sounds have only a specific identity or resemblance, and there is nothing numerically the same, but the cause, which produc'd them. In like manner it may be said without breach of the propriety of language, that such a church, which was formerly of brick, fell to ruin, and that the parish rebuilt the same church of free-stone, and according to modern architecture. Here neither the form nor materials are the same, nor is there any thing common to the two objects, but their relation to the inhabitants of the parish; and yet this alone is sufficient to make us denominate them the same. But we must observe, that in these cases the first object is in a manner annihilated before the second comes into existence; by which means, we are never presented in any one point of time with the idea of difference and multiplicity; and for that reason are less scrupulous in calling them the same.

Secondly, We may remark, that tho' in a succession of related objects, it be in a manner requisite, that the change of parts be not sudden nor entire, in order to preserve the identity, yet where the objects are in their nature changeable and inconstant, we admit of a more sudden transition, than wou'd otherwise be consistent with that relation. Thus as the nature of a river consists in the motion and change of parts; tho' in less than four and twenty hours these be totally alter'd; this hinders not the river from continuing the same during several ages. What is natural and essential to any thing is, in a manner, expected; and what is expected makes less impression, and appears of less moment, than what is unusual and extraordinary. A considerable change of the former kind seems really less to the imagination, than the most trivial alteration of the latter; and by breaking less the continuity of the thought, has less influence in destroying the identity.

We now proceed to explain the nature of *personal identity*, which has become so great a question in philosophy, especially of late years in *England*, where all the abstruser sciences are study'd with a peculiar ardour and application. And here 'tis evident, the same method of reasoning must be continu'd, which has so successfully explain'd the identity of plants, and animals, and ships, and houses, and of all the compounded and changeable productions either of art or nature. The identity, which we ascribe to the mind of man, is only a fictitious one, and of a like kind with that which we ascribe to vegetables and animal bodies. It cannot, therefore, have a different origin, but must proceed from a like operation of the imagination upon like objects.

But lest this argument shou'd not convince the reader; tho' in my opinion perfectly decisive; let him weigh the following reasoning, which is still closer and more immediate. 'Tis evident, that the identity, which we attribute to the human mind, however perfect we may imagine it to be, is not able to run the several different perceptions into one, and make them lose their characters of distinction and difference, which are essential to them. 'Tis still true, that every distinct perception, which enters into the composition of the mind, is a distinct existence, and is different, and distinguishable, and separable from every other perception, either contemporary or successive. But, as, notwithstanding this distinction and separability, we suppose the whole train of perceptions to be united by identity, a question naturally arises concerning this relation of identity; whether it be something that really binds our several perceptions together, or only associates their ideas in the imagination. That is, in other words, whether in pronouncing concerning the identity of a person, we observe some real bond among his perceptions, or only feel one among the ideas we form of them. This question we might easily decide, if we wou'd recollect what has been already prov'd at large, that the understanding never observes any real connexion among objects, and that even the union of cause and effect, when strictly examin'd, resolves itself into a customary association of ideas. For from thence it evidently follows, that identity is nothing really belonging to these different perceptions, and uniting them together; but is merely a quality, which we attribute to them, because of the union of their ideas in the imagination, when we reflect upon them. Now the only qualities, which can give ideas an union in the imagination, are these three relations above-mention'd. These are the uniting principles in the ideal world, and without them every distinct object is separable by the mind, and may be separately consider'd, and appears not to have any more connexion with any other object, than if disjoin'd by the greatest difference and remoteness. 'Tis, therefore, on some of these three relations of resemblance, contiguity and causation, that identity depends; and as the very essence of these relations consists in their producing an easy transition of ideas; it follows, that our notions of personal identity, proceed entirely from the smooth and uninterrupted progress of the thought along a train of connected ideas, according to the principles above-explain'd.

The only question, therefore, which remains, is, by what relations this uninterrupted progress of our thought is produc'd, when we consider the successive existence of a mind or thinking person. And here 'tis evident we must confine ourselves to resemblance and causation, and must drop contiguity, which has little or no influence in the present case.

To begin with *resemblance*; suppose we cou'd see clearly into the breast of another, and observe that succession of perceptions, which constitutes his mind or thinking principle, and suppose that he always preserves the memory of a considerable part of past perceptions; 'tis evident that nothing cou'd more contribute to the bestowing a relation on this succession amidst all its variations. For what is the memory but a faculty, by which we raise up the images of past perceptions? And as an image necessarily resembles its object, must not the frequent placing of these resembling perceptions in the chain of thought, convey the imagination more easily from one link to another, and make the whole seem like the continuance of one object? In this particular, then, the memory not only discovers the identity, but also contributes to its production, by producing the relation of resemblance among the perceptions. The case is the same whether we consider ourselves or others.

As to *causation;* we may observe, that the true idea of the human mind, is to consider it as a system of different perceptions or different existences, which are link'd together by the relation of cause and effect, and mutually produce, destroy, influence, and modify each other. Our impressions give rise to their correspondent ideas; and these ideas in their turn produce other impressions. One thought chaces another, and draws after it a third, by which it is expell'd in its turn. In this respect, I cannot compare the soul more properly to any thing than to a republic or commonwealth, in which the several members are united by the reciprocal ties of government and subordination, and give rise to other persons, who propagate the same republic in the incessant changes of its parts. And as the same individual republic may not only change its members, but also its laws and constitutions; in like manner the same person may vary his character and disposition, as well as his impressions and ideas, without losing his identity. Whatever changes he endures, his several parts are still connected by the relation of causation. And in this view our identity with regard to the passions serves to corroborate that with regard to the imagination, by the making our distant perceptions influence each other, and by giving us a present concern for our past or future pains or pleasures.

As memory alone acquaints us with the continuance and extent of this succession of perceptions, 'tis to be consider'd, upon that account chiefly, as the source of personal identity. Had we no memory, we never shou'd have any notion of causation, nor consequently of that chain of causes and effects, which constitute our self or person. But having once acquir'd this notion of causation from the memory, we can extend the same chain of causes, and consequently the identity of our persons beyond our memory, and can comprehend times, and circumstances, and actions, which we have entirely forgot, but suppose in general to have existed. For how few of our past actions are there, of which we have any memory? Who can tell me, for instance, what were his thoughts and actions on the first of *January* 1715, the 11th of *March* 1719, and the 3d of *August* 1733? Or will he affirm, because he has entirely forgot the incidents of these days, that the present self is not the same person with the self of that time; and by that means overturn all the most establish'd notions of personal identity? In this view, therefore, memory does not so much *produce* as *discover* personal identity, by shewing us the relation of cause and effect among our different perceptions. 'Twill be incumbent on those, who affirm that memory produces entirely our personal identity, to give a reason why we can thus extend our identity beyond our memory.

The whole of this doctrine leads us to a conclusion, which is of great importance in the present affair, *viz.* that all the nice and subtle questions concerning personal identity can never possibly be decided, and are to be regarded rather as grammatical than as philosophical difficulties. Identity depends on the relations of ideas; and these relations produce identity, by means of that easy transition they occasion. But as the relations, and the easiness of the transition may diminish by insensible degrees, we have no just standard, by which we can decide any dispute concerning the time, when they acquire or lose a title to the name of identity. All the disputes concerning the identity of connected objects are merely verbal, except so far as the relation of parts gives rise to some fiction or imaginary principle of union, as we have already observ'd.

Daniel Dennett (born 1942), Austin B. Fletcher Professor of Philosophy and director of the Center for Cognitive Studies at Tufts University, is a widely read contemporary American philosopher, best known for his extensive work in the philosophy of mind and cognitive science. Dennett's many books include Elbow Room: The Varieties of Free Will Worth Wanting *(Cambridge, MA: MIT Press, 1984);* The Intentional Stance *(Cambridge, MA: MIT Press, 1989);* Consciousness Explained *(Back Bay Books, 1991);* Darwin's Dangerous Idea *(New York: Simon & Schuster, 1995);* Kinds of Minds: Toward an Understanding of Consciousness *(New York: Basic Books, 1996);* Brainchildren: Essay on Designing Minds *(Cambridge, MA: MIT Press, 1998); and* Freedom Evolves *(New York: Viking, 2003). In addition, the volume Dennett edited with Douglas Hofstadter,* The Mind's I *(New York: Basic Books, 1981), is a fascinating collection of essays and comments on philosophy of mind; anyone interested in the subject will find it a challenging treat to both the reason and the imagination. "Where Am I" is a delightful work of fiction that gives a hard shake to our traditional idea of personal identity and pushes us to look at the issue in an altogether new light. Whether any traditional account of personal identity can survive the stresses of Dennett's tale is a question you may find yourself pondering long after you finish the essay. Originally presented as a lecture at the Chapel Hill Philosophy Colloquium, it was first published as the final chapter in Dennett's* Brainstorms: Philosophical Essays on Mind and Psychology *(Montgomery, VT: Bradford Books, 1978).*

Where Am I?

Now that I've won my suit under the Freedom of Information Act, I am at liberty to reveal for the first time a curious episode in my life that may be of interest not only to those engaged in research in the philosophy of mind, artificial intelligence, and neuroscience but also to the general public.

Several years ago I was approached by Pentagon officials who asked me to volunteer for a highly dangerous and secret mission. In collaboration with NASA and Howard Hughes, the Department of Defense was spending billions to develop a Supersonic Tunneling Underground Device, or STUD. It was supposed to tunnel through the earth's core at great speed and deliver a specially designed atomic warhead "right up the Red's missile silos," as one of the Pentagon brass put it.

The problem was that in an early test they had succeeded in lodging a warhead about a mile deep under Tulsa, Oklahoma, and they wanted me to retrieve it for them. "Why me?" I asked. Well, the mission involved some pioneering applications of current brain research, and they had heard of my interest in brains and of course my Faustian curiosity and great courage and so forth. . . . Well, how could I refuse? The difficulty that brought the Pentagon to my door was that the device I'd been asked to recover was fiercely radioactive, in a new way. According to monitoring instruments, something about the nature of the device and its complex interactions with pockets of material deep in the earth had produced radiation that could cause severe abnormalities in certain tissues of the brain. No way had been found to shield the brain from these deadly rays, which were apparently harmless to other tissues and organs of the body. So it had been decided that the person sent to recover the device should *leave his brain behind.* It would be kept in a safe place where it could execute its normal control functions by elaborate radio links. Would I submit to a surgical procedure that would completely remove my brain, which would then be placed in a life-support system at the Manned Spacecraft Center in Houston? Each input and output pathway, as it was severed, would be restored by a pair of microminiaturized radio transceivers, one attached precisely to the brain, the other to the nerve stumps in the empty cranium. No information would be lost, all the connectivity would be preserved. At first I was a bit reluctant. Would it really work? The Houston brain surgeons encouraged me. "Think of it," they said, "as a mere *stretching* of the nerves. If your brain were just moved over an *inch* in your skull, that would not alter or impair your mind. We're simply going to make the nerves indefinitely elastic by splicing radio links into them."

I was shown around the life-support lab in Houston and saw the sparkling new vat in which my brain would be placed, were I to agree. I met the large and brilliant support team of neurologists, hematologists, biophysicists, and electrical engineers, and after several days of discussions and demonstrations, I agreed to give it a try. I was subjected to an enormous array of blood tests, brain scans, experiments, interviews, and the like. They took down my autobiography at great length, recorded tedious lists of my beliefs, hopes, fears, and tastes. They even listed my favorite stereo recordings and gave me a crash session of psychoanalysis.

The day for surgery arrived at last and of course I was anesthetized and remember nothing of the operation itself. When I came out of anesthesia, I opened my eyes, looked around, and asked the inevitable, the traditional, the lamentably hackneyed postoperative question: "Where am I?" The nurse smiled down at me. "You're in Houston," she said, and I reflected that this still had a good chance of being the truth one way or another. She handed me a mirror. Sure enough, there were the tiny antennae poling up through their titanium ports cemented into my skull.

"I gather the operation was a success," I said. "I want to go see my brain." They led me (I was a bit dizzy and unsteady) down a long corridor and into the life-support lab. A cheer went up from the assembled support team, and I responded with what I hoped was a jaunty salute. Still feeling lightheaded, I was helped over to the life-support vat. I peered through the glass. There, floating in what looked like ginger ale, was undeniably a human brain, though it was almost covered with printed circuit chips, plastic tubules, electrodes, and other paraphernalia. "Is that mine?" I asked. "Hit the output transmitter switch there on the side of the vat and see for yourself," the project director replied. I moved the switch to OFF, and immediately slumped, groggy and nauseated, into the arms of the technicians, one of whom kindly restored the switch to its ON position. While I recovered my equilibrium and composure, I thought to myself: "Well, here I am sitting on a folding chair, staring through a piece of plate glass at my own brain. . . . But wait," I said to myself, "shouldn't I have thought, 'Here I am, suspended in a bubbling fluid, being stared at by my own eyes'?" I tried to think this latter thought. I tried to project it into the tank, offering it hopefully to my brain, but I failed to carry off the exercise with any conviction. I tried again. "Here am *I*, Daniel Dennett, suspended in a bubbling fluid, being stared at by my own eyes." No, it just didn't work. Most puzzling and confusing. Being a philosopher of firm physicalist conviction, I believed unswervingly that the tokening of my thoughts was occurring somewhere in my brain: yet, when I thought "Here I am," where the thought occurred to me was *here*, outside the vat, where I, Dennett, was standing staring at my brain.

I tried and tried to think myself into the vat, but to no avail. I tried to build up to the task by doing mental exercises. I thought to myself, "The sun is shining *over there*," five times in rapid succession, each time mentally ostending a different place: in order, the sunlit corner of the lab, the visible front lawn of the hospital, Houston, Mars, and Jupiter. I found I had little difficulty in getting my "there"'s to hop all over the celestial map with their proper references. I could loft a "there" in an instant through the farthest reaches of space, and then aim the next "there" with pinpoint accuracy at the upper left quadrant of a freckle on my arm. Why was I having such trouble with "here"? "Here in Houston" worked well enough, and so did "here in the lab," and even "here in this part of the lab," but "here in the vat" always seemed merely an unmeant mental mouthing. I tried closing my eyes while thinking it. This seemed to help, but still I couldn't manage to pull it off, except perhaps for a fleeting instant. I couldn't be sure. The discovery that I couldn't be sure was also unsettling. How did I know *where* I meant by "here" when I thought "here"? Could I *think* I meant one place when in fact I meant another? I didn't see how that could be admitted without untying the few bonds of intimacy between a person and his own mental life that had survived the onslaught of the brain scientists and philosophers, the physicalists and behaviorists. Perhaps I was incorrigible about where I *meant* when I said "here." But in my present circumstances it seemed that either I was doomed by sheer force of mental habit to thinking systematically false indexical thoughts, or where a person is (and hence where his thoughts are tokened for purposes of semantic analysis) is not necessarily where his brain, the physical seat of his soul, resides. Nagged by confusion, I attempted to orient myself by falling back on a favorite philosopher's ploy. I began naming things.

"Yorick," I said aloud to my brain, "you are my brain. The rest of my body, seated in this chair, I dub 'Hamlet.'" So here we all are: Yorick's my brain, Hamlet's my body, and I am Dennett. *Now*, where am I? And when I think "where am I?" where's that thought tokened? Is it tokened in my brain, lounging about in the vat, or right here between my ears where it *seems* to be tokened? Or nowhere? Its *temporal* coordinates give me no trouble; must it not have spatial coordinates as well? I began making a list of the alternatives.

1. *Where Hamlet goes, there goes Dennett.* This principle was easily refuted by appeal to the familiar brain-transplant thought experiments so enjoyed by philosophers. If Tom and Dick switch brains, Tom is the fellow with Dick's former body—just ask him; he'll claim to be Tom, and tell you the most intimate details of Tom's autobiography. It was clear enough, then, that my current body and I could part company, but not likely that I could be separated from my brain. The rule of thumb that emerged so plainly from the thought experiments was that in a brain-transplant operation, one wanted to be the *donor*, not the recipient. Better to call such an operation a *body* transplant, in fact. So perhaps the truth was,

2. *Where Yorick goes, there goes Dennett.* This was not at all appealing, however. How could I be in the vat and not about to go anywhere, when I was so obviously outside the vat looking in and beginning to make guilty plans to return to my room for a substantial lunch? This begged the question I realized, but it still seemed to be getting at something important. Casting about for some support for my intuition, I hit upon a legalistic sort of argument that might have appealed to Locke.

Suppose, I argued to myself, I were now to fly to California, rob a bank, and be apprehended. In which state would I be tried: in California, where the robbery took place, or in Texas, where the brains of the outfit were located? Would I be a California felon with an out-of-state brain, or a Texas felon remotely controlling an accomplice of sorts in California? It seemed possible that I might beat such a rap just on the undecidability of that jurisdictional question, though perhaps it would be deemed an interstate, and hence Federal, offense. In any event, suppose I were convicted. Was it likely that California would be satisfied to throw Hamlet into the brig, knowing that Yorick was living the good life and luxuriously taking the waters in Texas? Would Texas incarcerate Yorick, leaving Hamlet free to take the next boat to Rio? This alternative appealed to me. Barring capital punishment or other cruel and unusual punishment, the state would be obliged to maintain the life-support system for Yorick though they might move him from Houston to Leavenworth, and aside from the unpleasantness of the opprobrium, I, for one, would not mind at all and would consider myself a free man under those circumstances. If the state has an interest in forcibly relocating persons in institutions, it would fail to relocate *me* in any institution by locating Yorick there. If this were true, it suggested a third alternative.

3. *Dennett is wherever he thinks he is.* Generalized, the claim was as follows: At any given time a person has a *point of view*, and the location of the point of view (which is determined internally by the content of the point of view) is also the location of the person.

Such a proposition is not without its perplexities, but to me it seemed a step in the right direction. The only trouble was that it seemed to place one in a heads-I-win/tails-you-lose situation of unlikely infallibility as regards location. Hadn't I myself often been wrong about where I was, and at least as often uncertain? Couldn't one get lost? Of course, but getting lost *geographically* is not the only way one might get lost. If one were lost in the woods one could attempt to reassure oneself with the consolation that at least one knew where one was: one was right *here* in the familiar surroundings of one's own body. Perhaps in this case one would not have drawn one's attention to much to be thankful for. Still, there were worse plights imaginable, and I wasn't sure I wasn't in such a plight right now.

Point of view clearly had something to do with personal location, but it was itself an unclear notion. It was obvious that the content of one's point of view was not the same as or determined by the content of one's beliefs or thoughts. For example, what should we say about the point of view of the Cinerama viewer who shrieks and twists in his seat as the roller-coaster footage overcomes his psychic distancing? Has he forgotten that he is safely seated in the theater? Here I was inclined to say that the person is experiencing an illusory shift in point of view. In other cases, my inclination to call such shifts illusory was less strong. The workers in laboratories and plants who handle dangerous materials by operating feedback-controlled mechanical arms and hands undergo a shift in point of view that is crisper and more pronounced than anything Cinerama can provoke. They can feel the heft and slipperiness of the containers they manipulate with their metal fingers. They know perfectly well where they are and are not fooled into false beliefs by the experience, yet it is as if they were inside the isolation chamber they are peering into. With mental effort, they can manage to shift their point of view back and forth, rather like making a transparent Necker cube or an Escher drawing change orientation before one's eyes. It does seem extravagant to suppose that in performing this bit of mental gymnastics, they are transporting *themselves* back and forth.

Still their example gave me hope. If I was in fact in the vat in spite of my intuitions, I might be able to train myself to adopt that point of view even as a matter of habit. I should dwell on images of myself comfortably floating in my vat, beaming volitions to that familiar body *out there.* I reflected that the ease or difficulty of this task was presumably independent of the truth about the location of one's brain. Had I been practicing before the operation, I might now be finding it second nature. You might now yourself try such a *trompe l'oeil.* Imagine you have written an inflammatory letter which has been published in the *Times*, the result of which is that the government has chosen to impound your brain for a probationary period of three years in its Dangerous Brain Clinic in Bethesda, Maryland. Your body of course is allowed freedom to earn a salary and thus to continue its function of laying up income to be taxed. At this moment, however, your body is seated in an auditorium listening to a peculiar account by Daniel Dennett of his own similar experience. Try it. Think yourself to Bethesda, and then hark back longingly to your body, far away, and yet *seeming* so near. It is only with long-distance restraint (yours? the government's?) that you can control your impulse to get those hands clapping in polite applause before navigating the old body to the rest room and a well-deserved glass of evening sherry in the lounge. The task of imagination is certainly difficult, but if you achieve your goal the results might be consoling.

Anyway, there I was in Houston, lost in thought as one might say, but not for long. My speculations were soon interrupted by the Houston doctors, who wished to test out my new prosthetic nervous system before sending me off on my hazardous mission. As I mentioned before, I was a bit dizzy at first, and not surprisingly, although I soon habituated myself to my new circumstances (which were, after all, well nigh indistinguishable from my old circumstances). My accommodation was not perfect, however, and to this day I continue to be plagued by minor coordination difficulties. The speed of light is fast, but finite, and as my brain and body move farther and farther apart, the delicate interaction of my feedback systems is thrown into disarray by the time lags. Just as one is rendered close to speechless by a delayed or echoic hearing of one's speaking voice so, for instance, I am virtually unable to track a moving object with my eyes whenever my brain and my body are more than a few miles apart. In most matters my impairment is scarcely detectable, though I can no longer hit a slow curve ball with the authority of yore. There are some compensations of course. Though liquor tastes as good as ever, and warms my gullet while corroding my liver, I can drink it in any quantity I please, without becoming the slightest bit inebriated, a curiosity some of my close friends may have noticed (though I occasionally have *feigned* inebriation, so as not to draw attention to my unusual circumstances). For similar reasons, I take aspirin orally for a sprained wrist, but if the pain persists I ask Houston to administer codeine to me *in vitro*. In times of illness the phone bill can be staggering.

But to return to my adventure. At length, both the doctors and I were satisfied that I was ready to undertake my subterranean mission. And so I left my brain in Houston and headed by helicopter for Tulsa. Well, in any case, that's the way it seemed to me. That's how I would put it, just off the top of my head as it were. On the trip I reflected further about my earlier anxieties and decided that my first postoperative speculations had been tinged with panic. The matter was not nearly as strange or metaphysical as I had been supposing. Where was I? In two places, clearly: both inside the vat and outside it. Just as one can stand with one foot in Connecticut and the other in Rhode Island, I was in two places at once. I had become one of those scattered individuals we used to hear so much about. The more I considered this answer, the more obviously true it appeared. But, strange to say, the more true it appeared, the less important the question to which it could be the true answer seemed. A sad, but not unprecedented, fate for a philosophical question to suffer. This answer did not completely satisfy me, of course. There lingered some question to which I should have liked an answer, which was neither "Where are all my various and sundry parts?" nor "What is my current point of view?" Or at least there seemed to be such a question. For it did seem undeniable that in some sense *I* and not merely *most of me* was descending into the earth under Tulsa in search of an atomic warhead.

When I found the warhead, I was certainly glad I had left my brain behind, for the pointer on the specially built Geiger counter I had brought with me was off the dial. I called Houston on my ordinary radio and told the operation control center of my position and my progress. In return, they gave me instructions for dismantling the vehicle, based upon my on-site observations. I had set to work with my cutting torch when all of a sudden a terrible thing happened. I went stone deaf. At first I thought it was only my radio earphones that had broken, but when I tapped on my helmet, I heard nothing. Apparently the auditory transceivers had gone on the fritz. I could no longer hear Houston or my own voice, but I could speak, so I started telling them what had happened. In midsentence, I knew something else had gone wrong. My vocal apparatus had become paralyzed. Then my right hand went limp—another transceiver had gone. I was truly in deep trouble. But worse was to follow. After a few more minutes, I went blind. I cursed my luck, and then I cursed the scientists who had led me into this grave peril. There I was, deaf, dumb, and blind, in a radioactive hole more than a mile under Tulsa. Then the last of my cerebral radio links broke, and suddenly I was faced with a new and even more shocking problem: whereas an instant before I had been buried alive in Oklahoma, now I was disembodied in Houston. My recognition of my new status was not immediate. It took me several very anxious minutes before it dawned on me that my poor body lay several hundred miles away, with heart pulsing and lungs respirating, but otherwise as dead as the body of any heart-transplant donor, its skull packed with useless, broken electronic gear. The shift in perspective I had earlier found well nigh impossible now seemed quite natural. Though I could think myself back into my body in the tunnel under Tulsa, it took some effort to sustain the illusion. For surely it was an illusion to suppose I was still in Oklahoma: I had lost all contact with that body.

It occurred to me then, with one of those rushes of revelation of which we should be suspicious, that I had stumbled upon an impressive demonstration of the immateriality of the soul based upon physicalist principles and premises. For as the last radio signal between Tulsa and

Houston died away, had I not changed location from Tulsa to Houston at the speed of light? And had I not accomplished this without any increase in mass? What moved from A to B at such speed was surely myself, or at any rate my soul or mind—the massless center of my being and home of my consciousness. My *point of view* had lagged somewhat behind, but I had already noted the indirect bearing of point of view on personal location. I could not see how a physicalist philosopher could quarrel with this except by taking the dire and counterintuitive route of banishing all talk of persons. Yet the notion of personhood was so well entrenched in everyone's world view, or so it seemed to me, that any denial would be as curiously unconvincing, as systematically disingenuous, as the Cartesian negation, "non sum."

The joy of philosophic discovery thus tided me over some very bad minutes or perhaps hours as the helplessness and hopelessness of my situation became more apparent to me. Waves of panic and even nausea swept over me, made all the more horrible by the absence of their normal body-dependent phenomenology. No adrenaline rush of tingles in the arms, no pounding heart, no premonitory salivation. I did feel a dread sinking feeling in my bowels at one point, and this tricked me momentarily into the false hope that I was undergoing a reversal of the process that landed me in this fix—a gradual undisembodiment. But the isolation and uniqueness of that twinge soon convinced me that it was simply the first of a plague of phantom body hallucinations that I, like any other amputee, would be all too likely to suffer.

My mood then was chaotic. On the one hand, I was fired up with elation of my philosophic discovery and was wracking my brain (one of the few familiar things I could still do), trying to figure out how to communicate my discovery to the journals; while on the other, I was bitter, lonely, and filled with dread and uncertainty. Fortunately, this did not last long, for my technical support team sedated me into a dreamless sleep from which I awoke, hearing with magnificent fidelity the familiar opening strains of my favorite Brahms piano trio. So that was why they had wanted a list of my favorite recordings! It did not take me long to realize that I was hearing the music without ears. The output from the stereo stylus was being fed through some fancy rectification circuitry directly into my auditory nerve. I was mainlining Brahms, an unforgettable experience for any stereo buff. At the end of the record it did not surprise me to hear the reassuring voice of the project director speaking into a microphone that was now my prosthetic ear. He confirmed my analysis of what had gone wrong and assured me that steps were being taken to re-embody me. He did not elaborate, and after a few more recordings, I found myself drifting off to sleep. My sleep lasted, I later learned, for the better part of a year, and when I awoke, it was to find myself fully restored to my senses. When I looked into the mirror, though, I was a bit startled to see an unfamiliar face. Bearded and a bit heavier, bearing no doubt a family resemblance to my former face, and with the same look of spritely intelligence and resolute character, but definitely a new face. Further self-explorations of an intimate nature left me no doubt that this was a new body, and the project director confirmed my conclusions. He did not volunteer any information on the past history of my new body and I decided (wisely, I think in retrospect) not to pry. As many philosophers unfamiliar with my ordeal have more recently speculated, the acquisition of a new body leaves one's *person* intact. And after a period of adjustment to a new voice, new muscular strengths and weaknesses, and so forth, one's *personality* is by and large also preserved. More dramatic changes in personality have been routinely observed in people who have undergone extensive plastic surgery, to say nothing of sex-change operations, and I think no one contests the survival of the person in such cases. In any event I soon accommodated to my new body, to the point of being unable to recover any of its novelties to my consciousness or even memory. The view in the mirror soon became utterly familiar. That view, by the way, still revealed antennae, and so I was not surprised to learn that my brain had not been moved from its haven in the life-support lab.

I decided that good old Yorick deserved a visit. I and my new body, whom we might as well call Fortinbras, strode into the familiar lab to another round of applause from the technicians, who were of course congratulating themselves, not me. Once more I stood before the vat and contemplated poor Yorick, and on a whim I once again cavalierly flicked off the output transmitter switch. Imagine my surprise when nothing unusual happened. No fainting spell, no nausea, no noticeable change. A technician hurried to restore the switch to ON, but still I felt nothing. I demanded an explanation, which the project director hastened to provide. It seems that before they had even operated on the first occasion, they had constructed a computer duplicate of my brain, reproducing both the complete information-processing structure and the computational speed of my brain in a giant computer program. After the operation, but before they had dared to send me off on my mission to Oklahoma, they had run this computer system and Yorick side by side. The incoming signals from Hamlet were sent simultaneously to Yorick's transceivers and to the computer's array of inputs. And the outputs from Yorick were not only beamed back to Hamlet, my body; they were recorded and checked against the simultaneous output of the computer program, which was called "Hubert" for reasons obscure to me. Over days and even weeks, the outputs were identical and synchronous, which of course did not *prove* that they had succeeded in copying the brain's functional structure, but the empirical support was greatly encouraging.

Hubert's input, and hence activity, had been kept parallel with Yorick's during my disembodied days. And now, to demonstrate this, they had actually thrown the master switch that put Hubert for the first time in on-line control of my body—not Hamlet, of course, but Fortinbras. (Hamlet, I learned, had never been recovered from its underground tomb and could be assumed by this time to have largely returned to the dust. At the head of my grave still lay the magnificent bulk of the abandoned device, with the word STUD emblazoned on its side in large letters—a circumstance which may provide archeologists of the next century with a curious insight into the burial rites of their ancestors.)

The laboratory technicians now showed me the master switch, which had two positions, labeled *B*, for Brain (they didn't know my brain's name was Yorick) and *H*, for Hubert. The switch did indeed point to *H*, and they explained to me that if I wished, I could switch it back to *B*. With my heart in my mouth (and my brain in its vat), I did this. Nothing happened. A click, that was all. To test their claim, and with the master switch now set at *B*, I hit Yorick's output transmitter switch on the vat and sure enough, I began to faint. Once the output switch was turned back on and I had recovered my wits, so to speak, I continued to play with the master switch, flipping it back and forth. I found that with the exception of the transitional click, I could detect no trace of a difference. I could switch in mid-utterance, and the sentence I had begun speaking under the control of Yorick was finished without a pause or hitch of any kind under the control of Hubert. I had a spare brain, a prosthetic device which might some day stand me in very good stead, were some mishap to befall Yorick. Or alternatively, I could keep Yorick as a spare and use Hubert. It didn't seem to make any difference which I chose, for the wear and tear and fatigue on my body did not have any debilitating effect on either brain, whether or not it was actually causing the motions of my body, or merely spilling its output into thin air.

The one truly unsettling aspect of this new development was the prospect, which was not long in dawning on me, of someone detaching the spare—Hubert or Yorick, as the case might be—from Fortinbras and hitching it to yet another body—some Johnny-come-lately Rosencrantz or Guildenstern. Then (if not before) there would be *two* people, that much was clear. One would be me, and the other would be a sort of super-twin brother. If there were two bodies, one under the control of Hubert and the other being controlled by Yorick, then which would the world recognize as the true Dennett? And whatever the rest of the world decided, which one would be *me*? Would I be the Yorick-brained one, in virtue of Yorick's causal priority and former intimate relationship with the original Dennett body, Hamlet? That seemed a bit legalistic, a bit too redolent of the arbitrariness of consanguinity and legal possession, to be convincing at the metaphysical level. For suppose that before the arrival of the second body on the scene, I had been keeping Yorick as the spare for years, and letting Hubert's output drive my body—that is, Fortinbras—all that time. The Hubert-Fortinbras couple would seem then by squatter's rights (to combat one legal intuition with another) to be the true Dennett and the lawful inheritor of everything that was Dennett's. This was an interesting question, certainly, but not nearly so pressing as another question that bothered me. My strongest intuition was that in such an eventuality *I* would survive so long as *either* brain-body couple remained intact, but I had mixed emotions about whether I should want both to survive.

I discussed my worries with the technicians and the project director. The prospect of two Dennetts was abhorrent to me, I explained, largely for social reasons. I didn't want to be my own rival for the affections of my wife, nor did I like the prospect of the two Dennetts sharing my modest professor's salary. Still more vertiginous and distasteful, though, was the idea of knowing *that much* about another person, while he had the very same goods on me. How could we ever face each other? My colleagues in the lab argued that I was ignoring the bright side of the matter. Weren't there many things I wanted to do but, being only one person, had been unable to do? Now one Dennett could stay at home and be the professor and family man, while the other could strike out on a life of travel and adventure—missing the family of course, but happy in the knowledge that the other Dennett was keeping the home fires burning. I could be faithful and adulterous at the same time. I could even cuckold myself—to say nothing of other more lurid possibilities my colleagues were all too ready to force upon my overtaxed imagination. But my ordeal in Oklahoma (or was it Houston?) had made me less adventurous, and I shrank from this opportunity that was being offered (though of course I was never quite sure it was being offered to *me* in the first place).

There was another prospect even more disagreeable: that the spare, Hubert or Yorick as the case might be, would be detached from any input from Fortinbras and just left detached. Then, as in the other case, there would be two Dennetts, or at least two claimants to my name and possessions, one embodied in Fortinbras, and the other sadly, miserably disembodied. Both selfishness and altruism bade me take steps to prevent this from happening. So I asked that measures be taken to ensure that no one could ever tamper with the transceiver connections or the master switch without my (our? no, *my*) knowledge and consent. Since I had no desire to spend my life guarding the equipment in Houston, it was mutually decided that all the electronic connections in the lab would be carefully locked. Both those that controlled the life-support system for Yorick and those that controlled the power supply for Hubert would be guarded with fail-safe devices, and I would take the only master switch, outfitted for radio remote control, with me wherever I went. I carry it strapped around my waist and—wait a moment—*here it is*. Every few months I reconnoiter the situation by switching channels. I do this only in the presence of friends, of course, for if the other channel were, heaven forbid, either dead or otherwise occupied, there would have to be somebody who had my interests at heart to switch it back, to bring me back from the void. For while I could feel, see, hear, and otherwise sense whatever befell my body, subsequent to such a switch, I'd be unable to control it. By the way, the two positions on the switch are intentionally unmarked, so I never have the faintest idea whether I am switching from Hubert to Yorick or vice versa. (Some of you may think that in this case I really don't know *who* I am, let alone where I am. But such reflections no longer make much of a dent on my essential Dennettness, on my own sense of who I am. If it is true that in one sense I don't know who I am then that's another one of your philosophical truths of underwhelming significance.)

In any case, every time I've flipped the switch so far, nothing has happened. *So let's give it a try. . . .*

"THANK GOD! I THOUGHT YOU'D NEVER FLIP THAT SWITCH! You can't imagine how horrible it's been these last two weeks—but now you know; it's your turn in purgatory. How I've longed for this moment! You see, about two weeks ago—excuse me, ladies and gentlemen, but I've got to explain this to my . . . um, brother, I guess you could say, but he's just told you the facts, so you'll understand—about two weeks ago our two brains drifted just a bit out of synch. I don't know whether *my* brain is now Hubert or Yorick, any more than you do, but in any case, the two brains drifted apart, and of course once the process started, it snowballed, for I was in a slightly different receptive state for the input we both received, a difference that was soon magnified. In no time at all the illusion that I was in control of my body—our body—was completely dissipated. There was nothing I could do—no way to call you. YOU DIDN'T EVEN KNOW I EXISTED! It's been like being carried around in a cage, or better, like being possessed—hearing my own voice say things I didn't mean to say, watching in frustration as my own hands performed deeds I hadn't intended. You'd scratch our itches, but not the way I would have, and you kept me awake, with your tossing and turning. I've been totally exhausted, on the verge of a nervous breakdown, carried around helplessly by your frantic round of activities, sustained only by the knowledge that some day you'd throw the switch.

"Now it's your turn, but at least you'll have the comfort of knowing *I* know you're in there. Like an expectant mother, I'm eating—or at any rate tasting, smelling, seeing—for *two* now, and I'll try to make it easy for you. Don't worry. Just as soon as this colloquium is over, you and I will fly to Houston, and we'll see what can be done to get one of us another body. You can have a female body—your body could be any color you like. But let's think it over. I tell you what—to be fair, if we both want this body, I promise I'll let the project director flip a coin to settle which of us gets to keep it and which then gets to choose a new body. That should guarantee justice, shouldn't it? In any case, I'll take care of you, I promise. These people are my witnesses.

"Ladies and gentlemen, this talk we have just heard is not exactly the talk *I* would have given, but I assure you that everything he said was perfectly true. And now if you'll excuse me, I think I'd—we'd—better sit down."

Study Questions

1. What are some specific practical issues that are closely related to the problem of personal identity?
2. Discuss the bodily continuity standard for personal identity.
3. What is the continuity standard for personal identity?
4. Describe Hume's view on the problem of personal identity.
5. What is Derek Parfit's position on personal identity?
6. Discuss the pros and cons of the life-narrative view of personal identity.
7. From the Locke reading, describe Locke's standard for personal identity.
8. How would Hume criticize Locke's view on personal identity?

Exercises

1. One of the first examples discussed is offered by Selina: A deeply reflective person completes a living will specifying that if her rational capacities are permanently impaired, then she wants no lifesaving medications. But when a disease destroys her reasoning abilities, she becomes very happy; indeed, she appears much happier than at any previous time in her life. If she develops a life-threatening infection that could easily be treated with antibiotics, should we treat her or instead follow the instructions in the living will?
2. In the dialogue, no one offers a direct answer to the preceding question. Given their views, how do you think each of them would answer?
3. An ancient and famous philosophical example related to questions of identity is the "Ship of Theseus." Theseus is a great Athenian hero, and in honor of his great exploits, the people of Athens preserved his ship and sailed it in a yearly celebration. Over the years, of course, parts of the ship had to be replaced. When parts were thrown away, replacement parts—made from

similar materials—were used to make repairs. Eventually, over many years, every part of the ship has been replaced. Is this still the Ship of Theseus?

4. Several models of free will were discussed in Chapters 8 and 9: the libertarian model (Campbell), simple compatibilism (Hume), deep compatibilism (Frankfurt), and rational compatibilism (Wolf). Which of those views would fit best with the *narrative* model of identity? Which of those views would be *least* compatible with the narrative model of identity?

5. Suppose that my own "life narrative" contains a number of self-serving distortions, distortions that I have come to believe are true. For example, in my life narrative I drop my physics major—to the profound disappointment of the physics faculty, who see a great future for me in physics—in favor of philosophy, because I am fascinated by the deeper questions about the meaning of life. In fact, I switched to philosophy because I couldn't pass calculus, and my physics professor gently suggested I try a different major. Can this distorted narrative still suffice to establish a continuing personal identity?

6. Is there a single defining standard for personal identity? Or is personal identity instead a "cluster concept," in which several factors—bodily continuity, coherent memories, a sense of personal identity, friendly recognition by the family dog—contribute to establishing personal identity, with no single factor being definitive?

7. Add one more step to Dennett's delightful story, "Who Am I?" Suppose that Dennett's brain is destroyed, but the computer and the new body continue to function, and none of Dennett's friends can tell any significant difference. Did Dennett die? Is this computer-driven body still the same Dennett? Is he more or less like Dennett? Can we settle this question by inquiry and reasoning, or will it require some sort of *stipulation*?

Glossary

Life narrative: An ongoing autobiographical account of one's life that gives continuity and sense of personal identity to the episodes of one's life experience.

Additional Resources

Many of the resources suggested for Chapter 5 are also relevant here.

The classical sources for the problem of self-identity are John Locke, Chapter 27 of the second edition of his *Essay Concerning Human Understanding*, 1694; Bishop Joseph Butler, *The Anatomy of Religion*, first appendix, 1736; David Hume, *Treatise of Human Nature*, Book I, Part IV, 1739; and Thomas Reid, third essay in *Essays on the Intellectual Powers of Man*, 1785.

Among the most influential contemporary philosophers on personal identity are Sydney Shoemaker, *Self-Knowledge and Self-Identity* (Ithaca, NY: Cornell University Press, 1963), *Identity, Cause, and Mind* (Cambridge, U.K.: Cambridge

University Press, 1984), and *Personal Identity*, with Richard Swinburne (discussed shortly); and Derek Parfit, *Reasons and Persons* (Oxford, U.K.: Clarendon Press, 1984). Thomas Nagel's "Brain Bisection and the Unity of Consciousness" is also well known. Originally published in 1971 in *Synthese*, Volume 22, pp. 396–413, it is available in the collection of essays by Nagel entitled *Mortal Questions* (Cambridge, U.K.: Cambridge University Press, 1979), as well as in several anthologies.

Harold W. Noonan, *Personal Identity*, 2d ed. (London: Routledge, 2003) is a superb introduction to the issues surrounding personal identity. Originally published in 1989, it has been updated to include recent work (especially the biological theory of identity).

John R. Perry, *A Dialogue on Personal Identity and Immortality* (Indianapolis, IN: Hackett, 1978), is a very readable introduction to the question of personal identity and includes discussions of many of the traditional problems associated with personal identity and its application to the question of individual immortality. Also, John Perry's *Personal Identity* (Berkeley, CA: University of California Press, 1975) is an excellent anthology that brings together both classical and contemporary writings on the question of personal identity; Perry's introduction to the volume is a very helpful brief guide.

In *Personal Identity*, by Sidney Shoemaker and Richard Swinburne (Oxford, U.K.: Basil Blackwell, 1984), Swinburne argues for dualism while Shoemaker defends materialism; their essays and their comments on the opposing arguments make a very interesting study of some of the key issues related to personal identity.

An excellent volume of contemporary essays, *Identity, Character, and Morality*, edited by Owen Flanagan and Amélie Oksenberg Rorty (Cambridge, MA: MIT Press, 1990), draws connections between identity issues and ethical questions (especially questions concerning moral responsibility).

A very good collection of essays on the subject of personal identity is *The Identities of Persons*, edited by Amélie Oksenberg Rorty (Berkeley, CA: University of California Press, 1976). *Personal Identity*, edited by Raymond Martin and John Barresi (Oxford, U.K.: Blackwell Publishers, 2002), is another good collection. It opens with an excellent historical essay by the editors and contains important recent papers on the subject.

Bernard Williams is always fascinating and is one of the best philosophical writers; for his views on personal identity, see his *Problems of the Self* (Cambridge, U.K.: Cambridge University Press, 1973).

A good collection of articles on artificial intelligence by one of the leaders in the field is John Haugeland's *Mind Design* (Cambridge, MA: MIT Press, 1981). It was specifically designed (as Haugeland notes) as a sequel to Alan Ross Anderson's *Minds and Machines* (Englewood Cliffs, NJ: Prentice-Hall, 1964), which contains many of the classic papers in this area.

Eric T. Olson argues for a *biological continuity* view of personal identity: "[O]ne survives just in case one's purely animal functions—metabolism, the capacity to breathe and circulate one's blood, and the like—continue." His book, *The Human Animal: Personal Identity without Psychology* (New York: Oxford

University Press, 1997), considers a variety of thought experiments and poses some original ones as well.

One of the most interesting and insightful writers from the life-narrative approach to personal identity is Ronald Dworkin; see especially his *Life's Dominion* (New York: Knopf, 1993). A leading advocate of that approach is Alasdair MacIntyre; see his *After Virtue: A Study in Moral Theory* (South Bend, IN: University of Notre Dame Press, 1981), especially the section entitled "The Story-Telling Animal."

A very extensive and thorough bibliography of material on personal identity—including links to material available online—can be found at *http://www.philosophy .ucf.edu/mind.html.*

Notes

1. This point was raised by Charles B. Daniels, "Personal Identity," in Peter A. French, ed., *Philosophers in Wonderland* (St. Paul: Llewellyn Publications, 1975).
2. Ronald Dworkin, *Life's Dominion* (New York: Knopf, 1993), p. 210.

Chapter *12*

The Nature of Humans

in which Sarah, Selina, and Ben sort out—
but do not settle—their differences

Selina and Sarah were already drinking coffee when Ben arrived, dropped his book bag on the floor, his coffee cup in front of his chair, and his announcement squarely on the table. "I've finally figured out what your problem is, Selina."

Selina raised her eyebrows. "So you finally looked in a mirror?"

Ben laughed and turned toward Sarah. "She keeps that knife sharp, doesn't she? By the end of the semester I'll be one solid scar." Then, turning back toward Selina, "No, I'm just a minor annoyance. Your big problem is that you're a control freak."

"Thanks a bunch, Ben; I love you, too."

Control and Understanding

"I don't mean control freak in that way," said Ben; "I mean that your great desire is to gain *control* of events, to be able to accurately predict and manipulate phenomena. And you refuse to leave room in your conceptual scheme for anything that can't be brought within your scientific system of control and prediction. That's your problem, Selina, because there is more in heaven and earth than is dreamt of in your philosophy, and more in heaven and earth than can be dealt with through scientific prediction and control."

"Perhaps you're right, Ben." Selina made reply. "Perhaps there is more in heaven and earth than is dreamt of in my philosophy, more than can be explained by the methods of science."

"Selina, are you alright?" Sarah was amazed. "That's the mildest response I've ever heard from you. Ben comes in and throws down a challenge, and you meekly concede his point without the slightest struggle?"

"Not at all," Selina replied. "I conceded nothing. Granted, there *may* be more in heaven and earth than can be dealt with through scientific method. But we'll never know that until we *try*, will we? The history of science is filled with phenomena that were regarded as beyond the scope of scientific explanation, phenomena for which we now have solid scientific explanations. Comets were messengers from God, cosmic signals of mystical significance; only priests and prophets could interpret these harbingers of divine wrath or godly favor. Or at least that's what they were until Edmund Halley studied earlier sightings of comets and combined that data with Newton's laws of motion to predict the return of the comet that is named after him. Bubonic Plague was a mark of God's righteous judgment upon a city or country, and people rushed out to burn witches in an effort to placate God's retributive wrath. The scientific study of disease showed that the plague germs were carried by fleas; once we found that out, we could prevent the terrible disease—and also, incidentally, save a lot of 'witches' from being burned at the stake. The human hand was inexplicable by natural processes, requiring the intervention of a divine designer; or so it was thought, until Darwin gave a simpler and more fruitful account. Seizures were clear evidence of demonic possession, and those who suffered seizures were condemned and ostracized. Study of the brain has now provided an understanding of what causes seizures and has enabled us to prevent them. Hurricanes were evidence of God's wrath. Apparently, some

---

One impulse from a vernal wood
May teach you more of man,
Of moral evil and of good,
Than all the sages can.

Sweet is the lore which Nature brings;
Our meddling intellect
Mis-shapes the beauteous forms of things:
We murder to dissect.

Enough of science and of Art;
close up those barren leaves;
Come forth, and bring with you a heart
That watches and receives.

William Wordsworth,
"The Tables Turned"

---

people still think that: Pat Robertson, the television evangelist, announced that his prayers had convinced God to turn His wrath away from the Eastern seaboard and steer a hurricane off the Atlantic coast. But most people find the scientific explanation of weather systems more plausible than Reverend Robertson's persuasive powers with a deity. So maybe you're right, Ben. Perhaps there are some things that science will never explain. But the only way we'll know is by *trying* to explain them scientifically. Sometimes we fail. Sometimes we repeatedly fail. But that prompts us to change some of our basic assumptions and develop new hypotheses, leading to new scientific breakthroughs—new paradigms, in Thomas Kuhn's terminology. Of course, there's another approach: Give up, insist that it is 'beyond scientific explanation,' beyond our understanding, it must be left in the realm of mystery. I don't see much value in such a failure of nerve."

"But even if most phenomena are subject to scientific explanation," Ben answered, "something is lost when we try to make *everything* a subject for science. William Wordsworth said it best: You murder to dissect."

"Not so." Selina shook her head. "Look, take something wonderful, like, uh. . . ."

"Like falling in love," Sarah suggested. "That's something wonderful, and tough to analyze, even tougher to predict and control."

"Yeah," Selina agreed, "Falling in love. That's a good case. It is wonderful. I try to do it at least once a week."

"Selina!" Ben's voice was wounded.

"Sorry, Ben. Just teasing. You're my one and only. But you must have known you were gonna get some grief for walking in and announcing that you 'know what my problem is.' The nerve of some men. I would use men as an example, except they don't fit: They're too easy to predict and control, and besides, they're not that wonderful."

"Alright," Ben said, "you've had your fun, or your revenge—maybe both. But yeah, take Sarah's example: How would you do a scientific analysis of love?"

"Actually, scientists are already working on that," Selina replied. "Indications are that it has something to do with scent. But probably a combination of factors: the environment where the encounter occurs probably plays a part, sexual attraction is obviously an element, no doubt a whole range of psychological states to examine. What causes people to fall in love? Scientists don't yet know. But we will. Or at least I believe we will. Someday we'll do an analysis of Reuben and Rachel, take a DNA sample, run a smell test, check their alcohol levels, and predict that Reuben will fall in love with Rachel 47 minutes after he meets her and Rachel will return his love about an hour after that. And I gotta tell you, I don't think it will be nearly as tough a scientific puzzle as predicting the path of Halley's comet."

Sarah shook her head. "I don't know, Selina. I mean, I like science, and scientific research. But it seems to me that a scientific analysis of falling in love might take some of the romance out of it. Can't we keep a little mystery?"

"Or a *lot* of mystery, would be my preference." Ben agreed with Sarah. "I don't want any 'romance scientist' predicting when I'm going to fall in love. Not that any scientist will ever be able to do that. But even if they could, it seems to me something science should keep out of its test tubes."

"Come on, guys. What sort of explanation would you prefer? Cupid twangs his magic bow? Two halves of a single soul find each other in mystical embrace? Not very helpful. When science explains something, it doesn't destroy it. Halley's comet is still beautiful and awe inspiring, and the fact that we can predict its coming and going doesn't alter that. Falling in love is a wonderful thing"—Selina smiled at Ben—"and will remain so even when we can understand its causes and predict its course. And think of what positive effects might follow. People not only fall in love; sadly, they often fall *out* of love as well, and homes are wrecked, divorces take a terrible psychological toll, children get hurt. If we could understand the causes of falling in love, perhaps we could also learn what causes the destruction of loving relationships and take effective steps to prevent that from happening. Gaining a scientific understanding of something doesn't diminish our pleasure and delight; to the contrary, it may well enhance it."

Belief in God

"Alright," Ben said, "I'm not denying that we often gain significant advantages from scientific explanations. It's true that some phenomena we thought beyond the reach of science have yielded to scientific inquiry. But

---

No theory changes what it is a theory about. Nothing is changed because we look at it, talk about it, or analyze it in a new way. Keats drank confusion to Newton for analyzing the rainbow, but the rainbow remained as beautiful as ever and became for many even more beautiful. Man has not changed because we look at him, talk about him, and analyze him scientifically. His achievements in science, government, religion, art, and literature remain as they have always been, to be admired as one admires a storm at sea or autumn foliage or a mountain peak, quite apart from their origins and untouched by a scientific analysis. What does change is our chance of doing something about the subject of a theory. Newton's analysis of the light in a rainbow was a step in the direction of the laser.

B. F. Skinner, *Beyond Freedom and Dignity*
(New York: Alfred A. Knopf, 1971), p. 213

there's at least one aspect of humans that can't be reduced to or explained by simpler mechanical processes: our souls, our spirits, our spiritual dimension."

"Yeah, you've got me there, Ben. I'll never be able to give a scientific explanation for the soul," Selina shook her head, "but perhaps one day we'll be able to give a scientific explanation for the mass delusion that causes so many otherwise intelligent people to believe in such nonsense. In fact, I think we have a pretty good start on an explanation already."

"What explanation is that, Selina?" Sarah was curious. "Sigmund Freud's analysis of God in terms of a super father figure?"

"No, I'm not a Freudian," Selina replied, "but I do think that the best explanation comes from psychology. From behavioral psychology, or cognitive behavioral psychology. Psychologists like Martin Seligman."

"I remember studying about Martin Seligman," Ben said. "He did research on learned helplessness. He placed dogs in restraining harnesses, so that they couldn't escape, and exposed them to repeated shocks. He then took the dogs out of the restraining harnesses and placed them in shuttle boxes: boxes with two compartments, separated by a small wooden barrier. The floor of the shuttle box compartment where he placed the dogs was electrified, and the dogs were then shocked. They easily could have jumped over the barrier into the other compartment and thus escaped the shock: Dogs not previously shocked in the restraining harness did exactly that. But the dogs that had suffered repeated shock in the restraining harness did not try to escape: They gave up, cowered in the box, and waited for the shock to end. The dogs were dragged over the barrier into the other side of the shuttle box where there was no shock; but when placed again in the shock section, they still would not try to escape, but stayed where they were and cowered. They had to be dragged over the barrier again and again, repeatedly encouraged to escape, until finally they got over their helplessness and started to escape on their own."

"Yeah, that's exactly it, Ben," said Selina. "You obviously made good use of your psychology classes."

Sarah shook her head. "I remember reading about Seligman's experiments. I found them really fascinating, but I always felt guilty about it. Frankly, I don't think it's right to expose dogs to severe shocks and cause them to experience the sort of suffering that was involved in Seligman's experiments. Still, I think the experiments teach us something very important: When people give up and don't try, we tend to be disgusted with them. We say, 'That person's useless, he won't even try; if he would just try, he could do it; but how can I help him if he won't even try?' That's a lesson we need to remember when we work with women who won't make any effort to escape a husband who inflicts abuse on them, and students who give up quickly on math problems, and long-term impoverished people who make no effort to 'help themselves.'"

Selina nodded. "I agree with you, Sarah: the experiments bother me, also. The dogs not only suffered severe shocks, but also—according to Seligman's own report—became severely depressed. And that's a misery in itself, in addition to the shock. But as you said, what we learned from the experiment was very important: Not only did we learn that when our efforts repeatedly fail, learned helplessness results; we also learned that learned helplessness has awful results: It leads to lethargy, depression, weakened immune systems and thus greater vulnerability to disease."

"Alright, I agree with you about the importance of preventing a sense of helplessness. But," Sarah continued, "how does that explain belief in God?"

"I remember when I stopped believing in God. Frankly, I found it liberating. Suddenly I could question everything, think anything, no ideas were off limits. It still feels liberating: Go wherever the evidence leads, with no set of beliefs immune from challenge. Still, there's one thing I miss." Selina sipped her coffee. "I remember, when I was a kid, if someone was sick and there was nothing I could do to help, or there was some tragedy in India that bothered me, but there was nothing I could do to alleviate the suffering—well, there was always something I *could* do, something important, something that kept me from feeling helpless. I could always pray. I had a direct line to this personal superhero, God, Who would listen to my prayers; and if I prayed hard enough, He might step in and correct the problem. And sometimes He did! With powers like that, I *never* felt totally helpless. And even if I didn't always feel that the control was entirely in my hands, at least I didn't think I was totally hopeless, that the outcome was in the hands of fate. In short, belief in God is a good way to avoid a sense of learned helplessness, a way to keep from falling into total despair when there's really nothing you can do. Maybe that's why belief in God is often strongest among the oppressed and powerless and impoverished: It's not as good as genuine powers of control, but it's a lot more adaptive than utter hopelessness and helplessness."

"Okay, Selina, so belief in God works well, at least for some important purposes." Sarah was intense. "If a theory works well, helps us live better, isn't that a reason to consider it true? Some people might suppose that a theory is true in case it 'matches what is really there'; but contemporary scientists like yourself recognize that the notion of a correct theory 'mapping reality' is naive. After all, there are always many possible theories that can 'fit the facts.' The question is, Which theory guides us best. As William James says, 'On pragmatistic principles, if the hypothesis of God works satisfactorily in the widest sense of the word, it is true. Now what-

I firmly disbelieve, myself, that our human experience is the highest form of experience extant in the universe. I believe rather that we stand in much the same relation to the whole of the universe as our canine and feline pets do to the whole of human life. They inhabit our drawing-rooms and libraries. They take part in scenes of whose significance they have no inkling. They are merely tangent to curves of history the beginnings and ends and forms of which pass wholly beyond their ken. So we are tangents to the wider life of things. But, just as many of dog's and cat's ideals coincide with our ideals, and the dogs and cats have daily living proof of the fact, so we may well believe, on the proofs that religious experience affords, that higher powers exist and are at work to save the world on ideal lines similar to our own.

William James, *Pragmatism* (New York: Longman, Green, 1907), pp. 143–44

ever its residual difficulties may be, experience shows that it certainly does work. . . .'[1] James thought the belief works best in the form of 'meliorism.' That is, it works best as a belief that stands between the *pessimistic* belief that evil and destruction will inevitably triumph (and our efforts are therefore useless, and we are ultimately helpless); and the *optimistic* belief that a good, omnipotent God will automatically make everything turn out right (and our efforts are irrelevant). James's meliorism maintains that God is a strong (but not omnipotent) force for good, and the ultimate outcome still hangs in the balance. Thus, our own actions and efforts make a difference in whether evil wins or good triumphs. And God remains a force for good even when the outlook is darkest—so the struggle is never hopeless. That's a very useful belief: It encourages our best efforts and guards us from falling into helplessness or hopelessness. In short, it works well, guides us effectively. And what better standard could there be for a true belief?"

"Or maybe the reason it works so well," Ben replied, "is simply because there is a real God—not just a useful belief, and not James' melioristic God, but an omnipotent God over all—and God does hear and answer prayer."

"Yes, that's certainly a simpler explanation," Selina countered, "all you have to add to your explanatory scheme is an all-powerful deity with a mysterious nature that is beyond our understanding. Why don't you throw in some woodland elves and sugarplum fairies while you're at it? And witches and ghosts and goblins, as well; then we can explain everything."

"I didn't say anything about ghosts and goblins and things that go bump in the night, Selina. Just because I believe in God, that doesn't mean I believe in all those other things."

"But Ben," Selina replied, "if you believe in God, you don't *need* all those other things: God can 'explain' everything. Once you allow mysterious beings to infect your explanatory system, then *everything* becomes easy to explain. That's the problem: The explanations become too easy, and nothing can possibly refute them, no prediction is crucial. If the prediction doesn't come out as you anticipate—well, God's ways are not our ways, God is mysterious. It may provide comfort, but it doesn't provide anything in the way of real explanation. Besides," Selina turned toward Sarah, "if we're judging theories on the basis of which set of beliefs works best and guides us most effectively, my belief in empirical science wins hands down over miracles and mysteries and deities. Science guides us to all sorts of new and valuable discoveries and really enables us to make things happen: cure disease, combat epidemics, overthrow repressive regimes, design better social systems, predict new phenomena. The religious illusion of the power of prayer may have some benefits; but *genuine* control exercised by our own powers has a lot more. When the world is a place of disorder, and we can't understand the causes of disease or the paths of comets or changes in the weather, and they all seem chaotic and unpredictable, we may need belief in God to give us some sense of control and order. After all, an illusory sense of control is better than a sense of total helplessness. But with genuine scientific control and improved knowledge and effective predictions, we gain a stronger and more legitimate sense of power if we eliminate the illusions."

"Okay, kids, end of round one," Sarah intervened, "go back to your respective corners and drink your coffee. Anyway, your argument started me thinking about some other possible differences in your views. One difference is obvious: Ben believes in God, believes in souls, and Selina does not. Selina is a thorough naturalist, and Ben insists on the reality of a transcendent, nonnatural dimension. That's no small difference, of course. But I was thinking about how it relates to another basic question: How do you see humans in relation to the rest of the natural world? In particular, are humans radically different and distinct from everything else in the world, or is there a basic continuity and just differences of degree?"

Are Humans Special?

"If Ben believes humans have souls and spirits," Selina asked, "doesn't that automatically mean that he believes in a radical difference between humans and the rest of the world, between humans and other animals, for example?"

"Not necessarily," answered Sarah. "St. Francis certainly believed that humans have immortal souls, but he did not believe in a radical break between humans and the rest of God's creation. He preached to humans, but also to birds, and even to a wolf—a wolf that repented of its vicious attacks and converted to Christianity, at least according to legend. And Spinoza believed in God, but viewed God and the natural world as all one: There is nothing outside of God's infinite attributes, so there is no radical break between God and humans or between humans and the rest of the world. And the Hindu religion takes a similar perspective. And from the other direction, there are those who deny any nonnatural aspects of the world—who deny souls and spirits and deities altogether—but still believe that there is a marked difference between humans and the rest of the world, between humans and other animals: Humans are special and distinct and unique because we alone have reason, or because we alone have ethical codes, or because we alone have language. So the distinction between naturalists and those who believe in a non-natural dimension is one thing; the question of how humans are related to other animals is quite another."

"Alright," Selina nodded, "so it's a separate question from the naturalist–transcendent distinction. But I have a hard time seeing how a scientific naturalist could suppose there is a sharp divide between humans and other animals. After all, humans and chimps split apart only six million years ago: just the blink of an eye, on the evolutionary time scale. We share over 98% of our DNA with chimpanzees, and we are more closely related to chimpanzees than they are to either gorillas or orangutans. Unless humans have some divine stamp of approval that God denied our great-ape cousins, I can't imagine how humans are 'different in kind' from other animals. There are differences, sure: We are a different species. But the similarities are much more evident than the differences."

Ben frowned. "Alright, I do believe humans have souls, and *only* humans have souls. But leave that aside for the moment. There are other reasons, not dependent on any religious doctrine, for marking a clear line between humans and other species."

"Wait a minute, Ben, not so fast, back up a second." Selina held up her hand to signal halt. "Go back to that souls thing. There's something

---

Even if one supposes that a key difference between humans and other animals is that the former have souls and the latter do not—the position of the Catholic Church—that does not justify cruel treatment of animals. Cardinal Bellarmine, a prominent Roman Catholic theologian, drew precisely the opposite conclusion: Since animals do not have immortal souls, wrongs done to them will not be rectified in the afterlife; therefore, nonhuman animals should be treated with even greater concern than humans.

[Argument developed by Bernard E. Rollin, *Animal Rights & Human Morality*, revised edition (Buffalo: Prometheus Books, 1992), p. 29]

that confuses me; maybe you could help me out. You say that *only* humans have souls? Chimpanzees and gorillas and orangutans do not; and, of course, any ancestors common to both humans and chimpanzees do not have souls, right?"

"Right," Ben answered, though somewhat uneasily.

"So what about our not-so-distant ancestor *Homo erectus*? Did it have a soul? Or did it have only a half soul? Or maybe a 'protosoul'? At exactly what point of development did the line that veered off from chimpanzees get souls? And assuming the evolutionary process was gradual, was there some particular point at which souls emerged? One generation lacked souls, but at the next tiny evolutionary step the species had souls? Junior gets a soul, but Mom and Dad are soulless?"

Ben put his hands to his temples and shook his head slowly. "Selina, I have no idea. I guess whenever God decided the time was right."

Selina raised her coffee cup: "A salute to God; He is always such a convenient solution."

"Alright, I knew you were never going to buy the 'humans have souls' answer," Ben said. "But look, there are other reasons for believing that humans are uniquely different—different in *kind*—from all other animals."

"Go ahead, Ben," Selina smiled. "I can't *wait* to hear what sets us apart from every other element of the entire evolutionary process."

"Actually, I've been thinking about this a lot," Ben continued. "Some philosophers contend that its reason that makes humans special and unique, right, Sarah?"

"Reason is a perennially popular philosophical candidate, Ben, quite right," Sarah agreed.

"Yeah, but I don't think reason marks the dividing line," Ben continued. "In the first place, I don't think humans are really all that smart. When philosophers talk about humans as *rational*, they tend to idealize our rational practices. In fact, we often reason and plan badly, we act on motives that we don't admit to ourselves while using 'reason' to justify a decision actually made on the basis of prejudice or superstition. Second, other animals—chimpanzees, for example—are a lot smarter than we used to think. They use tools, they transmit cultural practices, they make elaborate plans, they form alliances, they practice deception, and—though some still dispute it—they can apparently learn at least a rudimentary language and even teach it to other chimpanzees."

"Wow, Ben!" Sarah's eyes were wide. "That was impressive! I didn't know you knew that much about chimpanzees; and I would have never guessed that you would allow any sort of comparison of chimpanzee intelligence with human intelligence."

"Not so long ago I would have thought there was no legitimate comparison," Ben said, "but then I started reading a lot of the research on chimpanzee intelligence and social relations and abilities. It changed my perspective, I admit."

"But if you acknowledge that there's no huge gap between the intelligence of humans and the intelligence of some other animals, then why hang onto the belief that humans are somehow special and different?" Selina frowned. "You're not going back to that old stuff about souls, are you?"

"I do believe in souls, as you well know," Ben replied, "and I don't think that souls are 'old stuff.' But as I said, there are other reasons for maintaining that humans are distinctive, separate, special. But the difference is not simply a difference in intelligence."

"So how about morality?" Sarah asked. "Many people make that the clear division: Only humans can act morally (or immorally)."

"Yeah," Selina said, "and some people think that is a very implausible claim. If humans can act morally, then it seems hard to deny that other animals also act morally. If a human cares for and comforts a friend, we count that as morally good behavior. Chimpanzees, and maybe some other species as well, exhibit the same sort of behavior. If we're going to count it as moral in humans, it seems that simple consistency requires that we count analogous chimpanzee behavior in the same moral category."

Darwinism insists that features evolve gradually, and something as important as morality should have been present in our (very recent) shared ancestors. Furthermore, if morality is as important biologically to humans as is being claimed, it would be odd indeed had all traces now been eliminated from the social interactions of other high-level primates.

Michael Ruse,
Taking Darwin Seriously
(New York: Blackwell,
1986), p. 227

"You know, Sarah, I gotta go along with Selina on this one. I've been thinking a lot about this over the past few months, reading some books on chimpanzee behavior." Ben pulled a couple from his backpack and opened them on the table. "And I've gradually come around to the view that other animals *can* be moral actors—at least some other animals in some circumstances. Roger Fouts gives an example that occurred in his dealings with Washoe, one of the earliest chimpanzees to learn American Sign Language. Washoe and several other chimps were living on an island, surrounded by a high fence and a moat filled with water. Chimps are deathly afraid of water: They are poor swimmers and swiftly drown in deep water. One morning, a new chimpanzee, Penny, was introduced to the colony. At one point in the early afternoon, Penny panicked, leaped over the fence, and splashed into the moat. She thrashed about in the water for a moment, but would obviously soon drown.

Washoe leaped the fence, and with one hand gripping a post, she slid far down the muddy bank until she could reach Penny and pull her to safety. Had she slipped, or had her leap over the high fence carried her slightly farther into the water, Washoe would have drowned along with Penny. Roger Fouts"—Ben flipped the pages to a passage he had underlined— "describes his own reaction after Penny and Washoe were rescued from their precarious perch on the slope of the moat:

> While Penny was calming down, I had time to gather my wits, and to let the enormity of what I'd just seen sink in. Washoe had risked her own life to save another chimpanzee—one she had known for only a few hours.[2]

Of course, Washoe had to act swiftly to carry out her daring rescue, and obviously she did not spend a lot of time contemplating her moral duty to Penny. But in exactly similar circumstances, had Washoe and Penny been humans, we would not hesitate to say that Washoe acted morally—that, indeed, her act had been one of moral heroism. Simple consistency seems to demand the same conclusion, whether Washoe is a chimpanzee or a human." Ben opened the second book. "Along similar lines, Frans de Waal tells about one of his favorite chimps, named Mama, who was a very effective peacemaker in her group:

> Mama enjoys enormous respect in the community. Her central position is comparable to that of a grandmother in a Spanish or Chinese family. When tensions in the group reach their peak, the combatants always turn to her— even the adult males. Many a time I have seen a major conflict between two males end up in her arms. Instead of resorting to physical violence at the climax of their confrontation, the rivals run to Mama, screaming loudly.[3]

Maybe Mama was simply doing this because she disliked fighting and enjoyed a peaceful and harmonious community. But if a human patched up quarrels and prevented violent conflict for exactly the same motives, we would certainly count the human behavior as moral—unless, perhaps, we were strict Kantians, who believed that the *only* genuine moral acts are those done purely from devotion to moral principle, with no element of affection or care or inclination. There's a lot in Kant's ethics that I like, but I don't believe that all moral behavior must be purely rational. If we take such an austere view of moral behavior, then not only chimps, but also most humans, will fall outside the moral sphere."

"Ben, you are on the side of the angels," Selina exclaimed; "or rather, you are on the side of naturalism, which is even better! You agree that there is no sharp line between human intelligence and the intelligence of other animals, and you include at least some animal behavior within the sphere of morality. It sounds to me that you have given up any idea of a sharp dividing line that distinguishes humans from other species."

"Sorry to disappoint you, Selina, but I'm afraid I'm still on the side of the angels. There is a basic and important distinction between humans and the rest of the natural world, but the distinction isn't a simple one. Rather, it requires a special combination of higher reason, ethical principle, and willpower."

Selina shook her head. "Ah, Ben, so close, so close. You had your fingers closed around the naturalism prize, and you couldn't quite hold on. How could you have slipped back into the realm of mystery and special human powers after being so close to the goal?"

"Wait a minute, Selina," Sarah said. "I want to hear this. Ben's distinction sounds interesting."

"Many mistakes are interesting, Sarah," Selina said; "falsehoods often glitter. But that doesn't make them true."

"Be fair, Selina. Don't reject Ben's account until you at least hear it."

"Yeah, Selina, be fair. You should at least give my view a hearing."

"Okay, I'm waiting to hear: Fill me in on all the sordid, mysterious details," Selina said, taking a long drink of coffee.

"I'm not sure she's listening with an open mind, Ben," Sarah said, "but at least she's listening. And so am I. Tell us why humans are uniquely different from everything else in the world."

"Okay, it's not because humans have a monopoly on intelligence or even on reason: Other animals also engage in intelligent behavior and use reason; and besides, our own rationality is far from perfect. And it's not because we are the only animals that act freely: Other animals also make free choices, especially if you think of free choice the way the compatibilists do, as following your own wishes. And it's not because humans are the only animals that act morallly: Washoe and Mama act morally, and probably other animals as well. None of those traditional elements separate humans from other animals. But if you link them together, you get a special result; you might say that the whole is greater than the sum of its parts. Humans do have special intellectual powers. Even if we grant that chimpanzees can learn language and that they can make plans, humans still have a power of thinking in terms of higher level principles that remains uniquely human. As bright as chimps are, they don't write laws, and there is nothing comparable to our arguments about whether various principles are consistent with one another, no development of higher order mathematics, no legal debate over rules and precedents and exceptions. I'm not saying that such human activities of sequential, rule-based reasoning are necessarily better than what chimps can do. Roger Fouts, who has done extensive research with chimpanzees, believes that the key difference is that humans reason better *sequentially*, using higher order rules, but that chimpanzees are superior in *simultaneous* processing skills, the sort of reasoning required to function effectively in a dense jungle environment in which threats appear swiftly and from all sides. Simultaneous processing enables chimps to read multiple cues—such as 'body language' and facial gestures—simultaneously, as a coherent whole.[4] Maybe Fouts is right; that's a question for psychologists and biologists to resolve. But in any case, humans do possess a special ability to think in terms of moral rules and higher order principles and to reflect on our deep approval or rejection of principles. Only humans can follow an ethical rule, can act a particular way because they believe they *ought* to act that way, and that they *ought* to act that way because they have objectively reasoned that this ethical *principle* is correct. Alright, maybe that's not the highest form of ethical behavior: Maybe Kant was wrong, and ethics based on affection rather than rationally derived rules is superior. But whatever you think about that, following an ethical *principle* because you believe it to be the *right principle* remains an important element of ethics; and that capacity is uniquely human."

Ben paused. Selina still looked skeptical, but at least she was listening. Ben sipped his coffee and continued. "It runs even deeper than that. Humans can reflect on our deepest rules and commitments and reflectively approve or disapprove of them. For example, I can set my highest goal as one of enriching myself and key all my efforts to accumulating wealth. Thus, I might decide that—in the interests of that highest goal— the best means to that end is to cheat my employees out of their pensions

---

Interestingly enough, Ben's view of the special distinctive nature of humans seems to be shared by chimpanzees raised in human families, without being around other chimps; except that the chimps unhesitatingly include themselves among the special class of humans. Washoe and Lucy were two chimpanzees raised in human families that always used American Sign Language (ASL) with them. The chimps soon became quite proficient at it, and they regarded themselves as human. When they categorized the world, they divided it into people (including humans, among whom they placed themselves) and all other animals (e.g., dogs, cats, black bugs, other chimpanzees). Roger Fouts, who has devoted his career to the study of chimpanzees and language, describes another chimp. Viki Hayes was raised in a human family and had no contact with other chimpanzees: "Viki loved to sort things, and one day she was sorting photographs into two piles: humans and animals. When she came to a picture of herself, Viki put it in the same pile with Dwight Eisenhower and Eleanor Roosevelt. But when she came to a picture of her chimpanzee father, she put him in with the cats, dogs, and horses."

Roger Fouts and Stephen Tukel Mills, *Next of Kin: What Chimpanzees Have Taught Me About Who We Are* (New York: William Morrow and Company, 1997).

and reduce health insurance for their families. But I can also stop and reflect on whether that overall *goal* is worthwhile, whether I really approve of being a person wholly driven by greed. And even if accumulating great wealth *is* my strongest desire, I can morally disapprove of that desire and resolve to change my character and desires, or at least to *combat* my strongest desire. For example, if my self-examination reveals that I am sexist and that my deepest desire is to subjugate women and treat them as inferior, I might still decide that such a character is morally repulsive and resolve to struggle against it. That's the third and final element in what makes humans distinctive: our special human power of contracausal free will. If I overcome my strongest desires and reshape my character by my moral choice, then I must exert the willpower to combat my desires. In fact, the higher level of ethical reflection which calls into question my basic desires is essential for the exercise of this special power of contracausal free will. It's that special unique human combination— deeper levels of sequential rational reflection, a higher level of rule-governed ethical reflection, and a special power of free will—that gives humans a unique distinctiveness and sets us apart from the rest of the natural world."

Sarah applauded. "Quite a theory, Ben! Your account pulls together three traditional grounds for drawing a clear line between humans and nonhumans: Humans have reason, act ethically, and have free will."

Selina shook her head. "It is an amazing theory. It's amazing that anyone could seriously suggest it. Ben, you could *never* believe such a thing if your thoughts had not been slanted and biased by religious dogmas and a desire to preserve the special privileged status of humans. You have three grounds for suggesting that humans are uniquely different from other animals: a difference in intelligence, a difference in the capacity for engaging in ethics, and a difference in the possession of free will. None of them are very strong, so you string them together, and you suppose that you've created a difference that is significant. Doesn't work, Ben: A chain is only as strong as its weakest link, and every link of that chain is faulty. And if you were not striving to save your traditional religious belief in the great gulf between humans and the rest of the world, you would never find such an argument plausible."

"So who are you to criticize my motives?" Ben smiled, but it looked a little forced, and there was an edge of anger in his voice. "Here you are criticizing my argument for drawing a clear line between humans and other animals. But you claim that other animals are basically similar to humans, and then you want to go into pharmacological research, and who do you think will be the test subjects for all those drugs and vaccines you want to develop? Researchers now want to use chimpanzees for biomedical research specifically because they are *genetically* and biologically so *similar* to humans; but then they claim it's still alright, because they aren't humans. And you claim there's no essential difference between humans and other animals, but you want to do research that will involve killing a multitude of laboratory animals. Maybe my arguments are biased, but at least I'm no hypocrite."

Selina's voice grew louder. "Yes, I want to do pharmacological research, but I'm no hypocrite! I am firmly opposed to all animal testing. In the first place, I think it's stupid: We can get more reliable results from *in vitro* cellular testing, without using any lab animals. And besides, tests on other species aren't a good way of testing drugs for ultimate human use: There are too many diseases that behave very differently in different species, and there are many drugs that do almost no harm to other animals, but cause significant harm to humans. But even if we *could* get valuable results from tests on laboratory animals, it would still be wrong: It's no more legitimate to test a drug on or purposefully infect a chimpanzee or a white mouse or a dog than it is to force the same thing on an unwilling human. Whatever the differences between an average human and an average chimpanzee, clearly there are some unfortunate humans whose mental capacities are well below those of a normal chimp. If we think it's wrong to use such humans for painful and dangerous tests, it's rank inconsistency and raw prejudice to suppose it's okay to do those tests on the chimps. I want to do research, because I love doing research and because I want to relieve suffering, but I will never participate in causing suffering to chimpanzees and dogs and cats and lab mice in the hope of *maybe* relieving suffering in humans. In fact, I nearly flunked my anatomy lab because I refused to kill a laboratory rat for dissection. So don't call me a hypocrite. Maybe some researchers are, but I am not."

"Alright, children, you're both in time-out." Sarah quickly intervened. "Don't you remember what we all agreed on? No use of ad hominem fallacies. Selina, it doesn't matter what Ben's motives are or what desperate psychological needs he is trying to meet by drawing a distinction between humans and other animals. Ben gave an *argument*, so his motives don't matter: The argument has to be judged on its own merits, not on the merits of the arguer. And Ben, you're just as bad. Even if Selina were a hypocrite—and she certainly is *not*—that would be irrelevant. She gave an *argument* against your argument, and you have to answer her argument. It doesn't matter whether her character is virtuous or vicious, hypocritical or highly principled. Okay, in addition to her criticism of your argument, she also used an ad hominem fallacy. But"—Sarah wagged her finger at both of them, in an exaggerated scolding gesture—"two wrongs don't make a right."

Ben looked a bit shamefaced and put his hand on Selina's. "You're right, Sarah. I'm sorry, Selina. I got carried away. You're certainly no hypocrite: You're the most principled person I know. I may not agree with all your principles, but there's no doubt that you sincerely strive to live by your principles. If anyone has the courage of her convictions, then it's my lovely Selina."

"It was all my fault," Selina replied, as she squeezed Ben's hand. "I had no right to question your motives. I don't always agree with you, either. But I know very well that the positions you take are careful and well thought out, and you don't just blindly follow anyone's tradition." The two shared a very long kiss.

"I think I prefer you guys when you're fighting and lobbing fallacies at each other," Sarah said. "When they say 'Make love, not war,' that's not meant literally—at least not here in the coffee shop."

"Sarah, you've been sitting over there like the cat that swallowed the cream," Selina said, "sipping on your coffee and watching sedately as Ben and I hammer each other. And watching us kiss and make up, right? You becoming a bit of a voyeur, roomie?"

"Not voluntarily, trust me," responded Sarah. "It's just that I share my coffee break with a bunch of exhibitionists. I mean, really, why do you suppose the university gives you dorm rooms?"

Selina laughed. "Anyway, girl, it's time to choose up sides. Do you agree with me that humans fit squarely within our natural world, or are we part of some special distinct realm, as our friend Ben suggests?"

"Actually, Selina, some people believe that humans are special and distinct, though we are still part of the natural world. But certainly, there are many who make the distinction between humans and other species as part of a *larger* difference between the natural and nonnatural realms. On that view, humans may have one bodily foot in the world, but the other—whether it's a special mental substance or an immaterial soul—belongs to a very different sphere."

"Yes, Sarah, all that is very nice," Ben said, "but it doesn't answer Selina's question. So tell us: Which side are you on?"

Holism

"I'm not trying to duck the question, guys. But you know, there's another alternative. I'm not sure that I completely agree with it, but I think Spinoza's view has its charms. Perhaps there are special human qualities, perhaps there is a God; but there is no separation between special human qualities and the natural world, no separation between natural and supernatural or natural and nonnatural. Everything is part of one whole: Mind and body, god and the world, all are aspects of one system; we might see them in different ways, from different perspectives, but ultimately, they are all part of one unified whole. From that viewpoint, the question of whether humans are uniquely different from other species loses much of its significance." Sarah was paging through her notebook, looking for a favorite quotation she had written there. "The logician Raymond Smullyan expresses it well, from a Taoist point of view:

> The confusion is largely caused by your bifurcation of reality into the "you" and the "not you." Really now, just where do you leave off and the rest of the universe begin? Or where does the rest of the universe leave off and you begin? Once you can see the so-called "you" and the so-called "nature" as a continuous whole, then you can never again be bothered by such questions as whether it is you who are controlling nature or nature who is controlling you.[5]

So maybe when you ask whether humans are special and distinct, you are asking the wrong sort of question, viewing the problem from too short a perspective."

No man is an island, entire of itself; every man is a piece of the continent, a part of the main; if a clod be washed away by the sea, Europe is the less, as well as if a promontory were, as well as if a manor of thy friends or of thine own were; any man's death diminishes me, because I am involved in mankind; and therefore never send to know for whom the bell tolls; it tolls for thee.

John Donne,
Devotions upon Emergent Occasions,
1624, no. 17

Selina shook her head. "Look, Sarah, I don't wish to knock your Taoist reflections, and I certainly do not mean to cast aspersions on your philosophical hero, Benedict Spinoza. Heaven forbid! I would sooner poke a grizzly bear in the eye than insult a philosophy major's favorite philosopher. Still, lovely as all this sounds, I can't see how it washes any windows or chops any wood or gathers any crops. We're all part of one great being, everything is really one, we are all united into one great whole. It's inspiring; and I fervently wish that everyone could somehow embrace that wonderful idea. But if we really want to understand our world, that requires something other than warm ideas about all being one. We need controlled studies that make specific detailed comparisons between distinct groups, in specifically defined circumstances. In one sense, perhaps we're all one, but it's also essential to isolate the specific gene that causes Tay–Sachs disease, and to identify the particular virus that causes human immunodeficiency disease, and to focus narrowly on the bacteria that produce the different varieties of disease. And we must attend carefully to the detailed causal histories that shape one man to a life of violent crime and his brother to a life of gentle virtue. Perhaps we are all one, from that elevated perspective Spinoza adopts; but if we are to understand our immediate grubby world we must focus on individuals and particulars and the detailed differences among them."

"We probably won't resolve our differences on the best way to view the world," Sarah said, "or if we do, it will probably require more than one cup of coffee."

"Yeah, and Ben and I will never see the world from the same angle," replied Selina. "Or if we do, it will probably require more than one lifetime."

"It's a curious thing, isn't it," Ben reflected. "Here we are, three brilliant, thoughtful people, considering the same arguments, examining the same evidence, yet coming to such different conclusions. Contracausal free will seems perfectly obvious to me and perfectly ridiculous to Selina; and you, Sarah, believe in free will—though what you call free will is nothing like what I would count as free will—yet you *reject* moral responsibility. Selina cannot quite imagine anyone believing that there is a mental substance in addition to the physical, and I can't believe that anyone doubts it; and again, Sarah takes a third view, that they are different perspectives on a single whole. Selina believes there is nothing outside the natural empirical world, and I am certain there is a transcendent realm of souls and God and miracles that are inexplicable in natural terms. And again, Sarah thinks there is another perspective that encompasses both."

The Importance of Perspectives

"Maybe our differences are not so surprising after all," Sarah replied, "when you consider the different perspectives we take. It's hard to find any clear points of agreement because whatever 'simple facts' there might be get viewed and interpreted in light of our different outlooks and theoretical beliefs. That's not to say that such views can't change, can't be rejected in favor of opposing theories and new perspectives. There are certainly cases of 'conversion.' Selina, after all, once saw the world as a Christian theist, and now she's a dedicated atheist. John Dewey rejected the Kantian absolutism he favored as a young man in favor of naturalism. William James rejected a rather austere empiricism in favor of a pragmatic view that left him room for otherworldly beliefs. Radical young reformers sometimes become reactionary old people. But it's not like changing a small detail; it's more like a paradigm shift, a total change in perspective, a Gestalt switch. Your basic viewpoint, what you consider as evidence, even what you consider a significant issue, is colored by that outlook. When a plane crashes and one hundred people are tragically killed, nonbelievers see evidence that there is no loving, all-powerful

God watching over us. When one child on that plane survives, believers see evidence of God's divine grace. Ben regards his strong intuitive sense of God's presence as evidence for God's existence. When Selina feels 'intimations of immortality,' as Wordsworth calls them, she is likely to look for their origin in our natural evolutionary history or our psychological nature. If she hears voices from God, she'll check for a chemical imbalance in her brain."

Selina laughed. "If I hear voices from God, I'm giving up vodka. If that doesn't work, then I'll get a brain scan and seek appropriate drug therapy."

"So what Ben counts as evidence of divine presence, Selina will count as evidence of psychological malady. Not surprising that such differences run deep."

"Alright, we've looked at several basic issues that distinguish our perspectives," Ben said. "Sarah is more of a holist: she tends to see the world as interconnected, everything ultimately part of one greater whole. I guess Selina and I are more individualistic: I'm somewhat more individualistic when it comes to political views—but maybe I'm changing, okay?—while Selina takes a more individualistic approach to science: The best way to learn about the world is to break it down into its simplest elements. So individualism vs. holism, that's one important element of worldviews. And then, of course, there's the natural-vs.-transcendent difference: Selina is certain that everything can ultimately be explained in naturalistic, non-miraculous terms, and I'm equally certain that there's a realm of truth that is beyond the natural realm. And then there's that issue of whether humans are uniquely different from the rest of the world or whether we are just another element that differs only in degree. Any other basic elements of competing perspectives?"

Rationalism and Empricism

"One that philosophers have traditionally regarded as the most basic of all," Sarah answered, "the distinction between rationalists and empiricists."

"Ah, yes," said Selina, "that most fundamental of philosophical categories! But really, Sarah, is it such a clear distinction for contemporary philosophers? After all, even dedicated empiricists like myself recognize the importance of rational thought in constructing scientific theories. No contemporary scientist thinks you can just pick up the raw facts and fit them together into an adequate explanation; rather, you start by devising a theory, a hypothesis, that seems most *reasonable*, and then you test the theory by means of experiments and observations. And though there are probably still a few pure rationalists lost in the philosophical fun house, they don't seem to survive in the natural world. So is the rationalism–empiricism distinction still really useful?"

"Selina," said Ben, "step outside your chemistry lab for just a moment, and stare deep into the loving eyes of your favorite rationalist."

"Oh, yes," Selina laughed, "I forgot. Rationalists are an endangered species, but we are fortunate to have one here at this very table. Maybe we ought to put him in the zoo: fix up a special natural-state exhibit, have a room with a comfortable leather chair and the collected works of Plato."

Sarah smiled "Rationalists aren't such rare birds, Selina. Maybe you don't meet them in the science labs that often, but step out into the world and you'll find the woods are full of them."

"Is that true, Sarah?" Ben looked reassured. "Frankly, I was starting to feel like the last surviving member of the species. I wasn't sure there were enough of us left to form a breeding population."

"Don't worry about that," Selina reassured him, "I'm confident that rationalists can mate with empiricists."

"I'll take your word for it, Selina," Sarah responded. "Let's not have any empirical proof right here in the coffee shop. To get back to what we were talking about before Selina's imagination got the better of her, there certainly are plenty of rationalists—along with lots of empiricists, of course, some of them rather vocal. But there are very few *pure* rationalists or *pure* empiricists. Perhaps Plato was a pure rationalist: He seemed to think that the only *real* knowledge was the knowledge gained by the light of pure reason. And Kant was certainly a rationalist when it came to ethics. But the classical rationalists—Descartes and Leibniz—believed that although reason is the source of the most fundamental and important truths, we still require empirical observation to learn some significant truths about the world. And empiricists such as Hume and Locke believed there was an important role for reason in both philosophy and scientific investigation—and Locke, though not Hume, believed that reason was the source of our knowledge of ethics. Still, there remains an important basic difference between the rationalist and empiricist perspectives: Empiricists agree that there are important things to be known by reasoning: the truths of mathematics and geometry, in particular—but they hold that basic to our knowledge of the world is sensory data we gain by observation and testing. It's important to formulate interesting testable hypotheses about the world; but ultimately, those hypotheses must be subjected to confirmation or falsification through our empirical observations. Thus, the cornerstone—the touchstone—of our knowledge is our sensory observations. In contrast, the rationalists may agree that there are some mundane truths known by observation, but the deeper reality and the more important universal truths must be sought by means of pure reason. Perhaps the clearest place to mark the difference is in ethics. Rationalists tend to believe that we know the truths of ethics through reason and that no empirical observation could either establish or refute ethical truths. It's true that cruelty is wrong, even if a survey shows that most people favor cruelty and even if we discover that cruelty is a successful survival strategy. Many empiricists hold the view that, on the contrary, ethics is set not by universal principles of reason, but instead through our feelings, and often they hold that there is no real *truth* of ethics at all, since ethical claims cannot be established by observational testing—though, as already noted, some empiricists, such as Locke, place ethics in a different category and treat it rationally."

"I'm not knocking the rationalist–empiricist distinction," Selina said, "but isn't it basically the same as the distinction between nonnaturalism and naturalism?"

"Not quite," Sarah replied. "Certainly, those who favor nonnaturalism are likely to be rationalists rather than empiricists, since they believe there is something beyond and more important than what can be known through empirical observation. But on the other hand, not all rationalists are nonnaturalists: A rationalist might believe that the most basic and important way of knowing about the world is through our remarkable capacity of reason, but the only world there is happens to be the natural one. For example, someone who thought that mathematics is the single key to understanding the universe, and that we can know the essential structure of the natural world through mathematical reasoning, and that, by discovering the secret mathematical order of the universe, we could unlock the secrets of the natural world would·hold such a rationalist–naturalist view. And finally, an empiricist might believe that the only real *knowledge* we can gain is based on sensory observation of the natural world, but also believe that there is a further *non*natural world that we believe in by faith, although we have no genuine *knowledge* of its existence."

"Alright, let's keep the distinction between empiricists and rationalists," Selina agreed. "We need to draw a clear distinction between the hardworking empiricists and the dreamy castles-in-the-sky rationalists."

Ben laughed. "So does that cover the range of philosophical differences? Rationalism vs. empiricism, nonnaturalism vs. naturalism, holism vs. individualism, determinism vs. nondeterminism, human uniqueness vs. the continuity of species: Selina and I disagree on just about all of them, don't we?"

Selina smiled. "Yeah, I guess it's true that opposites attract. But really, it's not surprising that we disagree on almost all of them, is it? I mean, once we've split on something like naturalism vs. nonnaturalism, it's not surprising that we would disagree on most of the others, also."

"I suppose so," Ben answered, "but are there anymore of these fundamental philosophical differences, Sarah?"

Simple Realism

"Well, there's one we've talked about without really choosing sides: the
distinction between those who are simple realists or direct realists, on the
one hand, and those who believe that theory and preconceptions color
everything we think, on the other."

"Hey, that's an important distinction, Sarah." Ben smiled. "It seems
to me that we *do* know some things just as they are in themselves. I know
that this is a table"—Ben banged the table with his fist—"and I know it
more certainly and directly than I could ever know any *theory* about it. Of
course, it's made up of subatomic particles—I believe that from my
physics class. And in another culture or in a different language, we might
call it by another name; and if you put a cushion on it and a back, maybe
it will become a very large chair. But right now, this moment, at this place,
this is certainly a table."

"Easy, Ben," Selina laughed. "You start shouting about how you
know that this is a table, they're going to come and take you away."

Ben smiled. "That would be the supreme injustice: Selina is denying
that we know that murder is wrong, and Sarah is saying how this table is
really part of the one great Whole—and I get locked up for saying that
this is a table! We simple realists certainly come in for lots of abuse."

"Do you really believe in simple realism, Ben?" Selina looked quizzi-
cal. "Or are you just being difficult?"

Ben laughed. "I'm not really sure. It does seem to me that some of our
knowledge is simply clear and direct: maybe of the table, more likely of
basic truths of ethics, maybe a direct intuitive experience of God's goodness. But I won't mention that last one: It'd probably send Selina right
over the edge. Still, it's clear that overall perspectives and viewpoints do
shape the way we experience the world and what we count as evidence. So
I'm not at all sure on this one."

"Actually, this is one of those distinctions that tend to cut across the
others," Sarah said. "Some rationalists believe in direct realism, and so
do some empiricists, though, of course, there are big differences in what
they think we can know directly. And of course, many empiricists and
rationalists reject direct realism. But there's one other basic difference
that you might consider. At least, it's a difference that William James
mentions. James talks about all these different basic divisions, and he
divides them into two groups. On the one side he places the 'tender-
minded,' who typically believe in rationalism, religion, monism (or

> *Tender-minded and tough-minded people, characterized as I have written them* *down, do both exist. Each of you probably knows some well-marked example of* *each type, and you know what each example thinks of the example on the other* *side of the line. They have a low opinion of each other. Their antagonism, when-* *ever as individuals their temperaments have been intense, has formed in all ages a* *part of the philosophic atmosphere of the time. It forms a part of the philosophic* *atmosphere to-day. The tough think of the tender as sentimentalists and soft-* *heads. The tender feel the tough to be unrefined, callous, or brutal. Their mutual* *reaction is very much like that that takes place when Bostonian tourists mingle* *with a population like that of Cripple Creek.*
>
> William James, *Pragmatism* (New York: Longmans, Green, 1907), pp. 12–13

holism), and free will; on the other side—he calls them the 'tough-minded—are those who favor empiricism, atheism or agnosticism, plural-ism (individualism), and determinism."

"Yeah," Selina exulted, "tough-minded—that's us, Baby!"

"Actually," Sarah laughed, "James himself favored most of the views on the 'tender-minded' side of the list; though basically he thought his pragmatic approach could accommodate both. But anyway, there was another characteristic on James's list: He thought that the tough-minded tended to be pessimists, while the tender-minded were optimists."

Pessimism vs. Optimism

"No way!" Selina was outraged. "We tough-minded types are famous optimists! After all, we believe that we can make discoveries and cure dis-eases and improve the world through our own powers. We don't wait for God to do it for us. We don't regard criminal acts as the inexplicable results of human free will; instead, we believe that there are causes of vio-lent behavior, and by studying them empirically, we can discover them and change them. God didn't make the world for our benefit, but we evolved in this world, so we are reasonably well adapted to it, and we have the natural capacities to live successfully in it. That doesn't mean we won't screw it up: We also have some serious flaws, and we might well blow ourselves up and go the way of the dinosaurs. But we have the *ability* to make things happen, to change things for the better, to make our lives and our worlds a better place. The future isn't guaranteed to turn out right: There's no benevolent God keeping an eye on everything and preparing a perfect future. But that's part of the fun: What happens is really up to me and up to us. Whether we succeed or fail, thrive or perish—in nuclear destruction or global warming—is largely a matter of our own efforts and ingenuity. And our own stupidity, on some occasions. That's enough for this tough-minded empiricist: I don't need pie-in-the-sky-by-and-by-when-I-die; there are plenty of projects, challenges, and opportunities in the here and now. Enough to keep me busy and interested and enthusiastic for a full, rich lifetime, and that seems to me enough optimism for anyone."

"Wow!" Sarah lifted her cup in salute. "That is one *optimistic* empiricist. Actually, you're not the only one, Selina. The French philosophes of the 18th century—philosophers like Diderot, La Mettrie, D'Holbach—were typically enthusiastic empiricists, and they generally rejected religion and otherworldliness and souls, but they were profoundly optimistic about their ability to make the world better through science and knowledge. Actually, I think the main reason William James thought of the tough-minded as pessimists is because he tended to treat tough-minded *determinism* as the equivalent of *fatalism:* Our fate is fixed, and there is nothing we can do to change or improve it. Also, he—along with many others of that very early 20th-century period—was disturbed by the idea that (according to a strict materialist view) the cosmos would eventually run down and the Earth and everything in it would be utterly destroyed: All our ideas, efforts, and hopes would ultimately be completely extinguished. The fact that it would not occur for many millions or even billions of years made no difference to James: If the world would *ultimately* meet such an end, then he considered that a very depressing and pessimistic perspective."

There is the sting of it, that in the vast drifting of the cosmic weather, tho many a jeweled shore appears, and many an enchanted cloud-bank floats away, long lingering ere it be dissolved—even as our world now lingers, for our joy—yet when these transient products are gone, nothing, absolutely nothing remains, to represent those particular qualities, those elements of preciousness which they may have enshrined. Dead and gone are they, gone utterly from the very sphere and room of being. Without an echo; without a memory; without an influence on aught that may come after, to make it care for similar ideals. This utter final wreck and tragedy is of the essence of scientific materialism as at present understood. . . . The notion of God, on the other hand, however inferior it may be in clearness to those mathematical notions so current in mechanical philosophy, has at least this practical superiority over them, that it guarantees an ideal order that shall be permanently preserved. . . . Materialism means simply the denial that the moral order is eternal, and the cutting off of ultimate hopes; spiritualism means the affirmation of an eternal moral order and the letting loose of hope.

William James, *Pragmatism,* pp. 54–55

Selina shook her head. "So, the cosmos will burn itself out in a few billion years. Somehow, that doesn't throw me into pessimistic despair. A few billion years seems quite long enough for me."

Ben laughed. "That's the trouble with you empiricists: You're so shortsighted; you can't seem to see beyond a few billion years. Still, I think there's something in what James says: The rationalist, nondeterminist, spiritualist view does seem to me more optimistic. Sometimes the world looks pretty bleak. Belief that there is some higher power, some higher truth, that is permanent and positive—that seems to me ultimately a more optimistic point of view."

"And," Selina replied, "it seems to me a crutch for those who are afraid to face the world as it is and stake the future on their own struggles. Sorry, Ben, that sounded sort of harsh, didn't it? I didn't mean it that way. It's just that I hate the idea that we empiricists are pessimists. That seems a terrible slander, Sarah. William James wasn't being fair to us tough-minded sorts."

"To be perfectly honest, Selina," responded Sarah, "I'm not sure that the optimism–pessimism distinction is a function of philosophical views—though, obviously, William James and a lot of other philosophers would disagree. If you want to know why one person is a pessimist and another an optimist, I think psychology probably offers better explanations than philosophy. In any case, I agree with you: Pessimists and optimists seem to fall in equal numbers into the tender-minded and tough-minded categories. So I have doubts about James's pessimistic–optimistic distinction. Still, I think James is right on at least one point. At the beginning of his lectures on pragmatism, he quoted"—Sarah found the page in her notebook—"a passage from G. K. Chesterton:

> There are some people—and I am one of them—who think that the most practical and important thing about a man is still his view of the universe. We think that for a landlady considering a lodger, it is important to know his income, but still more important to know his philosophy. We think that for a general about to fight an enemy, it is important to know the enemy's numbers, but still more important to know the enemy's philosophy. We think the question is not whether the theory of the cosmos affects matters, but whether, in the long run, anything else affects them.

Be patient toward all that is unsolved in your heart and try to love the questions themselves like locked rooms and like books that are written in a very foreign tongue. . . . Live the questions now. Perhaps you will then gradually, without noticing it, live along some distant day into the answer.

Quoted at the beginning of Hilary Putnam's *Realism with a Human Face*, edited by James Conant (Cambridge, MA: Harvard University Press, 1990); quotation is from Rainer Maria Rilke, *Letters to a Young Poet*

I agree with James on that; except that I think it's equally important to know a *woman's* view of the universe as well. And in any case, I know a great deal more about my friends Selina and Ben than I knew before we started meeting for coffee. And more about my own views also. Some of what I know is that I'm not quite sure what some of my own views are, but that's an interesting thing to know, too. Anyway, I'm glad my philosophical beliefs are not set in stone: Much of the philosophical fun is in trying new ideas and finding your own conclusions. Oh, by the way, I've been working out some new ideas about free will, based on stuff we've been studying in psych. But I guess that will have to wait for tomorrow."

Study Questions

1. What explanation does Selina offer for the widespread belief in God?
2. Discuss the pros and cons of the claim that humans are special and distinct from all other species.
3. What role does our basic perspective play in the way we answer controversial questions?
4. What is simple realism?
5. Compare and contrast William James's "tough-minded" and "tender-minded" individuals.

Exercises

1. Which of the following is most definitive of your view? That is, which one is most *firmly* set in place and helps to fix the others? Your view that humans are (or are not) distinctively apart from the world? Or your views about ethics? Or your views about free will? Or your view concerning the nature of human intelligence? Or your view concerning God? Or your view concerning personal identity? Or your views on individualism vs. holism?
2. Of the views listed in Exercise 1, which could you most *easily* change? That is, on which question could you change your answer while making the *fewest* revisions in your other beliefs?
3. Ben and Selina have some basic disagreements on many issues. Of all their disagreements, which one do you think will cause them the *greatest problems* or cause the *most conflict* if they remain together?
4. Selina appeals to the work of Martin Seligman on learned helplessness as part of her explanation for widespread belief in the existence of God. One of the major arguments in support of moral responsibility is based on effort: We aren't responsible for our talents and circumstances, but we are morally responsible for our *efforts*—or lack thereof—to do the very best with the talents we have. What are the implications of Seligman's research for that argument?
5. William James divides philosophical *temperaments* into two basic categories. One side (which he calls "tough-minded") typically consists of empiricists, naturalists, nonreligious people, determinists, and individualists (as opposed

to holists). The opposing ("tender-minded") side comprises rationalists, non-naturalists (idealists), religious individuals, believers in free will, and holists. But as James also points out, few of us are purely one or the other. Do your own views fall more on the tough-minded or tender-minded side?

If you hold views that are primarily on one side, but one or two of your beliefs fall on the other (e.g., you are generally "tough-minded," but you also believe in free will), do you experience that as a *tension* in your belief system?

Glossary

Learned helplessness: According to Martin Seligman and other psychologists, the state of extreme passivity and helplessness (often accompanied by severe depression) that is caused by long-term experience of having no control over one's environment, especially when the environment is experienced as aversive.

Meliorism: A theological view favored by William James according to which God is a powerful force on the side of good, but not all powerful (so that human efforts may be essential for good to triumph).

Transcendent: Anything that lies outside or beyond the realm of possible human experience, or anything beyond the natural world; often contrasted with *immanent* events, occurring within the natural realm.

Additional Resources

A good survey of distinctive philosophical systems can be found in Leslie Stevenson and David L. Haberman, *Ten Theories of Human Nature* (New York: Oxford University Press, 1998). Another book offering a comparative view of a different set of positions is Roger Trigg, *Ideas of Human Nature: An Historical Introduction* (Oxford: Blackwell, 1988). For a more continental orientation, see Peter Langford, *Modern Philosophies of Human Nature* (Dordrecht, the Netherlands: Martinus Nijhoff Publishers, 1986).

William James (see his *Pragmatism*, available in many editions) was very interested in comparative philosophical systems. A system favored by the biologist E. O. Wilson is described in his *Consilience: The Unity of Knowledge* (New York: Knopf, 1998).

For more on learned helplessness, see Martin E. P. Seligman, *Helplessness: On Depression, Development, and Death* (San Francisco: Freeman, 1975); and Christopher Peterson, Steven F. Maier, and Martin E. P. Seligman, *Learned Helplessness* (New York: Oxford University Press, 1993).

Kai Nielsen, "Naturalistic Explanations of Theistic Belief," in Philip L. Quinn and Charles Taliaferro, eds., *A Companion to Philosophy of Religion* (Oxford: Blackwell, 1997), offers interesting ideas about the sources of religious belief and the effects of a naturalistic analysis of belief.

Frans de Waal has written extensively and clearly on intelligence in nonhuman animals, especially primates. See *Chimpanzee Politics* (London: Jonathan Cape, 1982); *Peacemaking among Primates* (Cambridge, MA: Harvard University Press, 1989); *Good Natured* (Cambridge, MA.: 1996); *The Ape and the Sushi Master: Cultural Reflections of a Primatologist* (New York: Perseus Books, 2001); and (with Frans Lanting) *Bonobo: The Forgotten Ape* (Berkeley, CA: University of California Press, 1998). A fascinating, but disturbing, book by a psychologist who has been deeply involved in teaching language to chimpanzees and in struggling to protect chimpanzees is Roger Fouts's (with Stephen Tukel Mills) *Next of Kin: What Chimpanzees Have Taught Me About Who We Are* (New York: William Morrow, 1997).

To learn more about the work of Roger Fouts, visit *www.friendsofwashoe.org*. The website for the Great Ape Project is excellent, with many links; go to *www.greatapeproject.org*.

Notes

1. William James, *Pragmatism* (New York: Longman, Green, 1907).
2. Roger Fouts (with Stephen Tukel Mills), *Next of Kin: What Chimpanzees Have Taught Me About Who We Are* (New York: William Morrow, 1997), p. 180.
3. Frans de Waal, *Chimpanzee Politics* (London: Jonathan Cape, 1982), p. 56.
4. Fouts, op.cit., p. 350.
5. Raymond Smullyan, "Is God a Taoist?" in *The Tao is Silent* (New York: Harper & Row, 1977).

Credits

Index